The Psychology of
Music Performance Anxiety

The Psychology of Music Performance Anxiety

Dianna T. Kenny

Professor of Psychology and Music,
Australian Centre for Applied Research in Music Performance
Faculty of Arts
The University of Sydney

OXFORD
UNIVERSITY PRESS

OXFORD
UNIVERSITY PRESS

Great Clarendon Street, Oxford OX2 6DP

Oxford University Press is a department of the University of Oxford.
It furthers the University's objective of excellence in research, scholarship,
and education by publishing worldwide in

Oxford New York

Auckland   Cape Town Dar es Salaam   Hong Kong   Karachi
Kuala Lumpur Madrid Melbourne Mexico City   Nairobi
New Delhi Shanghai Taipei Toronto
With offices in
Argentina Austria Brazil Chile Czech Republic France Greece
Guatemala Hungary Italy Japan South Korea Poland Portugal
Singapore Switzerland Thailand Turkey Ukraine Vietnam

Oxford is a registered trade mark of Oxford University Press
in the UK and in certain other countries

Published in the United States
by Oxford University Press Inc., New York

ISBN 978-0-19-958614-1

Printed and bound by CPI Group (UK) Ltd, Croydon, CR0 4YY

Whilst every effort has been made to ensure that the contents of this book are as complete,
accurate and up-to-date as possible at the date of writing, Oxford University Press is not
able to give any guarantee or assurance that such is the case. Readers are urged to take
appropriately qualified medical advise in all cases. The information in this book is
intended to be useful to the general reader, but should not be used as a means of
self-diagnosis or for the prescription of medication.

For

Patrick, Christina and Giselle

with love

Foreword

It is often said that both optimists and pessimists contribute to society: the optimist invents the airplane and the pessimist the parachute. In this sense, there is optimism and pessimism in every performing musician. On one hand, performers strive to advance their art, seeking out new perspectives, new works, new interpretations, and new media to engage their audiences in distinctive and meaningful ways. On the other, they must consider the beliefs, traditions, and standards against which their performances are judged, take steps to meet or reject expectations, and then accept the consequences of their actions. Finding a successful balance between these parameters is no trivial matter, and when viewed in the context of the modern music profession, with its intense competition, shifting employment landscape, and seemingly endless supply of "note perfect" recordings, it is no wonder that individual musicians struggle to think and feel more positively about performing.

Understanding performance anxiety is one of the most important challenges facing performance scientists today. Not only does it present a complex picture, characterized by great diversity in its causes and differences of scale in its expression, but it has personal and professional implications for each musician who experiences it. Moreover, misconceptions about performance anxiety, among both scientists and musicians, and the pernicious ways in which some musicians seem to "treat" it— through quiet suffering, outright denial, or even substance abuse, for instance—has historically tended to confuse the matter and hinder scientific enquiry.

Nonetheless, great strides have been made in recent years to further our knowledge of the causes, symptoms, and treatments of music performance anxiety. There is no better analysis of these advances than this groundbreaking volume. Comprehensive in its scope and rigorous in its handling of the topic, *The Psychology of Music Performance Anxiety* offers new theoretical perspectives and indispensable practical insights. This book is unique in a number of ways. First, it brings clarity to the concept of anxiety. Drawing on literature from philosophy and diverse psychological perspectives, it analyzes and integrates the extensive empirical and clinical research into anxiety and the anxiety disorders and their possible relationships to music performance anxiety. Second, it tackles the vexed question of the nature of music performance anxiety: is music performance anxiety a dimensional construct that differs only in degree of severity between musicians or is it more usefully conceptualized in terms of discrete subtypes that require different treatment approaches? Kenny argues that the methods of investigation, nomothetic and idiographic, each have valuable insights to contribute, as do the range of theoretical perspectives she covers. Detailed clinical examples are provided to highlight the intensely personal suffering experienced by musicians with severe music performance anxiety. Third, the book reviews the literature on performance and performance psychology and identifies the circumstances under which peak and optimal performance may be attained. Fourth, there is a detailed review of available treatments and a comprehensive discussion of the various psychological theories and empirical support that underpin these treatments. Finally, amid the rigorous argumentation regarding the theoretical and empirical issues surrounding music performance anxiety, the voices of musicians are clearly heard throughout the book, thus making it accessible to a wide readership of researchers, psychologists, musicians, teachers, and students.

What is clear is that performing music can be a deeply enriching experience. Despite this, negative thoughts about performing are common among musicians, even for those at the highest of international levels. Enrico Caruso once remarked: "Of course I'm nervous. The artist who boasts he is never nervous is not an artist—he is a liar or a fool" (cited in Rushmore, 1971, p. 72). In a more exaggerated fashion, the pianist Vladimir Horowitz retired from public performance on four separate occasions throughout his long career: from 1936–1938, 1953–1965, 1969–1974, and 1983–1985. Apparently "highly neurotic" and beset by feelings of inadequacy, he simply could not satisfy himself that he was "living up to his potential. Was he a great musician or a mere entertainer?" (Schonberg, 1992). The experiences of Caruso and Horowitz, among others covered in the book, suggest that even eminent musicians can have persistent doubts about their performing skills. More importantly, they also demonstrate that exceptional performances are still possible in the face of such difficulties.

Gradually, science is shedding a brighter light on music performance anxiety and on effective methods for managing it, allowing performers to re-focus their attention on the exhilarating opportunities and enjoyment that performing music affords. Regardless of scientific advances, however, this can be a challenging personal journey, one that requires knowledge, determination, hard work and, perhaps above all else, an open mind. *The Psychology of Music Performance Anxiety* has opened up the field to intense and rigorous scrutiny, provided a solid theoretical and conceptual grounding on which future researchers can build, and has most certainly delivered a clearer way forward.

Rushmore, R. (1971). *The singing voice.* New York: Dodd, Mead & Company.
Schonberg, H. (1992). *Horowitz: His life and music.* New York: Simon & Schuster.

Aaron Williamon
Royal College of Music
London, 2011

Preface

At a particular point in the conceptualization of my book on music performance anxiety, I was reminded of a passage from a remarkable early paper, The psychic mechanism of hysterical phenomena (Freud, 1893), in which Freud muses:

> ... even I myself am struck by the fact that the case histories which I am writing read like novels and, as it were, dispense with the serious features of the scientific character ... [but] focal diagnoses and electrical reactions are really not important in the study of hysteria, whereas a detailed discussion of the psychic processes, as one is wont to hear it from the poet ... allows one to gain an insight into the course of events of hysteria (p. 50).

At the time of writing in 1893, Freud was in the very early stages of his struggle to understand a pervasive psychological phenomenon of his day—hysteria. Without wishing to draw an immodest parallel between Freud's struggles to understand hysteria and my own struggle to understand music performance anxiety, I felt almost from the outset of its conceptualization that 'the serious features of the scientific character' were not only premature but stifling in my attempts to understand the lived experience, the phenomenology of music performance anxiety, in all its manifestations, in younger and older, amateur and professional, vocal and instrumental, solo and orchestral/choral musicians.

Although most of my early formal training in psychology was based on the principles of learning theory, and most of my clinical practice in the paradigms of the cognitive behavior therapies, with maturity, experience, and exposure to other ways of understanding the 'Johnian quality of John' (Allport, 1955) I became aware that while these orientations provided an excellent basis from which to commence the Herculean task of understanding human behavior and assisting people to change, there were vast caverns of conscious and unconscious experience that needed to be understood and worked with in the pursuit of a 'cure' or, as newer age psychoanalysts and psychotherapists prefer, an authentic existence. Many psychologists have long understood that 'Stimulus-response psychology and conditioning theory cannot get along without Freud's internal mental world ...' (Mahl, 1968, p. x). However, they have not always had the loudest voices, and the field has been impoverished by the imbalance and consequent neglect of the internal mental world.

Accordingly, I have painted a large canvas. I have drawn on my own experiences of severe music performance anxiety as well as all the sources of knowledge currently available. I offer a number of ways to characterize music performance anxiety using psychiatric taxonomies, epidemiology, and different theoretical perspectives. These include learning theory, psychoanalytic theory, attachment and relational theories, emotion, psychophysiological and neurochemical theories of anxiety, performance psychology and the psychology of peak performance. We need all these perspectives in order to enhance our understanding of the hybrid nature of the music performance anxieties and the musicians who inhabit them, the wide range of underlying causes, their varied manifestations and often unpredictable consequences and outcomes. It is simultaneously a work of synthesis and speculation. Many of the hypotheses presented in this book await empirical and clinical confirmation or revision.

The first and final chapters are devoted to the musicians themselves, in which they have shared their stories and struggles, and offer their advice and wisdom. They have raised their voices in praise of their art and provided moving insights into the creative yet often painful act of music making. Above all, they have shared themselves with us. For this profound act of courage, I am deeply grateful.

Allport, G. W. (1955). *Becoming: Basic considerations for a psychology of personality*. New Haven: Yale University Press.

Freud, S. (1893). The psychic mechanism of hysterical phenomena. In R. M. Hutchins (Ed.). *The major works of Sigmund Freud* (Vol. 54, pp. 25–31). Chicago: University of Chicago: Encyclopaedia Britannica.

Mahl, G. F. (1968). Gestures and body movements in interviews. In J. M. Shlien (Ed.). *Research in Psychotherapy* (Vol. 1, pp. 295–346). Washington DC: American Psychological Association.

Dianna T. Kenny
5th February 2011

Acknowledgments

I offer my deepest appreciation and respect to the many musicians who have shared their knowledge, experience and narratives with me, struggled in therapy to overcome their anxieties, and who so generously contributed their time to help me understand their experience of music performance anxiety. The eight orchestras of Australia—Adelaide Symphony Orchestra, Australian Opera and Ballet Orchestra, Melbourne Symphony Orchestra, Opera Victoria, Sydney Symphony Orchestra, Queensland Symphony Orchestra, Tasmanian Symphony Orchestra, West Australian Symphony Orchestra—were partners in this undertaking to better understand music performance anxiety and I thank both management and musicians for their wonderful support and trust.

The data for the research on tertiary performing arts students reported in Chapter 5 was collected at the National Institute of Creative Arts and Industries (NICAI), Auckland University, New Zealand. I thank Professor Sharman Pretty (former Dean) and Professor Jennifer Dixon (current Dean) of NICAI and my research associates, Justine Cormack, violinist with the NZ trio, and Rosemary Martin, PhD student in dance, for their collaboration and assistance.

This work was supported, in part, by an Australia Research Council (ARC) Grant LP0989486 to Dr Bronwen Ackermann, Professor Dianna Kenny and A/Professor Tim Driscoll, with industry partners, the Australia Council for the Arts (ACA) and the eight orchestras of Australia. I thank the ARC, ACA and my co-investigators for their financial and collegial support respectively.

Dr Steven Arthey, clinical psychologist, was a generous and knowledgeable colleague who conducted the therapy for some of the musicians involved in our studies and whose insights contributed to theorizing music performance anxiety from the perspective of intensive short term dynamic psychotherapy.

Tom Jones, clinical psychologist, friend and intellectual companion since student days, provided the cognitive behavior therapy formulations for the two musicians discussed in Chapter 8, and stimulating discussion on the efficacies of different psychological interventions.

A/Professor Stephanie McCallum, one of Australia's finest pianists, gave generously of her insights into piano pedagogy, performance practice and management of music performance anxiety.

Dr Peter Lorenz made helpful comments on beta-blockers in the pharmacotherapy section.

Dr Diana Wong, an infinitely patient guide, taught me that '*The dragon cannot be slain in effigy.*'[1] She also taught me different ways of knowing, including ways of knowing myself - important lessons that helped shape some of the ideas in this book.

---

1 Freud, S. (1912a). The dynamics of transference, Standard Edition, 12, 99–108, p. 108 (Alternative translation: "It is impossible to destroy anyone *in absentia or in effigie*").

To the staff at Oxford University Press, Charlotte Green and Martin Baum, my thanks for your encouragement, interest, and support for this project. Thanks also to the production staff, Abigail Stanley at Oxford University Press and Priya Sagayaraj at Glyph International, for their efficiency and professionalism in preparing the manuscript for publication.

Contents

Figures

Tables

Boxes

At some time in the future our attempts at explanation will be felt to be just as metaphorical and symbolical as we have found the alchemical one to be . . . the investigator of the future will ask himself, just as we do, whether we knew what we meant

Jung, 1955, p. 919.

Chapter 1

Phenomenology of music performance anxiety

One of the most exhilarating experiences I know of is performing in public, especially when there is a magnificent piano under my fingers, great music in my head, and the feeling that there are no technical obstacles

Reubart, 1985, p. 1.

So begins Reubart's book on mastering the anxiety associated with playing the piano from memory. Sadly, not all performers feel so positive and energized about performing in public. For some, performances are characterized by fear and dread, and experienced as an overwhelming challenge that must be endured. Frederic Chopin (Zdzisław Jachimecki, 1937) was one such performer:

> I am not fitted to give concerts. The audience intimidates me, I feel choked by its breath, paralyzed by its curious glances, struck dumb by all those strange faces.

Chopin was not alone in his antipathy to public performance. Some other unlikely sufferers of music performance anxiety (MPA) include Maria Callas, Enrico Caruso, Pablo Casals, Luciano Pavarotti, Leopold Godowsky, Vladimir Horowitz, Ignacy Paderewski, Arthur Rubenstein, and Sergei Rachmaninoff (Ostwald, 1994; Schonberg, 1963; Valentine, 2002).

What are the factors that produce such vastly different performance experiences? This is the question that this book will attempt to answer. A comparison of the two descriptions of performance experience given in these opening lines provides some first clues. You will notice that in Reubart's description, he is focused on his own sensory and subjective experiences: the emotional high of exhilaration, the physicality of his fingers stroking the keys of a magnificent piano, the auditory perception of 'inner music', and the feeling of motor coordination and freedom that provides the solid technique through which his musical intentions are realized. There is no mention of an audience or a performance venue or his reaction to these. We get a sense of heightened awareness and connectedness between musician and the music. Reubart's account is present (there is no past or future) and focused on the act of giving birth to the music in his head.

Chopin's attention, by contrast, is focused outwards, onto the audience. He appears to be acutely aware of every nuance of their behavior, their curious glances, their strangeness such that he feels intimidated, and he concludes that there is a very poor fit between his temperament and the art of performing. He conveys a sense that performing overwhelms and depletes him: he feels choked, paralyzed, and struck dumb. Why was Chopin so averse to public performance? He was a child prodigy, an acclaimed composer and acknowledged virtuoso, yet he gave few public concerts, preferring composition and piano teaching to displaying himself in public. Georges Sand, his lover, provides some insight into his character in her descriptions of his insecurities and anxieties when composing, efforts that were accompanied by emotional torment and bouts of weeping and complaining when he could not choose among his musical ideas (Zdzisław Jachimecki, 1937). Of course, Chopin was also very ill with pulmonary tuberculosis for most of his adult life, a condition that left him feeling exhausted and gasping for breath. This could also have contributed to his feelings of choking; he may therefore have felt this sensation both physically, due to his illness, and emotionally, due to his performance anxiety.

This is not to suggest that a performer who focuses on the audience will necessarily suffer performance anxiety or render an impaired performance. Attunement with one's audience can enhance performance, producing its own rewards. The relationship between a performer and his audience is a very personal experience that arises through a complex interaction between the musician, his past experiences, the current performing context, and the nature of the audience. Louis Armstrong, universally acknowledged as one of the greatest jazz trumpeters of all time, explained his relationship between his music making and his audience thus:

> I never tried to prove nothing, just wanted to give a good show. My life has always been my music, it's always come first, but the music ain't worth nothing if you can't lay it on the public. The main thing is to live for that audience, because what you're there for is to please the people.[1]

Mozart was a consummate manipulator of his audience, always mindful of their responses to his music. He took great delight when he had correctly anticipated their reactions, as the following excerpt from a letter to his father, Leopold, on the occasion of the premiere of his 'Paris' symphony in 1778, shows:

> Just in the middle of the first Allegro there was a passage which I felt sure must please. The audience were quite carried away—and there was a tremendous burst of applause . . . Having observed that all last as well as first Allegros begin here with all the instruments playing together and generally *unisono*, I began mine with two violins only, piano for the first eight bars—followed instantly by a *forte*; the audience, as I expected, said 'Hush' at the soft beginning and when they heard the *forte*, began at once to clap their hands (Mozart, 1778/1985).

In his long eulogy for the great Australian pianist, Geoffrey Tozer, the former prime minister of Australia, Paul Keating, a champion of Geoffrey, shows particular insight, perhaps gained from his own experience as a prominent public figure, into the importance of the audience for performing artists:

> [Tozer's] early death at age 54 reminds us of the death of Maria Callas at the age of 53. Performing all their lives, both artists finally reached the stage of wondering what it is all about. After operating constantly at a level of high achievement, they needed the spiritual

---

[1] Retrieved from http://tinpan.fortunecity.com/riff/11/quotes.html (6.6.09).

sustenance of audiences and friends. They needed the acclamation to stir the genius in them. When the acclaim stopped, both of these people turned towards an inner, more human life, with a lower premium on the art (Keating, 2009).

Keating speaks of the 'spiritual sustenance' that an audience provides and that when this sustenance in the form of 'acclamation' ceases, performers must look inward to sustain themselves. There is an inference that some artists, like Tozer and Callas, are not able to provide themselves with inner sustenance and that this failure contributed to their early deaths. Callas's highly publicized and difficult relationship with her mother that ended in estrangement provides some clues as to why Maria may have been unable to nurture herself in the absence of external acclaim. In an interview for *Time* magazine in 1956, Maria said:

> My sister was slim and beautiful and friendly, and my mother always preferred her. I was the ugly duckling, fat and clumsy and unpopular. It is a cruel thing to make a child feel ugly and unwanted . . . I'll never forgive her for taking my childhood away. During all the years I should have been playing and growing up, I was singing or making money. Everything I did for them was mostly good and everything they did to me was mostly bad.

Underlying psychological vulnerabilities that result in, among others, high levels of performance anxiety will be a recurring theme in this book.

Music performance anxiety does not afflict only classical musicians. Popular musicians also suffer from it. It is not just the lifestyle of a popular musician that accounts for the widespread drug and alcohol abuse among this group. Take, for example, the lyrics of the song below that point to the emotional difficulties experienced by musicians in this genre. Although there is not one psychologist among the members of the pop group, The Band, they have captured, better than any text I have read on the subject, the essence of music performance anxiety through the poignant words of their song, 'Stage Fright' (The Band, 1970). The left column presents the song's lyrics; the right column identifies the central characteristics of the experience of music performance anxiety that they capture.

Lyrics	Feature of MPA
See the man with the stage fright	*Extreme anxiety associated with performance*
Standin' up there to give it all his might	*Maximum personal investment*
He got caught in the spotlight	*Fear of exposure*
And when he gets to the end	
He wanna start all over again	*Perfectionism*
Now deep in the heart of a lonely kid	*Underlying psychological vulnerability*
Suffered so much for what he did	*Psychological costs of performing*
They gave this cowboy his fortune and fame	*Ambivalence about a performing career*
Since that day, he ain't bin the same	*Loss of self*
I got fire water on my breath	*Self-management via self-medication (with alcohol)*

Lyrics	Feature of MPA
And the doctor warned me I might catch my death	*Physical/psychological health consequences*
Said you can make it in your disguise	*Phenotypical presentation (hide one's fear)*
Just never show the fear that's in your eyes	*Fear as the basic underlying emotion*
And as he says that easy phrase	*Glib advice from others*
Take him at his word	
And for the price that the poor boy pays	*Consequences of performance*
He gets to sing just like a bird	
Your brow is sweating and your mouth gets dry	*Somatic symptoms of anxiety*
Fancy people go drifting by	*Valued but feared audience*
The moment of truth is right at hand	*(Reality based?) catastrophizing; evaluative threat*
Just one more nightmare you can stand	*Extreme emotional distress*

The song paints a picture of a young man dedicated to his craft (he invests 'all his might'), but at great personal cost (he experiences 'stage fright'). He bravely faces that which he most fears (the spotlight), but is rarely satisfied with his performance. He has a perfectionistic standard to which he aspires, but rarely attains (when he gets to the end, he wants to start all over again). He is psychologically vulnerable (he is lonely; perhaps he has had little support, encouragement, or understanding; and hence he suffers alone). His musical success has brought him 'fortune and fame' but his emotional life has suffered (fear is his constant companion, but he must never show it). He has never been the same since he attained success (there is a suggestion that something of himself has been lost). This creates a conflict for him: performing is both the prized and the feared object. He manages his emotional distress by self-medicating with alcohol. Every performance is accompanied by the somatic symptoms of intense anxiety (his brow is sweating and his mouth is dry); he worries about the audience reaction to his performance ('Fancy people go drifting by'), afraid that he may be exposed as a fraud and a failure (when he is confronted with the 'moment of truth'). Despite the intense emotional distress and worry that he experiences, he steels himself for his next performance ('Just one more nightmare'). This is the cycle of music performance anxiety for many performers.

Now compare the words of the song 'Stage Fright' with these verbatim accounts of performance experiences by musicians. They come from the whole spectrum of performance attainment—from those just embarking on their professional careers to those who have attained international status as a performing artist.

Transcript 1

I was performing in my last recital for my music degree in front of about 50 colleagues and staff members from the university. The venue was a large recital room at the university. It was a piece for cello and piano but the piano part was minimal and the cello part required long, slow, lyrical playing.

I was poorly prepared. I had not had a lesson on the piece with my teacher, and I had had only a quick rehearsal with the pianist. I was very nervous, and because it was an assessment, I had to sit in the room for two hours while other students performed, so I did not get the opportunity to warm up. When I started to perform, my right hand shook uncontrollably for the whole eight minutes of the performance and I was incredibly embarrassed. I tried to play a very difficult slow piece where every shake in the bow is magnified 100 times and it was, and probably still is, one of the most embarrassing moments of my life. Having to sit there during this performance and just watching your hand shake and feeling very unable to do anything about it . . . Afterwards, no one mentioned it besides my teacher. All of my friends and colleagues just pretended it didn't happen. Even now, eight years later, I feel sick thinking about that performance. It made me lose confidence in myself; I lost my nerve and mental strength. Soon afterwards, I started taking beta-blockers in all my performances.

(Male cellist, aged 19 years)

Transcript 2

I played a concert in the Royal Albert Hall in front of an audience of 3,000 people. The concert was also broadcast live on BBC radio. My performance went very well. I played very accurately, but also with great freedom and expression. Lots of people I respected complimented me on my performance afterwards. The CEO of the orchestra told me that I was the highlight of the concert, and many musicians in the audience told me that I had given an inspired performance. So did the conductor. This performance enhanced my reputation, made me feel very good about myself, and I got a great review in the *Sunday Times*.

(Male cellist, aged 23 years)

Transcript 3

I think it has probably been five or six years in the making of me suffering from a growing level of performance anxiety. It comes and goes; sometimes I have good performances, sometimes I do a good audition and have success, but other times it is absolutely crippling and I cannot even play and I guess in the last year it has really become quite bad and it has reached a point were it is making me very unhappy. I have recently been pulling out of auditions and the ones I have attended lately—it wasn't good at all, it was my muscles. I could barely move my arms I was so, so nervous, really, and I thought, well, I don't really want to do this any more so I am going to put the cello away and get a job doing something else . . . if I could, in an ideal world, if I could get rid of the anxiety and the nerves, I would love to be a cellist and a musician and I think when I play well I am actually good at it and I think I am good enough to be at the professional level but at the moment it's just not possible because of the stress and the pressure that I am putting on myself. Now I am at the point of actually making the decision to put the cello away and stop doing it altogether.

(Male cellist, aged 27 years)

If the reader is a performer or a music teacher, such accounts of performance experiences may sound very familiar. The young performer in transcript 1 had what appears to be a very aversive fear conditioning (see Chapter Six) experience that subsequently necessitated, in his judgment, the ingestion of beta-blockers in all subsequent performances in order to avoid repeating what he described as the 'the single most embarrassing experience of my life.' What psychological vulnerability could account for so severely negative an emotional reaction and prolonged post-performance rumination, such that, eight years after the event, he continues to feel sick when he recalls it?

This reaction is not infrequent among performers and is one to which we will return later in this book.

The performer in transcript 2 had what is commonly described as a 'flow' experience. Flow, also described as an autotelic experience, has the characteristic of being 'so engrossing and enjoyable . . . it is worth doing for its own sake even though it may have no consequence outside itself. Creative activities, music, sports, games, and religious rituals are typical sources for this kind of experience' (Csikszentmihalyi, 1999, p. 824). The play of young children also has this autotelic quality. Attainment of this state is the goal of all performing artists.

Flow experiences and performance anxiety co-occur. Anais Koivisto, a young actor who suffers from extreme performance anxiety, described both intense anxiety and its unwanted consequences and flow in her acting career. 'I don't know how much longer I can go on like this . . . Everything feels physically hard.' She described moving in a jerky and uncontrolled way, and of having her muscles freeze during rehearsals. She said it was hard to smile. Worst of all for an actor, her voice would go into her chest, silencing her. 'But acting is not always like this for me. Sometimes, it is lovely, sublime, wonderful, easy—like surfing when you hit the barrel of a wave and suddenly you are gliding over glassy water' (*Theme* magazine, in Nicholson & Torrisi, 2006).

During a state of flow, the person has a sense of spontaneous, effortless performance and total immersion and focus on the activity to the exclusion of other environmental or internal stimuli. Such states are, paradoxically, the culmination of discipline, dedicated practice, concentration, and perseverance: they occur when the challenges are matched with the necessary underlying skills and the honing of those skills to achieve mastery. They may also have a very long gestation period, as so graphically described by Carl Jung, a Swiss psychiatrist and psychoanalyst, who developed a method (later known as Jungian psychology) of understanding the human psyche in terms of dreams, art, mythology, religion, and philosophy. Hobson (1953) describes the process whereby Carl Jung produced his seminal work, *Symbols of transformation* (1911), thus:

> This work proved to be a critical turning point in Jung's life and work. By his own account he was 'literally struck dumb', as if by an 'explosion', unable to understand or formulate material which came upon him like a 'landslide' (Jung, 1952, pp. xxviii and xxvi; 275).

Jung (1963) later maintained:

> . . . [my fantasies] operated like a catalyst upon the stored-up and still disorderly ideas within me. Gradually there formed out of them, and out of the knowledge of myths I had acquired, my book *The psychology of the unconscious* (p. 158).

And again:

> All my works, all my creative activity, [have] come from initial fantasies and dreams which began in 1912, almost fifty years ago. Everything that I accomplished in later life was already contained in them, although only in the form of emotions and images (p. 184).

Our cellist reported that he 'played very accurately, but also with great freedom and expression.' Note that he first commented on his technical mastery of the work before the sense of abandonment to the music. The following is an account of the state of flow described by a composer: 'You are in an ecstatic state to such a point that you feel as though you almost don't exist . . . My hand seems devoid of myself, and I have nothing to do with what is happening. I just sit there watching in a state of awe and wonderment. And the music just flows out by itself' (Csikszentmihalyi, 1975, p. 44). Similarly, Steptoe (2001, p. 291) identified a state of flow in the post-performance interview of baritone, Thomas Allen, who said, following a production of *Don Giovanni* in Japan, 'I could have walked over the housetops I was so high.' When the producer came backstage to congratulate him, Allen picked him up and carried him across the stage, 'Oh! I could have run up Mount Fuji.'

The performer in transcript 3 refers to a chronic state of severe music performance anxiety that has been building over many years and has reached such a peak that his muscles are no longer able to perform the biomechanical tasks required for performance. His emotional state is such that feelings of nervousness overtake all other emotions in the performance setting. However, he clings to the hope that 'in an ideal world' he can overcome his anxiety and fulfill his dream of becoming a professional cellist. The dilemma he currently faces is whether to give up playing the cello altogether because he cannot control his anxiety. Playing his instrument is making him very unhappy and he feels that he is no longer able to perform well because of his psychological state. This cellist has been in a state of indecision for many months, unable to choose his future path. What forces keep him oscillating between the two choices? Some psychologists refer to this state as ambivalence, a state described by Dollard and Miller (1950) as an approach–avoidance conflict. The response tendency of approach towards a goal (in this case, continuation of his professional cello career) is instigated by a combination of drives and internal motives (in this case, the desire to express oneself through musical performance) and external stimulation from the environment, such as encouragement from friends and family, and the occasional positive feedback that he still receives from some of his performances. The response tendency of avoidance is an aversive motivational state such as pain or fear or shame that acts as a danger signal to cease the approach. Our cellist has reached the stage of being so overcome by fear of performing that his muscles 'would no longer cooperate.' It is interesting that in reports of both states of flow and extreme anxiety, there is a perception or experience of some form of dissociation—the composer's 'hand seems devoid of myself' when he is in the flow state; Jung 'was struck dumb;' when overcome by anxiety, the cellist's 'muscles will no longer cooperate.'

I wonder whether the reader will be surprised to learn that the three transcripts above belong to the same musician. They represent accounts of some of his musical experiences over the course of his musical training and career, from the senior years of his Bachelor of Music degree to early international success and to a state of such crippling anxiety that he has reached the point of packing away his cello and giving up his aspirations of a career as a professional cellist. Such accounts alert us to the dynamic nature of music performance anxiety and its coexistence with experiences of peak performance. For some performers, the ratio of peak to impaired performances becomes very low and we then wonder what factors maintain a performer in an essentially aversive situation for such a long time. We will be drawing on explanations from both learning and psychodynamic theories to understand these questions.

The experience of intense music performance anxiety is not limited to early-career musicians. Very experienced musicians who have enjoyed success at the national level and many highly accomplished and successful international performers continue to experience an aversive level of performance anxiety throughout their careers, despite repeated success, critical acclaim, and objectively assessed superb performances.

The following is an account from a professional orchestral clarinettist who experienced music performance anxiety in its various forms throughout her career.

> Apart from . . . instances of situational music performance anxiety that had a debilitating impact on my control and ability to perform, I experienced . . . anxiety before most solo performances . . . Initial onset always occurred one month before a performance [and] heightened acutely 48 hours before performances, particularly solo performances. Along with my chronic music-related anxiety was . . . a mildly simmering undercurrent of cognitive unease and emotional tension throughout my personal life and performing career . . . The thought of any type of important performance (particularly solo, juried auditions) would infuse my entire waking moments with a pervasive anxiety, a sense of restlessness and unease that I could not rationalize away. I could not rest. I was not consciously aware of being in a state of anxiety as indicated by my thoughts and behavior. However, I developed an uncontrollable state of tension, contraction and spasm in the muscles of my lower face including my mouth, chin, jaw and throat . . . which I understood to be a somatic manifestation of my inner world. Through embodying my anxiety, I had taken MPA to a new level of debility that spread to non-musical areas of my life, adversely affecting my confidence in self-expression and verbal communication on a continuous daily basis for many months.
>
> (Female orchestral clarinettist, aged 45 years)

The phenomenology of performance anxiety is similar for internationally acclaimed performers, as the following examples will show. Tatiana Troyanos was one of the greatest mezzo sopranos of her time. She had a stellar career at the Metropolitan Opera for 17 years. Despite her magnificent voice, exceptional musicality, and love of her craft, she suffered extreme performance anxiety that plagued her throughout her career (Myers, 2002). In an interview with Robert Jackson in *Opera News* in 1982 (Myers, 2002), she said, 'I need tension onstage . . . the right kind, because the other kind is frightening. Certain things never go away. There are things within me that I live with and channel into exciting performances. I have this do-or-die determination, probably to overcome past difficulties, insecurities, fears.'

To what might Tatiana be referring in this statement? One possibility is that her parents, both aspiring opera singers, but incompetent in both marriage and parenting, gave her up for adoption at the age of seven or eight years (Myers, 2002), an experience that must have left her with a deep sense of betrayal, abandonment, and insecurity. She channeled both her formidable talent and deep anxieties into her performances. However, as she progressed through her career, she canceled greater numbers of concerts as she became increasingly unable or unwilling to continue to face the paralyzing anxiety that accompanied her performances. This brief biography alerts us to the role of underlying psychological vulnerabilities in the experience of performance anxiety, a theme to which we will return repeatedly in this volume.

The consequences of debilitating performance anxiety were also encapsulated by Robert Silverman, a concert pianist and Professor of Piano at The University of British Columbia:

> I am not blessed with a natural piano technique and no matter how long or hard I practiced, I could never attain the secure feeling that my fingers would work well (or even passably) at any given performance. Almost invariably, my initial 'warming-up' period during a concert was sheer torture; particularly during concerto appearances, I often felt a total disconnection between my hands and mind . . . inner tensions disable my natural coordination . . . it was a short step to the conclusion that if I could reorient my practicing toward the goal of bringing as much as possible of my knowledge of piano playing into a state of consciousness, the stage fright might be alleviated somewhat, since, for all my nervousness, I did, after all, know how to play the piano (Reubart, 1985, p. viii).

Silverman subsequently developed new practice techniques that eventually reduced his performance anxiety to tolerable levels. However, he cautioned that 'every pianist's stage fright is as unique as his fingerprints' (p. ix), a point which will already have become clear in the preceding pages. In this account, uncertainty about technical mastery appears to have played a major role in the genesis of performance anxiety.

One of the puzzles about music performance anxiety is that despite intense pre-performance distress, performance breakdowns are relatively infrequent occurrences in professional musicians. Although performers will sometimes report that their performance did not reach their subjectively prescribed standard because they felt too anxious, those listening to the performance are often not aware of any decrement in performance quality. An interesting study investigated the effects of the female hormonal cycle on the perceived voice quality of young female classical singers. Singers who reported that their voices were severely affected by their hormonal cycle completed voice recordings of specific vocal tasks on the first day of the cycle and again in mid cycle. These recordings were randomly presented to both the singers and expert vocal pedagogues to ascertain whether significant differences in vocal quality were perceptible between the two vocal samples. Singers, but not pedagogues, were able to accurately identify the timing of the recordings. Although the singers recognized the vocal strain required to produce a quality sound during menstruation, discernible differences were not detected by expert listeners (Ryan & Kenny, 2009).

However, performance breakdowns can and do occur. The Beatles are probably the most successful pop group of all time. Despite this, one of its members, George Harrison, suffered intense performance anxiety that did not abate throughout his long career. It was probably fueled to some extent by the constant comparisons with the extremely talented John Lennon and Paul McCartney, who were both prolific songwriters and excellent guitarists. In his book, *Here, There and Everywhere*, Geoff Emerick (2006), the Beatles' sound engineer, recounted a story about George trying to perform his guitar solo for his song 'Taxman'. As often happened to George when the pressure was on, he struggled for two hours to play the part. George Martin, the Beatles' producer, eventually insisted that Paul play the solo, as they could not take more studio time waiting for George to get it right. On another occasion, during one of their last live performances, for the BBC show *Our World*, which was transmitted live around the world via satellite, the Beatles played John Lennon's song, 'All You Need Is Love'.

George Harrison was reluctant to agree to a live broadcast because he was worried about making a mistake during his four-bar guitar solo. Such was his anxiety that he specifically requested that the cameras not focus on him during his solo 'either because he did not have confidence in his playing, or because he felt it was likely that he would replace the part later' (Emerick, 2006, p. 207).

Most people associate performance anxiety with physical or physiological symptoms, which are collectively called somatic anxiety; so far, our accounts have focused primarily on the somatic and behavioral consequences of music performance anxiety. However, performance anxiety has other dimensions, including a cognitive dimension, which is highlighted with great clarity in this comment from Claudio Arrau, an internationally acclaimed concert pianist, in response to a question about how he handled errors in his performances:

> I used to think it was the end of the world. It sometimes took months for me to recover. I wanted to be perfect, divine—beyond any flaw or memory mistake. But that always produces the opposite effect. Now I don't get so upset . . . You know what would happen in my very early years if something went wrong? I gave up. I kept playing but I gave up. As if the rest didn't count (Arrau in Horowitz, 1982).

There are several features in Arrau's account that are typical of people who express their anxiety cognitively. First, there is catastrophic thinking (for Arrau, one mistake meant 'the end of the world'); then post-performance rumination (he took months to recover from a performance with which he was not happy); next, unrealistic goal setting and extreme perfectionism (he wanted to be 'perfect, divine—beyond any flaw or memory mistake'); and finally, he showed an inability to take pleasure or comfort in the positive aspects of the performance (the 'rest didn't count').

Perfectionism, although not extensively studied in the performing arts, appears to be both an etiological and maintaining factor in anxious performance. One of the reasons for this is that the performing arts are exacting disciplines. There is always 'the promise of the perfect wave; the perfect performance. The possibility that just on the other side of these frightful, disorienting feelings, we might discover the most perfect version of ourselves' (Nicholson & Torrisi, 2006). Like anxiety, perfectionism can exert both a positive and negative effect on performance. Taken to extremes, it can be debilitating. For example, Barbra Streisand gave up live performance for 27 years after she forgot the words to a song in a concert in Central Park in 1967 (BBC News, 2006). She had a famous comeback in 1994 at Madison Square Garden. She told the audience she now relied on a teleprompter to make sure she does not forget the words (5 October 2006). At an ABC news interview with Diane Sawyer (22 September 2005) she said that she was now 'less afraid' after having avoided live performances for nearly three decades due to debilitating stage fright caused by forgetting the words at the 1967 concert. Streisand described the experience as:

> [s]taggering . . . I couldn't come out of it . . . It was shocking to me to forget the words. So, I didn't have any sense of humor about it . . . You know, I didn't make up words . . . [S]ome performers really do well when they forget the words. They forget the words all the

time, but they somehow have humor about it. I remember I didn't have a sense of humor about it. I was quite shocked . . . I didn't sing and charge people for 27 years because of that night . . . I was like, 'God, I don't know. What if I forget the words again?'

Streisand also reported feeling extremely hurt by bad reviews.

You know, I can't remember my good reviews. I remember negative ones. They stay in my mind. So, that says a lot about my upbringing or, you know, a feeling of self-worth when I was younger. Now, I can sort of look at it and see that's kind of funny. But, you know, it is true even today.

Sawyer asked her if her voice can still do everything she wants it to do. Streisand responded:

You know, I always think I can't do it. If I try to sing it . . . the beginning of a record, let's say . . . 'Ooh, my God!' . . . And then as I sing, it just sort of opens up, and I thank God for this gift that I have. Because I'm surprised myself.

You will have noticed that both Troyanos and Streisand understood that psychological vulnerabilities from their early lives had a role to play in their anxious response to performance, despite their prodigious talent and palpable success. Streisand sees the link as 'kind of funny'—probably an oblique reference to the discrepancy between her feelings of low self-worth on the one hand and her unparalleled success on the other, but acknowledges that 'it is true, even today.' She remains afraid that she can't do it, despite incontrovertible objective evidence to the contrary. Neither Streisand nor Arrau could take comfort in the positive; Arrau dismissed his entire performance if he made one error; Streisand cannot hold positive reviews in mind but remembers all her negative reviews. Our orchestral clarinetist not only held her anxiety in mind, she embodied it; it had become so much a part of her that she no longer had any conscious awareness of feeling anxious, a point to which we shall return later in this book. She, like Troyanos and Streisand, recognized that her anxiety mirrored her 'inner world,' and that although it manifested its worst consequences during music performance, it 'spread to non-musical areas of my life, adversely affecting my confidence in self-expression and verbal communication on a continuous daily basis.'

Personal vulnerabilities can have a devastating effect, not only on the capacity to perform, but on the global quality of life of the performer. Cat Power, an indie rock singer, canceled her US tour in 2006 because of anxiety. She routinely hides her face in her hair, performs covers rather than original songs for fear no one really wants to hear her work, and sings with her back to the audience. One of her fans wrote: 'She is so painful to watch, I wonder why she bothers playing live.' Cat gives some clues as to the source of her anxiety:

People who drink habitually don't realize they're doing it, because it was part of their upbringing. Everybody from my immediate family to my grandparents to my great-grandparents—there were always severe alcoholic and psychological problems. If your parents gave you fire to play with when you were two, you'd be standing in fire by the time you were an adult. [Before my most recent hospital stay] I was drinking from the time I woke up in the morning until the time I went to bed. When something bad happens, you go to the bar and turn off your emotions. I never realized that I'd gotten to the point of such depression. So that's why I can't drink anymore. I need to be able to face things.

(Chan Marshall, aka Cat Power)[2]

From these accounts of subjective performance experiences and performance anxiety, we have already gained some insights into the latter's complex nature. What theory or theories can account for such differences in the performance experiences of musicians? It is clear that the construct of music performance anxiety is multidimensional and multi-causal. For our young cellist, a very painful and embarrassing musical performance experience appeared to have played a major role in the development of his anxiety. However, as we shall later see, such reactions occur in those who are already psychologically vulnerable; for Tatiana, serious underlying psychological vulnerabilities that she attempted to sublimate in her performances gradually overwhelmed her to the point that she became increasingly unable to perform; and for Robert Silverman, concern about his technique created significant somatically expressed anxiety (i.e. 'a total disconnection between my hands and mind') such that pre-performance warm-up routines were 'sheer torture.' Both he and Streisand returned to performance and achieved some degree of mastery over their anxiety—Silverman through practice techniques and routines, and Streisand through the use of physical supports (teleprompter).

We now begin the difficult task of providing plausible theoretical scaffolding around these experiences such that they may eventually inform a more inclusive theory of the etiology of music performance anxiety, its different phenotypes, treatment, and ultimately prevention. By carefully attending to the descriptions of performance experiences of performers themselves, and through the judicious application of psychological theory, I hope in this book to elucidate the nature and causes of, and hopefully treatments for, this complex and often career-destroying phenomenon.

Summary

In this chapter, the phenomenology (i.e. lived experience) of music performance anxiety in all its manifestations—somatic, cognitive, and behavioral—as experienced in classical, jazz, and popular musicians, both instrumentalists and vocalists, was presented. We discovered that music performance anxiety is no respecter of musical genre, age, gender, years of experience, or level of technical mastery of one's art. We compared the experiences of performers who find performance exhilarating with those whose anxiety deprives them of joy in performing and started to explore some of the differences in their respective behavior, perception, and focus that maintain or exacerbate their anxiety. We also speculated about the presence and nature of personal vulnerabilities in very anxious musicians that are expressed, not just in their musical performances, but which pervade their lives. Tatiana Troyanos, Maria Callas and Barbra Streisand are examples of consummate artists who were affected in both their performing and private lives by psychological vulnerability. We discussed the role of aversive performance experiences in triggering what for some musicians becomes a

---

[2] http://www.spinmag.com/articles/spin-interview-cat-power.

lifelong fear of performing. The role of perfectionism in causing and maintaining anxiety in performance was introduced. Finally, we learnt that anxious musicians can experience exhilaration in some of their performances—an experience described as 'flow'—and that it is for such experiences that anxious musicians remain in the field of music performance. We concluded the chapter with an understanding that the construct of music performance anxiety is multidimensional and multi-causal and that we must go in search of theories to explain this complex phenomenon and its different phenotypes in order to inform treatment and eventually to contribute to its prevention, at least at extreme levels, because some anxiety (arousal) is needed to render an exciting performance.

Chapter 2

Conceptual framework

[I]n every occasion of living an individual is different from what he was before or what he will be after the occasion

Hadley Cantril, 1956, p. 5.

A wide range of disciplines in the sciences (biology, physiology), humanities (literature, history, philosophy), and social sciences (anthropology, sociology, and psychology) have made unique contributions to our understanding of human behavior. In this book, I will be drawing on different perspectives in order to explain the many facets of music performance anxiety that have emerged in the empirical and clinical literature. No one theory appears able to account for all the observed phenomena and the field is too young to attempt a synthesis. I will therefore rely on the phenomenology of music performance anxiety, examples of which were presented in the opening paragraphs of the book, and details of which are further discussed in Chapters Eight and Nine, to identify commonalities and differences in the experiences of those who suffer from this condition, and to identify some unifying guiding principles that may enhance our understanding—hopefully resulting in the development of effective treatments.

Although I will draw on the dominant paradigms in psychology and psychiatry throughout this book, I do so with caution because of the inherent limitations in their methods and theorizing about our subjective experiences and psychological states. For example, the prevailing emphasis on diagnostic categories for psychological conditions has both advantages and disadvantages, and these will be covered in more detail in our discussion of the diagnostic classification systems currently in use, and how music performance anxiety may usefully be classified within this system. Most people would agree that it is essential to correctly differentiate psychoses from other psychological disorders. Since the major form of treatment for the various psychotic illnesses is pharmacotherapy and since different drugs produce differential effects on different conditions, few would argue that careful diagnosis should precede prescription of medication. However, for other psychological ills, the argument with respect to the use of a classificatory system is not so clear, and this is reflected in recent developments to achieve a synthesis in psychological therapies for a range of emotional disorders (Barlow, 2008a). Before we embark on a detailed discussion of this issue, we will review some of the philosophies and methods underpinning psychology that have influenced theory and therapy, in order to explicate the concepts and models on which I rely in this book to further our understanding of music performance anxiety.

Philosophy, psychology, and psychological perspectives

The disciplines of psychiatry and psychology were founded on Cartesian dualism (i.e. the belief that mental phenomena are non-physical), which has formed the basis of our attempts to understand the nature of our world and how we function in it. It has permeated the concepts, both implicit and explicit, and methods of study in the discipline, and hence needs explication. Cantril (1956) expressed concern that the young discipline of psychology had been 'saddled with René Descartes' conception of the nature of man in terms of a mechanistic determinism' (p. 4) in which the world is divided into two basic substances: *res cogitans* (minds, thoughts) and *res extensa* (bodies, the material world) (Descartes, 1989; Stolorow, 2006). In his opening lecture in the Benjamin Franklin Lectures for 1953, Hadley Cantril (1956) made this remark:

> As a psychologist accepts the challenge of beginning discussions on 'A Portrait of Western Man' and reviews the accumulated data of his discipline, he must in all honesty confess at the outset that in the brief history of his science the subject of man as a living, striving, anxious, hopeful, curious, valuing, prayerful organism has been somewhat neglected (p. 3).

Modern psychology is replete with Cartesian dualities: mind–body; mind–brain; cognition–affect; reason–desire; subject–object; internal–external. These dualities have polarized psychology, in both its concepts and methods, despite early warnings that 'Stimulus-response psychology and conditioning theory cannot get along without Freud's internal mental world' (Mahl, 1968, p. x). For example, we have relied on a nomothetic (the study of groups or populations) as opposed to an idiographic (in which the focus is on the study of the individual) method (Molenaar & Campbell, 2009); a categorical as opposed to dimensional understanding of human characteristics (Barlow & Nock, 2009); and a spatial as opposed to a temporal conceptualization of the self (Mitchell, 1993). Dissenting, but often unheeded, voices have called for an examination of the philosophical underpinnings of the discipline of psychology. For example, Gordon Allport (1955) addressed the need for an idiographic approach to understanding human behavior:

> Individuality . . . is a legitimate object of curiosity . . . [A]ll of the animals in the world are psychologically less distinct from one another than one man is from other men . . . [W]hen we are interested in guiding or predicting John's behavior, or in understanding the Johnian quality of John, we need to transcend the limitations of a psychology of species, and develop a more adequate psychology of personal growth.

The struggle to understand the 'Johnian quality of John' has major implications for understanding the anxious quality of anxiety for different individuals and, by extension, the quality of music performance anxiety in individual musicians, who, as we saw in the opening pages, may have very different subjective experiences of this phenomenon.

More than fifty years later, we see the same call for an idiographic, temporal, and dimensional approach to the study of a psychology of personal growth. Compare how closely these two statements align with those of their predecessors and with each other, given that they derive from authors working in very different ways with human beings, the first as research psychologists and the second as an interpersonal psychoanalyst. Molenaar and Campbell (2009) concluded that:

> It is helpful to conceive of a human being as an integrated dynamic system of behavioral, emotional, cognitive, and other psychological processes evolving over time and place (p.112) . . . Psychological processes like cognitive information processing, perception, emotion, and motor behavior occur in real time at the level of individual persons. Because they are person-specific . . . their analysis should be based on intraindividual variation (p.116).

Similarly, Mitchell conceived of the 'self' not as a spatial construct that resides in the mind, 'a place where things happen' (p. 101), but as:

> recurring patterns of experience and behavior . . . [S]elf refers to the subjective organization of meanings one creates as one moves through time, doing things, such as having ideas and feelings, including some self-reflective ideas and feelings about oneself . . . [S]elves change and are transformed continually over time; no version of self is fully present at any instant, and a single life is composed of many selves (pp. 101–2).

Recall the three excerpts from the cellist in Chapter One, in which he described his very different performance experiences and experiences of self as a performer over time. Without a temporal perspective, one gains a very incomplete picture of the 'subjective organizations of meanings' that occur in 'every occasion of living.'

The more recent disciplines of cognitive neuroscience and neurobiology have provided evidence for the inseparability of mind and body, for which Freud (1962) had an intuitive understanding: 'the ego is first and foremost a bodily ego' (p. 20). Research from these disciplines asserts that feelings represent a person's interpretation of their bodily states, and that reason, to be truly rational, requires awareness and understanding of the emotional signals that derive from bodily states. In *Descartes' Error*, Damasio (1994) asserts that we can no longer think about ourselves as either disembodied minds or mindless bodies. Rather, we are embodied minds: 'the brain is the body's captive audience' (p. 158).

Developing this understanding further, Stolorow (2006) argued that attempts to dichotomize human experience as subjective (internal) or objective (external), or intrapsychic or interpersonal are misguided and constrain genuine understanding of experience. For example, he argued that the initial danger situation that signals anxiety—helplessness in the face of overwhelming affect—is an internal experience. When the infant learns that an external object (such as a parent or other caregiver) can alleviate his distress, the danger situation becomes one of fear of the loss of the love object or fear of the loss of love from the love object, which are interpersonal experiences. When the love object is internalized (that is, a mental representation of the caregiver is developed 'in mind' as either a nurturing or punishing object), the experience once again becomes internal. Mitchell (1993), a relational psychoanalyst, similarly argues that all personal motives have a long relational history:

> The very capacity to have experiences necessarily develops in and requires an interpersonal matrix . . . [T]here is no experience that is not interpersonally mediated. The meanings generated by the self are all interactive products (p. 125) . . . If the self is always

embedded in relational contexts, either actual or internal, then all important motives have appeared and taken on life and form in the presence and through the reactions of significant others (p. 134).

Philosophers like Heidegger (1962; original work published 1927) also challenged the Cartesian position by arguing that humans are engaged and contextually embedded. According to Heidegger, we are all 'beings-in-the-world,' part of an indissoluble system of mutual influence. Freud's concept of anxiety as a signal for a danger situation thus becomes a being-in-danger, in which the person's experience of endangerment is understood as part of the larger person–world system. Freud (1926) conceptualized anxiety as both an affective signal for danger and the motivation for psychologically defending against the (perceived) danger. Freud proposed four basic danger situations: the loss of a significant other; the loss of love; the loss of body integrity; and the loss of affirmation by one's own conscience (moral anxiety). When an individual senses one of these danger situations, motivation for defending against the anxiety is triggered. Freud also distinguished between traumatic (primary) anxiety, which he defined as a state of psychological helplessness in the face of overwhelmingly painful affect, such as fear of abandonment or attack, and signal (secondary) anxiety, which is a form of anticipatory anxiety that alerts us to the danger of re-experiencing the original traumatic state by repeating it in a weakened form such that measures to protect against re-traumatization can be taken.

In the case of musicians with performance anxiety, the danger signal relates both to early danger experiences, such as pressure and/or failure to perform well (and perhaps not just in the musical performance setting) under conditions of evaluative threat, which are internalized, and current experiences of performance and performance anxiety, which are interpersonal and occur between the performer and the audience, but which are understood and interpreted within the framework of the earlier, internalized anxiety experiences. By simultaneously attending to both sets of danger experiences—the internalized past and the interpersonal present—sense can be made of the performer's current experiences of endangerment in the performance setting.

Definitions of anxiety and their contribution to definitions of music performance anxiety

[T]he problem of anxiety is a nodal point at which the most various and important questions converge, a riddle whose solution would be bound to throw a flood of light on our whole mental existence (Freud, 1916–1917/1973, p. 393).

Singers and wind players may find it interesting that the derivation of the word 'anxious' comes from words meaning 'pressing tight,' 'strangling,' and 'constriction,' and unlike our modern use of the term 'anxiety,' it originally denoted disquiet and sadness (Marks, 1987). The sensation of strangling associates anxiety with the throat and the source of vocal function. Sadness is associated with poor posture, consequent poor breathing habits (Bartley & Clifton-Smith, 2006), and hence impeded performance, to which the breathless, choking voices of terrified actors or singers, or the weak, breathy tone of anxious wind players attest.

Anxiety occupies a central place in most psychological disorders, including music performance anxiety. Indeed, the anxiety disorders are the most frequently diagnosed psychological conditions in both adults (Antony & Stein, 2009; Antony & Swinson, 2000c; Flint, 1994) and children (Antony & Stein, 2009). Almost every discipline in the humanities and social sciences has discussed the nature of anxiety and its causes and many have attempted to distinguish it from its close conceptual neighbors, stress, activation, arousal, worry, and fear. Because it is the central concept in this book, we need to agree on its definition, characteristics, and functions. Failure to do so has hindered the development of the field of study in music performance anxiety and needs an urgent remedy. In his seminal review of the state of the art in music performance anxiety research, Brodsky (1996) stated:

> as the constructs of anxiety, stress and tension . . . lack a standardized definition, these have often been subject to assessment by each experimenter's personal definition . . . with no conformity among the medical professional or research community concerning diagnostic criteria . . . [P]erforming arts medicine does not seem to be closer today (than ten years ago) regarding the nomenclature of these symptoms, how to measure the degree of severity of symptomatology or how to evaluate the incidence of MPA (pp. 89–90).

Anxiety: biological and environmental interactions

Biological basis of anxiety

In *On the Origin of Species by Means of Natural Selection* (Darwin, 1859) and *The Expressions of the Emotions in Man and Animals* (Darwin, 1872), Charles Darwin questioned whether anxiety was innate or learned. Darwin had more than a scientific interest in the subject; he himself suffered the anguish of panic attacks with agoraphobia. Darwin has in his history a profound psychological vulnerability that, like Tatiana Troyanos, may have contributed to the development of his anxiety disorder. His mother died when he was eight years old and he was subsequently sent to boarding school, two events that are likely to have produced severe anxiety in which the loss of his mother was compounded by his removal from his family and his familiar environment.

Cannon (1929) codified Darwin's observations that humans and animals responded to potentially dangerous or life-threatening situations with a stereotypical set of physiological responses that became known as the general adaptation syndrome or the 'fight–flight–fright (freeze)' response. This ancient alarm system clearly has survival value. When an alarm response is triggered, the cooperative relationship between the sympathetic and parasympathetic divisions of the autonomic nervous system is disrupted and the homeostatic balance of the organism is disturbed. The sympathetic branch of the autonomic nervous system prepares the body for 'flight-or-fight' activity, which includes acceleration of heart rate and respiration (in extreme cases, hyperventilation), slowing of digestion, dilation of blood vessels in the muscles in readiness for action, constriction of blood vessels in other parts of the body, pupil dilation, loss of peripheral vision, and auditory exclusion. In combination, this alarm system mobilizes the organism for fighting or escaping (flight) the danger (Gleitman, Fridlund, & Reisber, 2004).

The third arm of this alarm system, which is controlled by the parasympathetic division of the autonomic nervous system, produces tonic immobility, a set of responses described as 'freezing' or 'playing dead.' When this pattern of behavior occurs during a performance, it is described as 'stage fright' (Coyle, 2006), a topic to which we will return later. In some situations, in some people, sympathetic and parasympathetic alarm responses may become activated together, resulting in the anxious performer experiencing a mixture of symptoms, some stemming from sympathetic and some from parasympathetic activation (Mornell, 2002). These physiological changes can have cognitive consequences for the performer. For example, changes in blood circulation and chemicals transported in the blood may cause confused thinking, loss of concentration, memory lapses, and feelings of agitation and unreality (Bartley & Clifton-Smith, 2006), as described by some of the performers in the opening paragraphs of Chapter One, and as you shall see in more detail in Chapter Six.

Although there is a degree of automaticity in these types of responses, animals respond to threat in complex ways. Some animals will flee unless cornered, others will stand perfectly still or change color to protect themselves from imminent danger. A threat from another animal does not always result in immediate fight or flight. During a period of heightened awareness prior to fight or flight, both people and animals interpret behavioral signals from the potential threat, and may respond with indifference or play as well as fight, flight, or fright (Foa & Kozak, 1986b). According to Foa and Kozak (1986b), animal fear originates in a predatory defense system but the social fears of humans originate in a dominance/submissiveness system. Submissiveness could perhaps be construed as a way of 'playing dead' socially with a threatening person, particularly when the feared person can also deliver aversive consequences. In this two-tier system, people may respond to external threats by using a primitive predatory defense system, but the process whereby people learn to become submissive or socially anxious has until recently been thought to be learnt. However, more recent evidence shows that social engagement behaviors also have a neurobiological basis (Porges, 2001).

Historically, the autonomic system was conceptualized as two opposing but balanced processes: the sympathetic and the parasympathetic nervous systems. To recapitulate, the sympathetic system, associated with the fight-or-flight response, is activated by the perception of threat and acts to raise heart rate and metabolism, and shift energy to the brain and muscles. The parasympathetic system is associated with ordinary functioning, when one is calm and not experiencing threat or danger. A more recent theory, called the polyvagal theory (Porges, 2001; 2007) explains the reactions of the autonomic nervous system in safe and unsafe situations, including social situations. According to this theory, during evolution an increasingly complex neural system developed in order to regulate the different neurobehavioral states needed to deal with environmental challenges, from survival on the one hand to positive social-emotional engagement on the other. The physiological states underlying all survival-related behaviors are associated with specific neural regulation pathways or circuits. Porges showed that the autonomic nervous system is not a system in balance, but a hierarchy composed of three neural circuits that have evolved over time, each with its own behavioral strategy that can override the other two. Under increasing levels of threat, people move to the circuits that have an older evolutionary history.

Social behavior and communication are mediated by one of the two branches of the vagus nerve responsible for innervating the parasympathetic nervous system. In mammals, the vagal system is split into two systems, called the dorsal and ventral systems. The dorsal vagal system is part of the neural substrate for the 'freeze' response, described above. The ventral system is connected to facial, vocal, and neck muscles, and forms part of the social engagement system, a newer threat response system that is only present in (social) mammals.

The three circuits and their associated behavioral strategies described in the polyvagal theory are:

1 *Freeze response.* This response is controlled by the older part of the vagus nerve system (the dorsal system of the parasympathetic system), which is responsible for regulating the heart (blood pressure) and the smooth muscles responsible for digestion (stomach) and breathing (lungs, diaphragm). This system responds to threat by fostering immobilization by depressing heart rate and metabolic activity such that the organism 'plays dead.'

2 *Flight or fight.* This response depends on the functioning of the sympathetic nervous system which increases metabolic output and inhibits the dorsal vagus system to foster mobilization of the organism to face the threat.

3 *Communication (social engagement).* The third circuit is controlled by the newer part of the vagus nerve system (the ventral system of the parasympathetic system). It regulates the somatic muscles of speech and eating—larynx, pharynx, and esophagus—and processes associated with attention, motion, emotion, and communication. It also regulates the heart and the bronchi to promote calm and self-soothing states; but it can also rapidly regulate cardiac output to respond to environmental contingencies and is associated with cranial nerves that regulate sociability via facial expression and vocalization, necessary for functioning in a social environment. The social engagement system is closely related to stress reactivity through its neurophysiological connections with the hypothalamic-pituitary-adrenal (HPA) axis (the neuroendocrine system that controls stress reactions and constitutes the common pathways that mediate the general adaptation syndrome (GAS) (Gaab, Sonderegger, Scherrer, & Ehlert, 2006; Selye, 1955).

The polyvagal theory provides the basis for a relatively new psychological theory called intensive short-term dynamic psychotherapy that may have promise in the treatment of performance anxiety, although it has not specifically been evaluated for this condition. It will be described more fully in Chapter Seven.

There is one other feature of anxiety that requires comment. Is anxiety contagious? How do groups of animals or humans respond to a common threat, such as a fire, a flood, or the events of 9/11? Using an animal model of a natural predator-and-prey relationship between the barn owl and the vole, Eilam and Izhara (2010) tested the communal group response to a common threat. The results showed that while individuals respond to an apparently equal danger with varying degrees of anxiety, when a group is placed under a common threat, the group members display the same level of anxiety, appearing to adopt an acceptable code of conduct, in this case, an acceptable level of anxiety, that overrides individuals' natural tendencies to experience high, moderate or low anxiety. When the group comprised all females or all males, each group showed similar levels of heightened anxiety when exposed to the threat. However, if the group contained both males and females, only the females showed heightened anxiety, while the males remained relatively calm. The researchers explained this effect in evolutionary terms: males must protect the nest and to do that they must remain calm. This study has two interesting implications for orchestral musicians. First, orchestral musicians comprise a mixed male and female group exposed to a common threat, such as a difficult or incompetent conductor. Second, it has been my experience in talking and working with professional musicians that they are reluctant to talk with each other about their emotional difficulties in general and performance anxiety in particular. When I ask them why they feel unable to talk with each other, they say that there is an underlying fear that performance anxiety is contagious among performers. If someone talks to a colleague in the orchestra about their anxiety, both the speaker and listener fear that the anxiety will be transferred from one to the other, and further, that the anxiety will increase. It would be interesting to explore the group anxiety levels of musicians in orchestras to ascertain whether they respond in the same way as a community of voles, and to test their belief that performance anxiety is contagious among orchestral musicians.

Environmental origins of anxiety

According to learning theorists, anxiety is a conditioned response, that is, a learnt form of fear. In this model, fear is defined as a primary aversive drive, called an unconditioned stimulus. The word 'unconditioned' denotes that one does not have to learn how to be afraid—it occurs spontaneously in a fear-arousing situation. Mowrer (1939) described the theory thus: 'anxiety is a learned response, occurring to signals (conditioned stimuli) that are premonitory of (i.e. have in the past been followed by) situations of injury or pain (unconditioned stimuli)' (p. 565). Anxiety was thought to be 'conditioned' (i.e. learnt) in three ways: through classical conditioning, operant conditioning, or observational learning. These methods are reviewed in Chapter Six. The original theory, called the classical theory of fear acquisition, has subsequently undergone major revisions to incorporate the role of cognitions in fear conditioning and is now called the neo-conditioning model (Rachman, 1991). These changes will be discussed in more detail in Chapter Three. Although at first the conceptualizations of anxiety offered by the psychodynamic and learning theory schools appear quite different, they do have some fundamental commonalities that may be usefully employed in developing effective treatments for musicians with performance anxiety.

The commonly accepted current definition of anxiety is expressed in the following:

> Anxiety is a unique and coherent cognitive-affective structure within our defensive motivational system. At the heart of this structure is a sense of uncontrollability focused on future threats, danger, or other potentially negative events . . . Accompanying this negative affective state is a strong physiological or somatic component that may reflect activation of distinct brain circuits such as the corticotrophin releasing factor system (Barlow, 2000, p. 1249).

The similarity between Freud's definition of anxiety and that proposed by Barlow is striking. Each refers to anxiety as both an affect (emotion) and a defensive-motivational system whose function is to protect against what Freud called helplessness in the face of overwhelmingly painful affect and what Barlow describes as a sense of uncontrollability about possible future threats. Freud and Barlow offer possible clues to the experience of anxiety in music performance: it may be a defense against experiencing or re-experiencing overwhelmingly painful affect or a fear of the possibility of facing an intolerable future threat. The future threat may be the fear of an impaired performance and/or the fear of experiencing painful affect, such as shame or humiliation following an impaired performance. It is the time frame that differs in the two definitions: Freud refers to previous experience and Barlow to anticipated experience. However, to be afraid of a possible future experience, one would need to have had a previous experience on which to base this future-oriented fear. Hence, the experience of anxiety is simultaneously internal and intrapsychic, external and interpersonal, and past and future oriented. Psychoanalytic theorists would argue that the emotions aroused by previous internalized experiences are projected into current and future experiences, thus setting up a situation in which the earlier traumatizing experiences are repeated in each subsequent performance even when the original traumatizing factors of the original experiences may no longer be present (Malan, 1979). We will return to this in our discussion of possible etiologies in music performance anxiety in Chapter Six.

Recent research suggests that anxiety may not be a unitary phenomenon; there may be distinctive dimensions within the concept of anxiety along which anxious people differ. These include anxious apprehension and anxiety sensitivity. A distinction is also made between trait (general anxiety proneness) and state (situational) anxiety.

Anxious apprehension

Anxiety is the apprehension cued . . . by a threat to some value that the individual holds essential to his existence as a personality . . . [I]ts special characteristics . . . are the feelings of uncertainty and helplessness in the face of the danger. The nature of anxiety can be understood when we ask what is threatened in the experience which produces the anxiety (May, 1977, p. 180).

The identification by Rollo May that apprehension is the key element in anxiety has been widely accepted in subsequent scholarship on anxiety, including the definition provided by Barlow earlier. Anxious apprehension is today defined as a future-oriented mood state that is accompanied by a feeling of helplessness and a shift in the focus of attention to oneself, in which a negative affective state and negative cognitions about one's inability to cope are prominent. Physiological arousal, in the form of generalized autonomic reactivity and hyper vigilance prepares the person to deal with the (perceived) threat (Barlow, 2002a). Negative self-evaluative focus and disruption of attention to the task may result in performance impairment, which in turn increases arousal and accompanying negative affective and cognitive states. Even when performance is not impaired, the performer experiences the performance situation as aversive, as it triggers a negative affective state that feels uncontrollable.

Anxious apprehension is both an emotional and a cognitive process. Highly anxious people engage in a number of related cognitive activities such as hyper vigilance for threat-related stimuli (Eysenck, 1991), reduced cue utilization with narrowing of attention to mood-congruent cues (Easterbrook, 1959), attentional bias to threat-relevant stimuli and self-evaluative concerns (Puliafico & Kendall, 2006), (implicit) memory bias (i.e. showing better memory and more neural activity for words describing threatening bodily sensations) (Pauli *et al.*, 1997), and interpretive bias (i.e. anxious people are more likely to interpret ambiguous material as threatening) (Foa & Kozak, 1986a).

Anxiety sensitivity

The concept of anxiety sensitivity arose as part of expectancy theory, which proposes that a number of basic fears combine to determine an individual's overall level of anxiety in anticipation of a stressful event. These include: (i) fear of negative social evaluation (embarrassment); (ii) fear of injury, pain, or death (danger); (iii) fear of loss of mental, emotional, or physical capacities (loss of control) and (iv) fear of anxiety symptoms themselves (anxiety sensitivity) (Moore, Chung, Peterson, Katzman, & Vermani, 2009). Anxiety sensitivity is the fear of arousal-related sensations that arise from beliefs (catastrophic thinking) that the sensations themselves are dangerous or harmful (Stephenson & Quarrier, 2005; Taylor, Jang, Stewart, & Stein, 2008). Moore *et al.* (2009) have shown that anxiety sensitivity and event expectancy (i.e. the likelihood that a particular event will occur) combine in an additive fashion to determine the amount of anxiety that one will experience in a social situation.

Trait anxiety and anxiety sensitivity are different constructs, the former predicting a general proneness to respond anxiously to threatening stimuli, with the latter predicting proneness that is specific to the experience of the symptoms of anxiety (not the anxiety-producing stimuli per se) (Reiss, Peterson, Gurskya, & McNally, 1986). These symptoms include the fear of physical sensations, fear of mental events, and fear of publicly observable symptoms. In trait anxiety, the feared stimulus is regarded as dangerous; in anxiety sensitivity, it is the anxiety reactions themselves that are feared. Stephenson and Quarrier (2005) assessed the prevalence of anxiety sensitivity in 67 tertiary students, together with their levels of state and trait anxiety as predictors of performance anxiety. Anxiety sensitivity was found to be a more important predictor of performance anxiety than trait anxiety.

The anxiety-sensitivity dimension of anxiety may account for individual differences in the degree to which people respond fearfully to events and to their risk of developing an anxiety disorder, because it amplifies the anxiety-producing properties of stimuli (Taylor, 1999). Three related dimensions of anxiety sensitivity have been identified: physical, cognitive, and social concerns. People with physical concerns believe that sensations such as breathlessness will lead to physical collapse; those with cognitive concerns believe that difficulties in concentrating or rumination will lead to mental incapacitation; and those with social concerns believe that observable indicators of social anxiety such as blushing or trembling will result in social rejection. Recent research with twins has found that anxiety sensitivity is heritable in women but not men and that severe anxiety sensitivity is more strongly associated with genetic factors.

For women, a combination of genetic and environmental factors influenced all three dimensions of anxiety sensitivity, but for men, only environmental influences were identified (Taylor *et al.*, 2008). However, environmental factors are important in etiology, particularly early learning experiences related to sex-role socialization. Women score highest on physical concerns compared with cognitive or social concerns while men showed the opposite pattern: they had higher scores on cognitive and social concerns and lower scores on physical concerns. On the total score for anxiety sensitivity, using the Anxiety Sensitivity Index (Peterson & Reiss, 1992), women consistently score higher than men (Stewart, Taylor, & Baker, 1997). The findings with respect to gender differences in anxiety sensitivity and its heritability in women but not men may account for the fact that more women suffer from anxiety disorders than men. Assessments of anxiety sensitivity during childhood (between 7 and 14 years), using the Child Anxiety Sensitivity Index (CASI) (Silverman, Fleisig, Rabian, & Peterson, 1991) were found to predict the development of panic disorder at 16–30 years. Children with high anxiety sensitivity appear to have reactions similar to those of high anxiety-sensitive adults. Children high in anxiety sensitivity worry about bodily manifestations of anxiety and their possible associations with illness, embarrassment, or loss of control (Vasey & Dadds, 2001). Similarly, Hayward *et al.* (2000) found that anxiety sensitivity is a specific predictor of panic attacks in adolescents.

Recent work has identified a relationship between aspects of perfectionism and heightened anxiety sensitivity, particularly those aspects of perfectionism associated with self-presentation. Further, interpersonal perfectionism was hypothesized to be related to both fear of negative social evaluation and panic attacks (Flett, Greene, & Hewitt, 2004). This will be taken up again in the section on perfectionism.

State and trait anxiety

Since the 1960s, anxiety has been understood as a two-factor structure, consisting of state and trait components. Spielberger (1972) defines trait anxiety as 'relatively stable individual differences in . . . the disposition to perceive a wide range of stimulus situations as dangerous or threatening' (p. 39). State anxiety is understood to be a transitory emotional state characterized by heightened tension and apprehension, while trait anxiety refers to relatively stable individual differences in anxiety proneness; that is, in differences between people in their tendency to respond to situations perceived as threatening with elevations in anxiety-state intensity. State anxiety more closely resembles fear, while trait anxiety refers to the propensity of the individual to feel chronically worried or apprehensive. It may be a concept interchangeable with stress, although stress can involve both state and trait anxiety, depending on whether the stressor is acute or chronic. Individuals with high trait anxiety perform worse than those low in trait anxiety in circumstances that involve evaluation of performance and/or the threat of failure (Deffenbacher, 1986; Spence & Spence, 1966); but more of that later. Situations become stressors for people only if they are construed as threatening or unmanageable. The cognitive appraisal of the situation is the critical element in defining an event or situation as stressful, except in circumstances that would be experienced as stressful by almost everybody, such as natural disasters and war (Eysenck, 1997).

Stress, arousal, activation, fear, and anxiety

Terms such as stress, anxiety, arousal, activation, and fear tend to be used interchangeably. Anxiety/stress is universal, and appears in both common and unique forms in most cultures around the world. It is a somewhat paradoxical construct. It is simultaneously rational and irrational, normal and abnormal, induced by everyday hassles and major life crises. It can be uplifting or devastating in its effects. Stress appears to have supplanted the term 'anxiety' in everyday usage. However, it is best to assign to each concept a precise definition.

Stress

Stress serves a somewhat paradoxical function for humans, since it is both necessary for survival and strongly associated with susceptibility to disease, and with disease severity and prognosis (Auerbach & Gramling, 1998). Hans Selye (1907–1982) is commonly credited with introducing stress as a field of study. He identified two types of stress: distress, the experience of unpleasant or excessive demands or negative emotions arising from these; and eustress (literally 'good stress') such as excitement, anticipation, and passion (Selye, 1955).

The term 'stress' remains poorly defined in the literature, particularly the performance anxiety literature where the terms 'stress,' 'anxiety,' and 'fear' are used interchangeably (Templeton, 2003). Even in mainstream psychology and health psychology journals, the word 'stress' sometimes refers to a stimulus (i.e. an event that causes discomfort), a response to that stimulus, or the physiological consequences of the response to the stimulus (Kemeny, 2003). The term is also used to describe an objective, quantifiable, environmental demand, more accurately labeled a 'stressor,' and as a subjective cognitive appraisal of environmental conditions. Stress is more properly defined as an environmental demand that requires a coping response. Arousal signals that the person is feeling stressed (either positively or negatively), and anxiety is the emotional reaction evoked in an individual in response to a stressful situation that is perceived as threatening or contains demands that are perceived to be excessive or unachievable (Gaudry & Spielberger, 1971).

The underlying assumption in stress research is that there tends to be a universal response to all stressors. Cannon labeled this the flight-or-fight response (discussed earlier), which is triggered by the release of a neurotransmitter called noradrenaline by the sympathetic arm of the autonomic nervous system under conditions of immediate threat, which results in an 'adrenaline rush.' This unified response to stress was called the generality model of stress. More recent research has resulted in a revision of early conceptualizations of stress and the stress response. It shows that organisms can respond with highly idiosyncratic emotional and physiological responses to specific stress conditions. This is called the specificity model of stress (Kemeny, 2003). In the case of acute psychological stressors, such as performance anxiety, a different biological system is activated—the hypothalamic–pituitary–adrenal axis—whose stimulation by perceived stress can result in the release of the stress hormone, cortisol, into the blood, saliva, and urine. This process is slower acting than the autonomic nervous system, and occurs over minutes rather than seconds. Interestingly, the peak cortisol response occurs 20 to 40 minutes prior to the perceived stressful event and returns to baseline levels between 40 and 60 minutes after the stress has abated (e.g. when the performance has ended) (Kemeny, 2003). However, for some musicians, their response to the performance setting resembles that more commonly identified with responses associated with an immediate threat to survival, and it is these musicians who report the most severe forms of music performance anxiety.

Exposure to stress may have some beneficial effects on functioning and performance, provided that the stress exposure is not so demanding of resources as to leave the performer depleted or assured of failure each time they experience that particular stress. Experiencing success under stress enables the learning of important coping and problem-solving skills. This in turn enhances self-efficacy, our belief that we are able to succeed at particular challenges, which in turn leads to persistence in coping with future stressors. Stress may motivate us to achieve and it may fuel creativity (Dienstbier, 1989).

Arousal/activation

It is important to distinguish physiological arousal from somatic anxiety. Physiological arousal refers to the intensity of behavior that varies on a continuum from deep sleep to intense excitement or fear. Synonymous terms for arousal include 'activation' (Champion, 1969) and 'alertness' (Cox, 2007). Arousal is initially non-directional and may denote either a positive or negative experience. Changes in arousal levels are reflected in changes in functions governed by the autonomic nervous system, such as changes in heart rate, blood pressure, respiration, sweating, muscle tension, digestion, urination, body temperature, and other body functions that to some extent are involuntary, and by the hypothalamic–pituitary–adrenal axis, in the case of psychological stressors. The arousal response is initiated by any sensory stimulation from the environment and/or from the cerebral cortex (Cox, 2007). If arousal is associated with a positive affective quality, the person will report a feeling of excitement or anticipation; if arousal occurs as a result of some perceived threat in the environment, the person will experience somatic anxiety. Physiologically there may be a high degree of overlap between these conditions (Mornell, 2002). With training, some degree of conscious control of autonomic nervous system function is possible (Bartley & Clifton-Smith, 2006; Cox, 2007).

Fear

While it is difficult to disentangle the terms 'stress' and 'anxiety,' the term 'fear' is much clearer in its usage. With few exceptions (e.g. Borkovec, 1976; Wolpe, 1958), most writers on the subject make a clear distinction between fear and anxiety. The term 'fear' is reserved for an event that denotes immediate danger, in contrast to anxiety that denotes the feeling of being 'troubled in mind about some uncertain event' (from the Latin 'anxius') (Marks, 1978). Karen Horney (1937) has expressed the distinction thus:

> Fear and anxiety are both proportionate reactions to danger, but in the case of fear the danger is a transparent, objective one and in the case of anxiety it is hidden and subjective. That is, the intensity of the anxiety is proportionate to the meaning the situation has for

the person concerned, and the reasons why he is thus anxious are essentially unknown to him (p. 38).

Freud (1973) made a further distinction between anxiety ('*angst*'), fear ('*furcht*') and fright ('*schreck*'):

> Anxiety relates to the state and ignores the object, while fear draws attention precisely to the object. It seems that fright, on the other hand . . . lays emphasis . . . on the effect produced by a danger which is not met by any preparedness for anxiety. We might say, therefore, that a person protects himself from fright by anxiety (p. 443).

This statement by Freud is prescient of the polyvagal theory because of its implicit acknowledgement that anxiety operates on a hierarchy, with sympathetic arousal as the more adaptive form of responding to danger, and with fright (or freezing) as less adaptive.

Emotion, cognition, and anxiety

Once viewed as separate disciplines, recent formulations of cognition and emotion now acknowledge that 'the neural circuitry of emotion and cognition interact from early perception to decision making and reasoning' (Phelps, 2006, p. 28). Originating in a neurobiological system, emotion is a multi-component process, comprising our affective experience (i.e. feeling states such as happiness, anger, and surprise); a set of expressive behaviors (i.e. innate patterns of responding such as facial expression and bodily postures), and cognitive appraisal (how events are perceived and interpreted may determine the type and intensity of the emotional response) (Barlow, 2002a; Lazarus, 1984; 1991a; 1991b). Cognitive appraisal is a complex process that involves assessment of the demands of the situation such as an impending performance, the personal resources that can be accessed to meet the demands, the possible consequences of the performance, and the meaning of those consequences to the individual (Smith, Maragos, & van Dyke, 2000).

Early theories asserted that anxiety was primarily a cognitive process in which danger is exaggerated, misperceived, or misinterpreted: see, for example, Beck and Clark (1997); Mandler (1984); Spielberger (1985). These theories state that anxiety is experienced primarily as a result of distorted cognitions that arise from faulty information processing that triggers inappropriate motor, physiological, and affective responses. More recent formulations of anxiety and the anxiety disorders give primacy to emotion:

> Common to the anxiety disorders is the emotion of anxiety and associated cognitions related to present and future threat of harm, physiological arousal when confronted with anxiety-relevant stimuli and behavioural tendencies to escape from or avoid anxiety triggers and to prevent anticipated harm (Foa *et al.*, 2005, p. 1788).

Izard (1993) attempted an integrative theory of emotion involving four subsystems: neurobiological, motor/behavioral, physiological/motivational, and cognitive. These four systems combine with environmental contingencies, learning, and individual characteristics to produce emotional experience. Thus, anxiety is defined as a complex (learned) emotion in which fear is combined with other emotions such as anger, shame, guilt, and excitement (Izard, 1977). The 'development of an anxious person-ality results from the interaction of learning with basic emotions, resulting in stable affective-cognitive structures that are trait-like' (Barlow, 2002b, p. 42; Izard & Blumberg, 1985).

Neuroscience has further elucidated the complex relationship between anxiety and cognitive and emotional processing. Brain structures such as the amygdala and hypothalamus, associated with the processing of emotion, are mostly subcortical, while the structures responsible for cognitive function are mostly cortical. The discov-ery of precise locations in the brain for emotional and cognitive processing has given rise to the view that these systems are modular and functionally specialized. However, there are regions in the brain, called hubs, in which there is a high degree of connectiv-ity between the emotional and cognitive processing centers. These hubs regulate and integrate the flow of information between systems (Pessoa, 2008). Although emotional processing often occurs outside conscious awareness, produces fast, invol-untary, autonomic responses, and guides decision making, these systems also interact with cortical systems and require cognitive resources (Dvorak-Bertsch, Curtin, Rubinstein, & Newman, 2007).

The amygdala, until recently, was associated primarily with affective functions, in particular, fear processing, but has now been shown to be involved in processes such as attention and associative learning, which are cognitive functions. The level of acti-vation of the amygdala, which plays a critical role in the processing of emotional information, may be moderated by the cognitive load, such as the amount of working memory required to perform a task, or when attention is directed to another task. Thus, changes in the direction of attention and cognitive demands of a task affect the degree of activation in the amygdala, which in turn reduces the intensity of emotional responses such as fear (Pessoa, 2008). More recent research has also shown that the amygdala is capable of storing and retrieving memories for specific fears; in other words, it can discriminate among different fear-conditioning experiences such that when one fear experience is reactivated through exposure and modified, another similar, but different, experience will be retained and stored unchanged, and will be reacted to with fear, as in the original fear-learning situation. Thus, disruption to one type of fear memory will not disrupt or reduce other fear memories (Debiec, Diaz-Mataix, Bush, Doyere, & LeDoux, 2010). This research may have significant implications for the management of performance anxiety, suggesting that each fear-learning experience may need to be recalled and modified before a decrease in overall fear responding to the performance situation can be achieved.

Emotions, moods, and traits

We also need to understand the distinction between emotions, moods, and traits. These three concepts can be distinguished on temporal and level-of-awareness dimensions. Emotions are the shortest of the three in duration, are complex and spontaneous, and more difficult to control compared with moods or traits. Moods have a longer duration than emotion but will eventually abate, while traits are enduring characteristics of a person. Emotions are in the forefront of awareness: you can usually identify without too much difficulty whether you are happy, sad, or angry; moods may be preconscious and less easy to articulate, while traits are partially genetically determined and unfold unconsciously, in the sense that they are developed in early life through an interaction between genetics, temperament, and experience in processes that are out of our awareness (LeDoux, 1996).

Emotions, but not cognitions, always involve bodily reactions, such as changes in respiration, heart rate, movements or postures, and non-verbal vocalizations and facial expressions (Sauter, Eisner, Ekman, & Scott, 2010). Ekman (2003) has identified a small number of body movements that reliably accompany emotional reactions to what he termed the 'basic' emotions, that is, innate emotions that are common to all humans (LeDoux, 1998), such as anger, disgust, fear, joy, sadness, and surprise. These emotional body postures or movements do not have to be learned because they are 'preset' or hardwired and automatic, and have been observed universally across cultures. These include moving towards an object that has triggered anger or enjoyment; freezing when fearful; turning away when disgusted; postural slumping when sad; looking down at an object of contempt; fixating our attention when surprised; relaxing our body posture when relieved; and laughing when highly amused. Recently, the expression of pride, comprising an open posture and a slight smile with the head tilted slightly back has been added to this list (Tracy & Robins, 2008). All other emotional bodily actions are learned and presumably can be unlearned (Eckman & Shean, 1997).

Worry and rumination

Worry is a thin stream of fear trickling through the mind. If encouraged, it cuts a channel into which all other thoughts are drained (Arthur Somers Roche).[1]

Just as universal emotions such as anxiety can become problematic because of their intensity, frequency, and duration, cognitions can become problematic in the same way. Rumination is the process whereby cognitive appraisal becomes excessive, and instead of the process of cognitive appraisal supporting adaptive outcomes, rumination exacerbates depressed mood, fails to result in adaptive problem solving and inhibits instrumental behavior. It deserves special attention because of its strong association with both anxiety and depression and its manifestations in some forms of performance anxiety, although this latter association has not been well documented. However, clinical experience has alerted me to the importance of rumination in performance anxiety. Recall, for example, Claudio Arrau's comment that it took him months to recover from a concert in which he had made an error. Barbra Streisand took 27 years to recover from one episode of forgetting the words of one of her songs in a live concert. We can only imagine the intensity of the ruminative thinking that must have occurred over this period and which is barely hinted at in her comment, 'I couldn't come out of it . . . It was shocking to me to forget the words.' Similarly, the cellist also engaged in prolonged post-performance rumination such that eight years after the event, he continued to feel sick when he recalled the performance that caused him such embarrassment. There are further graphic

---

[1] Retrieved 4/11/10 from http://thinkexist.com/quotes/arthur_somers_roche/.

examples provided in the detailed analysis of performance-anxious musicians presented in Chapter Eight.

Rumination is defined as 'a mode of responding . . . that involves repetitively and passively focusing on symptoms of distress and on the possible causes and consequences of these symptoms. Rumination does not lead to active problem solving to change circumstances surrounding these symptoms' (Nolen-Hoeksema, Wisco, & Lyubomirsky, 2008, p. 400). Rumination is distinguished from other forms of thinking by its perseverative quality rather than by the actual content of the thoughts, which tend to be negatively valenced and involve feelings of hopelessness, pessimism, and self-criticism. Unsurprisingly, rumination saps people's motivation and initiative. In dysphoric (i.e. chronic low-mood) people, rumination amplifies their problems and leads to appraisals that these are overwhelming and unsolvable. Although ruminators are able to generate suitable solutions to problems, they express less confidence in the possible outcomes of the proposed solution and need more time to commit to, and are less likely to implement the proposed solution (Lyubomirsky, Tucker, Caldwell, & Berg, 1999).

Although people prone to ruminate have higher levels of general anxiety (Nolen-Hoeksema, 2000), anxious individuals are more likely to worry than ruminate. Worry has been defined as:

> a chain of thoughts and images, negatively affect-laden and relatively uncontrollable . . . an attempt to engage in mental problem solving on an issue whose outcome is uncertain but contains the possibility of one or more negative outcomes: consequently worry relates closely to the fear process (Borkovec, Robinson, Pruzinsky, & DePree, 1983, p. 10).

This definition alerts us to the idea of a chain of thoughts. People who worry excessively often engage in what is described as catastrophic chaining, that may commence with a speculative concern. An anxious musician may go through a chain of this nature:

> I have not practiced the last five bars of the coda of the sonata as well as the other sections. I am not going to play that section well. I am going to worry about the recapitulation and the coda from the minute I sit down at the piano on stage. That means that I am not going to play any of the sonata well. I may as well not turn up to the concert. I will only make a fool of myself. I will probably ruin any chance I have of a career in music.

Worry is one of the defining features of generalized anxiety disorder but is present in most of the anxiety disorders (Barlow, 2002b). It is the perceived uncontrollability of the worry—that is, the belief that the worry is out of one's control and one cannot do anything about it—that distinguishes it from normal worry. Worry and rumination share many features: they are both perseverative, self-focused, over-inclusive, negatively valenced thoughts that result in cognitive inflexibility, decrements in attention, motivation, and problem solving, and consequently performance deficits such as failure to implement solutions (Nolen-Hoeksema et al., 2008). However, worry tends to be future oriented and focused on possible threats, while rumination is focused on past events and content is related to questions regarding self-worth, meaning, and loss. The goal of worry is to anticipate and prepare to deal with possible threats, and to avoid negative affect. Worry occurs predominantly as inner speech (i.e. talking to oneself) rather than in imagery, and it has been speculated that worry may be an attempt to avoid more acute distress by blocking the imagery, which requires emotional processing, that is associated with the worrying thoughts. Worry interferes with emotional processing and reduces the flexibility of responding (Bentz & Williamson, 1998). The goal of rumination is to understand the meaning of events and is a substitution for action (Nolen-Hoeksema *et al.*, 2008).

Summary

In this chapter, we have built the conceptual framework from which to theorize music performance anxiety. We reviewed some of the philosophies, such as Cartesian dualism, and research methods such as nomothetic (study of groups or populations) and idiographic (study of the individual) approaches underpinning psychology in order to explicate the concepts and models on which I rely in this book to further our understanding of music performance anxiety. We then examined definitions of anxiety, recognizing its central role in most psychological disorders. We explored both its biological and environmental origins and discussed some of the key theories of anxiety, in particular, the general adaptation syndrome, the generality and specificity models of anxiety, the polyvagal theory and conditioning models derived from learning theory. Critical components of anxiety—anxious apprehension and anxiety sensitivity—were identified and their roles in the genesis of the anxiety disorders were discussed. The two factor structure of anxiety, comprising trait and state components was described. The definitions of common terms such as stress, anxiety, arousal, activation and fear were elaborated in order to bring some conceptual clarity to our later discussions. This was followed by a discussion of recent formulations of cognition and emotion as multi component processes with common roots in the neurobiological system. Current theorizing has replaced the central role assigned to cognitions in the genesis of the anxiety disorders, giving primacy to emotion, although the integrated action of cognition and emotion was understood as a complex interaction between neurobiological, motor/behavioral, physiological/motivational, and cognitive systems involving both cortical and subcortical brain structures. Emotions, moods and traits were distinguished along three dimensions—their temporal characteristics, level of awareness and degree of involvement of bodily states. We ended our discussion with an analysis of the characteristics of two cognitive phenomena involved in anxiety disorders—worry and rumination. In the next chapter, we will examine the differences between normative experiences of physiological arousal, somatic anxiety, fear, worry, and rumination, and their occurrence within the context of a psychological disorder, for which, without treatment, the sufferer may experience significant impairment in either occupational or social functioning or both.

Chapter 3

The anxiety disorders

Anxiety is fear of one's self
Wilhelm Stekel.[1]

Because anxiety is a universal emotion, it can be difficult at times to discern the point at which 'normal' anxiety becomes pathological and at what point it is appropriate to diagnose an anxiety disorder. Similarly, because music performance anxiety is also highly prevalent (if not ubiquitous) among performing musicians, the same diagnostic dilemmas apply. However, performance anxiety in general, and music performance anxiety in particular, receive either scant or no attention in diagnostic taxonomies, so an additional question posed to researchers and clinicians who study or work with people who suffer high levels of performance anxiety is deciding whether such people suffer from a unique condition known as performance anxiety or whether their performance anxiety is a manifestation of another underlying anxiety disorder or other psychopathology.

Normal fear is generally considered to be a precursor of pathological anxiety and the development of an anxiety disorder. In its normal state, fear motivates defensive behaviors such as fight (approach) or flight (avoidance) as adaptive responses to danger. During normal fear processes, activity in fear-related brain circuits increases to assist the individual to face the threat and decreases once the danger has passed. During psychosocial stress, the fear circuits activate, but instead of reducing their activity, they become hyper-excitable; vigilance increases, attention to threat-relevant stimuli heightens and generalizes, and, eventually, activation of the fear circuits occurs independently of triggering stimuli in a process called neural sensitization or kindling (Rosen & Schulkin, 1998). One of the key differences between normal fear and pathological anxiety is that fear is cue-specific and anxiety is non-specific or 'free-floating,' denoting a state that is chronically present.

In this section, we will gain an understanding of the nature of the anxiety disorders most relevant to music performance anxiety, how they are classified, their defining features, and their commonalities and differences. We will then attempt to locate music performance anxiety within the spectrum of the anxiety disorders.

Diagnostic and Statistical Manual of Mental Disorders (DSM-IV-TR)

The Diagnostic and Statistical Manual of Mental Disorders (DSM) is published by the American Psychiatric Association (APA) and provides diagnostic criteria for

---

[1] Retrieved 4/11/10 from http://thinkexist.com/quotes/wilhelm_stekel/.

mental disorders. The criteria for the relevant mental disorders presented in this book are taken from the 2000 'text revision' (DSM-IV-TR) (American Psychiatric Association, 2000) of the fourth edition of the DSM (1994). At the time of writing, the DSM V was in preparation and is due for release in 2011. Two other major diagnostic manuals are used internationally. The first is the International Statistical Classification of Diseases and Related Health Problems (ICD). Its classifications are similar to those found in the DSM. The other, less commonly used, is the Psychodynamic Diagnostic Manual (PDM Taskforce, 2006), which is used by practitioners practicing some form of dynamic psychotherapy.

In these diagnostic systems, mental disorders are classified into categories that present prototypical or defining features of each disorder. However, as will become clear throughout this book, there is considerable overlap between diagnostic categories. Comorbidity, the co-occurrence of two or more disorders, is very common. Most disorders can be described along a continuum of severity from mild to moderate to severe. For many of the disorders, symptoms must be sufficient to cause 'clinically significant distress or impairment in social, occupational, or other important areas of functioning' (American Psychiatric Association, 2000). The DSM-IV-TR organizes each psychiatric diagnosis into five levels (axes) relating to different aspects of the disorder or disability (see Box 3.1).

Categorical versus dimensional conceptualizations of mental disorders

Although it is beyond the scope of this book to discuss the criticisms of the categorical classification of mental disorders, it is useful to identify and briefly discuss some of the more fundamental concerns, particularly as some of these issues are relevant to our conceptualization and understanding of music performance anxiety. Some of the key concerns include the poor reliability of current classifications, the high rates of comorbidity among the current categories of disorder, especially the anxiety and mood disorders, which are of most relevance to our concerns with music performance anxiety, and the application of thresholds on the number, severity, and duration of symptoms that are needed to qualify for a diagnosis, which may result in the loss of potentially significant clinical information that could be used in treatment planning

Box 3.1 The five axes of DSM-IV-TR disorders

Axis I: Clinical disorders, including depression and the anxiety disorders.
Axis II: Underlying personality disorders such as avoidant personality disorder, dependent personality disorder, obsessive–compulsive personality disorder, mental retardation.
Axis III: Acute medical conditions, such as brain injuries, and physical disorders that may cause symptoms similar to those in the mental disorders.
Axis IV: Psychosocial and environmental factors contributing to the disorder.
Axis V: Global Assessment of Functioning or Children's Global Assessment Scale for children under the age of 18 (on a scale from 100 to 1).

(Brown & Barlow, 2005). Given that there is so much overlap between categories of disorder, some researchers have argued that a complaint-based approach might be more appropriate (Krueger, Watson, & Barlow, 2005; Maser & Akiskal, 2002). Brown and Barlow (2005) argue that, in the interim, it might be useful to consider the introduction of dimensional severity ratings to the existing diagnostic categories and criteria sets, which would allow consideration of individual differences in symptom severity to be recorded and to capture some symptoms that currently fall below the threshold for inclusion in the symptom set because they do not significantly impair social or occupational functioning, but may still, nevertheless, have clinical significance for treatment planning and prognosis.

Although there is some consensus regarding the dimensionality of some disorders, there is, as yet, no agreement on the identification of optimal dimensions that could be used. For the mood and anxiety disorders, with which we are primarily concerned, the dimension of trait-negative affect-neuroticism has been proposed. The dimensional argument is based on the evidence that families of disorders, such as anxiety and depression, are founded on the same core vulnerabilities in temperament and personality and the clinical observation of high comorbidity and symptom overlap between some families of disorders. There is also recent evidence from clinical outcome studies that failure to attend to the broader behavioral phenotypes results in sub-optimal or overly specific outcomes. These results have led to the conclusion that 'cognitive behavioral treatment is effective in addressing the symptoms and maintaining processes of panic disorder with agoraphobia but did not result in substantial reductions in general predispositional features (e.g. neuroticism) leaving patients vulnerable to the emergence or persistence of other disorders' (Brown & Barlow, 2005, p. 553). This argument was made many years ago by psychodynamic therapists who referred to symptom substitution as the process that occurs when core psychopathology is ignored in favor of addressing the symptoms alone (Paolino, 1981). These predispositional features have been the subject of large epidemiological studies. For example, in a community sample of 2,365 adolescents, negative affectivity was found to be a major non-specific risk factor for both panic attacks and major depression (Hayward, Killen, Kraemer, & Taylor, 2000).

The focus on presenting symptoms precludes consideration of the context in which the behavior (symptom) occurs, the situational (i.e. factors in the environment), or relational (i.e. problems in the individual's relationships with significant others) determinants of behavior and the underlying etiology of the symptoms (Spitzer & Wakefield, 1999). To some extent, problematic symptoms may represent an adaptive response to a maladaptive environment. In music performance anxiety, one also needs to consider the nature of the task and how task characteristics interact with behavioral, situational, and relational factors that combine to cause anxiety. We will return to these issues in our discussion of music performance anxiety in Chapter Four.

Having made the argument for a dimensional approach, it is also important to consider the usefulness of a categorical or typological approach. This will become evident later when we discuss the possible existence of subtypes of social anxiety disorder, of which performance anxiety may be, for some individuals, a specific concern that is likely to respond to brief therapy compared with those who present with a picture of more generalized or pervasive anxiety, for which a different approach may be warranted. Definitions and defining criteria for the anxiety disorders most likely to co-occur or to be present in the symptom constellation of music performance anxiety are presented below.

Generalized anxiety disorder (GAD)

GAD is a relative newcomer to the taxonomy of anxiety disorder, first appearing in the DSM-III-R (American Psychiatric Association, 1980) to describe residual anxiety states that did not comfortably fit with the more specific diagnostic criteria of other anxiety disorders. It is characterized by the presence, for at least six months' duration, of chronic feelings of excessive worry and anxiety without a specific identifiable cause. Individuals with generalized anxiety disorder often feel tense, restless, and fatigued. They report worrying about minor issues, daily events, or possible future harms. These feelings are accompanied by physical complaints such as elevated blood pressure, increased heart rate, muscle tension, sweating, shaking, nausea, diarrhoea, and insomnia. GAD frequently occurs comorbidly with panic disorder and social phobia, tends to be persistent, and follows a chronic course, with remission rates of 0.15 after one year and 0.25 after two years. The probability of becoming asymptomatic from all symptoms was found to be only 0.08 (Yonkers, Massion, Warshaw, & Keller, 1996).

In many ways, the descriptors for GAD resemble those for people with high trait anxiety, discussed in Chapter Two. GAD is relatively stable, as are personality traits, with early age of onset and lifelong course. People with GAD, like those with high trait anxiety, do not have specific foci for their anxious responding, but focus on a range of social and physical threats. Because GAD closely resembles 'normal' anxiety, in that the cognitive content of the anxious thoughts and beliefs appears similar to those with high trait anxiety, it is difficult to define a cut-off for the disorder (Rapee, 1991). Box 3.2 presents the diagnostic criteria for generalized anxiety disorder.

Social phobia (social anxiety disorder)

Anxiety disorders are the most prevalent mental health condition, and social anxiety disorder is the most commonly occurring anxiety disorder. It is problematic because of its early onset (50% before the age of 11 years), its persistence into adulthood, and the fact that it is a risk factor for both depressive illness and substance abuse (Stein & Stein, 2008). The central feature of social anxiety disorder is the occurrence of intense anxiety when performing a task that is scrutinized in some way by others (Hofmann & Barlow, 2002). Several theories have attempted to account for the central theme in social phobia—the fear of negative evaluation (Beck, Emery, & Greenberg, 1985; Leary, 1983; Rapee & Heimberg, 1997; Schlenker & Leary, 1982; Strauman, 1989). These theories propose that a discrepancy between the motivation to make a desired impression and the perceived (in)ability to make that impression triggers anxiety. Dysfunctional cognitive schemas, comprising negative core beliefs and assumptions regarding oneself and others are activated during the appraisal phase of a threatening event. The individual then assesses his/her ability to cope with the situation by following rigid rules and enacting safety behaviors, such as avoiding or escaping the

Box 3.2 Diagnostic criteria for generalized anxiety disorder (GAD)

Diagnostic criteria for 300.02 generalized anxiety disorder are as follows:

A Excessive anxiety and worry (apprehensive expectation), occurring more days than not for at least six months, about a number of events or activities (such as work or school performance).

B The person finds it difficult to control the worry.

C The anxiety and worry are associated with three (or more) of the following six symptoms (with at least some symptoms present for more days than not for the past six months). Note: Only one item is required in children.

   1 Restlessness or feeling keyed-up or on edge

   2 Being easily fatigued

   3 Difficulty concentrating or mind going blank

   4 Irritability

   5 Muscle tension

   6 Sleep disturbance (difficulty falling/staying asleep, or restless unsatisfying sleep).

D The focus of the anxiety and worry is not confined to features of an Axis I disorder, e.g. the anxiety or worry is not about having a panic attack (as in panic disorder), being embarrassed in public (as in social phobia), being contaminated (as in obsessive–compulsive disorder), being away from home or close relatives (as in separation anxiety disorder), gaining weight (as in anorexia nervosa), having multiple physical complaints (as in somatization disorder), or having a serious illness (as in hypochondriasis), and the anxiety and worry do not occur exclusively during post-traumatic stress disorder.

E The anxiety, worry, or physical symptoms cause clinically significant distress or impairment in social, occupational, or other important areas of functioning.

F The disturbance is not due to the direct physiological effects of a substance (e.g. a drug of abuse, a medication) or a general medical condition (e.g. hyperthyroidism), and does not occur exclusively during a mood disorder, a psychotic disorder, or a pervasive developmental disorder.

perceived threat. The result is an anxiety response, which feeds back into the core beliefs and assumptions in a vicious cycle.

The term social phobia—the word 'phobia' comes from the Greek (φόβος), meaning 'fear'—made its first appearance in the 1980 edition of the DSM, and was intended to describe people who reported fear of a specific situation such as public speaking. This definition was expanded in the DSM-III-R (1987) to include a generalized subtype that recognized individuals who expressed a more pervasive social anxiety. This two-part typology was criticized by Heimberg, Hope, Dodge, & Becker (1990) who argued that a tripartite typology consisting of generalized, non-generalized, and specific (circumscribed) forms better reflected the clinical presentation of people with social phobias. Although the DSM-IV (1994) did not reflect these subtypes, as you will see from Box 3.3 below, evidence is mounting that supports such a model (Blote, Kint,

Box 3.3 Diagnostic criteria for social phobia

Diagnostic criteria for 300.23 social phobia are as follows:

A A marked and persistent fear of one or more social or performance situations in which the person is exposed to unfamiliar people or to possible scrutiny by others. The individual fears that he or she will act in a way (or show anxiety symptoms) that will be humiliating or embarrassing. Note: In children, there must be evidence of the capacity for age-appropriate social relationships with familiar people and the anxiety must occur in peer settings, not just in interactions with adults.

B Exposure to the feared social situation almost invariably provokes anxiety, which may take the form of a situationally bound or situationally predisposed panic attack. Note: In children, the anxiety may be expressed by crying, tantrums, freezing, or shrinking from social situations with unfamiliar people.

C The person recognizes that the fear is excessive or unreasonable. Note: In children, this feature may be absent.

D The feared social or performance situations are avoided or else are endured with intense anxiety or distress.

E The avoidance, anxious anticipation, or distress in the feared social or performance situation(s) interferes significantly with the person's normal routine, occupational (academic) functioning, or social activities or relationships, or there is marked distress about having the phobia.

F In individuals under age 18 years, the duration is at least six months.

G The fear or avoidance is not due to the direct physiological effects of a substance (e.g. a drug of abuse, a medication) or a general medical condition and is not better accounted for by another mental disorder (e.g. panic disorder with or without agoraphobia, separation anxiety disorder, body dysmorphic disorder, a pervasive developmental disorder, or schizoid personality disorder).

H If a general medical condition or another mental disorder is present, the fear in Criterion A is unrelated to it, e.g. the fear is not of stuttering, trembling in Parkinson's disease, or exhibiting abnormal eating behavior in anorexia nervosa or bulimia nervosa. Specify if: Generalized: if the fears include most social situations (also consider the additional diagnosis of avoidant personality disorder).

Miers, & Westenberg, 2008). This evidence will be discussed in more detail in the section on focal music performance anxiety. Box 3.3 presents the diagnostic criteria for social phobia as it occurs in the DSM-IV-TR.

Specific phobia

The word 'phobic' is applied to people who display an intense and persistent (and to the objective observer, irrational) fear of certain objects, people, activities, or situations. Phobic people actively avoid contact with the feared stimulus. In severe cases, contact with the feared object may trigger a panic attack, and for others it may impair daily functioning because of the efforts required to avoid or escape the feared object or situation. Specific phobias have a one-year prevalence of 4.4% (Kessler *et al.*, 2005a). Onset usually occurs in childhood or adolescence. Women are twice as likely to suffer from specific phobias as men (Antony & Swinson, 2000c). Box 3.4 presents the diagnostic criteria for specific phobia.

Panic disorder (without agoraphobia)

Panic disorder is one of the more serious anxiety disorders and may occur with (about 36% of cases) or without agoraphobia (from the Greek, meaning 'fear of open spaces'). Panic attacks are usually described by sufferers to 'come out of the blue,' that is, they are not expected and appear to occur without obvious triggers. They are usually accompanied by an urge to flee, with all the attendant physiological systems arousal that is associated with the fight–flight response. In addition, the sufferer experiences a sense of dread and foreboding of threat or danger, risk of death, loss of control, or public humiliation. Attacks can last from seconds to hours, and intensity and specific symptoms can vary between sufferers and within sufferers over time. Symptoms include all those physiological responses associated with activation of the sympathetic nervous system, in addition to catastrophic cognitions of fear of dying or going crazy, embarrassment and humiliation, and the need to retreat to a safe place. Anticipatory anxiety develops in response to the experience of panic attacks, in which the person worries about recurrences of the panic attacks and accordingly changes his/her behavior, often maladaptively and avoidantly, in order to prevent their recurrence (Barlow, 2008b). Onset tends to be in early adulthood, unlike in specific phobias or social anxiety disorders, where onset can occur in childhood and adolescence, although many adults with panic disorder report that their first panic attack occurred in adolescence (Hayward *et al.*, 2000). Women are about twice as likely as men to suffer from panic attacks (Antony & Stein, 2009). Box 3.5 presents the diagnostic criteria for panic disorder without agoraphobia.

Obsessive–compulsive disorder

Obsessive–compulsive disorder (OCD) is an anxiety disorder characterized by recurrent, unwanted thoughts (obsessions) and/or repetitive behaviors (compulsions) such as hand washing, counting, checking, or cleaning. Engaging in obsessional thoughts or performing behavioral rituals provides temporary relief. Attempts to prevent the performance of these rituals lead to an increase in anxiety, which is temporarily relieved

Box 3.4 Diagnostic criteria for specific phobia

Diagnostic criteria for 300.29 specific phobia are as follows:

A Marked and persistent fear that is excessive or unreasonable, cued by the presence or anticipation of a specific object or situation (e.g. flying, heights, animals, receiving an injection, seeing blood).

B Exposure to the phobic stimulus almost invariably provokes an immediate anxiety response, which may take the form of a situationally bound or situationally predisposed panic attack. Note: In children, the anxiety may be expressed by crying, tantrums, freezing, or clinging.

C The person recognizes that the fear is excessive or unreasonable. Note: In children, this feature may be absent.

D The phobic situation(s) is/are avoided or else endured with intense anxiety or distress.

E The avoidance, anxious anticipation, or distress in the feared situation(s) interferes significantly with the person's normal routine, occupational (or academic) functioning, or social activities or relationships, or there is marked distress about having the phobia.

F In individuals under age 18 years, the duration is at least six months.

G The anxiety, panic attacks, or phobic avoidance associated with the specific object or situation are not better accounted for by another mental disorder, such as obsessive–compulsive disorder (e.g. fear of dirt in someone with an obsession about contamination), post-traumatic stress disorder (e.g. avoidance of stimuli associated with a severe stressor), separation anxiety disorder (e.g. avoidance of school), social phobia (e.g. avoidance of social situations because of fear of embarrassment), panic disorder with agoraphobia, or agoraphobia without a history of panic disorder. Specify type: animal; natural environment (e.g. heights, storms, water); blood-injection injury; situational (e.g. airplanes, elevators, enclosed places); other (e.g. fear of choking, vomiting, or contracting an illness; in children, fear of loud sounds or costumed characters).

by re-engagement in the problematic behavior. The most common rituals include cleaning, (hand)washing, checking, and ordering. OCD occurs in children, adolescents, and adults, with a lifetime prevalence of about 1%–2% (American Psychiatric Association, 2000; Rasmussen & Eisen, 1994). Box 3.6 presents the diagnostic criteria for obsessive–compulsive personality disorder.

Depression

Although the literature has focused primarily on the anxiety disorders with respect to understanding music performance anxiety, the possible presence of depression

Box 3.5 Diagnostic criteria for panic disorder without agoraphobia

Diagnostic criteria for 300.01 panic disorder without agoraphobia are as follows:

A Both (1) and (2):

  1 Recurrent unexpected panic attacks

  2 At least one of the attacks has been followed by one month (or more) of one (or more) of the following:

  a persistent concern about having additional attacks

  b worry about the implications of the attack or its consequences (e.g. losing control, having a heart attack, 'going crazy')

  c a significant change in behavior related to the attacks.

B Absence of agoraphobia (i.e. anxiety about being in places or situations from which escape might be difficult (or embarrassing) or in which help may not be available in the event of having an unexpected or situationally predisposed (e.g. outside the home alone; being in a crowd or standing in a line; being on a bridge; or traveling in a bus, train, or automobile) panic attack or panic-like symptoms.

C The panic attacks are not due to the direct physiological effects of a substance (e.g. a drug of abuse, a medication) or a general medical condition (e.g. hyperthyroidism).

D The panic attacks are not better accounted for by another mental disorder, such as social phobia (e.g. occurring on exposure to feared social situations), specific phobia (e.g. on exposure to a specific phobic situation), obsessive–compulsive disorder (e.g. on exposure to dirt in someone with an obsession about contamination), post-traumatic stress disorder (e.g. in response to stimuli associated with a severe stressor), or separation anxiety disorder (e.g. in response to being away from home or close relatives).

in the presentation should not be overlooked, if for no other reason than that the anxiety disorders frequently co-occur with depression. The extent and patterns of co-occurrence (comorbidity) will be discussed in the next section. Box 3.7 presents the diagnostic criteria for dysthymic disorder, a disorder where depressed mood is pervasive, but at a less debilitating level compared with a major depressive disorder.

Major depressive disorder is a clinical condition characterized by one or more major depressive episodes (see Box 3.8). It is also known as clinical depression, major depression, unipolar depression, or unipolar disorder. It is characterized by pervasive low mood, low self-esteem, and loss of interest or pleasure in undertaking normally enjoyable activities. The condition has significant negative impacts on family, work or school life, social functioning, sleep, eating habits, and general health. It occurs twice as frequently in women as in men.

Box 3.6 Diagnostic criteria for obsessive–compulsive personality disorder

Diagnostic criteria for 301.4 obsessive–compulsive personality disorder

A pervasive pattern of preoccupation with orderliness, perfectionism, and mental and interpersonal control, at the expense of flexibility, openness, and efficiency, beginning by early adulthood and present in a variety of contexts, as indicated by four (or more) of the following:

1 Is preoccupied with details, rules, lists, order, organization, or schedules to the extent that the major point of the activity is lost.

2 Shows perfectionism that interferes with task completion (e.g. is unable to complete a project because own overly strict standards are not met).

3 Is excessively devoted to work and productivity to the exclusion of leisure activities and friendships (not accounted for by obvious economic necessity).

4 Is over-conscientious, scrupulous, and inflexible about matters of morality, ethics, or values (not accounted for by cultural or religious identification).

5 Is unable to discard worn-out or worthless objects even when they have no sentimental value.

6 Is reluctant to delegate tasks or to work with others unless they submit to exactly his or her way of doing things.

7 Adopts a miserly spending style toward both self and others; money is viewed as something to be hoarded for future catastrophes.

8 Shows rigidity and stubbornness.

Relationships and comorbidities among DSM-IV diagnoses

Comorbidity is the term used to describe a condition that meets criteria for more than one disorder. Cormorbidity appears to be common for several mental health problems, in particular, anxiety and depression (Andrews, Henderson, & Hall, 2001). In the Australian National Mental Health Survey, 4.4% of respondents met criteria for two disorders, and 3.8% for three or more. People who qualify for multiple diagnoses often have underlying personality difficulties, which, unless recognized, make treatment difficult and often unsuccessful. The most frequent personality patterns evident in people with multiple anxiety diagnoses are those with avoidant and obsessive compulsive personality styles (Turner, Beidel, Borden, Stanley, & Jacob, 1991). Avoidant or phobic personalities display a pervasive pattern of social inhibition, feelings of inadequacy, and hypersensitivity to negative evaluation. They tend to avoid people, relationships, and situations in which they fear criticism, disapproval, rejection, or humiliation. They demonstrate very poor self-concept and view themselves as inferior to other people (American Psychiatric Association, 2000). They may fear not only external phenomena but also their own internal states. People with obsessive–compulsive

Box 3.7 Diagnostic criteria for dysthymic disorder

Diagnostic criteria for 300.4 dysthymic disorder

A Depressed mood for most of the day, for more days than not, as indicated either by subjective account or observation by others, for at least two years. (Note: In children and adolescents, mood can be irritable and duration must be at least one year.)

B Presence, while depressed, of two (or more) of the following:

1 poor appetite or overeating

2 insomnia or hypersomnia

3 low energy or fatigue

4 low self-esteem

5 poor concentration or difficulty making decisions

6 feelings of hopelessness.

C During the two-year period (one year for children or adolescents) of the disturbance, the person has never been without the symptoms in Criteria A and B for more than two months at a time.

D No major depressive episode has been present during the first two years of the disturbance (one year for children and adolescents).

G The symptoms are not due to the direct physiological effects of a substance (e.g. a drug of abuse, a medication) or a general medical condition (e.g. hypothyroidism).

H The symptoms cause clinically significant distress or impairment in social, occupational, or other important areas of functioning. Specify if: early onset: if onset is before age 21 years; late onset: if onset is age 21 years or older. Specify (for most recent two years of dysthymic disorder): with atypical features.

disorder engage in ritualistic obsessions (intrusive and persistent ideas, thoughts, impulses, or images that are anxiety provoking) and/or compulsions (repetitive behaviors such as hand washing, ordering, checking, or mental acts such as praying, counting, repeating words silently) that are extremely time consuming and/or cause distress and/or significant impairment in functioning. Compulsions aim to reduce the stress and anxiety caused by the obsessions or to prevent the occurrence of a dreaded event or situation (American Psychiatric Association, 2000). In people with anxiety disorders who have these underlying personality styles, treatment of the presenting problem only is likely to be unsuccessful until these entrenched patterns are addressed. Estimated comorbidity of an Axis I (anxiety and mood disorders) and a personality disorder (Axis II) diagnosis ranges from between 66% to 97%. Given the entrenched and maladaptive nature of the behavioral patterns in people with personality disorders, it is not surprising that such people are difficult to treat and often respond poorly to treatment, particularly when only a symptom-based approach (i.e. dealing with the

Box 3.8 Diagnostic criteria for major depressive episode

Diagnostic criteria for 296.xx major depressive episode

Five (or more) of the following symptoms have been present during the same two-week period and represent a change from previous functioning; at least one of the symptoms is either (1) depressed mood or (2) loss of interest or pleasure.

1 Depressed mood most of the day, nearly every day, as indicated by either subjective report (e.g. feels sad or empty) or observation made by others (e.g. appears tearful). Note: In children and adolescents, can be irritable mood.

2 Markedly diminished interest or pleasure in all, or almost all, activities most of the day, nearly every day (as indicated by either subjective account or observation made by others).

3 Significant weight loss when not dieting or weight gain (e.g. a change of more than 5% of body weight in a month), or decrease or increase in appetite nearly every day. Note: In children, consider failure to make expected weight gains.

4 Insomnia or hypersomnia nearly every day.

5 Psychomotor agitation or retardation nearly every day (observable by others, not merely subjective feelings of restlessness or being slowed down).

6 Fatigue or loss of energy nearly every day.

7 Feelings of worthlessness or excessive or inappropriate guilt (which may be delusional) nearly every day (not merely self-reproach or guilt about being sick).

8 Diminished ability to think or concentrate, or indecisiveness, nearly every day (either by subjective account or as observed by others).

9 Recurrent thoughts of death (not just fear of dying), recurrent suicidal ideation without a specific plan, or a suicide attempt or a specific plan for committing suicide.

problems associated with the Axis I disorder) is undertaken (Muran, Safran, Samstag, & Winston, 2005).

Among the Axis I diagnoses, the highest rates for comorbidity occur between the different anxiety disorders and between anxiety and depression, especially in clinical settings and in individuals with more severe agoraphobia. Patients with more pervasive anxiety disorders such as generalized anxiety disorder frequently receive additional anxiety diagnoses of social phobia and/or simple phobia (Sanderson, DiNardo, Rapee, & Barlow, 1990), and/or panic disorder (Yonkers *et al.*, 1996). In one study, for patients with generalized anxiety disorder, 90% had a lifetime history of another anxiety disorder and 83% had at least one other anxiety disorder diagnosis at the time of intake (Yonkers *et al.*, 1996). Social phobia, the condition of most interest in the context of music performance anxiety, often precedes the onset of other mental health conditions (Brown, Campbell, Lehman, Grisham, & Mancill, 2001). Social phobia and generalized anxiety disorder have been reported in 15%–30% of individuals with panic disorder, in 2%–20% of those with specific phobia, and in 10% of those with obsessive–compulsive disorder.

Approximately one-third of anxiety disorder patients are likely to receive an additional diagnosis of a mood disorder such as dysthymia or major depression (Brown *et al.*, 2001; Sanderson *et al.*, 1990). For example, in one sample of anxiety-disordered patients, 37% also qualified for a comorbid diagnosis of depression (McLaughlin, Geissler, & Wan, 2003). Comorbidity rates vary depending on the nature of the anxiety disorder. Reported rates for an anxiety disorder accompanied by a comorbid major depressive disorder vary widely, from 10% to 65% in individuals with panic disorder (American Psychiatric Association, 2000). In approximately one-third of individuals with both disorders, depression precedes the onset of panic disorder. In the remaining two-thirds, depression occurs coincident with or following the onset of panic disorder. A subset of individuals may treat their anxiety with alcohol or medications, and some may develop a substance-related disorder as a consequence.

On reflection, it is not surprising that there are high rates of comorbid presentations in people suffering from anxiety and depression. Both conditions share common features, such as negative affect, irritability, decreased energy, and performance deficits (Alloy, Kelly, Mineka, & Clements, 1990; Watson & Kendall, 1989), and/or shared biological and psychological vulnerabilities, such as expectations of uncontrollability, unpredictability, and helplessness, and respond to these with increased physiological arousal and hyper-vigilance (Barlow, 2002a; Watson, Clark, & Carey, 1988). Co-occurrence of a major depressive disorder is also common in children and adolescents with an anxiety disorder (Ford, Goodman, & Meltzer, 2003), with rates varying between 25% (Costello, Mustillo, Erkanli, Keeler, & Angold, 2003) and 73.1% (Lewinsohn, Zinbarg, Seeley, Lewinsohn, & Sack, 1997). Young people with comorbid disorders have a poorer prognosis than those with a single disorder (Kessler *et al.*, 2005a; Kessler, Chiu, Demler, & Walters, 2005b).

Figure 3.1 (from Stein & Stein, 2008, p. 1118) presents a schematic representation of the possible relationships between the major anxiety disorders and other conditions such as major depression. The focus of our discussion is the anxiety and mood disorders, but the complete presentation includes other conditions (schizophrenia, autism spectrum disorders, body dysmorphic disorder) that are of less interest to students of music performance anxiety and will not be discussed in this book, although they are included here for completeness. We will return to this schematic representation after our discussion of performance anxiety to see where the performance anxieties might fit within this conceptualization.

Summary

In this chapter we examined the construct of anxiety in greater detail and reviewed the various diagnoses within the Diagnostic and Statistical Manual of Mental Disorders (DSM-IV-TR) of the American Psychiatric Association (APA), which included anxiety as a central feature of the disorder. These included generalized anxiety disorder

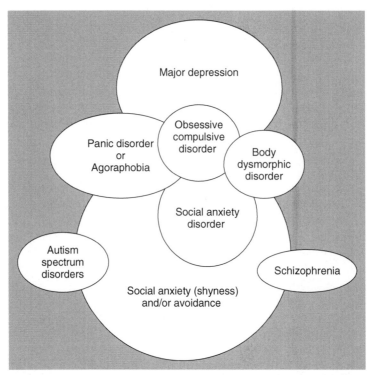

Figure 3.1 Conditions that commonly overlap with social anxiety disorder (social phobia). Reprinted from *The Lancet*, *371*, Stein, M.B., and Stein, D.J., Social Anxiety Disorder, 1115–25, Copyright (2008), with permission from Elsevier.

(GAD), social phobia/social anxiety disorder (SAD), specific phobia, panic disorder, and obsessive–compulsive disorder (OCD). We briefly examined the issues related to categorical versus dimensional conceptualizations of mental disorders, and how these disorders are classified, their defining features and their commonalities and differences. We discovered that comorbidity, the co-occurrence of two or more disorders, is very common, and that high rates of comorbidity point to the possible artificiality of categorical classifications of psychological disorders. Depression and its various manifestations (e.g. dysthymia and major depression) are common comorbid conditions with the anxiety disorders. We then reviewed the anxiety disorders in the DSM in the context of the characteristics of music performance anxiety. In the next chapter, we will attempt to define music performance anxiety and locate possible subtypes of music performance anxiety on a schematic map of the spectrum of the anxiety disorders.

Chapter 4

Defining music performance anxiety

Of course I'm nervous. The artist who boasts he is never nervous is not an artist—he is a liar or a fool

Caruso, 1964.[1]

The experience of anxiety is no stranger to the majority of people whose brief is to perform in front of others. In many ways, as Shakespeare asserts, life itself is a performance—'*All the world's a stage, And all the men and women merely players*'—but for some, center stage or center court is a threatening and frightening place to be, and playing one's part is made difficult by the experience of unwanted emotions, thoughts and behaviors. Like Jaques in Shakespeare's *As You Like It*,[2] one's part may be sad and unrewarding.

Performance anxiety is a disorder that affects individuals in a range of endeavors, from test taking (Elliot & McGregor, 1999), mathematics performance (Ashcraft & Faust, 1994), public speaking (Blote *et al.*, 2008; Merritt, Richards, & Davis, 2001), sport (Hall & Kerr, 1998; Hanton, O'Brien, & Mellalieu, 2003), and the performing arts in dance (Tamborrino, 2001), acting (Wilson, 2002), and music (Kenny, 2006; Osborne, Kenny, & Holsomback, 2005; Ryan, 2003, 2005). Prior to 1994, performance anxiety was not included in the classificatory systems of psychological or psychiatric disorders. In the DSM-IV (American Psychiatric Association, 1994) and DSM-IV-TR (American Psychiatric Association, 2000), performance anxiety is briefly discussed in a section on differential diagnosis in social phobia.

> Performance anxiety, stage fright, and shyness in social situations that involve unfamiliar people (a potentially hostile audience) are common and should not be diagnosed as Social Phobia unless the anxiety or avoidance leads to clinically significant impairment or marked distress. Children commonly exhibit social anxiety, particularly when interacting with unfamiliar adults. A diagnosis of Social Phobia should not be made in children unless the social anxiety is also evident in peer settings and persists for at least 6 months (American Psychiatric Association, *2000*, p. 300.323).

Accurate naming of a phenomenon is a first and essential step in its analysis and eventual understanding. The field of music performance anxiety has certainly suffered for

---

[1] Cited in Rushmore, 1971, p. 72.
[2] Jaques (Act II, Scene VII, lines 139–40) from William Shakespeare, *As You Like It*.

want of a name and definition, without which Jung's (1955) prescient question as to whether investigators of the future will know what we meant throws out a challenge to the field to achieve greater conceptual clarity. Surprisingly, not all agree with the need for clarity. Brandfonbrener (1999), for example, somewhat impatiently asserts: 'call it performance anxiety, stage fright, or musical performance anxiety, I think we all understand what we mean' (p. 101). However, the literature on music performance anxiety does not appear to have reached such consensus. While it shows that many researchers use the terms 'stage fright,' 'performance anxiety,' and 'music perform-ance anxiety' interchangeably (Brodsky, 1996; Papageorgi, Hallam, & Welch, 2007; Salmon, 1990), there is not always agreement as to the meaning of these terms. Brodsky (1996), for example, places 'stage fright' at the extreme end of his proposed continu-um of severity of music performance anxiety, while Fehm and Schmidt (2005) argue that stage fright denotes a less severe level of stress than performance anxiety. The German translation of 'stage fright' is *Lampenfieber*, which, literally translated, means 'light fever,' a phrase that graphically denotes the behavioral manifestations of the trembling and perspiration that often accompany a fever in a nervous performer in the spotlight (Mantel, 2003, p. 20). How do we compare the severity of these physio-logical symptoms with those of anxiety, a term that carries stronger emotional and cognitive associations than a 'fever'? In its English translation, the word 'fever' becomes 'fright,' thus denoting extreme and sudden anxiety.

To reduce confusion surrounding the use of the term 'stage fright,' several authors have called for all terms other than 'music performance anxiety' to be discarded (Salmon, 1990). Senyshyn (1999), for example, argues that stage fright refers to the sudden, intense fear or alarm felt on stage that is likely to lead to performance breakdown, which is a relatively rare event (Hardy & Parfitt, 1991), and thus this term fails to capture the experience of the majority of musicians whose level of anxiety is less than this or which, though severe, rarely leads to performance breakdown. It is clear that Senyshyn is using the term stage fright to denote the most extreme form of performance anxiety.

In the next section, we will critically examine some of the most frequently used definitions of music performance anxiety, before attempting to reach a consensus definition on which the remainder of this book may safely be based. Probably the most cited definition was offered by Salmon (1990), so we will start there. He offered this definition of music performance anxiety:

> the experience of persisting, distressful apprehension and/or actual impairment of performance skills in a public context, to a degree unwarranted given the individual's musical aptitude, training, and level of preparation (p. 3).

This oft quoted definition of music performance anxiety as 'the experience of persist-ing, distressful *apprehension* and/or actual impairment of performance skills in a public context, *to a degree unwarranted given the individual's musical aptitude, training, and level of preparation*' (my emphasis) needs critical analysis. There are a number of components to this definition. Firstly, it correctly refers to 'distressful apprehension,' akin to Barlow's anxious apprehension (see Chapter Six), which may or may not be accompanied by performance impairment. However, the definition becomes prob-lematic when it states that a diagnosis of music performance anxiety only applies if the apprehension is not consistent with musical aptitude, training, and preparation. Research shows that musicians of all ages, levels of aptitude, training, experience, and preparation report music performance anxiety (Brotons, 1994; Cox & Kenardy, 1993; Kenny, 2009b; Simon & Martens, 1979; Tamborrino, 2001; Wesner, Noyes, & Davis, 1990; Wolfe, 1989). Secondly, this definition appears to reserve the diagnosis for accomplished musicians (however defined at each level of musical development), who have had sufficient training and practice for their performance. It further implies that if there were little musical aptitude, insufficient training, or inadequate preparation, whatever apprehension is felt by musicians in these circumstances cannot be described as music performance anxiety. However, these factors are causally implicated in some but not all cases of music performance anxiety for musicians at all levels of accomplishment and experience.

Brodsky (1996) lamented as recently as 1996 that the:

> constructs of anxiety, stress and tension . . . lack a standardized definition . . . and that few studies about MPA have actually dealt with performance anxiety per se. With no conformity among the medical profession or research community concerning diagnostic criteria and research methodology, performing arts medicine does not seem to be closer today (than 10 years ago) regarding the nomenclature of these symptoms, how to measure the degree or severity of symptomatology, or how to evaluate the incidence of MPA (p. 89–90).

Performance anxiety had not been classified in any DSM up to and including DSM-IV (1994). In the DSM-IV-TR (2000), performance anxiety is briefly discussed in a section on differential diagnosis in social phobia:

> Performance anxiety, stage fright, and shyness in social situations that involve unfamiliar people are common and should not be diagnosed as Social Phobia unless the anxiety or avoidance leads to clinically significant impairment or marked distress (2000, 300.323).

It is somewhat disturbing that even the DSM does not attempt to differentiate between performance anxiety, stage fright, and shyness in social situations. The statement above, however, implies that social phobia is the more debilitating condition; as such, a definition is only warranted if the anxiety or avoidance that is characteristic of the diagnosis of all four conditions results in impairment or distress.

Ten years after the definition offered by Salmon (1991), Steptoe (2001) suggested that music performance anxiety consists of four components, 'the primary component [of which] is affect or feeling, i.e. feelings of anxiety, tension, apprehension, dread or panic, which forms the central experience of performance anxiety' (p. 295). The other three components comprising music performance anxiety in Steptoe's definition are cognitions (loss of concentration, memory failure, misreading of the score); behaviors (failures of technique and loss of posture, tremors and trembling); and physiological reactions (disturbances in breathing, salivation, heart rate, gastrointestinal function) and hormonal imbalances (release of excessive epinephrine, cortisol). He distinguishes stage fright from music performance anxiety in the following ways: (i) stage fright occurs in other performing arts such as ballet and drama; music performance anxiety refers only to musicians; (ii) stage fright implies distress in front of large audiences whereas music performance anxiety can occur in intimate settings, such as auditions, where the audience consists of one or two adjudicators; (iii) stage fright refers to a sudden onset of intense feelings of fear whereas music performance anxiety can build gradually over days or weeks before a performance. These distinctions are not very helpful in advancing our understanding of either construct. For example, stage fright, in its strict definition, can occur in musicians, even though the term is also applied to other performing arts. The intense fear triggered by being on stage can be experienced as the culmination of the gradual build-up of tension and anxiety in the weeks or months before a performance. Steptoe rightly points out that an essential element of the experience of music performance anxiety is not so much the presence or size of the audience, but the evaluative nature of the performance situation, and to this I would add the stakes, that is, the possible consequences of that evaluation.

The lack of a clear definition of music performance anxiety and the failure to make explicit the criteria that distinguish music performance anxiety from other anxiety disorders, including its close relatives, specific phobia and social phobia, if such distinctions exist, are a theoretical impediment to the field that compromise identification of those who need treatment and hinder the development of appropriate treatments. In view of the current unsatisfactory definitions of music performance, I have recently offered a new definition (Kenny, 2009b), which I will discuss in detail later in this chapter in the section on music performance anxiety as a social anxiety disorder, because I will argue that although music performance anxiety is frequently equated with social anxiety and social anxiety disorder, there are significant differences between these conditions.

Constructions of music performance anxiety

A number of assumptions underpin the currently available definitions of music performance anxiety and these need to be explicitly articulated and critiqued in order to progress the quest for a usable working definition of the concept.

Music performance anxiety as a dimensional construct

Brodsky argued that MPA is more helpfully understood as occurring on a continuum of severity to differentiate what he describes as 'normal everyday healthy aspects of stress and anxiety that are intrinsic to the profession' (1996, p. 91) from the severely debilitating symptoms of 'stage fright,' which he defines as an experience close to panic. Figure 4.1 demonstrates the proposed relationship between various descriptors of performance anxiety and their relative severity.

Notwithstanding the intuitive appeal of Brodsky's conceptualization of music performance anxiety as dimensional, the dimensionality of music performance anxiety awaits empirical verification. It is possible that the condition is better understood as a series of distinct subtypes, as I will argue later in this chapter. However, these formulations are based only on clinical experience and also require empirical verification.

| Career stress ⟹ tension in performance ⟹ performance anxiety ⟹ stage fright |

Figure 4.1 Relationship between various descriptors of performance anxiety and their relative severity.

Neither the dimensional nor the subtype conceptualizations can currently be argued empirically. They remain hypotheses awaiting empirical examination. Both arguments are presented for the reader to consider and to stimulate interested researchers. It is, of course, possible that these conceptualizations are not mutually exclusive. Many musicians experience some degree of career stress and tension in performance but are able to manage these experiences comfortably within their available resources. My proposed subtype formulations occur on the latter two dimensions of Brodsky's scale—music performance anxiety and stage fright. These conceptualizations will be discussed in the coming sections, but first let us examine the strength of the argument that music performance anxiety is a form of occupational stress, whose origin arises primarily in the organization of the work of the performing musician.

Music performance anxiety as occupational stress

Music—what a noble art, what a terrible profession (Hector Berlioz).[3]

Occupational stress was initially explained and managed within a psycho-medical model. In this model, personality deficits or vulnerabilities were considered to be causal, or at least precursors to the experience of occupational stress. The stressor and strain approach, on the other hand, attributed the cause of psychological and behavioral strain to work stressors (see, for example, the Scandinavian school (Levi, 1999)). This approach focused primarily on work characteristics and the epidemiology of occupational health. Rather than treating the individual, the focus of intervention is work reform. Sternbach (1995) described the working conditions of professional musicians as generating a 'total stress quotient' that far exceeds that observed in other professions. Like elite athletes, performing artists must maintain their skills at peak form, endure many hours of solitary, repetitive practice, constantly self-evaluate their performances and subject their public performances to close scrutiny. In addition, their workplace throws up many challenges that must be coped with on a daily basis. The stressors endorsed as moderately or severely stressful by more than 50% of a large sample of orchestral musicians from the Fédération Internationale des Musiciens (FIM Survey, 1997, in Steptoe, 2001) were, in order of frequency: working with a conductor who saps your confidence (73%); playing an orchestral solo (73%); illegible music (65%); disorganized rehearsal time (65%); problems with instrument (63%); making a mistake when performing (63%); incompetent conductor (61%); incompatible desk partner (61%); having medical problems that affect work (57%); and playing in a cold venue (55%).

In two early reviews of occupational stress, Cooper (1983, 1985) summarized and categorized six groups of organizational variables that may cause stress in the workplace. These are:

i factors intrinsic to the job (e.g. heat, noise, shift work)

ii relationships at work (e.g. conflict with co-workers or supervisors, lack of social support)

---

[3] Evans, A. (1994, p. 137). *The secrets of musical confidence: How to maximize your performance potential.* Sydney, Australia: Harper Collins.

iii role in the organization (e.g. role ambiguity)

iv career development (e.g. lack of status, lack of prospects for promotion, lack of a career path, job insecurity)

v organizational structure and climate (e.g. lack of autonomy, lack of opportunity to participate in decision making, lack of control over the pace of work)

vi home and work interface (e.g. conflict between domestic and work roles; lack of spousal support for remaining in the workforce).

Although these variables were developed in non-musical workplaces, any musician reading the six areas outlined above could readily associate them with a musical career, whether as an orchestral musician (Kenny & Ackermann, 2009), a popular or portfolio musician (Cooper & Willis, 1989), or as a choral artist (Kenny, Davis, & Oates, 2004).

Performing musicians face numerous occupational stressors in the physical, social, and psychological domains that must be addressed if their musical careers are to be both rewarding and sustainable. Ironically, although musicians simultaneously report the highest levels of job satisfaction, they also suffer the highest levels of exhaustion, psychosomatic complaints such as stomach aches, headaches and sleep disturbance (Kivimaki & Jokinen, 1994). Brodsky (1996) reports on three further studies that attest to the hazardous occupational environment of musicians—two of which identified musicians in the top five occupational groups most at risk of early death and mental illness respectively.

Physical and psychological stressors exert reciprocal and synergistic effects on the musician, and careful analysis of the intrinsic characteristics of the performer and the extrinsic demands on the musician must be made in order to develop appropriate interventions. Several large epidemiological studies have shown high physical injury rates among musicians (Manchester, 2006). Performer-related risk factors for injury include poor posture, poor physical condition, inadequate instrument set-up, long hours of playing, insufficient rest breaks and inefficient movement patterns (or poor technique) (Ackermann & Adams, 2004; Kenny & Ackermann, 2009). Musicians may suffer injury from a wide array of non-performance-related causes such as lifting and carrying awkward or heavy instruments and suitcases (when on tour), demanding work schedules, sitting on poorly designed orchestral chairs, temperature variations (Manchester, 2006), demanding repertoire and poor visibility of music scores (Horvath, 2002). However, the majority of musicians' injuries are overuse injuries (Dawson, Charness, Goode, Lederman, & Newmark, 1998) with soft-tissue symptoms predominating (Pascarelli & Hsu, 2001). Musicians of all ages and levels of skill are vulnerable to injury, but the risk increases as hours of playing increase. Older musicians more typically develop degenerative conditions (i.e. conditions that include a gradual deterioration in the structure of a body part, with a consequent loss of the part's ability to function) while younger musicians suffer more from performance-related musculoskeletal pain (Warrington, Winspur, & Steinwede, 2002). Prevention is the best form of management for occupational overuse injuries (Melhorn, 1998). Key factors in injury prevention include awareness of correct postural requirements, technique and biomechanics involved in playing one's instrument, and maintaining overall good physical condition that is achieved by warming up, stretching (Zaza, 1994), and strength and endurance training (Marieb, 2001).

Various ergonomic interventions aimed at reducing physical load include hand-splint adaptations for the trombone to assist with reach difficulties (Quarrier & Norris, 2001), development of polymer drumsticks with reduced vibration characteristics (Zaza, Fleiszer, Main, & Mechefske, 2000), a neck strap to carry the weight of the clarinet and bassoon that may effectively reduce strain on the thumb (Chesky, Kondraske, & Rubin, 2000), and many other instrument design modifications such as angle-headed flutes, key extensions on vertically held wind instruments, and remodeling of viola or guitar bodies (Norris, 2000). Instruction on good lifting technique is important for musicians who may injure their lower back as a result of carrying heavy or awkwardly shaped instruments (Fjellman-Wiklund, Brulin, & Sundelin, 2003).

Many organizations are deterred from major changes in the organization of work as a means of preventing stress due to the cost and disruption of implementing such strategies and the relatively small numbers of employees manifesting stress conditions that impair occupational functioning at any one time in any one workplace (Cooper & Payne, 1992). Many employees work under similar conditions of stress; why, then, do only a few succumb to occupational stress (however defined) in any given organization?

Occupational stress is a complex, multilayered phenomenon that requires a systemic or ecological analysis using multiple perspectives. Established definitions of occupational stress, such as that presented by the National Institute for Occupational Safety and Health (NIOSH, 1999) as the 'harmful physical and emotional responses that occur when the requirements of the job do not match the capabilities, resources, or needs of the worker' does not encompass, for example, causes located in the organization of work, dysfunctional organizations, problematic interpersonal relationships, or workplace inequities. The ecological view argues that social structures and processes affect people through psychological processes and that there is a dynamic reciprocal influence of social and psychological processes (Marmot, 1986). The systemic issues need to be named, addressed, and changed if some of the workplace factors that impinge on musician well-being are to be effectively addressed (Kenny, 2000a; Kenny & McIntyre, 2005).

Musicians are required to work in a pattern akin to shift work, be available to travel to performance venues, leave their families while on tour, adjust to changing time zones, live at close quarters with colleagues and peers, and cope with financial insecurity (Kenny & Ackermann, 2009). Frequently reported psychosocial issues while on tour or working on contract with interstate and overseas orchestras include loneliness, homesickness, sexual frustration, and relationship breakdown. Occupational issues include language barriers, unfamiliar backstage arrangements at concert venues, and variable quality of dressing rooms. In addition to these psychological and occupational stressors, there is the physical stress associated with moving instruments and luggage, setting up on different stages, adjusting to differently shaped chairs at every venue, sleeping in different beds with different pillows, coping with jet lag, general fatigue, and lack of sleep. New injuries or pains are frequently reported by professional musicians on tour as a direct result of these factors (Ackermann, 2002).

For the reasons outlined above, it can be difficult to differentiate between the occupational and physical stressors and psychological problems that may arise in individual musicians and which require individualized psychological intervention.

Individuals vary in their capacity to cope with such stressful working conditions. However, since not all performers suffer the same degree of psychological distress or report the same levels of occupational stress, individual differences in a range of psychological characteristics and responses to the performance situation are likely to account for variations in the degree to which musicians experience symptoms. For example, difficulties in coping may be compounded for those who are also highly anxious, who lack confidence in their abilities and who engage in unhelpful strategies to deal with their anxieties, such as the regular consumption of alcohol and licit (e.g. beta-blockers) or illicit (e.g. marihuana) drugs. The presence of physical problems, outlined above, may add to the anxiety of anxious musicians, who fear that their performance will be compromised by pain or overuse symptoms.

Occupational stress begins early in musical careers, as a study by Barney, Dews, and Williams (1989) shows. The ten issues of concern in a sample of music students from three tertiary-level music schools included stress, pre-performance anxiety, impatience to progress their musical career, burnout, job insecurity, conflict between music and one's personal life, inadequate practice facilities and depression. However, a study conducted by Chesky and Hipple (1997) on 359 tertiary-level majors that explored their alcohol use using the Young Adult Alcohol Problems Screening Test (YAAPST) found that music majors had significantly lower lifetime use of alcohol, lower past-year use of alcohol, and lower past-year severity of use. Music majors also reported fewer difficulties on the Problem Check List (PCL) compared with non-music majors. After adjusting for age and gender, no significant differences were found between music and non-music majors on a measure of performance anxiety (Performance Anxiety Inventory, or PAI). Music majors reported more confidence in their ability to concentrate and study and higher self-esteem than non-music majors. The differences between the groups were sustained after adjusting for age (the music majors were older) and gender (only 30% of the music majors were female). It is possible that even with all the occupational hazards that accompany a career in music, being able to play a musical instrument at a high level may bestow some advantages on the social-emotional adjustment of tertiary-level music students.

Only three studies have attempted to untangle the relationships between occupational stressors and state, trait, and music performance anxiety in professional musicians (Cooper & Willis, 1989; Kenny, Davis, & Oates, 2004; Steptoe, 1989). Steptoe surveyed career stress in 65 orchestra musicians and 41 advanced music students to ascertain the relationship, if any, between what he defined as career stress, which roughly corresponds to our concept of occupational stress and what he termed 'stage fright,' defined as 'perceived tension and exaggerated beliefs concerning the importance and consequences of any particular performance' (p. 3). His results indicated that career stress and stage fright were not independent, but appeared to co-vary in a positive direction. Those who had more career stresses also suffered greater levels of stage fright.

Kenny and colleagues assessed 32 operatic chorus artists from Opera Australia and found that they had significantly higher trait anxiety on the State Trait Anxiety Inventory (STAI–S; STAI–T) (Spielberger, 1983) than the normative sample. Their scores on occupational roles and personal strain subscales from the Occupational

Stress Inventory–Revised (OSI–R; Osipow, 1998) scale also exceeded those of other occupations. Does higher trait anxiety result in higher scores on the occupational roles and personal strain questionnaires of the OSI–R or does the sensitizing occupational environment of musicians foster greater anxiety? Although the issue regarding which factor, if either, played a causal role could not be answered in this study, it did provide some evidence that occupational stress appears to be a separate source of stress from trait anxiety and music performance anxiety, since scores on the occupational roles scale of the OSI–R predicted none of the scores on the three anxiety measures employed in the study: STAI; Cox and Kenardy (1993) Music Performance Anxiety Scale (CK–MPA); Kenny Music Performance Anxiety Inventory (K–MPAI, 2004). There were no differences on any of the anxiety measures between chorus artists who scored in the higher and lower ranges on the Occupational Roles Questionnaire (ORQ) of the OSI–R. This suggests that occupational stressors are different to and separate from trait and performance anxiety and need to be addressed separately. Further investigation of the relationship between occupational stress and trait and performance anxiety is needed.

With respect to occupational stressors, chorus artists were most concerned with role ambiguity and their physical working environment. Their major concerns included an unclear sense of what is expected of them, how they were evaluated, and what they needed to do to advance in their profession. Some also reported conflicting expectations from different supervisors (e.g. conductor, chorus master). Concerns about the physical environment related to issues such as the level of dust, noise, and inappropriate heat and cold in their working environment, as well as concerns about their erratic work schedules were also reported. Mean scores on role insufficiency and role overload were the next two most elevated scales on the OSI–R. Some chorus artists described a less than ideal fit between their skills and the job that they performed, with some citing underutilization of their skills, lack of recognition for their efforts, and concern about lack of career progression. Role overload issues focused on their perceived increasing workload and tighter deadlines. Although average scores on these sub-scales of the OSI–R for this occupational group were higher than for other occupations, they remained within the normal range with respect to the severity of their self-reported occupational concerns.

The operatic chorus artists demonstrated a greater reservoir of personal resources than the normative sample. They scored significantly higher than other occupational groups on self-care and recreation. They reported engaging in a variety of non-work activities that they found relaxing and satisfying. As a group, they were more likely to engage in regular exercise, have sufficient sleep, be careful with their diet, avoid harmful substances such as alcohol and drugs, and practice relaxation techniques. This is not surprising in a group of singers. The vocal instrument is delicate and requires special care to maintain it at optimal function. Most also reported adequate social support and coping resources. It was interesting to note that those engaging in more personal resources behaviors as defined in the OSI–R were also those who had the highest scores on trait anxiety. It is possible that the most anxious members of the group used their personal resources as an adaptive way of coping with their high anxiety.

The third study (Cooper & Willis, 1989) reported on the outcomes of interviews with 70 British male popular musicians, the aim of which was to ascertain the most frequent sources of stress that they experienced. Popular music encompasses styles such as rock, punk rock, jazz, blues, soul, funk, rap, reggae, country, heavy metal, ska, Brit pop, Gothic, and electronica, among others. The interviews painted a sobering picture of an occupation that suffers significant distress, to which performance anxiety made a major contribution. The quoted portions of the interviews reveal difficulty doing both live gigs ('I'm very open to vibes . . . if I see someone who . . . isn't sympathetic to the way I play, then that's me finished . . . it's a great help if you feel there's a sympathetic audience' 'You get on stage, and somehow, 50% of your technique seems to have disappeared' p. 26) and studio work ('In the studio, when the red light goes on and you've got to turn it on—I can't . . . jazz music is improvised and spontaneous, and it's fleeting really and you can't create to order—it's impossible' p. 26). Underlying the music performance anxiety were stresses associated with the lifestyle of a popular musician, the struggle to earn a living, the excessive demands of the industry on the musicians ('when you are in the recording studio, you are expected to be able to deliver perfection' p. 25), and the absence of a caring social network ('Promoters—your usual business associates—have no interest in musicians as people' p. 24). In addition, work overload ('a major stress is lack of sleep, due to recording sessions during the day and gigs at night' p. 28), work underload, lack of career development, low job satisfaction, financial insecurity (the need to do 'bread and butter gigs' to earn a living that are unchallenging, unstimulating, and boring—'for creative, skilled people, they can be like cancer' p. 29), difficult relationships at work, including from fellow musicians ('fear of attack by others, stress caused by the inevitable and often deliberate pressures asserted by other musicians'), and the impact on family and social life that results from constant travel and working non-standard hours, all figured large in the experiences of this group of popular musicians.

Raeburn (2007) identified almost the same concerns facing popular musicians as Cooper and Willis (1989). She lists the following as significant occupational stressors for popular musicians: rejection; financial uncertainty; work pacing and lifestyle demands associated with touring and promoting that often compete with an individual's needs; periods of boredom alternating with periods of intense work (i.e. 'feast or famine'); isolation from family and friends; increased exposure to alcohol and drugs; depersonalized sex on the road; increased exposure to pathogenic beliefs about creativity requiring self-destructive or extreme behaviors; increased exposure to audience, critics, or cultural projections and objectification; conflicts between career and family roles; concerns related to ageing in a youth-oriented market; and ongoing issues with the tension between artistic identity and commercial acceptance (p. 5). In her subsequent papers, Raeburn (1999, 2000) draws attention to the large number of premature deaths among popular musicians, most of whom had substance abuse in their profiles. She suggests that for psychologically vulnerable musicians who have difficulty with self-esteem and self-regulation, their work culture contributes to early death because it reinforces health risk-taking behaviors, and treats them like income-generating commodities whose role is to satisfy capricious and ever changing consumer demands.

Music performance anxiety as a focal anxiety disorder

There has been a strong tendency in the theorizing about music performance anxiety to understand it as a focal condition that resides in an otherwise healthy, functioning musician. This may well be an accurate conception for those whose music performance anxiety is mild and easily self-managed. Conversely, the level of performance anxiety may be severe and described as panic by those musicians who experience it, but remain confined to very specific situations such as auditions or infrequent requirements to play solo, if the musician is usually a *tutti* musician in an orchestra, as is the case with orchestral section leaders. However, there are also some theoretical issues that need resolution with respect to this conceptualization. The question of dimensionality, discussed earlier, is one such issue. The other key issue is whether music performance anxiety can exist as focal anxiety—that is, are there musicians who suffer significant levels of music performance anxiety but experience no other significant anxieties in any other areas of their lives? A highly accomplished violinist with 25 years' experience playing in a premier national orchestra described what appears to be focal music performance anxiety thus:

> I do a lot of teaching, a lot of conducting and lots of pre-concert talks and strangely enough, I don't get nervous about any of that. I don't get nervous at all about talking in public, I don't get nervous about conducting, or I get a little nervous, but I don't have panic attacks like I get when I perform . . . For me, it's almost like a learned response that I can't shake off. But for performing, it can hit me, really smash me.

Here is the account of another musician, also a *tutti* violinist in a premier national orchestra with 13 years' experience:

> Recently, two or three years ago, an associate principal position came up and I thought, well, I'll do this audition just as a challenge and to have something to work towards, and I went and did that. And I thought that I was going to be fine. I felt really prepared, and then I can remember driving down in the car and thinking, 'Oh, what happens if I suddenly get nervous?' because I didn't think that was going to happen, and then when I went in and played that day, I had an out-of-body experience. It was that bad that I couldn't actually play, and I got stopped. And it was just a nightmare. It really did feel terrible. I felt like my brain was just not connected with what I was doing. I was so wound up with . . . well, I don't know. It was just really odd. I just wasn't in control of what was going on. It wasn't that I was looking down, not that kind of out-of-body experience, but I felt like I just hadn't been all there. In retrospect, I was aware that when people were talking to me just before I went in, I wasn't focused. I wasn't aware of it at the time, but when I look back and think, I can remember [. . .] saying that to me . . . Yes, it felt just as if I wasn't in control at all. I was surprised . . . At that moment, yes, I was just probably panicking. It was a shock, because I play the violin every day and then suddenly not being able to play it—that was a shock. I don't get nervous playing the violin, not in the orchestra.

Both musicians described what appear to be highly circumscribed experiences of music performance anxiety. Both give vivid descriptions of the severity of these experiences. Hence, it appears that focal anxiety can be experienced as mild or severe—it has a dimensional quality to it. Both indicate that their panic in these focal situations did not generalize to other performance experiences.

There is thus anecdotal and clinical evidence that indicates that music performance anxiety can be focal, but the current state of the field does not yet permit an empirical answer to this question. We must therefore turn to the general anxiety literature for clues; in particular, to the research on public speaking anxiety, the most common performance fear identified in the general population, in which the question as to whether this form of anxiety may be focal or circumscribed has been examined in some depth.

Several researchers have investigated the question regarding the nature of public speaking anxiety, a form of performance anxiety, with respect to its location on the social anxiety spectrum and whether it is a distinct subtype of social anxiety or whether it occurs in a dimensional model, in which the differences between public speaking anxiety and social anxiety are qualitatively rather than quantitatively different (Blote et al., 2008). To be identified as a distinct subtype, it would need to display qualitative differences from social anxiety. Evidence for the subtype was presented by Hook and Valentiner (2002), who reported that individuals with performance anxiety show less fear than those with generalized social anxiety in most social situations, but more fear than the former group with respect to specific public performance situations. A subsequent review (Hofmann, Heinrichs, & Moscovitch, 2004) found further support for the subtype hypothesis; specific performance anxiety in public speaking but not social interaction anxiety was associated with physiological arousal akin to panic. Further, the heritability patterns for the two conditions also differed—relatives of people suffering social anxiety were more likely also to suffer from social anxiety, but no such familial pattern was found for performance anxiety.

Similarly, Eng, Heimberg, Coles, Schneier, and Liebowitz (2000) identified three groups of socially phobic individuals, one group of which consisted of those with only public speaking anxiety. There was also a group with pervasive social anxiety and a group midway between the specific and pervasive groups. All three groups displayed a high level of anxiety in public speaking situations. Furmark, Tillfors, Stattin, Ekselius, and Fredrikson (2000) also found strong evidence in a large community sample of a tripartite model of social anxiety, consisting of generalized, non-generalized, and specific social anxiety. The specific subtype was the most frequently encountered (7.7% of the sample), of which 40% reported only public speaking anxiety. However, as with Eng and colleagues, Furmark and colleagues found that all three groups reported public speaking anxiety as one among many of their social anxieties. Together, these studies indicate that performance anxiety can occur as a specific subtype of social anxiety. Evidence for a similar subtyping has also been reported in adolescents (Piqueras, Olivares, & Lopez-Pina, 2008).

Given the evidence for a specific subtype of a particular, but common, performance anxiety, one could cautiously extrapolate that the same subtype may exist for music performance anxiety. It is interesting that no heritability patterns were identified for the specific subtype, perhaps suggesting that such conditions may be more situationally determined than the more pervasive subtypes, where generational transmission through modeling of anxious behavior as well as genetic factors appears to be an important etiological factor.

If we continue the account of the second focally anxious musician above, we will see that there may be strong situational determinants to focal performance anxiety.

> I guess I was underprepared for the actual circumstances. I thought being prepared within my own playing was enough, but really, I needed to be prepared for playing by myself, as a soloist. And I didn't really attend to that . . . So yes, I think I was underprepared for that side of it, whereas I felt prepared on my instrument, if that makes sense.

This violinist had been a *tutti* musician for the 13 years of her professional life as a musician. She felt very unprepared and was taken by surprise by the demands of the audition setting that required her to play solo; hence her very extreme anxiety response to the audition situation.

The special case of the audition

It is almost a truism to say that musicians are more likely to feel anxious under conditions of evaluation, such as competitions, jury performances, and concerts or recitals than they would under practice conditions. Audition anxiety is understood as a situation of extreme overarousal/overstimulation coupled with a response repertoire or capacity that is insufficient to reduce the level of arousal (Robson, Davidson, & Snell, 1995). Brotons (1994) examined this question to determine whether musicians' physiological and psychological responses and behaviors are affected by jury compared with non-jury performances and whether the type of jury mattered, i.e. whether it was an open jury (both performer and adjudicators were known to each other) or double-blind (neither performer nor adjudicators were known to each other). Results showed significant increases in heart rate and state anxiety between jury and non-jury performances but no differences between open and double-blind jury conditions. Because of the realistically based anxiety-provoking stimuli in an audition, one must exercise caution in describing audition anxiety as a focal music performance anxiety.

Auditions almost always appear at the top of any music performance anxiety hierarchy. For many musicians, auditions are the only circumstances in which they report that their anxiety becomes unmanageable. Professional musicians are much more likely to use beta-blockers for auditions than for most other performance settings (Fishbein, Middlestadt, Ottati, Strauss, & Ellis, 1988). Below is an example of a musician describing his use of beta-blockers for an audition.

> I remember doing an audition for a job once and I tried beta-blockers. It had a discernible effect; it didn't stop me from being nervous but it certainly quelled some of the effects of being nervous like my legs were not quite so shaky. Getting nervous, which I must admit, sometimes it's unpredictable, sometimes it doesn't happen at all and I don't understand it. I can understand why it does happen but when it doesn't happen I don't understand what the difference is. So even when I took the beta-blockers—the only time I've ever taken it—I was still nervous but the anxiety effects weren't there.

The audition experience can be unexpectedly harrowing, even for very experienced and accomplished musicians.

> I had been acting in the principal's job for a lot of the past two, three years because the principal was very sick during this time and had to have a lot of time off work. I assumed the major responsibility for my section. When the principal finally left, the job was advertised and I had to audition for the position that people said I had filled very well over that

time frame. I hadn't done an audition in years, but I thought I would be OK because, of course, I knew the repertoire and had performed the required works hundreds of times. But come the audition, my body went haywire; I felt a sort of paralysis in my bowing arm and lost the fine control of the bow that has always been second nature to me. That threw me and although I kept going and got through it, we all knew that I had blown it. I didn't get the job . . . if I allow myself to think about it, I feel bloody angry that I had to go through that.

Below is a comment from a professional musician who acts as an adjudicator. Because he frequently recalls his own harrowing experiences as a student auditioning for jobs, he uses his empathy to support students whom he assesses.

I am very sensitive . . . I do a lot of auditions and I'm well known as someone who makes anyone who comes to do an audition for me feel as comfortable as possible. I make it as non-threatening as possible, and if I see things going slightly awry, then I stand up and stop them playing, and then tell them a joke. I'll do anything to make sure that I get the best out of the student . . . And I do see people, students, getting nervous in front of me and then I find that quite hard to watch, knowing my own demons with auditions. I'm very strong about trying to put that right as soon as possible.

Music performance anxiety as social anxiety or social anxiety disorder (social phobia)

Humans and primates appear to be biologically predisposed to associate fear with angry facial expressions (Ohman, 1986). Social phobia, in which there is an exaggerated fear of being watched or judged, may have its origins in this biological predisposition, which no doubt has survival value for some species. It is also possible that it could originate in the context of a poorly integrated personality whereby hostile or aggressive aspects of the self are disowned and projected onto external figures (Baumeister, Dale, & Sommer, 1998).

There is debate in the literature as to whether music performance anxiety represents a form of social phobia. Some researchers argue that both conditions are centrally organized around fear of negative evaluation (Barlow, 2002a; Wilson, 2002), while others argue that performance anxiety may be part of a larger constellation of symptoms representing social phobia (social anxiety disorder) (Hook & Valentiner, 2002; Turner, Johnson, Beidel, Heiser, & Lydiard, 2003). The classification of social phobia into generalized (i.e. anxiety experienced about interpersonal interactions generally), non-generalized (i.e. anxiety experienced only in settings in which the individual is being scrutinized), and specific (i.e. anxiety is reserved for a very few performance situations) subtypes (Turner et al., 2003) may assist in the clarification of music performance anxiety as a form of the specific social phobia subtype. This specific social phobia subtype may be equivalent to music performance anxiety as a focal anxiety disorder if music performance under conditions of threat or scrutiny is the only situation in which anxiety symptoms are manifested.

There are a number of reliable differences in the way that highly performance-anxious people think about performance situations compared with low-anxious people, and some of these characteristics are also shared by people with social anxiety.

High performance-anxious individuals, compared with low performance-anxious individuals, show:

i stronger negative expectancies before the event

ii stronger negative bias in their retrospective self-evaluations of performance

iii stronger expectation that their performance will be judged negatively by their examiners/audience

iv stronger concerns about the consequences of a poor performance

v heightened responsiveness to changes in reactions of judges or audience

vi failure to derive comfort from evidence that they have handled the situation skill-fully (Wallace & Alden, 1997).

In addition to the shared behavioral characteristics of those with performance anxiety and social anxiety, Gorges, Alpers, and Pauli (2007) assessed whether perfectionism, self-focused attention and absorption characterized each condition in a sample of 142 classically trained instrumental students and professionals. All of the subscales of the Leibowitz Social Anxiety Scale (Stangier & Heidenreich, 2004) were moderately (r = 0.50) correlated with the measure of music performance anxiety, but only the subscale 'performance anxiety' remained significant in a regression analysis. Cox and Kenardy (1993) and Osborne and Franklin (2002) reported a similar strength of association. Social anxiety predicted 24% variance of music performance anxiety. Public self-focus, perfectionism, and perception of the audience as benign explained a further 15% variance. None of the other factors assessed—absorption, private self-focus, fear of social interaction, or socially oriented perfectionism—predicted music performance anxiety. Hence, there is evidence that only the performance anxiety component of social anxiety is associated with music performance. This and other research prompt a closer examination of the research on both social anxiety and music performance anxiety since they indicate that there may be significant differences between the two conditions. Accordingly, I offered a new definition of music performance anxiety that is more consistent with current knowledge of the condition and which aligns with research on the anxiety disorders in general and social phobia in particular.

> Music performance anxiety is the experience of marked and persistent anxious apprehension related to musical performance that has arisen through underlying biological and/or psychological vulnerabilities and/or specific anxiety-conditioning experiences. It is manifested through combinations of affective, cognitive, somatic, and behavioral symptoms. It may occur in a range of performance settings, but is usually more severe in settings involving high ego investment, evaluative threat (audience), and fear of failure. It may be focal (i.e. focused only on music performance), or occur comorbidly with other anxiety disorders, in particular social phobia. It affects musicians across the lifespan and is at least partially independent of years of training, practice, and level of musical accomplishment. It may or may not impair the quality of the musical performance (Kenny, 2009b, p. 433).

You will notice that the definition distinguishes performance anxiety from social phobia. Although the two conditions share common features, in particular the nature of the faulty cognitions that underpin anxious responding such as those described above (e.g. likelihood and consequences of negative evaluation), there are also significant differences between social phobia and music performance anxiety. Those with performance anxiety are more likely than those with social phobia to have higher expectations of themselves (Abbott & Rapee, 2004); greater fear of their own evaluation of their performance, as opposed to fear of the scrutiny of others in social phobia (Stoeber & Eismann, 2007), although the latter is also present in music performance anxiety; a higher degree of post-event rumination (Abbott & Rapee, 2004); and a continued commitment to the feared performance situation, as opposed to avoidance of or escape from the feared situation in social phobia (Powell, 2004b).

Further, although performing music is described as a social event involving evaluation akin to situations feared by people with social phobia (Antony & Swinson, 2000b), in social phobia the feared task is not usually cognitively or physically demanding and is usually already in the behavioral repertoire of the person with social phobia or social anxiety; that is, social anxiety is not generally associated with social or behavioral skills deficits (Hofmann, Gerlach, Wender, & Roth, 1997). Many of the core symptoms of social anxiety, such as eating food in a restaurant, engaging in social interactions at parties or at work, signing one's name on a document in a bank, or, for men, urinating in a public toilet, are not complex cognitive or motor tasks that need hours of practice to perform. Musical and sports performances, on the other hand, require complex skill acquisition, intensive practice, mental and physical rehearsal, coordination, and great demands on cognitive capacity and memory. Thus, musical performance makes multiple simultaneous demands on the cognitive (Kenny & Osborne, 2006), attentional (Erickson, Drevets, & Schulkin, 2003), affective (Kenny, 2005a), conative, kinesthetic (Altenmüller, Gruhn, Liebert, & Parlitz, 2000), and motor systems (Kenny & Ackermann, 2009). Ericsson, Krampe & Tesch-Römer (1993) estimated that a 22-year-old violinist making her concert debut will have practiced for about 15,000 hours to perfect her art.

Performance anxiety may also be associated with failure of task mastery (Wilson, 2002) or attempts to perform tasks that exceed the capacity of the performer (Fehm & Schmidt, 2005), circumstances that rarely present in social phobia, except, to some extent, for more performance-based tasks, such as public speaking. In one study, Craske and Craig (1984) asked a group of expert judges to rate the piano performance of conservatory piano students, who were asked to rate their subjective level of distress before and after performances involving playing alone and with an audience. The students were divided into high- and low-anxious groups. Results generally confirmed that high levels of anxiety were associated with lower judge ratings of performance quality. However, although both high- and low-anxious pianists rated their subjective distress prior to the no-audience performance as the same, the highly anxious performers received lower ratings for performance quality than the non-anxious performers. The non-anxious performers also received higher performance quality ratings during their audience performance compared with their no audience performance, suggesting that slightly heightened anxiety may have had a facilitating effect on pianists who experienced generally low levels of trait anxiety.

In social phobia, the audience is often imaginary—in psychoanalytic terms, a projected aspect of oneself; that is, the socially phobic individual may fear that everyone is watching and judging them, when the reality may be that the person has not been noticed in the feared social setting. For the artistic or sports performer, the audience is 'real' and performers are usually correct in their assessment that people are watching and judging them (Brotons, 1994). Onto this reality of audience scrutiny, anxious musicians project their own perceptions about the nature of the audience. This is not to say that people with social phobia have a less serious condition. My purpose in making these distinctions is to highlight the differences between social phobia and music performance anxiety, and to point out that although they share some characteristics, the conditions are not the same and hence may need different or adjunctive theoretical conceptualizations, management, and intervention. In particular, aspects of the feared stimulus, the music performance, must form an integral part of the theoretical formulation and treatment of music performance anxiety.

Other key differences between social phobia and music performance anxiety are that people with music performance anxiety are more likely to be concerned about their own ability to competently perform the task rather than others' perceptions of their performance. Further, they are more likely to remain in the threatening performance situation than people with social phobia, who will typically engage in escape and avoidance behaviors in the feared setting. It therefore seems worthwhile at this point to comment on the characteristics of performance settings and other situational factors that are likely to exacerbate the experience of music performance anxiety.

Situational factors influencing the occurrence and experience of music performance anxiety include the presence or absence of an audience and its size, status, and perceived competence (Craske & Craig, 1984; Fredrikson & Gunnarsson, 1992; Hamann, 1982; LeBlanc, Jin, Obert, & Siivola, 1997; Ryan, 1998). Larger audiences whose members are respected by the performer for their status in the field and expert knowledge of their repertoire will elicit more performance anxiety than audiences without these characteristics. Moreover, the size of the performance ensemble influences the level of anxiety, with solo performances eliciting the highest anxiety, followed by small ensembles, orchestras, and teaching settings (Cox & Kenardy, 1993; Jackson & Latane, 1981; Kenny, 2004; Kenny *et al.*, 2004). LeBlanc *et al.* (1997) showed a strong linear increase in perceived anxiety, heart rate, and performance quality assessed by judges' ratings in student musicians as the performance setting changed from performing alone in a practice room to performing with one observer present to performing for a peer group and being told that the performance was taped. Females performed better in the last performance condition but reported higher anxiety and had higher heart rates than males.

Music performance anxiety as panic disorder

Below is a statement by a young Donny Osmond about the nature of his performance anxiety.

> Once the fear of embarrassing myself grabbed me, I couldn't get loose. It was as if a big bizarre and terrifying unreality had replaced everything that was familiar and safe. In the grip of my wildest fears, I was paralyzed, certain that if I made one wrong move, I would literally die. The harder I tried to remember the words, the more elusive they became. The best I could do was not to black out, and I got through the show, barely,

telling myself repeatedly, 'Stay conscious, stay conscious' (Osmond, 1999; Osmond & Romanowski, 1999).

Note the extreme combination of emotional and cognitive anxiety ('fear of embarrassing myself' and 'making one wrong move') and somatic anxiety (paralysis and fear of blacking out—hyperventilation). Fear that grips him is like a 'big bizarre and terrifying unreality' in which he feels 'paralyzed' and afraid he would 'literally die' if he made a mistake. These are the kinds of statements made by people who suffer from panic disorder. Refer to Box 3.5 in which the symptoms of panic disorder are discussed and note the degree to which Donny's comments fit with the diagnostic picture. However, it is inadvisable to make clinical judgments on fragments of public interviews. This issue will be revisited in Chapter Eight, where detailed transcripts of narratives of severely performance-anxious professional musicians are analyzed in more depth, and where a new way of conceptualizing extremely severe music performance anxiety is considered. However, it is of interest to note that some researchers differentiate panic from other emotional disorders, and argue that panic attacks (also known as false alarms—see Barlow, 2002) are not necessarily implicated in a clinical disorder. These issues will be covered in more detail in Chapter Six.

Differential diagnosis of music performance anxiety

Let us return to the classification of the anxiety disorders presented by Stein and Stein (2008) earlier (noting that this representation does not tell the whole story because of the possible comorbid occurrence of underlying Axis II disorders). From the foregoing discussion, it is now possible to speculate with respect to the typological classification of music performance anxiety and its locations in this diagnostic space. Three possible types are proposed: a focal anxiety disorder that is the result of specific conditioning experiences; a disorder that is either a manifestation of social anxiety/ phobia or is comorbid with this condition; and a third, more serious, type of performance anxiety that may be accompanied by depression as well as panic, and a pervasive problem with the sense of self and self-esteem. These are represented in Figure 4.2. A typological classification suggests that there are disjunctions between conditions in the typology—these conditions do not just differ with respect to severity but are somehow qualitatively different from each other and perhaps require different therapeutic approaches. I am particularly interested in the third proposed type—the most serious manifestation of the condition—and will devote considerable time to this form of music performance anxiety in Chapter Eight.

Comorbidity and music performance anxiety

Because music performance anxiety has not been assigned a diagnosis in the psychiatric classification system, there has not been a systematic body of research exploring the issue of comorbidity with respect to music performance anxiety; nor has there been general discussion in the music performance anxiety literature. The main focus of possible comorbidities with music performance anxiety has been its co-occurrence with social anxiety (social phobia), so our attention will be addressed in that direction in the following section.

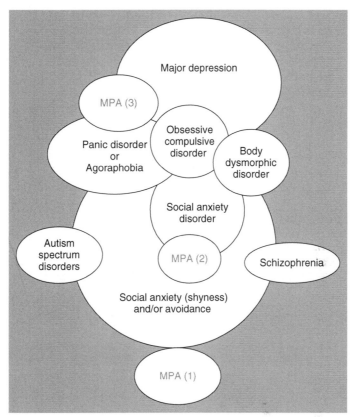

Figure 4.2 The three proposed subtypes of music performance anxiety MPA (1) focal music performance anxiety; MPA (2) as (or with) social anxiety/social anxiety disorder; MPA (3) as panic disorder with or without depression. Adapted from *The Lancet, 371*, Stein, M.B., and Stein, D.J., Social Anxiety Disorder, 1115–25, Copyright (2008), with permission from Elsevier.

Social anxiety (social phobia)

There is evidence for comorbidity between social phobia and other anxiety disorders and musical performance anxiety. Clark and Agras (1991), for example, found that 95% of a sample of college and adult musicians with high music performance anxiety qualified for a diagnosis of social phobia. Cox and Kenardy (1993) reported on 32 performance-anxious music students with respect to the presence of social phobia and the effects on their anxiety in different performance settings. While performance setting alone was a critical factor with respect to performance anxiety, the presence of social phobia amplified these effects.

Other evidence from child and adolescent musicians, in whom heightened performance anxiety was found in those showing probable and possible diagnoses of social phobia (Osborne & Kenny, 2005), strengthens the claim that these two conditions may share some common roots. These studies also suggest that music performance anxiety should not be considered in isolation. Careful diagnostic assessment is needed to identify those with comorbid conditions, since comorbidity indicates a more serious course of illness (Kessler, Stang, Wittchen, Stein, & Walters, 1999; Wittchen, Stein, & Kessler, 1999). However, comorbidity studies beg the question: If music performance anxiety is a social phobia, how can someone diagnosed with music performance anxiety have a comorbid social phobia? Perhaps the differential diagnosis should be between a specific social phobia, where the condition is only manifested in music performance, and other more generalized manifestations of social phobia that are consistent with the DSM-IV-TR. In a book that is generally considered the authoritative text on the anxiety disorders (Barlow, 2002a), performance anxiety is treated as a (specific) social phobia. However, the chapter on social phobia (social anxiety disorder) opens with an account of the severe music performance anxiety of Donny Osmond (a pop singer), which conflates the two conditions. (I have earlier argued that the quoted material indicates the possible presence of panic disorder). In a subsequent paper entitled 'Etiology and treatment of social anxiety,' Bitran and Barlow (2004) reproduce a figure presented in Barlow (2002a) as a model of the etiology of social phobia, but rename it as a model of social phobia and performance anxiety. This is unfortunate; any subsequent definition of music performance anxiety must resolve these diagnostic issues.

Other comorbidities

There is very little research on the presence of other comorbid conditions and music performance anxiety, although clinical experience alerts us to their presence. One unpublished study provides some insights. Using the Composite International Diagnostic Interview–Auto (CIDI–A; World Health Organization, 1997), Osborne (1998) assessed concurrent psychological disorders in musicians with music performance anxiety. Results showed that specific phobia, generalized anxiety disorder, panic disorder with/without agoraphobia, and major depressive disorder (but not dysthymia) were frequently comorbid. One-third of those with severe performance anxiety had comorbid generalized anxiety disorder. Depression, obsessive–compulsive disorder or traits, generalized anxiety disorder, and panic disorder are all candidates that need to be assessed in the diagnostic work up of a severely performance-anxious musician.

Psychological characteristics of people who suffer from anxiety

Clinical experience tells us that music performance anxiety is a dynamic process involving a complex interplay between the musician, the music, and performance settings over time. The tendency in the current literature to list the frequently occurring characteristics of those who are more likely to suffer from music performance anxiety (Papageorgi et al., 2007) or the settings in which anxiety is likely to be at its worst (Brotons, 1994) tells us something about the common descriptors of the condition but does not capture the essence of the subjective experience; nor does it provide sufficient clues as to the causative factors that underlie the development and maintenance of the condition in individual musicians, and the complex interplay between all of the observed characteristics.

Further, although nomothetic (i.e. large population-based) studies that identify commonalities among ostensibly homogenous groups of people have provided valuable information about the relationships between causal and outcome variables, and efficacy of treatments for health problems, clinicians often question the applicability of such findings to people seeking assistance with psychological difficulties in clinical settings. While findings from nomothetic studies can be very useful in providing foci for psycho-educational and preventive programs, clinical research and practice need to be supplemented with idiographic approaches (research that intensively studies individuals over time) to identify sources of inter-subject variability and factors that may account for such variability. Sigmund Freud was an idiographic researcher, as are subsequent clinicians/researchers, particularly within the psychodynamic school (Malan, 1979; Malan & Osimo, 1992). They provide rich and novel information and insights that nomothetic researchers can subject to verification. Failure to include both nomothetic and idiographic methods in the study of human behavior makes theories and treatments blunt instruments (Barlow & Nock, 2009).

Another problem with taking an enumerative approach to understanding the distinguishing features of high- and low-performance-anxious people is that many of the identified characteristics overlap such that some may be synthesized into meta-traits or characteristics that account more economically for the available variance in an outcome of interest than a number of individual characteristics considered alone. Trait anxiety, neuroticism, negative affectivity, and introversion; and self-concept, self-esteem, self-efficacy, and locus of control are good examples of oft discussed factors that could usefully be synthesized into meta-constructs.

With these provisions in mind, we will briefly review the literature on the key characteristics that commonly occur in people who suffer from performance anxiety (I will also add a couple of my own that have not previously been described). I will argue later that many of the characteristics described in the following pages can more usefully be understood holistically as an underlying characterological organization that has arisen as a result of the combined impact of underlying biological vulnerabilities, thwarted developmental processes resulting from early empathic failures (such as failure to provide sufficient support, understanding, or respect for the emerging autonomous self) of significant caregivers (parents and teachers) (Mitchell & Black, 1995) and/or particular (anxiety-) conditioning experiences. These experiences are intensified in the brutal competitive environment to which many young musicians are exposed, often prematurely, during their formative years, which renders them vulnerable to the experience of shame, inadequacy, and fear of exposure. Such speculation can only be validated via an idiographic approach, since the measurement of psychological characteristics via self-report questionnaires (that produce high or low scores) provide no information about causal factors or the processes or experiences to which the individual has been exposed and which need to be made explicit in therapy, understood, and worked through. Notwithstanding, in the following sections we will discuss the frequently occurring characteristics in anxious people and, where available, the evidence for such characteristics in musicians.

Trait anxiety, neuroticism, negative affectivity, introversion, and behavioral inhibition

Objective circumstances rarely account for more than 20% of the explained variance in well-being (Kozma, Stone, & Stones, 1999). Personality factors, particularly neuroticism (trait anxiety), are considered to be the most important mediators/moderators of stress reactivity (Creed & Evans, 2002). Trait anxiety, the propensity of individuals to respond anxiously across a broad range of situations and experiences, is considered one of the major dimensions of personality in most contemporary theories of personality (Eysenck, 1997). The American Psychiatric Association (2000) lists 12 disorders that are primarily disorders about the amount of anxiety experienced and the maladaptive responses to those anxiety reactions. Negative affectivity, a construct synonymous with Eysenck's construct of neuroticism, was defined by Watson, Clark and Carey (1988) as a temperamental sensitivity to negative stimuli; that is, as a summary term for individual differences in negative emotionality (subjective distress, discomfort, dissatisfaction) and poor self-esteem. However, it is almost a tautology to argue that those individuals high in negative affectivity are more likely to experience greater depressed mood, anxiety, and stress than those with high positive affect, since dispositional characteristics are to a large extent defined by their concomitant affective states.

Various theories have attempted to account for individual differences in trait anxiety/negative affectivity, including the role of heredity (about 31% of individual differences in neuroticism are due to heredity) and physiological variability, particularly in the septo-hippocampal system, and/or cognitive systems, where reliable differences have been observed in the degree of attentional resources that are allocated to threatening stimuli in the environment, as well as to their own behavior, cognitions and physiological activity by those high in trait anxiety (Eysenck, 1991, 1997).

Recently, a temperamental factor called behavioral inhibition has also been associated with the subsequent development of anxiety disorders (Chorpita, Albano, & Barlow, 1996; Chorpita & Barlow, 1998). Behavioral inhibition refers to the propensity to avoid unfamiliar events and people. Individual differences in behavioral inhibition may occur, in part, as a result of high reactivity in the septo-hippocampal region and amygdala that enhances fear responses to novelty and unfamiliarity. When confronted with the unfamiliar, young children will cease their play behavior and seek to re-establish proximity to their caregivers. Even when proximity is re-established, children with this disposition remain vigilant of their surroundings and avoid novel objects or unfamiliar people (Fox, Henderson, Marshall, Nichols, & Ghera, 2005). Behavioral inhibition has two key components—reactivity and self-regulation. Reactivity refers to one's physiological and behavioral responses (e.g. intensity and speed of responding) to sensory stimuli. Over time, children learn to regulate their responding through cognitive processes such as voluntary attentional control and response inhibition (Chorpita, Brown, & Barlow, 1998). Hence, both the initial level of reactivity to certain stimuli and the way in which the child responds to or regulates their reactivity determine the level of later behavioral inhibition exhibited in particular situations. High levels of negative reactivity may become associated with negative affect that predisposes disengagement from novel situations associated with negative affect.

Children showing high levels of early behavioral inhibition are more likely to be lonely, anxious, and/or depressed (Fox *et al.*, 2005).

Anxious children and adolescents use both cognitive and behavioral avoidance as a means of coping with their anxiety. Avoidance reduces their exposure to possibly corrective behavioral experiences that in turn could change maladaptive (anxiety-producing or anxiety-maintaining) cognitions. It is difficult to acquire new skills or to experience mastery over previous failures if one avoids situations in which those experiences occur. The behavioral and cognitive repertoire thus becomes increasingly impoverished due to the lack of exposure to new opportunities and failure to revisit old opportunities to master previous failed attempts.

Evidence in musicians

In a Norwegian study (Kaspersen & Gotestam, 2002), 126 conservatory students completed a short, specially designed MPA questionnaire in addition to the Positive and Negative Affect Schedule (PANAS) (Watson *et al.*, 1988), which provides measures of positive and negative affectivity—measures of trait affectivity and neuroticism. Anxiety prior to and during a musical performance was positively associated with higher levels of negative affectivity.

In another study of 43 second- and third-year vocal studies students at the Guildhall School of Music, UK, the mean trait anxiety scores for the female but not the male students were significantly elevated compared with undergraduate norms; however, their scores were still within the normal to low range and showed no significant difference with their male student counterparts (Kokotsaki & Davidson, 2003). It is interesting that the pre-performance state anxiety scores were elevated compared with the norms, the during-performance scores were the same as the norms, and the post-performance scores were lower than the norms, but again, all scores were within normal limits. Similar results were reported by Nagel, Himle, and Papsdorf (1989). However, only generic measures of state and trait anxiety, i.e. the STAI (Spielberger, 1983), were used and such tests may not be sensitive enough to detect specific issues associated with music performance anxiety (Kenny & Osborne, 2006).

Coping style

Personality and coping are closely related concepts. Indeed, Eysenck (1988) defined personality as a function of coping style. Some theories of coping ascribe dispositional status to coping styles; for example, Miller (1992) described 'monitors' and 'blunters'; Rotter (1966) 'internals' and 'externals'; Carver, Scheier, and Weintraub (1989) optimists and pessimists. Current conceptualizations posit that personality characteristics, especially optimism (Carver & Scheier, 1999), neuroticism, and extraversion (McCrae & Costa, 1991) exert a significant impact on coping. In addition to personality dispositions or traits, coping is also influenced by the actual or appraised characteristics of the stressful environment, particularly its controllability and predictability, and by the social resources available to the individual in the coping enterprise (Folkman & Moskowitz, 2000). Coping has unfortunately assumed an amorphous, multivariate dichotomous character. The literature is replete with studies comparing problem-focused and emotion-focused coping (Lazarus & Folkman, 1984); direct and indirect coping

(Parkes, 1994); active and passive coping (Peter & Siegrist, 1997); behavioral and avoidance coping (Cushway & Tyler, 1994); positive and negative coping (Burke & Greenglass, 2000); and meaning-based coping, dichotomized into situational and global meaning (Folkman & Moskowitz, 2000). Are all these forms of coping describing different coping constructs? Which classification of coping is better, and how do we decide? Each of these forms of coping has been associated with a formidable array of equally nebulous and ill-defined, global, non-specific adaptational outcomes (Weber, 1997) such as stress, negative affect, and psychological distress, some of which could be argued to be tautological since, for example, negative affect is both a determinant of coping style and an outcome of coping. It is not surprising that a number of researchers have declared the field to be disappointing, if not barren, sterile and trivial (Lazarus, 1999) in terms of its theoretical and clinical contributions to psychological adaptation under conditions of stress.

Fear of negative evaluation

Fear of negative evaluation is a core component of social anxiety disorder (social phobia) and by extension, music performance anxiety. Why does it play such a central role in the performance anxieties, particularly as young performers approach adolescence? During adolescence, cognitive capacity undergoes rapid development, moving from the ability to understand only the material world and the present, to a capacity to engage in abstract thinking and to project oneself into the future.

Recent research on brain development shows that the brain continues to grow throughout adolescence and into the early twenties, prompting some researchers to advocate an extension of adolescence to the mid twenties (Sowell, Thompson, Tessner, & Togam, 2001). Three distinct processes of brain development have been identified: proliferation—an increase in the brain's gray matter or unmylenated cells in response to genetic, hormonal, and environmental stimuli; pruning—elimination of unused nerve fibers and stimulation and strengthening of 'preferred' connections; and myelinization—the covering of nerve fibers with myelin (a substance that insulates the nerve fibers and makes them more efficient in conducting sensory, pain, and cognitive stimuli). The development of formal operational thinking is associated with the activation of these processes in the prefrontal cortex of the brain, the last part of the brain to undergo development and change, and the part responsible for skills such as organizing thoughts, weighing consequences, assuming responsibility, and interpreting emotions.

Not everyone achieves formal operations, the capacity for hypothetical, logical, and abstract thought. Formal operational thinkers have the capacity for hypothetico-deductive reasoning, the ability to detect logical flaws in arguments, recognizing that problems may have more than one solution, thinking abstractly about concepts such as justice, gravity, and religion, constructing and testing hypotheses, dealing simultaneously with different aspects of a problem, and thinking about the future and about the process of thinking itself.

Formal operational adolescents apply their newly developed cognitive skills to self-reflection and because this is a new and intense process consuming much emotional and cognitive energy, adolescents can often appear self-centered. Because adolescents are focused on themselves, their thoughts and expanding sense of intellectual power, they come to perceive themselves as being 'center stage.' Formal operational adolescents are often characterized by four cognitive qualities, as follows:

1 **Adolescent egocentrism**

This describes a tendency to focus on oneself to the exclusion of others. There is a belief that no one can understand what they are thinking, feeling, or experiencing because these are unique and not previously experienced by others, especially parents. There is a heightened sensitivity to actual or perceived criticism, self-criticism, and self-doubt.

2 **Invincibility fable**

Arising from adolescent egocentrism, the invincibility fable is the erroneous belief that one is not subject to the negative consequences of common risky behaviors, such as unprotected sex, substance abuse, reckless driving, and thrill-seeking activities.

3 **Personal fable**

The personal fable is an egocentric belief that one is destined to achieve greatness through outstanding accomplishments in one's chosen field; it is sometimes accompanied by the fantasy that one's parents are inadequate and inferior, and possibly not one's biological parents.

4 **Imaginary audience**

The imaginary audience is the egocentric belief that others are constantly thinking or talking about one, or if present, scrutinizing one, leading adolescents to pay exaggerated attention to their appearance (Piaget, 1970).

Anxious adolescents, through the mechanism of social avoidance, do not resolve their imaginary audience cognitions, which appear to be one mechanism through which their social anxiety is maintained. While some musicians abandon their careers as a result of unmanageable anxiety (the ultimate social avoidance), a great number also stay and fight. This group of musicians does not engage in social avoidance, but often continues to suffer very distressing music performance anxiety, even in the absence of performance breakdowns. It would be interesting to ascertain the nature of the imaginary audiences in quitters and stayers and whether different constructions of the imaginary audience are related to persisting with or abandoning one's musical career. A second question would be to identify the maintaining factors of performance anxiety in the absence of performance breakdown and whether these are associated with a particularly harsh (internalized) imaginary audience.

Self-concept, self-esteem, self-efficacy, and locus of control

I know with myself, it is an area of my personality that I cannot come to terms with. I don't feel worthy as a human being. I have to validate who I am from the outside, from other people rather than from myself. I can't give that to myself. My parents never delighted in my achievements. I was always in the shadow of my older brother. He was two years older than me and he was smart, motivated, conformist, always did well. I could never measure up. I was rebellious. I left home at 17 years to escape the shadow, but I guess there is always a shadow hanging over me (Professional male orchestral musician).

Self-concept (one's view of oneself) and self-esteem (one's approval of oneself) are central concerns of psychologists and are among the most studied phenomena in psychology. Self-efficacy (one's belief in one's capacity to achieve outcomes) is a relative latecomer but it has also enjoyed a central role in personality theory and social psychology since Bandura introduced it in the 1970s (Bandura, 1977b). Bandura (1991) subsequently extended his general theory of self-efficacy to explain individual differences in people's capacity to cope with anxiety. One's belief that one can effectively cope with anxiety-arousing objects, events, or people will influence both anxiety reactions and actual behavior in the anxiety-arousing situation. Although individuals may display a general tendency to be high or low in self-efficacy, self-efficacy can be highly specific and one can show high self-efficacy in one area, for example, reading, and low self-efficacy in another, such as mathematics. Self-efficacy is the outcome of complex learning experiences that are acquired either directly through repeated success or failure at specific challenges, through the degree of somatic arousal that occurs in given situations and one's response to that arousal, through vicarious encounters or observation, and through modeling or verbal persuasion by people who are highly valued (Bandura, Cioffi, Taylor, & Brouillard, 1988). Perceived coping inefficacy is accompanied by high levels of subjective distress, autonomic arousal, and catecholamine secretion (Bandura, Taylor, Williams, Mefford, & Barchas, 1985).

Self-efficacy is closely related to one's perceived control over the environment. Those who have a low sense of control often attribute cause to chance or events outside their control. They are said to have a low locus of control or an external locus of control. Those who attribute outcomes to their own efforts are said to have an internal or high locus of control (Rotter, 1966). A diminished sense of control is strongly associated with the experience of negative emotions. Early and prolonged experiences of uncontrollability are one developmental pathway to the chronic experience of negative emotional states that constitute a psychological vulnerability for the subsequent processing of life events as outside one's control. The family environment is strongly implicated in the development of control-related emotions and cognitions in children. A necessary condition for healthy development is a secure and predictable relationship with at least one primary caregiver (Bowlby, 1980). This is dependent on the capacity of the caregiver to respond sensitively to signals from the child and the effectiveness of the child's attempts to influence the caregiver. Early disrupted attachments will result in anxious attempts to recover contact with the caregiver; chronic disruptions from an insensitive caregiver that are not repaired result in withdrawal and depression, signaling that the child has abandoned attempts to influence the caregiver (Rutter, 1980). Attachment representations (internal working models of the attachment relationship) of either secure (control enhancing) or insecure (control diminishing) attachment are carried forward into adulthood, influencing responses to subsequent relationships and experiences. The attachment relationship constitutes the primary method by which children develop a sense of controllability and predictability, and this early learning generalizes to all other domains of experience, creating the needed dynamic links between models of negative emotion (affectivity), locus of control, and self-efficacy (Chorpita, 2001).

Both anxiety disorders and depression share a common risk factor related to the perceived degree of control that one experiences over one's environment. The (perceived) degree of control is related to the experience of helplessness and hopelessness. When one experiences uncertainty about one's capacity to control outcomes (uncertain helplessness), one experiences anxiety; the experience of certain helplessness results in both anxiety and depression. When the degree of helplessness is overwhelming and covers a range of situations in which there is an expectation that the outcome will certainly be negative, the individual will experience hopelessness and depression (Chorpita, 2001).

More recently, an integrative concept, core self-evaluation (CSE), which synthesizes a number of concepts such as self-esteem, locus of control, generalized self-efficacy, and (low) neuroticism, has been shown to have both heuristic value and predictive validity. The first order of business in creating a new, broad, latent construct of this kind is to demonstrate that the four core traits load on a common factor, that the construct can be measured reliably and that it predicts better than its components used separately key outcomes such as greater life and job satisfaction, higher motivation and persistence, lower stress, success, and higher quality of life, among others. Judge (2009), who developed this construct, reviewed its current status with respect to work success assessed by income and prestige. He demonstrated that CSE may account for differences in work success for people who have other characteristics in common, such as high parental educational achievement and high grade point average. This construct may usefully be applied in the study of music performance anxiety and may contribute to our understanding of why musicians with an outstanding level of musical skill differ in the degree of success that they experience and the level of discomfort they feel in pursuing their art.

Perfectionism

Socrates: *The wise man will always be found attuning the harmonies in his body for the sake of the concord in his soul.*

Glaucon: *By all means, if he is to be a true musician.*

Plato: *I take the speaker and his speech together, and observe how they sort and harmonize with each other. Such a man is exactly what I understand by 'musical'—he has tuned himself with the fairest harmony, not that of a lyre or other entertaining instrument, but has made a true concord of his own life between his words and his deeds, not in the Ionian, no, nor in the Phrygian nor in the Lydian, but simply in the Dorian mode, which is the sole Hellenic harmony* (Laches, 188d, in Plato, Book IX of *The Republic*, 360 BC).

Perfectionism is a multidimensional human characteristic, the complexities of which are far too great to unravel in a brief section in this book. The interested reader is therefore referred to the excellent work of Flett and Hewitt (2002) and Tangney (2002), who provide a detailed and scholarly analysis of the field. In this section, the key issues of definition, impact, and measurement of this construct will be covered briefly.

Music performance requires a high level of skill in a diverse range of skill areas including fine motor dexterity and coordination, attention and memory, aesthetic and interpretative skills. To achieve prominence requires the attainment of near perfection, demanding years of training, solitary practice, and constant, intense self-evaluation. One would therefore imagine that being perfectionistic in professions such as the performing arts or sport would be an advantage. Intuitively, performance in areas of endeavor requiring perfection should be enhanced in perfectionists. One would expect perfectionism to be adaptive or facilitative of high performance quality. However, the trait of perfectionism has a somewhat paradoxical effect, with research showing that individuals who are high in perfectionism and who tend to be cognitively preoccupied with attaining perfection in their performances may be more vulnerable to impaired performance, have difficulty concentrating on their performance, and experience higher dissatisfaction with their performances (Flett & Hewitt, 2005). Perfectionists expend a great deal of energy on the process of evaluation, develop rigid ideas regarding what constitutes success and failure, and perceive success as all-or-nothing, as demonstrated by Claudio Arrau's comment that one error wiped out his whole performance. Perfectionists tend to equate a perfect performance with self-worth and an impaired performance with worthlessness (Shafran & Mansell, 2001). Consequently, perfectionists fail regularly, thus rendering themselves prone to chronic anxiety and depression, as well as embarrassment and shame.

One of the problems in the study of perfectionism is that different researchers have identified different dimensions of perfectionism and there appears to be no currently accepted set of factors that define this construct. For a more detailed discussion of this issue, see Slaney, Rice, and Ashby (2002). A number of scales have attempted to capture the multidimensional nature of perfectionism. The Frost Multidimensional Perfectionism Scale (FMPS: Frost, Marten, Lahart, & Rosenblate, (1990, 1991) proposes six dimensions of perfectionism: excessive concern over making mistakes, high personal standards, perception of high parental expectations, high parental criticism, the doubting of the quality of one's actions, and a preference for order and organization (1990, p. 449). Barlow's (2000, p. 1249) definition of anxiety, which incorporates a 'sense of uncontrollability . . . a state of helplessness . . . because *one is unable to obtain desired results or outcomes*,' has much in common with the definition of perfectionism given by Frost *et al*. However, the six dimensions do not appear to be stable across samples. One Australian study (Khawaja & Armstrong, 2005) developed a shorter version retaining 17 of the original 35 items that had two strong dimensions— functional and dysfunctional perfectionism.

Another measure of perfectionism is the Multidimensional Perfectionism Scale (Hewitt & Flett, 1991). This proposes three dimensions: self-oriented perfectionism (excessive striving and demanding of self), other-oriented perfectionism (demanding perfection from others), and socially prescribed perfectionism (the perception that other people demand perfection from oneself). These three dimensions show different relationships to the different dimensions of anxiety (Flett & Hewitt, 2005). For example, socially prescribed perfectionism is the dimension linked most closely with state and trait anxiety, especially under conditions of ego threat (Flett, Endler, Tassone, & Hewitt, 1994). It is also more strongly associated with the cognitive-worry and autonomic-arousal components of state anxiety, but again only under conditions of high ego involvement. There is growing evidence, as indicated in the earlier discussion of social anxiety, that many socially anxious people may be perfectionists and that their high performance standards and concern with mistakes contribute to their social distress and self-criticism (Alden, Ryder, & Mellings, 2002). Socially prescribed perfectionism is most strongly associated with fear of negative evaluation, as it is associated with the imagery of an evaluating, disapproving other (Tangney, 2002). These three dimensions of perfectionism are also differentially associated with the self-conscious emotions of shame, guilt, embarrassment, and pride, which are emotions associated with self-evaluation (Tangney, 2002). Guilt is an emotion associated with a particular behavior, which leads to the need to confess, apologize, and/or make reparation. Shame, by contrast, is an emotion focused on a defective self, which leads to a feeling of exposure, worthlessness, and a desire to shrink and hide. Feelings of shame may arise both in the presence of others (i.e. it may have an audience) or alone, in which case the person is concerned with how their defective self might appear to others. Embarrassment is the most socially focused of the self-conscious emotions, always occurs in the presence of others, and is less intense than feelings of shame, involving a lesser sense of the severity of the transgression. Socially prescribed perfectionists appear to suffer more shame, embarrassment, anxiety, and depression than either of the other two forms, possibly because they perceive their standards and goals to be externally imposed, unlike self-oriented perfectionists, who select more achievable goals and are more domain-specific in their application (Tangney, 2002). The perception of the external imposition of goals and standards heightens one's sense of uncontrollability and hence anxiety. With respect to music performance, the standards may be imposed, not only by perceived significant others, but by the availability of perfect recordings of the repertoire against which the performer and the audience compare a live concert performance.

A third scale, the Perfectionistic Self-Presentation Scale (Hewitt *et al.*, 2003), explores the interpersonal components of perfectionism that include the need to present a flawless image to others (perfectionistic self-promotion) or to hide flaws or mistakes from others (non-display of imperfection) or reluctance to communicate such flaws (non-disclosure of imperfection). These interpersonal aspects of perfectionism have been significantly associated with anxiety sensitivity, low self-esteem, reduced sexual satisfaction and eating disorders.

Yet another partitioning of the construct of perfectionism was explored recently in a study on the relationship between accuracy, response bias, and time taken to complete a proofreading task (Stoeber & Eysenck, 2008). In a sample of 96 university students, perfectionistic standards were associated with high rates of incorrectly detected errors, called false alarms, and reduced efficiency in completing the task; discrepancy perfectionism, on the other hand, defined as perceptions that one is failing to meet perfectionistic standards and expectations for oneself, was associated with fewer correctly detected errors, that is, hits, and a conservative response bias.

Aspects of perfectionism are associated with a range of other characteristics, including higher anxiety, lower confidence and a failure (rather than a success) orientation to one's performances. One study of high-school athletes found that those who were extreme perfectionists tended to have an ego orientation characterized by self-focused attempts to protect a vulnerable self-esteem rather than a task orientation with an emphasis on mastery (Hall, Kerr, & Matthews, 1998). When this pattern is combined with low self-esteem, lack of success is experienced as a severe threat to the 'self.' An obvious factor that should be considered but which is often overlooked is the actual level of skill possessed by the performer and the degree to which this matches his/her performance aspiration. Insufficient ability to meet performance demands in perfectionistic individuals is likely to have a number of negative outcomes including heightened anxiety, pervasive fears of failure and self-doubt, and dissatisfaction with performance (Flett & Hewitt, 2005).

Perfectionism has often been noted in the anxiety disorders, in particular, disorders characterized by social anxiety. However, studies examining the relationship between perfectionism and social anxiety have been inconclusive (Alden *et al.*, 2002). Alden and colleagues have resolved some of the anomalies by noting that maladaptive self-appraisal is inherent in social anxiety but that the tendency to compare oneself against high standards is independent of social anxiety. People who are socially anxious tend not to set unrealistically high standards for themselves; rather, they perceive themselves as falling short of others' expectations. Hence, perfectionism measures that assess high standards do not correlate well with measures of social anxiety, while those assessing maladaptive evaluations do (Alden *et al.*, 2002).

Evidence in musicians

> *I try hard not to judge my fellow musicians. They each have their own story. I try not to be judgmental, but I am very judgmental against myself. I always have the feeling that I am letting someone down. For example, if I play a wrong note, it means that I am not doing my best, and I have ruined the performance. This feeling of disappointment might last a whole day, 24 hours, but then I have to move on and think about the next concert. Sometimes, you have euphoria after a concert—you put your heart and soul into your performance. If you play well, you are buzzing for 24 hours. If you have given a bad performance, you have a sense of disappointment, of despair . . . but that is part and parcel of being a performer* (Professional male orchestral musician).

Mor, Day, Flett and Hewitt (1995) investigated perfectionism in professional classical musicians. They found that performers with higher personal standards of perfection ('I must work to my full potential at all times') and social standards of perfection ('The people around me expect me to succeed at everything I do') and low personal control experienced more debilitating performance anxiety, somatic anxiety, and less goal satisfaction than those performers who did not score highly on these items.

Another study, conducted by Sinden (1999), assessed a sample of 138 university-level instrumental music students, using Frost's Multidimensional Perfectionism Scale (MPS) (Frost *et al.*, 1990), and reported a significant relationship between dimensions of perfectionism (high concern over mistakes, high doubts about actions, and low personal standards) and performance anxiety. In a subsequent study, Kawamura,

Hunt, Frost and DiBartolo (2001) found that maladaptive perfectionism was related to a social anxiety/trait anxiety/worry factor. One would expect that for elite performers, there would be a close relationship between anxiety and perfectionism. In a study of operatic chorus artists, Kenny, Davis, and Oates (2004) found that perfectionism was associated with high trait anxiety and music performance anxiety. Although perfectionism was highly correlated with the Kenny Music Performance Anxiety Inventory (K–MPAI), it did not add to the prediction of K–MPAI in the regression analysis after the influence of state and trait anxiety, and solo and choral musical performance anxiety were considered.

The relationship between perfectionism, using the Frost Multidimensional Perfectionism Scale (MPS) and MPA, using the Music Performance Anxiety Inventory for Adolescents (MPAI–A) was examined in adolescent musicians (Osborne & Kenny, 2005). Although the original MPS had six subscales, in our sample, factor analysis produced only two factors—a general perfectionism factor (15 items) and a need for neatness and organization scale (three items), which together accounted for 37% of the total variance in music performance anxiety. The total perfectionism scale had a modest correlation with the total MPAI–A ($r = .213$, $p < .001$) but was a poor predictor of music performance anxiety.

A recent study (Stoeber & Eismann, 2007) cautions against a globally negative picture of the role of perfectionism in music performance. In a study of 146 adolescents attending high schools for the musically gifted, four dimensions of perfectionism were examined: striving for perfection; negative reactions to imperfection, a component of the dimension of perfectionistic concerns; and perceived pressure from parents and teachers to be perfect. The four dimensions of perfectionism were highly intercorrelated. The most significant findings were that perfectionistic strivings were associated with intrinsic motivation, effort, and achievement. Negative reactions to their perceived imperfection were associated with higher distress, higher performance anxiety, somatic complaints, and emotional fatigue. Interestingly, perceived pressure from parents or teachers was not significantly associated with performance distress. These results suggest that by the time young musicians have reached middle adolescence (average age of this sample was 16 years) they have internalized the pressures and demands for perfectionism from significant others such as parents and teachers, and no longer need the external pressure to provide extrinsic motivation.

Further investigation of the role of perfectionism in the development and maintenance of music performance anxiety in adolescent musicians is required. More attention should be given to the role of actual and perceived pressure to be perfect from parents and teachers in the development of the different forms of perfectionism described in Stoeber and Eismann (2007), and the role that both extrinsic and introjected (internalized) perfectionism play in subsequent music performance anxiety, a phenomenon that has been described by (Kirchner, 2003a, 2003b) as 'self-generated expectations' (p. 80). Later in this volume, I will present the results of studies of tertiary performing arts students and professional musicians who identify 'pressure from self' as one of the key causes of their music performance anxiety (see Chapter Five).

Narcissism and shame

> *What would you think if I sang out of tune?*
> *Would you stand up and walk out on me?*
> *Lend me an ear and I'll sing you a song,*
> *And I'll try not to sing out of key,*
> *I get by with a little help from my friends.*[4]

The word 'narcissism,' which literally means self-love or self-esteem, has entered the lay lexicon as a pejorative term whose psychological definition is often misunderstood. The term originated in Ovid's *Metamorphoses* in which Narcissus was so consumed by pride that he chose a life of never-ending self-reflection and forfeited the possibility of a meaningful romantic relationship. Freud (1914) viewed narcissism as a normal developmental process 'related to the instinct of self-preservation, a measure of which may justifiably be attributed to every living creature' (pp. 73–4). Normal functioning is narcissistic; that is, we all engage in a tendency to overvalue ourselves. This notion of overvaluing the self has been demonstrated experimentally in research on optimism bias, a concept that describes a tendency to engage in overly positive self-appraisals that include exaggerated perceptions of control or mastery, and unrealistic optimism with respect to susceptibility to risk (Emmons, 1987; Taylor & Brown, 1988). Recall our earlier discussion of adolescents 'invincibility fable' (Piaget, 1970). Narcissism is depleted by emotional investments in other people and is enhanced when one receives love from others or approval from one's own, internalized ego ideal (Freud, 1914). Narcissistic injury occurs when parents use their children to gratify their own narcissistic needs or to humiliate them for failure to conform to parental desires, rather than understanding, accepting, and nurturing their children as separate individuals. Some parents are only able to view their children as extensions of themselves, and thus cannot provide an environment in which they can become autonomous individuals (Auerbach, 1990). Shame is closely related to narcissism and both must be understood in the context of two underlying processes—the evaluation of the self and object relations (the process through which our internalized images of important others interact with our external relationships). According to Auerbach (1990, p. 556),

> The central components of the shame experience are the feelings of exposure, whether in one's own eyes or those of others, and the wish to hide. That which is exposed, which elicits shame or related affect, is a failing of the self.

Note the common features in this definition of shame to that provided above by Tangney in the context of its association with perfectionism. Auerbach offers an etiological explanation. Shame as an affect is present in infancy, and can be observed in the behavior of lowering of the head and eyes, the turning away of the face in response to disruptions of parent–infant interaction; in particular, failures of parental responsiveness to an excited, interested, or joyful baby. Eventually, children who have developed the capacity for self-awareness, and who experience repeated parental empathic

---

[4] Lyrics by John Lennon/Paul McCartney. Published by © Northern Songs/Sony/ATV Music Publishing. All Rights Reserved. Used by Permission.

failures, associate their feeling of shame to characteristics of the self; that is, the core of shame is 'the eye turned inward to discover in the midst of interest or enjoyment hidden faults and defects' (Auerbach, 1990, p. 557). Auerbach concludes:

> Thus, when parents accept their children as they are and allow them a private zone for self-exploration without parental scrutiny, children . . . remain relatively unashamed in the face of potential exposure and . . . tolerate the experience of shame when such feelings do occur. . . In contrast, narcissistic vulnerability and shame proneness develop when parents, because of their own needs, either cannot for the most part accept or affirm . . . the child's authentic or spontaneous gestures or cannot allow the child a private zone. Under these circumstances, the experience of selfhood becomes painful and precarious. The assertion of individuality becomes an occasion for shame because shame attaches to any actions that bring looks of anger, sadness, distress, or disapproval to parental eyes. When the shame that results from the devaluing exposure of the child's individuality becomes too painful, the child attempts to regain parental love and approval, to establish a restitutional sense of fusion by destroying his or her uniqueness and presenting instead a more acceptable façade . . . self-esteem becomes riddled with shame, and the sense of shame becomes not a respect for others but a false-self compliance, a destruction of one's own experience to avoid others' withering glares (p. 558).

Erik Erikson (1968) also identified the emergence of shame early in life in response to inadequate parenting. He proposed that dialectical conflict was the basic mechanism that influenced development throughout the lifespan. He developed an eight-stage theory of psychosocial development, outlining the developmental challenges that had to be reached at each stage before progressing to the next. The first stage, which occurs in the first year of life, was termed 'Trust vs Mistrust.' Adequate primary care for the infant's basic needs results in trust and hope. Failure to provide adequate care, both physical and emotional, will result in mistrust and fearfulness. The second stage, between 1 and 3 years of age, Erikson termed 'Autonomy vs Shame and Doubt.' The provision of freedom within limits allows the developing toddler to explore the environment and to develop autonomy and self-assertion. Excessive restrictions or disapproval result in shame, doubt, and excessive conformity.

It is not difficult to see how such shame experiences can give rise to social phobia and performance anxiety, and how shame might be at the heart of obsessional post-performance ruminations about mistakes made during a performance. A perform-ance is a public display of self, a mode of expression that cannot be hidden or taken back. The repeated re-enactment of a faulty performance may be an attempt to undo the performance and redo it or to deal with the shameful exposure of inadequacy and defi-ciency. The fear of re-experiencing shame (i.e. the exposure of an inadequate or defi-cient self) while performing may constitute, for some vulnerable musicians, the underlying concern associated with performance anxiety.

Although there has been a long-standing interest in the emotions of narcissism (pride) and shame within the psychoanalytic literature and among influential devel-opmental theorists like Erik Erikson, broad interest in what have become known as the self-conscious emotions only entered mainstream psychology with the publication of Tangney and Fischer's seminal text on the subject, *Self-conscious emotions: The psychology of shame, guilt, embarrassment and pride* (1995). This work is summarized and updated in Tangney (2002). Since then, an extensive body of work has developed to answer some basic questions about the nature and origins of this group of emotions and how they differ from the more basic emotions of fear, anger, and joy. It is now generally acknowledged that this set of emotions plays an integral role in motivating and regulating behavior. Goffman (1959) went so far as to assert that every social act and every decision about social acts have at their core the avoidance of shame and embarrassment. This group of emotions is more cognitively complex than the basic emotions and critically involves the self because these emotions require the capacity to form stable self-representations, to self-reflect, to make causal attributions, and to make judgments about whether one's behavior deviates from an internalized ideal.

Evidence in musicians

At the time of writing, the only references to narcissism or shame and indeed any of the self-conscious emotions in the etiology or maintenance of music performance anxiety have in the psychoanalytic writing on music performance anxiety, which is covered in Chapter Six. I have mentioned them here in the hope that future researchers will bring these concepts into mainstream research and consider these factors in both the causes and treatments of music performance anxiety. Examination of transcripts that describe (mostly unrealistic) perfectionistic strivings, excruciating embarrassment or shame following a flawed performance, and the persistence of such feelings many months or even years after the event, as in the excerpt from the interview with Claudio Arrau and in the example of our cellist in the opening sections of the book, prompted my interest in the role of narcissism and shame in music performance anxiety. An additional prompt occurred in the form of recent interest in the relationship between social anxiety (social phobia) and narcissism and shame and the foregoing discussion of the relationship between perfectionism and shame and perfectionism and social anxiety. Schurman (2001, p. 5004), for example, explored the relationship between social phobia, shame, and two narcissistic subtypes: the more familiar form characterized by grandiosity, exhibitionism, extroversion, and self-centeredness and the less familiar form characterized by hypersensitivity, shyness, introversion, avoidance, and anxiety about rejection. Schurman (2001) reported a close association between social anxiety and shame, with higher levels of social anxiety being accompanied by stronger feelings of shame; and between social anxiety and the second, but not the first, narcissistic subtype. Performers with this second type of narcissistic personality organization may be particularly vulnerable to the experience of more intense shame and hence the development of the more severe forms of performance anxiety.

Although not directly addressing the question of music performance anxiety, an interesting speculative article (Raeburn, 2007) explores the role of pathogenic or toxic shame in the life of the American country music singer, Johnny Cash, as presented in his autobiography and the 2006 film depicting his life, *Walk the Line*. In this article, Raeburn distinguishes between healthy shame and toxic shame:

> A healthy sense of shame is a source of personal power—it acknowledges that to be human is to be limited, provides humility, connects one with his or her core dependency needs,

and allows people to ask for help when necessary. Toxic shame, on the other hand, becomes a core identity of worthlessness and a motivator of self-destructive and addictive behavior. Toxic shame is the byproduct of insecure attachments and shame-based family rules and systems and is transferred across generations unconsciously and procedurally via criticism, rejection, invalidation, verbal or physical abuse, and other forms of emotional abandonment (p. 3).

The consequences of toxic shame are described as follows:

> Toxic shame . . . becomes a core identity of worthlessness . . . If healthy shame implies 'I made a mistake,' toxic shame says 'I am a mistake.' It [is] the original motivator of self-destructive and addictive behavior as the person experiences him- or herself as an object of contempt and needs to disassociate from that experience. Often, this disassociation takes the form of being 'more than' or 'less than' human, both of which defend against authentic experience. Bradshaw states, 'The most paradoxical aspect of neurotic [toxic] shame is that it is the core motivator of the superachieved and the underachieved, the Star and the Scapegoat, the Righteous and the Wretched, the Powerful and the Pathetic' (p. 5).

She argues that the popular music industry, which is more focused on creating and satisfying ever-changing consumer demands, thereby ensuring continuing profit, has always taken precedence over the welfare of the musicians or their need to write and perform 'authentic' music that validates them as musicians and as people. There are continuing concerns over financial security and maintenance of one's hard-earned position on the charts. Raeburn quotes a comment attributed to Hunter S. Thompson about the nature of the music industry:

> The music business is a cruel and shallow money trench, a long plastic hallway where thieves and pimps run free, and good men die like dogs. There's also a negative side (p. 5).

All of these characteristics of the music industry expose vulnerable musicians to continuous shame experiences that may eventually be medicated by substance abuse (Raeburn, 2007).

Summary

In this chapter, we tackled the very difficult task of defining music performance anxiety, recognizing that accurate naming of a phenomenon is a first and essential step in its analysis and eventual understanding. We took as our starting point that most forms of performance, including test taking, mathematics, public speaking, and sport, as well as the performing arts in dance, acting, and music carry the risk that some performers will experience a severe form of performance anxiety in their execution. We noted that to date, performance anxiety has not been classified within the DSM and that even among music researchers, there is no consensus regarding the definition of music performance anxiety. The term 'stage fright' has been used interchangeably, somewhat unsatisfactorily, with the term 'music performance anxiety.' We examined a number of definitions of music performance anxiety and their robustness within the framework of current evidence. In attempting to capture the essence of the condition, we reviewed current conceptualizations of music performance anxiety as a dimensional construct, as occupational stress, as a focal anxiety disorder, as social anxiety or social anxiety disorder (social phobia), and as a panic disorder. We also reviewed the comorbidity of music performance anxiety with other disorders, in particular social anxiety disorder. In the final section of the chapter, a number of frequently observed characteristics of people who suffer performance anxiety were reviewed. These included trait anxiety, neuroticism, negative affectivity, introversion, and behavioral inhibition; fear of negative evaluation; low self-concept, self-esteem, self-efficacy, and locus of control; perfectionism; and narcissism and shame.

Chapter 5

Epidemiology of music performance anxiety

> *All the world's a stage,*
> *And all the men and women merely players . . .*
> William Shakespeare.[1]

Epidemiology of the anxiety disorders

The anxiety disorders are the most frequently occurring mental health problems in both adults (Kessler *et al.*, 2005a) and children and adolescents (Cartwright-Hatton, McNicol, & Doubleday, 2006). About 29% of the adult population report an anxiety disorder, 12.5% a specific phobia or a social phobia (also called social anxiety disorder) (12.1%) over their lifetime (Kessler *et al.*, 2005a). In the National Comorbidity Survey Replication (NCS-R) (Ruscio *et al.*, 2008), comprising a nationally representative survey of 9,282 people over 18 years of age, 24% respondents identified at least one lifetime social fear, the most common of which were public speaking (21.2%) and speaking up in a class or meeting situation (19.5%). Despite interest in social phobia subtypes (Hook & Valentiner, 2002), a specific examination of the types of fears reported and how they clustered together revealed no subtype distinction between performance-based fears and interactional fears. The distinction was more usefully made between levels of severity along a single dimension, with people reporting more individual fears showing greater severity of the condition and more social and occupational impairment than those describing fewer fears.

Rates of anxiety disorders in children prior to the NCS-R study varied widely—between 2.6% and 41% (Achenbach, Howell, McConaughy, & Stanger, 1995; Cartwright-Hatton *et al.*, 2006; Costello *et al.*, 2003; Sugawara *et al.*, 1999; Velting, Setzer, & Albano, 2004). Ruscio *et al.* (2008) showed a strong relationship between the number of fears reported and earlier age of onset. Those reporting more than five fears had earlier onset, between early childhood and mid adolescence, compared with those with fewer fears who showed later onset, typically in the mid twenties. The same relationship was observed for avoidance of social situations, with those with fewest fears least likely to engage in avoidance behaviors compared with those with more than five fears.

---

[1] Jaques (Act II, Scene VII, lines 139–40), *As You Like It*.

Comorbidity was very common, with two-thirds of those suffering between one and four social fears qualifying for at least one other diagnosis. The comorbidity rates increased with the greater number of social fears; there was a 90% comorbidity rate in those who reported more than 11 social fears (Ruscio *et al.*, 2008). Shared vulnerability factors such as low positive affect may account for the high comorbidity between social anxiety and mood disorders (Brown *et al.*, 2001). People with lifetime social phobia are three times more likely to have a major depressive disorder and dysthymia (chronically depressed mood) and were six times more likely to have bipolar disorder (Kessler *et al.*, 1999). Based on a number of NCS studies, Kessler concluded: 'The combination of high prevalence, early onset, chronicity, impairment, risk of secondary comorbidity, and low probability of treatment makes social phobia an important disorder from a public health perspective' (p. 565).

Women are 85% more likely to develop all forms of anxiety disorders than men (Ginsberg, 2004). For example, women have nearly twice the average rate of generalized anxiety disorder, agoraphobia and panic disorder compared with men (Gater *et al.*, 1998). Cross-cultural gender patterns for anxiety disorder prevalence are consistent with studies conducted in Western countries (Ollendick, Yang, Dong, Xia, & Lin, 1995). Women are also more likely to report a specific animal or situational phobia (e.g. lightning, enclosed spaces, darkness, flying, and heights) than men, although equal proportions of men and women report high levels of fear of injections, dentists, and injuries (Fredrikson, Annas, Fischer, & Wik, 1996). The same patterns of gender distribution of anxiety disorders in adults are evident in younger females, with girls consistently showing higher rates (1.5 to 2 times) than boys (Ford *et al.*, 2003). The foci of anxiety are also different for boys and girls, with girls' anxiety more strongly focused on fears of their own inadequacy and concern with competence (Kashani, Orvaschel, Rosenberg, & Reid, 1989).

In 75% of cases, the onset of mental health disorders occurs before the age of 24 years (Insel & Fenton, 2005). However, caution must be exercised before pathologizing the anxiety and fears of young children, in whom some degree of fear and anxiety is developmentally normative, age specific and transitory (Gullone & King, 1992; Gullone, King, Tonge, Heyne, & Ollendick, 2000). Age of onset of an anxiety disorder varies with the subtype of the disorder; onset of anxiety disorders is generally earlier than for other mental health problems, with median age of onset at around 11 years (Kessler *et al.*, 2005a). There appears to be a childhood peak at 9–10 years of age (4.6%); by age 12, less than 1% of children have a diagnosable anxiety disorder, but this rate rises during adolescence, reaching a peak of about 1.6% by age 16 years. Rates of social anxiety disorder (social phobia) are low in childhood (0.08–0.9%) (Almqvist *et al.*, 1999; Sugawara *et al.*, 1999) and increase in adolescence (1.5%) (Essau, Conradt, & Petermann, 1999; Kashani & Orvaschel, 1990; Lewinsohn, Hops, Roberts, Seeley, & Andrews, 1993), with 7.3% lifetime incidence (Wittchen *et al.*, 1999). Simple phobia is more common, with estimates between 2% and 3% in children and 3% to 4% in adolescents (Anderson, Williams, McGee, & Silva, 1987; Kashani & Orvaschel, 1990; Lewinsohn *et al.*, 1993).

Some anxiety conditions, such as specific phobias, receive a diagnosis as early as 6 years of age (Lewinsohn, Gotlib, Lewinsohn, Seeley, & Allen, 1998). Generalized anxiety disorder makes an early appearance in childhood but can also be diagnosed for the first time in adulthood (Hoehn-Saric, Hazlett, & McLeod, 1993). Anxiety disorder rates decrease with age (Alonso *et al.*, 2004; Andrews *et al.*, 2001; Kessler *et al.*, 1994), with generalized anxiety disorder and phobias accounting for most anxiety later in life (Flint, 1994).

The phenomenology of the presentation of anxiety disorders in children and adolescents changes with increasing age, from a pervasive, ill-defined, and family-oriented presentation to more focused interpersonal, in particular peer, concerns. Unlike other anxiety disorders such as separation anxiety, social anxiety increases with age for both males and females as they enter adolescence (Kashani *et al.*, 1989).

Epidemiology of music performance anxiety

It is not difficult to imagine that most performers, by the very nature of their profession, would be affected by the 'general stresses related to having to perform under conditions of high adrenalin flow, anxiety, fatigue, social pressure, and financial insecurity' (Lehrer, Goldman, & Strommen, 1990, p. 48). Powell (2004b) estimated that approximately 2% of the US population suffers from debilitating performance anxiety (including public speaking, test taking, 'stage fright' in performing artists and athletes, and writer's block). About one-third of sufferers have other comorbid conditions, including another anxiety disorder (usually generalized anxiety disorder or social anxiety) (Sanderson *et al.*, 1990); 10% to 15% of those with a social phobia also have depression (Kessler *et al.*, 1999). Powell (2004b) acknowledges that some of those presenting with performance anxiety have underlying psychological conflicts that require psychotherapy, but estimates that about two-thirds of those presenting with concerns about performance anxiety to his university's mental health clinic did not qualify for either Axis I or II diagnoses. He describes these cases as performance anxiety (or what I have identified as focal performance anxiety).

Since not all performers suffer the same degree of music performance anxiety, or indeed report the same levels of occupational stress, individual differences in a range of psychological characteristics are likely to account for variations in the degree to which musicians experience symptoms. However, no category of performer is exempt from the experience of music performance anxiety. Whether a child, adolescent, or adult musician, whether amateur or professional, experienced or inexperienced, solo or ensemble, instrumentalist or singer, performers of all types and ages may suffer from music performance anxiety.

A note of caution is needed before we commence our discussion of the epidemiology of music performance anxiety. Unlike the anxiety disorders, the field of music performance anxiety has not yet developed universal, reliable, and valid assessment instruments for the assessment of music performance anxiety. Many of the available population studies of musicians have used instruments especially designed for a particular study. Few of these instruments have been published or validated and it is rare for scoring criteria or cut-off scores to have been developed. In such circumstances, we cannot be confident that each questionnaire is identifying the musicians with the same level of performance anxiety nor whether the proportions identified would be the same if another instrument had been used. It is therefore important to keep these limitations in mind when reading the following sections.

Adult musicians

Orchestral musicians

Researchers continue to rely on estimates of the prevalence of music performance anxiety from studies of professional orchestral musicians conducted between ten and twenty years ago. Several early international reviews of music performance anxiety among professional orchestral musicians remain our best source of the frequency and severity of music performance anxiety. However, these surveys need to be interpreted cautiously because the original questionnaires used are difficult to obtain and research was less rigorous than it is today in its requirements with respect to validating research instruments and assessing their reliability. Further, and probably more importantly, conceptualizations of music performance anxiety assessed in these early surveys were symptom focused and none attempted to assess the degree to which high scorers on these self-report questionnaires had other comorbid psychological conditions. In addition, very little demographic information was available on the musicians completing these surveys, so vulnerable subgroups, if they existed, could not be identified.

Nonetheless, most of the available studies indicate that the phenomenon is widespread and problematic (Steptoe, 2001; Steptoe & Fidler, 1987). The advantage of these early surveys was that they were population studies that recruited very large samples from orchestras internationally. This type of survey is much more likely to give an accurate estimate of the prevalence of music performance anxiety than clinical samples, which would run the risk of overestimating the magnitude of the problem, given that such a sample would be self-selected—only those seriously affected by anxiety would present to clinicians for treatment. Not surprisingly, in view of the methodological limitations of these early studies outlined above, estimates have varied about the extent of the problem in orchestral musicians. Notwithstanding these limitations, estimates of severe and persistent music performance anxiety range from 15% to 25% (Fishbein *et al.*, 1988; James, 1997; van Kemenade, van Son, & van Heesch, 1995). In the Fishbein *et al.* study, 19% of women and 14% of men reported that their anxiety was severe. A Dutch study found that 59% of musicians in symphony orchestras reported intermittent or less severe forms of performance anxiety that were nonetheless severe enough to impair their professional and/or personal functioning, with 21% reporting that they experienced performance anxiety at a severe level (van Kemenade *et al.*, 1995). The International Conference of Symphony and Opera Musicians (ICSOM) National US survey distributed to 48 orchestras (2,212 respondents) reported that 82% of American orchestral musicians experienced medical problems and 24% of musicians frequently suffered stage fright, defined in this study as the most severe form of music performance anxiety; 13% experienced acute anxiety and 17% experienced depression, 14% sleep disturbance, and 10% severe headaches (Lockwood, 1989). James (1998), in a survey of 56 orchestras, found that 70% of musicians reported that they experienced anxiety severe enough to interfere with their performance, with 16% experiencing this level of anxiety more than once a week. In a study of

19 Canadian orchestras, Bartel and Thompson (1994) reported that almost all professional orchestral musicians (96%) reported stress related to their performance. The most recent study, the FIM (Fédération Internationale des Musiciens) Survey, conducted in 1997 and reported in Steptoe (2001), showed that 70% of the 1,639 musicians completing the survey sometimes experienced anxiety before their performances that was severe enough to impair the quality of their playing. Specifically, 67% reported rapid heartbeat, 56% sweating hands, 56% muscle tension, 49% loss of concentration, and 46% trembling and shaking. Even in the world's most prestigious orchestras, such as the Vienna Symphony orchestra, 58% of members reported 'nervous stress' prior to performances and 24% reported high levels of tension before performing (Schulz, 1981).

The most recent population survey of orchestral musicians was conducted by Ackermann, Kenny, and Driscoll (unpublished), who surveyed all eight premier state orchestras, including two opera and ballet (pit) orchestras in Australia. The sample comprised 357 of these musicians, a number representing half of the total possible sample. Musicians completed a very comprehensive baseline survey that included the Kenny Music Performance Anxiety Inventory (K–MPAI, 2009a), a 40-item questionnaire based on Barlow's emotion theory of anxiety. (The psychometric properties of this instrument are discussed in the section on assessment.) In this group of highly skilled professional orchestral musicians, 44.8% reported significantly increased muscle tension prior to or during a performance; 41.2% reported significantly increased heart rate such as pounding in their chest. Only 43.4% were confident that they would perform well in stressful performance situations, while 37.3% reported that their level of worry and nervousness about their performance interfered with their focus and concentration.

Operatic choral artists

One study showed that opera chorus artists are also prone to high levels of performance anxiety. In the first study of its kind, Kenny, Davis, and Oates (2004) found that scores indicating high trait anxiety, as measured by Spielberger's State Trait Anxiety Inventory (STAI), were approximately three times (50%) more prevalent among opera chorus artists than among the normative sample for the test (15%). The strong association between trait anxiety and music performance anxiety found in student musicians appears to be prevalent even among experienced, professional operatic chorus artists (Kenny et al., 2004; McCoy, 1999). Reaching an acknowledged level of excellence through selection into a prestigious opera company did not appear to protect against the heightened experience of (trait) anxiety. Perhaps living and working in an environment of constant social evaluative threat—the chorus artists in this study were required to re-audition for their place in the opera chorus every year—may heighten musicians' anxiety. Alternatively, it may be that musical giftedness and higher trait anxiety are related in some way that needs further exploration. A similar study of members of seven semiprofessional choirs (N = 201) reported high levels of music performance anxiety, with greater anxiety for solo as opposed to ensemble performances. Singers with college music training reported less frequent, but not less severe, performance anxiety than those who had no musical training at college level.

The conductor was identified as a major factor in choral singers' experience of performance anxiety (Ryan & Andrews, 2009).

College (tertiary-level) musicians

Few studies have compared the levels of anxiety experienced by highly accomplished professional musicians with those of tertiary-level music students or amateur musicians. One such study (Steptoe & Fidler, 1987) reported that student musicians studying at the Royal College of Music, UK, had higher scores on an adaptation of Speilberger's State Anxiety Inventory compared with orchestral musicians who were members of the world's most prestigious orchestras. Steptoe cautions that such results do not necessarily lead to the conclusion that music performance anxiety decreases over time as musicians move through their careers, but rather that the most anxious musicians have not sustained a career in music and have left the profession. Anecdotal evidence from Chapter One alerts us to a third possibility: that anxious musicians who stay in the profession may become more anxious over time. We need prospective longitudinal studies to ascertain the levels of anxiety experienced by musicians over the course of their careers.

Available studies exploring the levels of music performance anxiety in tertiary-level music students all draw similar conclusions to those reported for adult professional musicians. In a sample of 126 Norwegian conservatory music students, 36.5% reported that their music performance anxiety was so problematic that they felt the need for help to manage it. Significantly more women (53%) than men (11.8%) reported a need for help in this area. Only 5.6% reported no anxiety prior to a performance and 8% reported no anxiety during a performance. Forty per cent of the sample reported significant anxiety in other situations, mostly of a social nature (Kaspersen & Gotestam, 2002). Other similar studies conducted with tertiary-level music students provide estimates that are consistent with rates reported by professional musicians. Schroeder and Liebelt (1999) surveyed 330 German music students (age 20–23 years) and found 22.8% with high levels of performance anxiety. Wesner, Noyes, and Davis (1990) found that 21% of their sample of 302 music students reported high levels of performance anxiety; 16.5% reported that the level of anxiety had a negative impact on their careers.

Adolescents

Compared with adult orchestral musicians, similar percentages of child and adolescent orchestral musicians report music performance anxiety (Britsch, 2005). Fehm and Schmidt (2005), in their sample of 15- to 19-year-old gifted musicians found that 32.5% reported that performance anxiety exerted a strong negative influence on their performance, with 9.5% reporting that it had a detrimental effect on their musical career. When these researchers combined reports of at least moderate impairment and at least moderate distress, they identified that 34% of students suffer a clinically relevant level of severity of performance anxiety.

These students also present the same cognitive concerns and describe similar patterns of physiological arousal regarding their music performance (Ryan, 1998, 2003).

Severity and frequency of music performance anxiety in adolescents appear to be unrelated to years of training or level of skill attainment, as assessed by musical grade (Rae & McCambridge, 2004).

The realization that music performance anxiety may manifest in childhood and adolescence, just like other anxiety disorders, necessitated the development of a robust measure of music performance anxiety for this age group (Kashani & Orvaschel, 1990). This measure, the Music Performance Anxiety Inventory for Adolescents (MPAI–A) (Osborne & Kenny, 2005) is discussed later in this volume. Osborne, Kenny, and Holsomback (2005) used this scale to assess the degree of music performance anxiety experienced by high-school-aged music students attending Australian high schools specializing in the performing arts. It was also validated on a younger sample of 84 11- to 13-year-old band musicians from the United States. As predicted, girls scored higher on the MPAI–A than boys; and those in the age group 14–19 showed the highest levels of music performance anxiety of the three age groups assessed. This study also showed that those who aspired to become professional musicians reported the lowest levels of music performance anxiety.

Children

Until recently, little attention has been paid to music performance anxiety in children, although several studies have acknowledged that children experience anxiety in other performance-evaluative contexts such as sport and test taking (Fleege, Charlesworth, Burts, & Hart, 1992; Hembree, 1988; Kass & Gish, 1991; Passer, 1983; Scanlan & Lewthwaite, 1984; Simon & Martens, 1979; Smith, Smoll, & Barnett, 1995; Terry, Coakley, & Karageorghis, 1995; Zatz & Chassin, 1985). The presence of music performance anxiety in children was first identified incidentally by Simon and Martens, whose main focus was sports performance anxiety (Simon & Martens, 1979). In the course of their study of 749 9- to 14-year-old boys that compared anxiety in test, sport, and musical activities, the greatest anxiety was reported by boys performing solo on a musical instrument. Performing with a band was responsible for the highest anxiety among 11 group activities, including team sports. One of the largest studies to date examining music performance anxiety in child performers in elementary school was conducted by Wang (2001), who found that in his sample of 1,033 students, 23% reported high levels of performance anxiety that impaired their performances.

A series of studies (Ryan, 1998, 2003, 2004, 2005, 2011) has explored music performance anxiety in children. They found that many children, including 3–4 year-olds, display similar constellations of physical and physiological symptoms of music performance anxiety as adult musicians and that performance anxiety is negatively correlated with self-esteem and performance quality. In a study of 12-year-old sixth-grade children performing in a piano recital, Ryan (1998) found that performance anxiety was negatively related with self-esteem, that children's heart rates rose significantly through each stage of the recital (sitting stage side, walking onstage, performing), and that over half of the children exceeded the 50th percentile on anxiety norms.

Ryan (2004) has also observed gender differences in the way that boys and girls of this age responded to performance stress. Girls' heart rates followed a steady rise from baseline through each stage of the recital while boys' heart rates remained relatively low, even when next in line to play, until they were actually on stage, at which time their heart rates spiked rapidly, exceeding the girls' heart rates. For girls, there was a direct relationship between the degree of anxiety experienced and performance quality; for the boys, those with high heart rates immediately prior to performing displayed few anxious behaviors but had impaired performances. Boys with lower heart rates prior to performing, on the other hand, displayed more anxious behaviors but performed better.

A number of other studies have confirmed the different anxiety response patterns between girls and boys, with girls showing greater synchrony than boys between behavioral, physiological, and psychological responses (LeBlanc *et al.*, 1997; Osborne *et al.*, 2005; Rae & McCambridge, 2004). Desynchrony between physiological, behavioral measures and performance may be explained by both the polyvagal theory (Porges, 2001) and different socialization experiences of boys and girls. Polyvagal theory argues that people who express their anxiety in the striated muscles are actually less anxious than those whose anxiety is expressed in their smooth muscles, although such people may not display anxiety as obviously as those whose anxiety is a result of arousal of the sympathetic nervous system. Western culture approves the expression of psychological vulnerability in girls more so than boys, and it is therefore possible that boys learn to suppress overt expression of anxiety at an early age (Stewart *et al.*, 1997).

The experience of music performance anxiety in child musicians has also been shown to increase with audience size and perceived importance of the performance, a relationship also frequently observed in research with adult musicians (LeBlanc *et al.*, 1997). In one study, Ryan (2005) assessed performance anxiety in 173 children in grades three through seven. Children completed the trait and state form of the State Trait Anxiety Inventory for Children during a regular school day and the state form again on the day of a major school concert. Results indicated that state anxiety was significantly higher on the day of the school concert and was related to children's level of trait anxiety, findings that again concur with research on adult musicians.

Ryan and Boucher (2011) recently examined performance stress in 66 children aged 3–4 years, attending two daycare centers that staged musical performance events for parents. Prior to performances, the children were assessed psychologically, using specially constructed questionnaires, physiologically via cortisol secretions, and behaviorally via videotapes of their anxious behaviors during performances. Measures were taken at baseline and following two concerts. In the first study of its kind with such young children, it was found that even at the preschool level, children experience performance stress as indicated by a rise in cortisol levels and an increase in anxious behaviors. Cortisol levels were significantly lower before the second concert compared with the first, indicating that exposure to performance and increased performance opportunities have a mitigating effect on physiological anxiety responses (as assessed by cortisol levels). A similar pattern was observed for the behavioral measures of anxiety, with a sharp increase from music lesson to the first concert followed by a decrease in the second concert. Children also responded with greater anxiety when the performance occurred in an unfamiliar setting. There were no gender differences in anxious responding for these children, in contrast to frequently observed gender differences for older children and adolescents (Ryan, 1999, 2000, 2004, 2006; Kenny & Osborne, 2006; Osborne & Kenny, 2005). This is an important study, demonstrating that automatic anxiety responses to performance situations are present from a very early age and that these performance experiences may lay down templates for subsequent reactions to music performance experiences throughout life. They provide an important prelude to the discussion in Chapter Eight, of the phenomenological experiences of extremely anxious musicians, many of whom were precocious and gifted in their musical development, and, as a result, thrust into performance situations that may have caused them intolerable levels of anxiety.

Self-reported causes of music performance anxiety

Two studies have reported on the self-identified causes of music performance anxiety. Both samples were presented with a list of possible causes of music performance anxiety and asked to select all those that played a role in their music performance anxiety experience. From the selected list, participants were then asked to rank, in order of importance, the factors that contributed most to their experience of music performance anxiety. In the first study (Kenny, 2009a), using a sample of New Zealand tertiary-level music and dance students, music students identified inadequate preparation for the performance as the most likely cause of their anxiety, whereas the dance students identified 'pressure from self' as the most important cause (see Table 5.1). 'Pressure from self' was ranked second by the music students. In the second sample, 357 professional orchestral musicians from the eight premier orchestras in Australia ranked their perceived causes of music performance anxiety. Their rankings are listed in Table 5.2. When all perceived contributing factors to music performance anxiety were included, 'pressure from self' was reported as one of the causes of music performance anxiety in 66% of the tertiary-level performing arts students (Table 5.1) and in 88% of the orchestral musicians (Table 5.2).

Two of the striking features of the results for the orchestral musicians are the number of items endorsed as contributing to their music performance anxiety and the even spread of the items ranked first, that is, the factor perceived to be the primary cause of their music performance anxiety. These results indicate that careful assessment of each musician's anxiety profile must be obtained, so that targeted treatment for each of the concerns can be addressed in therapy. Possible reasons for treatment failure include the lack of treatment specificity and sensitivity (the 'one size fits all' approach to therapy) and the failure to address a wide enough number of factors that contribute to the development and maintenance of music performance anxiety. Although both students and professional musicians selected 'pressure from self' as the first ranked cause most frequently, the pattern of perceived first causes of music performance anxiety diverges for the next rankings. For example, professional musicians identified not knowing how to manage the physical arousal of performance as the second-highest cause of their anxiety—a selection made by none of the music students. Longitudinal studies are needed to ascertain whether perceived causes of music performance anxiety remain stable or change over time.

Table 5.1 Frequencies and percentages of selection, and items ranked 1 from 21 causes of performance anxiety in music and dance students (n = 151)

All ranked causes of music performance anxiety	N	%	Ranked 1
Pressure from self	100	66.2	21.2
Inadequate preparation for performance	75	49.7	16.4
General lack of confidence in self	64	42.4	8.6
Attempting repertoire that is too difficult	64	42.4	7.3
Excessive physical arousal prior to or during performance	63	41.7	7.3
Bad performance experience	50	33.1	7.3
Concern about audience reaction	71	47	6
Technical flaws that cause uncertainty	83	55	4
Concern about reliability of memory	71	47	4
Lack of confidence in yourself as a musician	46	30.5	4
Negative thoughts/worry about performing	63	41.7	3.3
Bad performance feedback	33	21.9	2.6
Generally high level of self-consciousness	45	29.8	2
Tendency to be anxious in general, not just in performance	28	18.5	2
Pressure from or competing with peers, other musicians	53	35.1	1.3
Generally low self-esteem	21	13.9	0.7
Inadequate support from people close to you	18	11.9	0.7
Not knowing how to manage physical arousal	34	22.5	0
Not knowing how to manage negative thoughts/worry about performing	33	21.9	0
Pressure from teacher	28	18.5	0
Pressure from parent(s)	17	11.3	0

Assessment of anxiety

The experience of anxiety involves one or more of the following components:

  i physiological arousal (elevations in heart rate, respiration, perspiration, etc.)

  ii subjective feelings of discomfort (the emotion or affect of anxiety)

  iii disturbed cognitions (worry, dread and rumination)

  iv overt behavior (shaking, trembling, posture, muscle tension).

To this list, for performance anxiety, I have added a fifth dimension, which I call 'embodied anxiety.' The idea of embodied distress comes from a number of sources, including Porges (2001, 2007) who proposed the polyvagal theory discussed in Chapter Two, and the application of this theory in the form of a highly structured psychoanalytic psychotherapy called intensive short term dynamic psychotherapy

Table 5.2 Numbers, percentages, and first-ranked causes among 22 causes of music performance anxiety in orchestral musicians (N = 357)

All ranked causes of music performance anxiety	N	%[a]	Ranked 1
Pressure from self	297	88.1	29.4
Not knowing how to manage physical arousal	149	46.1	23.5
Inadequate preparation for performance	205	62.5	18.9
Tendency to be anxious in general, not just in performance	119	36.1	16.8
Health issues	146	43.7	16.5
Negative thoughts/worry about performing	252	75.9	14.2
Inadequate support from people close to you	87	27.3	12.9
Excessive physical arousal prior to or during performance	258	77.7	11.7
Lack of confidence in yourself as a musician	163	51.3	11.2
Attempting repertoire that is too difficult	205	61.7	9.7
Concern about reliability of memory	187	56.8	9.5
Bad performance experience	257	77.4	9.4
Concern about audience reaction/Fear of negative evaluation	228	67.5	9.2
Pressure from conductor or section leader	141	43.1	8.9
Pressure from or competing with peers, other musicians	195	59.8	8.7
Generally low self-esteem	111	35.1	8.7
Not knowing how to manage negative thoughts/worry about performing	144	45.1	8.5
Technical flaws that cause uncertainty	237	71.8	8.3
General lack of self-confidence	192	59.1	8
Generally high level of self-consciousness	176	54.5	4.7
Negative performance feedback	104	32.9	3.8
Pressure from parent(s)	37	11.7	3.3

[a]valid percentages are given to account for missing values; multiple response data

(ISTDP), which will be discussed in Chapter Seven. This form of psychotherapy pays particular attention to the way in which individuals express or discharge their anxiety. Its founder, Habib Davanloo (2005), observed that some very highly anxious individuals do not appear anxious—that is, they do not show the typical behavioral manifestations of anxiety that we generally associate with anxiety, but express their anxiety through the smooth rather than the striated muscle system or through cognitive or perceptual distortions such as spacing out, losing concentration, and visual blurring amongst others. Performers who experience anxiety in these ways sometimes report that they do not feel or appear anxious but their bodies malfunctioned or misbehaved during performance.

There are three principal ways in which anxiety is assessed. These are:

i   psychophysiological measures (e.g. heart rate, blood pressure, respiration, muscle tension)

ii self-report (e.g. questionnaires, checklists, or interviews to assess affect and cognition)

iii behavioral observation (e.g. observers code for behaviors such as facial expression, heavy breathing, tremors, perspiration, postural orientation, nail biting, eye blinks, pacing, hand wringing).

However, it is important to note that these forms of assessment are not interchangeable. A number of researchers have noted with puzzlement the disjunction between these different forms of anxiety assessment, but explanations for this have generally been unsatisfactory. Although concordance between the different measures of anxiety increases with increasing severity of anxiety, the highest correlations between physiological measures and subjective, self-report measures did not exceed 0.38, which is considered to be a modest association between two variables (Craske & Craig, 1984).

Possible explanations for this discordance between the various measures of anxiety was provided by Weinberger, Schwartz, and Davidson (1979), who showed that inconsistencies in physiological responsiveness between low- and high-trait-anxious people (i.e. between people prone to react anxiously in a wide range of situations) were accounted for by a subgroup in the low-trait-anxious self-reporters who had high scores on measures of social desirability. Social desirability is a phenomenon that reflects people's need to gain approval by appearing in a culturally appropriate and acceptable manner by providing descriptions of the self or by presenting oneself in terms that would be judged as desirable or favorable. Put simply, social desirability is the tendency to give responses that make the individual look good (Holden & Passey, 2009). This subgroup was classified as 'repressors' by Weinberger and colleagues. Physiological reactivity was subsequently assessed for these three groups. Results indicated that the 'true' low-trait-anxious group (low scorers on both social desirability and anxiety measures) had the lowest physiological reactivity, followed by the 'true' high-trait-anxious group, followed by the repressors. This innovative work has been replicated many times in many different domains, showing that humans are susceptible to defensive and self-presentation biases in most areas of human endeavor, a phenomenon that is heightened when people are asked to self-report undesirable traits or characteristics (Thomas, Turkheimer, & Oltmans, 2003).

In a recent study of 67 music students from six Swiss music universities, Studer and colleagues (Studer et al., 2011) studied the prevalence of hyperventilation and its association with music performance anxiety. Hyperventilation is defined as breathing in excess of metabolic requirements (Gardner, 1996). The advantage of this study was its conduct in a naturalistic setting, with three sets of measurements taken at baseline, prior to a non-audience performance, and prior to a performance with an audience. Self-report measures of both affective (STAI–S) and physiological (Nijmegen Questionnaire, a checklist for 14 hyperventilation symptoms: van Dixhoorn & Duidenvoorden, 1985) experience were collected simultaneously with measurements of cardio-respiratory activation, including heart rate, percentage of ribcage contribution to a breath, ventilation, tidal volume variability, number of sighs, end-tidal carbon dioxide (CO_2) (the measure of hyperventilation), and heart rate variability (HRV). Students were divided into high and low anxious groups according to their scores on the STAI–S. At baseline, there were no differences on any of the physiological measures between the high- and low-anxious students. Further, there was no difference between the high- and low-anxious students on the physiological parameters prior to the two performance conditions, a finding consistent with previous research (Craske & Craig, 1984). These results are interpreted to indicate that stressful performance situations result in general activation (readying the person to meet the challenge) and that such activation is not necessarily related to anxiety. While musicians with higher STAI–S scores showed a greater increase in self-perceived physiological symptoms from the non-audience to audience performances, there were no differences in actual physiological activation compared with lower STAI–S score musicians. The high-anxious students also showed a greater tendency to hyperventilate in the audience performance than low-anxious students; lower-performance-anxious musicians tended to hypoventilate, while moderately performance-anxious musicians showed both reactions. The measure of hyperventilation was not associated with any of the other physiological variables assessed, again providing evidence of some degree of disjunction between the various measures of performance anxiety.

Researchers in the health area have long known about the unreliability of self-report measures in assessing psychological well-being or predicting health outcomes. Such measures are unable to differentiate those who are genuinely psychologically healthy from those who maintain 'a facade or illusion of mental health based on denial and self-deception,' and that 'clinically derived assessment procedures that assess implicit psychological processes may have advantages over self-report mental health measures' (Cousineau & Shedler, 2006, p. 427). These researchers used the Early Memory Index (EMI), an implicit measure of mental health/distress and compared its capacity to predict health outcomes against a range of standard self-report measures that assessed mental health, perceived stress, life events, and mood. The EMI showed stronger associations with health service utilization and illness onset than any of the more standard self-report measures. One of the key reasons that standard self-report measures are limited in this way is that the relevant psychological processes may be implicit, that is, they are not available to awareness and thus, cannot be directly reported upon. A great many cognitive and affective processes, including memory, cognition, affect, motivation, and attitudes can be implicit (Wilson, Lindsey, & Schooler, 2000).

This short discussion demonstrates the complexities involved in psychological assessment, and the assessment of music performance anxiety is no exception. In fact, my clinical experience suggests that musicians are reluctant to report on their own music performance anxiety to their colleagues and other musical peers, and indeed some have reported that their partners often do not know the extent to which they suffer from the condition. Caution is therefore warranted in the interpretation of all forms of self-report, either oral or written (via questionnaires or 'paper and pencil' tests). You may be wondering about how one can interpret the many thousands of studies that have used self-report as a primary form of data collection, or whether self-report studies should be discontinued in the future in favor of other forms of data collection. You will recall our discussion in Chapter Two about different types of research and research questions and how methods of enquiry need to be matched to the purpose of the investigation. With respect to investigations into music performance anxiety, you will note in Chapter Eight that I have elected to use a method of enquiry that, while time consuming, has yielded very rich data that would not otherwise be accessible to the researcher. This is the use of unstructured and semi-structured narrative data, in which I invite musicians to engage in a conversation with me about their experience of music performance anxiety. These conversations are subjected to a rigorous analysis from a number of theoretical perspectives using independent reviewers—but more of this later. For now, keeping all the cautions above in mind, we will briefly review the current situation with respect to the assessment of music performance anxiety using traditional self-report measures.

Assessment of music performance anxiety

Reliable and valid assessment instruments are needed in order to progress research into music performance anxiety. A review of the English-language research literature identified 20 music performance anxiety self-report measures, developed for specific research projects with college and/or adult musicians. Most measures were generic (i.e. not specific to any musical instrument), although some were specifically created for pianists (e.g. Piano Performance Anxiety Scale) and string players (e.g. Stage Fright Rating Scale). Most of these scales assessed music performance anxiety as an enduring quality in musical performance (i.e. as a characteristic or trait of the individual) while others assessed music performance anxiety in the performing context—e.g. Music Performance Anxiety Questionnaire (MPAQ), Performance Anxiety Self Statement Scale (PASSS), and the State Emotion Questionnaire (SEQ) and were therefore measures of situational anxiety. Spielberger's State Trait Anxiety Inventory–State subscale is often used in conjunction with these music-performance-anxiety-specific scales to assess both enduring anxiety (trait anxiety) and anxiety that occurs in the performance situation under particular conditions (state anxiety) (Spielberger, 1983).

Many of the available music performance anxiety scales are adaptations of existing anxiety measures. For example, Appel's Personal Report of Confidence as a Performer (PRCP) was adapted from Paul's Personal Report of Confidence as a Speaker (Paul, 1966); Cox and Kenardy's Performance Anxiety Questionnaire (PAQ) (Cox & Kenardy, 1993) was adapted from Schwartz, Davidson, and Goleman's (Schwartz, Davidson, & Goleman, 1978) Cognitive-Somatic Anxiety Questionnaire (cited in Cox & Kenardy, 1993); the Performance Anxiety Inventory (PAI) was based on Spielberger's 1980 Test Anxiety Inventory (Nagel *et al.*, 1989); and the Achievement Anxiety Test Scale (Alpert & Haber, 1960) was modified by both Sweeney and Horan (Sweeney & Horan, 1982), and Wolfe (Wolfe, 1989) into the Adaptive–Maladaptive Anxiety Scale (AAS–MAS). The most recent scale, the Kenny Music Performance Anxiety Inventory (K–MPAI) (Kenny *et al.*, 2004; revised 2009a) was constructed to specifically address each of the components of Barlow's emotion-based theory of anxiety disorders (Barlow, 2000). Only the K–MPAI, PRCP and PAI assess all three components—cognitive, behavioral and physiological—now commonly believed to comprise music performance anxiety and other anxiety disorders (Barlow, 2002a; Hardy & Parfitt, 1991; Lang, Davis, &

Ohman, 2000; Morris, 2001). However, only the K–MPAI assessed underlying psychological vulnerability. Five of these scales were reproduced in full in the journals in which they were published to facilitate future research (K–MPAI; Musician's Questionnaire; PAI; PAQ–Cox and Kenardy, and PAQ–Wesner, Noyes and Davis) (Cox & Kenardy, 1993; Wesner *et al.*, 1990). Factor analytic studies have been reported on the MPAQ, AAS-MAS and Trait Anxiety Scale.

A critical review of the psychometric data on these scales presented in the articles was conducted using criteria adapted for self-report measures from McCauley and Swisher's review of language and articulation tests (McCauley & Swisher, 1984; Osborne & Kenny, 2005). This review indicated that subject numbers in the various research studies were small (20–53). Although Wesner, Noyes, and Davis had the largest sample (N = 302) and described their sample thoroughly, they provided no results other than percentages for gender, age group, and category of musician as impaired/unimpaired who endorsed various symptoms of music performance anxiety (Wesner *et al.*, 1990). This evaluation procedure also indicated that the reporting of basic psychometric properties such as internal and external reliability for these scales was limited or absent. Internal reliability refers to the extent to which a measure is consistent within itself, that is, that all items are measuring the same construct or psychological factor. External reliability refers to the extent to which a measure varies from one use to another. This is assessed using the test–retest method— testing the same person again after a period of time on the same test to determine whether they obtain similar scores on both testing occasions. Very few of the tests reported measures of internal or external reliability. No single measure satisfied all the criteria, although the K–MPAI met most of the criteria and reported the best psychometric properties. Table 5.3 summarizes the results.

An expanded 40-item version of the K–MPAI has recently been developed and tested on tertiary-level music students (Kenny, 2009a) and professional orchestral musicians (Kenny, unpublished). Principal axis factoring (with varimax rotation)[2] of the K–MPAI revealed, for the tertiary-level music students (n = 159), 12 underlying factors, which can be subsumed under the following categories:

i   early relationship context (subscale 7: generational transmission of anxiety; subscale 4: parental empathy)

ii psychological vulnerability (subscale 1: depression/hopelessness; subscale 9: controllability; subscale 11: trust; subscale 12: pervasive performance anxiety)

iii proximal performance concerns (subscale 3: proximal somatic anxiety; subscale 2: worry/dread (negative cognitions); subscale 6: pre- and post-performance rumination; subscale 8: self/other scrutiny; subscale 10: opportunity cost; subscale 5: memory reliability).

---

[2] *Factor analysis* is a statistical procedure used to uncover the underlying dimensions of a set of variables or items. It reduces a data set from a larger number of variables to a smaller number of factors. Principal axis factoring is one method of factor analysis. Rotation procedures attempt to clearly separate and identify the underlying factors in a set of items.

Table 5.3 MPA self-report measures meeting each of nine psychometric criteria[1]

	Criterion	N measures (N = 20)	Measures
1	Description of normative sample	9	MPSS, PAQ–WND, PAQ–CK, PASSS, AAS–MAS, MPAS, TAS, SAS, PMCI
2	Sample size	2	PAQ–WND, MPAQ
3	Item analysis	12	PRCP, PAQ–WND, K–MPAI, PI, MPAQ, PAI, SSQ, AAS–MAS, MPAS, TAS, SAS, PMCI
4	Means and standard deviations	10	PRCP, PAQ–WND, PAQ–CK, SES, PASSS, K–MPAI, PAI, AATS, PPAS, AD
5	Concurrent validity	15	PAQ–WND, PAQ–CK, K–MPAI, PI, SEQ, MPAQ, SSQ, AATS, PPAS, AD, AAS–MAS, MPAS, TAS, SAS, PMCI
6	Predictive validity	0	—
7	Test–retest reliability	0	—
8	Description of test procedures	17	PRCP, MPSS, PAQ–WND, PAQ–CK, SES, PASSS, K–MPAI, MPAQ, PI, SEQ, PAI, SSQ, AATS, PPAS, AD, AAS–MAS, MPAS
9	Description of tester qualifications	0	—

[1] From Osborne & Kenny (2005). Originally printed in and reprinted here with permission from: Psychometric review of language and articulation tests for preschool children by R.J. McCauley and L. Swisher. *Journal of Speech and Hearing Disorders, 49*, 34–42. Copyright 1984 by American Speech-Language-Hearing Association. All rights reserved.

The factor structure and factor loadings obtained for the tertiary level music and dance students are presented in Table 5.4.

Table 5.5 presents the number and percentages of orchestral musicians endorsing each item on the Kenny Music Performance Anxiety Inventory (K–MPAI). The factor structure and factor loadings obtained for the 357 professional musicians, who were all members of one of the eight premier state orchestras in Australia are presented in Table 5.6.

The factor structure and factor loadings obtained for the 357 professional musicians, who were all members of one of the eight premier state orchestras in Australia are presented in Table 5.6. The factor structure of the two samples is similar for the six major factors—somatic anxiety, worry/dread, depression/hopelessness (psychological vulnerability), parental empathy, memory and generational transmission of anxiety. Further factor analyses with other large samples of musicians will need to be undertaken to confirm the stability of the factor structure of the K–MPAI.

These results provide evidence of a complex structure for music performance anxiety that is consistent with the emotion-based theory of the anxiety disorders. These data indicate that management and treatment of music performance anxiety will need to take account of multiple factors in its etiology and maintenance, with a broader focus than proximal performance concerns that occupy the cognitive behavioral therapies. For example, 27% of musicians did not generally feel in control of their lives; 30% did not feel that their parents were responsive to their needs; 38% did not feel that their parents listened to them; 35% did not find it easy to trust people;[3] 59% remained committed to performing even though it caused significant anxiety. These issues are related to the quality of attachment that these musicians experienced in early life and will be taken up again in Chapter Eight. However, a brief word about the importance of control in the expression and development of negative emotions is warranted. Strong associations have been established between experiences of uncontrollability and the development of psychological vulnerability for anxiety and depression (Barlow, 2000; Chorpita & Barlow, 1998).

MPA measures for children and adolescents

Ryan (1998) and Maroon (2003) developed research-specific measures to assess music performance anxiety in younger musicians, but neither presented any data on their psychometric properties. Only one self-report measure of music performance anxiety for school-aged children and pre-tertiary adolescent musicians has been published in the public domain. This is the Music Performance Anxiety Inventory for Adolescents (MPAI–A; Osborne & Kenny, 2005) (see Table 5.7; in the questionnaire the instructions to students were: 'Please think about music in general and your major instrument and answer the questions by circling the number which best describes how you feel').

Data from 381 talented young musicians aged 12 to 19 years attending schools of performing arts were used to investigate the factor structure, internal reliability, construct, and divergent validity of the MPAI–A. Construct validity is demonstrated when the scale successfully measures the psychological factor of interest, in this case music performance anxiety. It is evaluated using statistical methods that show wheth-er a common factor can 'explain' the pattern of results underlying several measure-ments using different observable indicators. One such method is internal reliability or consistency that is assessed using Cronbach's alpha. The closer the value approaches 1, the higher the internal consistency. Cronbach's alpha for the full measure was 0.91. Another statistical method, factor analysis, identified three factors which together accounted for 53% of the variance in the items (i.e. the ability of one item or factor to predict another item or factor on the test). The first factor, *Somatic and cognitive features,* accounted for 43% of the variance. The majority of items loading on this factor consisted of those describing the physical manifestations of performance anxi-ety immediately prior to and during a performance. Two items related to worry and fear of making mistakes. The second factor, *Performance context,* accounted for 6% of the variance, and described the preference performers have for either solo or group contexts and the nature of the audience. The third factor, *Performance evaluation,* contained items relating to the performance evaluations of both the audience and

---

[3] These items relate to attachment quality. Approximately 65% of children in the general population have a secure pattern of attachment, with the remaining 35% divided between the insecure classifications (Prior & Glaser, 2006).

Table 5.4 Factor structure of the revised K–MPAI for tertiary-level music students

Factor	1	2	3	4	5	6	7	8	9
1. Depression/hopelessness (Psychological vulnerability)									
I often feel that I am not worth much as a person	.665								
Sometimes I feel depressed without knowing why	.646								
I often feel that I have nothing to look forward to	.602								
I often feel that life has not much to offer me	.542								
I often find it difficult to work up the energy to do things	.474								
Sometimes I feel anxious for no particular reason	.460								
I worry that one bad performance may ruin my career	.426								
I am often concerned about a negative reaction from the audience	.335								
I find it easy to trust others (-)*	.332								
2. Worry/dread (Negative cognitions)									
Thinking about the evaluation I may get interferes with my performance		.630							
During a performance I find myself thinking about whether I'll even get through it		.613							
I often prepare for a concert with a sense of dread and impending disaster		.600							
Even in the most stressful performance situations, I am confident that that I will perform well (-)*		.586							
My worry and nervousness about my performance interferes with my focus and concentration		.540							
Even if I work hard in preparation for a performance, I am likely to make mistakes		.417							
3. Proximal somatic anxiety									
Prior to, or during a performance, I experience increased heart rate like pounding in my chest			.761						
Prior to, or during a performance, I experience shaking or trembling or tremor			.609						
Prior to, or during a performance, I feel sick or faint or have a churning in my stomach			.582						
Prior to, or during a performance, I get feelings akin to panic			.573						

Table 5.4 (continued) Factor structure of the revised K–MPAI for tertiary-level music students

Item	Loading
Prior to, or during a performance, I have increased muscle tension	.425
Prior to, or during a performance, I experience dry mouth	.411
I remain committed to performing even though it terrifies me	.399
4. Parental empathy	
My parents were mostly responsive to my needs (-)*	.836
My parents always listened to me (-)*	.704
My parents encouraged me to try new things (-)*	.660
5. Memory	
When performing without music, my memory is reliable (-)*	.901
I am confident playing from memory (-)*	.802
6. Pre and post performance rumination	
After the performance, I replay it in my mind over and over	.619
I worry so much before a performance, I cannot sleep	.524
7. Generational transmission of anxiety	
One or both of my parents were overly anxious	.638
Excessive worrying is a characteristic of my family	.624
As a child, I often felt sad	.431
8. Self/other scrutiny	
I am concerned about my own judgment of how well I will perform	.638
After the performance, I worry about whether I played well enough	.413
I am concerned about being scrutinized by others	.323
9. Controllability	
I generally feel in control of my life (-)*	.609
I never know before a concert whether I will perform well	.478

*These items were reverse scored.

Table 5.5 Items from the Kenny Music Performance Anxiety Inventory (2009a), and the numbers (n = 357) and percentages of professional orchestral musicians who agreed with each item (arranged in order of % agreement)

No	Items from Kenny Music Performance Anxiety Inventory	Frequency	%
1	I generally feel in control of my life	261	73.0
9	My parents were mostly responsive to my needs	251	70.3
2	I find it easy to trust others	233	65.3
23	My parents always listened to me	222	62.2
40	I remain committed to performing even though it causes me significant anxiety	210	58.8
38	I am concerned about being scrutinized by others	182	51.0
33	My parents encouraged me to try new things	179	50.1
39	I am concerned about my own judgment of how I will perform	169	47.3
20	From early in my music studies, I remember being anxious about performing	160	44.9
30	Prior to or during a performance, I have increased muscle tension	160	44.8
35	When performing without music, my memory is reliable	159	44.7
17	Even in the most stressful performance situations, I am confident I will perform well	155	43.4
22	Prior to or during a performance, I experience increased heart rate like pounding in my chest	147	41.2
25	After the performance, I worry about whether I played well enough	147	41.2
29	One or both of my parents were overly anxious	144	40.3
26	My worry and nervousness about my performance interfere with my focus and concentration	133	37.3
5	Excessive worrying is a characteristic of my family	131	36.7
37	I am confident playing from memory	127	35.6
7	Even if I work hard in preparation for a performance, I am likely to make mistakes	108	30.3
36	Prior to or during a performance, I experience shaking or trembling or tremor	106	29.7
3	Sometimes I feel depressed without knowing why	103	28.9
15	Thinking about the evaluation I may get interferes with my performance	101	28.3
32	After the performance, I replay it in my mind over and over	99	27.7

Table 5.5 (*continued*) Items from the Kenny Music Performance Anxiety Inventory (2009a), and the numbers (n = 357) and percentages of professional orchestral musicians who agreed with each item (arranged in order of % agreement)

No	Items from Kenny Music Performance Anxiety Inventory	Frequency	%
4	I often find it difficult to work up the energy to do things	94	26.3
11	I never know before a concert whether I will perform well	91	25.5
12	Prior to or during a performance, I experience dry mouth	86	24.1
8	I find it difficult to depend on others	84	23.5
10	Prior to or during a performance, I get feelings akin to panic	78	21.8
19	Sometimes I feel anxious for no particular reason	77	21.6
16	Prior to or during a performance, I feel sick or faint or have a churning in my stomach	76	21.3
18	I am often concerned about a negative reaction from the audience	74	20.7
27	As a child, I often felt sad	67	18.8
21	I worry that one bad performance may ruin my career	63	17.7
24	I give up worthwhile performance opportunities due to anxiety	62	17.4
14	During a performance I find myself thinking about whether I'll even get through it	52	14.6
34	I worry so much before a performance, I cannot sleep	51	14.3
28	I often prepare for a concert with a sense of dread and impending disaster	47	13.2
13	I often feel that I am not worth much as a person	46	12.9
6	I often feel that life has not much to offer me	36	10.1
31	I often feel that I have nothing to look forward to	32	9.0

performer, the consequences of those evaluations (particularly when a mistake is made), and difficulty concentrating in front of an audience when performing. This factor accounted for 3% of the variance. Construct validity was demonstrated by significant positive relationships with social phobia (measured using the Social Phobia Anxiety Inventory (Beidel, Turner, & Morris, 1995, 1998), and trait anxiety (measured using the State Trait Anxiety Inventory) (Spielberger, 1983). The MPAI–A demonstrated convergent validity by virtue of a moderate to strong positive correlation with the adult measure of music performance anxiety. Discriminant validity was established by a weaker positive relationship with depression, and no relationship with externalizing behavior problems. Osborne, Kenny, and Holsomback cross-validated the Music Performance Anxiety Inventory for Adolescents (MPAI–A), indicating that

Table 5.6 Rotated factor[1] structure of the *Kenny Music Performance Anxiety Inventory* with Cronbach's alpha[2] for 357 professional musicians

α	Factor	1	2	3	4	5	6	7	8
.908	**1. Proximal somatic anxiety and worry about performance**								
	Prior to, or during a performance, I feel sick or faint or have a churning in my stomach	.748							
	Prior to, or during a performance, I experience increased heart rate like pounding in my chest	.744							
	Prior to, or during a performance, I get feelings akin to panic	.726							
	Prior to, or during a performance, I experience shaking or trembling or tremor	.648							
	Prior to, or during a performance, I experience dry mouth	.640							
	During a performance I find myself thinking about whether I'll even get through it	.637							
	Prior to, or during a performance, I have increased muscle tension	.629							
	My worry and nervousness about my performance interferes with my focus and concentration	.537	(.468)					(.374)	
	I worry so much before a performance, I cannot sleep	.520	(.438)						
	I often prepare for a concert with a sense of dread and impending disaster	.519	(.355)						(.354)
	I remain committed to performing even though it causes me significant anxiety	.448							
.862	**2. Worry/dread (Negative cognitions/ruminations) focused on self/other scrutiny**								
	After the performance, I replay it in my mind over and over		.776						
	After the performance, I worry about whether I played well enough		.727						
	I am concerned about being scrutinized by others		.694						
	I am often concerned about a negative reaction from the audience		.574						
	I worry that one bad performance may ruin my career		.574						
	I am concerned about my own judgment of how I performed		.523						
	Thinking about the evaluation I may get interferes with my performance		.520						
	Even if I work hard in preparation for a performance, I am likely to make mistakes		.396					(.352)	
.849	**3. Depression/hopelessness (Psychological vulnerability)**								
	I often feel that I have nothing to look forward to			.687					
	I often feel that life has not much to offer me			.683					
	I find it difficult to depend on others			.676					

Table 5.6 (continued) Rotated factor[1] structure of the *Kenny Music Performance Anxiety Inventory* with Cronbach's alpha[2] for 357 professional musicians

α	Items						
	I often find it difficult to work up the energy to do things	.659					
	I find it easy to trust others (-)*	.645					
	Sometimes I feel depressed without knowing why	.622					
	I often feel that I am not worth much as a person	.551					
	I generally feel in control of my life (-)*	.507					
.754	**4. Parental empathy**						
	My parents always listened to me (-)*		.846				
	My parents were mostly responsive to my needs (-)*		.824				
	My parents encouraged me to try new things (-)*		.719				
	As a child, I often felt sad		.464				
.920	**5. Memory**						
	When performing without music, my memory is reliable (-)*			.929			
	I am confident playing from memory (-)*			.926			
.720	**6. Generational transmission of anxiety**						
	One or both of my parents were overly anxious				.793		
	Excessive worrying is a characteristic of my family				.774		
	Sometimes I feel anxious for no particular reason		(.367)		.440	(.423)	
.588	**7. Anxious apprehension**						
	I give up worthwhile performance opportunities due to anxiety					.703	
	Even in the most stressful performance situations, I am confident that I will perform well (-)*					.497	
	I never know before a concert whether I will perform well				(.420)	.462	
n/a	**8. Biological vulnerability**						
	From early in my music studies, I remember being anxious about performing						.497

* Reverse scored items [1] Only factor loadings > .35 are displayed

[2] Cronbach's α (alpha) is a statistical measure of the internal consistency or reliability of a set of scores used to assess a homogenous group of individuals.

Table 5.7 Music Performance Anxiety Inventory for Adolescents

What I think about music and performing	Not at All; Hardly ever		About half the time			All or most of the time	
1 Before I perform, I get butterflies in my stomach	0	1	2	3	4	5	6
2 I often worry about my ability to perform	0	1	2	3	4	5	6
3 I would rather play on my own than in front of other people	0	1	2	3	4	5	6
4 Before I perform, I tremble or shake	0	1	2	3	4	5	6
5 When I perform in front of an audience, I am afraid of making mistakes	0	1	2	3	4	5	6
6 When I perform in front of an audience, my heart beats very fast	0	1	2	3	4	5	6
7 When I perform in front of an audience, I find it hard to concentrate on my music	0	1	2	3	4	5	6
8 If I make a mistake during a performance, I usually panic	0	1	2	3	4	5	6
9 When I perform in front of an audience I get sweaty hands	0	1	2	3	4	5	6
10 When I finish performing, I usually feel happy with my performance	0	1	2	3	4	5	6
11 I try to avoid playing on my own at a school concert	0	1	2	3	4	5	6
12 Just before I perform, I feel nervous	0	1	2	3	4	5	6
13 I worry that my parents or teacher might not like my performance	0	1	2	3	4	5	6
14 I would rather play in a group or ensemble than on my own	0	1	2	3	4	5	6
15 My muscles feel tense when I perform	0	1	2	3	4	5	6

Margaret S. Osborne and Dianna T. Kenny, The Role of sensitizing experiences in music performance anxiety in adolescent musicians, *36*(4), copyright © 2008 by Sage Publications. Reprinted by permission of Sage.

the test is valid and reliable using a sample of American children playing in school bands. The MPAI–A can potentially benefit music educators by providing a basis for preventive action and by enabling them to monitor overall levels of music performance anxiety as well as specific anxiety symptoms in vulnerable students. Ryan and Boucher (2011) are in the process of developing assessment tools for very young children engaged in musical performance.

Summary

How common is music performance anxiety? Does it occur with equal frequencies among male and female performers; adult, adolescent, and child musicians; classical and popular musicians; orchestral and choral musicians; professional and amateur musicians? These are the questions to which we turned our attention in the first part of this chapter. The common perception that children do not experience performance anxiety was dispelled by the work of Ryan and colleagues. The self-reported causes of music performance anxiety were assessed for tertiary-level and professional orchestral musicians. Both groups ranked 'pressure from self' as either the first or second most prominent cause of their anxiety. Two of the striking features of the results for the orchestral musicians were the number of items endorsed as contributing to their music performance anxiety and the even spread of the items identified as the primary cause of their music performance anxiety. These results indicate that careful assessment of each musician's anxiety profile must be obtained, so that targeted treatment for each of the concerns can be addressed in therapy. In the second part of the chapter, methods of assessment of music performance anxiety were reviewed. Analysis of the existing assessments highlighted the complexity of this undertaking, particularly in view of the fact that different forms of assessment measurements—physiological, subjective feelings of discomfort (the emotion or affect of anxiety), cognitive (worry, dread, and rumination), and overt behavioral (shaking, trembling, posture, muscle tension)—are not interchangeable. Many of the available music performance anxiety scales are adaptations of existing anxiety measures, assess symptoms only and have no theoretical basis. New measures—the Kenny Music Performance Anxiety Inventory (K–MPAI) for adult musicians and the Music Performance Anxiety Inventory for Adolescents (MPAI–A) for adolescent musicians—have attempted to address shortcomings in existing measures by attending to relevant psychometric properties of robust tests and providing a theoretical rationale for the items. Much work is required in the area of assessment of music performance anxiety.

Chapter 6

Theoretical contributions to understanding music performance anxiety

While understanding the characteristics of people who suffer from music performance anxiety is helpful, it is important that such observations and measurements are theoretically driven. Without theory, such observations remain descriptive rather than explanatory and make it difficult, if not impossible, to develop appropriate ways to conceptualize and treat the condition. In this chapter, we will explore the range of theoretical approaches that are established in other areas of psychological functioning and which may have something to offer to advance our understanding of music performance anxiety and its treatment. I will commence with the psychoanalytic theories because these constitute the original theoretical attempts to understand ourselves and they formed the basis on which all other subsequent theories developed.

Psychoanalytic/psychodynamic theories

> . . . *he merely told*
> *the unhappy Present to recite the Past*
> *like a poetry lesson till sooner*
> *or later it faltered at the line where*
> *long ago the accusations had begun,*
> *and suddenly knew by whom it had been judged,*
> *how rich life had been and how silly,*
> *and was life-forgiven and more humble,*
> *able to approach the Future as a friend*
>   W.H. Auden.[1]

Psychodynamic theories hold to the principles of psychic determinism, which means that there is a lawful regularity in mental life and that all behavior has one or more causes; and multiple determination—that the same (unconscious) motive can result in diverse behaviors and that a given behavior may be a function of multiple motives (Malan, 1979; Malan & Osimo, 1992).

All psychodynamic theorizing is underpinned by five tenets:

i A proportion of one's mental life—including thoughts, feelings, and motives— is unconscious, (occurs outside conscious awareness). These unconscious wishes, motives and feelings exert a significant impact on behavior, can lead to

---

[1] 'In Memory of Sigmund Freud' from *Another Time*, Random House (1973).

problematic symptoms such as anxiety, and cause concern and distress to individuals who may not understand the source of their symptoms or the reasons for their behavior.

ii Inner conflict is inevitable and ubiquitous because people must find a way to meet their needs within the constraints imposed by communal living. People can also experience conflicting emotions towards the same person or situation, resulting in the need to find compromise solutions.

iii Childhood experiences lead to the development of stable personality patterns and these in turn affect the way people relate to themselves and others.

iv These childhood experiences are mentally represented within, are enacted in new relationships, and underpin the development of symptoms, including anxiety.

v Personality development involves the development of the ability to self-regulate both impulses and emotions, and the achievement of a mature, autonomous self (Westen, 1998).

Within psychodynamic theory, anxiety can be understood in two main ways. The first, Freud's (1926) concept of the danger situation, has been briefly described earlier (Chapter Two). It has a central position in his theorizing, which will be outlined briefly to provide an appropriate context in which to understand the role of anxiety in psychological functioning generally and in music performance anxiety in particular. The central tenet of Freud's psychoanalytic theory is the concept of the unconscious, from which he derived two corollary concepts: hidden meaning and repression (Billig, 2006). The unconscious refers to the existence of thoughts and feelings of which we are not aware that motivate our strivings and behavior. The contents of the unconscious are usually experienced as painful or forbidden and have been repressed by the individual; that is, excluded from consciousness, in order to reduce the pain, guilt, or conflict caused by the repressed (unwanted) experience. However, the excluded material continues to influence behavior because it is so emotionally charged that it demands expression. The individual will often experience intense anxiety and may express the repressed thoughts or feelings in subtle or symbolic ways. Such behavior has a hidden meaning that must be uncovered and consciously re-experienced, worked through, and understood (McNally, 2003; Trippany, Helm, & Simpson, 2006). Thus, the overt behavior is a disguised, more acceptable manifestation of a hidden meaning. Hidden meanings and repressed thoughts and feelings are uncovered in psychoanalysis or psychodynamic therapy using the therapist's interpretations of the patient's behavior and communications during the therapy session (Durbin, 2006). Interpretations are based on the analysis of free associations (i.e. the encouragement by the therapist for the person to say whatever comes into his/her mind, without censoring any thoughts or feelings), resistances (i.e. reluctance to face the feared thoughts, feelings or impulses), dreams, and transference, a process whereby the patient transfers onto the therapist thoughts and feelings s/he has for other significant (and problematic) others in his or her life (Gabbard, 2006).

According to Freud, our personality is an organized energy system of forces and counter forces whose task is to regulate and discharge aggressive and sexual energy in socially acceptable ways (Gramzow *et al.*, 2004). He proposed that personality consists of three structures, which he termed id, ego, and superego (Mayer, 2001). At birth, the person is all 'id'—a series of impulses that seek gratification. As the child develops, so does the ego, the reality tester, the rational part of the personality that mediates between the demands of the id and the limits imposed by reality. Gradually, the child learns to delay immediate gratification, to compromise, accept limits, and cope with inevitable disappointments. Between the ages of 4 and 6, the superego develops. The superego is formed out of the internalized (introjected) values of parents (or significant other caregivers) and society, and becomes the person's conscience from which an ego ideal, the standard by which one measures oneself, is formed (Kilborne, 2004). It is the role of the ego to regulate the primitive impulses of the id and the relentless and punishing superego. In order to achieve this regulation, we employ a series of defense mechanisms of which repression, discussed above, is the most fundamental. However, to live comfortably with our repressed wishes and fantasies, second-line defenses (sublimation, rationalization, projection, and displacement) may be called into play (LeCroy, 2000).

Sublimation refers to a socially adaptive way of dealing with aggressive and sexual energy. Sport and competition are two examples. If sublimation fails, we may then resort to denial and refuse to recognize the real nature of our behavior. For example, an excessively flirtatious female may deny her sexual intent or an alcoholic may deny he has a drinking problem. Rationalization is the process of giving an intellectually plausible explanation for one's behavior that denies its true motive. Projection is a defense mechanism whereby an individual attributes those characteristics, motives, or behaviors that he cannot accept in himself to other people. For example, an ambitious, competitive individual may criticize his colleagues for being overly ambitious and competitive. In displacement, we deflect our feelings onto the wrong target. A man angry with his boss will come home and shout at his wife and children. A child who is angry with his teacher may become aggressive and defiant towards his mother. Sometimes people are so afraid of the intensity of their feelings they will behave in the opposite way, as a means of keeping powerful impulses under control. This is called reaction formation. For example, someone who is afraid of being dependent may behave in a defiant, individualistic, and independent fashion. A very aggressive or critical individual may behave passively or compliantly. These behaviors are usually rigidly adhered to because the person fears a slight loosening of control will result in the breakthrough of the repressed impulses (Beattie, 2005). People who resort to such defensive behavior may experience intense anxiety and it is this feeling of discomfort that motivates the individual to seek help.

Because the discipline of psychology was dominated for much of the 20th century by the behaviorist school, whose focus was the study of overt behavior, the study of both conscious and unconscious processes was neglected (Locke, 2009). However, there has been a gradual re-emergence of interest in mental processes within mainstream psychology over the past 20 years, particularly with respect to the unconscious mind (Bargh & Morsella, 2008), unconscious memories (Greenwald, 1992), selective attention (see Paulhus, Fridhandler, & Hayes, 1997 for a review), self-deception (Baumeister et al., 1998), positive illusions (Taylor & Brown, 1994), and the repression or denial of impaired attachment (Fonagy, Steele, & Steele, 1991) on coping and adaptation.

Cramer (1998) argues that both coping (conscious and intentional processes) and defense mechanisms (unconscious and unintentional processes) are adaptational processes of equal status in determining the outcomes of responses to stressors, and both should assume equal status in explanatory models.

Although providing a strong foundation for theorizing about human behavior, Freud's classical theory has undergone significant modifications in recent years. It is beyond the scope of this text to discuss in detail the myriad theories that have had their origins in Freud's pioneering work. However, we will discuss in depth two of these developments: attachment-based psychotherapy (Bowlby, 1980, 1988; Wallin, 2007) and self-psychology (Kohut, 1971, 1977, 1984) in Chapter Eight, when we discuss the issues faced by severely anxious musicians.

Attachment and relational theories of anxiety

Attachment theory is a developmental theory that attempts to explain how normal development becomes derailed by problematic or impaired attachment relationships in early life. The developmental psychopathology perspective is a useful, heuristic organizational framework through which the development, maintenance, progression, or remission of psychological disorders can be understood. It has developed in response to the failure of simpler models to account for the complexities that underpin both normal and pathological development (Cicchetti & Cohen, 1995). This model is underpinned by three major principles, which are summarized below:

i **Multideterminism:** Many factors in complex interactions contribute to both healthy and abnormal development. Two broad classes of factors, called protective and risk factors, combine to determine both the nature of the difficulties that affect development and the eventual expression and outcome of those difficulties. Protective factors reduce risk and enhance development, while risk factors compromise development and increase risk for psychopathology. For example, the loss of a parent during childhood (risk factor) may be offset to some degree by the availability of alternative secure attachment figures (protective factor). Risk and protective factors have different effects at different stages of development. For example, behavioral inhibition (that is, shy, avoidant behavior) towards unfamiliar adults in childhood predicts fear of negative evaluation in adolescents (Vasey & Dadds, 2001).

The cumulative risk for development of a psychological disorder is the ratio between risk and protective factors. In the case of the development of music performance anxiety, the young musician may be high in negative affectivity as a result of either a genetic vulnerability to anxiety proneness or as a result of inadequate parenting. Repeated stressful exposure to performance situations may increase anxiety, which in turn increases the risk of performance impairment, an event that will be experienced as punishing, which in turn increases anxiety for subsequent performances.

ii **Multifinality:** A single factor may be associated with multiple outcomes depending on the organization of the system in which those factors operate. For example, a child prone to anxiety is less likely to develop an anxiety disorder if s/he has parents who are attuned to her vulnerabilities and provide needed environmental supports that encourage coping under conditions of stress than a child with the same anxiety proneness who has parents who are themselves anxious and who model anxious behaviors to their children.

iii **Equifinality**: A given outcome may be reached by multiple pathways. For example, there are several possible pathways to the development of social anxiety disorder (SAD). SAD may develop slowly in temperamentally shy children due to a genetic vulnerability such as heightened anxiety sensitivity and behavioral inhibition; it may develop as the result of modeling of anxious behaviors and/or transmission of anxiety-provoking information; or it may arise as a result of one or more aversive conditioning experiences in otherwise normally functioning children.

Factors such as gender differences in anxiety proneness, age at which the child's development has been compromised by the onset of an anxiety or other disorder, the level of developmental competence reached prior to the onset of the disorder, the environmental response to the disorder, and the degree of loss of vital developmental experiences brought about by the disorder all influence the trajectory and outcome of the disorder (Vasey & Dadds, 2001).

The development of secure attachments

The development of secure attachment through high-quality parent–child relationships in early life has a significant impact on later mental health and illness. Attachment is defined as a 'relationship that develops between two or more organisms as they become attuned to each other, each providing the other meaningful stimulation and arousal modulation' (Field, 1996, p. 545). The critical features of recent definitions of attachment include its capacity for arousal reduction through the caregiver's prompt response to distress and negative affect, the reinstatement of a sense of security following arousal, and the open and synchronous responsiveness to infant communications (Zeanah, 1996; Zeanah & Fox, 2004). Margaret Mahler and colleagues (Mahler, Pine, & Bergmann, 1975; Mahler, 1972) described this process of attachment development and how secure attachment is related to the development of autonomy and self-concept. The process is schematically represented in Figure 6.1.

Prior to about four months of age, infants react to people in the same way, that is, they show indiscriminate attachment to all caring figures. By about four months of age, infants will smile and vocalize more with their mothers than other adults, behaviors that indicate that differentiation between the mother and other caregivers is occurring. Most infants experience separation anxiety and stranger anxiety, commencing from between six to nine months of age (Goubet, Rochat, Marie-Leblond, & Poss, 2006). During this phase, infants will cry when mother leaves, and cling to her when she reappears. Infants will also show a fear of strangers and a reluctance to be held by them. Intense attachment to mother continues to about three years of age, although with increasing mastery over their environments, infants will also attach to other significant figures, such as grandparents, siblings, and daycare workers. Infants thus develop a 'hierarchy of attachment' to several people, but mother is usually always at

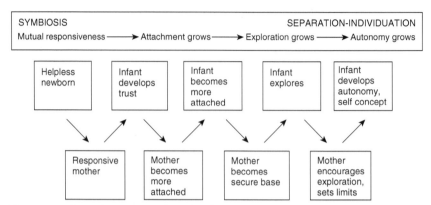

Figure 6.1 Schematic representation of Mahler's model of attachment, autonomy, and the development of self-concept.

the top of that hierarchy (Grossmann & Grossmann, 2005). As cognitive development proceeds and person permanence and object permanence develop (i.e. belief that a person or object continues to exist when out of sight), infants learn to accept mother's temporary absences because they now understand that she will return.

John Bowlby (1907–1990) and Mary Ainsworth (1913–1999) were key figures in the study of attachment. Like Freud, Bowlby and Ainsworth believed that attachment was based on the survival needs for nourishment from their mothers (Ainsworth & Bell, 1970; Bowlby, 1980). However, Harry Harlow (1906–1981), working with rhesus monkeys, showed that physical contact is the most important element in promoting infant attachment to a caregiver (Harlow & Zimmerman, 1959). Ainsworth developed a research technique to assess the quality of attachment in infants and young children, called the Strange Situation (Ainsworth & Bell, 1970). From her observations of infant behavior in this situation, Ainsworth distinguished secure and insecure attachment, which was based on the mother's degree of sensitivity to the needs of her infant. Later studies showed that paternal sensitivity also promotes secure attachment in infants (Cox, Owen, Henderson, & Margand, 1992). Interestingly, the quality of maternal caregiving predicts attachment quality more accurately for younger children, indicating that other factors come into play as children get older. One of these factors is child-rearing practices. Diana Baumrind (1971) identified three patterns of child rearing: authoritarian (emotionally cold parents set rigid rules and strict limits), permissive (emotionally distant parents set few rules and show poor limit setting), and authoritative (emotionally warm parents negotiate rules and set flexible limits). Children with authoritative parents are more likely to become socially competent, happy, and high-achieving compared with children with parents who are permissive or authoritarian (Steinberg, Darling, & Fletcher, 1995). Attachment security is stable through to adulthood, indicating its importance in providing a secure foundation for later development.

Insecure attachment and attachment disorders arise when there is an absence of a significant attachment relationship, or when a significant attachment relationship is lost and not replaced (as in the case of maternal death) or as a result of maternal deprivation (mother is insensitive, unresponsive, neglectful, or abusive) in the absence of other compensating relationships. Children with early insecure attachments have significantly poorer peer relations, greater moodiness, and more symptoms of depression and anxiety compared with securely attached children (Elicker, Englund, & Sroufe, 1992). Family adversity, child temperament and characteristics, ineffective parenting, and insecure attachment combine in complex ways to influence adaptation throughout the lifespan (McEwen, 2003).

Attachment quality is multidetermined and includes the social context into which both parents and their children are born. Innate characteristics of parents, their early life experiences, including relationships with their own caregivers, interact with current life experiences, such as a supportive or abusive partner or financial stress, to influence the level of psychosocial adjustment achievable, their ability to cope, and the emergence of psychopathology. All of these factors contribute to the quality of parenting that they are able to provide to their children. The quality of attachment is determined by the quality of parenting and by the presence and quality of compensatory relationships that are available to the child. Object relations (i.e. internal working models or mental representations of relationships) and available resources, both material and personal, determine the way in which experiences are appraised, and these factors form the basis for the development of the coping repertoire of the individual. From this repertoire, behavioral attempts to cope with challenges emerge, and the outcome of this coping behavior is either resilience (positive coping under conditions of risk) or vulnerability (maladaptive coping, including the development of psychopathology). The child then transfers these experiences into their parenting of the next generation of children. We will be revisiting attachment theory in Chapter Eight in more detail, when we discuss the phenomenology of severe music performance anxiety in professional musicians. Kenny (2000b) has developed a schematic representation that attempts to integrate the developmental, attachment, and coping literatures to include all the factors responsible for the trajectories of resilience and vulnerability. A schematic representation of the model is presented in Figure 6.2.

Behavioral theories of anxiety

Behavioral theories (Bandura, 1969; D'Zurilla & Goldfried, 1971; Wilson, 1995; Wolpe & Lazarus, 1966) have made a major contribution to the understanding of the laws that govern human behavior. However, they are a 'psychology of species' and of themselves may not be adequate to explain the anxious quality of anxiety in each individual sufferer, or the performance anxiety quality of performance anxiety in anxious musicians. However, such theories still have much to offer with respect to understanding how maladaptive behavior arises, that is, how it is learned, maintained, or extinguished (removed from the behavioral repertoire). All those whose profession it is to interact with people should have a working knowledge of behaviorism, or learning theory, so we will take some time in this section to understand its basic principles.

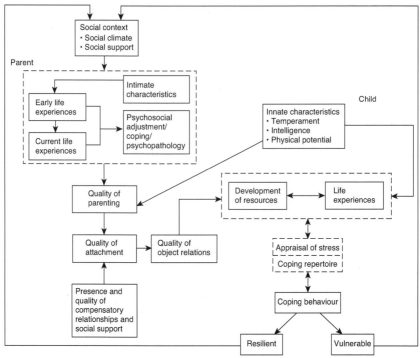

Figure 6.2 A model of the generational transmission of resilient and vulnerable behavior (Kenny, 2000). Reproduced from D.T. Kenny, J.G. Carlson, F.J. McGuigan, and J.L. Sheppard (2000), *Stress and Health: Research and Clinical Applications* (pp. 73–104), with permission.

Classical conditioning

Classical conditioning (Pavlov, 1927) describes a learning situation in which neutral objects are paired with noxious events, called unconditioned stimuli, in such a way that the neutral objects take on the properties of the noxious unconditioned stimuli, thereby producing the same reaction that would normally be elicited by the noxious stimuli alone.

The types of responses that are classically conditioned are automatic behaviors, like reflexes, or innate emotions like fear, which can be elicited by any conditioned stimulus that is associated with the original environmental event, the unconditioned stimulus, that automatically produced the (fear) response. The strength of the fear or other automatic response is determined by the number of repetitions of the association between the fear-producing stimulus and the experience of fear or pain and by the intensity of the fear or pain experienced in the presence of the conditioned stimulus.

John B. Watson, an early learning theorist, identified three stimuli that innately induce fear. These are pain, noise, and sudden loss of support (Watson & Rayner, 1920). He claimed that all other fears were learned through the process of classical conditioning. However, we know that other stimuli, such as darkness, dead or mutilated bodies, or snakes can all produce fear without our having to have had prior experience with these stimuli. These are examples of evolutionary fears, that is, fears that we are biologically primed to learn because they either pose a threat to our survival as a species or challenge us with our mortality (Ohman, 1986).

This 'classical' conditioning theory has undergone revision in recent years to account for the findings that even the simplest forms of conditioning appear to have a cognitive component, that conditioning can occur in the absence of a close temporal association between the stimulus and the response, that individuals show marked differences in their propensity to undergo fear conditioning; that is, they show differences in anxiety sensitivity, and the identification of a phenomenon called vicarious conditioning, whereby a person may become conditioned to the stimulus–response association simply by observing another person undergo such conditioning. This process is called observational learning (Olsson & Phelps, 2004). In addition, some people fail to acquire fear in situations that would normally be considered to be highly fear inducing, for example, during air raids. Fear can also be acquired through the transmission of verbal information that conveys a threat (Olsson & Phelps, 2004), and through social contagion, particularly in naïve, isolated, and poorly educated people (Rachman, 1991).

One of the most troubling facts for classical conditioning theory is that many people presenting with anxiety or phobic symptoms cannot recall an aversive conditioning experience. It is now assumed that in such cases, noncontiguous conditioning is likely to have occurred. Since people are less likely to make connections between stimuli and responses that are temporally separated, they report that they cannot remember any conditioning experiences. Similarly, the fact that some people do not develop conditioned fear in circumstances in which one would expect this to occur can be explained by a process called blocking. This refers to the fact that a stimulus will not become a conditioned signal even if it is repeatedly paired with an unconditioned stimulus unless it has some value. This situation occurs when there is already a conditioned stimulus associated with the unconditioned stimulus (fear-arousing event). The conditioning of a second conditioned stimulus is blocked by the existing conditioned stimulus because it provides no added value in predicting the onset of the unconditioned stimulus over and above that predicted by the first conditioned stimulus (Rachman, 1991). These phenomena indicate that simple contiguity between stimulus and response is insufficient to account for conditioning. Conditioning is now understood to be a process whereby people and animals learn about the relationships between events. This means that stimuli are not equally likely to become conditioned. People already have a relationship with stimuli in their environment and they seek to form a coherent representation of their world through attending to stimulus–response associations.

The history of the stimulus influences the conditioning process. Previous benign experiences with a stimulus may be sufficient to prevent fear conditioning following one aversive experience with the same stimulus. Conversely, a previously neutral stimulus may become aversive through its temporal association with an intense anxiety or fear response. For example, if, as a young performer, you suddenly experienced a range of physiological symptoms such as butterflies in the stomach, limb tremor, or perspiration as you mounted the stage, the stage may become a conditioned stimulus for your unconditioned response of physiological arousal. Your response (physiological arousal) to mounting the stage was unconditioned because it occurred automatically (for reasons upon which we will speculate later). After such an experience, there is a risk that every time you mount a stage in the future, you may experience a similar response to the one you experienced on that first occasion. The stage and your response to it become conditioned, because prior to your first experience on stage, you did not experience fear when you saw a stage. It is puzzling why such responses persist in some people, particularly when no negative consequences arise from their appearances on stage and their performances go well. Recall, for example, the intense performance anxiety of Tatiana Troyanos presented in Chapter One. To explain such observations, we need to turn to other theories of human behavior. You will recall from our discussion of psychodynamic theories that such a response may arise for different reasons in different people; for example, fear of exposure, fear of negative evaluation from an audience perceived as threatening, worry about technical mastery, and/or because there may be a specific biological vulnerability that creates a nervous system that is overreactive to situational stressors.

If this fear persists, some people can learn to reduce it by replacing it with a response incompatible with the fear response, for example, a relaxed attitude. This process of learning to replace one conditioned response with another, more adaptive, response is called systematic desensitization, a therapeutic procedure used extensively to treat a range of anxiety-related problems, and one that we shall discuss further in the chapter on treatment. However, for this technique to be effective, it may be necessary to assist the individual to understand and change faulty cognitions, reassess practice and pre-performance routines, and/or bring unconscious fears into awareness so that they can be processed and understood. Systematic desensitization can be achieved in several ways—in imagination (called imaginal systematic desensitization), in the real-life setting that triggered the original conditioning experience (called in vivo systematic desensitization), and now, with the advent of advances in technology, in virtual reality scenes (Muhlberger, Wieser, & Pauli, 2008). More detail on these techniques will be covered in Chapter Seven.

Operant conditioning

In operant conditioning (Skinner, 1953), the person must make a response, i.e. operate on his environment, in some way. If the response is followed by a reward, called positive reinforcement, then that response is more likely to occur again in a similar situation. However, if the response is punished, the occurrence of the response becomes less likely in future. A third consequence of responding, that of preventing an unpleasant event from occurring, is called negative reinforcement. This consequence increases the probability of the response occurring in the future (Skinner, 1969). In operant conditioning, the consequences of a particular response determine the probability of its reoccurrence.

Behavior must never be viewed in a vacuum. One must consider the setting in which the behavior occurs, the nature of the task to be learned, the characteristics of the person performing the behavior, the reinforcement contingency, and the characteristics of the person dispensing the reinforcement, in particular, how important this person is to the learner. The principles of operant conditioning describe the relationship between behavior and environmental events, both antecedents and consequences that influence behavior. This relationship, referred to as a contingency, consists of three components:

i antecedents (stimulus events that precede or trigger the target behavior)

ii behaviors (responses, usually the identified problem behavior)

iii consequences (outcomes of the behavior, i.e. what actually happened immediately after the problem behavior occurred).

Conducting a functional analysis of behavior is the first step in designing a behavioral change program. The aim of a functional analysis is to identify factors that influence the occurrence and maintenance of a particular (problem) response. This includes an assessment of the physical (where the behavior occurs) and social (who is present) environment in which the behavior occurs.

A functional analysis consists of three components:

i selecting the target behavior;

ii identifying current contingencies;

iii measuring and recording behavior.

This process should not be confused with other explanatory models that may seek to explain behavior in terms of a medical diagnosis or a personality trait. Behavior change programs are more concerned with the nature of our interactions with the environment than with our nature per se. Once the contingencies have been identified, it is important to measure and record the occurrence of the target behavior before and after treatment to determine whether the intervention has had the desired effect in reducing unwanted behavior, increasing desirable behavior or changing the circumstances under which behavior is performed.

Obviously, not all people will react in the same way to a given set of consequences. Although classical and operant conditioning have been helpful in understanding some human behavior, they are not sufficient to account for all our learning, such as why we find different consequences reinforcing or punishing. The early behaviorists viewed conditioning as a process determined solely by environmental experience and reinforcement contingencies. Neither model assigned a role to cognitive processes in the conditioning process, and viewed the person as a passive recipient of environmental experience.

Dollard and Miller (1941) were the first behaviorists to note the importance of imitation in learning. Bandura (1969) later elaborated this idea into social learning theory, a very influential model in developmental psychology, which recognized that cognitive factors influenced the impact that reinforcement has on behavior. Bandura's research demonstrated that we can learn by observing others (observational learning), that what we learn depends on the importance we attach to the behavior and the significance of the model to the observer. Such learning can occur even when neither the observer nor the model is rewarded for the behavior. Because parents are very significant models for their children, social learning theory helps us to understand how children acquire complex ideals, characteristics, and ways of relating to others. Children identify with and imitate their parents' behavior. This process is so powerful that children will often repeat in their own adult lives the behaviors and relationships of their parents (Taubman-Ben-Ari, Mikulincer, & Gillath, 2005). Just watching another person, particularly a parent, react anxiously to an event or being told that something is threatening and dangerous can produce anxiety responses in the observer. These are the mechanisms whereby parents can transmit their own anxieties to their children. Parents who are anxious are more likely to have children with an anxiety disorder (Woodruff-Borden, Morrow, Bourland, & Cambron, 2002). As we shall see later, many of the most anxious musicians discussed later in this book report having parents with anxiety disorders and other disorders that produce anxiety in their children through a process of anxious attachment (see Chapter Eight).

Modern learning theory and the etiology of the anxiety disorders

The shared feature underlying all recent models of behaviorism or learning theory is the concept of reciprocal determinism, the idea that internal cognitive processes, environmental events, and behavior are interdependent and influence each other. These recent models have moved closer to psychodynamic models in an attempt to account for the many complexities in human behavior that are not easily explained by the original mechanistic models that focused on overt behavior.

In a recent paper in *American Psychologist*, Mineka and Zinbarg (2006) have synthesized recent developments in learning theory that contribute to a more sophisticated understanding of individual differences in responses to conditioning experiences and to the development of an anxiety disorder. Although some of these issues were canvassed in the scholarly literature over 20 years ago (Rescorla, 1988), the changes to learning theory have not had adequate uptake within clinical research and practice. The key additions to the theory will be summarized below, given their importance to our understanding of the etiology of music performance anxiety.

One of the key questions with respect to the development of an anxiety disorder is why some individuals who are exposed to aversive conditioning experiences do not develop abnormal fear reactions or phobias. Part of the explanation lies in the genetic contribution to fear conditioning which may be mediated through personality variables such as high trait anxiety and behavioral inhibition (i.e. timidity and shyness). These so-called vulnerability factors affect the speed and strength of conditioning and, in fact, predict the onset of multiple specific phobias. A number of theories now include vulnerability and dispositional factors in the etiology of psychological disorders, most notably for our purposes, Barlow's triple vulnerability model, which we will deal with shortly.

Previous learning or conditioning experiences are now understood to play a central role in the onset of anxiety disorders. The terms 'attachment' (Bowlby, 1980) and 'attachment quality' (Schore & Schore, 2008) are not concepts that appear in the experimental/animal learning psychology literature. However, the concepts 'previous learning' and 'conditioning experiences' taken together refer, at least in part, to attachment, which describes the pattern of emotional learning that occurs in the context of early primary relationships and which has a profound impact on later learning and social and emotional adjustment. Specifically, early experiences that signal control and mastery over one's environment are protective against the development of all forms of psychopathology, including the anxiety disorders (Chorpita *et al.*, 1998). It is a shame that the two literatures do not communicate to form a more unified and coherent theory of human behavior. I will be discussing attachment theory later in this volume because of its relevance to understanding musicians with very severe music performance anxiety (see Chapter Eight). In attempting to account for the development and course of anxiety disorders, modern learning theory has expanded its original and exclusive focus on overt behavior to include a consideration of temperamental vulnerabilities, learning history, and the contextual variables that occur before and after stressful learning events. I will limit the discussion here to the role that these factors play in the development of the specific and social phobias and in panic and panic disorder as these anxiety disorders are most relevant to our understanding of music performance anxiety.

Early learning histories underpin the development of vulnerability and resilience (also called which is defined as invulnerability the capacity to cope in adverse circumstances). The degree to which a child is vulnerable or resilient has an impact on their response to traumatic or stressful life events and these responses determine the short and long term consequences of the traumatic experience. When these learning histories are considered in the context of individual temperamental vulnerabilities, predictions can be made about who is likely to develop a phobia amongst people who have all had similar relevant conditioning experiences. For example, Susanna and Geraldine, two talented 15-year-old piano students learning from the same teacher, competed in the same eisteddfod, playing the same repertoire. Both experienced significant performance breakdowns that ended their chances of success in the eisteddfod. Susanna subsequently developed an intense anxiety about performing in future eisteddfods and this fear gradually generalized to most performance situations. Geraldine, on the other hand, while mortified by her performance failure at the eisteddfod, recovered sufficiently to compete in another section of the eisteddfod two days later and did not develop any significant anxieties about performing in public. Why did these two young performers have such different reactions to their performance breakdowns in the eisteddfod? It may help to know that Susanna was temperamentally shy and introverted, lacked confidence in her pianistic ability and had not had much public performance experience. Geraldine was what her mother called a 'born performer' and delighted in playing for anyone who asked her. She was a happy child with an easy-going temperament and a realistic self-confidence in her pianistic abilities. Susanna's mother, somewhat socially anxious herself, was unable to conceal her anxiety for her daughter prior to her performance and was overly solicitous. Geraldine's mother kissed her daughter good luck and hoped that she had fun performing. Knowing both the learning history and the temperamental vulnerabilities of these two young pianists now starts to make sense of the very different outcomes of the same aversive experience.

In addition to the transmission of genetically based vulnerability, modeling of social anxiety occurs in families and this is followed by social reinforcement of similar behavior in the children (Antony & Rowa, 2008; Bitran & Barlow, 2004). Susanna's learning history included observing her mother struggle in socially demanding situations, which could result in vicarious conditioning of anxious responding. The impact of prior experiences also affects the response to subsequent aversive experiences. Susanna's previous performance experiences were anxiety laden while Geraldine had a reservoir of positive performance experiences in her learning history. The number of non-traumatic exposures to a performance situation is protective against the development of severe anxiety in a subsequent potentially traumatizing situation.

Probably one of the most critical factors that determine whether a specific or social phobia will develop is the degree to which the person feels control over the aversive situation. Animal studies have demonstrated that uncontrollable (but not controllable) electric shock increases submissiveness and exaggerated fear responses and that repeated experiences of social defeat produce the phenomenon known as 'learned helplessness' (Alloy *et al.*, 1990). There is growing evidence that perception of uncontrollability is strongly associated with the development of social anxiety (Armfield, 2006; Mineka & Zinbarg, 2006).

In a critique of Mineka and Zinbarg (2006), Olatunji, Forsyth, and Feldner (2007) argued that modern learning theory is still problematic because it does not give due recognition to the role of emotional regulation, which consists of actions such as reappraisal, distraction, avoidance, escape, and suppression in fear learning. They state:

> fear-related learning is a normative and ubiquitous experience among humans ... Emotional regulatory processes share a common goal: to minimize the frequency, intensity, duration, or situational occurrence of internal feeling states (e.g. anxiety), associated thoughts, and physiological reactions . . . (p. 258) However, it is when individuals down regulate (i.e. suppress, avoid, escape) conditioned emotional responses in a rigid fashion that such learning becomes problematic (p. 257).

Olatunji *et al.* (2007) further argued that emotional regulation disorders provide an explanation as to how fear learning shifts from normative to disordered. They describe a four stage process whereby people:

i   deny that they will experience unwanted or aversive emotions, thoughts, or physical sensations

ii are unwilling to acknowledge these unwanted emotions, thoughts, or physical sensations

iii actively seek to alter their form and frequency of occurrence

iv engage in rigid strategies to accomplish points 1, 2 and 3.

They conclude that:

> anxiety disorders are not entirely a function of fear learning; rather, they are a function of what people do with conditioned fear . . . [T]emperamental vulnerabilities . . . fear learning . . . and neuroticism or uncontrollability will contribute to the etiology of anxiety disorders only in cases where persons engage in excessive/inflexible emotional regulation in the context of contingencies that demand approach (p. 260).

It is worthy of note that there is now experimental evidence to show that active suppression of aversive thoughts and feelings does not provide relief from the associated emotions but appears to make them worse (Feldner, Zvolensky, Stickle, Bonn-Miller, & Leen-Feldner, 2006). Further, emotional regulation is now considered one of the important outcomes of learning theory-based therapies (Eifert & Forsyth, 2005).

Cognitive theories of anxiety

Conditioning and cognitive theories have traditionally been conceptualized as incompatible, mutually exclusive methods for understanding behavior. The dichotomizing of these two theoretical approaches is another example of the unhelpful and essentially ill-informed dualities that have arisen in psychology, other examples of which were discussed in Chapter Two, which described the conceptual framework for this book.

Much of the research on anxiety has focused on the central etiological role of faulty cognitions in the genesis and maintenance of anxiety disorders (Beck & Clark, 1988; 1997; Mandler, 1984; Spielberger, 1985). Theorizing in music performance anxiety has, to date, followed a similar route (Kenny, 2009b; Kenny & Osborne, 2006; Lehrer, 1987; Steptoe & Fidler, 1987; Wolfe, 1989). This conceptualization needs to be broadened to account for all the manifestations of music performance anxiety, as we shall see later. Nonetheless, faulty cognitions have been found to be present in both adult (Papageorgi et al., 2007) and adolescent musicians (Kenny & Osborne, 2006; Osborne, Kenny, & Cooksey, 2007) who suffer high levels of music performance anxiety.

Aaron Beck is the best known name in the field of cognitive therapy for anxiety and depression. Although the cognitive therapies are aligned with the learning theories, it may surprise you to learn that Aaron Beck trained as a psychoanalyst and was greatly influenced in his theoretical formulations about the role of cognitions in anxiety generation and maintenance by his training in psychoanalytic therapy approaches. He developed a schema-based theory of anxiety, which has much in common with psychoanalytic notions of the unconscious. Beck and Clark (1988) defined a schema as follows:

> Cognitive structures [i.e. schemas] are functional structures of relatively enduring representations of prior knowledge and experience [that] guide the screening, encoding, organizing, storing and retrieving of information. Stimuli consistent with existing schemas are elaborated and encoded, while inconsistent or irrelevant information is ignored or forgotten . . . [T]he maladaptive schemas in the anxious patient involve perceived physical or psychological threat to one's personal domain as well as an exaggerated sense of vulnerability (pp. 24–6).

Beck and Clark argued that the different anxiety disorders were characterized by different maladaptive schemas. For example, in the generalized anxiety disorders, the focus is on a wide range of normal situations that pose a threat to one's self-esteem; for people with panic disorder, bodily sensations and mental phenomena are interpreted catastrophically; for people with simple phobias, danger is assigned to specific avoidable situations. The foundations for these schemas are developed in early life and reinforced over time as more attentional resources are directed to the sources of perceived threat. Thus, these schemas influence cognitive functioning by focusing the individual's attention on aspects of their internal and external environment that confirm their schemas of threat or danger.

Two of the major consequences of this process of schema development and consolidation are that anxious people may become very rigid and narrowly focused in their perceptions and cognitions. Two of the most prevalent and serious cognitive distortions, as they are called, are attention binding and catastrophizing. Attention binding refers to a preoccupation with danger and an involuntary focus on danger and threat-related stimuli, including words, environments, and situations. Catastrophizing has a number of elements that include predicting the worst outcome for events and overestimating the frequency of occurrence of such events. Anxious people are vulnerable to cognitive distortions that result in the interpretation of neutral events as dangerous, or mildly threatening stimuli as catastrophically dangerous (Eysenck, 1997). You will be familiar with many music performance-based catastrophic thoughts; for example, 'One mistake will ruin my whole performance,' 'You are only as good as your last performance,' 'If I make a mistake during performance, I don't deserve my position in this orchestra,' 'Everyone can play this better than me' and so on.

Substantial evidence confirms the existence of schema-congruent processing in people with anxiety, including those with performance anxiety (Armfield, 2006). These schemas are activated in times of stress and people may not be aware that they have developed such rigid cognitive processes until a relevant situation arises or until they start to challenge them with the support of a psychologist. More recent theorizing about the cognitive origins of anxiety builds on this framework. For example, Newman and Beck (2010) describe a specific type of schema that they call the 'cognitive triad,' which comprises people's beliefs about themselves, their social network, and their future that influences the onset and severity of emotional disorders. They argue that when people experience high levels of maladaptive emotional distress, it is generally underpinned by problematic, stereotypic, and biased interpretations related to this cognitive triad of self, world, and future. For example, people with anxiety disorders may view themselves as more vulnerable and others as more capable than they are. These others are perceived to be critical of them. The future is perceived to be a series of disasters waiting to happen. Particular types of cognitive processing, sometimes referred to as cognitive styles characterized by biases in attention, memory, interpretation, and repetitive negative thoughts increase a person's vulnerability to developing an emotional disorder (Mathews & MacLeod, 2005).

Cognitive theories are not without their critics, because no theory is without flaws, and a number of issues have been identified with a purely cognitive approach to understanding human behavior. These include, until recently, the neglect of emotions; the neglect of consciousness (and the unconscious); the failure to consider the contribution of embodiment (the physical body) to cognition; and the failure to recognize that human thought and action are socially embedded (Clark, 2008). Consequently, there has been an explosion of research and theory development in the cognitive theories of the anxiety disorders to incorporate these elements into theory and practice. The literature is too vast to be covered here but many of the newer models have relevance for the performance anxieties, as they share, with all other anxiety disorders, a central role for worry. For a comprehensive review of recent theorizing in and evidence for the newer cognitive models, the interested reader is referred to Behar, DiMarco, Hekler, Mohlman, and Staples (2009). Below is a table taken from this review that summarizes the models, their key components, and their implications for therapy. The five models are: Avoidance model of worry and GAD (AMW) (Borkovec, 1994); Intolerance of uncertainty model (IUM) (Dugas, Letarte, Rheaume, Freeston, & Ladouceur, 1995); Meta-cognitive model (MCM) (Wells, 2002); Emotion dysregulation model (EDM) (Mennin, Heimberg, Turk, & Fresco, 2002); and Acceptance-based model (ABM) (Roemer & Orsillo, 2002). The models cluster into three types: cognitive models (i.e. IUM, MCM), emotional/experiential models (i.e. EDM, ABM), and an integrated model (AMW). A summary of treatment components is presented in Table 6.1.

Table 6.1 Summary of treatment components for each of five 'new wave' therapies

Theoretical model	Theoretical components	Key intervention components
Avoidance model of worry and GAD	Cognitive avoidance	Self-monitoring
	Positive worry beliefs	Relaxation techniques
	Ineffective problem-solving/emotional processing	Self-control desensitization
		Gradual stimulus control
	Interpersonal issues	Cognitive restructuring
	Attachment style	Worry outcome monitoring
	Previous trauma	Present-moment focus
		Expectancy-free living
Intolerance of uncertainty model	Intolerance of uncertainty	Self-monitoring
	Negative problem orientation	Intolerance of uncertainly education
	Cognitive avoidance	Evaluating worry beliefs
	Beliefs about worry	Improving problem-orientation
		Processing core fears
Metacognitive therapy	Positive beliefs about worry	Case formulation
	Type 1 Worry[1]	Socialization
	Negative beliefs about worry	Discuss uncontrollability of worry
	Type 2 Worry[2]	Discuss danger of worry
	Ineffective coping	Discuss positive worry beliefs
Emotion dysregulation model	Emotional hyperarousal	Relaxation exercises
	Poor understanding of emotions	Beliefs reframing
	Negative cognitive reactions to emotions	Emotional education
		Emotional skills training
	Maladaptive emotion management and regulation	Experiential exposure exercises
Acceptance-based model of GAD	Internal experiences	Psychoeducation about ABM
	Problematic relationship with internal experiences	Mindfulness and acceptance exercises
	Experiential avoidance	Behavioral change and valued actions
	Behavioral restriction	

[1] Type 1 worry is focused on non-cognitive events such as external situations or physical symptoms.

[2] Type 2 worry is associated with ineffective strategies aimed at avoiding worry via attempts at controlling behaviors, thoughts, and/or emotions such reassurance-seeking, checking behavior, thought suppression, distraction, and avoidance of difficult situations.

From Behar, E., DiMarco, I. D., Hekler, E. B., Mohlman, J., & Staples, A. M. (2009). Current theoretical models of generalized anxiety disorder (GAD): Conceptual review and treatment implications. *Journal of Anxiety Disorders, 23*(8), p. 1014.

Evidence for dysfunctional cognitions in the development of music performance anxiety

In the context of music performance anxiety, an anxious musician might come to view him/herself as a fraud or a sham who does not have the necessary musical talent or skills to occupy the position that they hold in their orchestra; they perceive their peers as more capable than they and that the audience is critical of them. They are on the alert to find signs of their incompetence, and fear that they will experience a perform-ance catastrophe at their next performance. These cognitive triads set up vicious cycles, in which the fear of a performance catastrophe may result in avoidance of expe-riences that could disconfirm their catastrophic predictions and support their self-esteem and adaptive learning. Instead, their maladaptive (avoidant) response to their anxiety reinforces their cognitive distortions, heightens their distress, increases feel-ings of uncontrollability and unpredictability in the performance setting, and increases symptoms, avoidance, or both. The task of cognitive therapy is to challenge this closed, pathological system and replace it with one that is more open and adaptive.

Research shows that for some musicians, similar patterns become established early in a musical career. For example, Osborne and Kenny (2005a) found a curvilinear trend in music performance anxiety levels in adolescent musicians that was consistent with the development of formal operational thought, a characteristic cognitive change associated with the progression from childhood to adolescence (Piaget, 1970). These changes include an increase in retrospection and self-evaluation. Formal operational thought tends to develop in areas in which the adolescent is greatly interested and involved. The cognitive skill of formal operations allows adolescents to imagine other people's thoughts, which can lead some to mistakenly believe that others are as preoccupied with their thoughts and appearance as the adolescents themselves. This can create anxiety and self-criticism in some adolescents (Kenny, 2000b). Given that adolescents are also more likely to evaluate themselves in terms of academic and other achievements (Heaven, 2001), the increasing levels of music performance anxiety with age in the high school years is consistent with other research on adolescent cognitive development.

Negative cognitions may have a more important role in causing performance disrup-tion than physiological or behavioral components of anxiety (Bruce & Barlow, 1990; Kenny & Osborne, 2006). In music performance anxiety, arousal appears to be subject to cognitive appraisals that determine the subsequent emotional response, that may or may not optimize performance, depending on how it is interpreted by the performer (Salmon, 1990). Although Craske and Craig (1984) found that neither the behavioral, physiological, or cognitive systems uniquely defined the music performance anxiety state, particular cognitive styles contributed strongly to anxiety maintenance.

Musicians with high music performance anxiety show higher fear of negative evaluation than low music performance anxious musicians. The two most critical cognitions predicting music performance anxiety in solo music performances related to the consequences (e.g. 'My career is ruined,' 'If I make the slightest mistake, they'll think I'm incompetent and I'll get thrown out of school') and likelihood of negative evaluation (e.g. 'The audience expects me to play at a higher standard than I can play, and they'll be disappointed in me') (Osborne & Franklin, 2002). On the other hand, musicians who are able to control their music performance anxiety at moderate levels do so, in part, by using realistic self-appraisal, e.g. 'I'm bound to make a few mistakes, but so does everyone.'

Osborne and Kenny (2008) tested two hypotheses related to the genesis of music performance anxiety in young musicians: first, that music students who reported a negative music performance experience would self-report higher levels of music performance anxiety than those who had not had previous negative performance experiences; and second, that negative cognitions would be more predictive of adolescent music performance anxiety than the somatic and emotional components of this sensitizing experience. Two hundred and ninety-eight music students from high schools specializing in the performing arts were asked to provide written descriptions of their worst performance experience, what happened, and how they felt, specifying their age at the time, audience characteristics, and any events that occurred subsequent to the performance. Descriptions were classified according to six domains: situational and behavioral factors, affective, cognitive, and somatic symptoms of anxiety, and outcome of the performance. Accounts were scored in each domain and a total score was calculated. Scores were summed to provide a linear scale that was compared with self-report of music performance anxiety, measured using the Music Performance Anxiety Inventory for Adolescents (MPAI–A) (Osborne & Kenny, 2005b) and standardized trait anxiety scores, measured using the STAI.

This study used a methodology similar to Ryan's (2003) of open-ended questions, in which participants were asked to generate their own statements about their performance experience rather than respond to statements on questionnaires. In this way, we were able to access spontaneous cognitions of young musicians to ascertain whether they developed the same types of anxious cognitions as those typically observed in anxious adults. Results indicated that music performance anxiety was best predicted by trait anxiety and gender, and that the presence of negative cognitions in their worst-experience account improved the prediction of music performance anxiety over trait anxiety and gender alone. Females reported more emotional distress than males and had significantly higher total scores. These findings confirm patterns found in adult performers and across other forms of performance anxiety in children (e.g. test anxiety). This study highlighted cognitions as an important element to address in the treatment of music performance anxiety in young musicians. Figure 6.3 summarizes the degree to which the presence of negative cognitions about a poor performance experience adds to the prediction of music performance anxiety for both males and females. The number of negative cognitions (e.g. 'I was very worried about the performance,' 'My teacher had very high expectations of me,' 'I worried that my teacher would be disappointed in me,' 'The examiners were very intimidating and psyched me out') spontaneously produced in the worst-experience description were counted. In Figure 6.3, cognition is presented as a binary variable coded 0 for those producing 0–1 negative cognitions and 1 for those producing two or more negative cognitions in their account of their worst performance experience. (Note: Both MPAI–A and STAI–T scores are in their original units).

Osborne, Kenny, and Holsomback (2005) found significant differences in levels of music performance anxiety according to musical ability. Students who were less advanced

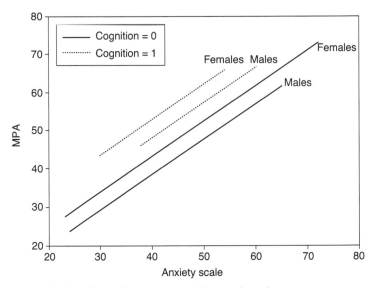

Figure 6.3 Prediction of MPA by anxiety, cognition, and gender.

in their musical training reported significantly lower MPA on the MPAI–A than more skilled performers of the same age (11–13 years). Further, students who reported that they wanted to be a professional musician had lower music performance anxiety scores compared with those who indicated that they did not know whether they wanted to be a professional musician or did not want to be a professional musician. It is possible that students reject or are uncertain of a career as a professional musician because of the discomfort associated with high music performance anxiety. It could also indicate that more accomplished students accurately perceive greater musical ability and competence than peers, which mitigates the levels of anxiety experienced during performance. Further research is needed to replicate and better understand these findings.

Emotion-based theories of anxiety

A number of theorists have proposed emotion-based theories of anxiety development. Lang (1979), for example, argued that anxiety is manifested in an individual whose fear structure is activated by a specific experience or event. A fear structure contains information, learnt and stored from past experiences, that alerts the person to (perceived) danger. Lazarus (1984, 1991a) contends that an affective stimulus alone cannot trigger emotion but has to be at least minimally processed before it can do so. The concept of cognitive appraisal is the central feature of Lazarus's theory. Cognitive appraisal, which is influenced by biological variability, temperament, learning experiences, and sociocultural factors, determines the emotional response (e.g. anxiety, anger, guilt, or shame) to given situations. Appraisal involves an assessment of goal relevance (whether anything is at stake), goal congruence (whether the encounter is appraised as harmful—or threatening if it is future harm—or beneficial), and goal content (the type of ego involvement required). Secondary appraisal involves the determination of the capacity to cope with the situation. The goal content of anxiety involves future threat associated with uncertainty about outcomes and consequences and hence is accompanied by a feeling of powerlessness (Lazarus, 1991b, 2000b). The threat is goal incongruent (i.e. the encounter is perceived as harmful) and under such circumstances, avoidance or escape are the preferred coping strategies.

Foa and Kozak (1986a) distinguished between normal (reality-based fears) and pathological fear structures. Emotional processing of the fear is required to alter the fear structure and reduce anxiety. For this to occur, the fear structure must be activated by direct exposure or through symbolic means (imagination). In this way, the fear will gradually reduce, as will the emotional engagement in the feared stimulus or situation, through a process called habituation. Exposure procedures underlie most current treatments for anxiety (Powell, 2004a; Powell, 2004b). Repeated and prolonged exposure to the feared situation promotes re-evaluation (corrective or fear-disconfirming information) of the meaning and consequences of the feared situation, as well as a reduction in emotional and physiological arousal. While this theory has been shown to be effective in the treatment of many forms of anxiety, including specific phobias, post-traumatic stress disorder, and agoraphobia, in the case of performance anxiety, repeated exposure to the feared situation (music performance), but without the skills and strategies to ensure success, is likely to have a deleterious effect on the performer, with potentially devastating consequences.

Barlow's triple vulnerability model

Barlow (2000) proposed an elegant emotion-based model of anxiety development that owes much to Lazarus, whose relevance to understanding performance anxiety has been discussed in detail elsewhere (see Kenny & Osborne, 2006; Kenny, 2006). Barlow's model proposes an integrated set of triple vulnerabilities that can account for the development of an anxiety or mood disorder. These are

i   a generalized biological (heritable) vulnerability

ii a generalized psychological vulnerability

iii specific life experiences that establish specific psychological vulnerabilities.

The generalized biological vulnerability infers a genetic contribution to the development of particular temperaments that have been labeled at various times 'neuroticism,' 'negative affect,' or 'behavioral inhibition.' The generalized psychological vulnerability is based in early experiences, in particular negative events that result in a sense that life is unpredictable and uncontrollable and that one does not have the necessary coping resources to manage such events. Uncontrollability is strongly associated with negative affect and subsequently anxiety and depression (Allen, McHugh, & Barlow, 2008). The first two processes (a biological vulnerability and a generalized psychological vulnerability based on early experiences) may be sufficient conditions for the development of anxious apprehension. Genetic predisposition and sensitizing early-life experiences may be sufficient to produce a generalized anxiety or mood (depression) disorder.

Barlow (1988, 2000, 2002a) argues that panic attacks, which he calls 'false alarms', may arise in response to stressful life events in people who experience high levels of general anxiety. However, panic may not have the same etiology as the generalized anxiety disorders, and at the very least, requires the experience of a specific psychological vulnerability whereby anxiety comes to be associated with certain internal (somatic sensations or intrusive thoughts) or environmental (social evaluation) stimuli that have become associated with heightened threat or danger through learning processes such as respondent or vicarious conditioning. These specific conditioning experiences, in addition to panic disorders, may also lead to the development of the more focal or specific anxiety disorders such as social phobia, obsessive–compulsive disorder or the specific phobias. Conditioning history is therefore a necessary component in anxiety disorder etiology (Field, 2006). Social evaluation may be accompanied by heightened somatic sensations (false alarms or fear responses in the absence of a real threat or danger) that become associated with a perceived increase in threat or danger, such as the fear of others' disapproval or rejection. Those perceiving most threat are likely to experience the greatest anxiety, and those who are most anxious are more likely to perceive the social evaluative context as more threatening.

What triggers false alarms? This is a complex question since it is likely that they are multidetermined. Barlow suggests that individuals who experience false alarms may have heightened neurobiological hyper-reactivity that triggers basic emotions such as fear or defensive reactions such as panic attacks. Recent research has identified different roles for different neural substrates in fear conditioning, such as the amygdala and hippocampus. (For a detailed review, see Phelps, 2006). This hyper-reactivity interacts with psychological triggers and is expressed as anxiety. Initially, false alarms appear uncued and unexpected; however, with prompting, 80% of people with panic disorder can recall a negative life event that preceded their first panic (Horesh et al., 1997). Sensitivity to anxiety appears to be normally distributed throughout the population, indicating that it is a dimensional rather than a categorical construct (Reiss, Peterson, Gursky, & McNally, 1986). Almost all the anxiety disorders are characterized by chronic hyper-arousal (Nash & Potokar, 2004). High anxiety sensitivity appears to be a risk factor for false alarms and subsequent development of panic attacks, particularly in individuals with high negative affect (Hayward et al., 2000). High anxiety sensitivity constitutes the first component (i.e. biological vulnerability) and negative affect the second component (i.e. psychological vulnerability) of the three-factor model.

Another possible explanation is that false alarms mimic the panic and distress evident in children who have experienced separation from their mothers, a phenomenon known as separation anxiety (Bowlby, 1980). The evidence for this proposition is not strong (Hayward et al., 2000). A more plausible explanation comes from the work of Ehlers (1993), who showed that people with panic attacks report observing more panic behaviors in their parents than people with other anxiety disorders and people with no anxiety disorder. Many people who develop anxiety disorders report early learning experiences as children during which their caregivers focused anxious attention on bodily sensations and communicated their beliefs regarding the danger surrounding these symptoms and sensations (Chambless, Caputo, Bright, & Gallagher, 1984).

This research points to several possible learning processes whereby false alarms may be conditioned in vulnerable individuals: respondent (classical) conditioning, observational (vicarious) learning or modeling, and information/verbal instruction

(Rachman, 1991), or instructed fear (Olsson & Phelps, 2004). The conditioning models were covered in Chapter Six, but we will revisit them here. You will recall that in classical or 'Pavlovian' conditioning (Pavlov, 1927), a neutral stimulus that is present during a fear-arousing experience (the unconditioned stimulus, or UCS) may acquire the capacity to elicit the fear response in the absence of the original fear-arousing experience. The neutral experience thus becomes a conditioned stimulus (CS) for fear through its paired association with the UCS. Fear in this circumstance is called conditioned fear because the neutral stimulus would not have elicited fear without its pairing with the UCS, that is, without undergoing conditioning. The strength of the relationship between the CS and the conditioned response (CR) depends on the number of pairings that have occurred between the UCS and the CR and the intensity of the fear invoked by the UCS. Internal somatic sensations may become conditioned stimuli (Gosch, Flannery-Schroeder, Mauro, & Compton, 2006), particularly in those who have heightened neurobiological hyper-reactivity and/or learning experiences that teach them to be anxious about their somatic sensations. Some specific phobias are apparently acquired in this way. A person may experience a false alarm of such intensity that learning in the situation in which the person experiences the false alarm takes place. Subsequently, the person comes to experience anxiety in the situation that was the location of the first false alarm. Anxiety then arises in anticipation of the occurrence of another false alarm in that conditioning situation or environment (Barlow, 2002a).

Other factors such as temperament, context, past experience, cognition (Field, 2006), and the evaluation of the unconditioned stimulus itself (Dadds, Davey, & Field, 2001) all play a part in (fear-)conditioning experiences. Although fear is conditioned in this way, it is avoidance learning (i.e. learning to avoid the feared stimulus) (Mowrer, 1947) that maintains the fear. Emotional conditioning, including fear conditioning, does not require conscious awareness of the temporal association between the UCS, UCR, and CR (Le Doux, 1996).

Classical conditioning models are not sufficient to account for all observed phenomena in fear and anxiety conditioning. You will remember our earlier discussion of Miller and Dollard (1941) who noted the importance of imitation in learning and how Bandura (1969) subsequently developed the observational learning paradigm to supplement existing conditioning models. Parents play a very important role in their children's learning, both intentional and incidental, because they are powerful and important figures in their children's lives. Parents of socially anxious children are themselves often socially anxious and interact with their children in ways that encourage the development of anxious apprehension in social situations, by discussing the potential threat in particular social situations and reinforcing their children's socially anxious behaviors such as avoidance of situations feared by their parents (Barrett, Rapee, Dadds, & Ryan, 1996). One critical element in vicarious learning of anxious or phobic responding is the strength of the fear response in the model, a phenomenon called 'emotional contagion' in which the observer reacts with the same intensity to a situation as the model even in the absence of any overt threat (Mineka, 1987). Some fear responses can be symbolically acquired; that is, emotional reactions attach to stimuli in the absence of aversive stimuli; they can be conditioned via a paradigm known as 'instructed fear', in which verbal instructions that there will be an aversive consequence in a given situation are sufficient to condition an emotional response to that stimulus (Ost, 1985).

Another learning paradigm that could condition false alarms is operant conditioning. This form of conditioning appears to be associated with true rather than false alarms and to be more common in people with non-generalized or specific social phobia who exhibit fear responses compared with those with the generalized subtype, who are more likely to exhibit anxiety (Barlow, 2002). The former group is more likely to attribute their fear of the social/performance situation to panic, whereas the latter group is more likely to attribute their anxiety to fear of negative evaluation (Heimberg et al., 1990). It should be noted that the shared feature underlying all recent models of conditioning is the concept of reciprocal determinism, the view that genetic and biological predisposition, internal emotional and cognitive processes, life experiences, environmental events, and behavior are interdependent and influence each other (Bandura, 1977a, 1991).

Psychophysiological and neurochemical theories of anxiety

Physiological self exists in the molecular and cellular interactions of the biological/physical context, while psychosocial self emerges from human relationships within a sociocultural context. Because of this, we cannot describe or measure one in terms of the other—they are incommensurate—yet each affects the other and we can gain useful insights into ourselves by recognizing the mutual influences (Booth, 2007, p. 165).

Our bodies are complex biochemical systems that are constantly changing and adapting to environmental demands. Living organisms are distinguished by their characteristic of 'autopoiesis,' that is, the process of continual self-generation and environmental adaptation (Maturana & Varela, 1987). As we have already discussed in earlier sections of this book, the body has a complex, coordinated, mostly automatic reaction to environmental stressors, particularly those that signal danger, and changes in endocrine secretions, digestive system, musculature, breathing, heart rate, and blood circulation occur simultaneously in response to this environmental threat. In addition to our five senses, which detect changes in the environment, we have an immune system, which behaves like a sixth sense, whose role is to detect differences between molecules that belong to our bodies and those that do not.

The immune system distinguishes between our 'biological self' and 'biological non-self' and then acts to expel 'non-self' components in order to maintain the biological integrity of the organism (Blalock & Smith, 2007). Remarkably, the immune and nervous systems work cooperatively to restore homeostasis or balance in an organism under threat. The brain communicates with the rest of the body through two overlapping pathways: (i) the 'hardwired' neurons of the autonomic and somatic nervous systems and their synaptic neurotransmitters such as serotonin, and (ii) the fluid-borne hormones (e.g. adrenaline and noradrenaline) of the neuroendocrine system located in the hypothalamic–pituitary–adrenal (HPA) axis (Booth, 2007).

Increased neuroendocrine activity, in the form of release of glucocorticoids and neuropeptides during fear responses, increases the excitability of fear circuits which underpin the development of pathological anxiety. These represent an exaggeration of the normal processes involved in anticipatory anxiety and anxious apprehension (Gunnar & Donzella, 2002). Associative learning processes are thought to be critical to the production of neural sensitization that leads to enhanced perception in response to threat and danger (Le Doux, 1996). To put it more simply, our neuro-immune system is responsive to environmental changes, and these changes are coordinated in response to our previous immune history, such that different people will respond to different environmental insults differently depending on what previous exposures and hence structural changes have occurred in their biological system (Booth, 2007).

In Chapter Four, I briefly discussed the concept of behavioral inhibition, a process that links biology and behavior within a developmental framework. Although it has its biological basis in an overactive amygdala, which enhances fear responses to novelty, the early caregiving environment is also influential in the development and expression of behavioral inhibition, a precursor to the development of anxiety disorders in older children (Fox *et al.*, 2005). Increased activity of the amygdala would be expected to result in increased activity across a number of response systems such as heart rate, cortisol secretion, and EEG recordings. Behaviorally inhibited children show higher heart rates and heart rate acceleration when placed in unfamiliar situations compared with uninhibited children. Children who were highly inhibited and insecurely attached (i.e. showing both biological and psychological vulnerability) showed a larger cortisol response in the Strange Situation compared with children who were also inhibited but securely attached (biological vulnerability only). Similarly, inhibited children, as opposed to uninhibited children, show asymmetrical activation in EEG (i.e. electroencephalograms or brain activity) in the right frontal region of the brain, indicating activation of the motivational system associated with withdrawal (Fox *et al.*, 2005).

This complex physiological self coexists with our psychosocial self that emerges from the dense relational matrix into which we are born (Mitchell, 1993) and through which we eventually discern 'me' and 'not me' (recall William James from Chapter Two), and become both participant (I) and observer (me) in our lives. We realize that the object that we have designated 'self' is also the means by which we observe the self, and hence we create a conceptual object called 'mind' in which we locate our thinking processes. Our psychosocial selves (and minds) are embodied within the physiological self that is conditioned by the social and cultural milieu in which it is enmeshed (Booth, 2007). Emotions arise in response to changes in our biological and social contexts and are conditioned through patterning and repetition of experiences over time. Because our emotions are necessarily embodied, they shape physiological processes in our physiological selves, in response to how the physiological self is perceived by our psychosocial self. If an event is perceived as a threat, a coordinated neuro-immune response called the 'fight or flight' response is triggered (see Chapter Two). The immune response to threat or illness triggers biochemical changes which in turn alter the body's neurochemistry, which in turn affects perceptual processes. It is not sensory experiences per se that affect psychosocial processes but the meaning ascribed to those experiences, which have arisen from our social history. Susan Greenfield, in *The Private Life of the Brain* (Greenfield, 2000), attempts to answer the question about how our unique personalities emerge from our anatomically identical physical brains. Greenfield uses the phrase 'personalized brain' to describe how this process comes about. Similarly, Booth (2007) states that 'we can consider body and mind as distinct but interactive domains of self-expression that work in concert to generate that which we each discern as our personal identity' (p. 173). However, this influence is not one way; there is a psychosocial feedback loop that affects our physiologies, just as our physiologies affect our psychosocial selves. Interpretations of environmental (both internal and external) events as stressful change our physiology; changing our interpretation can change our physiology. In anxiety and stress research, there is growing empirical evidence that emotionally expressive techniques can change physiology; and that changed physiology (through medications, for example) can alter perception and behavior.

The psychobiology of music performance anxiety

It will come as no surprise from the foregoing discussions that music performance is hard work, both physically and emotionally. In the only study of its kind to date, Iñesta, Terrados, García, & Pérez (2008) demonstrated this empirically. They used continuous heart rate recording as a tool for effort measurement in 62 professional musicians aged 15–71 years while playing their instruments in real time and across a range of different activities, including practice, rehearsals, and public concerts, to assess cardiac demand in diverse work settings. They used various measures of cardiac output, including heart rate (HR), Maximum Theoretical Heart Rate (MTHR),[2] and Maximum Theoretical Heart Rate percentage (%MTHR) to allow comparison across gender and age groups. Heart rate comparisons were made between rehearsal and public concert of the same repertoire; first concert versus second concert of the same repertoire. These comparisons were made for winds, strings, piano, and percussion. The overall cardiac demand of professional musicians was found to be significantly greater when compared with a sedentary occupation. Cardiac demand was significantly higher in concerts than in rehearsals performing the same musical repertoire. Wind players had the highest maximum heart rate during rehearsals (132, which represented 68% MTHR) but pianists had the highest maximum heart rate during concerts (167, which represented 86% MTHR). However, wind instrumentalists' HR was high during concerts (151, 79% MTHR) compared with strings (137, 72% MTHR). According to the American College of Sports Medicine, these MTHRs constitute an intensity of effort rated as hard (70–89%) (American College of Sports Medicine, 1998). There were no significant differences in heart rates between the first and second concert of the same repertoire. It is a shame that we have no measure of how these heart rates would have changed for very anxious musicians, given that the work of musicians in general carries an overall high cardiac demand.

An earlier study provides some insight into the effect of high anxiety on the psychobiology of music performance. Fredrikson and Gunnarsson (1992) assessed subjective, neuroendocrine, and cardiovascular functions in 19 music students from the Music Academy in Stockholm. They were classified into high- and low-anxious

---

[2] MTHR was calculated using the formula [220 – age in years].

performers and the parameters of interest were measured in private and public performance. Heart rate was higher in public but not private performance for high-anxious students. Interestingly, increase in neuroendocrine activation (adrenaline, noradrenaline, and cortisol) increased from private to public performance but were not different between high- and low-anxious students. It is possible that the method of categorizing the students into high (at least one episode of performance-related tremor) and low (no performance-related tremor) did not provide a sensitive enough division of the level of music performance anxiety experienced between the two groups.

In another study of 18 skilled pianists, Yoshie, Kudo, Murakoshi, and Ohtsuki (2009) assessed subjective, autonomic, and motor stress responses by measuring subjective state anxiety, heart rate (HR), sweat rate (SR), and electromyographic (EMG) activity of upper extremity muscles while they performed a self-selected solo piano piece under stressful (competition) and non-stressful (rehearsal) conditions. HR and SR increased from rehearsal to competition, as did EMG magnitude of proximal muscles (*biceps brachii* and upper trapezius) and the co-contraction of antagonistic muscles in the forearm (*extensor digitorum communis* and *flexor digitorum superficialis*). The authors concluded that:

> Although these responses can be interpreted as integral components of an adaptive biological system that creates a state of motor readiness in an unstable or unpredictable environment, they can adversely influence pianists by disrupting their fine motor control on stage and by increasing the risk of playing-related musculoskeletal disorders (p. 117).

Theories of performance: how to achieve optimal performance

> *Two things are necessary for a life in music: a clear idea of what you want to be, and the arrogance to pursue it. You can't walk onstage and say to the public, 'Excuse me, I'm here.' You must believe in yourself and make immediately clear to everyone, 'I'm going to play! LISTEN!'* (Isaac Stern).[3]

The increasing competitiveness and expectations of musical performance have led to gradually greater physical and emotional demands on performers at younger ages (Lieberman, 1991), comparable to those at the elite level of sport. Athletes and swimmers are always striving to create new world records in their chosen domains (Ericsson, Krampe, & Tesch-Romer, 1993; Ericsson & Lehmann, 1996). A parallel process has occurred in music performance. The following examples illustrate the increased expectations with respect to music performance capabilities that have occurred over time. When Tchaikovsky (1840–1893) wrote his violin and piano concertos, famous performers of the time refused to play them, claiming that the scores were unplayable. However, over the succeeding years, numerous violin and piano virtuosi have made playing his and similar scores commonplace, and indeed the concertos of Tchaikovsky

....

[3] Stern, I., & Potok, C. (1999). *My First 79 Years*. Cambridge, MA: Da Capo Press, p. 4.

are now considered part of the standard repertoire for concert pianists and violinists (Ericsson *et al.*, 1993). Even 12-year-old prodigies now perform these works (Horvath, 2002). Parallels exist in the repertoire for other instruments. The flute repertoire is instructive. Jacques Ibert's Flute Concerto (1932) was felt to test the upper limits of flute technique and musical expression when written for the celebrated French flute player, Marcel Moyse. However, the work is now routinely listed on examination syllabuses and is attempted by secondary-school students for competitive performances. Mozart's *Andante* K315 was written because the original dedicatee of the G Major *Flute Concerto* was felt to not fully have mastered the breath control and necessary legato technique of the middle movement of that concerto. Few performers would substitute this movement today and indeed the original slow movement is deemed well within the abilities of a talented 14–15 year-old student.

As we discussed in Chapter Four, performance anxiety can occur in a range of different human endeavors. However, music performance anxiety is a more complex phenomenon than other anxiety disorders because of its multifaceted nature. For example, optimal arousal in music performance is dependent on a large number of interdependent factors that include trait anxiety (Kenny *et al.*, 2004), state anxiety (Martens, Burton, Vealey, Bump, & Smith, 1990), music performance anxiety (Kenny & Osborne, 2006; van Kemenade *et al.*, 1995), personality characteristics (Peterson, 2000a; Seligman, 1991), cognitive capacity (Libkuman, Stabler, & Otani, 2004), cognitions (Sternbach, 1995), physiological arousal (McNally, 2002), task complexity (Tassi, Bonnefond, Hoeft, Eschenlauer, & Muzet, 2003), task mastery, including motor skill (Kokotsaki & Davidson, 2003; Sparrow & Newell, 1998), situational factors (Ackermann & Adams, 2004; Brotons, 1994; Horvath, 2002), and availability of working memory resources (Libkuman *et al.*, 2004). However, making lists of influential factors does not assist individual performers in achieving optimal performance. Both psychological theories and performance theories are needed. Performance theories are distinguished from psychological theories of performance anxiety in that their focus is on maximizing performance rather than alleviating psychological distress. It is often assumed that successful performance, once reliably achieved, will reduce psychological distress (Kenny *et al.*, 2004; Powell, 2004b; Wilson, 2002). This is not always the case, as we learnt in Chapter One and as we shall see later when we discuss some case studies of music performance anxiety in Chapter Eight. For now, our task is to understand the theoretical and empirical bases for theories of performance whose aim is to support the achievement of optimal performance.

Peak performance

There is some conceptual confusion between the many terms used to describe an episode of superior performance. However, for our purposes, we will define the terms 'peak experience' and 'flow' as subjective states of intense well-being and enjoyment and the term 'peak performance' as optimal functioning, what is referred to in sport as a 'personal best.' Peak performance (Harmison, 2006) is the focus of the following discussion. To achieve peak performance, both physical and psychological preconditions are required. It is not easy to precisely separate these preconditions in this way, as they are overlapping and interdependent, as illustrated by the title of an excellent paper on the subject, 'The mind of expert motor performance is cool and focused' (Milton, Solodkina, Hluštík, & Smalla, 2007). In this paper, Milton *et al.* state that expert performance is defined by a quality that far exceeds the quality of non-expert performance. It includes a capacity for intense focus on the required motor performance that precludes distractions or intrusions, and the capacity to reproduce a maximal level of performance consistently under a wide range of environmental contingencies, for example, from practice to a competitive event. In a study of novice and skilled golfers, Milton and colleagues assessed the brain processes underlying these performance outcome skills and found a significant decrease in the overall volume of brain activation accompanied by a relative increase in the intensity of activation of specific brain regions (parietal,[4] occipital,[5] and premotor[6] areas) necessary for the execution of the task in the skilled but not in the novice golfers. Because these differences in brain activation patterns between novices and experts were observed before they executed their golf shot, it was concluded that the quality of performance was due to the level of organization of neural networks during motor planning. Experts exhibited an economy of motor planning both at the level of central neural programming and subsequent motor unit activation that was not evident in novice golfers. It was argued that novices engage in more cognitive activity than experts to execute a motor skill that they are learning. Cognition will activate areas of the brain (cerebellum[7] and basal ganglia[8]) not specifically required for the execution of the motor task; similarly, if novices have more difficulty filtering out or excluding irrelevant information, their brains will also show activation in the limbic area, (posterior cingulate,[9] amygdala–basal forebrain,[10] complex and basal ganglia), which is, in fact, what occurred. These areas of the brain did not become active during the motor planning

---

[4] The parietal lobe generates movement plans (intention), chooses objects in the environment for further processing and generates visual attention to target objects, which are represented by activity proportional to their behavioral priority (Bisley & Goldberg, 2010).

[5] The occipital lobe contains the primary visual cortex responsible for visual processing and perception.

[6] The premotor cortex is part of the motor cortex, which is located in the frontal lobe. It is critical to the sensory guidance of movement and control of proximal and trunk muscles of the body. It is involved in learning, execution, and recognition and movement planning of the limbs (Altenmüller, Wiesendanger, & Kesselring, 2006).

[7] The cerebellum is a region of the brain involved primarily in motor control. It contributes to coordination, precision, and accurate timing of fine-tuned movements. It also has a role in attention and language, and in the regulation of fear and pleasure responses. Damage to the cerebellum impairs motor learning (Altenmüller & Gruhn, 2002).

[8] The basal ganglia are involved in motor control and learning, primarily in action selection and motor inhibition related to non-automated voluntary action (Altenmüller & Gruhn, 2002).

[9] The posterior cingulate is part of the limbic system that is activated by emotional stimuli. It may mediate interactions of emotional and memory-related processes.

[10] The basal forebrain is critical for cognitive-emotional behaviors/processes, including arousal, attention, sensory processing, reinforcement, associative learning, decision making, and memory. This circuitry influences the emotional, motivational, and cognitive state of an organism (Altenmüller & Gruhn, 2002).

of experts. Other research has shown that good learners who are highly skilled but who have not yet achieved the automaticity that defines expert performance also show activation in the posterior cingulate, demonstrating an inverse relationship between level of motor skill and degree of posterior cingulate activation—the lower the motor skill, the higher the activation (Tracy *et al.*, 2003). Activation of the limbic system suggested emotional activation of the kind seen in anxious performers when placed in a stressful performance situation. However, limbic activation in novices included regions not exclusively associated with emotional regulation, leading to the conclusion that the increased effort required by novices and their inability to filter out irrelevant stimuli contributed to their poorer performances.

What are the psychological characteristics associated with peak performance? These include: (i) feelings of high self-confidence and expectations of success; (ii) feeling energized yet relaxed; (iii) feeling in control; (iv) entering a state of intense concentration; (v) retaining a keen focus on the task; (vi) maintaining a positive attitude and thoughts about the performance; (vii) being determined and committed. States associated with a poor performance, by contrast, include self-doubt, loss of concentration and feeling distracted, maintaining a focus on the outcome of the competition, and feeling over- or under-aroused (Krane & Williams, 2006). A number of researchers have investigated the set of psychological skills essential to the achievement of a peak performance and collectively arrived at the following: (i) goal setting; (ii) imagery; (iii) focus and attentional control; (iv) automatic coping skills—thought control, arousal management strategies, and facilitative interpretations of anxiety (Andersen, 2009; Eysenck, Derakshan, Santos & Calvo, 2007; Hardy, Jones, & Gould, 1996a; Latham & Locke, 2007; Robazza, Bortoli, & Nougier, 1998; Rodebaugh, 2007). We will discuss some of these factors in the next chapter. For now, we will review some of the more influential theories of performance and available research, starting with the foundational theory of the relationship between arousal and performance, which has been canonized into law but has proved to be problematic for the field, as we shall see.

Optimal arousal and the Yerkes–Dodson Law

Probably the most quoted (and misquoted) figure in the history of psychology is the Yerkes–Dodson Inverted U curve (Yerkes & Dodson, 1908). As Figure 6.4 shows, the law states that a moderate level of arousal results in the highest level of performance. Arousal that is too low or too high impairs performance.

You may be surprised to learn that the curve was derived in experiments with mice, not humans. Secondly, the original relationship identified in these mice experiments was between stimulus strength and speed of habit formation under different conditions of punishment stimulus frequency for tasks varying in level of difficulty. From their original experiments, Yerkes and Dodson derived three graphs based on the curve's changing shape with respect to task difficulty. For easy tasks, the relationship between stimulus strength and habit formation (i.e. learning) was in fact linear, not U shaped. By the 1950s, researchers somewhat controversially extended these findings to define the relationship between arousal and performance (Broadhurst, 1957). The axes of the original graph were changed to depict a purported relationship between emotional

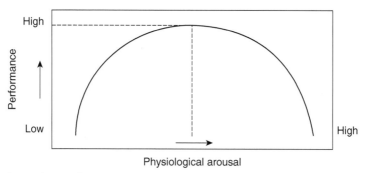

Figure 6.4 Yerkes–Dodson curve.

arousal and performance, but the exact nature of arousal was not strictly defined. It was understood to imply a unidimensional construct incorporating both psychological and physiological response systems, and was interpreted as mediating the relationship between a stimulus and response (Hardy & Parfitt, 1991). Over time, the conceptualization of this relationship expanded as one between stress and performance, arousal and performance and anxiety and performance. The central tenet of this relationship (however defined) was that low and high levels of emotional arousal have a detrimental effect on performance. Easterbrook's (1959) cue utilization theory was developed to explain the relationship between high levels of arousal and poorer performance. It states that at medium levels of arousal, people can attend to a wide array of cues, which decreases as arousal increases, thereby impairing performance.

However, there have been challenges to both the Yerkes–Dodson law and Easterbrook's theory in recent years, for example, the basic premise that restriction of information is necessarily detrimental to performance. Hanoch and Vitouch (2004) argued that high emotional arousal was adaptive in some circumstances precisely because it restricted the allocation of attention to essential information in the environment and reduced attention to peripheral or irrelevant information. They state:

> high arousal states allowed humans to respond more rapidly to certain contingencies that have arisen during our evolution. By 'overruling' conscious control and behavioral flexibility, high levels of arousal may trigger a phylogenetically 'old' route that practically secures certain behavioral output (e.g. flight reactions or 'freeze' reactions). From an evolutionary perspective, panic is not a detrimental imbalance of the system; rather it is a focus on the essential (p. 430).

You will recall our discussion of the biological basis of anxiety and the theories of Steven Porges presented in Chapter Two and note the similarities of these arguments with the polyvagal theory. However, the problem arises when these old routes are triggered in situations where fight or flight responses are not appropriate, such as in music performance. For this reason, Hanoch and Vitouch (2004) propose the concept of *arousal congruent performance*, which attends to the ecological rationality of emotional arousal, that is, the appropriateness of the amount and type of emotional arousal with respect to the task and the context in which the task is performed. Emotional arousal is no longer considered a unidimensional construct. There are different types of arousal: sympathetic (automatic), attentional, and electrocortical arousal and behavioral activation; and distinct emotions (fear, anger, joy, etc.), each with its own distinct physiological arousal pattern (Ekman, Levenson, & Friesen, 1983).

Notwithstanding the complexities of the relationship between arousal and performance, there are some general principles with which most would agree. These are:

i A high level of arousal is essential for optimal performance in gross motor activities requiring strength, speed and endurance.

ii A high level of arousal impairs performances requiring a complex series of movements, coordination, fine muscle movement and concentration (as in musical performance).

iii A slightly increased level of arousal over baseline is preferable for all motor tasks, including the activities of daily living (Wilson, 2002).

An optimal performance is determined by a complex interaction between person characteristics, task characteristics, and performance demands and setting. When all of these characteristics occur at an optimal level, the performer is said to be 'in the zone' (Young & Pain, 1999) or to have achieved a state of 'flow' (Marr, 2000). Another construct to describe peak performance is the 'individualized zone of optimal functioning' (IZO) (Hanin, 1986); that is, the performer has achieved the optimal level of pre-performance anxiety that results in a peak performance for that individual. Optimal pre-performance anxiety that creates excitement and enhances mental focus and alertness predicts performance quality (Turner & Raglin, 1991). The challenge for coaches and pedagogues is to discover the optimal pre-performance anxiety for individual performers, based on the interaction between the nature of the task, their temperament, skill level, performance experience, and physiology.

A number of other important interactions have been observed between the inverted U and task characteristics, including task complexity and task mastery. For example, optimal performance on simple tasks will increase as arousal increases, but will deteriorate on complex tasks after a moderate level of arousal is exceeded (Tassi *et al.*, 2003) (see Figure 6.5). This relationship was identified in the original experiments conducted by Yerkes and Dodson, but was subsequently lost and rediscovered nearly a century later.

However, the relationship between task complexity and task difficulty is by no means straightforward, and research using computer-based complex problem-solving tasks has failed to provide support for the proposition that increases in task complexity increase task difficulty (Greiff & Funke, 2008). In addition, task difficulty is related to the skill and experience of the performer, hence the degree of difficulty is not a fixed value but is dependent on performer skill, knowledge, and experience. Further, increases in task complexity may not lead to increases in task difficulty because those increases may not represent an increase in the cognitive complexity of the task, which is defined as the number of steps or processes needed to complete the most complex subtask of the problem (Stankov & Crawford, 1993). Cognitive complexity has therefore been proposed

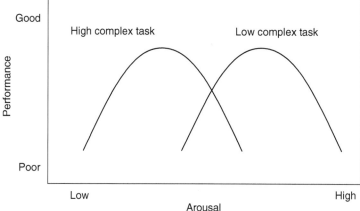

Figure 6.5 The theoretical relationship between physiological arousal and task complexity.

as a way to assess 'true' task difficulty. Music performance comprises much more than cognitive complexity—it also involves psychomotor complexity and a number of dimensions that are more ineffable, such as aesthetic and musical sensibilities. From the foregoing discussion it will have become clear that deriving general principles related to task complexity/arousal relationships is highly challenging, requiring interpretive and sensitive application in the area of music performance.

The Yerkes–Dodson law and music performance

It is unfortunate that even recent articles in music journals (e.g. Papageorgi *et al.*, 2007) continue to report the Yerkes–Dodson law in its original form, without reference to subsequent research that demonstrates the complexity of the arousal–performance relationship and its interaction with other significant intrapersonal, situational, and performance-related factors. Papageorgi, Hallam, & Welch (2007) propose a flawed conceptual framework for music performance anxiety that predicts impaired performance at low and high levels of arousal and optimal performance at medium levels of arousal. Their model further states that the level of arousal predicts adaptive (medium arousal) or maladaptive (low and high levels of arousal) behaviors during the performance and heightened or reduced self-esteem and other longer-term effects. Achieving optimal performance in any human endeavor is much more complex than this model asserts.

Focused attention increases when there are low to moderate levels of arousal, decreasing with very high levels of arousal (Mather *et al.*, 2006). When arousal is high, one's attention to peripheral cues in the situation is reduced and there is a greater focus on highly salient central cues (Libkuman *et al.*, 2004). The location of the curves on the continuum of low to high physiological arousal also depends on other factors, such as the performer's level of state and trait anxiety and interactions between state and trait anxiety and task mastery (Kokotsaki & Davidson, 2003). Different levels of arousal are optimal for different performers (Salmon, 1990). Those high in trait anxiety will require lower levels of arousal to achieve an optimal performance compared with low-trait-anxious individuals who need higher levels of arousal to achieve their best performance (assuming that the task has been learned to mastery). Performers need a certain amount of arousal or anxiety to maximize their performance. Increased anxiety can, under certain conditions, facilitate performance, especially for performers with high task mastery, which is associated with better adjudicator ratings (Steptoe & Fidler, 1987).

Figure 6.6 provides a schematic relationship between the degree to which the task has been practiced to mastery (automaticity) and the amount of physiological arousal needed to produce an optimal performance. However, even at ideal levels of arousal, low practice will produce a suboptimal performance. A well-practiced piece will be performed well at higher levels of arousal but will also suffer if arousal exceeds a certain optimal maximum (Kokotsaki & Davidson, 2003).

More experienced performers may need more anxiety in order to achieve peak performance (Steptoe, 1989; Wolfe, 1989). Therefore, we can distinguish between the positive aspects of anxiety, such as arousal and intensity, that enhance performance and negative aspects, such as apprehension and nervousness, that may impair performance (Mor et al., 1995).

These are issues that must be addressed when planning interventions for music performance anxiety and for musicians who wish to learn to manage their performance anxiety. Treatments for music performance anxiety need to promote sufficient relaxation to counteract the negative symptoms of excessive arousal, while maintaining sufficient arousal and concentration needed for an optimal musical performance (Brotons, 1994).

The story does not stop here, however, complex as it already seems. A number of other factors need to be understood about the attention, arousal, anxiety, and

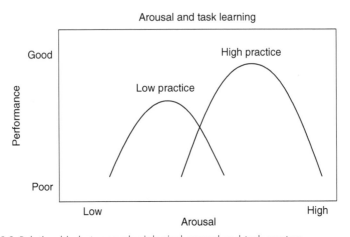

Figure 6.6 Relationship between physiological arousal and task mastery.

performance relationship. The first of these is that attention is not a unitary system, but a set of networks that are functionally and structurally independent (that is, each component of the attentional network involves activation of different parts of the brain) although they may work cooperatively. Attention consists of three main components: alerting, orienting, and executive control. Alerting is the process whereby stimuli are perceived and processed. Orienting requires the individual to select particular pieces of incoming information from among numerous sensory stimuli; while the executive control network attempts to resolve conflicts and control voluntary action in response to these incoming stimuli (Horvath, Herleman, & McKie, 2006).

Second, state and trait anxiety interact differently with different attentional systems. The two types of anxiety bias attention differently, although different researchers have offered different explanations for how this might occur. Williams, Watts, MacLeod, & Mathews (1997) argue that state anxiety increases the threat value assigned to a stimulus or situation, while trait anxiety orients attention to the source of threat. State anxiety is context dependent, while trait anxiety is less associated with situational stimuli and represents habitual cognitive biases in assessments of situations as dangerous or threatening. Results of a recent study showed a complex relationship between anxiety and attention. Trait anxiety was related to deficiencies in the executive control network, and state anxiety was associated with hyper-functioning of the alerting and orienting networks (Pacheco-Unguetti, Acosta, Callejas, & Lupiáñez, 2010). These results make sense in light of the above discussion on the different characteristics of state and trait anxiety, since alerting and orienting are situation-dependent tasks while executive control involves complex patterns of cognitive control.

The performance of high-trait-anxious individuals may be impaired by the less efficient functioning of the executive attentional system in high-demand situations. High state anxiety appears to heighten contextual sensitivity and vigilance processes, which may or may not affect performance. If at a manageable level, state anxiety may enhance receptivity to salient and relevant stimuli; however, if it rises above a threshold, it may impair performance by narrowing attentional focus too much.

Cognitive perspectives: attentional control theory

A number of theories have attempted to explain the relationship between anxiety and cognitive performance. These include cue utilization theory (Easterbrook, 1959), processing efficiency theory, and attentional control theory (Eysenck et al., 2007). Only attentional control theory will be covered in this section because it is the most heuristic and empirically supportable of this group of theories, although it incorporates elements from previous theories. Further, it is specifically concerned with attentional control in the context of anxiety during cognitive performance, and hence is of central relevance to our attempts to understand how anxiety might interfere with attentional control during music performance.

A number of theories posit the existence of two attentional systems: a goal-directed, top-down, attentional system influenced by cognitive processes such as knowledge, goals, and expectations; and a bottom-up stimulus-driven system that responds to stimuli (Corbetta & Shulman, 2002). Anxiety is thought to disrupt the balance between these two systems, increasing stimulus-driven processes and decreasing goal-directed processes (Eysenck *et al.*, 2007).

Anxiety is posited to exert its detrimental effects on cognitive performance by impairing five central executive functions. These are: (i) switching attention between tasks; (ii) planning subtasks to achieve a goal; (iii) selective attention and inhibition (i.e. focusing attention on relevant, and inhibiting irrelevant, information and processes); (iv) updating and checking the contents of working memory; (v) coding representations in working memory (Smith & Jonides, 1999). These functions have been subsequently updated, consolidated, and empirically confirmed by Miyake *et al.* (2000). Using complex statistical techniques, these researchers identified three control functions of the central executive. These are: (i) inhibition (i.e. the ability to use attentional control to prevent disruption to goal-directed behavior; (ii) shifting (i.e. the ability to shift attention appropriately according to task requirements); (iii) updating (i.e. encoding new representations into working memory). Research has shown that anxiety impairs the inhibition function because anxious people are more easily distracted by threat-relevant and other distracting cues, including worry, compared with low-anxious people. These effects are compounded when the demands (e.g. processing and storage) on working memory are high and for anxious people who have lower working memory capacity (Eysenck *et al.*, 2007).

The concepts of effectiveness and efficiency are also central to attentional control theory. Effectiveness refers to the quality of task performance; efficiency describes the relationship between the effectiveness of the performance and the effort or resources required to achieve the outcome—efficiency decreases with increasing use of resources. There are also some key assumptions for the theory, most of which now have some degree of empirical support. A fundamental assumption is that anxiety affects performance through its detrimental effect on attentional processes. For example, anxiety increases the allocation of attentional resources to threat-related stimuli, both internal (e.g. worry) and external (e.g. actual or perceived environmental threats), thereby reducing attention to (non-threatening) task-relevant stimuli (Fox, Russo, Bowles, & Dutton, 2001). Although highly anxious people report more worry than low-anxious people, and one would expect that high levels of worry would predict poorer performance, this is not always the case, because worry impairs efficiency more than effectiveness. This means that a person who worries excessively may still perform a task well but will require greater effort and/or resources to accomplish the task than someone low in worry (Bentz & Williamson, 1998). You may be wondering how anxiety might impair attentional control when there are no threatening, task-irrelevant stimuli present. One possible answer is that anxiety heightens attention to threat in a non-specific way; that is, the person becomes hyper-vigilant for threat in general and directs his/her attention over a wide range of stimuli, both internal and external. Maladaptive cognitive-attentional processes (e.g. worry, task-irrelevant thinking, negative self-preoccupation) have also been strongly implicated in poor test performance. Smith, Amkoff and Wright (1990) found that cognitive-attentional processes accounted for most of the variance in both performance on tests and test anxiety, but that both cognitive skills (e.g. study habits) and self-efficacy (i.e. the exercise of human agency—how a person influences his/her thoughts, behaviors, goals, and outcomes) measures added additional unique variance.

How might attentional control theory assist in our understanding of musical performance under pressure, particularly for anxious performers? Anxious performers compensate for reduced efficiency with additional effort and the use of compensatory strategies. For example, a number of very skilled musicians of my acquaintance have told me that they are prone to over-practice for an audition, even when they are required to perform works that have been in their repertoire for many years. Many have developed idiosyncratic pre-performance routines, use mental rehearsal and imagery, engage in mock auditions, visit the audition venue, and do a range of other activities in order to reduce the 'mental noise' they describe when preparing for the audition. There is considerable interdependence of the theories presented in this section, as you will discover when you learn about distraction theory and self-focused and explicit monitoring theories, which follow shortly.

The catastrophe model and multidimensional anxiety theories

I have briefly alluded to the many implications of the (mis)application of the arousal–performance relationship arising from the Yerkes–Dodson law in the previous section. A number of theories have subsequently been developed that have empirically tested the arousal–performance relationship. In addition to the inverted-U hypothesis, we have the three-systems model of fear (Lang, 1971), the multidimensional anxiety theory (Martens et al., 1990), the catastrophe model of anxiety and performance (Hardy, 1990; Hardy & Parfitt, 1991), Kerr's (1987) reversal theory (Gould & Krane, 1992), and optimal zones of arousal hypothesis (Hanin, 2000a). This is a difficult and complex area of research and space does not permit a detailed analysis of each theory. However, a brief overview of the most influential and empirically supported theories will be provided below, because of their obvious relevance and importance to managing music performance anxiety. Lang's foundational theory and two models that have received considerable attention in the sport performance literature, multidimensional anxiety theory (Martens et al., 1990) and the catastrophe model (Hardy, 1990; Hardy & Parfitt, 1991), will be briefly discussed in this section.

Lang (1971) proposed his three-systems model of fear after the failure of previous unitary models that had assigned primacy to cognition to account for experimental findings. His three components are behavioral, physiological, and verbal, which he proposed were interactive yet partially independent. The partial independence of each of the three systems was explained by the fact that none of the systems uniquely defined the anxious state and each system was not equally sensitive to stressors. Two dimensions of relatedness were identified between the three factors in Lang's model, the first, concordance–discordance and the second, synchrony–desynchrony. Concordance refers to the level of response equivalence between the three factors at any given time; synchrony refers to the rate of change of the three factors. Desynchrony could take the form of independence or inverse relationships between the factors. A number of studies have provided support for this theory. One applied to music performance anxiety will be described in more detail below.

Martens *et al.* (1990) identified two distinct and partially independent components of competitive sport anxiety: cognitive anxiety, related to concerns about the consequences of failure, and somatic anxiety, defined as a negative perception of the meaning of physiological arousal prior to performance. The theory states that these two forms of anxiety have different antecedents. Somatic anxiety is a conditioned fear response associated with the performance venue, and cognitive anxiety is associated with the perceived probability of success (or failure). The theory predicts that cognitive anxiety will remain high and stable prior to the event, but that somatic anxiety will be low until immediately before the event, once the performer has arrived at the performance venue. Using a time-to-event paradigm derived from this theory, a dissociation between these two forms of anxiety has been demonstrated in a number of studies. This relationship is illustrated in Figure 6.7. It shows that cognitive anxiety can be high and somatic anxiety low two days before the performance, with somatic anxiety rising sharply shortly before the performance. It is noteworthy that physiological arousal assessed by heart rate follows a similar time course to somatic anxiety (Hardy & Parfitt, 1991). Both cognitive and somatic anxiety reduce rapidly after the performance.

The catastrophe or cusp catastrophe model of anxiety and performance states that cognitive anxiety determines whether the effects of physiological arousal are small and smooth or large and catastrophic (Hardy & Parfitt, 1991). This theory generates four predictions, as follows:

i When cognitive anxiety is low, the relationship between physiological arousal and performance will follow the inverted-U shape.

ii If physiological arousal is high on the day of the performance, there is a negative relationship between cognitive anxiety and performance.

iii If physiological arousal is low prior to the event, cognitive anxiety enhances performance relative to baseline performance.

iv When cognitive anxiety is high leading up to the performance, the effects of physiological arousal on performance can be either positive or negative, depending on how high cognitive anxiety and physiological arousal are.

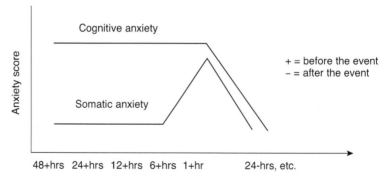

Figure 6.7 Time-to-event program (from Martens *et al.*, 1990, in McNally, 2002).

Thus, the principal thesis of the theory is that physiological arousal (somatic anxiety) results in a performance catastrophe only when cognitive anxiety is high.

Subsequent studies testing these models have provided mixed support. Recent studies attribute positive results in earlier studies to methodological limitations. For example, in a recent re-analysis of several studies using seven levels (13%, 25%, 40%, 50%, 75%, 89%) of maximum arousal, catastrophe theory's predicted precipitous drop in performance was not replicated (Landers & Lochbaum, 1998). Further, when cognitive anxiety was assessed as a continuous, as opposed to categorical (i.e. high/low), variable, the predictions of the catastrophe model were not replicated (Cohen, Pargman, & Tenenbaum, 2003). However, recent modifications to the theory have clarified some unresolved issues. For example, Hardy, Beattie, and Woodman (2007) added a third factor to their model, i.e. effort required to perform the task. They hypothesized that a performance catastrophe may be due to the relationship between cognitive anxiety and effort rather than or as well as cognitive anxiety and physiological arousal (experienced as somatic anxiety). In two studies that manipulated task difficulty as a way of increasing effort, and social pressure and ego threat instructions to manipulate levels of cognitive anxiety (worry), their findings supported a processing efficiency theory explanation of anxiety-induced performance catastrophes. They suggested that there may in fact be two cusp catastrophe models of performance: the original one citing the interactive effects of cognitive anxiety and physiological arousal on performance and a second model showing how interactions between cognitive anxiety and effort affect performance. In this model, high cognitive anxiety and high effort would predict a performance catastrophe.

Other factors also appear to mediate the relationship between somatic and cognitive anxiety and performance. The two related constructs of self-efficacy (Bandura, 1977a, 1991) and self-confidence are two such factors. In a study of 50 soccer players, the circumstances under which cognitive anxiety improves performance were investigated. All the high/low configurations of these three factors (cognitive and somatic anxiety and self-confidence) were compared. Players with low cognitive and somatic anxiety performed better if they were high in self-confidence. Those with high cognitive anxiety, low somatic anxiety, and high self-confidence performed better than the other four groups and were the only group who improved their performance. Finally, players who were high in both cognitive and somatic anxiety performed worse only if they were low in self-confidence (Orbach, 1999). In another study, performance showed gradual decline when participants' cognitive anxiety dominated over their self-confidence (Landers & Lochbaum, 1998). Similarly, contrary to the prediction of multidimensional theory, cognitive and somatic anxieties have been shown to co-vary rather than act independently. Further, the discrepancy between goal attainment in previous performances and goal aspiration for future performances may heighten both anxiety and motivation, provided that the goal discrepancy is not so great that the probability of success is perceived to be (or is actually) low, in which case anxiety will remain high but motivation will show a significant decrease. Another study examined the role of state anxiety in catastrophic decrements in performance in 60 dart throwers who were assessed for level of cognitive anxiety prior to dart throwing. State anxiety was manipulated by increasing the distance of throw. Participants with low cognitive anxiety showed gradual decrements in performance over larger distances, while those with high cognitive anxiety had more catastrophic performance decrements. Results highlight the importance of cognitive anxiety in motor performance (Ingurgio, 1999). More recent studies have identified other factors that affect the arousal–performance relationship. Experimental manipulations of the level of competitiveness created high state anxiety. Experimental manipulations of social pressure and ego threat instructions induced high levels of worry (cognitive anxiety). The results were explained in terms of processing efficiency of anxiety-induced performance catastrophes and indicated the complexity of the interrelationships of factors affecting performance. The amount of effort required for the performance interacted with cognitive anxiety to determine performance outcome (Hardy *et al.*, 2007).

Multidimensional anxiety theories and music performance

Craske and Craig (1984) tested Lang's three systems model using 40 advanced pianists, who were divided into two groups, anxious and non-anxious. Each participant performed alone and for an evaluative audience, during which continuous behavioral, physiological (heart rate), and self-report measures were obtained via video recording and telemetry. Results indicated support for Lang's theory. The anxious group showed greatly increased anxiety in the audience performance in all three systems; their response was synchronous. By contrast, the non-anxious group showed increases comparable to those in the anxious performers in physiological arousal but not the other two systems; their responses were desynchronous. Similarly, concordance between the three systems was evident in the anxious performers in the high-stress (evaluative audience) performance, while the non-anxious performers' three systems showed discordant relationships, consistent with Lang's multidimensional model of anxiety.

Self-efficacy theory predicts that anxiety will increase as self-efficacy decreases because low self-efficacy is accompanied by self-defeating thoughts, emotional distress, heightened arousal and reduced behavioral mastery (Bandura, 1991). In a test of the theory with piano students, Craske and Craig (1984) found limited support for the prediction. Self-efficacy measures did not show the inverse relationship predicted by the theory. In the non-anxious group, self-efficacy remained stable from performing alone to performing with an evaluative audience, but autonomic arousal increased from one condition to the other. In the anxious group, while all three systems increased between the two conditions, there was no loss of self-efficacy. It has been argued that actual skill and task mastery mediate the relationship between self-efficacy and anxiety (Rachman & Hodgson, 1974).

Miller and Chesky (2004) tested the predictions of the multidimensional anxiety theory (Martens *et al.*, 1990) using modified versions of the Competitive State and Trait Anxiety Inventory–2 (CSAI–2; CTAI–2) on musicians (71 college music majors, of whom 59 (83%) reported experiencing performance anxiety) by examining the intensity and direction of cognitive anxiety, somatic anxiety, and self-confidence over a series of performances at weekly intervals involving varying degrees of stress, such as studio lessons and jury performances. For all performance conditions, cognitive anxiety was higher than somatic anxiety. Higher cognitive anxiety scores were associated with lower scores for self-confidence. Although males and females reported similar levels of both somatic and cognitive anxiety, females reported more debilitating effects than males. Interestingly, teachers' perceptions of students' performance quality were higher than the students' own perception of their performances. Students reported higher anxiety for jury performances but their teachers' perceptions revealed consistent underestimation of the intensity of their students' anxiety. The study provided some support for the theory—that is, two distinct components of performance anxiety (somatic and cognitive) that varied according to performance demands and covaried with levels of self-confidence. Changes in cognitive or somatic intensity were also associated with whether the anxiety was perceived as facilitative or debilitative with respect to performance.

Reversal theory

A discussion of the arousal–performance relationship would be incomplete without a discussion of the role of personality variables that exert a stress-moderating effect on performance. In Chapter Two, we discussed the role of stable differences in cognitive style, coping strategies, social skills, and negative affectivity in moderating the degree to which individuals are adversely affected by negative life experiences. Most of the literature that has examined the relationship between personality factors and response to stress has focused on the positive linear relation between stressful events and disturbances of mood. Reversal theory (Apter, 1982) examines both the positive and negative aspects of the stress-moderating effects of particular personality characteristics. It proposes four pairs of opposite meta-motivational states that structure an individual's experience of his or her own motivation. Level or arousal (telic/paratelic) and quality of hedonic tone (feelings of unpleasantness/pleasantness) interact in ways that either enhance or impair performance. Reversal theory is so named because these states may shift suddenly and unexpectedly and such shifts have significant impacts on performance. Early theories that explored the relationship between arousal and hedonic tone posited a single homeostatic optimal arousal system (see, for example, Hebb, 1955). In reversal theory, two different phenomenological states or modes of information processing are proposed. Apter characterized people as telic dominant or paratelic dominant. The word 'telic' (from the Greek word *telos*, meaning *goal)* is characterized as serious, arousal avoidant, and goal directed. Arousal in telic-dominant people is experienced as unpleasant and anxiety producing because it is perceived to interfere with the achievement of the goal. Paratelic-dominant people are playful, arousal seeking, and spontaneous. The activity, as opposed to the goal, is the focal point and arousal is experienced as pleasant and exciting and increases the enjoyment of the activity. Low levels of arousal create boredom and listlessness (Martin, Kuiper, Olinger, & Dobbin, 1987). Thus, reversal theory accounts for both pleasant and unpleasant states of high arousal (excitement versus anxiety, respectively), as well as pleasant and unpleasant states of low arousal (relaxation and boredom, respectively). People tend towards one pole but fluctuate between them depending on environmental factors, such as frustration and satiation. Reversals have been tracked in golfers during tournaments (Hudson & Walker, 2002). The key differences between the states occur along the dimensions of preference for planning versus spontaneity, seriousness versus playfulness, and arousal avoidance versus arousal seeking. There are some similarities between these poles and those of extraversion–introversion (Eysenck, 1960) and sensation seeking. A series of studies that tested the predictions of reversal theory produced the following results:

i   Paratelic-dominant subjects show superior task performance in moderately stressful conditions compared with non-stressful conditions.

ii Telic-dominant subjects were more distressed on psychological and physiological measures in the moderately stressful condition compared with the non-stressful condition.

iii At very high levels of stress, both telic- and paratelic-dominant individuals showed a positive linear relationship between stressors and mood disturbance (Martin *et al.*, 1987).

In a recent test of the theory with respect to performance outcomes, Cromer and Tenenbaum (2009) assessed the relationship between perceived pressure, challenge perception, and level of determination in telic and paratelic individuals on task performance. Results showed that pressure had a minimal effect on performance regardless of participants' meta-motivational dominance. The authors concluded that paratelic individuals tried harder than telic individuals because they possess a particular form of intrinsic motivation that contributes to better performances.

Distraction theory

Several theories have been proposed that add to our knowledge and understanding of performance impairment, also called suboptimal performance and choking under pressure. Pressure is defined as the presence of situational incentives to perform well (Hardy *et al.*, 1996a). This may seem like an odd definition of pressure, which many people would associate with the word 'stress,' which is defined as the absence of sufficient resources to cope with a particular demand. However, the word 'pressure' in the performance context refers not to resources (such as skill, task mastery, etc.) but to the possible positive and negative consequences of the performance, the presence of a valued, evaluative audience, and ego-relevant threats. (You will note the association between distraction theory and research on goal setting presented in Chapter Seven).

Self-presentation catastrophes (i.e. stage fright), also described as 'choking' or 'freezing,' usually involve a panic-like reaction and result in performance impairment or breakdown, or the performer avoiding or leaving the scene. These extreme forms of performance anxiety do occur, however rarely, and require explanation. Distraction theory (Wine, 1971) and self-focus or explicit monitoring theory (Baumeister, 1984) have been proposed to explain the phenomenon of choking. Although we all wish to perform well under pressure, some performers experience performance pressure as an excessively anxious desire to excel at their performance. As a consequence, some will perform more poorly than expected given their level of skill and preparation.

Although there are still some unresolved issues regarding theories of choking, most researchers agree that it is fundamentally a problem of (in)attention. There are two key explanations for choking. Distraction theories propose that pressure creates a dual-task situation in which skill execution and anxiety about the performance compete for the attentional and working memory capacities needed for the performance (Beilock & Carr, 2001). Heightened anxiety shifts attention from the task to task-irrelevant information, thereby reducing available working memory for the task at hand. Pressure does not result in a uniform loss of performance capacity but is dependent on the nature of the task being performed. Tasks that rely heavily on working memory are more likely to be affected by performance anxiety or pressure to perform than tasks that are performed more intuitively or automatically (Maddox & Ashby, 2004). Distraction theory accounts best for complex cognitive tasks, such as mathematical problems that are not based on an automated or proceduralized skill representation, such as playing a concerto from memory. For the latter type of task, a decrement in working memory capacity may actually improve performance by forcing reliance on the automatic (i.e. over-learned) processes used to achieve skill mastery. Support for the theory comes from studies that show that high-anxious subjects perform worse than low-anxious subjects on tasks that are reliant on working memory, but performance differences are fewer on tasks not placing high demands on working memory (Calvo, Ramos, & Estevez, 1992). Choking is a relatively infrequent occurrence and is more likely to occur for only the most difficult problems that make large demands on working memory and that have not been highly practiced.

Self-focus or explicit monitoring theories

The one important thing I have learned over the years is the difference between taking one's work seriously and taking oneself seriously. The first is imperative and the second is disastrous (Fonteyn, 1976 , p. 16).

Self-focus or explicit monitoring theories of choking suggest that pressure-induced performance decrements result from the explicit monitoring and control of proceduralized knowledge that is best performed as an uninterrupted and unanalyzed whole. In other words, in contrast to distraction theory, self-focus theories hypothesize that pressure during performance raises self-consciousness and increases one's attention to the skill processes involved in the execution of the task. Such attentional focus interrupts or disrupts a well-learnt, automatic skill (Masters, 1992). Wulf (Wulf, McNevin, & Shea, 2001; Wulf & Prinz, 2001) also recognizes attentional shifts as problematic for the execution of skilled motor behavior. His constrained-action hypothesis proposes two types of attention: internal focus in which conscious attempts to control outcomes are made using kinaesthetic, kinematic, or somatosensory information, and external focus whereby automatic motor processes are harnessed to achieve an (complex motor) outcome, such as playing a concerto. In the music context, an external focus would be on the sound produced (Maas et al., 2008).

According to another theory, the schema theory of motor control (Schmidt, 2003), change in focus can be triggered by alterations in the habitual execution of the motor task, for example when pianists play on strange pianos that have a different action and sound quality to the instrument to which they are accustomed. These differences draw the performer's attention to sensory information as they try to adapt to the unfamiliar situation, such as the increased finger pressure needed for a piano with a stiffer action. Schema theory suggests that there are bodily memory representations of goal-oriented actions and their consequences based on past experience of motor performance in specific situations. These representations are called schema, which contain information about the relationships between the conditions, the motor commands generated, their sensory consequences, and the outcome of the movement process for given complex motor tasks. These schema are recalled, recognized, and adapted as required. When there is a mismatch between the expected and actual outcome of an action, the schema must be updated with the new sensory and movement information (Turner & Kenny, 2010).

The question arises as to whether one would expect expert performers to be more disrupted by unexpected changes in performance conditions than less experienced performers because they have more highly developed motor processes that are no longer plastic. Conversely, expert performers may be more able to adapt because their performance experience has resulted in the development of variants to their motor schemas encountered on multiple performance occasions that they can utilize once they have matched the current performance conditions to previous experience. In one study using Western contemporary singers, changes to habitual performance expectations resulted in a poorer performance (Turner & Kenny, 2010). Singers in this genre move freely during performance, unlike classically trained singers who maintain a relatively still posture. When the Western contemporary singers were asked to perform while standing still, none was able to maintain the sound pressure levels achieved in their normal performances that involved spontaneous movement.

Similar findings have been reported in studies that have investigated the influence of the learner's focus of attention, induced by instructions or feedback, on motor skill learning. Outcome studies have reported that directing performers' attention to the effects of their movements, i.e. maintaining an external focus of attention, is more beneficial than directing their attention to their own movements, i.e. maintaining an internal focus of attention. It is hypothesized that an internal attentional focus interferes with natural control processes in the motor system. In contrast, an external focus permits automatic control processes to regulate movements, providing support for the view that actions are controlled, to some extent, by their anticipated effects (Wulf & Prinz, 2001). These types of performance do not rely on conscious execution of the component skills and tasks that make up the total performance of skilled physical actions such as golf putting, tennis strokes, or music performance. Maximum consistency of performance is achieved by using motor loops that allow the performer to operate at a subconscious (non-cognitive) level; that is, automatically, integrating all of the components of the task into a single smooth action based on sensory and motor feedback. When this process works optimally, the performer is described as operating 'in the zone' or as experiencing 'flow.'

This account of choking has in common with the automatic execution model (Baumeister, 1984) the basic premise that choking occurs as a result of the inhibition of well-learned or automatic skills. However, they differ in their understanding of the mechanism involved. In a test of the two theories, using golf putting as the procedural skill and alphabet arithmetic as the non-proceduralized skill, Beilock and Carr (2001) found that those who trained under conditions of distraction (i.e. while simultaneously performing a word generation task) showed performance decrement in putting but not arithmetic when placed in a high-pressure post test. A group who trained while being filmed (i.e. trained under conditions of self-focus) performed better than the other groups. The researchers concluded that self-conscious training inoculates performers against choking under pressure. They concluded that performance pressure triggers explicit monitoring, which interrupts the performance of a proceduralized but not a non-proceduralized skill.

Distraction and self-focus in music performance

Performance anxiety may disrupt the normal functioning of feedback loops by making previously automatic actions conscious, thereby interfering with the smooth, integrated performance of the action. Thus, if, during the performance of an expert task such a playing a piano sonata from memory, the pianist switches to explicit monitoring of the performance, such as thinking, for example, 'I hope I remember the key change in the recapitulation,' this may hinder the processes underlying its automatic production, leading to performance impairment or breakdown.

Evidence to date supports the assertion that distraction theories of choking are more applicable to challenging cognitive tasks (such as mathematical problem solving), while explicit monitoring and automatic execution theories of choking apply more to tasks based on sensorimotor skills, such as sport performance. Music performance is a complex mix of both of these types of tasks. Learning a difficult musical piece involves a range of cognitive skills but ultimately is dependent on mastery of the automatic motor tasks required for executing the performance.

Wan and Huon (2005) tested both the distraction and self-focus (explicit monitoring) theories with a musical performance task, using the same method as that described by Beilock and Carr (2001). They taught 72 novice musicians some basic music skills under three conditions—single task (normal training conditions); dual task (distraction), and a video-monitoring condition, which focused their attention on step-wise skill acquisition—after which they were exposed to a high- or low-pressure performance test. Their results supported the explicit monitoring theory; they obtained the same protection against performance degradation under pressure in the video-training group as Beilock and Carr found for their golfers. Performers in this group actually improved their performance under pressure. Both groups of researchers argued that explicit monitoring is appropriate in the early development of a new task but as the task is learnt and becomes increasingly automated and proceduralized, attempts to monitor these proceduralized skills under pressure may disrupt the performance. As predicted, those in the normal training and dual task (distraction) group performed worse under high than low pressure at post test. A possible limitation of this study is the use of novice musicians. After just a few training sessions, it is questionable how much automaticity could be reached in a skill as complex as music performance. Subsequent studies might usefully address this very important question of protective training methods for highly skilled, highly anxious musicians.

Both theories of performance impairment may prove appropriate to music performance, perhaps at different stages of learning, that is, at the preliminary, non-proceduralized stage and at the later stage of skilled (i.e. proceduralized) performance. Future research can usefully explore these theories applied to music performance.

The mental health model of sport performance

So far in this section, we have dealt with a number of theories whose focus has been on performance and performance enhancement. The Mental Health Model (MHM) (Morgan, 1980) diverges from other performance theories by assigning a central role to mental health in sport performance. At its simplest, it states that there is an inverse relationship between psychopathology and sport performance. A number of studies have shown that between 70% and 85% of athletes can be correctly assigned to 'successful' and 'unsuccessful' (however defined) categories by virtue of their psychological health profile as measured by tests of personality and mood state (Raglin, 2001). It has a number of useful applications, including the prevention of staleness (overtraining) syndrome and the prevention of injuries. Morgan believed that the true value of the MHM lay in its use as a dynamic, idiographic assessment tool that repeatedly assesses athletes over a training period in order to monitor their mood and adjust their training load accordingly. In general, as training load increases, mood disturbances also increase and performance declines. About 10% of athletes show this pattern to such an extent that they are described as suffering from overtraining or staleness. In one study of Olympic canoeists, mood was monitored closely using the Profile of Mood States questionnaire over an intense training period prior to competition. Those who showed mood disturbance had their training loads reduced, while those who showed no mood disturbance had their training loads increased (Berglund & Stafstom, 1994). The researchers reported that they had no cases of staleness over the training season and several of the canoeists won Olympic medals.

In a prospective study of American Alpine skiers, May *et al.* (1985) found a strong positive relationship between depression, major negative life events, poor coping skills, and low social support and illness and injury later in the season. Athletes with poor mental health profiles were much more likely to be dropped from the team (50% vs 21%). Depressed athletes show performance decrement because depression has been associated with both deterioration of fine motor skills and increased response times (Sabbe, Hulstijn, & Van Hoof, 1996). Further, athletes with elevated anxiety and stress scores were at higher risk of injury due to excessive muscle tension and the effects of the many forms of cognitive dysfunction that occur in performers under stress. In another study of Olympic-level athletes, Meyers *et al.* (Meyers, Whelan, & Murphy, 1996) found that 85% of athletes who presented to the sports psychologists at the training center for performance enhancement services actually suffered from significant psychopathology. They argued for the development of reliable methods to identify vulnerable athletes in order to reduce the impact of psychological distress on their athletic performance and the much higher risk of illness and injury found in this group.

Theories of music performance anxiety

The vast literature on the etiology of the anxiety disorders and the foregoing discussion of theories of performance can usefully be used to build on research in music performance anxiety, to extrapolate potential etiological factors and to produce theories that can be subjected to empirical verification. Prior to embarking on this endeavor, it should be noted that theorizing about music performance anxiety lags far behind the anxiety disorders and sport performance and that the extrapolations presented here are intended as a stimulus for progressing research in this important but neglected area of anxiety management. Below I present some attempts at theorizing music performance anxiety. None of the theories—or perhaps they are more properly called hypotheses—has robust empirical support, but they provide a foundation for the development of studies to test them, as do further applications of the performance theories described in the previous section.

De Nelsky's theory

De Nelsky (1987) (in Robson *et al.*, 1995) proposed a model based on learning theory principles, as follows:

   i Much early reinforcement for outstanding performance.

  ii Performance becomes a major basis for self-esteem.

 iii Increasing competition with fewer and fewer rewards available.

  iv Highly critical judges provide much negative feedback concerning performance.

   v Perfection of performance becomes a primary goal.

  vi Highly practiced, automatic behavior becomes 'de-automatized'.

 vii Performer is obsessed more and more about possible negative outcomes.

viii Performance anxiety mounts.

  ix A positive feedback loop is established, which leads to ever-increasing amounts of performance anxiety.

Let us examine this sequence from a learning theory (operant conditioning) perspective. Step one involves positive reinforcement of a particular behavior. The effect of positive reinforcement is to increase the probability of the behavior reoccurring. If there is insufficient balance in the child's life, or if the parents perceive their talented child as a narcissistic extension of themselves, they will increasingly shape the child's behavior such that, if only outstanding musical performance is rewarded, self-esteem becomes contingent on musical performance. As the child progresses to performances outside the home and teacher's studio, they will be confronted with external judges who are more critical (inadvertently punishing) than their previous audiences. Rewards from parents will reduce if the child does not receive the praise of judges or fails to win competitions. The child will strive to restore his reinforcers by practicing more and setting increasingly unrealistic perfectionistic goals for his/her performance. Fear of negative evaluation directs attentional resources away from the task; errors become more probable; anxiety about errors further distracts attention from the task until finally, in some vulnerable young people, performance anxiety becomes intense, further impairing performance. The child is caught in an approach–avoidance dilemma. He remains in the field to recover his valued reinforcers (approach) but there is a pull to avoidance to escape the mounting emotional distress. Children will rarely give up on their attachment to parents, even bad parents, and their endless striving for love and recognition may keep them trapped in a maladaptive cycle, as we shall see later in Chapter Eight.

Montello's theory

I mix with some musicians whom I consider are natural performers, who have achieved an international standard. I see myself as a 'working musician.' I am in awe of people with perfect pitch, who can play anything from sight, who make music because they must . . . That is a significant part of my anxiety. I always feel inferior to other musicians whom I perceive as gods. I have to work very hard to maintain my standards in comparison. I am sure they work hard too, but there is always the comparison (Professional orchestral musician).

Based on her work with freelance professional musicians who were offered process-oriented group music therapy based on improvisation to explore their 'lived' experience of music performance anxiety, Montello and colleagues (Montello, Coons, & Kantor, 1990), using phenomenological analysis of their qualitative data, uncovered eight key factors that may contribute to music performance anxiety. These are (p. 295):

i   an 'inner critic'

ii   ambivalent association with primary instrument

iii   inadequate preparation for performance

iv   lack of commitment to performance

v   underdeveloped will and lack of focus related to performance

vi   discomfort in sharing one's music with an audience

vii   weak sense of self

viii   ambivalent relationship with the audience

All of these items, although somewhat lacking in precision, will by now be very familiar to those of you who have read thus far. An interesting finding of the study was that the majority of participants could identify a music-related trauma (not specified) early in life that had resulted in unresolved conflicts with respect to their personal and musical identity. Further, musicians who initially scored high on trait anxiety (STAI–T) but low on narcissism (as measured by the Narcissistic Personality Inventory (NPI): Raskin & Hall, 1981) showed the largest decrease in anxiety and the greatest improvement in confidence as performers. Montello *et al.* argued that the traumas triggered denial and dissociation of feelings associated with these early traumatic disruptions, against which anxiety was a defense. Those scoring high on the NPI were thought to be too highly defended to benefit from the therapy intervention, while those scoring lower were able to work through anxiety associated with earlier musical traumas and hence reduce current experiences of music performance anxiety. These conclusions are highly speculative, given the speculative nature of the theorizing, the small sample sizes in each study, and the small effect sizes reported for the treatment group compared with wait list and/or attentional controls in the second study.

Wilson's three-dimensional model of music performance anxiety

In another extension of the Yerkes–Dodson Law, Wilson (2002) developed a three-dimensional model in which three factors interact to determine the level of anxiety that will be experienced during performance. These are: (i) the trait anxiety of the performer; (ii) the degree of task mastery achieved of the works to be performed; and (iii) the degree of situational stress that accrues to the performance (presence, size, and characteristics of the audience; the 'stakes' of the performance: audition, solo recital, examination, etc.). The model makes similar predictions to those of Martens (1990) and Hardy and Parfitt (1991) with respect to the various interactions of these three factors.

Papageorgi, Hallam, and Welch (2007), drawing heavily on Wilson's model, proposed a conceptual framework for understanding music performance anxiety in which three sets of contributing factors are considered. These are: (i) performer susceptibility to experiencing performance anxiety; (ii) task efficacy; and (iii) performance environment. We note that this is a conceptual framework, not a theory. The model has not been tested empirically; further, its conceptual flaws are problematic, rendering its utility to the field questionable, as it is based on a faulty model of optimal arousal (see previous section). Further, there are confusions in the temporal dimension: susceptibility to anxiety, task efficacy, and performance environment are placed in the pre-performance conditions and are treated as temporally contemporaneous. However, anxiety proneness and previous performance (conditioning) experiences pre-date current task efficacy and appraisal of the performance setting and would presumably influence their appraisal of the performance setting. The model also indicates that the performer's psychological state prior to the performance is the result of cognitive appraisal, which, according to the model, predates level of autonomic nervous system (ANS) arousal. However, the level of ANS arousal is a factor that contributes to cognitive appraisal. The model is somewhat static and linear in conception and does not reflect the complex, dynamic interplay of all the salient causative and associated factors that impact a given performance.

Kenny's emotion-based model of music performance anxiety

Barlow's (2000a) model of anxiety is useful in aiding our understanding of performance anxiety in general and music performance anxiety in particular. In the case of young performers who are high in trait anxiety, that is, the expression of a generalized biological vulnerability, who come from home environments in which expectations for excellence are high but support for achieving excellence is low (generalized psychological vulnerability), exposure to early and frequent evaluations and self-evaluations of their performances in a competitive environment (specific psychological vulnerability) may be sufficient to trigger the physiological, behavioral, and cognitive responses characteristic of music performance anxiety. Anxiety may be triggered by conscious, rational concerns or by cues that trigger, unconsciously, earlier anxiety-producing experiences or somatic sensations. These may include earlier aversive performance incidents that may form the basis of the subsequent development of negative cognitions (Barlow, 2002a; Beck et al., 1985; Beck, 1995). Once anxiety has been triggered, the person shifts into a self-evaluative attention state, in which self-evaluation of perceived inadequate capabilities to deal with the threat, in this case the imminent performance, is prominent. The attention typically narrows to a focus on catastrophic cognitive self-statements that disrupt concentration and performance.

In this respect, music performance anxiety may share commonalities with social anxiety and in its extreme form appears similar to social phobia. One could argue that the conditions under which one performs, that is, the degree of social evaluative threat perceived by the performer, is the defining feature of social phobia. The third stage of Barlow's model, in which specific environmental experiences become conditioned in specific situations is necessary for the development of non-generalized and specific (social) phobias, and by extension, music performance anxiety.

A salient example from my casebook demonstrates this phenomenon for the development of music performance anxiety. A young oboe player completed his undergraduate and postgraduate oboe performance studies with distinction at a prestigious music school. He denied any experience of music performance anxiety, even in highly challenging environments such as his final senior recital. After graduation, he began attending for auditions to obtain a place in a national or international orchestra. He recounted that as many as 30 oboe players would present for audition for one position. The audition was an impersonal affair, with performances often conducted behind a screen to prevent the introduction of bias into the assessment process. Musicians were given less than five minutes to demonstrate their prowess, after which they were dismissed without comment. No feedback was given following unsuccessful auditions. Vulnerable performers would experience heightened anxiety about their performance in such situations because they have no means of evaluating their own performance, so musicians cannot learn from previous performances how to improve subsequent performances, except from their own critical appraisal of their performance, which may or may not have been accurate with respect to the reasons for the adjudicators' selection or non-selection. After many unsuccessful auditions, this musician reported the development of severe music performance anxiety expressed as anticipatory worry and dread, expectation of failure, and dry mouth (particularly problematic for wind players), accompanied by feelings of hopelessness and depression. Although remaining committed to the audition process, he described a loss of self-efficacy and decreased preparedness to invest the practice time necessary for a successful audition. Fortunately, his anxiety remained focused on the audition situation and did not generalize to other performance opportunities that came his way, including achieving several temporary contracts with prestigious national orchestras.

This case example illustrates a number of key components of the emotion-based theory of anxiety development, as well as something about his personality structure, sense of self and lack of agency, themes to which we will return later. The critical feature of this account is the sense of uncontrollability and unpredictability in a specific situation, in this case the audition, and the subsequent reporting of negative affect— anxiety, hopelessness, and depression. While unpredictability leads to anxiety, uncontrollability results in depression, although there is overlap between these two concepts and their consequences (Mineka & Zinbarg, 1996). Physiological arousal in the form of dry mouth added to the feeling of uncontrollability as wind players need to be well hydrated to perform; situational cues that evoke anxious responding, such as the coldness of the adjudicators; the impersonal and dehumanizing assessment procedures and the lack of feedback; attentional shift, whereby the focus is directed away from the performance task to a self-focus; and fear of negative evaluation and failure.

The process is as follows: 'Situational cues associated with negative affect result in a shift from an external to an internal focus of attention directed to somatic sensations, as well as the affective and self-evaluative components of the context, which result in further increases in arousal and anxiety' (Barlow, 2002a, p. 84). The audition example indicates the specificity of the situation in some cases of music performance anxiety. In this case, the audition process was objectively extremely aversive, fostering by its nature all the precursors to anxious apprehension and vulnerability to the development of a clinically significant anxiety disorder in a highly gifted, previously confident performer.

Below is an account from an advanced tertiary-level music student that illustrates other key dimensions of Barlow's emotion-based theory of anxiety.

> *I suffer from music performance anxiety. I only get it just before or on the day before a concert. I don't tend to think about it the week before. I don't sweat or get shaky or anything like that.* I am just so worried about what people will think *if it goes wrong. Once I go out there I concentrate so hard to relax and it goes the other way and then I end up being really casual about it and probably not concentrating enough. It got a lot worse once I started more serious music, when I left school at 18 and probably when I was performing at the academy because it was actual fellow musicians in the audience whereas before it had just been parents and friends. That was when I first started to think 'Oh god!' I don't know why it has turned out this way*—I've been lucky and never really had a bad experience. *Even if I made mistakes I wasn't really that worried about it. But now, before a concert, it's a complete nightmare.* I don't think there is anything I can do with it so I just leave it at that. *I go through my normal routine that I would any other day.* Before the concert I just wander round feeling nervous. *The biggest fear is making a mistake and other people noticing it.* I get really pissed off when I make any mistake, *especially in orchestral playing. It is not as bad playing in gigs and stuff especially when nobody knows you and people are not really listening* (Male clarinettist, aged 22).

There are a number of interesting features in this account. First, this young musician experiences a strong sense of uncontrollability and unpredictability in his concert performances. Although they are a 'complete nightmare,' he does not think that he can do anything about the anxiety and just 'leave[s] it at that.' He denies excessive physiological arousal and states that he has never had a bad experience (i.e. he does not remember any aversive musical performance experiences) that could have conditioned his present fear of performing. Note that he describes himself as 'lucky' not to have had such experiences, thus further demonstrating his overall sense of uncontrollability. This attribution of luck as responsible for positive outcomes demonstrates an external locus of control (Seligman, 1991), that is, the belief that one has no control over events in one's life. Only when he became 'serious' (i.e. personally invested) about music did he succumb to performance anxiety; that is, he began to conflate his self-esteem with his musical self-efficacy. In our experience working with young musicians, this is not an unusual (self-reported) trajectory (Osborne & Kenny, 2008), and is probably related to the development of self-reflective function[11] and the capacity for self-evaluation

---

[11] Self-reflective function presupposes a level of development where psychological separation/individuation has occurred (Fonagy, Gergely, Jurist, & Target, 2002).

and, inevitably, self-criticism that emerges in middle to late adolescence (Jackson & Lurie, 2006). The changing nature of the performance setting and the (perceived) increased demands from the audience ('before it had just been parents and friends,' now it is 'fellow musicians') also play a role in his anxious responding. He displays the typical fear of negative evaluation and excessively high (perfectionistic) expectations of his performance ('I get really pissed off when I make *any* mistake'). He also reports pervasive negative affect ('I just wander round feeling nervous'), attentional shift away from the task ('I concentrate so hard to relax and it goes the other way'), and situationally specific anxiety (anxiety occurs in orchestral playing but not in gigs because 'nobody knows you and people are not really listening'). Compare the above account with this account from a female pianist:

> *Everybody says that performance anxiety or having nerves before a performance is a good thing. Teachers and everybody say that. I suppose a little bit is OK but not the extent to which I feel it. I always experience it before I go on—there is always that incredible fear and worry that something will go wrong and if it does I get a massive panic attack. I fall apart and then I just panic completely. Before I go on, I get awful cramps in my stomach . . . like really bad period pain cramp . . . It's so awful I had to go to the doctor about it. It has always affected me like that and I need to go to the toilet all the time. Every single time I know it is going to happen* (Female pianist, aged 20 years).

Unlike our male clarinettist who denied somatic symptoms, for this pianist the level of physiological arousal was extremely aversive and dominated the account of her experience. This young woman no doubt suffers from neurobiological hyper-reactivity that triggers 'false alarms' (Barlow, 2002a; and see below) in even mildly anxiety-provoking situations. However, the nature of her physiological arousal is interesting. She reports panic, with symptoms arising in the sympathetic branch of the autonomic nervous system; and stomach cramps and diarrhea, which indicate that the anxiety is expressed through the smooth muscles of the parasympathetic branch of the autonomic nervous system. Her anxiety tolerance is very low because of the dual involvement of both systems simultaneously (Davanloo, 2005). There is also a strong emotional component: 'incredible fear and worry that something will go wrong,' that will trigger a 'panic attack' during which she 'fall[s] apart.' It is interesting that she describes her experience as panic, because there is a strong association between internal (cardiovascular, physiological, etc.) cues and false alarms in panic disorder (Dworkin, 1993) (note that Barlow states that panic reactions are false alarms—see Chapters Two and Six), compared with specific phobias in which the focus is on external cues, as in the case of the student at audition. This young woman may in fact have a comorbid panic disorder for which a differential diagnosis would be necessary. Conversely, her description of her music performance anxiety may be characterized as panic disorder. The conditioning of her response to the performance setting is very well established: 'Every single time I know it is going to happen.' Her commitment to the feared situation is compelling—she continues to perform despite this very disturbing account of her performance experience. Remaining in an objectively aversive situation is difficult to understand, but may be explained to some extent by Dollard and Miller's approach–avoidance gradient model, discussed in Chapter One. This young woman may explain her tolerance for these distressing symptoms by her love of music.

Alternatively, the behavior may be viewed as counter phobic, i.e. a feared situation is actively pursued in order to gain mastery over the fear rather than passively succumb to it (PDM Taskforce, 2006).

Research with child musicians demonstrates similar phenomena. For example, Osborne and Kenny (2008), using a retrospective recall method, explored the reports of young musicians' worst performance experiences with their scores on measures of trait anxiety and music performance anxiety. Here is one example of an account from a 13-year-old pianist sitting for a music exam: 'I had practiced until perfect and remembered scales beforehand. I walked in and got very nervous. I played three pieces OK but scales were terrible. I forgot the notes and fingering totally . . . I came out crying and felt like a failure.' Music students who reported a negative music performance experience scored significantly higher on the scale used to measure music perform-ance anxiety (MPAI–A) (Osborne et al., 2005) than those who did not report such an experience. Trait anxiety was also higher in the group recalling a worst performance. There was a positive linear association between trait anxiety and music performance anxiety. Caution is needed in the interpretation of these findings. It is possible that those young musicians who recalled a worst performance experience and/or provided the most detail in the recalled event (hence receiving higher anxiety scores for their account), may have been those with a greater propensity to experience anxiety because of their higher biological and/or psychological vulnerability. It is possible that low-anxious young performers may also have had similar 'worst performance' experiences but did not recall them or did not recall them in vivid detail because they did not appraise them in such a negative way as the highly anxious musicians, and hence the experience was not salient enough to be stored in long-term memory. However, the key point here is that there appears to be a universal phenomenology of the experience of music performance anxiety across the lifespan.

How can we explain these extreme reactions to musical performance in otherwise highly intelligent, musically gifted, socially competent young musicians? These accounts present vivid examples of emotional learning, the process whereby a stimu-lus (in this case, music performance) acquires emotional properties. These acquired emotional reactions are conditioned fear responses (Phelps, 2006). In humans, the fear response can be elicited automatically if we are confronted by a real and present danger that threatens our well-being. Fear triggers automatic emergency physiological reactions that were famously described by Cannon (1929) as 'fight or flight' responses that aimed at readying us to deal with the threat. Barlow (2002a) refers to these responses as 'true alarms' (p. 219). 'False alarms' (p. 220) are fear responses that occur in the absence of a real or present danger and are a defining characteristic of panic disorders and phobias, and, it seems, music performance anxiety. In my experience, many accounts of severe music performance anxiety contain very strong words associ-ated with fear and panic, as the accounts given here show.

We have discussed in the previous section explanations for the triggering of false alarms in the anxiety disorders and it is not a great leap of logic to conclude that the same or similar processes may be at work in music performance anxiety. In fact, all the background factors related to generally higher trait anxiety and heightened neurobiological hyper-reactivity are clearly evident in the self-descriptions of the young musicians presented above. We need more research to identify whether anxious musicians have heightened anxiety sensitivity, chronic hyper-arousal or high negative affect, factors that constitute the biological and psychological vulnerabilities described in Barlow's theory. We also have no information about the early life experiences of anxious musicians and the degree to which their early learning experiences as children included caregivers who focused anxious attention on bodily sensations and communicated their beliefs regarding the danger surrounding these symptoms and sensations. The possible learning processes—respondent (classical) conditioning, observational (vicarious) learning or modeling, and information/verbal instruction or instructed fear—whereby false alarms become conditioned in vulnerable people may also be useful to explore in anxious musicians; all are plausible, but as yet await empirical investigation.

Based on the foregoing discussion, I propose a conceptually modified model for the etiology and maintenance of music performance anxiety based on Barlow's model of the development of social phobia, as follows. In music performance anxiety, the stressful event is almost always described as a performance situation with an evaluative component such as a recital, concert, examination, audition, or eisteddfod. It may or may not involve an audience other than the examiner or adjudicator. The performance can be solo, orchestral, or choral (Kenny *et al.*, 2004). Figure 6.8 is a schematic representation of the pathways to and from music performance anxiety. The shaded area indicates the basic conditioning process for the development of anxious apprehension and hence generalized social phobia, or if a specific psychological vulnerability is present, a non-generalized social phobia. When anxious apprehension becomes focused on a complex musical performance, multiple factors, outlined earlier, need to be addressed in order to reduce the level of apprehension before the experience of too many alarms in the performance setting starts to condition the anxiety response to performing. Finally, the model emphasizes the iterative and mutually causal nature of the relationship between false and true alarms, a relationship that has not been discussed in the model for social phobia. I should mention that this theory focuses on the genesis and maintenance of severe anxiety responses in the performance setting. It assumes, for the purpose of explicating the theory, that other salient factors that contribute to performance anxiety such as adequate skill development and task mastery have been achieved.

In this model, both false and true alarms are the panic-like negative emotions and other forms of reactivity that have been conditioned in response to direct experience, stress, or conditioning in those with generalized biological and psychological vulnerabilities. The model accounts for the occurrence of severe music performance anxiety in musicians who have never experienced a performance breakdown. It appears that for those with a predisposition to experience heightened physiological and psychological arousal, the actual performance outcome is of secondary importance. These early experiences of either true or false alarms establish the propensity for anxious apprehension in performance situations. A number of outcomes of a performance become possible at this point. Repeated successful performances may eventually reduce the amount of anxious apprehension experienced before performances so that music performance anxiety does not persist, at least not at severe levels. However, if the

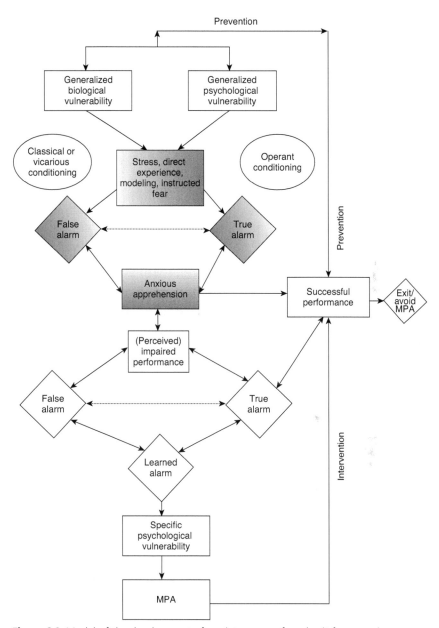

Figure 6.8 Model of the development of, maintenance of, and exit from music performance anxiety.

performance is impaired or is perceived to be impaired, the negative emotions and (cognitive) self-evaluation that follow may compound the anxious apprehension and trigger further alarms, which in turn increase the risk of impaired performance, in a vicious circle until the performance setting itself triggers conditioned alarms, even before the performance has taken place. Many performance settings, such as the audition process for orchestral musicians described above, are genuinely threatening, unpredictable, and uncontrollable and may have very little chance of success despite adequate preparation and task mastery. In these circumstances, performance is followed by actual negative consequences, such as non-selection at audition. If this sequence is repeated, the negative consequences will heighten anticipatory apprehension prior to subsequent performances. In music performance anxiety, true alarms and false alarms may become mutually recursive, such that successive performance impairments or successive exposure to genuinely threatening performance experiences increase subsequent true alarms, which in turn, increase the probability of subsequent performance impairments because of the interference effects that alarms exert on performance.

The model also attempts to account for those musicians who report intense feelings of music performance anxiety but do not experience performance impairment or breakdown. A false alarm involves the experiencing of anxious cognitive, emotional, and/or somatic anticipatory responses such as physiological arousal and/or dread and worry about a performance that is not subsequently impaired in performers who have not previously experienced performance impairment. However, these aversive anticipatory responses are contiguously associated with the performance situation and have been triggered by combinations of the biological and psychological vulnerabilities described in Barlow's theory. I would tentatively hypothesize that this subgroup of musicians may have comorbid anxiety disorders or be generally more vulnerable to the development of anxiety disorders than those whose music performance anxiety has been conditioned by true alarms in genuinely highly stressful performance settings.

Successful performances, despite their success, may still evoke alarm reactions, which, if repeated, become learned alarm responses triggered by the performance context. This, combined with the specific psychological vulnerability required for the development of a specific phobia, will thus become strongly associated with the performance situation, despite a lack of negative consequences, which under other circumstances would be extinguished because no aversive outcomes accrued. Hence, both classical and operant conditioning combine to produce learned alarms in psychologically vulnerable performers that, if not extinguished by appropriate interventions and performance outcomes, are likely to develop into music performance anxiety. It is possible, in certain individuals with particularly strong biological and/or psychological vulnerabilities, that no further impaired performances are needed to progress to music performance anxiety, since the learned alarm has become fully conditioned to the performance situation, as in our female pianist described earlier.

One feature of music performance anxiety that is not seen in other social phobias is the tendency of musicians to remain in the aversive situation, rather than engaging in avoidance or escape behaviors. One explanation is the strong personal investment in performing that musicians demonstrate, such that the approach gradient (the desire to remain in the field) remains stronger than the avoidance gradient (the desire to leave the field) (Dollard & Miller, 1950), even in situations that musicians describe as extremely aversive. If negative emotions become overwhelming and efforts to control them are unsuccessful, musicians may eventually leave the field (of music performance), and some may do so even if they have not experienced any serious performance breakdowns.

Given the known precursors to the development of the specific social/performance anxieties, it would be prudent to assess young musicians for generalized biological and psychological vulnerability and to implement preventive strategies early in their musical training. Education of parents and teachers in the etiology of these disorders and their prevention would also be useful. Strategies for prevention and psycho education for parents and teachers of young music students will be covered in the final chapter.

Summary

While understanding the characteristics of people who suffer from music performance anxiety is helpful, it is important that such observations be theoretically driven. In this chapter, all the major theories that have attempted to explain the etiology of anxiety and psychopathology in general are discussed and their defining principles summarized. Research pertaining to music performance anxiety, where available, was included for each theory. The discussion commenced with the psychoanalytic theories because these constitute the original theoretical attempts to understand ourselves and they formed the basis on which all other subsequent theories developed. Major offshoots of psychoanalytic theory are the attachment and relational psychotherapies. These were introduced in this chapter and will be taken up again in Chapter Eight. A brief discussion regarding the processes whereby children become securely or insecurely attached was provided together with a unifying model of the roles of developmental, attachment, and coping literatures. Next, the behavioral theories of anxiety and their primary conditioning models (classical and operant conditioning) were outlined. Cognitive theories of anxiety, which focus on the central etiological role of faulty cognitions in the genesis and maintenance of the anxiety disorders, have occupied a prominent place in theories of anxiety and its management over the past 30 years. Many recent variants of cognitive theories of anxiety have developed, including the Avoidance model of worry (AMW); Intolerance of uncertainty model (IUM); the Meta-cognitive model (MCM); and the Emotion dysregulation model (EDM). The emotion-based theories are gradually displacing the cognitive theories for their explanatory power with respect to the development of the anxiety and mood disorders. Barlow is a major figure in this framework and his triple vulnerability model shows promise in understanding the development and maintenance of performance anxiety. Cognitions and emotions occur in a physical body; hence the need to have some understanding of the psychophysiological and neurochemical theories of anxiety and the psychobiology of music performance anxiety. Theories of performance are essential to any discussion in the performing arts, as the achievement of peak performance is an important goal. Since many performance theories are based on misapplications of the Yerkes–Dodson Law, much discussion was devoted to the relationship between arousal and performance in this section of the chapter. This was followed by a critical review of a number of performance-based theories including the attentional control theory, the catastrophe and multidimensional anxiety theories, reversal theory, distraction theory, and self-focus or explicit monitoring theories. Finally, the few existing theories of music performance anxiety were outlined, including Wilson's three-dimensional model and Kenny's application of Barlow's emotion-based model.

Chapter 7

Treatment[1]

Technique without theory is blind; theory without technique is empty
Immanuel Kant.[2]

There has been an almost alarming proliferation of treatment approaches to the problems of living and these are developing ahead of the capacity of the research community to empirically validate their effectiveness. However, there have been a number of strong, empirical investigations into the efficacy of particular treatment approaches, and these will be considered in this chapter, along with descriptors of the major characteristics of each treatment approach covered. Of necessity, only the briefest coverage of each approach is possible in a book of this nature, and interested readers and practitioners will be referred to the respective literatures for more detailed descriptions. The treatment approaches covered in this chapter have been selected on the basis of their demonstrated or possible utility in the treatment of those who suffer from music performance anxiety. I will later argue that there is a group of performers who require special consideration with respect to treatment by virtue of long-standing difficulties with respect to their overall development that have made them susceptible to experience the most serious symptoms with respect to their performance anxiety.

Over the past 50 years, there has been a strong bias in the research and clinical communities towards the cognitive behavioral therapies, particularly for the anxiety disorders and depression. Pressure to provide cost-effective treatments for the growing numbers of people presenting to mental health providers has resulted in the development of short-term, symptom-focused, manualized therapies. However, a unitary focus on such treatment approaches may be counterproductive. There is increasing evidence for the efficacy of psychodynamically oriented therapies, and there are increasing concerns about the relapse rate at follow-up for people who have undergone a symptom-based cognitive behavioral treatment. Further, studies might show statistical differences before and after treatment, but these differences might not be clinically significant.

We will therefore start our discussion by identifying the range of possible treatments for music performance anxiety with a brief outline of the principal psychological therapies in most common use for which there is an evidence base. However, there may be problems with respect to the ecological validity of the evidence base for

---

[1] Portions of this text indicated by * are taken from Kenny, D.T. (2005). A systematic review of treatment for music performance anxiety, *Anxiety, Stress and Coping, 18*(3), 183–208, Taylor and Francis, reprinted by permission of the publisher (Taylor & Francis Group, http://www.informaworld.com).

[2] Attributed to Immanuel Kant. Alternative translation is: Experience without theory is blind, but theory without experience is mere intellectual play.

psychological therapies. These include the criteria for inclusion of participants in clinical studies and the outcome measures used. For example, many empirically supported treatments have been assessed on patient samples that rarely resemble the complex patients who present for treatment in clinical settings. By contrast, research-based clinical samples are selected on the basis that they have a primarily Axis I condition (as assessed using the DSM-IV-TR) and no Axis II condition (personality disorder) or other form of comorbidity (e.g. more than one Axis I condition) (Elliott, 1998). Westen and Morrison (2001) reported that 60%–70% of patients with multiple diagnoses were excluded from clinical trials of treatments for depression, panic, and generalized anxiety disorder, even though between 40% and 70% of patients with such primary diagnoses also have at least one other comorbid diagnosis. They therefore questioned whether the results of such trials can be replicated with clinic-based samples that include people with complex diagnostic presentations.

A similar concern with respect to the use of outcome measures in clinical trials has also been highlighted (Muran *et al.*, 2005). A study that evaluated the relative efficacy of four types of treatment for people with comorbid diagnoses showed that conclusions about the efficacy of the different therapeutic approaches changed depending on the nature of the outcome measure used. Self-report measures and other forms of questionnaires used to assess change may be specifically symptom based and may be too narrow in focus to allow a 'true' measure of clinical change to be evaluated, such as improvements in occupational or social functioning. Finally, a measure of patient drop-out should always be assessed as one form of outcome. A treatment may appear highly successful with 80% of participants showing remission of symptoms, but if only 15% of therapy starters completed therapy and were assessed at the end of the treatment program, different conclusions need to drawn about the efficacy of the treatment. Let's say that 100 people were enrolled in a treatment trial. Of the 15 people who completed therapy, 12 (i.e. 80%) showed benefit according to the outcome criteria used in the study. However, only 12% of the original 100 people who enrolled in therapy had a positive outcome. Researchers need to carefully assess the characteristics of those who completed the treatment and showed benefit, so that clinical resources are not wasted offering the therapy to people who are unlikely to benefit.

Psychoanalytic/psychodynamic therapies

The ultimate goal of psychotherapy is to assist each person with the task that is developmentally compelling for him or her—whether the task is the full flowering of the person's creativity or the attainment of some minimal awareness that one exists and deserves to stay alive (McWilliams, 1994, p. 68).

There is a group of therapies that are generally subsumed under the rubric 'psychoanalytic' or 'psychodynamic', and while these share many features in common, the newer wave of therapies differs in significant ways from the more classical therapies derived from Freud. Before we elucidate the characteristics of the newer therapies in this genre, it would be helpful to understand what most therapies of this type have in common. Blagys and Hilsenroth (2002) identified seven features of psychodynamic therapies that reliably distinguish them from other therapies, in particular, the cognitive behavioral therapies (CBT). These are summarized below.

i *Focus of therapy sessions is on affect and expression of emotion* in contrast to CBT's focus on cognitive factors such as thoughts and beliefs. This is based on the view that it is emotional and not intellectual insight that mediates change in therapy.[3]

ii *Exploration of attempts to avoid distressing thoughts and feelings* (often referred to as resistance and defenses in more classical terminology), whose aim is to discover the underlying emotions that are thought to be too painful to confront. In contrast, CBT focuses on faulty cognitions, called cognitive distortions, but does not explore the emotional substrate of these distortions.

iii *Identification of recurring themes and patterns* (called schemata or narratives, by which people make sense of their experience). CBT has a greater emphasis on specific antecedent and consequent events that together make up the reinforcement history of the individual.[4]

iv *Exploration of early life experiences,* particularly as they relate to current difficulties for which the patient has sought therapy. Significant attachment figures often take center stage in this exploration as these developmental relationships are repeated, frequently unknowingly, in current relationships. William Faulkner captured the essence of this process in his quip, 'The past is not dead . . . it is not even past.' By contrast, CBT has a focus on current difficulties and symptoms and eschews the relevance of past history in managing current problematic behaviors.

v *Focus on interpersonal relations,* both adaptive and maladaptive; these are sometimes called object relations to denote the mental representations that people build up of themselves (self-concept) and others in the process of their interpersonal relating with significant others. In CBT the focus is on the person's relationship with their current environment and symptoms, rather than on their relationships, either past or present.

vi *Focus on the therapy relationship.* The interpersonal relationship between the therapist and patient provides a fertile and potent learning opportunity since earlier and current problematic relationships are enacted in the relationship with the therapist. This brings the problem into the room and into the present, allowing it to be observed and worked with as it unfolds. The feelings that arise between patient and therapist are referred to as transference (the feelings that the patients project onto the therapist) and counter transference (the feelings stirred up in the therapist by the patient). In CBT, the therapist, while needing to be respectful of and empathic towards the patient, is not the central focus of the therapeutic contact, which remains firmly on the relationship between the patient and his symptoms.

---

[3] More recent CBT models increasingly include an emotional processing component.

[4] There are now schema-focused CBT approaches.

vii *Exploration of wishes and fantasies.* Psychodynamic therapies encourage open attention to all the passing thoughts and feelings that arise in the therapy hour, and encourage the patient to express them freely in a process known as free association. Such a process encourages wide-ranging self-reflection, allowing the emergence of a deep knowledge of self and others previously prevented by rigid defenses and attempts to protect against uncomfortable emotion. In many other therapies, including CBT, the therapist often formulates a treatment plan, hopefully in consultation with the patient, and then directs the content of the sessions according to this plan.

Psychoanalytic/psychodynamic treatment of anxiety

Many people who present to health services are given a diagnosis of depression, for which they are prescribed anti-depressants; or anxiety, for which they are prescribed anxiolytics, when the true diagnosis is 'unexpressed painful feeling for which the treatment is to express it' (Malan, 1979, p. 3). Psychodynamic therapy essentially involves the 'giving of insight through interpretation . . . to enable the person to face what s/he really feels, to realize that it is not as painful or as dangerous as feared, to work through it in a [therapeutic] relationship, and finally to be able to make use of real feelings within relationships in a constructive way' (p. 30). The aim of this emotional learning should be permanent, in that adaptive behaviors have replaced maladaptive attitudes and behaviors, and that these adaptive attitudes and behaviors can be generalized to new people and new situations in such a way that the learning becomes self-reinforcing.

Anxiety serves a very specific function in psychodynamic psychotherapy as a signal of internal distress and conflict that motivates human beings to adopt various defense mechanisms (e.g. repression, denial, displacement, projection, etc.; see Chapter Six), coping strategies, and compromise formations to avoid the experience of emotional pain or conflict and/or to control unacceptable impulses such as anger. Symptoms are often viewed as the incomplete expression of a wish or a need of which one consciously disapproves (Freud, 1923). The term 'compromise' indicates that one feels only partial satisfaction with the solution reached between the desire to express the repressed need and the repressing forces that prevent its expression. You will notice a compelling similarity in this description of the defense mechanisms and the model proposed by Olatunji *et al.* (2007) in Chapter Six to explain how fear learning shifts from being normative to pathological.

People may or may not be aware (in which case, we say that these feelings are unconscious) of their use of these mechanisms, which usually result in the development of maladaptive behavior(s) or troubling symptoms that both express the painful feelings in a disguised form while simultaneously defending against them. The tension and distress that this causes eventually motivate people to seek help. The task of the psychodynamic psychotherapist is to interpret the devices (i.e. defenses) used to protect oneself from experiencing the emotional pain or what one perceives to be unacceptable feelings; to help the person articulate the feared consequences of experiencing these painful or forbidden affects, which is the source of anxiety; and finally to help the individual understand the nature of the hidden feelings themselves. Both supportive

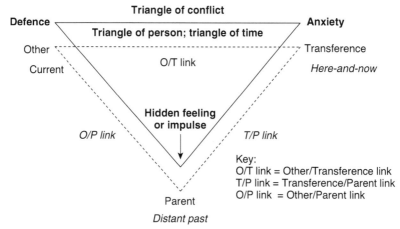

Figure 7.1 Triangles of conflict, person, and time, and the links between them that are made in psychotherapy. Adapted from *Individual Psychotherapy and the Science of Psychodynamics* (2nd ed.), Malan, D.H., Copyright (1979).

and expressive techniques are used to reduce internal conflict, to assist in emotional regulation, and to reduce anxiety to functional levels. This process was described by Malan (1979, p. 15) as the 'triangle of conflict.' The triangle of conflict is interpreted many times with respect to different important people in the individual's present and past. Such people include the therapist, onto whom the patient projects his/her fears and maladaptive modes of relating (a process called transference), current relationships with family, partners, colleagues, or friends, and finally people from the patient's family of origin such as parents and siblings. This triangle is called the 'triangle of person' or the 'triangle of time.' These two triangles and their relationship are represented graphically in Figure 7.1.

There is accumulating evidence that psychodynamic psychotherapy is effective for the treatment of emotional disorders, in particular, anxiety and depression (Shedler, 2010; Westen & Morrison, 2001). Shedler (2010) examined results from a number of meta-analyses examining the efficacy of psychodynamic therapies for common mental disorders, including anxiety and depression, most of which reported effect sizes[5] (median 0.75) that far exceeded effect sizes for antidepressant medications (0.17–0.31) and that equaled or exceeded the effects of cognitive behavioral therapy (median 0.62), particularly when longer-term outcomes were examined.

Relational and attachment-based psychotherapies

There have been many major developments in the field of psychoanalytic theory and practice over the past 100 years but it is beyond the scope of this book to enumerate and evaluate the great number of offshoots of the original theory. However, because of

---

[5] Effect size is a measure of the difference in outcome between a treated group and a control group. An effect size of 1.0 means that the average treated patient is one standard deviation healthier on the normal distribution (bell curve) than the average untreated patient (Shedler, 2010).

the potential importance of some of these newer and shorter variants of dynamic psychotherapy to the treatment of music performance anxiety, and to the mounting evidence with respect to their efficacy for other psychological disorders, I will briefly discuss two of these variants, the attachment-based psychotherapies and intensive short-term dynamic psychotherapy (ISTDP).

Attachment-based psychotherapy

Only a place marker will be provided here because a detailed overview of the attachment-based psychotherapies will be provided in Chapter Eight, where we discuss the more serious forms of music performance anxiety.

Intensive short-term dynamic psychotherapy (ISTDP)

Short-term psychotherapies share a number of common features, which include careful selection regarding suitability of patients, maintaining a therapeutic focus (as opposed to the free association of psychoanalysis), active therapist involvement (as opposed to the non-intrusiveness of analysts), the use of the transference (therapeutic) relationship and time-limited contracts. Most short-term psychotherapies use the triangle of conflict (feelings, anxiety, and defense) and the triangle of person (past, therapist, and current) (Malan, 1979; Malan & Osimo, 1992) to maintain the therapeutic focus (Davanloo, 2005).

The theoretical structure of ISTDP is similar to other models of dynamic psychotherapy. It also draws for its theoretical rationale on attachment theory (Bowlby, 1988; Schore & Schore, 2008), which has been covered in previous sections and will be dealt with again in more detail in Chapter Eight. The core therapeutic action in ISTDP is the 'patient's actual experience of their true feelings about the present and the past' (Davanloo, 1990, p. 2) and hence, although psychodynamic in theoretical structure, ISTDP is also an emotion-based therapy. You will observe the similarities between ISTDP and the unified protocol for the emotional disorders (Allen, McHugh, & Barlow, 2008) discussed later in this section.

The main areas of innovation of ISTDP lie in its therapeutic practices. Its founder, Habib Davanloo (2005), developed a technique to rapidly mobilize the unconscious therapeutic alliance in the service of removing the major resistances to change, which were not effectively removed through interpretation alone. He and his colleagues developed a highly structured approach to therapy that consists of eight phases:

 i inquiry and psychodiagnostic evaluation

 ii pressure

 iii challenge

 iv transference resistance

 v direct access to the unconscious

 vi systematic analysis of the transference

 vii dynamic exploration into the unconscious

 viii phase of consolidation.

In the initial intake phase (inquiry), it is important to clarify the degree of the patient's pathology, the severity of the resistances, and the way in which anxiety is discharged—through striated muscle, smooth muscle, or by cognitive or perceptual distortion (see our discussion of polyvagal theory in Chapter Two, on which ISTDP's understanding of anxiety and anxiety discharge is based). A related inquiry involves the understanding of the defenses that are dominant in the person's coping repertoire. Three of the most frequently occurring defenses are isolation of affect, repression, and projection. When the inquiry and the psychodiagnostic evaluation are complete, the therapist begins to challenge the patient by applying pressure to mobilize complex transference feelings toward the therapist. These are related to earlier, unsatisfactory primary relationships that have generated unconscious anxiety and defenses against the anxiety. The therapist's role is to block defenses as soon as they arise. The aim is to bring the resistances/defenses into the therapeutic relationship as soon as possible. Patients will sometimes respond angrily to the therapist for challenging their defensive coping strategies, thereby increasing their anxiety. The therapist maintains a focus on current problems, requesting specific examples that will mobilize an affective response. The type of anxiety manifested is constantly monitored to titrate the amount of pressure that the client can bear. If anxiety is expressed in smooth muscle or via cognitive or perceptual distortion, reduction of pressure to reduce anxiety is needed until the person recovers sufficiently to re-engage in the therapeutic process. As anxiety rises, so does resistance; the therapist's role is to point out and clarify the defenses that are recruited to prevent emotional experience and expression. The patient may become anxious that the therapist will hurt them as important people in their pasts have done (transference resistance). There is often a breakthrough of grief at this point (direct access to the unconscious). The next phase of therapy involves working through the emotions of grief, anger, and guilt, usually about the anger experienced towards a loved one, and other emotions that the patient has viewed as shameful and avoided. Davanloo stresses the importance of the therapeutic alliance, which enables the patient to cooperate with treatment, to collaborate with the therapist, and to face painful feelings.

Abbass, Hancock, Henderson, and Kisely (2009) conducted a Cochrane systematic review of short-term psychotherapies for the common mental disorders, including anxiety and depression, stress-related physical conditions, behavior disorders, and interpersonal/personality problems. A number of previous meta-analyses (systematic reviews) have yielded conflicting results. This review included only high-quality studies, called randomized controlled trials (RCT)[6] of the short-term psychodynamic psychotherapies. Twenty-three studies including 1,431 participants who undertook a therapy lasting not longer than 40 sessions (the average number was 15 sessions) were identified. Overall, treatment benefits were modest to moderate and these were generally maintained in short-term (immediately after therapy) and long-term

---

[6] A randomized controlled trial (randomized clinical trial) (RCT) is a scientific experiment designed to test the efficacy or effectiveness of an intervention. In RCTs, participants are randomly allocated to the treatment or control (no treatment) condition. To avoid bias, where possible, participants and researchers do not know to which group participants have been assigned.

(four years later) follow-up. Drop-out rates were lower compared with medication alone groups and occupational functioning was higher for the psychotherapy groups. The authors concluded that short-term psychodynamic psychotherapy for depression and anxiety (and other psychological problems) is promising, but the variability between studies and the range of treatments meant that only a few studies were available for each condition. While short term-psychotherapies were significantly better than minimal treatment and wait-list control groups, they did not appear to fare better than 'treatment as usual' groups. Treatment delivery and treatment quality were not always assured and these factors can significantly affect results. Larger studies of higher quality and with specific diagnoses are warranted.

Psychoanalytic/psychodynamic treatment of music performance anxiety

There has been considerable interest in the relevance and application of psychodynamic therapy to the problem of music performance anxiety (or stage fright, as it is sometimes described in this literature). Beginning at the inception of psychotherapy at the turn of the 20th century, musicians have sought the assistance of psychotherapists. For example, both Gustav Mahler and Bruno Walter consulted Sigmund Freud. Sergei Rachmaninov, Robert Schumann, and Anton Bruckner also received some form of psychotherapeutic support (Ostwald, 1987) during the course of their difficult and tortured lives. The work of Gabbard (1979, 1983, 1994), Weisblatt (1986), Ostwald (1987), Plaut (1990), and Nagel (1990, 1993, 2004) attests to the continuing interest in psychotherapy for the anxious musician. Gabbard (1979) argued that the universality of stage fright ('it is felt by all who dare to assert themselves before their fellows'; p. 384) must have multidetermined origins in normal developmental processes as well as in the reactivation of unconscious childhood conflicts based around pathological developmental experiences such as early traumata associated with guilt, shame, exhibitionism, fears about loss of control, and specific fantasies that arise in the unusual internal world of the gifted child.

The principal contribution of the psychoanalytic perspective to the treatment of music performance anxiety (and performance anxiety in general) is to provide an understanding of the meaning, both conscious and unconscious, of the performance situation to the performer. These conflicting meanings are expressed in characteristic symptoms that include panic, obsessional rumination before and/or after performances, and choking, blocking, and depersonalization during the performance. Choking was discussed in detail in Chapter Six. Depersonalization is the 'subjective sense of a split between one's observing and one's performing self; one's observing self perceives one's performing self as from a distance, operating lifelessly and mechanically' (Weisblatt, 1986, p. 64). An analytic understanding of music performance anxiety takes as its starting point that the performance situation stirs conflicting unconscious desires, wishes, or conflicts. The audience has a pivotal role in this process because of 'the universal propensity of performers to experience an audience as though it were a person from childhood, real or imagined' (p. 64). As for all causes of anxiety, music performance anxiety in its severe form is multiply determined. Weisblatt (1986) outlines four frequently occurring themes in musicians who suffer severe music performance anxiety. These are summarized briefly below:

Theme 1

i *Parental dynamic:*[7] Emotionally unavailable and unresponsive parents.

ii *Emotional consequence*: Musical talent is seen as a source of fulfillment for childhood grandiosity. Childhood fantasies of becoming a virtuoso and evoking in an audience the adoration and recognition that were denied in the relationship with parents.

iii *Meaning of performance anxiety*: Realistically knows that s/he will not become the great virtuoso of his/her childhood fantasies. While driven to performance by the need for adoration, the performer remains constantly fearful that s/he will humiliate him/herself by falling short of the idealized performance.

Theme 2

i *Parental dynamic*: Early parental devotion, subsequently withdrawn due to parental depression or other cause. Child grows up believing that strength and greatness are located in the parent and not the self.

ii *Emotional consequence*: The child strives to establish a tie to the 'right' parent and may transfer this striving onto his/her music teacher.

iii *Meaning of performance anxiety*: The audience is not the central source of anxiety but pleasing the idealized teacher.

Theme 3

i *Parental dynamic*: Parental relationship with child is characterized by underlying hostility and competitiveness

ii *Emotional consequence*: The unconscious meaning of performance is to triumph over the competitive parent. As a performer, there is a wish to overwhelm the audience so that they feel envious in relation to the performer as s/he did in relation to the parent.

iii *Meaning of performance anxiety*: To triumph over a parent brings with it guilt or fear of retaliation and hence considerable anxiety. This is the origin of the oft quoted but poorly understood concept of the 'fear of success' (Nagel, 1990). Plaut (1990) also comments on what he argues is often a central feature in performance anxiety—the wish to fail, which he defines as a need to alleviate unconscious guilt about performance success via self-punishment.

Theme 4

i *Parental dynamic*: The parent(s) approved of the child when compliant but withdrew love and support when the child asserted individuality.

---

[7] The word 'parent' is used generically. In each individual case, it could be a dynamic involving only the mother, only the father, or both parents.

ii *Emotional consequence*: If the parent(s) did not approve of a musical career, pursuit of that career in defiance of parental wishes generates anxiety.

iii *Meaning of performance anxiety*: Playing well will result in the loss of the parent; playing badly to appease the parent will result in a loss of the self.

There are no doubt other possible dynamics that underlie the development of severe music performance anxiety. However, the underlying overarching theme in the experience of music performance anxiety for some performers is that the loss or perceived loss of parental love may be recaptured in the applause of the audience. If the applause is not forthcoming, this may be experienced as a further loss of love and will reawaken the earlier trauma where parental love was lost or perceived to have been lost (Plaut, 1990). Practitioners and researchers of the future will need to systematically uncover the range of possible dynamics that result in performance anxiety through rigorous idiographic research methods that were discussed in Chapter Two in order to develop tailored individualized treatments for these anxious musicians. We will take these issues up again in Chapter Eight.

In her overview paper that encourages clinicians to think more broadly about the possible benefits of psychodynamic therapy for anxious musicians, Nagel seeks 'an approach to the theoretical understanding and treatment' of stage fright and suggests that any 'either/or' model be rejected in favor of an 'also/and' paradigm (Nagel, 2004, p. 39). Nagel poses and answers her question with respect to the paradoxical nature of performance anxiety and the need for a holistic approach to its treatment:

> Although one can conceptualize performance anxiety in the broader context of artist survival (economic, social, and emotional), there is a psychological paradox that is embedded in performance anxiety's potentially devastating effects on self-esteem and career satisfaction. If a musician desires a career in the performing arts, if he or she is well trained, well practiced, and of adequate talent, why would performance anxiety with its psychological and physical challenges undermine the ability to show in public what a musician can show in private? . . . musical performers' . . . egos develop in childhood side by side with their music lessons, all of which are in the constantly unfolding context of a unique life history (p.39).

Like Weisblatt, Nagel argues that the performer's life history and the unconscious conflicts associated with attachment, separation, rejection, competition, envy, loss, and the affects and fantasies they engender should be the focus of therapy, stating that for some musicians a focus on symptom reduction is unlikely to provide a sustainable benefit. Nagel alerts medical practitioners who consult with musicians to the possibility of somatization of psychological issues, that is, the displacement and conversion of painful feelings into physical symptoms that may result in an inappropriate focus on physical complaints and perhaps, in the extreme, unnecessary medications and even surgery. There is empirical support for such concerns (Spahn, Nikolaus, & Seidenglzanz, 2001).

Hayes (1975) offers an explanation of stage fright from a Jungian perspective. He states that it originates in:

> the experience of being detached from the herd. The anticipation of derisive laughter from the audience triggers an archetypal racial memory imprinted in all human beings of

the outcast, the stoned man, who has dared to assert himself as a creature in his own right, apart from the herd (p. 280).

These Jungian ideas are not too different from those of Plaut (1990), who argued that exceptional talent or creativity places one outside cultural norms and expectations, and that 'being an outsider inevitably carries the burden of vulnerability' (p. 59). A risk in the very early emergence of exceptional talent is that all of the young person's self-worth and self-esteem are attached to the area of talent. Any faltering steps in the area of talent risk derailing the young person's psychological equilibrium. Plaut also concurs with Weisblatt with respect to the importance of the performer's perception, or unconscious fantasies about his/her relationship to the audience, which give rise to music performance anxiety.

Ostwald (1987) alerted practitioners to the absence of attention to the specific issues of performing artists in the professional literature on psychotherapy for this group. This has still not been addressed in the intervening 30 years since his article was published. It is, however, essential that a sophisticated understanding of the artist's choice of modality for self-expression and a full history of previous experiences with teachers and mentors, performing history, perceived successes and failures, aspirations for the future, and fantasies about 'fame, status, wealth and immortality' (p. 135) be ascertained and addressed by the treating clinician. Oswald also suggests that attention be paid to the need of some performing artists to have a coach to assist them:

> in mental and physical preparation for playing, practicing and performing . . . to assist in assuming more ego control over the concert planning process . . . and to establish methods of practice that are less compulsive and involve a mental set of listening to oneself play rather than obsessing about the 17 things that might go wrong (p. 136).

There have been no formal studies, controlled case series or other forms of idiographic investigation into the utility of the psychodynamic therapies for the treatment of music performance anxiety. This is an area ripe for research. In Chapter Eight, we will commence this process by undertaking assessments of very anxious musicians, using in-depth interviewing and narrative construction to demonstrate how, for some musicians, their performance anxiety is integrally bound up with broader issues related to conflicts of the nature outlined by Gabbard, Nagel, Weisblatt, Ostwald, and Plaut.

Behavioral, cognitive, and cognitive behavioral therapy (CBT)

Three groups of therapies—behavioral, cognitive, and cognitive behavioral—are all based on the same principles, but use the available therapeutic techniques in different amounts. Although there are common and core elements to all good therapies, like psychodynamic therapies, the group of therapies collectively known as cognitive behavioral therapy have a number of relatively unique and distinctive activities that distinguish it from other forms of psychotherapy. We will therefore begin our discussion in this section by enumerating and evaluating the unique core elements that define this form of therapy. Blagys and Hilsenroth (2002) undertook just such a task for both the psychodynamic and cognitive behavioral approaches. The unique elements of psychodynamic therapy were outlined above, so, in similar vein, I will provide below a brief summary of the unique features of CBT based on their excellent review. These researchers identified six techniques/interventions that are unique to CBT when compared with the spectrum of psychodynamic-interpersonal psycho-therapies, as follows:

1 *The use of homework and out-of-session activities*

The rationale for the prescription of homework and out-of-session activities includes: opportunity to practice and consolidate skills learned in therapy; out-of-session practice of skills learned in the therapy room lead to generalization of those skills to the outside world; out-of-session activities assist in the maintenance of new learning after termination of therapy. These goals are consistent with the symptom-reduction focus of CBT approaches.

2 *Direction of session activity*

In contrast to psychodynamic approaches, cognitive behavioral therapists 'direct session activity by setting the agenda, using preplanned techniques at specific times during sessions, deciding what will be discussed prior to the session, and actively directing the patient toward specific topics . . . and tasks . . . In addition, cognitive behavioral therapists spend almost double the amount of time talking in the session compared with psychodynamic therapists, indicating a more active and directive stance' (p. 680).

3 *Teaching of skills used by patients to cope with symptoms*

This characteristic is related to point 2 above. Cognitive behavioral therapists view their role as psychoeducational, a term used to describe a teaching–learning process focused on developing new cognitions and behaviors that will assist the person to deal more effectively with their symptoms and to behave more adaptively. It follows that therapy will have a stronger behavioral task orientation in which a substantial proportion of the therapy time is devoted to teaching specific strategies for changing behavior.

4 *Emphasis on patients' future experiences*

While cognitive behavioral therapists are more likely to focus on patients' current and future behaviors, the difference in emphasis compared with psychodynamic approaches is not as stark for some of the other characteristics described here. Shorter psychodynamic approaches are also likely to have a primary focus on current and future experiences because there is not sufficient time to undertake an in-depth exploration of the past or childhood experiences. However, while psychodynamic approaches are generally interested in and focused to a greater or lesser extent on early conflicts and relationships, cognitive behavioral therapists rarely engage in discussion on these issues.

5 *Providing patients with information about their treatment, disorders, or symptoms*

Since cognitive behavioral therapists perceive their role as psychoeducational, it is not surprising that they would offer explicit explanations to patients about the treatment modality and the specific techniques that will be used to help them manage their symptoms. They will also often provide handouts about the treatment and recommend particular books for people to read. These therapeutic behaviors are very unlikely to occur in psychodynamically oriented therapies.

6 *An intrapersonal/cognitive focus*

Cognitive behavioral therapy is underpinned by the proposition that emotions and behavior are influenced by cognitions (i.e. beliefs or ideas about oneself and others). In CBT, therapists evaluate, challenge, and assist patients to modify false or distorted cognitions associated with their symptomatic behavior. Psychodynamic therapists also focus on the intrapersonal world of the patient but their focus tends more towards conflicts, impulses, fantasies, wishes, and expectations, which, although they are cognitive processes, are more emotionally charged than beliefs and attitudes; however, you will recall from our discussion of cognitions and emotions in Chapter Two that these processes are more closely intertwined than previously thought.

This spectrum of cognitive behavioral therapies (CBT) is the most researched of all psychological interventions and to date are considered the most effective treatments for a range of psychological disorders, especially depression and anxiety, although there have been recent strong challenges to this assertion (Shedler, 2010; Westen, 2002a). Because this group of therapies has dominated psychological practice, along with pharmacotherapy, for the past 50 years, we will begin this section with a cautionary tale.

> A careful examination of the scientific basis of the manualized short-term treatments so widely touted in recent years as 'empirically validated' suggests that, indeed, for many symptoms and disorders studied, notably depression and generalized anxiety (two of the most widespread problems with which patients present), the empirical support is only skin deep: it does not extend to the 60 to 70 percent of patients excluded from the average study; does not extend to the 50 to 70 percent of the patients who are included but who fail to improve; and does not apply to those patients who improved but who, two years after termination from brief therapies, can expect to relapse with as high rates as patients who received a placebo (Westen, 2002b, p. 919).

CBT is not suitable for everyone, as Westen argues, and it is important that an appropriate diagnostic history be taken of each person presenting for therapy so that a good match can be made between patient and treatment. A number of studies have concluded that the mechanisms of proposed change in the cognitive therapies may not in fact be the agents of change according to cognitive theory, which is a modification of distorted cognitions (Kazdin, 2007). Several researchers have concluded that successful therapies, whatever their appellation, are successful by virtue of adherence to critical elements of psychodynamic theory, which are the quality of the working alliance, a focus on emotional (re-)experiencing, discussion of interpersonal relationships, and exploration of past experience with early caregivers. Therapist adherence to these elements predicted positive outcome in both psychodynamic and cognitive therapies. Poor outcome was predicted by rigid adherence to a focus on cognitions (Ablon & Jones, 1998).

Behavior therapy for anxiety

Behavior therapy refers to the techniques based on classical conditioning, devised by Wolpe (1958) and Eysenck (1960) to treat anxiety. In current practice, the terms 'behavior therapy,' 'behavior change programs,' and 'behavior modification' are used interchangeably to denote therapeutic programs based on the principles of learning theory. Behavioral therapies focus primarily on changing the dysfunctional behaviors that arise when people feel anxious. Regardless of the orientation of specific programs, all behavior change programs operate on the following four tenets:

i Behavior can be explained by the principles of learning and conditioning.

ii The same laws of learning apply to all behavior, both normal and abnormal.

iii Abnormal behavior is the normal, lawful response to abnormal learning conditions.

iv Behavior, including thoughts and feelings, can be 'unlearned' and changed.

These four tenets underpin the four major theoretical models that have been derived from learning theory, and which have been described in Chapter Two. These are:

i Classical conditioning (Pavlov, 1927)

ii Operant conditioning (Skinner, 1953)

iii Observational (imitation) learning (Bandura, 1969)

iv Cognitive behaviorism (Beck, 1976; Ellis, 1984; Meichenbaum, 1977).

Behavior therapy in its purest form, as developed by Pavlov and Skinner, was developed within animal models and was initially applied to animal behavior. Because we cannot know what cognitive activity is occurring in non-human animals, early researchers had to rely on behavioral interventions and behavioral change as an indicator of responsiveness to the intervention. When we are discussing learning theory-based treatments for humans, the divide between behavior therapy, cognitive therapy, and cognitive behavioral therapy seems somewhat arbitrary. Even the simplest behavioral strategy has cognitive components because humans are sentient beings who have thoughts, beliefs, and attitudes about behavior.

Exposure, somatic management, and systematic desensitization
Exposure to the feared situation, object, person, sensations, or feelings is now considered to be the lynchpin of successful therapeutic interventions in this form of therapy. In its early form, it comprised two elements: teaching the patient how to relax in a process called deep muscle relaxation training that also involves breathing management, and then gradually introducing the person to their feared stimuli in graded steps, called the fear hierarchy, until they can tolerate the feared stimulus without triggering an anxiety response. This procedure is called systematic desensitization. Once the fear hierarchy has been mastered in the therapist's office, in a process called imaginal desensitization, people are encouraged to apply their new skills in the actual, anxiety-provoking situation (called in vivo desensitization). Recent developments in this form of treatment have used virtual reality to assist the individual to extinguish their fear responses, including music performance anxiety (Orman, 2003, 2004).

Exposure may occur in three ways: *in vivo*, which means that you confront the actual feared object; imaginal, which means that you confront the feared object in imagination; and interoceptive exposure, a procedure whereby the actual feared responses (i.e. physiological arousal) are induced under controlled conditions so that they can be managed and reduced in subsequent exposures. The feared sensations in panic attack can be induced by instructing the person to hyperventilate by breathing through a thin straw or engaging in vigorous exercise. In this way, individuals who suffer panic attacks can learn that their panic symptoms are the expected outcomes of normal activities such as exercise. Controlled inductions of such symptoms also teaches anxious people that they can exert control over these previously feared sensations (Arntz, 2002; Hecker, Fink, Vogeltanz, Thorpe, & Sigmon, 1998).

Behavioral treatments of music performance anxiety

Six studies have investigated the therapeutic effect of behavioral treatments on music performance anxiety, only two of which used samples specifically selected because they were high in music performance anxiety. Four of the six studies provided sufficient detail for some effect sizes to be calculated. The interventions assessed included systematic desensitization, progressive muscle relaxation, awareness and breathing, and behavioral rehearsal.* One of the first published studies of this kind was undertaken by Appel (1976), who assessed exposure-based behavior therapy involving systematic desensitization, muscle relaxation and counter conditioning, traditional musical analysis, and a no treatment control in 30 anxious volunteer graduate piano students. Behavior therapy reduced self-reported anxiety and both of the active treatments reduced errors in the piano recitals more than the control condition.

Kendrick, Craig, Lawson, and Davidson (1982) compared the efficacy of behavior rehearsal and cognitive behavioral treatments for music performance anxiety. The behavior rehearsal group did not show reductions in state anxiety or subjective stress, but they did show significant pre- to post-treatment improvements in performance quality and self-statements about performance anxiety (as measured by the Performance Anxiety Self-Statement Scale: PASSS). The behavior rehearsal group also showed greater pre- to post-treatment improvements in the visual signs of anxiety than controls, although the cognitive behavioral group showed an even greater improvement than the behavior rehearsal group on this outcome measure. Kendrick's study suggests that behavior rehearsal may be an effective form of treatment for music performance anxiety for some outcome measures (e.g. STAI, subjective stress scale) (Spielberger, 1983) but not others (e.g. self-efficacy and visual signs of anxiety) for which a CBT intervention was superior.*

Sweeney and Horan (1982) found that the behavioral technique of cue-controlled relaxation led to improvements in anxiety, music performance anxiety, heart rate, and performance quality in students suffering from music performance anxiety, but that CBT was not significantly more effective for these outcome measures than this simple behavioral treatment. Richard (1992) failed to find a therapeutic effect with cue-controlled relaxation but this failure may have been due to insufficient statistical power, given the very small sample size in his study.*

Reitman (2001) examined the therapeutic effect of two systematic desensitization procedures—music-assisted coping systematic desensitization and verbal coping systematic desensitization—in eight 75-minute group sessions, and home practice of relaxation (using tapes). He found that the treatment groups did not differ significantly from a waiting-list control group on any of the anxiety, heart rate, or performance quality outcome measures employed. However, Reitman's study is weakened by a very small sample size (18 subjects across three groups), and thus the lack of significance reported may reflect insufficient statistical power.

Five other studies (three of these are dissertations) assessed the efficacy of behavioral treatments for music performance anxiety on music students. Grishman (1989) and Mansberger (1988) used standard muscle relaxation techniques, Wardle (1975) compared insight/relaxation and systematic desensitization techniques, and Deen (1999) used awareness and breathing techniques. These studies indicated pre- to post-treatment improvements on self-report measures of performance anxiety (Deen, 2000); Grishman, 1989; Mansberger, 1988) and heart rate (Grishman, 1989; Wardle, 1969), but not performance quality (Deen, 2000; Mansberger, 1988; Wardle, 1975). Again, demand characteristics may have confounded these results due to the transparent nature of the research and the reliance upon self-report measures of music performance anxiety. Further, Mansberger (1988) obtained no pre-intervention measures.*

A recent study (Su *et al.*, 2010) examining the effects of a 10-minute relaxation breathing intervention conducted twice weekly for two months on 59 talented Taiwanese music students in grades 3 to 6 in reducing music performance anxiety in the lead-up to a music examination found that the technique had some efficacy in reducing self-reported music performance anxiety, as measured by the MPAI–A (Osborne *et al.*, 2005). However, these students were not screened for their level of music performance anxiety prior to enrolment in the trial and pre-testing showed that, as a group, their levels of anxiety on the MPAI–A were low. The variation in their self-reported anxiety levels over the four test times (two months, one month, 30 minutes and five minutes before the examination) showed little variation (39–43). There was a significant decrease in anxiety in the periods 30 minutes and five minutes before the examination, with a relaxation breathing intervention given after the 30-minute assessment. It is difficult to ascertain the clinical value of a three-point decrease on the MPAI–A. There were no effects for gender, grade, or instrument. The study would need to be replicated on a sample of students who tested high on the MPAI–A at pre-test to reduce the problem of floor effects in samples who were not high in anxiety at baseline.

Behavioral treatments (cue-controlled relaxation training, breathing, systematic desensitization, behavior rehearsal) appear to be at least minimally effective in the treatment of music performance anxiety but currently there is no consistent evidence indicating the superiority of any one type of behavioral intervention.

Cognitive therapy

Cognitive therapy is concerned with changing faulty thinking patterns that give rise to maladaptive behaviors, such as excessive muscle tension, avoidance of feared situations, or impaired performance, adaptation, and coping. In this therapy, people learn a skill called cognitive restructuring, which is a process whereby negative, unproductive, or catastrophic thinking is replaced with more rational, useful ways of understanding problem situations. Based on changed thinking patterns, people are often able to reassess or reappraise their feared situations in ways that make dealing with those situations more manageable. Key figures in the development of cognitive approaches to behavior change include David Meichenbaum (Meichenbaum, 1977), Aaron Beck (Beck, 1976; Beck *et al.*, 1985; Beck, 1995), and Richard Lazarus (Lazarus, 1984, 1991a, 1991b, 2000a). Rational emotive therapy, a cognitive therapy developed by Albert Ellis (1984, 2002), is perhaps the most extreme form of this type of therapy.

Cognitive therapy for anxiety

The principal focus of cognitive therapy is identifying, examining, and modifying maladaptive thinking styles through the process of teaching new skills such as rational responding, objective self-monitoring, formulating and testing personal hypotheses, behavioral self-management, and problem solving (Newman & Beck, 2010). Cognitive therapy has a strong educational focus and uses between-session homework and practice to reinforce and maintain the skills learnt in therapy in the outside world. The therapist is an active participant in the therapy, supporting the learning of their clients in the identification and modification of cognitive biases and distortions that result in maladaptive behavior and emotional distress and that interfere with problem solving.

A number of specific dysfunctional cognitive processes, called cognitive biases, cognitive distortions, cognitive errors, or logical errors, can be identified when an individual reports feelings of helplessness, hopelessness, anxiety, or a pervading sense of danger. There are seemingly endless ways that we humans can make ourselves feel miserable, and I sometimes wonder about the optimist who named our species *homo sapiens* (i.e. wise or knowing man). Some of these misery makers have been described by Newman and Beck (2010) and will be summarized below.

1 *Arbitrary inference*

Some people impulsively draw conclusions when there is insufficient evidence to support their conclusion and even in the face of evidence to the contrary. For example, a musician notices that the conductor looked in her direction with a frown on his face during rehearsal. She concludes that the conductor is critical of her playing and will report his dissatisfaction about her playing to the orchestra management.

2 *Selective abstraction*

Some people focus on a detail taken out of context, ignoring other, more salient features of the situation, and conceptualizing the entire experience on the basis of this circumscribed element. Musicians are particularly prone to use negative selective abstraction in assessing their musical performances. For example, Claudio Arrau, the pianist we discussed in Chapter One, denigrated his whole performance, which could comprise a two-hour recital, if he made just one mistake. He said the 'rest didn't matter'—that one mistake had wiped out his entire performance and any merit that it may have had.

3 *Overgeneralization*

This is a particularly common logical error and we can see countless examples of it in everyday life. You can recognize overgeneralizations in sentences starting with classes of people or things or the adverbs 'always' or 'never.' For example, 'All Germans are surly,' 'Women are neurotic,' 'Money is evil,' 'You always do the wrong thing.' An overgeneralization is a statement of belief of a general rule or principle that the person has derived from a set of very limited examples. Musicians are as prone as anyone to overgeneralizing. Examples include 'I never play well under pressure,' 'My bow arm shakes all the time,' 'I always forget the words.'

4 Magnification and minimization

Most cognitive errors do not occur in isolation and many are closely related. Magnification, which refers to the tendency to assign greater significance to negative events, evaluations, or assessments than to positive events, which are simultaneously minimized, is a close relative of selective abstraction. This pattern represents a systematic bias in thinking style that ensures that you can never feel happy with your achievements. A musician who auditions for a number of orchestras receives word that he has been accepted into one orchestra to which he has applied but has been rejected by two others for which he has auditioned. He becomes preoccupied with the rejections and ruminates as to the reasons that he has been rejected without taking time to celebrate his successful audition for an equally prestigious orchestra.

5 Dichotomous 'all or none' thinking

We all have the tendency at times to reduce our assessments of complex situations to 'either–or' or 'black versus white' algorithms. Although they have the effect of relieving cognitive dissonance,[8] cognitive load,[9] and uncertainty, such oversimplifications cause more problems than they resolve. This type of thinking is very evident in fundamentalist religious and political groups and takes the form of 'You are either with us or against us.' It stifles creative problem solving, and generates impasses and conflicts that cannot be resolved because such thinking prevents negotiation and compromise. This type of thinking can occur between couples, parents, and their children, between political leaders, and between colleagues. It can also occur within ourselves, where a harsh, punishing voice from the past continues to dictate to us in our adult lives. Imagine if members of a string quartet or other chamber group had members who were rigidly certain that the works in their repertoire could only be played one way—their way!

6 Diminished ability to engage in perspective taking (metacognition)

To achieve a mature level of cognitive function, people need to develop the capacity to perspective take, that is, to assess a problem from a number of different angles or from the point of view of other people, who might hold contrary views to one's own. In order to do this, we need to be able to think about our own thinking processes and to ask ourselves questions such as 'How did I arrive at that conclusion?' 'Are they any logical flaws in my argument?' 'Could I arrive at a different conclusion based on the same information?' The ability to think about the processes of one's own thinking is called metacognition (Davison, Vogel, & Coffman, 1997). Failures in perspective

---

[8] Cognitive dissonance is an uncomfortable feeling caused by holding conflicting ideas simultaneously (Lester & Yang, 2009).

[9] Cognitive load is the effort devoted to the processing, construction, and automation of schemas (Fitousi & Wenger, 2011).

taking and metacognition have been found to be present in both the mood and anxiety disorders, where people are often captive to their automatic (unconscious) reactions that do not allow them to achieve any distance or perspective on the problems confronting them. Part of the skill of metacognition is the ability to identify rigid, automatic patterns of responding, challenge them, and develop new, more flexible, creative and adaptive ways to manage the problem. It is worth recalling our earlier discussion about the poor outcomes for cognitive therapy if there is a sole focus on the cognitive dimension of treatment. Work with these cognitive distortions will yield better results if attention is paid to the quality of the therapeutic relationship and to emotional experience.

Cognitive therapy for music performance anxiety

Cognitive therapy is based on the principle that we have limited attentional resources to allocate to tasks and how that attention is distributed will affect task performance. In music, there are three main foci: the self, the audience, and the music. Before and during performances, musicians may focus relatively more or less on each of these three areas with thoughts such as 'I hope I don't have a memory lapse' (self-focus); 'The audience looks bored' (audience focus); 'I love the lilting melodies in this concerto' (music focused). It may not be surprising to learn that absorption in the task, in this case the music, tends to be associated with the lowest levels of performance anxiety (Wolverton & Salmon, 1991). Hence, the focus of cognitive therapy for music performance anxiety would be to shift attentional focus away from self and audience, and direct it towards the work being performed. Since much of the attentional focus on self and audience involves thought processes that are described as catastrophizing (e.g. 'One mistake and that's the end of my career,' 'The audience hates me'), shifting attentional focus from the self and the audience to the music will have the joint effect of making more cognitive resources available for the cognitive challenge of performing the work, but also of reducing the number of catastrophic thoughts. Steptoe and Fidler (1987) offer support for this assertion. In their study, musicians were asked what they were thinking just prior to a performance. Analysis of their self-statements indicated two broad classes—catastrophic and realistic appraisal (e.g. 'I might make a couple of mistakes but I can recover quickly and no one will notice'). Those who engaged in catastrophic thinking had higher music performance anxiety compared with those whose appraisals about the performance were more realistic. Similar results were obtained by Osborne and Franklin (2002). Further support is offered by a study that compared the effectiveness of attentional training with behavioral rehearsal, i.e. performance practice before the big concert in front of friendly and supportive audiences in reducing performance anxiety in pianists (Kendrick et al., 1982). Both groups were superior to a wait-list control, but attentional training was better than behavioral rehearsal in reducing anxiety levels prior to and during the performance. However, there were some methodological problems with this study, including issues related to program integrity.

Three other related cognitive strategies have been investigated as a means of reducing music performance anxiety. These are stress inoculation, positive self-talk, and the use of imagery. Stress inoculation, developed by Meichenbaum (1985), aims to increase mastery over one's fears in a three-step process as follows: (i) psychoeducation provides individuals with an understanding of the origin and maintenance of their fears; (ii) training in coping skills reduces the expression of anxiety in each of the 'channels' of anxiety expression—physical/autonomic, behavioral/motoric, and cognitive; (iii) application and practice of these new coping skills with a target fear consolidates and reinforces learning. In the cognitive application, catastrophic fears are 'reframed' into realistic appraisals that are less threatening and hence less anxiety arousing. Anxiety is interpreted as a signal that a situation needs attention (recall our discussion of Freud's concept of signal anxiety in Chapter Two) and that appropriate strategies need to be employed to deal with the situation. For example, in the cognitive domain, the performer may reinterpret autonomic arousal as normal, performance-enhancing excitement rather than as a signal for an impending performance disaster (Salmon, 1991). In the behavioral domain, the performer may be asked to visualize an anxiety-provoking performance situation such as an audition and rehearse in imagination, confronting the situation adaptively (if not successfully). Self-talk is a related strategy in which the performer focuses on his/her internal dialogue to identify negative self-statements ('I can't cope with this performance') and substituting these with more realistic, positive self-statements ('This concerto is difficult but I will master it with hard work').

Cognitive behavioral therapies

Cognitive behavioral therapy (CBT) is a combination of behavioral and cognitive interventions aimed at changing negative, maladaptive thinking patterns and problematic behaviors. CBT is focused and directive, usually of short duration and is action oriented; that is, it is not solely a 'talking therapy'—it relies on the client's record keeping, active participation, application via homework assignments, and evaluation.

Cognitive behavioral therapies have been developed in the past three decades (Butler, Chapman, Forman, & Beck, 2006; Kenny, 2005a; Lazarus & Abramovitz, 2004; Turkington, Dudley, Warman, & Beck, 2006) and are widely considered to be the treatment of choice for both the anxiety disorders in general (Rodebaugh, Holaway, & Heimberg, 2004) and for performance anxiety in particular (Birk, 2004; Kenny, 2005a). Empirical work to date indicates that combinations of cognitive and behavioral approaches show the best outcomes for these conditions, although sufferers are rarely 'cured' (Kenny, 2005a; Osborne et al., 2007).

Cognitive behavioral therapy (CBT) for anxiety disorders

Just as the psychodynamic psychotherapies are based on a number of foundational principles that identify them as psychodynamic therapies, cognitive behavioral therapies are also characterized by a number of distinctive features unique to this form of therapeutic intervention. Explicitly identifying the core features of particular therapeutic treatments is an important step in gaining clarification on which elements of a complex psychological therapy contribute to therapeutic outcome. Like most good therapies, CBT begins with an assessment phase in which the person recounts the story of their symptom onset to the therapist. Confirmation of diagnosis and severity may be assessed using questionnaires and rating scales. After the assessment phase, the

CBT therapist will provide some educational input about the person's condition. This is called psychoeducation and entails an explanation of the condition, how it developed, and what needs to occur to improve. Informed consent should be obtained prior to the commencement of therapy. The patient is invited to work collaboratively with the therapist to identify targets for treatment and which areas should take priority. The patient is also advised of his/her responsibilities in therapy, such as attending appointments, completing homework, diary keeping, and behavioral practice.

Most CBT interventions have four major components. These are:

i exposure to thoughts, objects, situations, and bodily sensations that are not dangerous but are feared, avoided, or endured with great distress

ii training in basic stress-management techniques

iii application and training in cognitive therapy techniques

iv training in specific skills that constitute areas of specific individual concern or weakness (e.g. assertiveness training, management of tremulous bow arm, or on-stage anxiety) (Sadock, Sadock, & Ruiz, 2009).

Cognitive behavioral and other combined interventions for music performance anxiety

Most of the available studies have been covered in the sections on behavioral and cognitive interventions, as the majority of studies compared a behavioral intervention with a cognitive intervention. The evidence for improvements in music performance anxiety following CBT is positive (for a detailed review, see Kenny, 2005c), although further studies with larger samples and less reliance on self-report measures would be useful. One should remember that treated performers may not achieve a level of anxiety similar to that experienced by those who do not suffer or who suffer minimally from the condition, even after treatment.

A number of studies have examined the effect of combining other treatment modalities, such as CBT with drug therapy, CBT with biofeedback, counseling, or relaxation. We will briefly review some of these studies here. It is important to keep in mind that most of these studies are old, and methodological problems preclude firm conclusions about some outcomes; however, they are useful as a guide to possible effective therapies and are included for completeness of coverage of the field of interventions for music performance anxiety. Clark and Agras (1991) found that cognitive behavioral therapy was superior to drug therapy with buspirone in the treatment of music performance anxiety, and also that improvement in performance quality, for which a strong effect size was found (1.64), was greater in a CBT + placebo group than in a placebo group alone. It should be noted that since buspirone has failed in studies of social phobia to separate from placebo, it is not appropriate to describe the CBT + buspirone as a combined treatment. Saying that CBT > buspirone in this context is not conceptually different from saying that CBT > placebo. Finally, Sweeney and Horan (1982) found that behavioral, cognitive, and cognitive behavioral treatments were all effective in treating students suffering from music performance anxiety, when compared with a control group, but that no significant differences were apparent between the three types of treatment. This was the case for improvements in general anxiety, music performance anxiety, and performance quality. The only difference between treatments was with respect to heart rate, where the behavioral and cognitive treatments alone led to greater pre- to post-treatment improvements than the combined CBT treatment, although it is not clear why.*

Nagel, Mimle, and Papsdorf (1989) provided 12 sessions of a combination of cognitive behavioral therapy (systematic desensitization, rational-emotive therapy, exposure) and thermal biofeedback to increase warmth in the hands of anxious undergraduate music students. They reported decreases in self-reported music performance anxiety and trait anxiety compared with a wait-list control. Similarly, Niemann, Pratt, and Maughan (1993) used a combination of muscle relaxation, breath awareness, performance coping imagery (six sessions) and biofeedback (six sessions) on 21 music students randomly assigned to treatment or wait-list control. Results indicated reductions in self-reported state anxiety prior to stressful performance situations. Unfortunately, both these studies did not have active control groups, so we cannot be sure of the role that attention played in the reported outcomes. Further, it is difficult to identify the effective component(s) in combined treatments of this nature, which is important to make interventions as cost effective as possible. Again, only self-report measures were used and there was no assessment of performance quality in either study. Finally, Sweeney-Burton (1997) was unsuccessful in reducing anxiety and improving musical performance following a similar behavioral + biofeedback intervention, but this study was conducted with music students who had not specifically been selected for their high music performance anxiety and thus the lack of significance may have been due to a floor effect.*

In summary, there is little evidence to suggest that combined treatment approaches enhance improvements in music performance anxiety over and above those offered by single treatments, but further research in this area is needed.

New wave cognitive behavioral therapies

Acceptance and commitment therapy and dialectical behavior therapy

In the past 25 years, there have been developments in the cognitive behavioral therapies for the mood (anxiety and depression) disorders that have resulted in the inclusion of mindfulness and acceptance principles in cognitive behavioral interventions. This involves a focus in the therapy not only on the content and management of unpleasant feeling states, but on the relationship that the individual has with his/her unpleasant internal and external experiences. Acceptance-based models of therapy acknowledge the universal experience of negative emotions and encourage the development of equanimity (acceptance) despite the content of current experience. There is some evidence to indicate that the way one responds to unpleasant states while experiencing anxiety or depression has an impact on the duration and intensity of symptoms and may also contribute to relapse after treatment (Thomsen, 2006). Mindfulness-based therapies (Kabat-Zinn, 2005) and acceptance and commitment therapy (ACT) (Hayes, Strosahl, & Wilson, 1999) and dialectical behavior therapy (DBT) (Linehan, 1993) are three examples of the 'new wave' or 'third wave'[10] cognitive behavioral treatments and these will be discussed briefly below. In addition to these, a group of therapies that attempt to formally integrate cognitive behavioral and psychoanalytic models has also been developed; these include the cognitive behavioral analysis system of psychotherapy (CBASP) and functional analytic psychotherapy (FAP) (Ost, 2008). Of these newer therapies, only mindfulness-based therapies have been applied to the problem of music performance anxiety, but the aim of the brief discussion of ACT and DBT is to encourage future researchers to consider such models if they prove efficacious in mainstream psychological research.

ACT and DBT both emphasize the importance of contextual and experiential change strategies in addition to the more traditional direct and didactic focus of first and second wave therapies. The third wave therapies share some features, which include a common focus on mindfulness, acceptance, defusion, the patient's values in life, relationships, the rationale for how the treatment works, the client–therapist relationship, and emotional expression[11] (Hayes, 2004). Ost (2008) has undertaken the first comprehensive comparison and meta-analysis of the third wave therapies. He reported effect sizes for ACT (.68) and DBT (.58). When ACT and DBT were compared with wait-list conditions, the effect sizes were large, 0.96 and 1.30 respectively, but in both therapies there were only two studies included in the calculation of effect size. Comparisons with 'treatment as usual' groups or other active treatments reduced effect sizes to the moderate range for both therapies. Ost (2008) concluded that the third wave therapies failed to meet the standards specified by the American Psychological Association to be considered empirically supported therapies. He was critical that studies in these therapies were less stringent than CBT studies. Finally, although effect sizes were moderate against treatment-as-usual comparisons, he recommended that they be directly compared with established empirically supported CBT studies to ascertain whether they added value to accepted treatments.

Mindfulness-based stress reduction (MBSR)

First, let us define our terms. The term 'mindfulness' and its practice originated in the Buddhist tradition in India over 2,500 years ago (Goleman & Schwartz, 1976). Mindfulness is the outcome of training in meditation techniques. It is understood to be a state of heightened awareness and focus on the reality of the present moment, with a mind that acknowledges and accepts the moment, devoid of feelings or thoughts or judgments about it (Bishop, 2002). It is a self-regulatory practice designed to train attention in order to bring mental processes under greater voluntary control (Walsh, 1995). There are different types of meditation, but most involve techniques for the focusing of attention, using an object of focus such as an image, an idea, a word, a phrase, or one's breath. Participants in meditation training workshops learn that thoughts and feelings are mental events, are not part of the self and do not necessarily

---

[10] The first wave was behavior therapy; the second wave was cognitive therapy.

[11] We discussed in Chapter Six evidence that active suppression of aversive thoughts and feelings do not provide relief from the associated emotions; on the contrary it appears to make them worse (Feldner *et al.*, 2006).

reflect reality (Kabat-Zinn, 2005). It was initially developed for use in chronic illness, to assist sufferers to reduce the amount of emotional distress they experienced as a result of their illness. Training involves between eight and 10 weekly group sessions and one full-day retreat. The groups are primarily psychoeducational and experiential in orientation.

In one of the first reviews of MBSR, Bishop (2002) was critical of the construct of mindfulness, stating that 'there have been no attempts to operationalize the central qualities [i.e. fully present in the moment, focused on reality, acknowledging and accepting reality] of mindfulness. However, each of the three dimensions emphasized in the literature seems to involve an aspect of attention regulation' (Bishop, 2002, p. 74). Bishop likens the components of mindfulness to constructs such as bare attention, sustained attention, attention switching, and attentional control. He also posits that mindfulness may constitute a metacognitive skill—the capacity to observe one's mental processes. Further, he identifies an attitude of 'nonstriving' in mindfulness that differs from a similar process, absorption, in that the latter involves immersion in experience whereas the former requires the observation of experience in a detached way, with an attitude of curiosity, openness, and acceptance. Bishop concluded that there was no evidence to support the construct of mindfulness:

> Convincing evidence in support of the construct validity would be obtained if experience with mindfulness meditation were to produce enhanced performance on cognitive tasks that require sustained attention and attention switching, termination of elaborative processing and awareness of stimuli (Bishop, 2002, p. 75).

Bishop identified only two controlled studies in non-clinical samples that showed that MBSR may be effective in reducing stress, anxiety, and dysphoria in the general population. However, he concluded that the available evidence, which was of a very low quality, was insufficient to support MBSR. In addition, he raised the important question of suitability for enrolment in MBSR programs. Since MBSR places great demands on attentional skills, Bishop speculated that any observed efficacy for this approach may be due to the self-selection of people high in the requisite skills pre-enrolment.

Several reviews have been conducted since 2002. The first, a Cochrane review of randomized controlled trials in which meditation therapy was used to treat the anxiety disorders (Krisanaprakornkit, Krisanaprakornkit, & Piyavhatkul, 2007), found only two studies that met inclusion criteria but neither was of high quality. The authors noted very high drop-out rates in both studies. In a subsequent review of studies using MBSR to treat anxiety and depression, Toneatto and Nguyen (2007) found no evidence that MBSR reliably reduced the symptoms of anxiety. They also noted the continuing poor quality of studies, and speculated that those that reported a positive effect could not reliably isolate mindfulness as the factor that contributed to the effect, suggesting that non-specific variables may have accounted for any improvements observed. Another study (Lee, Ahn, & Lee, 2007) reported positive results for participants suffering an anxiety disorder. However, the treatment program, comprising eight weekly one-hour sessions, included not only MBSR but also other interventions such as psychoeducation, exercise, relaxation, and hypnotic suggestion. Many of the participants were also taking anxiolytic medication. Van der Watt, Laugharne, and

Janca (2008) concluded that there was growing empirical support for the use of acupuncture, but not mindfulness-based meditation, for treating the anxiety disorders.

We need to exercise caution with respect to the conclusions that we draw from the available evidence, the quality of which precludes certainty about the efficacy of MBSR for the treatment of anxiety. Better studies are needed to assess efficacy in view of the fact that mindfulness-based meditative practices have been demonstrated to show increased cortical thickness in brain regions associated with attention and sensory processing, and left-sided anterior activation, which is associated with positive affect, suggesting that mindfulness practice may contribute to stress and anxiety reduction in people who do not find the practice of meditation too onerous (Kemper & Shannon, 2007).

Mindfulness-based treatments for music performance anxiety

Chang (2001; Chang, Midlarsky, & Lin, 2003) examined the effects of meditation training on 19 tertiary-level music students aged 18–41 years. The treatment group received eight weekly meditation classes and they were compared with an untreated control group before and after a concert performance on a range of cognitive and anxiety measures. The results of this study are difficult to interpret because the pre-performance anxiety scores were significantly higher for the treatment group and tests of significance were not conducted on change scores. However, there was only very modest support for the role of meditation in reducing performance anxiety. Because there was not an active control group, it is difficult to attribute the small changes to meditation over a placebo attention effect. Interestingly, there were no significant differences between the groups on measures of cognitive interference (i.e. mind wandering, intrusive thoughts) that the meditation intervention specifically addressed. A second study (Lin, Chang, Zemon, & Midlarsky, 2008) presents a rewritten paper using the same data as the 2001 dissertation, published in 2003, with a more detailed description of the meditation practice used—*Chan* meditation, which incorporates concentration and mindfulness—and the inclusion of an assessment of performance quality, which showed no significant difference between meditation and control groups. In assessing the relationship between performance quality and anxiety, the authors interpret results that showed a positive linear relationship between performance quality and anxiety to mean that the meditation group learnt to 'channel performance anxiety to improve musical performance' (p. 139). This statement is not supported by their data, firstly because there was no difference in performance quality between the two groups, and secondly because inspection of the scatter plots shows greater dispersion of state anxiety scores (25–70) than in the control group (35–55), with the three highest scorers for performance quality in the meditation group reporting anxiety in the low, middle, and high ranges. From the results of this study, we must conclude that there is insufficient evidence supporting the use of meditation in the treatment of music performance anxiety.

Yoga for music performance anxiety

A recent study that combined the use of yoga and meditation showed slightly more promising results (Khalsa, Shorter, Cope, Wyshak, & Sklar, 2009). Forty-five young adult professional musicians, average age 25 years, were randomized to a two-month yoga lifestyle intervention group: a group practicing yoga and meditation only; and a no-yoga practice control group. Each of the two yoga groups attended three Kripalu Yoga/meditation classes each week. Khalsa described Kripalu Yoga as follows:

> Kripalu Yoga is a complete yoga practice system incorporating classical yoga postures, multiple breathing techniques, and meditation. This style of yoga emphasizes introspective focus while coordinating breath and physical postures as a meditation in motion (p. 281).

In addition, the yoga lifestyle group also engaged in weekly group practice and discussion sessions. Participants were assessed at treatment end and one-year follow-up on measures of music performance anxiety, mood, performance-related musculoskeletal disorders, perceived stress, and sleep quality. The PAQ (Performance Anxiety Questionnaire) (Cox & Kenardy, 1993) was the measure of music performance anxiety used in the study. There were no differences on PAQ scores at end of the program for any of the three groups. However, there was a significant change over time for both the yoga groups, while no change occurred over time for the control group. No group differences were significant at long-term follow-up although the change achieved at end of program were maintained at follow-up for the yoga groups. Given that the intervention was intensive—three sessions per week over a two-month period—one would need to conclude that this approach does not appear to be a cost-effective way of reducing music performance anxiety in professional musicians, although such an approach may have broader health benefits.

Multimodal therapies

Several studies have been undertaken to assess multimodal therapies, defined as those therapies that simultaneously address the whole range of affected domains in performance anxiety. Indeed, cognitive behavioral therapies routinely address the three domains of affect, behavior, and cognition in their treatment protocols. However, for very severe performance anxiety, a more comprehensive approach is needed. Accordingly, Lazarus and Abramovitz (2004) have developed a multimodal approach for the treatment of performance anxiety that addresses seven domains, which they call BASIC ID. This acronym stands for behavior, affect, sensation, imagery, cognition, interpersonal relationships, and biological (including drugs) factors. They advocate attention to all of these modalities or domains in the treatment of people who experience severe performance anxiety. Under each heading the assessment process poses a series of questions aimed at developing targets for treatment. Examples taken from Lazarus and Abramovitz's (2004) model are given below.

Behavior: What are the self-defeating or maladaptive behaviors or performance deficits that need to be addressed?

Affective: What are the dominant affects—anger, anxiety, depression, sadness—and what generates these affects (cognitions, interpersonal conflicts)?

Sensation: Are there specific sensory complaints—tension, chronic pain, tremors, weakness? What feelings, thoughts, and behaviors are associated with these sensations?

Images/fantasies: What constitutes the self-image—are there specific failure images, traumatic experiences/memories, and are these connected to specific cognitions, behaviors, affects?

Cognitions: What are the underlying attitudes, values, beliefs, and opinions? Are there automatic thoughts that need identification?

Interpersonal: Who are the significant others in the person's life? Are these relationships adaptive/supportive/reciprocal?

Drugs: This is a broad domain that covers physical/biological aspects. Is the person healthy and fit? What role do medication and substance use (alcohol and illicit drugs) play?

One area not specifically included in this model is the environment or context in which the anxiety-provoking behavior needs to occur. Exposure to the actual performance venue and opportunity to practice the new skills *in situ* are key elements in successful behavior therapy (Antony & Swinson, 2000a). For some anxious performers, there may be a mismatch between the skill required for the task and the abilities needed to accomplish an outcome. It is important that people are encouraged to pursue skills in their area of strength wherever possible. An anecdote relating to the eminent French horn player, Barry Tuckwell, is instructive. Schooled in music from an early age, Tuckwell studied organ, piano, and violin, but did not feel a great affinity with any of these instruments. He was casually advised to try the French horn at age 13, and from that point, his life blossomed into a distinguished international career. He later recalled that the horn chose him. As we will see with some of our musicians in Chapter Eight, many started learning their instruments at a very young age, and their aptitude and parental desire resulted in a premature foreclosure of other career options that may have been more temperamentally suitable.

Not all performers presenting for treatment will require attention to all seven domains. However, all seven should be carefully assessed prior to developing a treatment plan, particularly in cases of severe performance anxiety. Assessment will reveal that performers become anxious for a range of different reasons but the core fears are the fear of making mistakes, fear of negative evaluation, and fear of exposure as a sham or an impostor, but more of this later.

Brain-based multimodal therapy

Linford and Arden (2009) have argued for a brain-based model of psychotherapy as an antidote to the medical model's reliance on psychotropic medication, the DSM (i.e. the need for diagnosis) and the so-called evidence-based therapies that took hold in the 1970s with the advent of Prozac (an antidepressant medication). They argue that, contrary to the current obsession with manualized treatments and the systematic application of a set of techniques, the methods employed by therapists were less related to therapeutic outcome as the common elements in all therapies, the basic one of which is exposure. Fritz Perls, the flamboyant Gestalt therapy practitioner, used the term 'safe emergency,' CBT therapists talk of exposure, and psychodynamic therapists aim to gradually expose repressed thoughts and feelings by providing a therapeutic environment in which the patient feels safe enough to relinquish their defenses in order to confront their emotional pain. Other common elements underlying successful treatment include therapist qualities of warmth, unconditional positive regard, respect, support, and confidentiality. Linford and Arden (2009) propose a brain-based therapy that 'incorporates current neuroscience, developmental psychology, psychodynamic theory, cognitive psychology and psychotherapy research' (p.19). They have coined the mnemonic BASE to describe their approach. Each of the elements will be described briefly below.

Brain. The brain grows and develops in response to interpersonal experiences of social appraisal and emotional regulation. Good mothers and good therapists assist in brain development and change. The discovery of mirror neurons provides a cellular-level explanation for the development of empathy, the capacity to grasp the minds of others. Further, brain structures change in response to chronic stress. For example, the hippocampus shrinks and the amygdala increases in volume. Amygdala overactivity has been linked to social anxiety disorder and some phobias.

Attunement. The brain has a profound need for relatedness to other brains, and a mother's capacity to attune to her baby results in implicit encoding of emotional rules by which individuals operate throughout their lives, including the management of painful content through resistance, defense, and numbing, among others. Therapies that encourage only the activation of the left hemispheric capacity for storytelling without activating the right hemisphere's emotional expectancies will be unsuccessful, because feelings must be experienced, not just talked about.

Systems. This model assumes that 'many psychological problems are down-stream effects of impairments in the brain's capacity to regulate the neurodynamics of stress' (p. 21). It is therefore important to consider the functioning of the whole organism, and an assessment of sleep, eating, and exercise habits, as well as the role of medications, is essential for healthy functioning.

Evidence. Positron emission tomography (PET) scans show that the brains (prefrontal cortex, hippocampus, anterior cingulate, and amygdala) of people change following successful psychotherapy. Similarly, changes in brain structures have been observed in people treated for an anxiety disorder.

This model appears to have a great deal of potential for the treatment of severe music performance anxiety because professional musicians with this condition experience chronic stress, which results in the release of high levels of the stress hormone cortisol, which in turn affects the functioning of the hippocampus and amygdala, leading to many of the symptoms described by anxious musicians—intense anxiety, cognitive disturbances such as confusion, loss of concentration, difficulties with memory, and a chronically elevated allostatic load.[12] However, the same caution applies to the multimodal therapies as those applied to the new wave cognitive behavioral therapies, that is, the need for empirical validation. These multimodal therapies are too recent as yet to have built up an evidence base. In bringing such treatments to the attention of music researchers, I am hopeful that an evidence base will be forthcoming in the near future.

---

[12] Allostatic load refers to the physiological costs of chronic exposure to fluctuating or heightened neural or neuroendocrine reactivity that results from repeated or chronic stress.

Other interventions for music performance anxiety

Music therapy

Montello (1989) and Montello, Coons, and Kantor (1990) assessed the effect of a 12-week music therapy intervention on freelance musicians suffering from music performance anxiety. The intervention consisted of musical improvisation, three musical performances in front of an audience, awareness techniques, and verbal processing of anxiety responses.* Participants became significantly more confident as performers and less anxious than waiting-list control subjects after the music therapy intervention. This form of therapeutic intervention was recommended as a way of reducing performance anxiety by helping musicians to: '(1) become more aware of the underlying dynamics of performance anxiety; (2) experience unconditional acceptance and support in a safe group environment; (3) bond with their music-selves; (4) transform anxiety through creativity (reparation); and (5) bond with others in the spirit of musical community' (p.4). Despite the small sample size, this study was methodologically strong, and included subjects with severe music performance anxiety. The results of a similar pilot study using a combination of music improvisation and desensitization with six female tertiary-level pianists (Kim, 2005) reported inconclusive results but was methodologically weak.

Brodsky and Sloboda (1997) investigated the efficacy of CBT alone, CBT while listening to music, and CBT + listening to music + vibro-tactile (music-generated vibration) sensations in the treatment of music performance anxiety over eight sessions of treatment. This study had no control group, was not conducted with a sample of music performance anxiety sufferers, relied only on self-report measures, and did not report the statistics required to clearly determine the nature of any group differences.* All treatments resulted in a reduction of trait anxiety but not music performance anxiety. However, at two-month follow-up, reductions in music performance anxiety were noted while trait anxiety scores returned to pre-treatment levels. Adding music to the treatment produced no additional benefits although it may have an effect on treatment acceptability for musicians to include a music component in the therapy.

Martin (2007) investigated the effect of six guided music imagery (GMI) sessions that emphasized images of mastery, strength, and protection on music performance anxiety in five self-referred tertiary-level music students. Music performance anxiety was assessed before and after the intervention using the Kenny Music Performance Anxiety Inventory (K–MPAI), Kenny's modification of the Cox and Kenardy Performance Anxiety Questionnaire, and structured interviews following end-of-year performance exams. There were trends on both measures showing reductions in performance anxiety after the imagery sessions for four of the five participants.

Youngshin (2008) assessed the impact of two music therapy interventions— improvisation-assisted desensitization and music-assisted progressive muscle relaxation (PMR) and imagery—on reducing music performance anxiety in 30 female college pianists who were randomly assigned to six sessions of one or other of the interventions. Pre- and post-test measures included a musical performance, visual analogue scales for MPA, stress, tension, and comfort, Spielberger's State Trait Anxiety

Inventory (STAI), and the Music Performance Anxiety Questionnaire (MPAQ) (Lehrer, Goldman, & Strommen, 1990). Participants' finger temperatures were also measured. Results indicated reductions on six measures for the PMR and imagery condition, and reductions on only two measures (tension and STAI) for the improvisation group. However, there were no statistically significant differences between the two approaches for any of the seven measures. The results are difficult to interpret because it is not possible to ascertain the unique contribution of the music component of the interventions over and above the desensitization and relaxation components.

The status of music-based therapies that include listening, music-guided imagery, and improvising is unclear as there are insufficient good-quality studies on which to base firm conclusions. Improvisation may have some efficacy for professional musicians in the light of the Montello findings and warrants further investigation, but should be used cautiously with less experienced musicians as they may have difficulty improvising and this may further add to their music performance anxiety.

Biofeedback

Biofeedback is a technique using electromyographic (EMG) feedback to assist anxious performers to reduce their muscle tension. EMG measures the strength of the electrical impulses occurring in muscles and produces traces of these impulses on a printout that can be easily visualized and understood. Other physiological data can be gathered in a similar way, including skin temperature, heart rate (ECG), and blood pressure. Using the visual feedback provided by printouts from biofeedback machines, individuals may learn to reduce their muscle tension or heart rate or increase their skin temperature or alter other physiological parameters. Studies conducted in the 1980s showed that biofeedback training could reduce muscle tension in specific muscle groups associated with playing the violin and viola (LeVine & Irvine, 1984) and that reduced tension resulted in improved performance quality (Morasky, Reynolds, & Sowell, 1983).

McKinney (1984) assessed peripheral skin temperature training using biofeedback on self-reported music performance anxiety and quality of musical performance in 32 male wind instrumentalists. He found that peripheral skin temperature training had no effect on peripheral skin temperature or anxiety levels assessed by the STAI–S. However, there was some evidence that biofeedback may be useful in improving performance quality (effect size = 0.83). This study was not conducted with subjects specifically selected because of their high level of music performance anxiety and effects may have been more pronounced with subjects suffering higher performance anxiety. Like Richard (1992, see below), the main effect of time (that is, repetition of the anxiety-provoking performance at post test) was the most salient result in this study, indicating that familiarity with the requirements of the task and practice effects were most effective in reducing performance anxiety.*

A more recent study (Thurber, 2007) explored the effects of heart rate variability (HRV), biofeedback training, and emotional self-regulation techniques on music performance anxiety and music performance on 14 student musicians who were randomly assigned to treatment and control groups. Treated students received four or five HRV training sessions of 30–50 minutes duration. Training included computerized bibliotherapy and training in emotional regulation. Each had a portable heart rate variability training device for home practice. Measures of outcome included the State Trait Anxiety Inventory (STAI), Performance Anxiety Inventory (PAI), Flow State Scale (FSS), average heart rate (HR), and heart rate variability (HRV). The study reported reductions on most of the anxiety measures following the combined biofeedback, bibliotherapy, and emotional regulation training. However, the study included multiple elements and it is not possible to determine how much each contributed to the effects. The study was small and used an inactive control group. The study would need to be replicated on larger samples using an active control group, testing one intervention at a time.

Ericksonian resource retrieval

This technique refers to the use of unconscious mechanisms within the individual's personal history to adapt to a current life challenge. Resources are defined as 'automated patterns of feeling, perceiving and behaving' (Lankton, 1983, p. 121). Resource retrieval is a process-oriented intervention that focuses on assisting the person to access their existing strengths rather than teaching him/her new skills. The basic structure of the technique involves identification of current life challenge, identification of relevant personal resource, cognitive and emotional re-experiencing and practicing of resource, and experience of the current challenge in the context of the cognitions and emotions related to the resource. Richard (1992) assigned 21 volunteer music students to one of three conditions: Ericksonian resource retrieval, cue-controlled relaxation, and a wait-list control. He found that Ericksonian resource retrieval reduced music performance anxiety at about the same rate as that of cue-controlled relaxation. However, repeated-measures analysis found that all three groups improved over time on measures of anxiety and confidence as a performer. Treatment and control groups did not differ in pre- to post-treatment improvements on self-reported music performance anxiety, performance quality, or performer confidence. Small subject numbers and attrition from the treatment conditions make the results difficult to interpret, and a larger replication with better compliance is needed to fully assess the potential of this technique in reducing music performance anxiety and in improving jury performances.*

Hypnotherapy

Only one study (Stanton, 1994) to date has assessed the therapeutic effect of hypnotherapy on music performance anxiety. In this study, a group of music students suffering from music performance anxiety were given two 50-minute sessions of hypnotherapy, while a control group of students discussed their performance and anxiety with their lecturer for a similar length of time. The Performance Anxiety Inventory (PAI) was administered pre and post treatment, and at six-month follow-up. A significant pre- to post-treatment reduction in music performance anxiety (as measured by the PAI) was found for the treatment group, but not the control group, and a further significant reduction was found at six-month follow-up. This study was weakened by the fact that the criteria for subject selection were somewhat subjective, with students selected by their lecturer for inclusion if they appeared to be prone to music performance anxiety. Stanton also suggested that some experimental subjects may have discussed the study with control subjects both during and after the treatment period, giving rise to a potential confound. In summary, Stanton's findings suggest that hypnotherapy may be efficacious in the treatment of music performance anxiety, but further methodologically superior studies are required. A note of caution should be introduced into this discussion. It is now understood that hypnosis is really self-hypnosis and the therapist is merely a facilitator who assists the individual to enter a state of self-hypnosis. Only about one in eight (12%) people are capable of entering a deep hypnotic trance; hence hypnosis as a treatment is unlikely to be of benefit to the majority of individuals (Powell, 2010).

Alexander technique

The Alexander technique is an educational process in which the student learns a set of skills that result in lessening of the areas of tension in the body, so that movement becomes easier and less effortful. The aim is to cultivate a more natural alignment of head, neck, and spine that has associated with it qualities of balance, strength, and coordination. The method aims to teach conscious and voluntary control over posture and movement and to undo involuntary muscle tension. The Alexander technique is a method for eliminating unwanted muscular patterns or habits that interfere with smooth performance. For a performer, the technique is a method for using kinaesthetic cues, the sensations of tension, effort, weight, and position in space, in order to organize one's field of awareness in a systematic way.*

Despite the enthusiasm with which this technique is marketed to performing artists, only one study to date has assessed the therapeutic effect of the Alexander technique on music performance anxiety. Valentine, Fitzgerald, Gorton, Hudson, and Symonds (1995) gave one group of music students 15 lessons in the Alexander technique, while a control group received no lessons in the technique. The treatment group showed improvement in musical and technical quality, and an increase in positive mood scores, while controls showed the opposite pattern of results. The treatment group also showed a decrease in anxiety and an increase in positive attitude to performance. These findings suggest that the Alexander technique may improve the quality of performance and mental state of the performer, and may help to modulate increased variability of heart rate under stress. However, the study had a weak design and we cannot be confident in the findings. Given the lack of good studies on Alexander technique in treating music performance anxiety, any conclusions must at this stage be tentative.

Lest we feel somewhat pessimistic about the current status of treatments for music performance anxiety, I will conclude this section with a summary of the effect sizes for eight of the studies reported in this chapter, calculated by McGinnis and Milling (2005). The studies were Appel (1976), Kendrick et al. (1982), Sweeney and Horan (1982), Nagel et al. (1989), Stanton (1994), Montello et al. (1990) (two experiments), and Clark and Agras (1991). Of the 11 effect sizes calculated, McGinnis and Milling found three in the medium range and two in the large range. The mean weighted effect size for the psychological treatments was 0.56 at post treatment and 1.36 at follow-up. These results indicate that treated participants achieved better results than 71% of controls at post test and 91% of controls at follow-up. Methodological limitations (i.e. non-standard assessment of music performance anxiety, haphazard or no screening of participants, poor treatment specification and fidelity, non-inclusion of active control groups, reliance on self-report, non-assessment of performance quality as an outcome, and no long-term follow-up, to name a few) of most of the studies conducted to date require that all results be treated with caution, but these calculations give rise to optimism that good, cost-effective treatments can be developed for music performance anxiety.

In summary, this review of treatment for music performance anxiety indicates that there is considerable scope for the development and evaluation of appropriate interventions. Many of the studies reported in this review constitute the only study of their kind for the treatment genre (hypnotherapy, Ericksonian resource retrieval, Alexander technique, and music therapy). Interventions leading to an improvement in performance quality, which is rarely assessed in these early studies, are most desirable, since they will have a self-reinforcing, confidence-enhancing effect on future performances, obviating the need for further treatment.

Emotion-based therapies

Emotions or affect, in particular, anxiety, constituted the primary focus of the early psychotherapies, beginning with Freud, who believed that the containment or relief of anxiety was the central determinant of a successful psychotherapeutic outcome (Freud, 1926). As we have learnt from the previous section, in the intervening years between Freud and the current day, a number of other foci have been considered in other therapeutic approaches. These include cognitions or thoughts (ruminations, worry, catastrophic thinking, delusions), behaviors (risk taking, impulsivity, behavioral manifestations of physiological arousal), and sensations and perceptions (somatization, psychogenic pain, perceptual distortions) (McWilliams, 1994). While all of these symptom constellations are important to consider in diagnosis, therapeutic planning, and treatment, there has been a recent return to the primacy of emotions/affects in many therapeutic approaches. We have already discussed how emotions are central to music performance anxiety, even though cognitive, behavioral, sensory, and perceptual symptoms must also be addressed. Interestingly, Allen *et al.* (2008) state that focus on 'any emotion [as] the target of treatment' (p. 222) is contrary to 'traditional protocols' (p. 221). This is a curious claim, given that emotion and the defenses against emotional experience have been the focus of all psychodynamic therapies since Freud! Perhaps the cognitive behavioral therapists are simply catching up with what has been known in other areas of psychological practice for over 100 years!

The rationale for the development of what they call a 'unified protocol,' that is, a generic emotion-based psychotherapy that has application across a wide range of psychological disorders (Allen *et al.*, 2008), is based on our previous discussion of the evidence supporting the commonalities in the etiology and symptomatology of the anxiety and mood disorders, the high rates of comorbidity among these conditions, the identification of underlying characterological dimensions such as high negative affect and low positive affect in people who suffer from one of the anxiety and/or depression disorder spectrum disorders, and their responsiveness to particular therapeutic interventions. This approach is summarized below. For a more detailed description, the interested reader is referred to Barlow (2008).

A unified protocol for the emotional disorders

The unified protocol for the treatment of emotion disorders was developed from an examination of all existing CBT protocols for emotion disorders, which were found to have three basic underlying change strategies. These are:

i altering emotion-based misappraisals of salient events

ii preventing avoidance of negative, emotionally charged internal and external triggers

iii modifying emotion-driven behaviors (Allen *et al.*, 2008, p. 220).

The treatment protocol aims to elicit and change behavioral responses to problematic emotions and emotional cues via accepted CBT interventions that include cognitive reappraisal and imaginal and *in vivo* exposure. The early stage of the protocol is focused on identifying how the patient avoids experiencing, expressing, and accepting the emotions that have motivated him/her to seek treatment. The task of the therapist is to support and tolerate intense emotional expressions in the client. You will recall that this is also one of the primary therapeutic foci for intensive short-term dynamic psychotherapy covered earlier in the chapter. A number of avoidance strategies may be identified, including denial of the emotion, suppression of the expression of the emotion, or other direct attempts to control emotion by avoidance. In dynamic psychotherapeutic terms, these behaviors would be identified as defenses against the forbidden or feared emotion. The use of medications during this type of treatment is strongly discouraged, firstly because those receiving medication in conjunction with CBT therapies are at higher risk of relapse and secondly, because the use of medications protects anxious individuals from experiencing their emotions and attendant physiological reactions in situations that would otherwise cause panic-like feelings or false alarms. Since the aim of the therapy is to elicit such emotional reactions, true exposure will be prevented by the effects of medication, thus preventing re-conditioning of the emotional responses in the problematic situations.

You will note with interest, as I did, the heavy focus on emotions in this unified protocol. Traditional cognitive behavioral therapies, as the term implies, did not focus on the emotions. Indeed, they did not figure at all in the treatment protocol except as a measure of change in processes such as systematic desensitization, in which patients rate on a scale from 0 to 100 the amount of anxiety that they are experiencing as they work their way through their fear hierarchy. Conversely, despite popular notions that psychoanalytic therapies are exclusively concerned with impulses, drives, and emotions, the cognitive dimension, at both the conscious and unconscious levels, has always been important in analytic theorizing and treatment. Indeed, Freud believed that a successful therapy required the uncovering of unconscious beliefs or core convictions that direct our behavior and our lives, often unconsciously (Freud, 1916–1917/1973). Hence, both cognitive and psychoanalytic therapies are now united in a mutual interest in both cognitions and emotions.

Although the development of an evidence-based unified protocol is a good idea, this protocol does not go far enough, as it is a compilation of the effective elements of the variations of treatments within cognitive behavioral therapy. Recent evidence suggests that we need to take a much broader approach to a unified protocol and include elements from other therapies that have been associated with positive therapeutic outcomes. Cognitive behavioral treatments have been slow to recognize the importance of the relationship between psychologist and client, in other words, the importance of the therapeutic alliance. A number of studies are now demonstrating that a failure to attend to the quality of the therapeutic relationship is associated with poorer clinical outcomes. In one study, Castonguay, Goldfried, Wiser, Raue, and Hayes (1996) assessed the relative contributions of CBT elements such as focus on distorted cognitions and common therapeutic elements such as the therapeutic alliance and the patient's emotional investment in therapy. They found that the latter elements were more predictive of successful outcome; in fact, sole focus on cognitive interventions for cognitive distortions was negatively correlated with treatment outcome. Other studies that have used a combination of techniques from psychodynamic therapy— for example, addressing the patient's early experience—and CBT were more effective than an intervention relying solely on CBT elements (Hayes & Strauss, 1998). It is possible that the positive effects of CBT are due to an 'unanalyzed idealizing transference'[13] (Powell, 2010), although this assertion will require empirical confirmation with respect to other elements that are central to the psychoanalytic psychotherapies (Shedler, 2010).

Transdiagnostic approach to the anxiety disorders

Despite the proliferation of diagnoses in successive diagnostic and statistical manuals of the American Psychiatric Association, researchers and clinicians now understand that the anxiety disorders share common underlying experiences, such as early life experiences (e.g. overintrusive, punishing, rejecting, overprotective parenting; developmental history where opportunities to predict and control aversive events were limited) that result in insecure attachment. Insecurely attached, anxious people also share some common cognitive processes. These include:

i selective attention (hyper-vigilant for threat)

ii memory bias

  i. selective memory (for bad events)

  ii. recurrent memory (intrusive memories of, for example, as bad performances)

  iii. overgeneralized memory (overgeneralized meanings given to past events lead to anxiety in the present)

---

[13] During development, the emerging self needs to merge with an idealized parent who provides a sense of safety and comfort. Gradually, the wish is simply to be near the source of such power and eventually, mature individuals are satisfied knowing that friends and family are available in times of need. An idealizing transference involves the attachment to another who has power or prestige that provides a means by which damaged self-esteem is recovered through the processes of idealization and identification (Kohut, 1977).

iii reasoning errors (i.e. cognitive distortions) (see Chapter Six)

iv rumination and worry (see Chapter Two)

v reinforcing metacognitions (e.g. 'Worrying helps me solve problems, prepares me for the worst, means I am a responsible person,' etc.)

vi avoidance and safety behaviors (including hyper-vigilance, checking, self-monitoring, thought suppression, distraction, reassuring self-talk, and chronic overactivity).

The five theoretical models presented in Behar *et al.* (2009) share some fundamental commonalities, including a central role for avoidance of internal affective experiences (i.e. thoughts, beliefs, and emotions), although they each have a different theoretical formulation. For example, the Avoidance model of worry (AMW), Emotion dysregulation model (EDM), and Acceptance-based model (ABM) view worry as an ineffective coping strategy to avoid emotional stimuli such as images, somatic activation, emotions, and other internal experiences. The Intolerance of uncertainty model (IUM) states that worry attempts to avoid uncertainty while the Meta-cognitive model (MCM) asserts that individuals try to avoid worrying about worry. All treatment components across the models include psychoeducation about GAD, self-monitoring, and an emphasis on training clients to cope with internal experiences. The emphasis on emotional processing in the newer wave of cognitive theories is, of course, reminiscent of psychodynamic therapy. Table 7.1 shows how the emphasis in treatment of the anxiety disorders has changed.

There are currently no applications of these newer models of the anxiety disorders to the management and treatment of music performance anxiety. I am hopeful that future researchers will be interested to pursue some of these potentially fruitful directions for performing artists.

Performance-based approaches

The man of virtue makes the difficulty to be overcome his first business, and success only a subsequent consideration (Confucius, from The Confucian Analects, 551 BC–479 BC).

We have just discussed in great detail the psychological approaches to the management and treatment of music performance anxiety. These approaches, while essential, are not complete because the performer's key goals relate to the quality of their performance rather than their mental state. Most performers who present for treatment have the dual goal of reducing their anxiety in order to be able to perform at their best and with enjoyment and pleasure. Therapists, coaches, pedagogues, and others who work with performers need to pay particular attention to performance-based approaches to improving performance. This is the subject of our next discussion. There is a great deal of pedagogical wisdom with respect to how to teach music; this section does not focus on specific teaching techniques for particular instruments, but rather on the theories and meta-skills that can be applied to the learning and performance of all complex performance tasks. Since sport psychology has again taken the lead in researching peak performance, we will begin with a brief overview of three indicative models that have been developed to enhance performance. This will be

Table 7.1 Traditional and contemporary cognitive behavioral therapy interventions

Traditional CBT	Contemporary CBT
Psychoeducation	Shared formulation and information
Cognitive reframing; structured problem solving	Cognitive strategies: disputing catastrophic thoughts; techniques to build metacognitive awareness; challenging metacognitions (Socratic questioning,[14] behavioral experiments)
De-arousal strategies: deep relaxation, breathing exercises, physical exercise	
Worry time; worry place; time management	
Hierarchical worry exposure	
Graded exposure to feared situations	Desensitization to distressing thoughts and emotions (exposure; mindfulness)
Elimination of reassurance seeking	
	Increasing tolerance of uncertainty (e.g. behavioral experiments; abandoning safety behaviors; exposure to uncertain situations)
	Imagery techniques

followed by a review of some critical elements considered essential to achieve outcomes that reflect the person's potential when s/he needs it most—under pressure. This quote from Garfield and Bennett (1984) encapsulates the key element of a good performance-based approach.

> The foundation of every peak performer's training is contained in a single word: *program*. I would like to emblazon this word on a billboard in letters nine feet tall to emphasize this point. Without the structure provided by a clear, step-by-step training program, the athlete can waste precious hours, or even years, seeking a path to excellence down cul-de-sacs where little or nothing is accomplished (p. 29).

Behavioral model of performance enhancement

At its most mechanistic, peak performance is achieved through the management of three key components: maximizing correct responses, eliminating incorrect responses, and encouraging maximal transfer from training to competition. As Suinn (2005) states: 'The most important outcome is reflected in performance under competitive conditions. Performance during practice sessions, no matter how perfect, is considered to be a sub-goal' (p. 313). These components occur against a background of the level

---

[14] Socratic questioning is disciplined, systematic questioning that explores complex ideas, issues, and problems, and uncovers and challenges assumptions, such as metacognitions and illogical thoughts.

of potential skill and the pace of acquisition of the skill, which are in turn influenced by the performer's genetic endowment, past exposure to training and performing, the quality of the coaching/teaching received, and so on. Any individual performance can also be affected on the day by a range of situational and environmental factors. Suinn (2005) advocates the use of behavioral techniques that address both the external (e.g. removal of the external cues, extinction of the conditioned emotional response to those cues, or conditioning new responses to such cues), and internal stressors (reducing emotional reactivity or rumination when errors occur) that interfere with optimal performance.

> Correct athletic responses involve those that make up the primary positive aspects of the sport: the motor skill itself, preparatory-arousal responses, cognitive or cue-instructional responses, and attentional/concentration responses. Incorrect athletic responses involve interfering motor habits, inappropriate arousal or conditioned emotionality, and negative cognitions. The transferability of responses from practice settings to competitive settings is a function of the nature of the practice and its similarity to game stimulus conditions (p. 314).

The principles of psychomotor learning and performance are relevant to human performance in general, and athletic performance is similar to other performing arts, including theatre, dance, music, and public speaking. Therefore the principles espoused in this behavioral model of performance enhancement are applicable to all performing arts since the primary goal is to transfer the skills learnt during preparation to the actual performance. Suinn's proposed techniques are packaged into an Anxiety Management Training (AMT) program (Suinn, 1990) that involves training in the direct use of relaxation under conditions of arousal in conjunction with cognitive restructuring to deal with problematic thoughts. This is an interesting approach that simultaneously addresses skill acquisition and anxiety—that is, anxiety management is an integral part of the training program. This approach achieves maximal transfer of training to the competitive environment because not only are the skills learnt to automaticity, but the emotional responses attached to those skills are embedded in the skill itself (Kenny, 2005b). Below is an account from a concert pianist that illustrates an example of what Suinn meant by embedding anxiety management training into performance preparation:

> Once you're anxious, it actually affects the tension in your muscles. A lot of my training has been in learning how to reverse the muscle response to anxiety. If I'm playing some very complex contemporary work with a score, if you're reading it, it's not prepared, it's prepared in a totally different way to say a solo recital, and you have to respond and it's technically very difficult and an extremely intellectually demanding work; if I'm doing that, people often say, 'Oh, you looked so relaxed.' And the reason why is because I'm consciously 'jelly fishing' my muscles in order to do it, because it makes it so much easier to do it . . . if my focus cuts out, the tendency is to panic so the muscles seize up but mine don't tend to for more than a micro second because my natural response to release the muscle kicks in. So in fact, when I'm more anxious, I'm constantly 'jelly fishing' because that's what I've trained myself to do; because that's the easiest way to get back my focus and calm.

Unifying model of psychological preparation for peak performance

Hardy, Jones, and Gould (1996b) developed a performance enhancement model with five components, as follows:

i fundamental foundational attributes—trait (sport) confidence, competitive trait anxiety, attentional style, task vs ego goal orientation, motivation and aspiration

ii psychological skills and strategies—goal setting, imagery and pre-performance routines

iii adversity coping skills and strategies—realistic appraisal, social support, recovery strategies, refocusing

iv ideal performance state—finding the optimal levels for emotions, cognitions, and arousal

v environment—physical (e.g. health and fitness, properly warmed up, properly rested, jet lag), social (e.g. social support before and during the competition), organizational (e.g. quality of pre-competition training), situational (performance venue characteristics, home crowd, accommodation, altitude, time zones).

When helping a performer to achieve a peak performance, all of these factors must be systematically addressed, deficits identified, and remedies found. Below is an account given by our concert pianist prior to an important solo recital where most of the five components described above went awry.

> I think the worst experience I've had was last year. I'd never really had a negative experience performing. I always found it incredibly exhilarating . . . I've always felt comfortable in the art of performing, and the little errors . . . that occur, little mishaps, might be greater or lesser according to various environmental reasons. Then last year, I gave a recital in [major city] and I realized now with hindsight that in the period before that recital I was depressed. My doctor has described it as reactive depression because I have to work with a psychopath . . . the impact of that was great . . . I was waking up in tears most mornings, I found myself unable to concentrate and unable to work at my normal standard, but I decided it was a question of crash through or crash. I was trying to treat myself, keep myself going. Then three days before I was due to fly out, I came down with a massive flu. I don't get the flu [laughs], I don't get sick in general, but this was the sort of flu where I couldn't get out of bed . . . shocking headache, I was absolutely exhausted. I literally could not get up to practice. So I thought, 'Right, well this is a problem—maybe I won't be able to do the concert.' I let the concert promoter know that I might not be well enough to get on the plane. The next day I got up and went to the piano, played through the program, it was fine. So I contacted them and said I would do it . . . I felt, 'If I don't stay on this horse, I'll never get back on it.' So I got on the plane [laughs] and I went over and they were very kind, they were very helpful, I had lots of rest. I was playing a huge work and it was a new performance for me, it was the Schumann Fantasy. It's a half hour long, it's extremely technically demanding as it requires consistent concentration in order to navigate its very complex sonata-style structure. I decided that given my particular physical and mental state at that point, I would have the music up in front of me. I've never played a solo recital with a score in front of me, and I found it really off-putting . . . and the performance was all wrong and I knew it was . . .

I was very distressed by the whole thing. I wasn't doing what I normally do. So my concentration just kept cutting out all the time. I found that very anxious making while I was playing. I thought that I would need to overhaul myself mentally to have another go at giving a full-length recital, which I had to do shortly after. So, luckily I got a second bite at that concert program about a month later at a smaller performance venue. It went much better the second time; I did it from memory and so on. So I could play it, I'm not talking about being totally incompetent, but I'm just talking about not being me. I knew it wasn't my top playing. So that's probably my worst experience and it was basically because I was sick and I know I don't get sick, so I knew I was sick because I didn't want to give the concert; I was not in the right frame of mind to give that concert.

You may find it instructive to review each of the five components of Hardy's model with this account in mind; you will be able to identify how personal and environmental contingencies can accumulate to either impair a performance or make the performance experience less positive than it could have been. Also look for the positive factors in this account that mitigated the very major physical and environmental challenges that had to be overcome. Even for very experienced performers, the demands of performance are such that careful attention needs to be focused on these five component factors prior to every performance.

Individual zones of optimal functioning (IZOF) model

Conducting nomothetic studies that identify factors that affect performance in a population is not a useful approach for assisting individual performers to optimize their performance (see Chapter Two for a detailed discussion). Hanin (2000a, 2000b) has developed a model, called the Individual Zones of Optimal Functioning (IZOF) model and an IZOF emotion-profiling assessment protocol that personalizes the application of the model. Successful athletic performance occurs when pre-competition anxiety approximates the ideal level (low, moderate, high) for that athlete. When this level strays outside the IZOF, performance suffers (see Harmison, 2006, for a review). However, anxiety is only one of many factors that affect performance, and Hanin's model attempts to address these through individual emotional profiling. The goal of this process is to assist athletes to identify (i) their individually relevant emotions; (ii) which emotions are most associated with their best and worst performances; and (iii) the relative intensity of these emotions as they affect performance. The psychologist devises a specific intervention to guide emotional regulation based on this emotional profile to support the athlete's performance aspirations. For example, if anxiety is found to be intense during worst performances, a program to address anxiety is devised that covers skills such as attentional control, cognitive restructuring, deep breathing, relaxation, and the use of energizing verbal cues. There has been some support for this model, although further studies are needed (Harmison, 2006). However, at a conceptual level, this model has much to recommend it, and applications for use in music performance seem warranted, given the very diverse reasons for their music performance anxiety given by professional musicians. One of the criticisms of the IZOF model is its inability to explain how anxiety can have both facilitative and debilitating effects on performance. It is to this very important issue that we will now turn.

Facilitating and debilitating effects of anxiety on performance

[I]f excitement is merely a form of anxiety that is expressed positively, then anxiety, under certain conditions, can be regarded as a salutary component of living . . . anxiety supplies essential creative energy . . . and that, instead of running away from anxiety, it is wisest to 'move through it,' achieving a measure of self-realization in the process (Reubart, 1985, pp. 12–13).

At first glance, most people will assume that anxiety is performance impairing and should be reduced to a minimum. This is not necessarily the case. Anxiety has a number of dimensions that have not always been conceptually or empirically addressed. By far the majority of studies have focused on self-reported anxiety and used rating scales and questionnaires such as the STAI–S to measure it. However, what these assessment tools measure is the performer's cognitive interpretation or perception of their anxiety state rather than the level of actual physiological arousal occurring at the biological level. Physiological arousal is non-specific—that is, the same physiological processes become activated under challenge of some kind, but the sensations of that arousal may be interpreted quite differently by different performers depending on their situational determinants and the personal history of the performer with respect to physiological arousal in the past. We therefore need to make a distinction between physiological arousal and somatic anxiety (see Chapter Two for a more detailed coverage of this topic).

What concerns us centrally in this section is the observation that anxiety can have both helpful and harmful effects on performance. Wolfe (1989), for example, noted that music performance anxiety can have both positive and negative effects on performance. He identified two adaptive and two maladaptive components of music performance anxiety. The adaptive components are arousal/intensity and confidence/competence, and the maladaptive components are nervousness/apprehension and self-consciousness/distractibility. Wolfe further described two processes that underpin maladaptive performance anxiety—the first related to performance deficits, such as inadequate preparation, poor technique, and lack of performance experience; and the other as an interference process in which anxiety hinders learning and hence preparation.

A more formal confirmation of the dual roles of anxiety on performance has been provided by Mor *et al.* (1995), who showed that performance anxiety can have both facilitating and debilitating functions and that these functions are negatively correlated. Facilitative (functional) anxiety readies the performer for the challenge ahead by directing preparatory arousal into effective task-oriented action; in debilitating anxiety, preparatory arousal is appraised negatively as anxious apprehension and attention is directed away from the task to self-focused negative affects and cognitions. One German study of 74 gifted 15–19-year-old musicians (Fehm & Schmidt, 2005) found that 73% perceived anxiety to have a negative influence on their performance, while 40% reported that it exerted a positive influence on their performance, with some reporting both effects. There was only a moderate negative correlation between the two dimensions ($r = -.38$) indicating that the facilitating and debilitating aspects of performance anxiety are not part of a single continuum.

Thus, the direction of anxiety, as either facilitative or debilitating, may be more important to performance quality than the intensity of the anxiety experienced. There are a number of studies in sports psychology that have reported the greater effect of direction than intensity of anxiety on sport performance (Gould, Greenleaf, & Krane, 2002). It remains an open question as to what factors mediate the perceived direction of physiological arousal, although a number of candidates have been identified, again in the sports literature. These include skill or task mastery, self-confidence (self-efficacy), perceived control (of the performance) (Hanton *et al.*, 2003), and perceived control of the anxiety symptoms (Rapee & Medoro, 1994). (You will recall our earlier discussion of the significance of uncontrollability in the etiology of the anxiety disorders.) One study has also shown a positive relationship between perceived control and anxiety direction in music performance anxiety (Mor *et al.*, 1995). Release of the stress hormones cortisol and catecholamine is to some extent affected by perceived control. If the stressor is perceived to be controllable, these hormones are not released (Davis, Donzella, Krueger, & Gunnar, 1999).

One study has attempted to unravel and clarify the complex relationship between perceived control of anxiety-related performance, perceptions of the direction and intensity of music performance anxiety, and circulating cortisol in a sample of 35 tertiary-level music students (Gill, Murphy, & Rickard, 2006). Prior to a performance examination, participants completed The Anxiety Control Questionnaire (Rapee, Craske, Brown, & Barlow, 1996) and provided a baseline measure of cortisol. Immediately following a short performance examination, participants provided a sample of saliva (for cortisol) and completed the Performance Anxiety Questionnaire (Cox & Kenardy, 1993) and a modified version of the Competitive State Anxiety Inventory (Martens *et al.*, 1990). Results showed that musicians experience high levels of anxiety and are generally more likely to interpret their anxiety as debilitative. However, those who reported high self-confidence were more likely to report their anxiety as facilitative. Perceived control over internal anxiety reactions, but not external events, was associated with lower intensities for both somatic and cognitive anxiety. Cortisol levels did not predict anxiety intensity or interpretation of anxiety as either facilitative or debilitative. Of interest was the finding that there was no relationship between any of these factors and performance outcome. More research is needed to clarify this relationship (Liston, Frost, & Mohr, 2003; McCormick & McPherson, 2003).

Goal setting

Goal setting theory states that the setting of specific challenging goals enhances performance. Like most other psychological relationships, the goal–performance relationship is not simple and many factors intervene to affect performance outcomes. Two key factors include the nature of the goal chosen and the person's self-efficacy or confidence that the goal can be attained. People with low self-efficacy may be less likely to choose or commit to a high-level goal compared with those high in self-efficacy who will choose increasingly higher-level goals after goal attainment. Factors that influence choice of goal include, but are not limited to, the degree of choice the person has in choosing the goal, the complexity of the tasks required to be performed, and the amount of effort and persistence required to achieve the goal (Latham & Locke, 2007). Teacher or parent behavior at the stage in goal attainment is also important. For example, in the early stages of learning, encouraging people to do their best has a more salutary effect on performance than specific goal setting. Setting interim or proximal goals and receiving feedback on those goals help to calibrate realistic longer-term goals that are both challenging and achievable (Latham & Locke, 2007). Framing a goal positively, that is, as achievable, increases the probability of goal attainment compared with negative framing of goals as difficult and unlikely to be achieved. Positive framing of errors as inevitable in the learning process has the same enhancing effect on performance compared with the more negative effect of framing errors as events that should be avoided (Andersen, 2009).

Goal orientation exerts a significant impact on goal attainment. People with a learning goal orientation focus on task mastery; errors are viewed as necessary and intrinsic to the process of learning. Those with a performance goal orientation choose tasks that will make them look good; they will avoid tasks they believe they cannot perform well (Horvath *et al.*, 2006). Striving to achieve learning goals results in superior performance compared with achieving performance goals, including failure avoidance (Heimerdinger & Hinsz, 2008).

Finally, and unsurprisingly, goal setting and goal attainment have an impact on subjective well-being. It appears that we humans love a challenge, because research has shown that goal attainment only enhances well-being if the goal was perceived to be difficult to attain (Cho, 2007). Sports researchers have known this for some time, because they have defined the characteristics of a worthwhile goal under the mnemonic SCRAM (i.e. the goal should be specific, challenging, realistic, acceptable, and measurable) (Mahoney, 1992).

Goal setting in music performance

In one of the only studies of its kind, Lacaille, Whipple, and Koestner (2005) applied to elite athletes and musicians the trichotomous theory of goal achievement (Elliot & Thrash, 2002) that was developed in the educational setting and found to predict achievement in the educational domain. The theory proposes two main types of goals—mastery goals and performance goals. Mastery goals pertain to the development of the requisite skills for the task. Performance goals are of two types—performance approach goals ('I want to have a perfect performance; I want to impress others; I want to do well relative to others'), which are directed toward the attainment of success and performance avoidance goals (e.g. 'I want to avoid making mistakes; I want to perform without embarrassing myself; I don't want to be the worst performer'), whose aims are to avoid failure. In the educational setting, mastery and performance approach goals are helpful to students, predicting task engagement and grade aspirations, while performance avoidance goals are detrimental and were associated with test anxiety and higher perceived threat. Lacaille *et al.* (2005) hypothesized that a focus on performance goals might not be helpful to musicians because of the high prevalence and frequency of performance anxiety in that profession. They speculated that non-achievement goals such as the intrinsic enjoyment of the music and being absorbed by the musical experience might be more helpful to anxious musicians.

Lacaille *et al.* (2005) compared 112 swimmers with 86 musicians aged between 14 and 30. Participants were asked to recall a peak performance and a catastrophic performance and then to complete a 12-item questionnaire on goals for their performance, based on Elliot and Thrash (2002). Musicians reported experiencing more anxiety than swimmers; they also reported that anxiety impaired their performance while swimmers reported performance-enhancing effects of anxiety. Musicians reported much higher anxiety during catastrophic performances than swimmers. There were no gender differences. For both groups, mastery goals were more likely to be associated with optimal performance. However, with regard to the performance goals, the results for swimmers and musicians diverged. Swimmers were supported by performance approach goals and undermined by performance avoidance goals. Musicians, however, were undermined by both types of performance goals and both were associated with catastrophic performances. Musicians benefited from focus on intrinsic goals that were unrelated to achievement, such as enjoying the music. These researchers concluded that pre-performance routines that focus on aesthetics and enjoyment while minimizing achievement goals were likely to be most supportive of musicians' performances. Interestingly, a similar approach has been recommended for actors. Since thinking negative thoughts produces physiological changes in the body, the Stanislavski School of acting recommends the focusing of thoughts away from negativity as one method during performance to control performance anxiety (Stanislavski & Rumyantsev, 1975).

Practice

The importance of good practice habits has received attention from many pedagogues (Davidson, 2004; Flesch, 1939; Fredrickson, 2002; Spohr, 1833). This is an important question because elite musicians spend an average of four hours per day in deliberate, concentrated practice (Ericsson *et al.*, 1993). Louis Spohr (1833), an eminent violin teacher, was one of the first to advocate that beginners should avoid unsupervised practice at commencement of training and recommended daily lessons with a teacher for the first few months to establish correct techniques and to avoid cultivation of bad habits. It is hard to imagine this being possible in today's world of competing commitments and economic constraints. However, the point is that it is easier to create good habits from the beginning than to undo bad habits once established. Rest breaks during practice and a gradual increase of practice duration should be part of the practice routine. Some teachers have recommended afternoon naps as a way of maintaining mental alertness in more accomplished students who are working towards a major performance and who are practicing several hours daily (Ericsson *et al.*, 1993). The physical health of the musician has been increasingly recognized as an area of concern (Ackermann, 2002). Performance-related musculoskeletal disorders occur and/or may become chronic as a result of sudden increases in practice time or intensity (Brandfonbrener, 2000; Horvath, 2002; Norris, 2000); routinely practicing for too long (Culf, 1998); practicing when already tired (Lieberman, 1991); or returning to practice too rapidly after an injury or without sufficient rehabilitation (Norris, 1993). It is also important that the period of rest used by performers following injuries or heavy workloads be appropriate, with excessive rest potentially being counterproductive because it reduces physical fitness and skill levels (Wynn Parry, 1998). Each instrument type has specific recommendations for practice routines. For example, a professional woodwind instrumentalist would split practice time into three segments: (i) work on tone (including sonority exercises); (ii) work on technique (including scales and studies); and (iii) work on music and scores (including orchestral excerpts and repertoire) (Crawford, 2003). Clear links between interpretative goals and the development of playing techniques are also an integral part of the practice routine. In order to give a successful performance, preparation includes conceiving of the performance in the player's mind well ahead of the performance date. Performers need to imagine how they would like the work to sound in the acoustic of the performance venue and for the particular audience for whom it will be performed (Fortune, 2007). There is a self-evident link between inadequate practice and music performance anxiety.

Pre-performance routines

Individuals take in cues from the environment and from their own movements to aid their performance. Preparing all aspects of the performance is helpful because performers have a finite capacity to attend to all the relevant cues in the performance setting. As arousal or somatic or cognitive anxiety increases, the range of cues to which one can attend reduces (Easterbrook, 1959). This is not necessarily problematic, as we discussed with respect to the misinterpretation of the Yerkes–Dodson Law in Chapter Six. However, at some individually optimal level of arousal, the most effective combination of attention to relevant cues seems to exist. Reduction in the use of appropriate cues will result in deterioration in performance quality. This process is called perceptual narrowing (Kahneman, 1973). High cognitive anxiety can result in preoccupation with extraneous stimuli (e.g. negative self-talk, focus on audience reactions) that are irrelevant to the performance task and which interfere with the attention needed to meet the challenges of the task. Hence, performance preparation such as visiting the venue and practicing in the performance setting may be helpful to anxious performers. Integrating performance setting cues into performance preparation reduces the demands on attention on the day of the performance. This may improve confidence, lower anxiety and enhance performance quality. Most musicians have their own instruments, to which they are accustomed. However, pianists must play the piano in the performance venue, and these instruments may have very different acoustic and mechanical properties from their own instrument. Young musicians can be adversely affected by having to accommodate to these differences in an already stressful performance situation. Practicing on the performance piano prior to the audition or recital can sometimes be very valuable in managing anxiety.

Most of the available studies on pre-performance routines have been conducted with athletes, so a brief summary of that literature may be helpful in directing attention to the type and relative usefulness of pre-performance routines for musicians. However, many of these studies are qualitative and have very small numbers of participants, leading to the conclusion that their effect on skilled performance in self-paced skills has yet to be confirmed (Lonsdale & Tam, 2008). Hanton, Wadey, and Mellalieu (2008) conducted in-depth interviews with eight elite athletes to ascertain what effect their pre-performance preparation strategies had on their performance anxiety.

The athletes reported using simulation training, cognitive restructuring, pre-performance routines, and overlearning of skills prior to important competitive events. Participants used each strategy in order to perceive their anxiety as facilitating performance. Cognitive restructuring and overlearning of skills were reported to reduce the cognitive symptoms of anxiety. These pre-performance preparation strategies were perceived to improve attentional focus, effort, and motivation in addition to controlling anxiety. Cotterill, Sanders, and Collins (2010) interviewed six international-level male golfers about their pre-performance routines. Using interpretative phenomenological analysis, the authors identified nine themes whereby pre-performance routines aid stressful competitive performance. These included deciding a priori how to allocate attention, the conscious use of psychological skills to support their performance, developing routines regarding shot selection, and other factors that prepared them for the competition. The nature of the pre-performance routines developed and practiced was dependent on personal and situational factors.

Many athletes and musicians have developed their own pre-performance routines and some contain superstitious behavior that has no instrumental value with respect to the required response. Jackson and Masters (2006) argued that ritualized behaviors in sport are common and occur in addition to or instead of more structured pre-performance routines because 'they provide temporary relief from pre-competition anxiety and act as thought suppressors in the moments preceding skill execution' (p. 621). Some empirical support for this assertion comes from a study that showed that pre-performance routines are effective if they maintain temporal and behavioral consistency (Lonsdale & Tam, 2008). These researchers examined the duration and specific pattern of behaviors exhibited by players before they made a free throw in basketball. Each player's pre-performance routine was documented and, for the target throws, each was classified according to whether players had adhered to the planned sequence or not. Results showed that players were more successful when they followed their dominant behavioral sequence (84% success) than when they deviated from their specific behavioral pattern (71% success). A more recent study with 60 experienced Australian footballers confirmed the role of pre-performance routines in minimizing choking (Mesagno & Mullane-Grant, 2010). The groups receiving pre-performance training in a range of psychological and behavioral components showed better management of increased state anxiety under pressure and improved performance compared with a control group who had received no such training.

Athletes and musicians often engage in superstitious behavior before a high-pressure performance. One study that investigated the effect of superstitious behaviors compared the efficacy of establishing a pre-performance routine with using a well-established routine based on idiosyncratic superstitious behaviors and not allowing players to use any form of pre-performance preparation. Contrary to predictions, the researchers (Foster, Weigand, & Baines, 2006) found no difference in effectiveness between pre-performance routines and superstitious behavior on the target behavior (basketball free throw). However, when the players used no routine at all, performance suffered compared with the structured pre-performance routine or enacting the superstitious behavior. Given the current evidence, it would be inadvisable to interrupt an existing pre-performance routine, even if it has no objective efficacy, if the performer has used it for a long time and believes that it assists performance.

Performance preparation in music performance

Stephanie McCallum, an eminent Australian pianist, described the elements required for the preparation and lead-up to a major solo recital.

> ... the tightrope that is a full-length memorized recital. That's a tightrope for any-one, it doesn't matter if you're Richter, Rostrapovich, or Pavarotti and you've done it 5,000 times. It is a very big outpouring of concentrated intellectual and creative energy. It takes a build-up of preparation, much like a sporting event, you have to peak at the right time. And you have to arrive on the stage in a condition where you're able to shed the physical symptoms of the adrenaline rush, but have the residue of concentration, very unusual high levels of concentration, which make you feel as though you are in a flow state where you're carried along by your brain. So it's partially a physical re-enactment of learned positions controlled by a creative impulse, which is held hostage to absolute con-centration. If your concentration goes, the creative impulse is destroyed because the panic of retaining the physical movements then becomes the major project. So one's goal is to reach a state of preparation where, when you're in this state of concentration, you don't have cut-outs—that is, a serious loss of concentration. It's a mental state of focus, which is like sitting someone down and you're going to tell them a story, and you have the story in your head. You know what it is you want to talk about. You're creating the story as you say it by the sentences that you construct and so on. You're trying to make an impression on the other person with the story, so you're emphasizing some things; you're considering the order in which the things come. It's a bit like that except that it is an infinitely more complex task than that because you're regurgitating an existing phenomenon, another's creation.

Compare Stephanie's description of the state of mind she enters after ideal prepara-tion for a major solo recital and this description of the definition of peak performance outlined in Chapter Six and the flow state:

> ... to achieve a state of complete clarity and purpose, even euphoria, through the capacity to concentrate intensely. It entails the capacity to shut out irrelevant stimuli and focus at great depth on the task at hand, often causing a person to lose the normal sense of time and self in which one is both actor and observer. Csikszentmihalyi believes the pleasure deriving from the flow state has an autonomous reality that must be understood on its own terms. Measurements of brain activity during flow states suggest that the flow may induce a special neurological state that is associated with a decrease in cortical activity (Pruett, 1987, p. 36).

The role of imagery in performance preparation

The spirit is the master, imagination the tool, and the body the plastic material... (Paracelsus, in Hartmann, 1973, p. 112).

In this section, we will briefly consider the role of imagery in teaching, learning, and performance. An image is defined as a recollection of a sensory experience (Günter, 1992); it is used in sport to imagine a desired behavior, such as shooting a goal in football or hitting a bull's eye in archery. Teaching through imagery is based on the idea that students can be assisted with the use of analogies involving similes, meta-phors, or images that may or may not reflect physical reality. The question of imagery has fascinated scholars through the ages. Aristotle, for example, appreciated the role of imagery in goal attainment (McMahon, 1973). The Egyptians believed in the power of visualization to cure disease (Samuels & Samuels, 1987). Today, several psychological practices, such as hypnotherapy, imaginal systematic desensitization, therapies conducted in virtual reality, and cognitive therapy all rely on the ability of patients (Lang, Cuthbert, & Bradley, 1998) and performers to imagine feelings, situations, and events (Holmes, 2005; Magrath, 2003–2004; Sisterhen, 2004).

Vocal pedagogy, by the very nature—both interior and invisible—of the vocal instrument to be trained, has relied on imagery as a central tool in communicating the technique required to achieve a beautiful tone (Tamborrino, 2001). Because of its complexity, vocal pedagogical methods have proliferated. Vennard (1958) attempted to bring some order to these methods and identified six main approaches, which he called demonstration, speech based, learning by singing, inspirational, mechanistic, and imagery. Most pedagogues would use a combination of some or all of these approaches. Learning by demonstration is now understood to work through the triggering of a sympathetic response via firing in the listener mirror neurons that are required to perform the demonstrated task. This effect is called the ideomotor principle, which is defined as the effect of behavioral enhancement that occurs in one's performance as a result of observing the movements of others (Sauser & Billard, 2006).

There has been a great deal of recent interest in the phenomenon of mirror neurons. It has challenged the long-held perspective that learning a new motor skill proceeds from declarative or propositional knowledge (i.e. 'knowledge of' or 'knowledge about' how to do something) to procedural knowledge (i.e. knowing how). Studies of the premotor cortices of monkeys showed that these mirror neurons discharged when the monkey actually executed a specific goal-directed action (i.e. grasping a piece of food) and when it observed the same or a similar action being executed. The same process has been observed in the human brain, not only in the execution of motor tasks but in mirroring emotions observed in other people and in anticipating an emotion such as anxiety. Most anxious people experience anticipatory anxiety whereby imagining being anxious in response to some future event produces similar physiological and physical activation in the body as if the event were actually occur-ring (Wulf & Prinz, 2001).

A recent functional magnetic resonance image (fMRI)[15] study showed that not only are mirror neurons involved in action recognition, motor imagery, and imitation of movements already in the motor behavior repertoire, but that the mirror neuron sys-tem is active in learning novel, complex actions. In this study, people who could not play a musical instrument learnt to play different guitar chords after observing an expert guitarist. Mirror neurons were active from observation of the model to the

---

[15] fMRI (functional magnetic resonance imaging) is a technique that measures the blood flow in the brain, which indicates areas of brain activity.

execution of the complex motor behaviors required to play the chords on the guitar (Buccino & Riggio, 2006). The same neurons activate when a motor behavior is executed, observed, and imagined (Filimon *et al.*, 2007). The Suzuki method of music pedagogy appears to be based on the brain's capacity both to learn novel behaviors through observation and to imitate existing behaviors. Humans can imitate from infancy but as yet, no specific neural substrate has been identified to account for this ability, although some researchers propose that actions may be represented in sensory format (Stocker & Hoffmann, 2004).

The research on mirror neurons supports the view, dating back to the great Italian master, Tosi, that one can produce a tone quality only as beautiful as one can imagine, suggesting that 'aural thought' triggers the vocal mechanism required to produce the desired sound (Patenaude-Yarnell, 2003). The inspirational approach also relies to some extent on imagery, since it encourages the singer to respond emotionally to the music via the imagination, which is stimulated by the lyrics and music, hence enhancing vocal quality (Günter, 1992). The debate between mechanistic (scientific) and empirical approaches continues today, with those favoring the empirical approach rejecting the mechanistic approach because, firstly, knowledge of vocal physiology does not produce a beautiful voice, and secondly, much of the musculature required for vocal production is out of conscious control. Empiricists favor an approach based on imagery that assists the student to access the correct vocal mechanisms required to produce certain sound qualities. This imagery may or may not be based on anatomical reality. Students may be assisted by using imagery to recollect previous sensory events or, indeed, produce new sensations that may subsequently assist vocal production (Ihasz & Parmer, 2006). Indeed, the ubiquitous use of terms like 'chest voice' and 'head voice' are nothing more than vocal images of the location of sound production and do not represent physiological reality (Burgin, 1973).

Recently, Moorcroft (2011) demonstrated the powerful performance-enhancing effects of imagery on vibrato characteristics in female classical singers. In her study, six female singers in the Western classical tradition recorded an eight-bar solo before and after three 25-minute interventions—a breathing imagery intervention, a Braille music code imagery intervention which involved the use of Braille script employed in the reading of music by the visually impaired which produced tactile, kinesthetic, and visual imagery related to music but unrelated to breath function; the third task was a non-imagery breath-related activity that required the completion of a cloze passage about breath function for singers. Acoustic and perceptual changes to the quality of the vibrato in the voices of the participating singers were assessed by the singers themselves and by a group of expert judges. The breathing imagery condition, but not the other two conditions, improved vibrato rate, bringing it closer to the 'ideal' rate; singers also perceived a better vocal quality and felt more warmed up in the breathing imagery condition. Judges were inconsistent in their ratings, as they are so often found to be in many studies of vocal quality (Kenny & Mitchell, 2007; Ryan & Kenny, 2009).

Studies of the use of imagery in sports performance show that imagery may influence warming up (Rushall & Lippman, 1998), performance anxiety (Hall *et al.*, 1998; Moritz, Hall, Martin, & Vadocz, 1996), and performance quality and outcome

(Barr & Hall, 1992; De Francesco & Burke, 1997). In music performance, motor imagery associated with simultaneous technical and emotional input can help to embed information securely in the memory. Introducing a more imaginative approach into performance practice has potential benefits for both motivation and memory retention (Holmes, 2005). Imagery may also assist less confident performers achieve heightened mental focus and a clearer perception of 'the perfect performance,' which may facilitate enhanced performance (Hall, 1995; Moritz *et al.*, 1996). Imagery may also enhance emotional connection with the music in performance (Peterson, 2000b) or the auditory, visual and, proprioceptive senses required for optimum technical function (Dunbar-Wells, 1999).

Pre-performance imagery may assist in focusing the mind on a thought or sensation that the performer associates with confidence. Others focus on the breath to calm anxiety and reduce automatic stress-related responses. These strategies serve simultaneously to distract the performer from the inner monologue of self-doubting and catastrophizing thoughts that can impair a performance (Liston *et al.*, 2003; Zinn, McCain, & Zinn, 2000). While imagery may be a useful tool in the performance preparation toolbox, it is not a substitute for solid, consistent practice to achieve mastery over the physical demands of the task at hand. Once the requisite competence has been achieved, confidence that one can perform the task at an optimal level under pressure appears to be one of the most important factors that contributes to consistently optimal performance (Moritz *et al.*, 1996). Below is an example of how a young bassoonist described her preparation for an audition, incorporating imagery into her protocol.

> Next week I am doing an audition. The required work is Stravinsky's Rite of Spring. It opens with a really high bassoon solo and nothing else is happening and it starts off very quietly. It's one of those pieces that everyone knows and it's a major bassoon excerpt when you do auditions, so it will be a stressful situation. I'm in the process of preparing for that now. I use a lot of visualization. While I practise it I imagine sitting in the hall doing the audition behind the screen and because I am doing it during my practice, I hope it won't feel like such a strange feeling when I get there.

Mental practice

A special form of imagery is mental practice, which is the imaginal or covert rehearsal of a skill in the absence of motor production of that skill (Ross, 1985). Mental practice presupposes mastery of the required motor skills and can be a useful adjunct, but never a substitute for motor practice. The less advanced the student and the more technically difficult the repertoire to be learnt, the more important is motor practice (Gabrielsson, 1999). Research in musical mental practice generally finds that mental practice is better than no practice, and that a combination of physical and mental practice appears to yield the best performance results. In one study of the effects of practice type (physical, mental, alternating physical/mental, and a motivational control) on piano performance in college musicians all three practice conditions required shorter learning times than the control condition. Physical and physical/mental practice were more efficient than mental practice alone (Coffman, 1990). Similar results were reported in a study of trombone students (Ross, 1985). In highly skilled musicians such as conductors, EMG patterns during mental rehearsal closely resembled EMG patterns during actual performance; similarly, in performers, mental imagery produced muscle activity in muscles required to execute the actual movements (Gabrielsson, 1999).

Research in clinical rehabilitation of stroke patients indicates that mental rehearsal facilitates physical practice, and that high rates of mental rehearsal were better than physical rehearsal alone (Allami, Paulignan, Brovelli, & Boussaoud, 2008). In a qualitative study of preparation and performance strategies used by elite pentathletes, content analysis of interviews showed that mental preparation was an important part of their routine. This took the form of competition simulation, mental practice, goal setting, emotion control, behavioral routines, specific technical strategies, attentional strategies, reaction to mistakes, and post-competition self-assessment (Bertollo, Saltarelli, & Robazza, 2009). Although there are, as yet, no empirical studies on the effect of mental practice as a strategy to reduce music performance anxiety by replacing negative cognitions prior to a performance with mental practice, it would seem a fruitful area to explore.

Pharmacotherapy for anxiety disorders

It is common knowledge within the music industry through international surveys and anecdotally that the use of drugs and other substances to manage performance anxiety occurs frequently. Because of the ethical constraints now in place to protect research participants, most of the available studies that assess the effects of particular classes of drugs on performing artists were conducted up to 30 years ago and many were not of the standard that is expected of research today, so conclusions from these studies need to be viewed cautiously.

In order to consider the proper role of pharmacotherapy for music performance anxiety, some understanding of the neuropsychology of anxiety would be helpful. This is a complex and difficult topic and space allows only for a summary of the main issues. For a more detailed treatment of the subject, interested readers are referred to Gray and McNaughton (2000). The primary thesis of this work is that anxiolytic (i.e. anti-anxiety) medication acts on the brain's septo-hippocampal system by impairing subcortical control of hippocampal 'theta' (rhythmical burst firing of cells) activity, which is this system's primary response to external arousal. Excess activity in the septo-hippocampal system will elevate the perception of environmental threat and increase the number of fear-arousing associations to these threats. There are other brain systems (i.e. neural networks) in addition to the hippocampal system responsible for theta activity and anxiolytic medications act on some, but not all of these systems. Further, there are many different types of arousal but not all are related to the generation of anxiety. However, some form of arousal is a necessary but not sufficient condition for the generation of anxiety.

Animal studies have shown that anxiolytic drugs produce the same behavioral effects as those seen in animals with lesions (damage) to the septo-hippocampal system (McNaughton & Gray, 2000), which is theorized to be the principal neural substrate of the behavioral inhibition system. This system is activated by conflict-generating stimuli such as punishment, the absence of reward when one was expected (called non-reward or extinction), novel stimuli (especially those that stimulate both curiosity and fear), and innate fear-inducing stimuli. The behavioral inhibition system processes and assesses each of these forms of stimuli before attempting to resolve the conflict through behavioral inhibition, increased arousal, or increased attention (Gray & McNaughton, 2000). Animal studies have led to the identification of a distinction between fear-related behaviors such as fight or flight, which occur under conditions of immediate threat (in the case of animals, the introduction of a predator into the field), and which permit an animal to leave the field, and anxiety-related behaviors, which in animal studies occur when a predator may or may not be present and the animal must engage in risk assessment to assess the level of danger, thus requiring the animal to enter a potentially threatening field. Blanchard, Griebel, Henrie, and Blanchard (1997) showed that fear and anxiety (as defined above) produce different behaviors associated with the degree of threat. Interestingly, Gray and McNaughton (2000) found that anxiolytic drugs affect anxiety-related behaviors but not the fear-related behaviors of avoidance, flight, and freezing.

The amygdala also has an important role to play in fear conditioning, as we discovered in Chapter Two, and is considered one of the higher centers of the hierarchical defensive system. The complex interplay between these brain systems is associated with unique behavioral tendencies. For example, activation of the amygdala alone produces a 'pure' fear response; activation of the hippocampus alone results in anxious rumination; activation of both the amygdala and hippocampus results in the constellation of behaviors that we call anxiety. The amygdala can also affect the septo-hippocampal system by its capacity to increase arousal (McNaughton & Gray, 2000).

Pharmacotherapy for music performance anxiety

Beta-blockers

Gates *et al.* (1985), Lehrer (1987), and Nubé (1991) have published reviews of the impact of beta-blockers on music performance anxiety and a brief overview of other drugs, such as anxiolytics (i.e. anti-anxiety) and antidepressants has been provided by Sataloff, Rosen, and Levy (2000). Packer and Packer (2005), although more recent, is only a case report with a summary of previous research. Harris (2001) reviews the use of beta-blockers in dancers. It is difficult to obtain an accurate estimate of the number of musicians using beta-blockers but several reports suggest the figure to be around 20%–30% (Fishbein *et al.*, 1988). Most musicians who report using beta-blockers use them for auditions, solo recitals, concerto performances, and difficult orchestral performances.

When people become stressed, the body produces a number of hormones, such as norepinephrine (noradrenaline) and epinephrine (adrenaline), which attach to adrenergic receptor sites, thus producing the physiological responses typical of an anxiety state. There are two types of receptor sites: alpha-receptors, which affect smooth muscle such as the intestines and constriction of blood vessels, and beta-receptors that affect skeletal muscle, causing trembling, shaking, or tremor, increased heart rate and dilatation of the bronchial tubes and blood vessels. There are two types of beta receptors, called beta-1, affecting the heart, and beta-2, that affect peripheral circulation and bronchi (Brandfonbrener, 1990). Beta-blockers bind to beta-adrenoceptors and block the binding of noradrenaline and adrenaline to these receptors, thereby blocking the physical effects of the fight-or-flight response, discussed in Chapter Two.

Beta-blockers were designed and developed for use in people with cardiac problems or following myocardial infarctions (heart attacks) to reduce or block the effects of the sympathetic arousal of the heart, including the lowering of blood pressure and cardiac output, in order to reduce the strain on the damaged heart muscle. The effect of beta-blockers is related to dose and individual sensitivity to the medication. The peak effect occurs at between one to one and a half hours after consumption. Beta-blockers have no sedative or calmative effect on the emotional symptoms or psychological effects of anxiety, such as sleep disturbance (although they can make you very sleepy), negative self-talk, or worry and rumination.

There is a wide range of beta-blockers available and these different forms of the drug have different effects on the different beta-receptor sites in the body. Metoprolol (Lopresor) and atenolol (Tenormin), for example, are beta-1 selective, which means they block only beta-1 receptors found primarily in the heart, but not the beta-2 receptors found in the smooth muscles in the lung and uterus. Beta-1-receptive beta-blockers act to decrease blood pressure, heart rate, and force of cardiac contraction. The beta-2 receptor-blocking drugs are preferred in the treatment of music performance anxiety, as opposed to the primarily cardioselective beta-blocking drugs. Propranolol (Inderal) is a beta-adrenoreceptor blocking agent which acts non-selectively on beta-receptors (β1 and β2) (MIMS, 2006). Inderal crosses the blood–brain barrier more easily than other forms of the drug, and thus may produce unwanted central nervous system side effects, such as mild lassitude, insomnia, and visual disturbances in 2% of patients. More serious side effects include severe nightmares and hallucinations. Psychiatric complications (depression, psychoses, psychotic reactions, and acute confusional states) may occasionally occur but are unlikely to be severe. It would, however, be wise to restrict treatment in patients who have suffered previous depressive illness (MIMS, 2006).

Because many of the somatic symptoms of performance anxiety are mediated through the activation of the sympathetic nervous system, beta-blockers have become increasingly popular among performers in recent years. In small doses, which minimize side-effects, Inderal appears to be the drug of choice for the management of performance anxiety (Brandfonbrener, 1990). Although now commonly used to assist people with severe performance anxiety, this usage is not listed in the MIMS as an indicator. However, available research shows that its use is widespread. For example, a survey of 2,122 orchestral musicians conducted by Lockwood found that 27% used propranolol to manage their anxiety prior to a performance; 19% of this group used the drug on a daily basis (Lockwood, 1989). In as yet unpublished research, a study of a sample of 357 orchestral musicians from the eight premier orchestras in Australia showed that 30% (n = 106) reported using beta-blockers to relieve their music performance anxiety. Of these, 45.5% reported that it was the most frequently or second most frequently used of their strategies to manage their music performance anxiety; 67% of the sample who used beta-blockers rated them as 'very effective' in controlling their symptoms, with a further 25% rating them as 'quite effective.' Only 5% (n = 18) reported using medications (e.g. Ativan®, Xanax®) other than beta-blockers to help control their music performance anxiety; 4% reported using antidepressants.

Beta-blockers appear to be most effective for those musicians who report primarily somatic manifestations of their anxiety (e.g. palpitations, hyperventilation, tremor, trembling lips, sweating palms, etc.) (Gates *et al.*, 1985; James & Savage, 1984) and less effective for those experiencing more cognitive or psychological effects, such as low self-esteem, social phobias, or generalized 'free floating' anxiety (Lehrer *et al.*, 1990). However, there is no clear indication that such drugs improve judge ratings of quality of performance (Brantigan, Brantigan, & Joseph, 1982; Gates *et al.*, 1985; James, Burgoyne, & Savage, 1983), although a more recent study found they did improve performance quality (Berens & Ostrosky, 1988) but not self-reported anxiety (Brantigan *et al.*, 1982) or stage fright ratings (Neftel *et al.*, 1982).

Nubé (1991) concluded that beta-blockers can be useful for specific impacts of performance anxiety such as the tremulous bow arm in string players, which inter-feres with both bow control and the quality of vibrato and hence tone quality of the instrument. However, he, like others (Packer & Packer, 2005), cautions that there is a cost–benefit effect in the use of beta-blockers for performers since they may also have adverse effects on other components of a performance such as rhythmic control and emotional connection to the music. Titrating the dose to precisely achieve the needed effects while minimizing the unwanted effects is very important, given the evidence that low doses may improve performance by managing problematic somatic manifes-tations while higher doses impaired performance in a sample of professional singers (Gates *et al.*, 1985). Sataloff, Rosen, and Levy (2000) cautioned against the use of beta-blockers for singers and wind instrumentalists, stating that these musicians require a similar level of stamina to athletes, including respiratory exertion that is 'sapped' by beta-blockers. Similarly, Packer and Packer (2005) identified a specific issue associated with regular prolonged use of beta-blockers and string players. In their case study report of a 26-year-old violinist who was prescribed atenolol (25 mg per day) for hypertension, it became increasingly difficult for him to sustain his vibrato technique or to produce a controlled vibrato. A music medicine specialist discontinued the atenolol and replaced it with an angiotensin-converting enzyme inhibitor for the hypertension, which led to a rapid improvement in this violinist's vibrato technique. Similar discussions regarding individual cases have occurred in instrument specific journals (Dalrymple, 2005).

Beta-blockers should only be used with medical supervision. The ICSOM study (Fishbein *et al.*, 1988) showed that those musicians taking beta-blockers for severe performance anxiety under medical supervision reported beneficial effects of the drug twice as frequently as those who were using these medications without medical super-vision (92% vs 46%). Further, beta-blockers should be viewed as a short-term adjunct to support those with severe music performance anxiety. If the anxiety is severe enough to require regular use, individuals should seek psychological treatment to assist with self-managing their condition. Beta-blockers are definitely contra-indicated in people with some heart conditions, asthma, diabetes, and Raynaud's syndrome. There are potential difficulties with drug withdrawal and unwanted side effects. Symptoms that have been reported in at least 10% of users include bradycardia, hypotension, cold extremities, gastrointestinal upset, sleep disturbance, and muscle fatigue. Some of the side effects of regular beta-blocker use are of particular relevance to musicians. In addition to the list given, these include dizziness, fatigue, headache, depression, short-term memory loss, dry mouth, muscle pain, and cramps. Long-term regular use may cause physical dependence, thus necessitating higher doses over time to achieve the same effects (Sasso, 2010). Propanolol can also exacerbate depression in vulnerable individuals (Steffenmeir, Ernst, Kelly, & Hartz, 2006).

Musicians need to understand that beta-blockers do not enhance musical performance. They relieve the problematic somatic symptoms that may impair performance quality, thus allowing the musician to play technically as well as their preparation has allowed. For example, beta-blockers reduce dry mouth in brass players and tremor in string players. These are physiological manifestations of anxiety that impair performance. By removing or reducing these troublesome effects, musicians will be able to play their instruments as well as they do under less stressful conditions where such symptoms do not arise. On the other hand, the dampening down of autonomic arousal may also dampen one's emotional response to the music and some musicians report not achieving the same level of commitment or intensity in their performances if they have taken a beta-blocker prior to the performance. Further, musicians whose performance anxiety is expressed primarily through emotional or cognitive symptoms cannot expect to benefit from beta-blockers. They will need to undertake some form of psychological therapy to obtain relief.

The debate about the advantages and disadvantages of beta-blocker use for music performance anxiety continues to be lively. The *New York Times* ran an article on the subject in 2004, presenting a story about the sacking of a flute teacher in Rhodes College in Memphis in 2003 for recommending the use of propanolol (Inderal) to her adult flute students, who suffered debilitating performance anxiety, as she had done until she commenced treatment with the drug (Tindall, 2004). The same article was reprinted a year later in the music journal, *The Horn Call* (Tindall, 2005). A more cautious appraisal of the role of beta-blockers and other drugs in performance management appeared a year later in the *International Musician* (Cox, 2006). Lederman (1999) summarized the arguments for and against the use of beta-blockers by performing artists, and realistically states that if the anxiety is truly debilitating, beta-blockers must be considered a viable treatment for the very distressed musician. I would add a caution here that the nature of the anxiety must be carefully assessed and, as stated earlier, if the anxiety is based in characterological dysfunction or is primarily cognitive in nature, beta-blockers are unlikely to effect any benefits for the performer. Birk (2004) cautions against the use of beta-blockers for specific phobias and performance anxiety because both specific phobia and performance anxiety are learned, while conceding benefits for most of the other types of anxiety disorders, such as generalized anxiety disorder and social anxiety disorder, which have been shown to have a strong heritable component and atypical brain function. The argument is that learned anxieties can only be extinguished by exposure, and the use of beta-blockers and benzodiazepines actually inhibit exposure and hence extinction (or reduction) of the anxiety response. You will recall our previous discussion that in music performance anxiety, avoidance is a much rarer coping strategy than for other anxiety disorders—musicians tend to face the music more doggedly than people with social anxiety face their social fears. Nevertheless, the essential argument is that CBT with exposure is currently considered best practice for the treatment of performance anxiety and that simultaneous use of beta-blockers or benzodiazepines would interfere with this therapeutic intervention.

Other prescription medications

It is unlikely that further studies of drug effects on music performance anxiety will be undertaken because ethical standards for research are much more rigorous than they were 30 to 40 years ago when these drug studies were conducted. This is a pity given the high usage of drug therapies by anxious musicians. However, there have been some well-controlled studies for social anxiety and a range of drugs have been assessed for efficacy for this condition. Given that music performance anxiety appears to have some characteristics in common and to be frequently comorbid with this condition, a short discussion of drug therapies for social anxiety would be useful. The most frequently used drug treatments for social anxiety are:

i monoamine oxidase inhibitors (MAOI) (antidepressant)

ii selective serotonin reuptake inhibitors (SSRIs) (antidepressant)

iii tricyclic and other antidepressants

iv benzodiazepines (tranquilizers, sedatives, hypnotics, muscle relaxants)

v beta-blockers.

In one methodologically robust study, Heimberg et al.(1998) assessed the relative efficacy of cognitive behavioral group therapy (CBGT), phenelzine (MAOI) therapy, educative-supportive group therapy (ES), and placebo. At the end of 12 weeks of therapy, those receiving CBGT and MAOI were equal in terms of improvement but superior to both ES and placebo conditions. However, at six-month follow-up, CBGT was superior to MAOI treatment, with 91% maintaining treatment gains in the CBGT group compared with 50% in the MAOI group.

Research evidence on the other drug classes listed in the previous paragraph are limited, although one study showed promising results for paroxetine (SSRI) and two studies showed benefits for clonazepam (benzodiazepine). However, both drugs have a risk of physical dependence, and discontinuation of the drug therapy resulted in high relapse rates. Similar conclusions were drawn for the use of tricyclic antidepressants in the treatment of social anxiety, although some studies reported benefit if participants clearly met criteria for the diagnosis (Ipser, Kariuki, & Stein, 2008). By way of clarification, it is important to state that there are many effective antidepressant medications for the treatment of depression (SSRIs, MAOIs, tricyclic antidepressants), and anxious musicians should be carefully assessed for comorbid depression. If present, prescription of an antidepressant may be helpful in improving overall psychological well-being. In the absence of depression, prescription of such medications for performance anxiety is not indicated since there have been no controlled studies of efficacy for their use in the management of music performance anxiety (Sasso, 2010). Similarly, and despite initial enthusiasm for the use of beta-blockers to treat social anxiety, their efficacy has not been supported by a number of studies, which showed that results were no better than placebo. However, the effects of beta-blockers may be better for people with non-generalized social phobia (which may parallel some forms of music performance anxiety) (Barlow, 2002a).

The evidence is accumulating against recommending the use of benzodiazepines and antidepressants for the treatment of performance anxiety (Birk, 2004). The benzodiazepines that include alprazolam (Xanax®), lorezapam (Ativan®), clonezapam (Klonopin®, Rivotril), diazepam (Valium) have well-documented side effects such as sedation, dizziness, and weakness, which are all anathema to a performing artist, in addition to longer-term problems such as tolerance and physiological addiction (Sasso, 2010). Performers themselves have reported a preference for beta-adrenoceptor blocking agents to anxiolytic drugs (e.g. diazepam) because of their reduced impact on central functions such as mental alertness and cognitive function (Lockwood, 1989).

In one of the more methodologically robust drug studies that used a double-blind, crossover design with placebo for music performance anxiety, assessing the relative benefits of nadolol and diazepam in a group of 33 tertiary-level music students, James and Savage (1984) found that nadolol reduced the rise in pulse rate caused by anxiety and improved those aspects of string playing that are adversely affected by tremor. However, neither drug influenced the subjective level of anxiety. Additionally, diazepam was associated with deterioration in performance quality. The authors concluded that beta-blockers can make a significant contribution to managing anxiety-induced disturbances of performance related to tremor, coordination, and judgment and are to be preferred over benzodiazapines.

Self-administered substances

Alcohol

> For many artists, actors and musicians, alcohol becomes their rocket fuel. And it eventually can burn them up. It didn't get me because . . . I suddenly became frightened of where I was going—down to Hell in a wheelbarrow (Anthony Hopkins).[16]

It is difficult to find the right place in a book of this nature for a discussion of the use of alcohol to control anxiety. However, since many musicians resort to alcohol in the hope that it will 'steady' their nerves, a paragraph of caution is warranted. Although we have survey evidence that many performing artists use alcohol and marihuana to manage their performance anxiety, there have been no formal studies into the effects of these substances on the quality of musical performance. Suffice it to say that the thousands of studies available on the impairing effects of these substances on many aspects of cognitive function, such as problem solving and complex behaviors like driving, indicate that musicians can expect no positive benefits for their music performance or health in general from the frequent use of such substances.

A number of epidemiological studies have established a strong link between alcohol use, alcoholism, and the anxiety disorders. For example, in 80% of cases of comorbid social anxiety disorder (SAD) and alcohol dependence, SAD had preceded the development of alcohol dependence. Comorbid SAD was also associated with greater severity of

---

[16] Cited in Falk (1989, p. 99).

alcohol dependence and abuse. However, and for reasons that are not clear, very few people with this comorbid presentation actually seek treatment (Schneier *et al.*, 2010). There are a number of explanations for the co-occurrence of these two disorders, but the obvious one is that people believe that the use of alcohol will reduce anxiety. In an interesting test of this hypothesis, Himle *et al.* (1999) found that alcohol did not, in fact, improve performance in socially challenging situations, such as giving a speech, in socially anxious individuals. A number of measures of social anxiety—subjective anxiety ratings, heart rate, and positive and negative cognitions—did not differ between the group receiving alcohol and the group receiving a placebo. These results were not influenced by previous drinking history. However, participants who believed that they had received alcohol prior to the task had lower ratings on negative self-perceptions than those who did not believe they had consumed alcohol prior to the task. One possible explanation for this finding is that people who believe that they received alcohol could externalize the reason for a poor performance to the alcohol rather than to any shortfall in themselves. The impairing effects of alcohol are well known, both in the short term, following excessive consumption or intoxication, and in the longer term, for habitual problematic drinkers. Short term deficits include decrements in verbal fluency, visuospatial skills, components of declarative memory, and psychomotor speed, which, with long-term use, may become permanent (Green *et al.*, 2010). Long term overuse of alcohol irreversibly damages the body's organs, particularly the liver and the brain.

Nicotine

Once begun, smoking is a notoriously difficult habit to break (Heishman, Kleykamp, & Singleton, 2010). Space does not permit a review of the well-documented health hazards of ingesting nicotine, including cancers in multiple organs, heart disease, lung diseases, vascular disease, hazards to unborn babies, and premature skin ageing (World Health Organization Study Group, 2007). Research has been undertaken to better understand the maintenance of smoking behavior, which appears to be at least partly related to the enhancement of arousal, attention, mood, cognition, and memory, and hence performance on speed and processing in information-processing tasks (Knott *et al.*, 2009). At low doses, nicotine stimulates the release of beta-endorphins, which are associated with a sense of calm and well-being. At high doses, nicotine prompts the release of noradrenaline, adrenaline and dopamine, which enhance both alertness and relaxation. Nicotine enhances memory via the increased release of two neurotransmitters involved with memory function, acetylcholine and vasopressin. However, all these effects are short lived (between 15 and 60 minutes); in order to maintain these transitory benefits of nicotine, continual ingestion of the substance is required. Nicotine withdrawal causes difficulty in concentrating and this is accompanied by deficits in task performance (American Psychiatric Association, 2000). Such effects have been observed in the laboratory between 30 and 120 minutes following onset of tobacco deprivation (Heishman *et al.*, 2010).

A recent meta-analysis of the acute effects of nicotine and smoking on human performance (Heishman *et al.*, 2010) has confirmed that nicotine exerts positive effects on fine motor skills, alerting attention accuracy and response time, orienting attention response time, short-term episodic memory accuracy, and working memory, with effect sizes ranging from 0.16 (weak) to 0.44 (moderate). The authors concluded that the beneficial cognitive effects of nicotine are likely to play a significant role in the initiation of smoking and maintenance of tobacco dependence.

I am not aware of any studies documenting the use of nicotine in anxious musicians, particularly pre performance. I hope that this brief exposition will be sufficient to dissuade musicians from consideration of its use. There are healthier alternatives to nicotine dependency, including regular aerobic exercise, which also increases the release of beta-endorphins, acetylcholine, and adrenaline. Aerobic exercise produces a relaxed alert state similar to that achieved from ingestion of nicotine; but unlike smoking, exercise does not simultaneously carry the serious risks of harm that smoking does (Rendi, Szabo, Szabo, Velenczei, & Kovacs, 2008).

Caffeine

Caffeine is a psycho stimulant chemical found in coffee, tea, soft drinks, and energy drinks and is the most widely used drug in the world (Astorino & Roberson, 2010), with 80% of Americans reporting daily consumption (Hammond & Gold, 2008). A number of studies have reported that caffeine has a positive impact on mood (Lara, 2010), cognitive function, particularly for longer, more difficult tasks involving low arousal (Lara, 2010), but also including selective attention, immediate and working memory (Adan & Serra-Grabulosa, 2010; Addicott & Laurienti, 2009), rapid visual processing and performance, including manual dexterity, psychomotor performance as indicated by a finger-tapping task (Harrell & Juliano, 2009), reaction times (Addicott & Laurienti, 2009), and muscular output and physical endurance in short-term exercise, particularly in elite athletes who do not normally ingest caffeine (Astorino & Roberson, 2010). The effects of caffeine on the attentional functions of alerting and executive control occur in a dose-response manner (up to 200 mg) (Brunye, Mahoney, Lieberman, & Taylor, 2010). Caffeine has therefore come to be regarded as a pharmacological tool to increase energy and effortful behavior in daily activities (Lara, 2010). However, the relationship between caffeine, mood, cognition, and performance is complex. Under varying conditions and tasks, it may have facilitatory or inhibitory effects on memory and learning; for example, it appears to aid passive but not intentional learning; tasks involving limited working memory but not tasks that depend heavily on working memory; with no effect on long-term memory. At low doses, caffeine improves mood and reduces anxiety, but at high doses, it increases arousal, including anxiety (Nehlig, 2010). Nehlig (2010) concluded that caffeine's indirect action on arousal, mood, and concentration contributed to its apparently cognitive-enhancing properties.

As with most drugs, caffeine has also been shown to have significant adverse effects. Tolerance may develop with habitual use and cessation may produce withdrawal effects, including fatigue (Addicott & Laurienti, 2009). Other researchers have pointed to the real risk of caffeine dependence, abuse, and addiction (Hammond & Gold, 2008; Joseph, 2001). Caffeine may also worsen conditions such as hypertension and heart arrhythmias. In addition, it may induce anxiety (Lara, 2010) or exacerbate the symptoms of the anxiety disorders and interfere with the effectiveness of anxiety medications (Hammond & Gold, 2008). Anxious musicians need to consider the anxiety-amplifying effects of caffeine, particularly prior to performance, and the fact that caffeine may interfere with the effectiveness of their anxiolytic (anti-anxiety) medications.

Complementary and alternative medicine (CAM)

Both prescription medications and non-prescription substances are expensive and have varied unwanted side effects. These are just two of the complex reasons why people in the Western world have increasingly turned to complementary and alternative medicine for relief from their afflictions. However, until recently, evidence for most complementary and alternative interventions used to treat anxiety and depression was either scant or of poor quality, making it difficult to know whether herbal and other natural remedies had any efficacy (van der Watt *et al.*, 2008). Herbs such as passionflower, kava,[17] and St John's wort,[18] the amino acid lysine[19] and magnesium[20] have all been candidates for reducing anxiety and enhancing mood and have been used for centuries in folk and traditional medicine. However, their effectiveness and safety have been the subject of scientific study only over the past 10–15 years (Kinrys, Coleman, & Rothstein, 2009). A meta-analysis of 24 studies—21 randomized controlled trials (RCTs) and three open-label, uncontrolled observational studies—examined five CAM monotherapies and eight combination treatments involving 2,619 participants, most of whom had been diagnosed with either an anxiety disorder or depression (n = 1786) (Lakhan & Vieira, 2010). Of the 21 RCTs, 71% (n = 15) showed a benefit for CAM. The authors concluded that there was strong evidence for the use of herbal supplements containing extracts of passionflower (3/3 RCTs) or kava (5/8 RCTs positive) and combinations of L-lysine and L-arginine as treatments for anxiety symptoms and disorders. The side effects were reported to be mild to moderate. They further concluded that combined supplements containing magnesium and other herbal combinations are promising but there was insufficient evidence at this time to draw firm conclusions about effectiveness (3/3 RCTs positive). However, magnesium as a monotherapy (i.e. taken alone) had results that were no better than placebo, leaving open the question that the other ingredients in the combined supplement produced the anti-anxyiolitic effects. Alternatively, magnesium could have synergistic effects when in combination with other herbs. St John's wort, as a monotherapy, showed insufficient evidence (1/4 RCTs positive) for use as an effective treatment to reduce anxiety.

---

[17] Kava is a drink that is prepared from the plant *Piper methysticum*.

[18] St John's wort (*Hypericum perforatum*) is derived from the flowering tops of a perennial shrub.

[19] Dysregulation of neurotransmitters such as GABA, serotonin, dopamine, and noradrenaline may cause anxiety. Amino acids such as L-tyrosine and L-tryptophan are precursors for specific neurotransmitters. Two other amino acids, L-lysine and L-arginine, may influence neurotransmitters involved in stress and anxiety. L-lysine acts as a partial serotonin receptor 4 (5-HT4) antagonist, decreasing the brain–gut response to stress as well as decreasing blood cortisol levels.

[20] Magnesium is a positively charged ion (a cation) that is involved in many important molecular functions in the body and has been linked to anxiety-related disorders.

Cannabis

In a recent newspaper article, 'I need pot to do my job',[21] Nigel Kennedy, internationally acclaimed concert violinist, admitted that he needed to smoke pot (cannabis) in order to do his job. After his apartment was raided by German police, he told a reporter from the German newspaper, *Das Bild*, 'I smoked a little grass. I can't do this job without it. I need it to relax.'

Observational studies in both animals and humans show that marijuana and other cannabis-derived substances affect mood and emotional reactivity that are dose dependent. At lower doses, the effects are anxiolytic; at higher doses, the effects are reversed, and anxiety and panic states are reported following ingestion (Gaetani *et al.*, 2009; Marco & Viveros, 2009). Because of its observed effects, and because the cannabinoid (CB) system is a neurochemical mediator of anxiety and fear learning in both animals and humans (Phan *et al.*, 2008), researchers have investigated the possible therapeutic uses of cannabis and its derivatives in the management of the anxiety and mood disorders. One approach has been to amplify the effects of the endogenous cannabinoids (EC), called anandamide, which elicit significant anxiolytic-like and antidepressant-like effects in rats and mice (Gaetani *et al.*, 2009). The anxiolytic effects of cannabidiol have also been demonstrated in other animal studies (Jiang *et al.*, 2005; Moreira *et al.*, 2006). These researchers argued that the EC system plays an important role in anxiety and mood disorders, and that future research could further investigate the possible pharmacological implications for the development of anxiolytic and antidepressant medications.

Another approach has been to investigate the use of cannabidiol (CBD), a major non-psychotropic constituent of cannabis. There has been much recent interest in this substance because of its many observed therapeutic effects that include anti-convulsive, anti-anxiety, anti-psychotic, anti-nausea, and anti-rheumatoid arthritic properties (Mechoulam *et al.*, 2002). In human studies, delta(9)-tetrahydrocannabinol (THC), the primary psychoactive ingredient in cannabis, significantly reduced amygdala (a critical brain region for threat perception) reactivity to social signals of threat but did not impair activity in the primary visual and motor cortices, thus demonstrating the anxiolytic function of THC (Phan *et al.*, 2008) without impairment in other brain systems. Phan *et al.* suggested that therapies targeting the cannabinoid system may be effective for the treatment of the anxiety disorders, including social anxiety.

In the first study of its kind, Crippa *et al.* (2011), using functional neuroimaging, explored the effect of cannabidiol on people with social anxiety disorder (SAD). There is a need to find effective therapies for SAD given the high prevalence of the condition, its poor response to current pharmacotherapies—only about 30% show a therapeutically meaningful response (Blanco, Antia, & Liebowitz, 2002)—and the high incidence of self-medication, including cannabis, for the relief of anxiety symptoms, particularly in people with SAD (Crippa *et al.*, 2009). In the Crippa *et al.* (2011) study, these researchers compared cannabidiol with placebo. The results suggested that cannabidiol reduces anxiety in people with SAD and that the anxiolytic effect was achieved via cannabidiol's activity in the limbic and paralimbic brain areas that are

---

[21] *Daily Telegraph*, Thursday 7 October 2010.

implicated in the symptoms of the anxiety disorders in general and SAD in particular. The authors argued that the earlier onset of action and fewer significant side effects of cannabidiol compared with current therapies for anxiety pointed to promising developments for cannabidiol in the treatment of the anxiety disorders. They cautioned that further double-blind, placebo-controlled long-term studies would be required to confirm its therapeutic use in humans.

Treatment of anxiety disorders in children and adolescents

The American Academy of Child and Adolescent Psychiatry published, in 2007, a practice parameter for the assessment and treatment of children and adolescents with anxiety disorders (Connolly & Bernstein, 2007). The aim of such parameters is to provide a set of recommendations based on a thorough review of the literature and outcomes of research that should guide the treatment decisions of clinicians working with young people with an anxiety disorder. The disorders covered in this publication include:

i separation anxiety disorder (SAD)

ii generalized anxiety disorder (GAD)

iii social phobia

iv specific phobia

v panic disorder (with and without agoraphobia)

vi agoraphobia (without panic disorder)

vii post-traumatic stress disorder (PTSD)

viii obsessive–compulsive disorder (OCD) (definitions for these disorders were given in Chapter Two).

Because of the complexities and multifactorial nature of both the etiology and presentation of the anxiety disorders in young people, a multimodal treatment approach should always be considered. This could include combinations of any of the following treatments that have been found to be efficacious in the treatment of anxiety and its disorders in adults: (psycho)education of parents and child, cognitive behavioral interventions, psychodynamic psychotherapy, family therapy, and pharmacotherapy.

Exposure-based cognitive behavioral therapy (CBT) has received substantial support for the treatment of child and adolescent anxiety disorders, in particular SAD, GAD, and social phobia (Compton et al., 2004). The essential elements in this therapy include:

i psychoeducation of parent and child about the origins, nature and course of anxiety, and the nature of the treatment

ii somatic management skills training (relaxation, breathing management)

iii cognitive restructuring (e.g. challenging negative expectations and modifying negative self-talk)

iv exposure (imaginal and in vivo exposure to the feared stimulus)

v relapse prevention (e.g. booster sessions, inclusion of parents and school in management of the anxiety) (Albano & Kendall, 2002).

Several studies have also supported the efficacy of group CBT for some young people with anxiety disorders (Flannery-Schroeder & Kendall, 2000; Manassis, Mendlowitz, & Scapillato, 2002). Individual treatment remains the preferred option for those with high levels of social anxiety and comorbid ADHD. Additional elements to this core set may be added to enhance treatment effects in particular groups of young people with anxiety disorders and these will be briefly discussed below. For children with social phobia, additional modules include social skills training and exposure to graded opportunities to practice social skills (Spence, Donovan, & Brechman-Toussaint, 2000). The use of group-based CBT may be useful for this purpose, since children with social phobia differ from non-anxious peers in having fewer friends, lower participation in peer activities, and more frequent use of avoidant coping (Beidel, Turner, & Morris, 2000).

Medication combined with some form of psychological treatment is indicated for those with moderate to severe anxiety symptoms that need to be brought under control quickly (Ollendick, King, & Chorpita, 2006). Severe anxiety symptoms in older youths may be a contra-indication for cognitive behavioral therapy alone, or SSRIs alone since a number of strong studies have predicted poor treatment response (Layne, Bernstein, Egan, & Kushner, 2003). This subgroup may need more intensive individual treatment, with additional components such as family therapy and social skills training if social phobia is a strong part of the symptom presentation. A more detailed discussion of the use of medication for youth anxiety disorders will be covered in the next section.

For young people with specific phobias, treatment focuses on graded exposure to the feared object or situation (Velting et al., 2004), cognitive modification of unrealistic fears, and participant modeling of approach behaviors to the feared object or situation. Similar additional components to the core set outlined above are recommended for panic disorder. These include interoceptive exposure, i.e. exposure to the physical sensations associated with panic such as dizziness, shortness of breath, tremor, and sweating, via exercises that induce these sensations under conditions of safety in which the child can experience these sensations and reprocess them as non-threatening. Education about the physiological processes that lead to these sensations is advisable before exposure (Ollendick, 1995). Other elements for inclusion in CBT for anxious young people include educational support (Last, Hansen, & Franco, 1998), parent training, parent management, and in cases where the parent is also anxious, therapy for parents (Chavira & Stein, 2002).

Despite the significant developments in the treatment and management of anxiety disorders in children and adolescents, CBT is not always effective and as many as 20%–50% of such young people will continue to meet criteria for their anxiety disorder at the end of treatment (Connolly & Bernstein, 2007). For this reason, other treatment modalities need to be considered. For example, there is mounting evidence that psychodynamic psychotherapy may be efficacious for anxious young people provided that the treatment intervention is sufficiently intensive (Muratori, Picchi, Bruni, Patarnello, & Romagnoli, 2003). Target and Fonagy (1994) reported that of 352 children treated for at least six months, 72% showed significant improvement on the Children's Global Assessment Scale. Rather than focusing directly on the symptoms per se as the target of treatment, psychodynamic psychotherapy addresses the core conflicts that have given rise to the symptoms. These may include anxious attachment to primary caregivers, anger or ambivalence toward attachment figures, and separation anxiety and dependence.

The danger with child-focused interventions is that core issues within the child's family may not be addressed, thus making maintenance and generalization of treatment gains difficult to sustain. A thorough assessment of the onset and etiology of the anxiety disorder may reveal a number of risk factors within the child's family that will need to be addressed during treatment. Chief among these are parental anxiety, which may be modeled inadvertently to children, and problematic parenting styles such as high maternal overinvolvement, excessive parental criticism, overcontrol and unrealistic expectations leading to damaging parent–child interactions (Cobham, Dadds, & Spence, 1998; Dadds *et al.*, 2001). In such cases, family therapy, marital therapy, and parent training and parent management may be necessary to achieve a good outcome.

The final decision for treatment modality will depend on a consideration of the following factors: psychosocial stressors, risk factors, severity and impairment of the anxiety disorder, comorbid disorders, age, gender and developmental functioning of the child, family functioning (including the presence of an anxiety disorder in one or both parents), and acceptability of the recommended treatment package to the family.

Medication for children and youth

Medication for children and youth suffering anxiety disorders should not be the first choice of treatment. However, medication may be indicated for young people whose anxiety is severe, whose functioning has been significantly impaired because of high levels of anxiety, or who have not shown a substantial response to psychotherapy (Birmaher, Brent, & Benson, 1998). SSRIs (e.g. fluoxetine, fluvoxamine, setraline, paroxetine) have demonstrated the most effective results for anxious young people with a range of anxiety disorders including GAD, social phobia and SAD (Birmaher *et al.*, 2003), and panic disorder (Masi *et al.*, 2001). They are generally well tolerated with few side effects that may include gastrointestinal symptoms, headache, and insomnia. However, positive family history of anxiety disorders, severity of illness, and presence of social phobia in young people with GAD and SAD reduced treatment efficacy of SSRIs. It should be noted that at the time of writing, the safety and efficacy of short-term but not long-term use of SSRIs for the treatment of anxiety disorders in young people had been established (Sakolsky & Birmaher, 2008). Although benzodiazepines have demonstrated effectiveness for the treatment of adults with anxiety disorders, controlled trials with children with anxiety disorders have not replicated the results for adults and should therefore be rarely recommended for use with young people (Connolly & Bernstein, 2007).

Summary

A daunting array of treatments has become available for the anxiety disorders and for psychological disorders in general over the past 30 years and choosing among them can be difficult for people seeking treatment. Empirical validation is required before treatments can be recommended. However, we need to exercise caution with respect to our definition of validation, which can be misleading given the complex methodological and statistical procedures involved in empirical studies. The chapter commenced with a review of the bias in the research and clinical communities towards the cognitive behavioral therapies, particularly for the anxiety disorders and depression. However, increasing evidence for the efficacy of psychodynamically oriented therapies has been forthcoming in recent years. An important issue in therapy selection is the degree of patient–therapy fit: different people respond better to different approaches, and indeed to different therapists. The basic tenets of the major therapeutic approaches were summarized and overall efficacy of particular approaches was reviewed, including, where available, different therapeutic approaches for anxious musicians. We began with the 'classical' psychoanalytic psychotherapies, moving to some recent developments, such as the relational and attachment-based psychotherapies, and intensive short-term dynamic psychotherapy (ISTDP), followed by the behavioral, cognitive, and cognitive behavioral therapies, including the 'new wave' of therapies such as mindfulness-based therapies, acceptance and commitment therapy (ACT) and dialectical behavior therapy (DBT). There has been recent interest in multimodal therapies that simultaneously address the whole range of affected domains in performance anxiety. Examples include BASIC-ID and brain-based therapies (BASE), unified emotion-based treatment protocols and transdiagnostic models identifying and addressing the common underlying characteristics of the anxiety disorders. Other music-specific interventions for music performance anxiety—music therapy, biofeedback, Ericksonian resource retrieval, hypnotherapy, and the Alexander technique—were then briefly reviewed. Performance-based approaches were discussed because performers who present for treatment have the dual goal of reducing their anxiety in order to be able to perform at their best, with enjoyment and pleasure. A number of models and factors were discussed, including the behavioral model of performance enhancement, the unifying model of pscyhological preparation for peak performance, the individual zones of optimal functioning (IZOF) model, the different functions of anxiety in performance models, and some key features of all performance models, such as goal setting, practice, pre-performance routines, imagery, and mental practice. The final section of the chapter was concerned with the vexed question of the role of medication in the treatment of music performance anxiety. I considered a range of prescribed substances, including beta-blockers, other prescription medications (monoamine oxidase inhibitors: MAOI), selective serotonin reuptake inhibitors (SSRIs), tricyclic and other antidepressants, benzodiazepines (tranquilizers, sedatives, hypnotics, muscle relaxants), and self-administered substances including alcohol, nicotine, caffeine, complementary and alternative medicines, and cannabis. The chapter concluded with a section on medications for anxious children.

Chapter 8

Severe music performance anxiety: phenomenology and theorizing

Music performance anxiety as a disorder of the self

We will now return to the discussion in Chapter Four as to whether music perform-ance anxiety is a dimensional construct or whether it is more helpful to view it as a group of disorders with specific subtypes. As stated earlier, there is no empirical evi-dence on which we can currently draw to assist us with this question. What follows in this chapter is a discussion in which I advance the proposal that there is a subgroup of anxious musicians who deserve special attention with respect to identification, diag-nosis, assessment, and treatment. This group is qualitatively different from those who report a focal anxiety or who can be classified within the social anxiety disorder spec-trum. This subgroup of musicians experience anxiety so pervasive and profound that it is experienced as a defining characteristic of their sense of self. In *The Analysis of the Self,* Kohut (1971), one of the first self psychological theorists, argued that a very early disturbance in the relationship with the mother, who is lacking in sufficient empathy and responsiveness to her baby's needs, or is in some other way either physically or emotionally absent or unavailable, prevents the development of true internal objects in the child; that is, strong and coherent mental representations of self and important others, thus creating in such individuals a severe narcissistic vulnerability that express-es itself in an insecure sense of identity, extreme sensitivity to hurts and slights, and catastrophic reactions to their own perceived or actual failures.

Winnicott (1965) described a similar phenomenon, in which an infant who suffers prolonged separation (or its emotional equivalent) from its mother experiences an overwhelming anxiety that leads to an inner void and a sense of emptiness and worth-lessness in later life. People who have had experiences of this type as infants or chil-dren have a core difficulty with identity and self-esteem. They therefore require sensitive mirroring of their experiences in order to manage the potentially overwhelm-ing anxiety they feel when ignored, criticized, or rejected or when they fail to meet their own expectations. This is because their personalities are organized around main-taining their self-esteem through affirmation from others, since they have not devel-oped the capacity for self-affirmation. This preoccupation with outward appearance and what others think of them gives rise to feelings of fraudulence, insufficiency, shame, and inferiority (McWilliams, 1994). People with this disorder are character-ized by a core difficulty with identity, self-esteem, a sense of inner emptiness, and for whom the continuity of a sense of self is fundamentally problematic. We will return to this theme later in the chapter when we work in depth with the subjective experience of very anxious musicians.

In the case of musicians with this type of psychological vulnerability, the performance situation holds many dangers. Sadly, music performance in our competitive, judgmental world is not always about the giving and receiving of pleasure, and is too often about the giving and receiving of criticism, competitiveness, and comparison. For vulnerable musicians, the performance situation can feel like an assault, coming both from within (in the form of harsh self-criticism and uncertainty) and from without, in the form of demanding parents, critical audiences, insensitive conductors, demeaning adjudicators, expectant teachers, and competitive peers. Thus, the performance situation may create a context that is experienced as dangerous and potentially annihilating for the vulnerable performer, an experience that resonates with the early overwhelming anxiety and sense of worthlessness that are central to those whose emotional deprivations were early, prolonged, and unrelieved.

Some musicians have responded skeptically when I have discussed the possible origins of their severe music performance anxiety in their early experiences with important others, perhaps long before they started studying music or learning their instrument. A very anxious musician, who had suffered lifelong anxiety and panic attacks as well as depression and suicidal feelings in relation to musical performance and 'life in general,' when asked about whether she would consider psychotherapy to help her to understand and manage her anxiety, replied:

> I would be interested in doing this, but I have always thought my problem is not important enough to do something about because I haven't had any sort of problem growing up. We had quite a privileged upbringing, private school, music lessons . . . I think people who have had a terrible traumatic childhood deserve the attention and therapy, of course. But nothing terrible happened to me. I probably just bring it [anxiety and panic attacks] upon myself.

The life history of this musician indicated that all of her siblings, who were all musicians, also suffered extreme forms of music performance anxiety, including panic attacks, and all had become poly drug users to manage their extreme anxiety symptoms. She described parents who were stern disciplinarians, who decided that all their children would be professional musicians like them, and which instruments they would play. The children were forced to enter many highly stressful competitions, eisteddfods, and auditions because 'it was good' for them, without being consulted about whether they wanted to do so or whether they felt that they could cope with the pressure. When asked whether she had discussed her concerns with her parents, she replied:

> I don't really like speaking to my parents about anything like that. My parents didn't understand it at all, because they've never experienced anything like that and they can't see what the problem is. They said, 'If you're a good violinist, then there shouldn't be any problem, so pull yourself together.'

The impact of these kinds of experiences on the developing child has been eloquently described by Wallin (2007) and Winnicott (1974). Wallin (2007) distinguishes between 'large-T trauma' such as the experience of being caught up in natural disasters, such as floods, fires, tsunamis, war or suffering physical or sexual abuse, abandonment, or parental mental illness or severe substance abuse, and 'small-t trauma,' also known as 'cumulative trauma' and 'relational trauma,' in which there are repeated, severe, and unrepaired disruptions to the relationship between parent and child, but which are likely to remain undetected and invisible to the outside world, since such families often appear to function very well, like the family of musicians I have just described. However, relationships in such families are painful and do not provide a psychologically safe environment in which children can manage their painful feelings. Winnicott (1974), in his paper 'Fear of breakdown,' captures the experience of small-t trauma thus:

> To understand this, it is necessary to think not of trauma but of nothing happening when something might profitably have happened. It is easier for a patient to remember trauma than to remember nothing happening when it might have happened (p. 45).

There is a large body of research that has explicated how one's relational experiences very early in life may affect, and indeed direct behavior, beliefs, emotions, and relationships throughout life. To understand the experience of severe music performance anxiety that cannot be understood in terms of failure of technical mastery or negative conditioning experiences that occur at a critical stage of a musical career, although these may also be prominent in the accounts of anxious musicians as we shall see, a more integrated approach is needed to fully understand the experience of these musicians.

Attachment theory offers the most heuristic and evidence-based insights into these musicians, and the attachment-based and relational psychotherapies may offer the best hope of treatment, although this assertion will need to be empirically verified. John Bowlby (1988) and Mary Ainsworth (1963) provided the research that underpinned the development of attachment theory. Attachment is defined as a biologically-based motivational-behavioral system whose goal is to ensure survival of the helpless infant. This system is characterized by three types of behavior:

i *Maintenance of the infant's physical proximity to its caregiver.* The infant will use behaviors such as crying, clinging, crawling, searching, and reaching for the attachment figure to attain physical closeness.

ii Using the attachment figure as a *'secure base'* (Ainsworth, 1963) from which to explore the environment. Observations of toddlers in parks highlight this function of attachment. With the parent sitting on a park bench, the young child will start to venture further afield, but will maintain some contact with the caregiver through turning, making eye contact, or vocalizing. S/he will periodically return to home base to receive reassurance before again venturing out on further explorations. If the attachment figure disappears, exploration will cease immediately and search behavior for the attachment figure will commence.

iii Return to the attachment figure as a *'safe haven'* when in danger or alarmed. Unlike some primates, who flee to a place, such as a burrow, to escape threat, humans seek safety in the company of a person or group with whom they are affiliated. Infants automatically seek their primary attachment figure (usually the mother) when feeling endangered.

Although he originally conceived it as a system whose outcome was protection from present danger, Bowlby (1988) later expanded his view of the role of attachment to include reassurance about the ongoing (emotional) availability of the caregiver. He had observed that a caregiver could be physically available to an infant, but if s/he were emotionally non-responsive, emotional development, and, if severe and prolonged, physical development, could be compromised. The final, critical step in the theory of secure attachment was that the infant's or young child's appraisal of the caregiver produced an experience of 'felt security,' defined as a subjective or internal experience of comfort and safety (Sroufe & Waters, 1977).

Mary Ainsworth (1963) investigated via observation of mother–infant dyads in controlled conditions the patterns of communication and relationship between mothers and their infants in order to understand the factors that resulted in either secure or insecure attachment, the outcomes of the child's expectations of the caregiver that are encoded as internal working models. Ainsworth identified three main forms of attachment, to which a fourth was added later by Mary Main (1995).

i *Secure attachment*: securely attached infants feel safe to explore and confident that their proximity and comfort-seeking behavior when distressed will be responded to appropriately. Mothers of securely attached infants are sensitive and responsive to their babies' signals, are quick to comfort them when distressed, and happy to let them explore safely. These mothers are characterized by sensitivity, emotional availability, acceptance, and collaboration with (rather than control of) their infant.

ii *Avoidant attachment*: avoidant infants show a very different pattern of communication with their caregiver. Unlike securely attached infants, avoidant infants do not acknowledge their mother's presence (i.e. they do not seek proximity) and they do not react with distress when she leaves. They appear calm and more interested in exploring the environment than in making contact with their mothers. Despite the apparent lack of distress, these infants have greatly elevated heart rates and circulating cortisol (stress hormone). These babies have learnt that any attempts to gain comfort and care from their mothers would be futile and hence their attachment behaviors have extinguished. Mothers of avoidant infants are characterized by inhibition of emotional expression, verbal and physical rejection of their infants, aversion to physical contact, and insensitivity to their infants' emotional signals and overtures.

iii *Ambivalent attachment*: Ainsworth identified two types of ambivalence—one characterized by anger and the other by passivity. Both types of ambivalent infants were too concerned about their mothers' whereabouts to feel free to explore and both responded with intense distress when she left them. However, when mother returned, angry infants in turn reconnected with their mothers but then rejected their approaches. Passive infants, overcome by feelings of misery and helplessness, made only token attempts to regain their mothers' attention. However, both angry and passive infants remained preoccupied with their mothers' whereabouts, even when they were present. Mothers of ambivalent infants were unpredictable in their availability to their children, insensitive to their emotional signals, and discouraged their children's development of autonomy, as evidenced by the inhibition of their exploratory behavior.

iv *Disorganized attachment*: infants showing disorganized attachment had parents who were simultaneously experienced as the safe haven and the source of danger. Following reunion after separation, disorganized infants showed a series of inexplicable and bizarre behaviors that included freezing, collapsing to the floor, and appearing dazed and confused. These behaviors came to be understood as the expression of opposing impulses to simultaneously approach and avoid their mothers. The majority of maltreated infants show this pattern of disorganized attachment, which occurs when the infant experiences the parent as frightening or frightened (for example, parents who are mentally ill, substance affected, or chronically depressed or anxious) (Main, Hesse, & Kaplan, 2005).

It will be evident from the foregoing discussion that the development of attachment styles is an interpersonal process that evolves in response to parents' caregiving style. Infants with secure attachment have mothers who are secure and autonomous with respect to their adult functioning and their experience of their own attachment relationships. For parents who have insecurely attached infants, three distinct patterns of adult states of mind with respect to attachment have been identified and these mirror the type of disordered attachment in their children.

Parents of avoidant infants tend to have a dismissing state of mind in which they minimize or devalue the influence of their own attachment experiences. Accordingly, they have difficulty trusting others. They may sustain long-term relationships but do not experience emotional intimacy in those relationships. They are, as Bowlby described, compulsively self-reliant and reluctant to feel or express emotions. Instead, such people tend to display excessive physiological arousal, as do avoidant infants, who display little overt distress when their mothers leave, but whose physiological arousal betrays their stress (Spangler & Grossmann, 1993). Dismissing parents ignore or suppress their infants' attachment needs, and such infants learn to live as if they had no such needs. These needs cannot be extinguished, but the use of minimizing or deactivating strategies, which support emotional distance, control, and self-reliance suppress the awareness of such needs.

Parents of ambivalent infants have a preoccupied state of mind, so called because their past unsatisfactory attachment experiences continually intrude upon their present life and relationships. They have a history of recurrent trauma or loss that remains unresolved, and they are hence too distressed by the past to effectively respond to the attachment behaviors of their children. The emotional life of such parents is governed by feelings of helplessness and fears of abandonment, disapproval, or rejection; hence, they are discouraging of their child's growing autonomy. In contrast to avoidant infants, ambivalent infants use hyper-activating strategies that amplify their affect in an attempt to secure the attention of their unreliably available parents.

Parents of disorganized infants are also described as unresolved/disorganized because they suffered repeated and painful trauma while simultaneously having no safe context in which to process and resolve their traumatic experiences. Responses to unresolved trauma include fear, emotional withdrawal, and dissociation. One way that people with such attachment experiences cope is to self-protectively split off unbearable states of mind from others that are more tolerable and able to be integrated into the developing sense of self. Children of such parents will often take on a controlling, parental role in an attempt to manage a frightening situation, in which the parent will unpredictably explode in physical or emotional abuse of their child.

Such experiences affect developing brain structures. You will recall from our discussion of the role of the amygdala in fear responding and the polyvagal theory in Chapter Two that the vagus, one of the cranial nerves originating in the brainstem, has three branches that respond selectively to environments that we consider safe, dangerous, or life threatening respectively. A number of other brain structures are involved in regulating the brain's danger response system, including the amygdala, which is involved in the fight-or-flight response, and which stores unconscious emotional memories. The hippocampus also contributes by moderating the reactions of the amygdala. It also interacts with the cortex to store explicit, linguistically retrievable memories (Le Doux, 1996). In children who have suffered severe emotional or relational trauma, the development of these brain structures may be compromised, with the result that the unchecked reactivity of the amygdala will produce extremely intense autonomic reactions in response to relatively minor internal or external triggers (Wallin, 2007). The extreme reactions of intense music performance anxiety in some musicians can now start to make sense in this context.

The psychological equivalent of the physical response to life-threatening situations—tonic immobility or 'playing dead'—is dissociation. Emotions are, in the first instance, bodily experiences. It is through the sensitively attuned attachment relationship that emotions are modulated, regulated, and understood. When such a relationship is absent or impaired, so too is the capacity for emotional regulation, including the capacity to accurately identify, name, and understand emotional experience, a process called mentalization (Fonagy *et al.*, 2002). Gunderson (in Bateman & Fonagy, 2004) defines it thus:

> [A] sense of self develops from observing oneself being perceived by others as thinking or feeling. The stability or coherence of a child's sense of self depends upon sensitive, accurate and consistent responses to him and observations about him by his caretakers. By internalizing perceptions made by others about himself, the infant learns that his mind does not mirror the world, his mind interprets the world. This is termed a capacity to mentalize, meaning the capacity to know that one has an agentive mind and to recognize the presence and importance of mental states in others (p. vi).

Without a capacity to mentalize, emotions are experienced only as somatic sensations (e.g. pounding heart, sweating, dry mouth, trembling, etc.) or physical symptoms (e.g. headache, gastrointestinal complaints, muscle tension, etc.) and are never fully comprehensible to the person experiencing these states. Emotional experiences that are too painful or traumatic, or are judged to be unacceptable to the primary attachment figure are split off or separated from other emotional states that are more 'acceptable' to the caregiver or tolerated by the individual and which can therefore be integrated into one's sense of self. The intolerable affects remain dissociated, undeveloped, and stored somatically, that is, in the body (Wallin, 2007). Individuals whose early attachment experiences were unsatisfactory develop multiple internal working models, some of which are defensively dissociated from others and from awareness, creating the risk of rapid shifts from manageable to overwhelming states of mind. Hence, failure of attachment relationships can undermine the development of cortical structures that are associated with both affect regulation and mentalization. The result is chronic hyper-arousal, such as that seen in severe anxiety, including severe music performance anxiety, which cannot be modulated by mentalizing or seeking comfort from an attachment figure (Schore, 2003). Such hyper-arousal is experienced to be outside one's control because the disturbed attachment experiences have resulted in the lack of a stable sense of self with the capacity for symbolic representation of one's own mental states. Hence, their affect remains intense, confusing, poorly labeled or understood, and, above all, unregulated.

The attachment system remains active during adulthood and continues to exert a significant influence on psychological and social functioning. Adults respond to perceived threats with activation of the mental representations of attachment figures laid down in infancy and childhood, as a means of coping with and regulating emotions (Ein-Dor, Mikulincer, Doron, & Shaver, 2010). When these attachment systems are faulty, their activation at times of stress and crisis is likely to result in emotional dysregulation of the type experienced by musicians whose music performance anxiety feels unmanageable. Such systems are not able to support the mitigation of distress or the attainment of felt security. Instead, distress is intensified and alternative, secondary attachment strategies involving either hyper-activation or deactivation of the attachment system are triggered (Main et al., 2005). People who experience attachment-related anxiety, that is, anxious attachment, in which the predominant concern is the unavailability of the attachment figure in times of need, will hyperactivate the attachment system in order to attract the attention of the emotionally absent caregiver. In contrast, those who experience attachment-related avoidance, that is, an avoidant attachment style, distrust their attachment figures and will deactivate the attachment system in favor of dealing independently with danger or threat (Ein-Dor et al., 2010). Those who are securely attached demonstrate both a strong sense that they can manage the threat and seek support from others to aid their own coping efforts. Anxiously attached individuals will catastrophize about the severity of the threat and will become insistent about their need for support to deal with it. Avoidantly attached individuals will minimize the threat and attempt to cope with it alone (Cassidy & Shaver, 2008).

These attachment systems are transmitted from parents to children; that is, a child's attachment security can be predicted with a high degree of concordance from their mother's state of mind with respect to attachment. A combination of quality of parent–child interactions and genetic factors (shared genes between parents and their children) mediate this intergenerational transfer of attachment quality (Ein-Dor et al., 2010). On average, about 65% of people are securely attached, 20% are avoidant, and 15% are anxious. These distributions remain relatively constant across the lifespan, from infancy to adulthood (van IJzendoorn & Sagi, 1999).

In light of the above discussion, it would be instructive to examine some accounts of severe music performance anxiety from professional classical musicians who participated in a phenomenologically oriented, open-ended, in-depth interview of their experience of music performance and its attendant anxieties with the author as interviewer. The accounts given below are stories or narratives derived from the interview about each musician's life experience and their understanding of their experience of music performance anxiety. The sample for this study was drawn from the population of professional performing orchestral musicians from the eight premier orchestras in Australia. There were nearly 800 musicians eligible to participate in a larger study that also involved an assessment of their mental and physical health and music-related injuries. Of this group, 400 volunteered to enter the study. Notices were sent via orchestra managers to all those interested in participating in the music performance anxiety interview study. Twenty musicians agreed to be interviewed. There were eight men and 12 women, with between four and 35 years of experience as a professional musician. Six reported a leadership role such as principal or assistant principal of their section. The following instruments were represented in the sample: violin, viola, cello, oboe, clarinet, bassoon, French horn, harp, trumpet, piano, and percussion. Although there were no exclusion criteria—all musicians were invited regardless of whether they suffered from music performance anxiety or not—16 of this group of 20 suffered very serious forms of anxiety, and it is on their stories I will focus in the next section.

Method of analysis

Before we interpret these narratives, we will begin with a note of caution about the method of analysis. You will remember from Chapter Two that within the psychology discipline's attempts to understand human behavior, there has been an oscillation between nomothetic and idiographic approaches, and that both methods have an important place in this complex enterprise. You will also recall our discussion in Chapter Five that highlighted the difficulties inherent in the reliance on self-report measures to gain an understanding of some psychological phenomena. With these issues in mind, a phenomenologically oriented narrative, which represents an idiographic approach, was, after careful consideration of possible frames of reference, determined to be the most appropriate method for data gathering of this kind. An analysis using the theoretical framework of attachment theory and a form of psychoanalysis called object relations, whose primary focus is the development of an understanding of a person's internalized relationships that have derived from their early attachment experiences with significant caregivers and others in their early lives was used to undertake a textual analysis of these interviews. Using this approach, it is hoped that severe forms of music performance anxiety can be illuminated, from both phenomenological and theoretical perspectives that may inform prevention, management, and treatment.

Psychoanalytic therapy reconstructs the stories an individual tells about him- or herself through a process of 'narrativization' of an experience that would otherwise 'linger as a traumatic lapse of meaning.' This process is termed 'narrative smoothing,' the practice of offering a 'home' for meaning: 'truth in the service of self-coherence' (Spence, 1986, p. 62). Spence asserts that a coherent self-narrative is a precondition for psychological well-being. Similarly, telling one's story to oneself or others is 'one of the essential constituents of our understanding of reality' (Butor, 1969, p. 26).

There are a great many psychotherapists who would support this view (Brandchaft, 2007; Mitchell, 1993; Sroufe & Waters, 1977; Stolorow, 2007). Indeed, in some psychotherapies, understanding the initial narrative and the subsequent reconstruction of that narrative, the process by which the individual asserts more control over the stories (as embodied in their internalized representations) that underpin their identity are the central goals of therapy (Schafer, 1978).

In his book, *Hope and Dread in Psychoanalysis*, Stephen Mitchell (1993) grapples with the diverse ways in which the self has been characterized in both literature and psychoanalysis. At one extreme, self is conceptualized as a spatial metaphor that is layered, singular, and continuous; at the other, as a temporal metaphor in which the self is understood to be multiple and discontinuous. Thomas Mann (1927), in *The Magic Mountain*, eloquently juxtaposes these two conceptualizations of self, foreshadowing the subsequent historical and theoretical interest in narrative as the form through which self is experienced:

> For time is the medium of narration, as it is the medium of life. Both are inextricably bound up with it, as inextricably as are the bodies in space. Similarly, time is the medium of music; music divides, measures, articulates time . . . Thus music and narration are alike, in that they can only present themselves as a flowing, as a succession in time, as one thing after another; and both differ from the plastic arts, which are complete in the present, and unrelated to time save as all bodies are, whereas narration, like music, even if it should try to be completely present at any given moment, would need time to do it in (p. 541).

More recently, McAdams (1997) examines ways in which the developing self seeks temporal coherence in the postmodern world. He argues:

> [M]aking sense of the modern self as it changes over time centrally involves the construction of self-narratives. Narratives, or stories, have the capacity to integrate the individual's reconstructed past, perceived present, and anticipated future, rendering a life in time sensible in terms of beginnings, middles and endings . . . [A] person's identity is not to be found in behavior, nor—important though it is—in the reactions of others, but in the capacity to keep a particular narrative going (p. 63).

Note the similarities in the constructs of 'keeping a particular narrative going' and Winnicott's notion of 'going-on-being.' Winnicott (1965) argued that the development of a continuous sense of self in time, which he called 'going-on-being' is developed in the non-intrusively receptive presence of another, who provides an experience that allows the baby to surrender to the flux of its experiences in time. Here we have the concepts of attachment, object relations, and the development of self-defining narratives coalescing into an experiential and theoretical unity.

Critics of the use of stories or narratives and case histories in psychotherapy as evidence argue that the case history genre is fiction because it involves unconscious and preconscious narrative smoothing on the part of the teller and the listener, the patient and the therapist. What is recorded in the interview/session may be biased in the direction of the theoretical frame under which the narrator/therapist operates (Smith, R. Harré, & van Langenhove, 1995). However, these are not insurmountable hurdles as there are safeguards against such biases. These include recording and verbatim transcription so that there is a complete record of the interview, the use of independent assessors of the narratives, and the development of case formulations from different perspectives.

There are a number of significant precedents for the use of narrative data in studies that explore the role of psychological factors in health outcomes. One such example is the 35-year longitudinal study that explored the effects of a pessimistic explanatory style, assessed via narratives of participants' life experiences, on medical outcomes (Peterson, Seligman, & Vaillant, 1988). Another is the 60-year longitudinal study of nuns that found the expression of positive affect in unstructured narratives in early adulthood was a strong predictor of longevity, with nuns with positive affect surviving nuns with negative affect by an average of 10.5 years (Danner, Snowdon, & Friesen, 2001). Cousineau and Shedler (2006) argued that narratives 'tap implicit psychological processes not accessible via self-report' (p. 428) because participants may not be aware of such processes, hence their implicitness, or may equally be unable or unwilling to disclose such processes directly, even if they were aware of them. Many individuals defensively deny emotional distress, and musicians are no exception. The majority of professional musicians with whom I have had contact report that even if they wanted to do so, they felt uncomfortable about disclosing the frequency and severity of their anxiety to colleagues or management for fear that such disclosures would either be contagious to their colleagues or receive a cold reception from management. Shedler, Mayman, and Manis (1993) called this defensive denial of distress, assessed via early memory narratives, 'illusionary mental health' (p. 1117) and found strong associations between denial and physiological reactivity.

The post-modern era supports the view that there are multiple 'worlds' and therefore 'multiple truths' (McAdams, 1997). Different frames of reference do not make a proposition untenable. But is there a 'right' version? Generally, a version is taken to be true or right if it is internally consistent. However, human experience and behavior are frequently not consistent. People behave in contradictory ways, believe contradictory propositions, love and hate the same person, feel anxious in some situations but not in others that appear, to the objective observer, more anxiety provoking. Is the benchmark of internal consistency appropriate for our endeavor to understand music performance anxiety or, indeed, any subjective experience? Musicians often report feeling anxious in one musical performance situation and not in others. Can objective, external factors that contribute to these different reactions be identified, or is the answer to be found in the subtle shifts in moods and perceptions of performers over time?

Worlds are constructed, not discovered, and are to some extent dependent on minds and language (Danzinger, 1997). Nonetheless, few would argue that phenomena exist before they are named. Is finding what is already there an act of construction of the thing found? For example, many people will report relief when a set of symptoms for which they have no name and no explanation is finally identified. Music performance anxiety has not reached the status of 'reification' of the other anxiety disorders. It has not found its way into the DSM. Can we therefore label it in the same way as other anxiety disorders? If so, will this advance its cause? Is music performance anxiety an 'entity' with a definable set of symptoms and consequences or is it a unique way of being-in-the-world in which the experience is inseparably constituted within the life world of the sufferer?

In the following sections, I will present, from the theoretical framework of attachment-related psychodynamic psychotherapy (Wallin, 2007), two accounts of these conversations that have been converted to narratives, allowing you, the reader, to answer the questions above to your satisfaction. Each case formulation will be followed by formulations prepared by two skilled practitioners who were blinded to the nature of the study or the musicians' presenting problems, one in ISTDP (intensive, short-term dynamic psychotherapy) (Davanloo, 1990, 2005) and the other in CBT (cognitive behavioral therapy) (Newman & Beck, 2010), who were presented with the case material and asked to prepare a case formulation with respect to the focus and content of their therapeutic interventions. For now, let us hear from Amanda.

Amanda's narrative: The thing I love is killing me . . . but do I really love it?

My parents are both orchestral violinists. There are four children in the family and we're all violinists, so we didn't get much choice. I never even imagined another career. We just always assumed that that's what we'd do, and that's what we all do. We're all violinists in orchestras. All I have ever done is music, the violin to be precise. I have been doing this all my life, except that I did take one and a half years off and that was because of performance anxiety. I was having panic attacks. I always have been a fairly anxious person and I used to take beta-blockers when I discovered them in about second year of the Con and otherwise I don't think I would've continued playing as a soloist, because I was too affected by nerves playing as a soloist. And I would never have passed an audition. I won some really big competitions taking beta-blockers and after I won a national competition, really soon after that, I fell apart, and I started having panic attacks all the time, especially at work. But then they started happening at home as well, just thinking about work. The whole thing—it was just so stressful, I was supposed to be so good [laughs] as a violinist . . . I thought there was something physically wrong with me. I went to heaps of doctors and had heaps of tests, and at work I started just not being able to continue playing because my heart would race so much and I couldn't think. I couldn't focus on what I was doing any more and I just had to leave the stage all the time. When I was having bad panic attacks sitting at the back of the second violins, it was not even that the audience could see me, but just the fact that I felt like everyone on stage was waiting to see whether I'd last the concert. So it was not even necessarily the music that I was playing, but the fact that I was physically there and would I still be there at the end of the concert—I found was a big, big problem for me. Wondering what people thought; what people would think.

This was so horrible and my parents didn't understand it at all, because they've never had anything like that and they can't see what the problem is. They would say, 'If you're a good violinist, then there shouldn't be any problem, so pull yourself together.' Anyway, I couldn't pull myself together. I went to a psychologist; I had brainwave-type training; I did rebirthing and anything I could think of, hypnosis; everything. Nothing helped and I just couldn't stand working . . . I just couldn't do it any more. So I resigned; for one and a half years, I just did nothing much. Then somebody put me on to Valium. I did another audition and I passed it and I got my job back; so I started working again but it was very hard and I still had the panic attacks most of the time. Then I started taking Aropax® but . . . eventually I got to such a state and I was so depressed and so miserable . . . I spiralled into a depression; a big depression.

If I have a solo concert, I take beta-blockers and Xanax® [alprazolam, marketed under the trade name Xanax® among others, is a benzodiazepine used to treat anxiety and panic disorder] because I found that, once I had panic attacks, I just couldn't control my nerves with beta-blockers. I had to have Xanax® as well to calm me down. But I still worry a lot; I'm just that sort of person. Another sister has had a lot of problems with the same sort of thing. She's on Aropax® [a group of medicines called selective serotonin reuptake inhibitor (SSRI) antidepressants] as well, with panic attacks at work. It's been a lifelong struggle for me. I just couldn't have been a musician unless it had been for the pharmaceutical industry. Because I just, I can't seem to do it on my own. I'm too worried and nervous . . . playing the violin especially, the tiniest bit of bow shake is just so detrimental to the performance.

I never got to a really bad stage fright until I was in my mid teens. After that it became so . . . I just couldn't really perform without some sort of drug. I was quite depressed as a teenager as well. I lost all the fun of being just a child performing, and it became serious [laughs]. It was preordained that I would be a violinist . . . I've got a photo of me at eight months old with a violin under my chin [laughs]. It wasn't a question of doubt that any of the four of us were going to be anything else apart from violinists. Not even another instrument was ever considered. There's been several times when I've felt really dreadful. I've felt very bitter about that . . . that I hadn't had any other choices. I was, I suppose, very abnormal in that I just did whatever I was told. I was never rebellious; I never spoke up for myself. I didn't dare question anything . . . But I do enjoy performing. That's the trouble. I am good at it but I just have this anxiety all the time. I should've had an outdoor job, or something where I can just relax more [laughs] and you're not so on the spot. I never wanted to do all the competitions and things. I just always felt I should do them; they were good for me. It's just a battle all the time. I never feel confident and happy. I need Aropax® even for rehearsals.

It's funny. My parents don't suffer at all and never have done, yet all four siblings suffer horribly. They really can't understand it. It's very hard to explain what panic attacks are like to somebody who has never had them, because you can't just pull yourself together. And, believe me, I've tried. It's not just a case of being nervous. It's a case of being unable to control your thoughts. I always feel like I'm being bombarded by thoughts and, when I take medication, I find that I can just focus on the one thing instead of having all these thoughts like I can't do it; I'm too scared to do it . . . it's like fireworks going off all around me.

I feel suicidal, basically. I just want to kill myself. I've often felt suicidal, to do with music. Just before the big competition that I won, I was very suicidal because the whole thing was just far too much for me to cope with. So I just wanted to . . . yes, I'd rather be dead. I can't explain, but I just . . . it's very, very severe anxiety. I just think there's no escape from it and I have to do it . . . Without the Aropax®, I really get so depressed and with the depression come the panic attack feelings again and once I start to have them, then that's pretty much the end for me because I just can't stand living with those. My suicidal thoughts are not just about performing, but life in general . . . about just getting through. It's terrible, but I have this feeling I just want to get through my life as fast as possible and so I'll be dead. Because it just seems too difficult. Just everything is difficult for me.

I don't really like speaking to my parents about it. My mother gets extremely defensive and I don't like any sort of conflict and she would get very, very upset and, believe me, it's not worth it. She always . . . they did what they thought was best and they would believe that and my parents are always right. They have never questioned why all four of their children have a serious anxiety problem.

I don't understand why I am like this. I remember telling a doctor once and she said, 'Why on earth do you do it? Why do this? If you need drugs why don't you do something else?' but I am actually very good at it. I don't know what else I would've done actually . . . that's the thing that I'm good at, but I'm just not emotionally made up for it, obviously.

Case formulation for attachment-based psychotherapy

One must be cautious in developing a case formulation from one in-depth interview. What follow are more in the nature of hypotheses and speculations about the possible dynamics underlying the distress and severe and intractable symptoms in these two anxious musicians. They are presented here to stimulate the interest of therapists who work with vulnerable musicians who present with core personality difficulties that will need to be addressed in the course of treatment for their music performance anxiety and to encourage careful assessment before choosing a therapeutic approach. Both of these musicians had already received various forms of psychological and pharmacological interventions whose failure to bring relief has compounded the sense of hopelessness about achieving a resolution of their symptoms.

Attachment style

There is probably sufficient material to permit the conclusion that Amanda's parents have a dismissing state of mind with respect to attachment, thus producing an avoidant attachment style in Amanda.

> My mother gets extremely defensive and I don't like any sort of conflict and she would get very, very upset and, believe me, it's not worth it. She always . . . they did, what they thought was best and they would believe that and my parents are always right.

False self formation

There has been considerable interest from a number of different theoretical perspectives in the concept of self and its pathological variant, the false self. For example, social interactionism (Mead, 1934), attachment theories (Bowlby, 1988; Sroufe & Waters, 1977), and cognitive developmental theory (Case, 1991; Piaget, 1970) all support the view that the self is a social construction that emerges from social and linguistic exchanges with significant others. All interpersonal processes carry risks of harm. False self behavior can be the outcome of interpersonal processes that do not validate the child's true self, thus resulting in the child's alienation from the core or 'true' self. Harter (1997) describes this process thus:

> Language can drive a wedge between two simultaneous forms of interpersonal experience: as it is lived and as it is verbally represented . . . The narrative that is constructed initially is highly scaffolded by parents who dictate which aspects of the child's experience parents feel are important to codify in the child's autobiographical memory, leading to potential misrepresentations of the child's actual experience . . . the falsified version of experience . . . contributes to the formation of a false self. Thus, displaying behavior to meet the needs and wishes of someone else incurs the risk of alienation from those inner experiences that represent one's true self (p. 84).

Amanda could not verbally represent her experience of panic to her parents:

> It's funny. My parents don't suffer at all and never have done, yet all four children suffer horribly. They really can't understand it. It's very hard to explain what panic attacks are like to somebody who has never had them . . .

A number of authors (Brandchaft, 2007; Kohut, 1984; Winnicott, 1965) have theorized about the origins of the false self in parental intrusiveness whereby children develop a false self based upon compliance with a conditionally loving or supportive parent. Such children develop 'contingent self-esteem' (Deci & Ryan, 1995), whereby they only feel worthwhile when they meet the demands of externally imposed standards. A range of caregiver behaviors in addition to conditional approval, including lack of attunement to the child's needs, empathic failure, lack of validation, threats of harm, and coercion all contribute to the development of a false self (Harter, 1997). Children respond to such interpersonal environments with attempts to be good and to please their parents. Superficially, such children may be viewed as developing well, but the consequences of false self development and feelings of inauthenticity are far reaching and may endure over a lifetime, as are evident in Amanda's story and Gerald's story below. A child's true self is fostered when caregivers are able to love and accept the child as s/he is, not only when s/he conforms to some externally imposed parental or social standard.

Parents like Amanda's make their love and approval contingent upon their child's acceptance of an externally imposed demand or expectation (e.g. becoming a violinist) and/or standard (e.g. 'You will be a successful, professional musician'). Such children display the behavior Amanda described—absolute compliance ('I just did whatever I was told'), a manifestation of false-self behavior.

Pathological accommodation

Words dry and riderless
the indefatigable hoof-taps
While
From the bottom of the pool, fixed stars
Govern a life.

Sylvia Plath.[1]

The false self is formed via a process called pathological accommodation. It is defined thus:

> [P]rocesses of pathological accommodation . . . emerge when the child is required preemptively to adhere to the needs of its primary [caregivers] at the expense of its own psychological distinctness. By repetitive patterning of the child's first reality [there] emerge . . . fixed belief systems. Systems of pathological accommodation are responses to [this] trauma . . . designed to protect against intolerable pain and existential anxiety . . . These earliest attachments exclude or marginalize spontaneous experience and metacognitive processes of self-reflection. The child's ability to process new information and, accordingly, to self-correct and grow are impaired as its emerging sense of self is usurped (Brandchaft, 2007, p. 667).

Note Amanda's comments on her experience of pathological accommodation:

> It wasn't a question of doubt that any of the four of us were going to be anything else apart from violinists. Not even another instrument was ever considered. There's been several times when I've felt really dreadful. I've felt very bitter about that . . . that I hadn't had any other choices. I was, I suppose, very abnormal in that I just did whatever I was told. I was never rebellious; I never spoke up for myself. I didn't dare question anything . . .

---

[1] 'Words' from *Plath: Poems*, published by Everyman's Library in 1998.

An extreme form of this process is evident in Amanda's description of her experience. She and her siblings were treated as narcissistic extensions of their parents. In its benign form, narcissistic extension is understood as parental pride, akin to the idea of 'a chip off the old block.' In its pathological form, children are placed in this role function to maintain their parents' self-esteem: the child feels responsible for the parent. Such children grow up confused about whose life they are actually living. Their failures are perceived as parental failures and as such, are subject to swift judgment, so that the child never enjoys the freedom to experience the self in safety (Miller, 1975). Such children are important to their parents, not because of who they are, but because they fulfill this self-esteem-maintaining function for their parents:

> The confusing message that one is highly valued, but only for a particular role that one plays, makes a child feel that if his or her real feelings, especially hostile or selfish ones, are found out, rejection or humiliation will follow. It fosters the development of the 'false self,' the presentation of what one has learned is acceptable (McWilliams, 1994, p. 175).

The movie *Shine*, which depicted the life of pianist David Helfgott,[2] presents an example of pathological accommodation in the arts. In David's case, it was his punitive, rigid, and dominating father who brutally imposed his will on David, who pathologically accommodated to his father by living out the identity imposed upon him by his father as his narcissistic extension who would fulfill his father's thwarted musical ambitions. There was also a more sinister requirement in David's case—to prevent the fragmentation of his father into incoherent rage that he vented on his entire family.

Feeling like an imposter or fraud

A theme that appears repeatedly and in many guises in musicians' narratives and in the transcripts of this sample of professional musicians is the feeling of being an imposter, a sham, or a fraud. This feeling is related to false self formation and pathological accommodation and arises in response to the need for narcissistic enhancement as a defense against core feelings of worthlessness (Harter, 1997; Kohut, 1984; Winnicott, 1965, 1974). There are possibly two very different pathways to the development of feeling like an impostor or sham. Children of highly critical parents may come to believe that regardless of their achievements, they will never meet the standard expected. The pervasive message is that one is either never good enough or is only good enough if meeting parental expectations, rather than their own. Conversely, there are parents, teachers, and education systems who overpraise children, teaching them that they can achieve whatever they desire. This situation may be equally damaging to children. Children are still being judged, even if the judgment is universally positive. This situation impairs the child's capacity to develop realistic self-esteem, and leaves them with an uneasy feeling that there is a false quality to the constant admiration. When confronted with the reality that they have limitations, they may feel like frauds and failures (Kaplan, 2009). Once the feeling of being an impostor is established, people, like this sample of anxious musicians, fear that they will be found out,

---

[2] These comments are based on the depiction of David Helfgott's family in the movie *Shine*. No judgment is made as to whether this depiction is accurate.

exposed, and ridiculed for their deception, leaving them in a constant state of anxiety and despair. Others use it to protect themselves from the pain of inevitable exposure—they can say to themselves when unmasked, 'I already knew that I was a sham.' People who describe such feelings may be perfectionists, who consider that a small error in their performance reveals their fraudulent status (Kaplan, 2009). The underlying emotion in this state of fraudulence is shame, a feeling of helpless vulnerability with the threat of exposure and with it the contempt of others. This is the constant underlying fear that accompanies every performance:

> In the shame-driven version of perfectionism, the compulsion expresses the terror of being exposed to the critical scrutiny of others, and exposed . . . as inadequate, empty, a sham (McWilliams, 1994).

I will return to this topic later where we discuss core themes that are common across very anxious musicians. For now, here is an example of how Amanda experienced it.

> I won some really big competitions taking beta-blockers . . . really soon after that, I fell apart, and I started having panic attacks all the time, especially at work and . . . in relation to performance . . . But then they started happening at home as well, just thinking about work. The whole thing—it was just so stressful, I think. Feeling that I was supposed to be so good [laughs] as a violinist and I just . . . I don't know . . . I started just not being able to continue playing because my heart would race so much and I couldn't think. I couldn't focus on what I was doing any more and I just had to leave the stage all the time . . . I just couldn't have been a musician, I don't think, unless it had been for the pharmaceutical industry [laughs].

Absence of play

The capacity of parents to play with their infants and children has been strongly associated with the development of secure attachment and the capacity to mentalize. Bateman and Fonagy (2004) have argued that the undermining of playfulness is one of the most serious deprivations of childhood, and, together with the other features of disordered attachment, leads to the development of severe personality pathologies. A child who has a violin put under her chin at the age of eight months has been given the message early that play is not valued; that there is no time for play. Instead of allowing the child to take the lead in a playful interaction, the anxious parent takes the lead, giving directions to the child, which the child anxiously attempts to follow, thereby crushing the child's initiatives and impairing the development of an agentive self that is so essential to the development of a sense of identity.

> The obsessive caregiver will keep scrutinizing the child for flaws and defects, and they then become enmeshed into a ritualistic system of 'fixing.' The center of the developmental stage is shifted from the child's vitalizing expressions to the caregiver's deadening, impinging, frightened, or abusive mismatch. Ever afterward, this sequencing will occur automatically beyond the influence of self-reflective awareness . . . the process results cumulatively in an 'overburdening' exhaustion . . . Well-being and happiness cannot be sustained within this system . . . The repetitive sequencing of such states of mind takes the form of obsessive brooding and self-reproach from which [such people] cannot free themselves when they are alone (Brandchaft, 2007, p. 674).

Many young musicians feel that their performance anxiety appears when they stop 'playing' with their music.

> I was quite depressed as a teenager as well. I lost all the fun of being just a child performing, and it became serious . . .

Music instruction is a fertile ground for ritualistic fixing and seeking after perfection. Note Amanda's comments about her experience of overburdening exhaustion:

> It's terrible, but I have this feeling I just want to get through my life as fast as possible and so I'll be dead. Because it just seems too difficult. Just everything is difficult for me.

Failure of mentalization and painful somatic responses to performance anxiety

[T]he ego is first and foremost a bodily ego (Freud, 1962, p. 20).

The infant's first experience of self is a bodily or somatic experience. The salient experiences include hunger and satiation, distress and comfort, cold and warmth, pain, and soothing touch. Damasio (1994) argued that the structures and operations of the body provide a stable source of experience upon which rest the foundation of the sense of self in a psychological sense. Similarly, as discussed earlier, Bowlby (1988) identified attachment as an essentially biological process in which the need for bodily protection was the underlying motivation for proximity seeking in the infant. Of critical importance is the relationship between secure attachment and physiological regulation and arousal. Recall, for example, our earlier discussion of the higher levels of physiological activation in infants who are insecurely attached to dismissing, preoccupied, or unresolved mothers. Bodily experience, like feelings and thoughts, may be denied, distorted, or dissociated. Emotional dysregulation is inevitably accompanied by some form of physiological hyper-arousal. Wallin (2007) points out that particular emotions automatically trigger specific biobehavioral responses. For example, anger triggers confrontation or inhibition; fear triggers flight or physical paralysis; helplessness triggers physical and emotional collapse. Schore and Schore (2008) state:

> If children grow up with dominant experiences of separation, distress, fear and rage, then they will go down a bad pathogenic developmental pathway and it is not just a bad psychological pathway but a bad neurological pathway. This is due to the fact that during early critical periods organized and disorganized insecure attachment histories are 'affectively burnt in' the infant's rapidly developing right brain (p. 12).

You will recall our discussion of the polyvagal theory in Chapter Two. When feelings are frightening, conflicted, or felt to be unacceptable, they create anxiety that is felt to be so intolerable that it must be defended against, denied, or dissociated. This level of chronically felt but unexpressed anxiety takes a physiological toll on the body, in the form of chronic hyper-arousal, excessive circulating stress hormones, and finally in the development of somatic symptoms or complaints. Somatization takes several forms, including tension in the striated muscles (the large muscle groups in the body), which is the most commonly experienced and best understood form. Others experience their anxiety in the smooth muscles and have symptoms such as nausea, cramps, abdominal pain, and bladder and bowel urgency. Our young pianist from Chapter Six expressed her anxiety through the smooth muscles. Others will experience cognitive-perceptual distortions, very evident in Amanda's account and in several of the other musicians. Amanda describes her severe mental confusion thus:

> [I]t's not just a case of being nervous. It's a case of being unable to control your thoughts. I always feel like I'm being bombarded by thoughts and, when I take medication, I find that I can just focus on the one thing instead of having all these . . . well, it's like fireworks going off all around me.

One of the key features of accounts of severe music performance anxiety is the extreme language used to communicate the intensity of the somatic or bodily discomfort experienced in the course of music performance-related panic. There will be numerous examples reported later, but for now, let us review some of Amanda's descriptors of her experience. She used phrases throughout her narrative such as: 'feeling immobilized by nerves,' 'I just have this anxiety that I've got all the time,' 'It's very, very severe anxiety. I just think there's no escape from it,' 'I really get so depressed and with the depression come the panic attack feelings . . . and once I start to have them, then that's pretty much the end for me because I just, I can't stand living with those.'

Chronic suicidality

Why become suicidal after reaching the pinnacle of her career, winning a prestigious national competition? We do not have enough information to select among a number of possible answers. Perhaps she felt she had nowhere to go after the ultimate achievement. Amanda had achieved what she (and her parents) had focused on for years. Her motivation and focus on this achievement evaporated under the intolerable stress that she experienced in the lead up to the competition and being subsequently confronted with feelings of inner emptiness, perhaps realizing in the achievement of the goal that the goal was not hers and she therefore did not feel it as a genuine achievement. In this context, chronic suicidality becomes comprehensible. Winnicott (1974) explains:

> Many men and women spend their lives wondering whether to find a solution by suicide, that is, sending the body to death which has already happened to the psyche . . . Death, looked at in this way as something that happened to the [person] but which the [person] was not mature enough to experience, has the meaning of annihilation (p. 45).

Below is how Amanda describes it:

> I feel suicidal, basically. I just want to kill myself. I've often felt suicidal, to do with music. Just before the big competition that I won, I was very suicidal because the whole thing was just far too much for me to cope with. So I just wanted to . . . yes, I'd rather be dead. I can't explain, but I just . . . it's very, very severe anxiety. I just think there's no escape from it and I have to do it . . . My suicidal thoughts are not just about performing, but life in general . . . about just getting through. It's terrible, but I have this feeling I just want to get through my life as fast as possible so I'll be dead. Because it just seems too difficult. Just everything is difficult for me.

It is noteworthy that the thoughts about suicide are very long-standing but have remained at the ideation level; that is, they have never been enacted into suicidal gestures or attempts. It is thus possible that her suicidal ideation is a consequence of turning her anger against her parents inwards and is therefore likely to be defensive in nature. It has perhaps become a distraction, a form of ruminative fantasizing that prevents her from thinking more adaptive thoughts and taking more adaptive action.

The puzzle of staying 'in the field'

Amanda displays the same disordered attachment in relation to her violin and her music making as she does with her parents. She has a passionate relationship with her violin and her music, yet her instrument and performing are also her persecutors.

> I remember telling a doctor once and she said, 'Well, why on earth do you do it? Why do this? If you need this drug, why don't you do something else?' but I am actually very good at it . . . I don't know what else I would've done actually and I think music does . . . if you fill out those questionnaires about what sort of career would be good for you, I was pointed in the musical artistic type direction so that's the thing that I'm good at, but I'm just not emotionally made up for it, obviously.

Case formulation for intensive short-term dynamic psychotherapy[3]

ISTDP views performance anxiety to be related to feelings about early attachment ruptures. Performance-anxious people do not experience their caregivers as unconditionally accepting of them. Now, in situations where evaluation, explicit or implicit, occurs, these patients have unconscious links between performance evaluation and evaluation from early attachment figures. As a result, complex feelings about these early attachment ruptures are triggered in performance situations and these begin to 'push up' from their unconscious—rage, guilt about the rage, grief, and love. The performance anxiety is a defensive maneuvre that occurs to keep these feelings out of conscious awareness. The conscious experiencing of these underlying feelings and the processing of the memories and fantasies attached to them result in the unconscious feelings no longer being triggered in performance situations, thus resolving the defensive component of the performance anxiety.

Amanda would be a good candidate for ISTDP. She has long-standing psychopathology with intense fears of rejection. Her panic attacks and depression (she collapses, takes to her bed, goes flat) indicate that she has a threshold at which point her feelings are internalized/somatized before she becomes consciously aware of them. She would need some graded ISTDP work (i.e. systematic desensitization to her feelings) to raise her threshold to the point where she could consciously experience her feelings (in particular the unconscious rage at her parents for their repeated empathic failures and demands for pathological accommodation). This unconscious rage may account for the chronic suicidality. It represents the internalization of her rage against her parents, which cannot be safely expressed. It may also be defensive, if self-defeating, in nature, a safe, familiar misery that prevents her active confrontation of pressing current issues. Amanda has an intellectual, externalizing defensive system, but at the same time, she is aware that the problems are within her. ISTDP would assist in the

3 This analysis was provided by Dr Steven Arthey, PhD, clinical psychologist, ISTDP practitioner, Melbourne, Australia.

rapid resolution of the overt symptoms, i.e. anxiety, depression, in approximately six to eight sessions. The underlying character pathology relates to passivity, compliance, and emotional detachment. This would take longer to resolve, but treatment should be completed in 15 to 20 standard sessions.

Case formulation for cognitive behavioral therapy[4]

Amanda expresses her difficulty well in saying that being an orchestral violinist is 'the thing that I'm good at, but I'm just not emotionally made up for it.' It is unfortunate that this insight did not lead to a more suitable career choice three decades earlier. On a surface level, she seems to have the catastrophic belief that she will panic and fail to complete a performance, even though, presumably, she is capable of performing reliably with the use of medications. On a deeper level, her dysfunctional thoughts relate to her belief that she can be nothing but a performing violinist. From her account, she still feels unable to take action that may displease her mother, and this inhibits her from rationally thinking about her options. She would probably meet criteria for a diagnosis of panic disorder. Multiple therapeutic approaches have already been attempted in this case, none of which has been entirely satisfactory. Generally speaking, a client's prospects of successful therapy decrease in proportion to the number of prior failed therapeutic attempts, so Amanda's prognosis is not good. The central cognitive component of therapy would systematically challenge her belief that she is likely to fail to complete a performance, as a result of panic. She may be helped to see that the evidence for this belief, so long as she takes suitable medication, is small. It will also be necessary to address her core beliefs that she must continue her performance career as a violinist, and the impossibility of disappointing her mother. Training in assertive communication, especially in relation to her mother, may also be helpful. Cognitive behavioral treatments for panic disorder in the general population have been widely studied and found to be effective. Depending upon the specific characteristics of her panic, Amanda could undergo systematic graded exposure to the situations that she has been avoiding, and to physiological states, such as hyperventilation, associated with panic. Training in relaxed breathing and in the ability to relax during performances may also help.

Certain factors should be considered before beginning therapy with Amanda. She has contemplated suicide; therapy must not push her beyond her limits of coping. It is possible that full and open consideration of the available options may result in her deciding to cease being a performing artist. Such a course of action may initially be highly stressful for Amanda, and also for her mother, although in time it may lead to a good recovery. As yet, the questions of whether it is better to be an unhappy performer or a contented non-performer is one which Amanda has not cared to fully consider.

Below is the second narrative, which we will compare with Amanda's, in order to identify similarities and differences in presentation.

---

[4] This case formulation was prepared by Thomas Jones, MClinPsych, clinical psychologist and CBT practitioner in private practice in Sydney, Australia.

Gerald's narrative: The monster inside

Part of the reason I'm responding to your study is because [pause] there are moments when being nervous about what I do have almost completely ruined my enjoyment of music. It's a monster so big that I can't do it without help. I just can't fight it, I just can't fight it any more and it's bigger than me . . . [sobs] . . . I did try to get help once. However, a lot of what she [the psychiatrist] offered to me helped me understand the nature of this condition, this state and to some extent what I could do to break it down but [pause] I just don't have the strength to be able to follow it through. It's a huge thing . . . the effect that the nervousness tends to have on me, it ruins my ability to concentrate and it tends to paralyze my mind to deal with the problem . . . It's now largely a conditioned response and I remember the psychiatrist recognizing it and suggesting ways I could decommission my response. But it's really hard to do that after [laughs] you've lived with it for 30 years. It's very hard to do. I wish I could get rid of it . . . It's such a powerful overriding state to be in that it's very hard for me to control it and to try and think of other things to do. Even now as we speak I feel short of breath, agitated, not at all comfortable . . . [sobs] . . . When it grabs me, I tend to lose my ability to focus. My attention freezes, which you certainly don't need when you're faced with a tricky passage or a long extended passage or an exposed section . . .

I think deep down I'm trying to examine, 'Why does this happen?' and it's partly my personality. I'm not a strong outgoing personality. I've never told anybody this before but I think it's to do with, somewhere deep down, I've got a lack of self-esteem and I measure that self-esteem against everybody else's opinion, and I keep thinking, 'I'm going to botch this and I'm going to go down in everybody's opinion,' so consequently it becomes a self-fulfilling prophecy. I genuinely believe that underneath it all I'm a really good musician and I've got no reason to feel a lack of confidence. I'm miles ahead of the game really, but for some reason I just genuinely don't believe it. I can't make myself believe it . . . I deeply believe I can cope with all these (musical) parts, I'm a professional, I know what I'm doing . . . I don't know why I feel that I'm going to botch it and I don't know why I start to psych myself out of it months beforehand . . . The more highly trained peers or audience that I have, the more it puts me under pressure and the worse I feel and I think it's to do with this esteem thing. I believe it's to do with they're going to see me for the sham that I am. I don't know why I feel like a sham. I'm in a privileged position where I play for this orchestra as section leader and on the face of it I'm the man. In theory I'm the best player in the state, in theory. I've got the job to prove it but by not proving it to myself I generally just don't believe it. So when I perceive that somebody's watching me who's in the know would see that I'm not actually any good, or not as good as I thought, then I feel like a sham . . .

For me as a professional musician, a wrong note is a catastrophe, a wrong note is an indicator that I'm not as good as I say I am. I'm not sure that my wife is aware just what a huge monster this is. I don't know if I wanna let her know, let anyone know . . . I am completely ruined by this monster and I don't know what to do . . . It's very easy to say, 'Don't be nervous, what have you got to be nervous about?' and it's absolutely true, there's just nothing for me to be nervous about because at the end of the day whether I play it well or whether I don't, it makes no difference. It's just not important in the greater scheme of things. But it assumes an importance because of this conditioned response and it's just so glib to say, 'You don't need to be nervous,' that does absolutely nothing at all. It's 1,000 times more powerful than the glibness of that statement . . .

Oh God, there was a bad conductor last year. It was just awful . . . [gasping] . . . You make an error, we all do sooner or later, but for me it's catastrophic . . . There was one instance in a concert last year where he suddenly, out of nowhere, completely and utterly ridiculed something I was doing, playing out of time or whatever it was. It was just in a tiny moment and it was really vicious, really uncalled for, really unprofessional on his part. Now I really genuinely don't mind if somebody pulls me up because I was doing something that wasn't appropriate, that is a conductor's job, to make sure I'm doing the right thing . . . my job is to comply with such demands when they're made of me . . . but it was in a very hurtful, personal, scathing, and unfair way. Everybody noticed it and there was a groan from everybody about the way he treated me and I was so completely upset . . . what meant nothing to him was devastating to me. Just terrible . . . [sobs] . . . I still haven't recovered . . . I'm still extremely wary of him and I dread the weeks that he comes . . . It's bad enough having this monster on my back of my own making without somebody like that making it worse . . . Part of the reason I felt so devastated about it was that he made me look like a sham in front of my peers. I know that I'm good at this; I know I can do it; I fight to really believe it, but I just can't believe it . . . I don't know what that is, I don't know where it came from, I don't know whether it's just part of my personality or if it's from my upbringing, maybe it is, I don't know, I don't know where it's come from and I don't know what to do about it . . .

I asked the Human Resources person for the orchestra whether I could get some help. She put some stuff in an envelope and put it in my pigeon hole about six months ago and I've carried it around in my bag ever since, unopened, waiting for the right moment when I can actually face it and open it and do something about it. I can't open the envelope because I know it's going to be a huge process. I know it's going to be difficult, and I know it's going to take a long time, and I probably won't like it, and I probably won't like what I have to do [pause] to face it . . . I was curious as to why I hadn't even bothered to open the envelope and look at it. It's not that I wasn't bothered . . . I was scared of it, and to my alarm it occurred to me that I'm beginning to think that I'd rather run away from this than face it. It's hard enough living like this as it is. I just don't want to open up another can of worms . . . I just want it all to go away. I just want it to stop. Thirty years of this is killing me. I absolutely love music, it's the only thing I've ever wanted to do, I'm fortunate enough to be good at it and for 30 years it's been seriously marred by this thing. I just want it to stop and maybe running away would do that, but I'm not going to do that [but] I feel so very lonely at times . . . Oh yes. Yes. I'm sitting here in my kitchen now, all by myself [pause] shaking [sobbing]. Nobody knows I'm doing that. Nobody cares [pause] and if I told somebody about it they'd look at me as if I was some kind of weirdo. 'What the hell are you doing that for? You've been performing for 35 years, what's the matter with you?'

Case formulation for attachment-based psychotherapy

How well do the themes identified in Amanda's narrative map onto Gerald's narrative? Let us examine each of the key headings applied to Amanda to assess the degree of concordance and the degree of divergence in the anxious experiences of these two musicians.

Attachment style

Below is Gerald's description of his father, which may justify a hypothesis that Gerald's father had an unresolved state of mind with respect to attachment, and that Gerald was insecurely (ambivalently) attached to his father:

> My father was a frustrated musician himself. My parents are just working-class people. My dad was a jazz piano player; he taught himself to play by ear. He was successful at it but

his personality didn't allow him to make a profession out of it. He's very highly strung, very nervous, a bit paranoid, he doesn't have any ability to stick at anything. He had piano lessons which he didn't last very long at because he cannot stick at anything. That's the story of his whole life. He's never been able to hold a job down. He left school when he was 14; he's an intelligent man, fantastic set of ears, a good musician but he had no formal training, he can't do it. He can't see anything through . . . he didn't give us that confidence to tackle things; we always worried that we would be failures, like him.

Gerald has a deeply ambivalent relationship with his father in which he is praising of his father's musicality and intelligence but critical of his inability to 'see anything through.' Gerald wonders whether he is, in fact, a failure like his father. He makes no specific mention of his mother other to say, in an impatient and dismissive response to a question about whether his parents were musicians, 'No, no, they're just working-class people.' We could speculate that Gerald's profound fears of being a sham and being exposed as a sham may relate to his perceptions of his father, whom he thought was a sham as a father and as a musician.

False self formation, pathological accommodation, and feeling like a fraud or a sham

There is considerable evidence in Gerald's narrative to indicate false self formation. Feeling like a sham or a fraud, an indicator of false self formation, is a pervasive feature of his narrative. Its converse, the defensive use of narcissistic enhancement, is also pervasive. Note these examples, in which Gerald attempts to explain his performance fears in front of a 'feared' audience:

The more highly trained peers or audience that I have, the more it puts me under pressure and the worse I feel and I think it's to do with this esteem thing. I believe it's to do with they're going to see me for the sham that I am. I don't know why I feel like a sham. I'm in a privileged position where I play for this orchestra as section leader and on the face of it I'm the man. In theory I'm the best player in the state, in theory. I've got the job to prove it but by not proving it to myself I generally just don't believe it. So when I perceive that somebody's watching me who's in the know would see that I'm not actually any good, or not as good as I thought, then I feel like a sham . . .

And his response to a conductor's negative public comment:

It's bad enough having this monster on my back of my own making without somebody like that making it worse . . . Part of the reason I felt so devastated about it was that he made me look like a sham in front of my peers . . .

There is an enormous amount of shame attached to his music performance anxiety and his fear of being a sham. This makes him vulnerable to the insensitive criticism of unthinking conductors. When he felt publicly exposed, shamed, and humiliated by the conductor in front of his peers, he was shattered by the experience and could not recover from it. Recall our earlier discussion in Chapter Four on narcissism and shame. Gerald's narrative fluctuates between painful expressions of low self-esteem and the crushing effects of exposure and shame and attempts to reassert himself in order to restore his confidence and feelings of self-worth. At times, these attempts appear grandiose and immature. Over his lifetime, he has not been able to stabilize his sense of self and he has oscillated between these two extremes in an exhausting effort to manage his fragile sense of self. Note the oscillations in these examples:

> I deeply believe I can cope with all these parts, I'm a professional, I know what I'm doing. I don't know why I feel that I'm going to botch it and I don't know why I start to psych myself out of it months beforehand.

> On the face of it I'm the man. In theory I'm the best player in the state, in theory. I've got the job to prove it and by not proving it to myself I generally just don't believe it.

Auerbach (1990) describes his situation thus:

> At a minimum, these circumstances create a vicious circle of painful individuality and low self-esteem, exposure and shame, compliance and other hiding maneuvers to escape embarrassment, and attempts, however painful, to reassert individuality and restore feelings of vitality (p. 559).

Perfectionism

Closely allied to the feelings of being a sham in very vulnerable musicians is their exaggerated perfectionism. Gerald states:

> For me as a professional musician, a wrong note is a catastrophe, a wrong note is an indicator that I'm not as good as I say I am.

Perfectionism is a form of defense expressed as chronic and brutal self-criticism following perceived failure to attain unrealistic goals. When these goals are not attained, perfectionists are left feeling inherently flawed rather than forgivably human. Perfectionistic strivings are an attempt to compensate for the perceived defects in the self (McWilliams, 1994).

Absence of play

Gerald recounted his early ability to 'play' with his music. He could 'muck around' and show off and revel in being a solo performer until his ability for social comparison and realistic self-appraisal developed.

> When I was [in] my last year at primary school, I'd always been a performer . . . I'd muck around on the ukulele and sing and do those sorts of things you do at primary school and always as a solo performer because I was good at it, and I remember in my last year I suddenly became aware that some of the other students were good at it as well . . . and it just upset my self-confidence . . .

After that, music became a deadly serious business; he could no longer enjoy the sheer emotional and visceral pleasure of making music. His emotional survival came to depend on his capacity to perform flawlessly, in such a way that he would not be exposed as a sham.

Failure to mentalize

One of the very salient features of Gerald's narrative is his reification of his music performance anxiety as the 'monster within.' This leads to a question about his relationship with his anxiety. Is he taking responsibility for it; that is, does he own the problem? Has he accepted and understood the problem or does he just perceive it as an alien intrusion in his life and wish it would go away? He does not know his own monster because it is part of him. A concept closely allied to the concept of self is the experience of agency, the sense in which the self is perceived as the center of initiative or action. We sometimes disclaim our actions (e.g. 'I acted out of character' 'That behavior was not me') and thus feel that our experiences or actions are happening to us rather than originating in us. Gerald lives the experience moment to moment; he related primarily in an emotional, uncontained, and distressed way. Even talking about his anxiety in the safety of his own kitchen makes him feel uncomfortable and agitated. He recalls highly charged, anxiety-provoking situations, such as the incident in which he was humiliated by the conductor, as if it were happening right now. His recall of that incident had the quality of post-traumatic stress, in which he was re-experiencing the trauma, rather than recalling it or recounting it. Gerald had not really processed that experience. He needs a reflective space in which he can start to mentalize about his feelings, in order to understand his actions as intentional, mediated by mental states and mental processes (Bateman & Fonagy, 2004).

Painful somatic responses to performance anxiety

There are a great many statements in Gerald's narrative that attest to his extremely painful somatic responses. Note these examples:

> It's such a powerful overriding state to be in that it's very hard for me to control it and to try and think of other things to do. Even now as we speak I feel short of breath, agitated, not at all comfortable . . . [sobs] . . . When it grabs me, I tend to lose my ability to focus. My attention freezes . . .
>
> It just becomes a huge battle to try and fight it, to try and fight it back and try and cope . . . Such a huge battle and at the end of it I'm left exhausted at the least, exhausted and having not enjoyed what I just did at all.

Social anxiety disorder

Examine an excerpt from Gerald's interview below in which I was exploring my hypothesis that he may have had a more generalized social anxiety disorder. It indicates the presence of significant social anxiety.

> *Dianna: You appear to feel uncomfortable when you're in company or when the spotlight is on you in any venue, not just in music performance.*
> Gerald: Yes. It's funny you should say that, I tend to avoid quite often going for drinks at the pub after a concert or something like that [long pause] because I believe I'm not very good at that sort of thing. Apart from the fact that I don't drink and maybe I'm not very interesting to talk to, or if I don't feel particularly talkative then there's not much point going. I'd just rather avoid the stress.
>
> *Dianna: Being in a group can be quite stressful?*
> Gerald: Yes. I don't find it that easy to fit in with them as other people do. It's kind of dependent upon confidence and a lot of people get a long way because of the way that they deliver what they do. I've been able to get where I am [pause] just on the quality of what I do.
>
> *Dianna: You don't have any of the bravado or the self-promotion that you see in a lot of other people . . .*
> Gerald: That's right. I'm good at it, but I'm not confident. I'm too scared to, I see these other people as being really good at pushing themselves even though they aren't necessarily

that good and I've had to fight harder to get where I am than they did, to get ahead of people. It's not a competition if you know what I mean but I had to fight really hard to get the work I do because I wasn't one of the crowd and because I didn't promote myself very well, because I can't.

Dianna: You were very dependent on your own ability to get you where you've got, not on your capacity to network or to big note or ...
Gerald: I'm hopeless at networking. Hopeless.

Dianna: So that puts a lot of pressure on your performance skills ...
Gerald: Yes.

Dianna: ... because you feel as if you are totally reliant on those to get you where you need to be with your music?
Gerald: And thank whoever, I can't thank whoever enough for giving me the ability that I have, and for making me as good at what I do as I am because without it plus having no confidence I would have got nowhere.

Dianna: The competence that you have has to compensate for the lack of confidence?
Gerald: Yes. That's why it gets really difficult when I'm faced with people listening or watching who are [pause] so full of bravado, but who are really good, who really understand what I'm doing. These are people for whom I have a great deal of respect because they don't need to talk the talk because they walk the walk. It really freaks me out.

The puzzle of staying 'in the field'

As for Amanda, there is an enormous tension between wanting to stay in the field of music performance and wanting desperately to escape from it. These tug-of-war experiences related to wanting and not wanting to do something demonstrate ambivalence, characterized as an approach–avoidance conflict (Dollard & Miller, 1950), mentioned in Chapter One. Amanda's suicidality represents her earnest wish to be free of her profound emotional distress with respect to performing. For Gerald, the theme of running away from it is present throughout his narrative. The intense ambivalence about running away is highlighted in these examples below. He states that running away would be a solution for his dilemma but he undoes the statement almost immediately:

I just want it all to go away. I just want it to stop. Thirty years of this is just killing me. I absolutely love music, it's the only thing I've ever wanted to do, I'm fortunate enough to be good at it and for 30 years it's been seriously marred by this thing. I just want it to stop and maybe running away would do that, but I'm not going to do that.

He is also afraid of obtaining help:

I was curious recently as to why I hadn't even bothered to open the envelope (containing a referral to a psychologist) and look at it. It's not that I wasn't bothered; it was almost like I was scared of it, and to my alarm it just occurred to me recently that now at the age of 51 I'm just beginning to think that I'd rather run away from this than face it. I've got maybe another 10, 15 years playing in the orchestra ahead of me; I could almost get away with it and never have to face it and fixing this thing.

Case formulation from the perspective of ISTDP[5]

Gerald is a highly anxious man with serious performance anxiety and moderate social anxiety. He seems to have mostly striated (i.e. voluntary) muscle anxiety, but may at times have cognitive perceptual disruption (CPD) when his anxiety becomes severe. This suggests that he may require some graded exposure to his underlying feelings. He has some awareness of underlying feelings and some connection to them with sadness as he recounted the difficulties his anxiety has caused in his life. He was also aware of his anger, expressed in his desire to punch the conductor. These are both positive signs of a shorter duration for treatment. Gerald does not seem to get depressed, although he is probably dysthymic, and he has some punitive superego (PSE) pathology with ideas of being a 'sham' and being inferior to others. He may have internalized his father's 'paranoia,' which was more likely to be very high social anxiety leading to severe avoidance behavior and his inability to stick at anything. It is possible that the word 'sham' originated with his father. Of the two transcripts, I think the violinist is likely to be the more unwell as she seems to have more PSE pathology and at least moderate depression. I estimate that Gerald would need around 10 sessions for resolution of his anxiety problems, but if the cognitive–perceptual disruption is severe, it might double treatment duration to 20 sessions.

Case formulation for CBT[6]

Gerald is able to clearly articulate dysfunctional beliefs, and is asking for a remedy that does not 'open another can of worms.' Thus, CBT rather than more insight-oriented therapy may appeal to him. He describes two main catastrophic dysfunctional thoughts, which are that 'a wrong note will make (high-status) people think I am a sham,' and 'a wrong note will lead to ridicule from a conductor.' Underlying these is the dysfunctional core belief that 'I am a sham.' These thoughts cause a great deal of anticipatory anxiety, and also rumination over perceived prior humiliation. From a CBT perspective, Gerald would need to be able to identify, then effectively challenge and dismiss these unhelpful thoughts whenever they occur. In therapy he would be assisted to recognize the linkage between these cognitions and the subjective and physiological experience of anxiety and to generate more helpful thoughts with which he can counter his fear-inducing thoughts. He would be encouraged to keep a daily written record of unhelpful thoughts and of his positive challenge thoughts. His positive challenge thoughts would include some of those that he can already identify, such as 'It's just not important in the greater scheme of things.' Gerald may also benefit from learning some behavioral skills such as relaxation, which he could use on a daily basis at home, and immediately before and during performances. During breaks in the score, he may be able to employ breathing-based relaxation techniques successfully without interfering with his performance. He may also be able to use

---

[5] This formulation was provided by Dr Steven Arthey, PhD, clinical psychologist, ISTDP practitioner.

[6] The CBT formulations were prepared by Thomas Jones, MClinPsych, clinical psychologist, CBT practitioner.

anxiety-reducing imagery, for example, picturing the conductor as a frightened, naked little man, instead of seeing him as a powerful bully. It is possible that Gerald may be unwilling or unable to apply himself to cognitive behavioral techniques, as they do require some willingness to directly tackle his unhelpful thoughts when 'I'd rather run way from this than face it . . . I just want it to stop.' If this is the case, psychoactive medication may be considered to augment the CBT or instead of CBT.

We have experimented with three case formulations for two of the narratives of severely anxious musicians. Clearly, these formulations have elements in common, and it would be difficult at this stage of our knowledge to be prescriptive about which approach would be more effective for each of these musicians. There has been no systematic case series or other form of treatment to guide our clinical choices at this time. All of the CBT studies have been conducted in groups on musicians with varying levels of performance anxiety. Shedler (2010), in grappling with the question regarding the appropriate application and effectiveness of psychological therapies for different disorders, reminded us of the verdict of the dodo bird in *Alice in Wonderland*: 'Everybody has won and all must have prizes' (p. 105). It is important to note that no study has convincingly shown differences between bona fide, active treatments that are intended to work, as opposed to differences between an active treatment and no treatment, or an active treatment and a sham treatment that was never intended to work. In comparisons between treatments that are intended to work with no treatment, significant differences in outcomes are generally reported. However, in comparisons between two active treatments that are both designed to have positive clinical outcomes, the differences will necessarily narrow, if not disappear. This is true for the literature on CBT as well as the literature on psychodynamic therapies. Whether the difference remains statistically significant after it narrows depends on a complex array of factors, including patient characteristics, program integrity, study quality, and the skill of the clinicians delivering the treatments. Another factor is the timing of the post tests. Psychodynamic therapies show a robust effect at long-term follow-up in which patients maintain gains made at the end of therapy and, indeed, continue to improve over immediate post-test levels on the criteria of successful outcome. This has not been the case for CBT treatments for anxiety and depression (Shedler, 2010). Overall, the psychotherapy outcome literature does not support claims that CBT is superior to psychodynamic treatment, nor indeed is the reverse true. Primarily, it supports the claim that doing something that is intended to be helpful is better than doing nothing, or doing something that is not intended to be helpful. This state of affairs should not deter efforts to understand music performance anxiety, develop empirically based case formulations and devise and evaluate well-grounded therapies for its management. During the time in which I was writing this book, we commenced a trial of ISTDP, the results of which will be presented at a later date.

Summary

In this chapter I raise the possibility that music performance anxiety at its most extreme might constitute a disorder of the self. It applies to a subgroup of musicians whose experience of anxiety is so pervasive and profound that it is experienced as a defining characteristic of their sense of self. Attachment theory is discussed at length before two narratives produced from transcripts of interviews are presented and reviewed from an attachment-based psychotherapy perspective, which posits that one's relational experiences in early life, and the subsequent quality of one's attachment experiences, may affect and, indeed, direct behavior, beliefs, emotions, and relationships throughout life. I argue that attachment theory offers the most heuristic and evidence-based insights into this subgroup of musicians and that the psychodynamic psychotherapies may offer the best hope of treatment. Commonalities are identified in the narratives of the two musicians from this perspective. A number of concepts are canvassed—attachment style, false sense formation, pathological accommodation, feeling like an imposter or fraud, the absence of play, the failure to develop a capacity to mentalize experience—resulting in painful somatic and emotional responses to their performance anxiety and the puzzle of staying 'in the field' in the face of such aversive experiences. Both narratives were then subjected to two alternative formulations—one from the perspective of ISTDP and the other from the CBT perspective.

Chapter 9

Common themes in the lives of performing musicians

O Cacophony, goddess of jazz and of quarrels,
Crack-throated mistress of bagpipes and cymbals,
Let be your *con brios,* your *capricciosos,*
Crescendos, cadenzas, prestos and *prestissimos,*
My head on the pillow
(Piano, pianissimo)
Lullayed by susurrus lyres and viols.

Sylvia Plath.[1]

Because this book is primarily about musicians for musicians, in this chapter I want to present the voices of the musicians without too much commentary, in order to encourage readers to identify relevant themes and issues that have been presented throughout this book in the words of the musicians themselves. These excerpts are taken from the set of 20 in-depth interviews[2] with orchestral musicians described in Chapter Eight. All interviews were audiotaped and transcribed in full. The aim of this analysis was to extract common themes in the transcripts that would provide a nuanced insight into the psychological lives of orchestral musicians. You will notice the insightful collective wisdom contained in their comments, a type of wisdom that has been called 'craft knowledge' in educational research. Craft knowledge is defined as 'professional knowledge gained by experience . . . but which is rarely articulated in any conscious manner' (Day, 2005, p. 21). These interviews were conducted using an essentially grounded theory approach[3] (Piantanida, Tananis, & Grubs, 2004) in which themes were permitted to emerge from the open-ended conversation rather than being explored a priori. The interviews were examined firstly as textual data from which significant and recurring themes emerged and exemplars coded. Only themes that

---

[1] 'Alicante Lullaby' from *Plath: Poems*, published by Everyman's Library in 1998.
[2] Details regarding gender, age, instrument, and years of experience have been omitted from the individual quotes in order to protect the identity of the participants, some of whom played low-frequency instruments such as harp, percussion, bassoon, and trombone. The participants constitute a very small group, easily identifiable within the relatively small world of professional musicians within the eight orchestras of Australia.
[3] Grounded theory is an inductive qualitative research method in which theory emerges from the data and moves from the specific to the general. Concepts are the key elements of analysis because theory is developed from conceptualization of the data, rather than the actual data.

appeared in at least 50% of the conversations are presented below. As themes emerged, the relevant literature was consulted, as were the in-depth analyses of selected transcripts presented in the previous chapter. This constant comparison method (Maykut & Morehouse, 1994) allows the importance and centrality of particular themes to be identified. Below I present a brief account of each of the main themes that emerged, with several verbatim exemplars from the musicians themselves.

Musical identity

Professional musicians are highly invested in their identities as musicians, and find it difficult to disentangle their self-esteem, that is, their view that one has intrinsic value, from their musical self-efficacy, the belief that one can perform well on one's instrument (Kemp, 1996). This high investment makes musicians and other high level performers, such as elite athletes, actors and dancers, more vulnerable to anxiety because of the perception that if they fail as performing artists, they also fail as people (Chesky & Hipple, 1997).

Many of the musicians interviewed had almost their whole identity and sense of self-worth invested in their musical identity. Below are some indicative examples.

> Music is my life, I don't do anything else. It was a deliberate decision to become a professional musician. I remember, I'm quite clear about this. When I was 14 I knew that that's what I was going to do. I didn't know in what shape or form but there was never any doubt. I never had to consider what my career options would be any more, it was always going to be that way and I went along for the ride from there on.

> You know you're a musician, you're an artist, you're not just 'Oh, I'm playing an instrument and somebody taught me to play it like this.' It's a real feeling of artistic input, so it's a total way of life really.

> We've got lots of scientists and doctors in our family. I just assumed that's what I would do. Be a scientist. Until I got to about 15 and I suddenly started identifying myself with the violin and I suddenly thought that I can't do anything else. That's what I really wanted to do . . . My job is so close to my heart . . . I guess I have that feeling that I am my job, which is rubbish, but if I can't do it then I'm hopeless. Yes, I identify so much of myself with playing the violin.

> My parents are both musicians, both professionals. I come from a family of five siblings and we all play music, so it's something I was bred into. I was playing the violin before I even knew what was happening; I think I started when I was 6. So right from a very early age, I was performing in public. I remember doing the little eisteddfod competitions before I was 10; probably when I was 8 or 9. My parents encouraged us to do music and to love it but it's not as if I was forced in any way to follow my parents' footsteps. I can't foresee having a career change . . . there's a few things I might like to do on the side, but I can't imagine not playing or performing.

> My life in general is the same as my musical life. I am complicated. I find that music is a big part of my life. It defines me—it is my life and my lifestyle. All my experiences as a musician are applied to my life in general. It makes me impatient and frustrated. I am not happy with my life. There are a lot of negative ruminations and it is hard for me to let go. If I perform badly, I practise like crazy for the next performance. But my anxiety is sky high. This can provide both a good focus point but can also be very destructive.

Compare this statement from an older musician who struggled successfully to separate her musical self from her 'human' self. It is interesting to note that the implicit conceptualization of a musician in this account is other than human, and therefore not permitted to make mistakes. Only by accepting her humanness was she able to accept that mistakes are made and survived.

> Music is not the main focus of my life now whereas when I was young, it was. I would think: 'I'm a harpist.' After about 20 years, I could say: 'No, I'm not a harpist, I'm a musician who plays the harp but that's not who I am; I'm actually a person.' My job doesn't define me, which in the beginning, when you're young, I think it does . . . Just hearing myself say 'I'm a harpist,' I think, 'Oh my God, what a thing to put on yourself—that I'm a violinist or a trumpeter or a flautist, my God, I'm a human being.' Being human allows you to make mistakes but also to be creative. I'm a human being.

Sense of self

Closely related to musicians' musical identity is the underlying sense of self.

> When I was about 12, I went to a concert and Joshua Bell, who was a very young man a the time, played a concerto. I'd never heard anything like it, and I thought, "Yep, that's it. That's for me." When I was in secondary school, I thought about doing engineering because I was good at science, but in the end, I thought, "No." But I never became a soloist, which was my dream. I think back and maybe I think I should've been less realistic, so to speak. But I took on the anxiety of my parents who wanted me to have a stable job, so instead of taking the risk of going overseas, I auditioned for orchestral positions. You need so much inner strength and self-belief to aim for a solo career, and you can't practice those things. They are either there or they're not.

> You have this feeling of being the only one who doesn't know how to deal with nerves and anxiety. I know it's not true but I remember that feeling from way back that I shouldn't be here and I've got to try and pretend that I know what I am doing. I mean I can play, I suppose I do deserve it but it's just that fraud feeling, I guess, and I don't really know where that comes from. I really can't convince myself that I can manage my nerves and so therefore I can't do my job properly. I clearly remember having those empty sorts of feelings . . . when I first started, that I'm not worthy of this. Even though I know I can play, I don't know that I can cope with it.

> I recently tried out for a principal's job in the [. . .] chamber orchestra. They were a great, great group to play with but I feel like I don't really deserve it because I can't manage it. I can't manage performing. I do manage but I feel like I can't do it how I want to be doing it. I don't feel comfortable at all.

> I'm a very shy person so for me performing wasn't easy . . . I was very scared when I played, even as a young person and that translated straight away into stiffness . . . Right from the beginning as a child I always had to have a pre-performance routine, because I wasn't one of those outgoing people, or quietly confident people, who, once they get on stage take over the world; they're just natural performers, it was never natural for me to perform though people looking at me playing out there at the front wouldn't have thought that. To them, even my own family, I was having a ball and it was a dream. They didn't know how tied up in knots I really was.

Internalized mental representations of parents

I have discussed in considerable detail throughout this book the far-reaching effects that the quality of early attachments and their disruption can have on the entire developmental trajectory that may continue throughout life. Until musicians enter a therapeutic relationship that encourages the exploration of their early life in relation to the development of their self-concept and performance anxiety, they are often dismissive of the idea that events that have occurred so long ago can have an impact on their current difficulties. Most are able to provide a narrative about their parents and even their relationship to their parents, but not understand the emotional impact that the internalized parent (if critical, neglectful, unreliable, or abusive) has on their current functioning.

> I actually didn't like entering competitions. There was always a lot of pressure about it and a lot of parents are very competitive, as if they were playing in the competition. I didn't like the whole atmosphere that it created, and I also didn't like having to go on stage all the time. My own nature is shy and I didn't enjoy the experience. But my parents and teachers said it was good for me and what can you say at 10 years of age when they are staring you down and saying you have to do it because they know what is best. I remember having quite a bad memory lapse in one competition and the adjudicator wrote that the piece was too difficult for me and I should not perform works that are beyond me. Those comments had a very negative impact on the way I felt about playing for a long time. Not so much having the memory lapse, but having this awful comment that has actually stayed with me until now. Those comments and the look of disappointment on my mother's face is etched very finely — that was 20 years ago but I can still recall every detail of it.

> My father was a scientist. He was totally absorbed in his world of science and test tubes; his laboratory was his world. I am the only person in my family to pursue the arts. My siblings and extended family are doctors and mathematicians and scientists. I remember when I was around 14 years, I was chosen to perform a big solo at a concert and my father promised he would come. At the last minute, just as we were all leaving for the concert, my father said that he had an idea and had to return to his laboratory to test it out. I still remember the disappointment I felt that he didn't come to my first big solo concert and that he did not seem to understand how hurt I was about it. Each time I get up to perform, I have a sense of that moment and wonder whether anyone wants to hear me play.

Generational transmission of music performance anxiety

Some of the musicians were able to reflect upon the effect that their own parents' anxiety had on their psychological functioning with respect to performance and their lives generally.

> My mum is a real worrier; she is wound up about everything. I am like that. She hides it well. It affects her different to me. I get cross and angry with myself and then it spreads to others. Mum bottles it up. She gets lots of headaches. I do too. I realized very early in high school that I was an anxious person . . . I get unhappy about very small things that only I would be unhappy about. My mum does not seem to have come to terms with her anxiety and I have not come to terms with my anxiety. I don't understand why it happens and when and why it doesn't happen. Sometimes I get nervous about the silliest things. She is like that, too.

Others described how they or their partners may have had an adverse effect with respect to the transmission of anxiety to their own children:

> My husband was a musician too. His whole family was very musical but they have huge mental health issues to deal with because they're extremely emotional and there's a hereditary problem with alcohol. He was an addictive personality, he had cigarettes, he got hooked on Valium and he was hooked on alcohol so they were real crutches for him that he needed to get out there and play . . . There is a strong anxiety thing through that side of the family . . . my daughter is a music graduate and she teaches privately. She's got an anxiety problem herself but she seems to be able to cope with performing. She hid it while she was at high school; it only came out when she had a breakdown when she finished school. She has panic attacks. It is quite severe and she's on medication; she has tried lots of different psychological therapies but she never could really get on top of it. I'm amazed she can get up and play at all. She's not a born performer either, and she didn't have good role models.

In the example below, this musician, whose story we discussed earlier, is reflecting on her approach to her own daughter's aspirations, and reveals her struggle not to repeat with her own daughter the experiences she had with her parents. Amanda is aware of the possibility of transgenerational impingement on her daughter but through conscious reflection is able to allow her daughter to make her own decision, something that she herself was denied.

> I've got the same problem now, because I've got a 15-year-old daughter and she's thinking about becoming a violinist, and I just don't know whether that's a good move or not. But at least it's entirely up to her whether or not she does it. I had to fight a slight battle with myself, thinking that I desperately wanted her to be a violinist but now I think, 'No.' I would rather she were happy at doing whatever she does. And I don't necessarily think she's going to be that happy being a violinist, because it can be quite a struggle.

Prevention of generational transmission of music performance anxiety

Generational transmission of anxiety is not inevitable, as the following excerpt shows. Even though this musician was very aware that both his parents, who were professional orchestral musicians, suffered performance anxiety severe enough to warrant the use of beta-blockers, he himself does not feel the need to resort to such measures to manage his own anxiety. It is possible that his experience of a secure attachment with his parents, who were able to discuss their own struggles with him honestly, without putting their anxieties into their son, was protective, in that it helped him to appraise the issue of performance anxiety as it related to his own performing career.

> My dad is a professional horn player and has at times really struggled with performance anxiety and used beta-blockers . . . he doesn't use them regularly, but if he's really having problems with confidence, just to get him through a certain performance. Playing principal horn that my dad used to play, it gets such exposed solos and those types of instruments are really vulnerable . . . it's a real test of the nerves . . . And I've seen that, and I don't know, somehow I've just thought it's obviously only a short-term fix. So I'm probably more prepared to tough it out and play badly on the odd occasion rather than to

take beta-blockers. I have discussed this a little with my dad. He doesn't enjoy taking them . . . it was just if there was a difficult solo passage or something didn't go well the night before and he had to come and do it again; when he was feeling really negative, those were the times he'd use them. My mother suffers from performance anxiety also. She doesn't play in the orchestra any more . . . She's now a full-time music teacher, teaches violin and piano. I think she takes beta-blockers if she's accompanying piano and has something really tricky to do. Seeing my parents suffering such high levels of performance anxiety such that they needed beta-blockers to cope with it . . . I guess it was sort of a reality check . . . that everyone finds it hard, and at any level . . . Well, I guess not everyone, but I mean the vast majority of people think, 'Gee, this job's hard,' and have self-doubt . . . I do too . . . I don't know how we escaped suffering more severely from performance anxiety. Maybe it's because we saw it happen. Yes, that's the only thing I can really think of, is that we performed a lot when we were little and we saw, for example, what was in our parents. Parents, when you're little, you think are completely infallible and pillars of strength, but we saw them really suffering and struggling. Maybe that's something that helped us think logically . . . well, logically is not the right word. I can't think of the word, but something like 'logically' about performance anxiety and what effects it has and how to not let it ruin things, or make life a lot more uncomfortable than it needs to be. Also, we talked about the issue with our parents. The fact that I know that they were nervous and that they took beta-blockers; they didn't try to hide it from us . . .

Onset of music performance anxiety

The majority of musicians interviewed for this study reported that their first memories regarding the onset of music performance anxiety occurred during adolescence. Although there is evidence that child musicians feel anxious prior to a musical performance (Ryan, 1998, 2004, 2005), these memories do not appear to be encoded in the same way as what appear to be much more salient experiences of music performance anxiety during adolescence. Adolescent musicians recall adverse musical performance experiences with a considerable degree of detail (Osborne & Kenny, 2008) and adult musicians recall these conditioning experiences during adolescence with a clarity and emotional 'present-ness' that resemble, in some instances, the flashbacks experienced by those who suffer post-traumatic stress disorder.

It is the characteristics of adolescent cognitive development, discussed in Chapter Two, that make the experiences during this period of development so salient. Many musicians report adverse memories of musical performances during this period of development as if they had happened yesterday. This phenomenon, called embeddedness, characterizes to some extent most young people during adolescence but it tends to be particularly stark, distressing, and persistent for those who have had unsatisfactory attachment relationships or have experienced other forms of emotional distress that have not been processed or resolved. Wallin (2007) defines embeddedness thus:

> [E]mbeddedness is context dependent, such that there are some events, some relationships, and some events in relationships that leave us feeling . . . swamped by overwhelming emotion [such that] we feel utterly unable in such contexts to . . . stand outside the experience and think about it . . . [T]he bridge from embeddedness to mentalizing is built on a foundation of affect regulation, recognition of intentionality and symbolic play (p. 139).

It is unfortunate that the simultaneous development of these intellectual capacities, the outcome of which is heightened self-consciousness and self-criticism as it becomes apparent that they are the object of others' scrutiny and evaluation, coincides with exposure on real and imaginary stages to real as well as imaginary audiences. This situation, in which there are actual or perceived adverse judgments co-occurring from within and without, can prove emotionally devastating to adolescents, particularly those who have not mastered earlier developmental challenges arising from unsatisfactory early attachment experiences (Harter, 1997).

Fear memories arising from these real and imaginary audiences are encoded and stored in the amygdala, in a process called memory consolidation. Once consolidation occurs, memories may be long lasting. When these memories are recalled later, they become subject to reworking and reappraisal, in a process called reconsolidation. Recent research has shown that the amygdala stores fear memories very specifically, and each memory stored will need to undergo its own specific reconsolidation in order to reduce the fear associated with that memory (Kindt, Soeter, & Vervliet, 2009).

Below is a sample of fear memories related to the onset of music performance anxiety experienced during the adolescence of these musicians with many years of professional music performance experience, who are reporting them between 20 and 40 years after they first occurred. You will note the intense language and affect used in these descriptions and the 'present' time quality that they display, memory features that are common to people who suffer from post-traumatic stress disorder (Greenberg & Wessely, 2009).

> I have always suffered from performance anxiety. The first time has always stayed with me. I had never experienced it before this. Maybe it was related to feeling self-conscious getting up in front of hundreds of people. This first time affected me very badly. I thought, 'WOW!' I did not know that my body could react in that way. At the end of every year, there is a combined schools' choral concert and to break up the vocal onslaught, there are a number of instrumental solos that are selected by audition. In year 11, I was selected as one of the soloists. In that performance, I really fell apart. I got really nervous and my body just let me down. It was really embarrassing. It was my first awakening to performance anxiety. I got a really dry mouth, the notes wouldn't 'speak' properly; my breathing was shallow and for the horn, you need to breathe deeply. I did not have the presence of mind to assess what was happening. I did not have any counter moves to counterbalance what was happening to me. I ke pt playing; I did not have a performance breakdown but the performance was bad and I felt very bad. I felt that I had disgraced myself. I was very down and very angry with myself and above all, I was very confused about what had happened and why it had happened. It was tough to accept that it had happened. I lost my sense of invulnerability. The feeling lasted a long time for me—days, weeks, I can't remember. It affected everything I did after that. I knew that anxiety would always be there after that concert and it has [been].

> The first time I remember suffering from performance anxiety [was] when I was about 12 years old. I had to perform a piece that I didn't want to play [laughs], I tried in vain to substitute it with something I liked, but my violin teacher insisted . . . And before that time I'd been playing in public at all sorts of concerts without a care in the world and when it came at me, it came as quite a shock and I think that memory's always stayed with me . . . I felt ashamed, I felt like I wanted to run away. I was playing the piece from memory, also,

I remember, and I forgot the music and I just froze . . . I can still picture myself on stage . . . I've had lots of worse experiences than that, but that one was the first one that I remember . . . I mean it was panic; it was a panic attack really . . . I have had feelings like that ever since, all the time . . . I take Inderal quite regularly and with that I can control it. Otherwise, I wouldn't be doing this job.

I never got to a really bad stage fright until I was in my mid teens. After that it became so . . . I just couldn't really perform without some sort of drug. I was quite depressed as a teenager as well. I lost all the fun of being just a child performing, and it became serious . . .

I remember that first time I had this horrible terror. I must have been in high school and I was put into a position at the last minute when I hadn't ever done it before. I was about 15 and I remember sitting on the outside of the first violins and I remember suddenly not being able to cope with it. I asked my friend if we could swap so I could be on the inside. It happened again when I was playing in the youth orchestra. The first year I was in the section sitting up the back and I just loved it. The second year I was suddenly leading or sitting in the front and I didn't quite know how to deal with it. I think I had that feeling that I really don't know what I'm doing but I am supposed to know. It's that fraud feeling.

I had an experience when I would've been about 19 or 20, and I went to one of these national music camps and I was in a chamber group and we were playing in one of the concerts that had practically the whole campus there. We were doing this piece by Mendelssohn with a huge first violin part that I was playing, and I somehow managed to work myself up into an enormous tizz about it, that this was so important and there were so many people watching who would know if I was any good or not. And I really worked myself up into such a state where I didn't actually eat properly for a couple of days and I felt sick . . . And you know, we did it and it didn't go well and it was a defining moment that I thought, 'Well, that was a bloody waste of energy, wasn't it?' And I guess that's probably the advice I'd give someone—that worrying about things doesn't actually help. I mean, worrying, if it motivates you to do better or to prepare more or to get on top of things better, that's great, but if it's become such a performance-inhibiting thing, why bother? And yes, obviously it's easier said than done to just switch off worrying about things; you can't. But for me, that experience of probably the most acute performance anxiety I ever had, I thought, 'That didn't help anyone.'

Music performance anxiety in older musicians

In Chapter Five, we explored the frequency and patterns of occurrence of music performance anxiety. As you will recall, music performance anxiety is no respecter of age, skill, or experience. The anxiety triggers, however, may be different for different groups of musicians, to which these accounts of older musicians attest.

One of our older players—he was a principal—was suffering very badly. We basically did a temporary job swap with another player to protect him and to alleviate his stress. When players get old, you can't control things the way you used to. He was unhappy about his playing and needed to alleviate his embarrassment. If you are not performing well in exposed parts, it is very difficult to live with. There is a real physical component to brass playing. It is harder as you get older. Tutti string players have more longevity than other types of players.

I just recently have decided to step down as principal trumpet with my orchestra, mainly to alleviate the level of stress I am experiencing. It was a difficult decision, because I enjoyed the leadership role, but I saw the last leader lose his ability as he got older and it was humiliating. He was in denial about his problem. I need to step down before that happens to me. I would like to be less wound up and to perhaps recapture the joy of playing before I retire.

Causes of music performance anxiety

I wonder whether it's more what your psychological make-up is . . . People who are extraverted seem to breeze through life; how they do that, whether they just naturally don't have things bother them or they're just big enough to say, 'Well I'm not going to let that bother me' . . . but I really believe it's 99% mental. Any performance, whether it's speaking or sporting, it's mental attitude. What makes somebody a hundredth of a second faster in the pool is just whether your body's working right on the day and that's all mental—being on top of the physical and how we play as a team; sports teams can play well together some times and not another time. Why do things click sometimes and not others? It's the concentration and the whole mindset and the collective will. I just think people need to be honest with themselves about where they're at and whether they want to still be there or not, whether they make any changes to what they do or whether they allow their anxiety to cripple them.

Phenomenology of music performance anxiety

I know that I am fundamentally totally lacking in basic feelings of self-confidence that give you a solid foundation on which to live your life. Piled onto those shaky foundations is my music performance anxiety so that I am always teetering on the edge, never centred or balanced or calm.

I use beta-blockers regularly. The main reason I started taking them is that they stopped me from shaking. I started about 30 years of age, because I got to the point of being a spring. It also freed up my ability to breathe deeply. Once I can do that, the anxiety decreases. Sometimes I forget to take them and I play just fine. Maybe they are now a placebo. But sometimes it hits me just before I start to play that I have forgotten to take my tablet. I then lock my body into a rigid posture to stop shaking. That has caused me a lot of shoulder and neck pain over the years. I have to take strong analgesics and visit the physiotherapist often to cope with this. I also get very bad tension headaches. I have, I suppose, what you would call embodied tension. I am wound up, stressed out, bundle of pain and nerves. It's a great life!

Unwanted effects of medication

I experience enormous anxiety before some concerts; in fact, I think I'd feel really weird if I didn't. In fact, yes, I got high blood pressure from extreme stress at work and the doctor put me on blood pressure tablets, and that wasn't me. I felt really bad about that but I did give a performance of the Schumann 'Fantasy' on blood pressure tablets. I just felt disembodied; it was fine, I did it from memory, it was fine, but it would bother me to be a performer if I had to do it like that all the time [laughs], because it takes away the adrenaline rush. Blood pressure tablets are beta-blockers and they just damp down your whole preparatory, psychological focus and everything; not your psychological focus but your excitement in the act of creation.

Conditioned responses—false alarms

Below are clear examples of Barlow's false alarms. You will recall from Chapter Six that panic attacks are 'false alarms' that appear uncued and unexpected and which become conditioned in particular stressful situations that are associated with heightened threat or danger in people who have a specific psychological vulnerability and heightened neurobiological hyper-reactivity. These examples highlight several of the key elements of false alarms—many of the musicians recognized the habitual, conditioned nature of the panic, but also commented that it seemed to 'hit' them out of the blue at the same time.

> . . . the exposedness of what I'm about to play or depending on who's watching, these [circumstances] set off this train of conditioned responses. It just becomes a huge battle to try and fight it, to try and fight it back and try and cope . . . Such a huge battle and at the end of it I'm left exhausted, exhausted and having not enjoyed what I just did at all [sobs].

> I have a massive problem in my head with playing softly in the orchestra and it feels to me that it really affects me physically and that I can't express what I am trying to do properly. I can get very stuck at the end of the bow because I'm worried about my bow shaking or not being in control with what I'm doing with the bow. Loud playing and difficult left hand passages don't worry me at all . . . but I can sit there in rehearsal for a concert that night and I'll think, 'Oh, no! That's going to happen there!' every time I look at [a soft passage]. I try not to think these horrible needy thoughts but I'm just so conditioned to think I'm really going to get stuck in the bow and everyone is going to think I am hopeless. I'm not going to feel I can express myself at all. It's like being in a straitjacket . . . So, I'm going through some sort of paralytic fit next to my desk partner and he doesn't even notice. I must look completely calm, I suppose, but I'm so used to feeling like I'm covering it up all the time and just getting through it . . . It's not like I don't enjoy playing but it's really starting to overtake how I feel about playing altogether and how I feel about playing in the orchestra.

> I always remember the first time it hit me. It was like being in an earthquake or a tsunami. I mean it was panic, I mean it was a panic attack, what I would quantify as a panic attack. I take Inderal® all the time now and that helps me to control it; I've never been comfortable performing. I couldn't do this job without medication. I did a lot of other things for a few years, but when I got back into music performance, playing in orchestras, I realised that I still had significant problems with my nerves. It's like a learned response now; I can't shake [it] off. When I am performing, it can hit me, yeah. It's not just during a performance; it can be in a rehearsal as well. It depends on how exposed I feel, where I'm sitting, all sorts of things, like if I have a big solo . . . I'm a great believer in doing good preparation but a panic attack will just take that all away. I tried a whole list of techniques described in that book, called The Inner Game of Music, by Barry Green . . . those things are good, but they don't work for me when panic absolutely overtakes me.

Unpredictability of panic attacks

> [Panic attacks] don't happen every concert, which terrifies me even more. With the pops concerts or even with chamber music, when I feel I can connect with the audience and with the people I'm playing with it's much less of a problem . . . But this whole thing of a big group being on stage and there's a sterile atmosphere, to me this is quite terrifying.

It's a strange thing . . . I just thought recently I hate the concert hall . . . I can't pinpoint what it is that sets me off on this path of a panic attack . . . there's so many factors like who you are sitting with. I don't like sharing a stand either because I feel physically constricted. Who you are sitting with; who's conducting; who's leading; what music you're playing—all that stuff. I do work on my technique a lot . . . I have lessons . . . I know what I am doing technically but then it gets to this point in the concert where it's almost like a blackout feeling, where you're in such panic . . . I've tried so many techniques for not allowing this to happen . . . In that moment, if it happens, I can't actually really think of anything except trying to get through it . . . I haven't actually succeeded in figuring out what actually happens in that moment or why.

I have not come to terms with my anxiety. I don't understand why it happens and when and why it doesn't happen. Sometimes I take beta-blockers and feel relaxed; I can also take them and still feel very nervous. Sometimes I get nervous about the most trivial things. Sometimes I will play a very difficult passage and not feel anxious. The anxiety is unpredictable. I think it would be better for me to understand this. I sometimes assess why I am playing so well and will conclude that my breathing is good, that I have a positive attitude, that I love the piece I am playing, that we have a good conductor. All these elements come into play.

Cognitive interference

Sight reading

As an orchestral musician a large part of what we do is dependent on our ability to sight read . . . I'm quite good at sight reading . . . however, being dependent on that when the chips are down and I'm feeling under pressure, my ability to sight read goes out the window. Not because I can sight read less but because I can't focus on what I have to remember to do the sight reading, I have to remember to read forward, read in advance. I just can't remember to do it because I'm so focused on feeling nervous.

Memory

One thing that used to make me very nervous is when I was playing solos in competitions, it was always from memory and I think that was one of the hardest things I found, which made me feel tense and worry about performing, was the big grim reaper of a memory slip or a memory lapse hanging over me. I think that's probably the thing that I associate most with performance anxiety, is that very thing . . . I haven't played from memory since I got the job in the orchestra. I can't think of a time when I've played anything from memory since my final recital at university . . . I do remember in university, both in my undergraduate and postgraduate courses, having memory lapses and occasionally falling in a heap. Yes, it happened. I almost expected, if I was playing really long pieces, that there was going to be a point where I floundered momentarily. And I guess once I did that more, you realise that you could actually, if you don't drop your bundle, you can actually recover from a small memory lapse. I just always found that playing from memory put me a lot more on edge than playing with the music.

Worry and rumination

Often I'll worry about things and usually that's in the before . . . it's not actually in the moment; like, the week before, I'll be worried about a certain programme. I don't know, I guess by worrying about it earlier, it means I do what it takes, that by the performance,

I don't feel the nerves, the butterflies and feeling tense. Yes, I guess I worry beforehand and then try and do what it takes to feel comfortable on the night.

It just seems so stupid to me, a stupid response, to something that I need to do, I need to be able to perform. That's what I do, that's what I'm paid to do . . . so it's a skill that I have to keep up and I have to do it and I want to do it, but I don't know why it has to be so damn difficult . . . I can cope with all these parts, I'm a professional, I know what I'm doing. I don't know why I feel that I'm going to botch it and I don't know why I start to psych myself out of it months beforehand.

Once I was a visiting player in another orchestra. We had a fantastic week of rehearsals but I started to worry about the solos on the night of the concert. I started to overthink immediately before going on stage. This really impaired my performance. Other people noticed that I did not play as well as in the rehearsals. I felt I should have sustained that high level of performance. There are lots of peaks and troughs in the graph of my anxiety and ruminations.

I realized very early in high school that I was an anxious person. That is why I practised obsessively because I was not happy with the results that I was hearing. I was conscious of what sounded good and not good. A lot of students are not good at self-assessment . . . I have always had a fear of sounding bad. I have a very acute ear but not perfect pitch. This is common in musicians, we are always self-analyzing. After concerts, I am always going over what went well and what did not go well . . . I find it very difficult to comfort myself after a bad performance. I need my own space; I can't be around people. This dominates my ability to enjoy my music . . . it takes me a long time to wind down after most performances. That first anxiety experience was a strong moment in my life.

Combined cognitive and physical interference

[I would like to] see the big musical picture but I am not easily able to do that . . . Not when I'm performing . . . I get so stuck in the little things about playing. About how I am feeling physically and what I am doing technically and, I guess, I'm trying to think of maybe too many things at once . . . Oh, my breathing is terrible and I try my best to delay the onset of the panic by breathing well. But, then again, I'm not actually sure what's happening, because I just try and get through it . . . I've noticed a few physical things like my right leg comes up like I'm trying to support the bow with the leg and I go into this claw-like position, my shoulder comes up . . . and I'm sure my breathing goes out the window.

What our teachers told us

No ordinary teacher will ever reach,
Those whom Time has failed to teach.[4]

[M]y main teacher was a Russian guy . . . he was just into playing the violin in the traditional way. He was not interested in anxiety or the like but he did once say to me just before a big concert, 'Oh, you look very stressed. Why be so stressed? You should smile and look for the pretty girls in the audience.'

My teacher was a very ordered and logical thinker when it came to violin playing and teaching . . . she had logical approaches to all aspects of playing the instrument, so that in moments of tension you figure out ways to get round it . . . she said that you should expect

---

4 Har ki namukht az guzashti ruzgar, Niz namuzad zi hich amuzgar (Transcription from Persian) Abu 'Abd Allah Rudaki, 9th-century Persian poet.

that when you play, you might be tight or your hands might get clammy or you're on edge . . . you approach all these things in your practice and think about it and then organize yourself so that you are prepared for all eventualities. It gave me confidence knowing that you've prepared it in a way that if something goes wrong, you can deal with it.

My teacher taught me never to leave anything to chance. For example, if you have to find a high note that's tricky to find, you've got to have a very ordered and methodical, relaxed approach to how you're going to find that exact spot on the instrument without getting flustered in the heat of the moment . . . practising at home can be very easy. You say, 'Oh yes, I know where that is. Yes, it should be right,' but in a performance situation when you're tense, that's not going to work . . . because at the last minute, you might question it, which is often what happens. But if you've got a complete, methodical approach to working out the spaces on the instrument and finding that note, it will work under pressure every time . . . like measuring the spaces with your fingers to find a top note rather than just winging it . . . measuring up with certain intervals and shifting it in a really sensible way. She was very sensible . . . She had a strategy for absolutely everything, so in times of pressure, the strategy was always there rather than the 'Whatever happens, happens' approach, which is what I had before, that you practise hard but then you just wing it, you just do it. But here, there's more, something to rely on in your hour of need. I don't do it as much these days, but yes, definitely sometimes I do think, 'What would my teacher say in a passage like this?'

One thing we'd aim for first, after covering all the basics like working out fingering or bowing so I could get through it . . . I would aim for fluency well before I aimed for perfection. I like to take a bigger-picture approach and not get bogged down on the first half page because it doesn't sound like a recording. I find that a negative way to do things; I find that you've got to get a whole picture, and then improve the whole picture rather than work on one corner of it until you feel sickened and angry and depressed. Work on the whole piece. My teacher was great like that. If I'd go to a lesson and I'd prepared 20 minutes of music, we'd work on 20 minutes of music, not the first two minutes. And then the next lesson, we'd work on that 20 minutes of music again, and you'd build it up on layers of detail . . . because I think if you focus with too much perfection on a small passage, it becomes a negative thing and you get worried about it. Yes, I found I respond better to a holistic approach to learning a piece, rather than taking a piece-by-piece approach.

The more I played, the more I learned to control those anxious moments. I learned to focus on the music, not on the unknown, not on what could happen. My teacher told me to get back on the horse as soon as possible after a performance disaster and it would sort itself out.

What we tell our students

I try to tell my students when they do exams that it doesn't matter what happens. If you don't get an A, it's no big deal. It's just on the day and you just move on, and I feel like that myself. Like, if you don't try something, you haven't tried it, and then if it doesn't work out, you go, 'Oh well,' and get on to the next thing. I would try to make them understand that it's not that important. It's not life and death and really, even if it does go badly, it doesn't really matter and you'll have another opportunity. But yes, I don't know how useful that is. I have got a student who has cried in every exam that she's done and I really haven't helped her a lot with that. I just kept making her do more. Yes, so I haven't got good strategies, I don't think, to handle them.

Situational factors that may exacerbate music performance anxiety

Conductors

Almost all of the musicians interviewed had a 'bad conductor story.' This is one area of professional music performance in which there is an obvious remedy that can be readily addressed in a cost-effective manner. There were two main concerns expressed, the first of which was the variability in tempi from rehearsal to performance or across performances that creates unnecessary stress in the musicians who must adjust their technique in response to faster and slower tempi. Secondly, conductors must be made aware of the potentially devastating effect their criticisms can have on performers. Those who are responsible for the development of conductor training courses in tertiary music institutions should seriously consider the introduction of additional courses in tempi and rhythm, and focused courses on understanding human behavior, human motivation, and risk factors for the development or exacerbation of anxiety disorders in orchestral musicians, including their own role as a risk factor. Below is a selection of the many interesting comments on this subject by orchestral musicians.

> A lot of things are totally out of our control and I've realized over the years that it's what your mind does with your situation that matters. You can be put in a really hard situation like where the conductor's tempos were impossible and you've got to change your fingering and readjust everything and then on the night it might be all back to slow again so it's an absolute nightmare really.

> Some conductors can't seem to stick to a tempo . . . it affects different instrumentalists differently. The stings might have to change their fingering for the faster tempos . . . the brass players have issues with the type of tonguing they have to do depending on the speeds but usually they can just say to the conductor, 'Look, you need to set a tempo and stay with it,' and they'll get away with it whereas the rest of us feel a bit more under the thumb; we're a bit more timid [laughs].

> I can't help that the conductor goes far too fast which meant I was never going to be able to play it the way I wanted, so you have to adjust. Some people might have just spent 20 million hours practising, trying to get it that fast—good luck if they can do it . . . You're working within limits and if you've got unrealistic things put on you and you only get a couple of days to practise before you have to perform . . . that can be a big problem if you let it . . .

> I used to sit there and tremble; my hands would shake because the conductor's looking at me, and how do you play when you're shaking so badly you can hardly keep the bow on your strings? Then I saw people being destroyed, their lives, their careers destroyed by a conductor because he'd pick on them or never give them a compliment and look at them and they shrivelled up inside and couldn't play and they had to walk away from their careers. I thought that's not right . . . A lot of things happen outside you and you've got a choice about how you react to that . . . when I'd see conductors speak horribly to somebody, I thought, 'They're not going to get the best result from that person by treating them like that.' So it turned everything around for me. Instead of me being a victim or feeling like I was at fault, suddenly I'm not under the thumb and I'm not scared because everything's going to go wrong. Rather, I am thinking that the conductor shouldn't be treating me like that. So he stops being a great big god up there to be feared; he is to be pitied because that's not the right way to get the result he's wanting. So he's a human too.

[Y]ou can build up resentment if you don't respect the musicianship or the skill of the conductor. You've got to try and pull something out of the fire without any help from them or even when they get in the way and make it impossible . . . and we see a lot of that here because we get a lot of not-so-good conductors and you've got to just try and make the music work in spite of the conductor.

Constrained by the ensemble

I love watching tennis but they make so many mistakes. Musicians are bred not to make mistakes . . . we've got so many variables in the orchestra . . . you have to acknowledge what restrictions you are placed under and accept them and then work within that. As a soloist you can go out there and play however you want, but in the orchestra you can't . . . You've got to be really flexible in an orchestra situation.

[Orchestral playing is] a different way of playing. And it's a different sound you make in orchestra . . . Some of the sounds, that soft playing sound, you would never make that sound in solo playing or chamber music . . . It's like one hair playing. The sound is meant to become a conglomerate sound, not a solo sound. It's strange . . . you are not trained to play with that sound. We're trained to be creative and take risks with the sound and decide musical issues . . . then you get into orchestra and everything is decided for you. But, then, I think it's an art to be able to play in orchestra properly. Yes, I think it's a strange job, to be honest. I mean I love it . . . but I just want to be able to feel comfortable.

In orchestra, I know people are judging a lot. It's silly to say they're not because they are. I guess I'm sitting playing with a bunch of people who I wouldn't normally choose to play with. Not because they can't play. Just because they are not the people I choose to play with and the fact they're probably the same with me. I just feel it's a strange atmosphere to play music that is so subjective that you are playing it with people who don't have the same subjective idea as yourself. It's almost a big pile of clashing subjectivity and emotion. People feel a lot of emotion when they play in an orchestra. It's an unnatural thing to be trained creatively and then plonk yourself in the section. Even though in a way it is creative, I guess, but not in a way that we as musicians want to be emotive and communicate to the audience. It's a sterile thing, the stage and the platform, a bunch of seats and it's really not comfortable for me.

Environmental challenges

Orchestral musicians can have a visual problem with trying to see the music, the conductor and the other players—you can't always see what's happening out the front when you've had to look at something else and the music. There's an awful lot of information to take in and you've got to listen like mad as well, have your ears pinned back to pick up all the cues. You can try and be with everybody because when you're stuck up the back it's not easy to play in ensemble very well from there.

Organization of work issues

I am seeing a psychotherapist to deal with work issues. There is an increasing divergence of managerial styles between managers and musicians—a polarization. There is a total lack of understanding or empathy from managers. It makes me feel uptight. I get very outspoken, I go into bat for other players; I worry about non-musical things and this decreases my ability to concentrate. I am very weary on a number of levels. I want to enjoy playing the horn, which I have not done in a lot of years. I am battling on many fronts—meetings, not having a say, not being listened to or heard. Our issues don't concern managers—things like workload, the acoustics of our venues, the environment. We do not trust our managers. We could be making nuts and bolts in a factory. Things like not being able to hear each other on stage is a big issue but they think we are just whingers, that we are just being temperamental musicians. There is no understanding of our work. Management don't understand their product. Musicians are not well paid. That is why we are very protective of our current conditions.

Music as an occupation

Music is the same as anything in life. I was passionate about it at the start but it is hard to retain the passion. It becomes a job, but I am grateful that I still have my health and my technique. There is no career path in music. I am still on the same salary scale 20 years later that I was on when I was 29 years old, when I reached the top of my pay scale. Lack of funding for the arts means that we sometimes have to play music that gets bums on seats. On those occasions, I just go through the motions; the music is not uplifting or inspiring. Music is not a glamorous profession.

Lack of peer support

We have to learn as individuals to take care of ourselves. There is camaraderie but no support when you are feeling vulnerable. There is a lot of unspoken stuff. If people are going through hard times, we will talk together, but there is a reluctance to get too personal. There is a fear that others' problems will rub off on you, especially music performance anxiety-type fears. Often you don't know that someone is suffering until they start unravelling.

I had a desk partner for five years who was a sociopath. Prior to having him as a desk partner, my performance anxiety was manageable, but after sitting next to him, I became extremely anxious because he took sadistic delight in exposing all my mistakes in different ways. I knew he was talking behind my back, criticizing me to other players. Sometimes, he left abusive notes in my locker, or said very horrible things to me when no one was listening. I eventually complained about him to management but because I could not prove anything or even that it was him leaving the notes, they did nothing. That was a really terrible time for me.

Self-help strategies: the wisdom of performing musicians

Healthy body, healthy mind

I've learnt . . . to be as rested as possible and to be as well as possible. You need to look after your health because you can't expect your body to respond when you are under a lot of pressure as soon as you get up to perform. You really owe it to yourself if you want to do a good job to be as fit and as healthy as you can be.

It gets harder as you get older in that your body needs more maintenance . . . to keep playing but I feel more on top of the emotional side now and because it's such a joy when you play, you get so much back, it's never felt like an almighty effort, it's been something that I've been pleased to rise to the challenges, I suppose, and find solutions for.

Yoga and breathing

I started doing Yoga for my back problems . . . and at the start I learnt to breathe and then I started incorporating breathing into my playing because breathing helps clear your mind and relaxes you at the same time, relaxes your hands and your whole body really.

[Y]oga breathing pre performance powers the mind to achieve a mental and physical still-ness but retain a state of alertness that gives you quiet confidence and stills the doubting voice in your head.

Meditation

Meditation gives you that feeling of peace but knowing that just simple deep breathing and concentrating on that breathing just for a little minute even before you play, or especially before you play, and while you're playing too, is magic. It automatically links in. A lot of players forget to breathe, so you're holding your breath while you're playing and afterwards you take in a big breath. I thought that was crazy because I've starved my body of the oxygen it needs to play, whereas if you can learn to breathe with the musical phrasing you're always getting breath in and then, from there, you can develop a relaxing, letting-go response.

Developing a secure technique

It was a long time coming before I really addressed it [music performance anxiety]. The first thing that worked for me was getting my technique right . . . I had to learn to play in a relaxed way which was half the trouble because nerves make you tight, so if you can concentrate on being relaxed, that takes half your brain away from being scared and it's concentrating positively on doing something other than being scared.

I've developed my technique of playing totally relaxed now. I haven't been a student for 30 years . . . but I keep developing my technique and learning from master classes and . . . watching everybody who plays my instrument and trying different things . . . I keep working on what I do.

Developing and then relying on muscle memory

The more experience you've had playing your instrument over many years, you can learn to trust your hands and your fingers that they know where to go. You can play with your eyes shut, you know you don't have to look. So many players never get out of that thing that I've got to look at every string otherwise how do I know where I am? At the end of each lesson my teacher said, 'Now go away and learn to play without looking' and that's the first thing I do with my students, in the first lesson, to play without looking because it's such a hindrance if you have to look all the time and it really frees you up to have the confidence to know your fingers know where to go so you're not worrying about every note and it's amazing how you can leap and fly like all the best acrobats.

My final teacher used to say, 'You should be able to go for a walk without your instrument and completely play the piece in your head. If you can't, you should figure out why and which bits are weaker, and work on those.' There are at least three types of memory when you're memorising a piece. You can remember what the page looks like; you can remem-ber what the piece sounds like; and you can remember your muscle movements and what it feels like to play the piece . . . In the end, I think it is the muscle memory that will carry you through if you get into trouble.

Adequate preparation

Make sure that your preparation is a long time out from when you actually have to per-form and even now in the orchestra I'm trying to look at music two or three weeks ahead of time just to prepare mentally and then do the fine-tuning of the technical nearer the time we've got to play because we do several programs at once so it's hard to keep all of them right up in the front of your mind. So I do a lot of back-of-the-mind sort of stuff holding stuff in there in a preparatory way and then put it away because it's still festering in the back of your mind and working on the immediate thing for this week, more in the technical sense because if you leave it to the week of the performance often you can get caught out and think, I need more weeks than this to get it into my hands, but also the mind will sort it out while you're sleeping. If you've fed the information in, in a relaxed state, it can sort it out.

The best thing for nerves is being better prepared physically . . . that gives you the confidence to not worry so much about awkward bits.

Strategizing

When I was learning big pieces of unaccompanied Bach, which is just you alone and they can go on for between 10 and 15 minutes and it can be really easy to get stuck or lost in a loop, or jump to the wrong place, I used to think of emergency points. I did not memorize the piece as one great, big, long thing and if I got lost, I'd have no clue where I was; I think of little navigation points where, if I really did flounder, I could regroup. You know, if necessary, I'd skip 10 bars and go to the next bit I remembered and just keep going like that, so that was one kind of strategy I would have; an emergency procedure.

My character is wound up. I am a worrier; I worry all the time, so my preparation is fastidious. Even these days, after 24 years of professional experience, I don't go into a performance without a Plan B, so if something went wrong, you would implement it. For example, if you are nervous and your mouth dries up, articulation becomes thick and muddy. So Plan B is to articulate with a harder definition. Plan B for shaking hands is to have some strong picture or image in your mind and to visualize something very relaxing, like lying on a float in the Caribbean with a gin and tonic. I visualize that scene just before I play the big horn solo in the slow movement of Tchaikovsky's Fifth Symphony. It doesn't work for everyone.

Developing personalized pre-performance routines

I know people who are vegetarian or a soloist who won't drink coffee, they're very particular about the sorts of foods they eat or whether they eat before or after a concert. There are a lot of people like that who have their own particular routine of what works for them. I've found a sugar burst, it only lasts a few minutes, just before a solo is a really good thing. I used to do chocolate but that's really bad for you so I've actually got some nutritional lollies that are actually quite good for that and I've got a sports drink which has slow-release energy and I only discovered by accident that was really useful for sparking your concentration which . . . takes about half an hour to kick in and it keeps you going and it's terrific stuff . . . to keep your concentration going, to keep your mind on the job.

Gaining cognitive control

Letting go of unrealistic perfectionism

[T]he way you struggle for perfection all the time . . . you're your own worst enemy because you're your hardest critic . . . if you're going to play in a cramped or frightened way you're going to destroy whatever it is you're trying to make, like the image or the mood or just being able to physically play.

There's very few times in your life you can say it's absolutely perfect and some people say perfection is impossible but you still have the striving for it. But if you're going to concentrate just on the negatives, you're not going to keep going. You're going to bomb out and not be in the job any more.

Replacing worry, rumination, and catastrophizing with self-instruction

There is a wealth of wisdom contained in the responses from musicians about how they have learnt to cope with severe cognitive anxiety. In the midst of what some of the musicians describe as paralysis, they work hard to find ways through it. I have included a range of examples that will hopefully be of interest to teachers and performing musicians alike. However, it is all summed up in the last comment of this section: 'I think a lot of people have trouble, myself included, with just trusting yourself, that you know how to do it.'

[J]ust concentrate on a physical aspect of your playing instead of worrying when's the first mistake going to be, which bothered me all my student years, when's the first mistake and then you can settle down after it . . . or you break a string and you think, nothing worse can happen, all that horrible stuff but now you can say, just watch your arm is at the right height or remember to curve. Aspects of techniques you need for a certain little troubled spot you're worried about and then remember to breathe through it.

You get up there and you're halfway through and then suddenly a nerve will hit and you think 'Oh my God, what will I do?' You have to block that thought, breathe and then concentrate on things like watch your elbow or just turn your hand or say, 'Look, there's that double stopping coming up.' It's some of those aspects of a particular technique that you're doing and that immediately stretches your mind off panicking about something going to go wrong and that gets you back on track really quickly.

[O]ne friend of mine, he's really incapacitated by nerves but he's got to be in the right frame of mind to take in any advice that you're trying to give. People like him are so busy thinking, 'Nothing will ever help me; I'm just stuck with where I am,' you can't really get through, make any sort of suggestions while they're not listening, but I do keep telling him, 'You can play twice as well as me and twice as fast as everyone else but you just destroy it because you let your mind say, "What if, what if it doesn't go right?"'

[Y]ou need things that take you out of the physical because you're dealing in a non-physical world through physical means. You're dealing in sound which is physical but it touches, it's the crossover between the physical and the emotional or the spiritual. It's so intangible and it's gone in a moment and we spend all our lives worrying about this thing that's lost within a split second and just seeing the ridiculousness of that and trying to be relaxed about what you do instead of being constantly worried about things going wrong.

I make sure that I write on top of my music things to think about before I start playing so I can snap myself out of mental paralysis. Little things like, 'Is the height of my seat correct?' 'Can I see the conductor and the music comfortably?' 'Have I thought of the speed?' 'Have I played through it, the first couple of bars in my mind before I actually start playing it physically?' I use things like that to get away from the effect of the paralysis . . . to have something else to think about rather than be paralyzed.

I don't switch off completely, but I think I have become better at not worrying about things so much, and not letting my mind and body respond in ways that are unhelpful to the performance, and trying to channel the worry into positive things. I'm no expert in this, but I think when you do get nervous, there are positives to it as well, that your concentration improves . . . I did a couple of workshops on it and I think someone said that feeling anxious is a defence mechanism, and it is your body's way of trying to help. Improved awareness and concentration are the positives that can go with that, rather than the shaky bow or sweaty hands or feeling sick [laughs]. I do from time to time get a shaky bow in really soft passages. That can also happen because of adrenaline, but yes, it does happen from time to time. The first thing I try to do is just not worry about it or say to myself, 'Oh my God, my bow is shaking. All the audience will know I'm nervous.' I try not to do that and I find that helps, and it means you get over it a lot quicker than worrying about, 'Oh, I'm nervous, what are people thinking?'

I try to remind myself that the people in the audience are there to enjoy themselves and they're not there to enjoy watching you suffer, and they want you to play as best as you can and there's no reason to be afraid of them, which I think is nearly always the case, you know, it's not an exam. They're not sitting there poised to criticize.

I tell myself that if I'm playing a really hard piece, you only have to do it for the first time once and after that it gets easier . . . so I feel that you just have to be stubborn and do the first performance of that piece, because next time it comes around, it's going to be easier and you know you can do it. And that, I think, goes for orchestral playing and also chamber music . . . the hardest pieces are really hard the first time you do them, but once you've done them and you feel more comfortable with them, you can then get out of your receded self-obsessed state and become more relaxed and communicative with the audience and also the other musicians around you.

I once heard a violinist say, 'What we do is ridiculous; we just scrape a wooden box with a stick.' I remembered that and I try to think of things in the simplest possible terms rather than say, 'There's 1,000 people watching and if I stuff up, it'll be the end of the world.' If you make a mistake, it's not a recording; it's gone. It's happened and it's over and the audience would've forgotten any mistake long before you do . . . If it is a recording, you get to do it again . . . stop letting your worry and self-doubt get in the way. I think a lot of people have trouble, myself included, with just trusting yourself, that you know how to do it.

Self-help books

I read the book called *The Inner Game of Music* and was able to implement the techniques and it just totally turned me around because even though you've had many years of experience and then suddenly you're exposed, you've got a tricky bit or whatever it is, to be able to recognize that your mind is your worst enemy, that you can use it constructively. If it's sitting there saying 'Look out for that,' or 'You can't do this,' all those negative things, in that book he actually attacks that and says how to turn that switch off, turn the negative off and go with the good; there's a lot of strategies in that book.

Obtaining emotional support

Sense of community

[Y]ou can actually feed off the other people's energy. You feed off the music, the sound that's happening and the emotion, all those things can pull you out of yourself if you're not feeling too hot or you're not feeling in the mood you can actually pull out of that by picking up on the vibes around you and letting those carry you forward, support you.

You can get jaded with things that happen around you . . . substandard conductors is mostly what we whinge about but the situation of having to tour, all those physical things that get in the way and things at work that annoy people but we always come together and we make great music and that's what keeps you going.

[W]here the orchestra thinks as one, that's really mind blowing; it's terrific and it raises everyone up out of themselves and you soar along on this great euphoria . . . It's many years of playing together and adjusting that you become like one and it's one of those things that takes your mind away from your own anxiety because of all those other things you've got to think about . . .

The orchestra is friendly . . . even when people were all going through crises of their own, it was like having an extended family which I'd grown up without. It was a novelty really, to have all these people that just because you were in the orchestra they were there to help, which was really good.

Focus on the music

You know what you want to do to craft a piece and perform it as you imagine but with your nerves getting in the way you end up just fighting to play the notes, which really kills the music. You have to let go of the nerves to be able to create what you want and to be free to risk all for the grand result. You wouldn't do it without training to do it. You don't jump off the deep end the first day out, you have to work up to it like gaining confidence in your ability to play that way. It's a gradual thing . . .

Music as therapy

Music as a comfort in life

You get on with life and in a way music carries you through all the other big life events. When my dad died I found music was a real comfort. Coming back to work after his funeral was a real comfort because that was very shocking, I didn't have any idea he was sick or anything. But I knew from my experience of music that I did not need to be frightened of my emotions and that music would really carry me through.

I'm an extreme worrier about all sorts of things. I get tied up in knots, because I'm on my own now and I'm just now beginning to resent that [laugh] but I'm fed up with having to always have the answers or find the answers or track things down or not have someone to talk things through so you make the right decisions. That's really bugging me . . . I've still got lots of problems but I'm using music as a haven from all of that so that performing is not the problem that it once was.

[A]nd music is . . . supportive and comforting to what else you are doing rather than being this big thing, this big stick that gives you the frights every time you do it.

Summary

This chapter was dedicated to allowing the voices of the musicians to be heard. The excerpts were taken from the set of 20 in-depth interviews with orchestral musicians described in Chapter Eight. Common themes from the transcripts of interviews revealed a nuanced insight into the psychological lives of orchestral musicians. There is a great deal of collective wisdom or 'craft knowledge' contained in their comments. Key themes emerged that included issues related to their musical identity and sense of self, their internalized mental representations of their parents, the generational transmission of music performance anxiety and its prevention through awareness and self-reflection, the onset and causes of music performance anxiety, and how music performance anxiety is manifested in older musicians. This is followed by varied accounts of the phenomenology of music performance anxiety, and their apt descriptions of false alarms. Accounts of the type and impact of cognitive interference, worry, and rumination they experience is informative, including effects on their ability to sight read and memorize their music. Some interesting insights follow on their experiences with their music teachers, and what they tell their students. We conclude with coverage on situational factors that may exacerbate music performance anxiety; conductors were the most frequently cited situational stressor! Others included the subservience to the ensemble (loss of individuality in orchestral playing), environmental challenges such as seating, issues related to the organization of work, lack of career progression, and their perceptions of music as an occupation. Finally, we hear about their self-help strategies, both physical and psychological, the importance of developing a secure technique, adequate preparation and ability to rely on muscle memory, strategizing in challenging situations, the role of pre-performance routines, and the importance of maintaining control of one's cognitions by letting go of unrealistic perfectionism. Obtaining emotional support when needed and experiencing the joy of music are the final pieces of advice that these experienced musicians have for other performers and students.

Chapter 10

Prevention and pedagogy

Early experience matters a lot in musical life, but so do time and experience. Children who are thought to start 'too late' or 'too early' are hamstrung by these stereotypes. Music starts when it starts, and its longevity is more a matter of its ties to the heart than to the mind. How children are treated by parents and teachers is as critical to the outcome of their musical lives as what they are taught

Pruett, 2004, p. 158.

Michael Hamburger's compilation of Beethoven's letters, journals, and conversations contain a letter to Czerny, who was piano teacher to his 11-year old nephew Carl (Hamburger, 1966). In it, Beethoven asks Czerny for patience otherwise he 'would accomplish less,' and to be 'kind, yet serious.' Beethoven continues:

> If once he has got the right fingering, plays in good time, with the notes fairly correct, then only pull him up about the rendering; and when he has arrived at that stage, don't let him stop for the sake of small faults, but point them out to him when he has played the piece through. I have always adopted this plan; it soon forms musicians which, after all, is one of the first aims of art and it gives less trouble both to master and pupil (pp. 153–4).

This book does not concern itself with the details of music pedagogy; indeed there is an abundance of such texts for interested teachers and scholars. I used this excerpt from Beethoven to illustrate a number of key points to which I wish to draw your attention in the prevention (or minimization) of severe music performance anxiety—that is, the environment and interpersonal relationships in which this teaching–learning occurs. Beethoven exhorts Czerny to be patient, kind, and serious, in order to maximize his nephew's learning. These are remarkable words from Beethoven, who was known for neither his patience nor kindness, but who clearly saw the benefits of establishing a safe and positive learning environment in which children could be 'formed into musicians.'

Prevention and pedagogy are two very important components in the musical education of young musicians, indeed of all students. I have argued in this book that both theorizing and treating music performance anxiety are in their formative stages. As is the case for other psychological treatments, even those that are well developed and researched, as they are for the anxiety disorders, affected individuals are rarely cured. We all face many challenges throughout life by virtue of being human in a complex world; those challenges are best negotiated by those who have secure attachments and have developed the resilience to confront obstacles with maturity and equanimity, including their music performance anxiety. In the next sections, I will briefly discuss some of the key principles whereby these outcomes can be achieved.

Parenting the musically gifted child

There is now a vast literature on giftedness and we have space only for a very brief discussion. First and foremost, children who are gifted are not physically, psychologically, or socioemotionally different from their peer group. They are children who have a particular gift in a specific domain, who, with application to the development of that gift, achieve an extremely high standard in the domain of their talent in a relatively short time. However, they have in common with all children of their age the need for secure attachment to primary caregivers, love, acceptance, and support for their overall development, in addition to an environment that supports the development of their special talent. Children whose gifts are nurtured more than the person with the gift may experience significant difficulties with their sense of self and self-esteem, as we learnt from musicians in the previous chapter.

There are many definitions of musical giftedness, but that of Greenacre (1971) has particular depth. She identified four essential features of giftedness: (i) greater sensitivity to sensory stimuli; (ii) unusual capacity for awareness of relationships between various stimuli; (iii) predisposition to an empathy of wider range and deeper vibration than usual; (iv) intactness of sufficient sensory motor equipment to allow the building up of projective motor discharges for expressive functions: for example, an earlier and greater reactivity to form and rhythm. Such children also experience their errors and shortcomings more acutely by virtue of the factors that contribute to their giftedness, so the capacity to learn to tolerate imperfection is a special skill that must be nurtured alongside their unusual musical gifts. Failure to develop a realistic appreciation that to be human is to be imperfect may set up lifelong worry and rumination about each performance that becomes a psychological burden with the capacity to undermine their enjoyment and even performance of their art, as we discovered in Chapters One and Two.

Pruett (2004) has provided what he calls a 'list of transcultural qualities of good enough parenting of children who happen to be musicians' (p. 154). You will notice the affinity of the items in his list with those characteristics described in the theories of attachment presented in various chapters throughout this book (Bowlby, 1987, 1988; Cassidy & Shaver, 2008; Schore & Schore, 2008; Wallin, 2007; Winnicott, 1965):

  i   sensitivity to children and their ever-changing needs

 ii   ability to make children feel loved, adored, and enjoyed

iii   devotion to sustaining strong values

iv   disciplining to teach, not punish

 v   affirmation of the child's uniqueness while expecting competence vi promotion of education (all—including musical) as a process, not an endpoint

vii sustaining an abiding presence through thick and thin

viii safeguarding the family's rituals and routines (p. 155).

Pruett (2004) reminds parents that while they are the first 'patrons' of their child's musical ability, they are parents first and foremost. Talent in any form can only be properly nurtured in an atmosphere of secure attachment with parents who see their children as people first and talented musicians subsequently. Similarly, Sloboda (1993) has identified a number of guidelines for parents of musically gifted children that allow them to provide a secure environment in which both the child and his/her gift can be nurtured. These include, but are not limited to the following:

i provision of emotional support for the child's evolving aspirations

ii provision of material support in the form of tuition fees, instruments, music, competition entry costs, travel to performance venues

iii support for less formal creative musical practices, particularly in the early stages of musical development. This means allowing the child to 'play' with their music. The form of play will differ depending on the child's age and interest. For younger children, musical play may comprise movement to the music, rhythm games, imaginative storytelling to different musical genres, exploring the different sounds that their instrument can make, and playing by ear their favorite 'pop' songs. Even accomplished adult musicians find new ways to play with their music to keep the process of artistic creation alive. For example, Yehudi Menuhin collaborated with the Indian sitar player, Pandit Ravi Shankar, to explore the possibilities of the music created where 'East meets West.' Simon Tedeschi, a classically trained concert pianist, is also interested in jazz music. He has teamed up with jazz pianist Kevin Hunt and jazz violinist Ian Cooper to explore jazz improvisation, to experiment with new sounds and rhythms, and to pursue his love of stride piano, a jazz piano style that evolved from ragtime.[1]

Teaching the musically gifted child

Weisblatt (1986) offers some psychoanalytic insights into the music student–teacher relationship. Teachers need to be not only excellent practitioners in their musical craft but also sensitive to the complexities that arise in the student–teacher relationship by virtue of the fact that musical performance is at the center of their interactions. If there are conflicts and anxiety inherent in musical performance, then the teacher assumes significant responsibility for assisting the student to navigate the treacherous rapids of his musical aspirations. For example, a child of precocious talent may harbor fantasies of grandiosity and unlimited success and admiration. The teacher needs to be alert to the student's underlying fears of humiliation if a performance exposes technical weakness. The teacher's sensitivity will assist the child to gradually let go of unrealistic fantasies and replace them with realistic aspirations. In the conversation reproduced

---

[1] Stride is characterized by a left-hand pattern comprising a single bass note or octave followed by a left-hand chord. This left-hand pattern supports the right hand melody.

below, Stephanie McCallum, concert pianist and piano pedagogue, makes a similar observation about assisting students to develop realistic musical aspirations. Teachers also need to be aware of the degree to which their students idealize them and to work with this dynamic effectively to support the student's growing confidence in their own internalized musical values and aspirations. Many teachers have also been performers and some have been disappointed by the non-realization of their own performance aspirations. In these situations, teachers need to be sensitive to the risk of feeling competitive with their talented students, responding to the student's natural competitiveness with anger or withdrawal, instead of supporting the student's growing self-assertion and autonomy as a person and a performer.

Further insights into the influence of a good teacher on musical outcomes have been provided by Rink (2002). For example, Davidson (2002) reported research showing that students with high musical achievement found their teachers to be entertaining and friendly as well as being proficient musicians. As the high-achieving students progressed through their music studies, the degree of musical competence they perceived in their teachers became more important. In contrast, students who stopped learning or had low levels of musical achievement were more likely to describe their teachers as unfriendly and incompetent.

Of course, one-on-one studio teaching is not sufficient to turn a music student into a confident performer. By examining Collier's biography (Collier, 1983) of Louis Armstrong, one of the greatest jazz trumpeters of all time, Davidson (2002) identified the essential elements that supported the development of his precocious talent, even though he did not have a designated studio teacher. Despite growing up in abject poverty on the streets of New Orleans, and spending his early years as a 'street kid,' there were a number of critical musical and personal experiences that interposed themselves to nurture Louis's musical gift. These included: (i) casual but frequent exposure to musical stimuli; (ii) many opportunities to freely explore jazz music and to develop performance presentation skills; (iii) experience of intense positive and aesthetic states in response to music; (iv) thousands of hours of practice, often on borrowed trumpets; (v) the availability of benign musical mentors, with whom Louis identified, and their provision of informal instruction and opportunities to engage in music making with them in an environment where trial and error and experimentation were a natural part of musical exploration and music making (p. 91).

In summarizing all the collective foregoing wisdom, we can conclude that children should be offered frequent, low-stress opportunities to perform almost from the beginning of their musical training. These performances should be presented in a positive, non-judgmental way, so that young performers can learn that performance is an integral, enjoyable, and manageable part of their musical education. Children should not be prematurely thrust into competitive environments whose focus is evaluation (such as auditions or competitions) unless it is made very clear to the student that no negative consequences will accrue to a poor performance. Repertoire should be well within the technical capacity of the student and the material should be over-learned to the point of automaticity. All of these strategies will enhance the student's sense of competence and control so that when confronted with critical performances, a strong sense of a competent self will guide a self-actualized performance.

The audition

No self-respecting book on music performance anxiety with a chapter on prevention and pedagogy could conclude without a section on audition management. Auditions can be a pivotal experience in the musical lives of aspiring professional musicians; it is the area that causes the most intense music performance anxiety and the most difficulty in managing.

Since the late 1970s players have been routinely auditioned behind curtains or screens in order to preserve anonymity and reduce bias. Candidates are prohibited from making any identifying sounds (like signature warm-ups on their instruments) and cannot talk, motioning only to an attendant if they desire a change to the music stand location. The attendant announces each performer by a candidate number and the panel votes by silent ballot after every candidate's performance, with a minimum of half the votes required to progress to the next round. In an effort to achieve a true representation of the sound quality of the player, curtains are no longer used since the level of sound absorption can mask the sound, making discrimination among players difficult. Sometimes the panel is seated behind a screen in the body of an auditorium so that the candidate can have the full stage to present his/her best performance.

Typical qualities assessed at orchestral auditions include strong rhythmic sense and good intonation. In the era of high-quality digital recording, the perfection of orchestral ensemble and tuning has increased dramatically. This has been reflected in the very high level of rhythmic sense and intonation required at orchestral auditions. In preparation, many players supplement good listening skills with mechanical aids such as a digital tuner (which shows the pitch of each note to a fraction of a hertz as it is played slowly) and the metronome. Repetitive slow practice of the repertoire with the aid of a metronome has been a staple of performance preparation for aspiring professional musicians since Franz Liszt.

In addition to rhythm and intonation, quality of sound is very important. Gianluigi Gelmetti, chief conductor of the Sydney Symphony, developed a 'Sydney sound' for the orchestra, marked by increasing the strength in the lower string complement and rearranging the double basses to sit at the back of the orchestra and hence reinforce the harmonic foundation to be clearly heard by the rest of the instruments. Oleg Caetani, chief conductor of the Melbourne Symphony, described the attributes sought in applicants on any instrument for that orchestra. He preferred a 'rich, defined and dark-hued' sound over a 'very light or beautiful' timbre and would seek this depth of tone even when the instrumentalist 'plays in pianissimo' (Fortune, 2007).

Robson, Davidson, and Snell (1995) have provided some very sensible guidelines with respect to managing auditions. A workshop based on the advice contained in this paper was prepared and presented to 92 students from the International Network of Performing and Visual Arts Schools (Gratto, 1998). This was a qualitative study that asked the students what new skills they learnt as a result of the workshop. It is difficult to ascertain from the paper whether students actually performed better during their auditions after participating. A more rigorous study on audition management techniques is needed to assess the objective outcomes of participation in such workshops. In the meantime, we need to rely on the craft knowledge of expert practitioners and common sense to support students and professional musicians through these difficult experiences. Accordingly, I will summarize the guidelines provided by Robson and colleagues here, together with own thoughts on the subject under some key subheadings.

Physical health

Physical conditioning

It is important that performing artists attend to their bodies. Playing an instrument is a physically demanding activity that requires good health and stamina to maintain over the course of a musical career. It is therefore recommended that a physical exercise program be incorporated into the regular schedule of all performing artists. For performers who have particular areas of persistent discomfort or pain, seeking advice from a physiotherapist or exercise physiologist to obtain a specific exercise program that will strengthen or remediate certain parts of the body is good prevention.

Fatigue

Obtaining sufficient rest is important, particularly before important or stressful events. Fatigue may lead to preventable errors or injuries. Some performers overextend themselves, taking on too many commitments prior to an audition, often as a way of distracting their attention from the mounting anxiety associated with the audition. It is important to recognize this pattern and address it appropriately.

Nutrition

High-performance fuels are required by performers, as they are for athletes, prior to a big performance or audition. Robson *et al.* recommend that two months before the event, fats in the diet be reduced to improve body shape and increase energy, and fibre be increased to protect against stress-related gastrointestinal disturbances such as irritable bowel. One week before the event, a high complex carbohydrate diet is advised. The meal immediately before the audition needs to be high energy but should not contain sugars, alcohol, or caffeinated drinks (see section on pharmacotherapy in Chapter Seven for reasons). They are also dehydrating—one of the common causes of fatigue. Anxiety is also dehydrating and hence it is advisable to drink plenty of water on the day.

Medication

In Chapter Seven I provided a detailed appraisal of the use of medications to manage performance anxiety. If medications are deemed necessary, it is important that performers do not wait for the day of audition, competition, or performance to take such medications for the first time. These need to be considered carefully in the relative calm of the preparation period and trialed several weeks before the date to determine the ideal dose to achieve the desired effects and to avoid unwanted side effects.

Psychological preparation

All the vulnerabilities discussed in this book start playing in stereo when one is facing a situation involving high-stakes evaluative threat. If the musician is highly self-critical and unsure of his/her ability, they will perceive their listeners to be the same—highly critical of their performance. Ruminating about what the adjudicators might be thinking tolls the death knell for a performance. Just as certain strategies are helpful to prepare oneself physically for a major challenge, it is important that the performer address psychological issues and 'condition' more adaptive, replacement strategies so that they will 'kick in' when needed during the stressful event.

Good musical preparation will go a long way to mitigating the debilitating effects of severe anxiety. All of the techniques and strategies outlined in the performance-based approaches in Chapter Seven are relevant here. Knowing that the notes are under your fingers; that your memory has been tested in rehearsal and in simulated performances; that your focus is on the music and the beautiful sound that you are creating for an audience to share with you can not only help you to perform at your best but will allow you, in the words of Mikhail Baryshnikov, 'to have pleasure while giving pleasure.'

Teachers need to be aware of their own mounting concern for the student and avoid communicating their anxiety to the student. They should also avoid being too critical in the pre-audition period as this will heighten the student's anxiety. Last-minute changes or coaching can be counterproductive and may disrupt the automated motor patterns that have developed in the preceding months. If an accompanist is needed, make sure you feel happy with the emotional and musical support they can offer, and have several rehearsals, some in concert format with your teacher, parents, and friends leading up to the date.

On the day, dress, think, and behave like a performer. Be sure to wear comfortable clothes and shoes that you don't have worry about. Make sure that the clothes are suitable for the weather conditions. Being too hot or too cold in a performance is distracting and excessive sweating from the heat and/or stiffness from the cold are challenges best avoided. Always leave plenty of time to reach the venue and know where you can park so additional pragmatic issues do not arise to tax your coping resources. Hopefully, you would have been able to visit the venue prior to the event so that you know the geographical location, distance, and time needed to travel, as well as getting some idea of the venue's acoustic and the seating arrangements of adjudicators and your own position. On arrival, enter into your own calm space and do not become involved in the hassles and bustle of pre-audition chaos. Go to a practice room and warm up, if possible. If this is not possible, sit in a quiet place and do some calm mental practice and use imagery to help you achieve the calm and focus needed to produce a peak performance.

Interview with Stephanie McCallum

I would like to conclude this book with excerpts from a conversation with Stephanie McCallum, concert pianist and piano pedagogue at the Sydney Conservatorium of Music, Sydney, Australia, recorded at The University of Sydney in August 2010. It contains musical wisdom, insight, and craft knowledge that transform my theoretical and technical talk into a language that speaks directly to musicians such that it serves as a fitting finale to this book.

Performance anxiety

Dianna: You mentioned to me that you have had success in helping very anxious students. Based on your own professional experience, if somebody came to you and said, 'I know I'm a good performer but my nerves are ruining my ability to perform,' what advice would you give?

Stephanie: I have a lot of students who come to me with RSI [repetitive strain injury] problems, which are clearly anxiety related. They come to me because they've been told, 'Oh, you should go to her, she has a really relaxed technique; she's really relaxed.' Before I take them on, I ask, 'What's your lifestyle like? What do you eat? How much do you exercise? Do you want to be a musician?'

Dianna: So you take a holistic approach to students from the start.

Stephanie: If I take them on, one thing I do early is to mark particular spots in their scores and say, 'At this spot, you release all your muscles.' . . . I like to get them thinking about releasing muscles all the time, and in fact the release of your muscles makes an enormous difference to the sound that you produce. So the release of muscles that I'm talking about with students is very often sound related rather than anxiety related. But, when I get students who are very, very anxious, then I will sometimes put in little conditioned responses for them in various spots of the score. I remember one girl, and this happens a lot at the conservatorium, where students come in from the country or small schools and they've been number one, and suddenly they're at the bottom of the heap. So they get RSI and they can't do their exams. I remember one really charming girl who was absolutely lovely, and I asked her these questions. And she said, 'Oh well, I have to admit, I eat total rubbish, I eat chocolate all the time, I never do any exercise and I don't have a regular routine.' And I said, 'Well, I will take you on if you clean up your act, get a decent diet and take up a sport.' And she said, 'Oh, I'll let you know.' She was ambivalent about it. She came back a couple of months later and said, 'I've taken up karate. I've never felt better, I love it. This is going really well, I'm going to become a black belt. My sensei says I have to eat organic, macrobiotic food.' [laughs] Within about six months, she was a totally transformed person; she'd got so excited about what I was talking to her about with her technique, sitting at a low stool, that she'd made one by sawing the legs off her piano stool [laughs]. She was a very enthusiastic convert. And although she was never going to be a solo performer, and that wasn't what she was aiming at, she just suddenly found the joy in playing again; she found that she could do it. She found that, given certain technical limitations on the size of the piece, she could be creative with what she was doing in the performance and it was very much related to her own state of mental and physical health.

Dianna: Did you talk to her specifically about anxiety?

Stephanie: Oh, absolutely! We talked through the whole issue of why she might be feeling anxious and why that would be a problem for her; we had a kind of CBT[2]-type piano session. But a lot of piano teaching is along these lines because it's a very demanding thing to do. If you're going to put yourself up there to be judged, it does take a fairly robust psyche.

---

2 Cognitive behavioral therapy.

Dianna: What do you tell your students about armoring their psyches for all the evaluation and judgment they're going to face as musicians?

Stephanie: I tell them that one person's opinion is one person's opinion and that the only opinion that is ever going to matter to them throughout their life is their own opinion. And that they will intrinsically know about their own playing, and with feedback from people they trust, like their teachers or their family and friends, about whether they're playing at their best or their worst, whether they're doing their best, they will intrinsically know that. That is in fact the most important thing because in a situation where you have judgment of a creative act, there will inevitably be criticism and there will inevitably be bitter disappointments about whether you got through to someone. But in the end, most people can critique their own playing far more effectively than anyone else; they're far harder on themselves usually, unless they've been given unrealistic ideas by their teachers or by people whom they trust.

Technique

Dianna: You were saying earlier that muscle relaxation is critical not only to performing but also to managing anxiety. To what muscles are you referring specifically?

Stephanie: The normal approach to the keyboard is to place your arm above the keyboard and then strike the keys with your fingers. That is an approach which dates back to the fortepiano in the 18th century, from a keyboard that had a very light weight to push down. But as the piano developed during the 19th century, the weight on the keys increased and the weight that we push down now on a single key is more than twice what it was then, even at the beginning of the 19th century, and obviously much more than during the 18th century. So the whole idea of the hand above the keyboard, with their finger movement, is actually totally inappropriate for a modern piano. And that causes most of the tension problems and anxiety problems related to modern technique. When students are taught to lift their fingers high, it's extremely damaging.

Dianna: That is how I was taught and I am sure many others will recognize this technique. What is your method?

Stephanie: You sit really low and use gravity, so you don't engage the bicep muscles. If you're trying to manage a cantabile sound, you just release the hand so that it's basically falling through the piano and then your movement is leverage; weightlifting, from the fingers, which is actually done not with individual fingers but through the whole hand on a triangular basis with this set of knuckles taking the strain. So the fingers are straighter, and they don't move much. In that way, you get leverage and to move, you use a push-off technique, like a trampoline. In a scale technique, you simply transfer weight. And to move position, you retain the integrity of the angle relationship to the key, but you get the momentum to move by making a circular pattern. So if you're going in one direction, you pull in the opposite direction and throw, so there's no tucking, no thumb tension at all, in fact the thumb is more often than not relaxed.

Dianna: Is this technique unique to you?

Stephanie: I learnt this style of playing from Ronald Smith. I've probably developed it myself over the decades. I'm in touch with various other Ronald Smith students. Some retain the technique and others have gone back to more conservative methods, I think just out of bad habit, quite frankly. At a conference I attended recently, I was talking to a woman called Rae de Lisle, who herself was an injured pianist and no longer performs. Her research area is focal dystonia,[3] and she's been working on technique for prevention of injury in pianists. What she's come up with is a technique similar to mine. She was fascinated when I was describing technically what I was doing because she could see that I was actually further along the path that she was moving towards. It's all against the received knowledge that a person of my sex and weight and build could play the repertoire that I habitually play with the level of sound I achieve.

Dianna: Yes, you are tiny.

Stephanie: . . . yes, and people will often comment on that. In fact, when I've played with orchestras, one guy, Graeme Skinner, who is a very good musician, was reviewing my performance, referred to the fact that my performance must have been amplified and, of course, I wasn't amplified. Interestingly, after I played in Perth recently, a tiny little student came up to me afterwards and she said, 'Oh, I'm so excited to have seen you play because now I know that when people say to me I can't make enough sound, I know they're wrong.'

Dianna: What a lovely comment. You have become her role model.

Stephanie: Yes, perhaps . . . Ron's technique is a very efficient use of your muscles. And obviously, it's absolutely critical that you're able to control the level of tension; you need very little tension except the tension required to hold certain things still at certain points.

Dianna: Do the shoulders ever come into it, if you're playing a very big work?

Stephanie: The shoulders basically need to be stable and balanced so that your head doesn't displace your weight. You need to have the weight hanging from your shoulder. Of course, you might lean in; when you play concertos you have to play really loudly, but I think the critical thing is stability of the hand.

Dianna: Do you think core stability makes a contribution?

Stephanie: Yes, how you sit at the keyboard is enormously important. You have to sit stably with your head supported. You see so many pianists who don't support their heads at all, so they've got this enormous weight flailing around at the top, destabilizing what they do with their arms.

The musical life

Dianna: How difficult is it for you to answer a question from one of your students, like 'Am I going to make it? Am I going to be a concert pianist?'

Stephanie: The whole concept of being a concert pianist is a totally outdated concept. If someone says something like that, I'd always say, 'Well, you're looking at being a pianist, you're looking at being a musician. Being a pianist is part of being a musician, it's not the

---

[3] Focal dystonia is a 'cortical sensory-motor mislearning syndrome caused by dysfunctional plasticity in the sensory and motor brain regions that causes 'degradation of sensory feedback and fusion of the digital representations in the somatosensory cortex', resulting in loss of voluntary control of highly trained sensory-motor skills and creating unwanted muscular contractions or twisting in affected body parts. It affects about one in 200 professional musicians (Altenmüller & Gruhn, 2002, p. 77).

whole thing. In order to make a success of any career, even a solo pianist's career, you will need to do many things and have a lot of different skills and expertise. You should embrace the opportunity to work on all those things, because limiting yourself and driving yourself like an automaton in a single direction without other input will kill it; it is self-defeating.'

Dianna: You would advocate a much broader view of the whole enterprise.

Stephanie: There's no doubt in my mind that the best pianists, even those who are solo pianists, are intelligent people with very lively intellectual lives. They usually also have talents to articulate what they're doing, they also quite independently do large amounts of research. Almost inevitably, in a really successful performance career, there will be activities like artistic direction, chamber music, various leadership roles, teaching. All these things will happen as part of being a musician. To think that you're going to go through your life, getting up and playing the Greig A Minor 20 times a year, it's not going to happen. I don't know that it ever has happened. I think it's a bit of a chimera. People say, 'Oh, there are only half a dozen people in the world who have a real career as a solo pianist.' Well, I would say I doubt if there's that many, because a career will always have many strands.

Dianna: You've talked about your preparation and the amount of intense concentration and technical mastery that's required; do you ever feel that you come to a point where you say, 'I've had enough, this is really too demanding of all of my personal resources'?

Stephanie: No. I've been very fortunate in the breadth of what I do. I do think it must be literally killing to get up and play the Greig A Minor 20 times a year, and I know there are people who do this. Thibaudet, for example, must have played the Ravel Concerto 20 times a year, every year for a decade. How you could do it, I do not know. I learn enormous amounts of new repertoire and I have an unusually large repertoire and I very rarely fixate on particular works. I don't pull out the same work over and over, though I have revisited key works in my life and I always find it really interesting to come back to something after a decade and see how your whole concept of it has changed. But I think the role that I play for myself as an explorer on piano repertoire is infinitely interesting. I can't imagine getting sick of it, but I do think it needs to be balanced, it's not something I would want to do to the exclusion of all else. I know that lots of orchestral musicians get totally bored with their work. Particularly groups like violas: they just can't hack playing the same stuff over and over; it becomes a chore.

Dianna: What do they do?

Stephanie: Oh, I don't know, I think they do teaching or they quit. Some people go into conducting or things like that if they're interested enough in the broad aspect of music.

Dianna: There seems to be a group of *tutti* musicians who don't get anxious but they are dying of boredom . . .

Stephanie: Yes, that's right.

Dianna: . . . and then there are the other group who are incredibly anxious to the point that their anxiety is threatening all the time to end their careers.

Stephanie: I think the level of anxiety can relate to the level of responsibility, and obviously a solo pianist has ultimate responsibility; there's no one else to blame. Also, the focus of the attention of the audience is totally on you. That's an unusual situation for a person, you can think in lots of environments that is very unusual. Even in music, it's very unusual; so I think that makes an enormous difference. If you're in the *tutti*, you virtually have no responsibility. Your responsibility is to follow like a sheep, so you're not in a creative act, you're in a running-through-someone-else's-pen act.

Dianna: It's interesting; I'm working with a violinist at the moment who says that the fact that she isn't able to create the music . . .

Stephanie: . . . drives her nuts. I think that's what drives people out of it. I've done a bit of work, sitting up with the bad boys in the brass section of the orchestra, where the keyboard players sit. And honestly, in that sort of environment, it is like a school class-room. You get this kind of ambience—the headmaster out the front and all these little subservient people obeying without question. I can see that you'd have to be a special orchestra for that not to develop. I know there are orchestras that do avoid that, where you get this wonderful sense of a giant chamber group all contributing to a common goal; but it's rare, I think, very rare.

Dianna: What effect do you think that has on musicians who are essentially orchestral musicians?

Stephanie: Well, I think it depends on their level of creativity. Some people need more autonomy, have the capability for more autonomy and therefore need it. I think it depends on your capabilities, quite frankly.

Dianna: What about a musician who feels like they're being held back from being creative, they're just being told what to do, how to play, when to play . . .

Stephanie: Well then, I would have thought an orchestral position would be really problematic; they would need to move into chamber music. That's why a lot of orchestral players do supplement their work with chamber music and teaching so that they have autonomy in that area, but they can also move into soloistic roles or conducting roles. Many of them wouldn't do that because of anxiety. You can't have everything, you've got to accept responsibility for what you do and that's going to create anxiety. If you want to hand the responsibility over to someone else and not be so anxious, well then, you don't get the autonomy. The person who takes the responsibility has to be allowed to have their head.

Dianna: It's a complex question though, isn't it?

Stephanie: Oh yes. And there are so many different roles, and they really are so different. I've obviously done a lot of solo work mainly as a recitalist, but also as a concerto player and that's a really interesting relationship. You walk into a group of people with whom you don't normally work and you're often working with a conductor who's a complete stranger, and you get one rehearsal or something like that. So it's a very stressful situation and it's really interesting talking to people like Stephen Hough, people who do this all the time and their stories of turning up in some city and within half an hour they're on the stage doing the concert—unbelievable.

Dianna: Without a rehearsal?

Stephanie: Well, with half an hour's sound check or whatever it is, or a rehearsal where the conductor says, 'We're going to start at bar 54,' and this kind of thing. There's not much allowance made for being human, so it is a very stressful thing. Then there's the role of the chamber musician, which, depending on the level of difficulty of the work that you're doing, can be even more stressful because if you're playing an extremely virtuosic role, but you don't have the autonomy of the rubato or other creative expression, you have to fit in with what everyone else is doing—that can be extremely stressful, even though you don't have the stress of the memorization and you don't have the stress of everyone's attention being on you, it's more focused. So that's a different kind of anxiety. Then there are things like accompanying a singer or just doing an um-pa-pa type of effect, it's a totally different thing. And playing in the ballet, which I played with, playing actually in a small orchestra, large ensemble-type thing, where the conductor is taking the rap and also the conductor is coordinating with dancers; that's another whole ball game. Did I feel any anxiety what-soever in those things? No, not a shred, because I can play the piece and everything else is someone else's problem. I just do my best. If I make a mistake, tough. You're just not in that sort of exposed space; you're protected by all sorts of things.

Dianna: Does that exposure, especially if you know there are very knowledgeable people in the audience, or it's a very prestigious venue like the Wigmore Hall or the concert hall at the Sydney Opera House, have an impact on anxiety levels?

Stephanie: I find one of the things that make me feel . . . not nervous, but makes me feel very exposed or very responsible, is getting a really big fee. If I'm getting a really big fee, I think, 'God. Fronting up and just playing the piano and they're going to give me all this money, better be bloody good.' But I don't think it actually has any effect on my performance, I think for every performance I want it to be my best performance.

Dianna: Doesn't matter where it is or who the audience is . . .

Stephanie: Doesn't matter where or who, no.

Dianna: That's the internal critic you were talking about.

Stephanie: Exactly. You play for yourself; you play for your own idea of the music. I once had to come up with 25 words for a marketing promo about why I play music. I came up with something along the lines of, 'In playing the piano, there is the possibility of transcendence of intellectual delight and the creation of beauty. You don't need any other reasons for playing the piano.'

Dianna: That sounds like your creed or manifesto in a way.

Stephanie: Well, it's not even my creed; it's the only reason for doing it. Why would anyone put themselves through it otherwise?

Dianna: Yes, I think I was getting at that point in my previous question, that it's so effortful and so demanding.

Stephanie: Yes. And yet, what is satisfaction in life but overcoming extremely demanding hurdles? Really, that's how people gain satisfaction in life. If you don't put yourself out there, you don't get the buzz. And I guess it probably is something of an addiction.

Dianna: Which, the performing or the buzz?

Stephanie: The buzz. It involves extraordinary levels of adrenaline highs and lows. I can imagine it must be like people who sail around the world solo or climb Mount Everest, I'm sure it's the same kind of thing. You set yourself a task and you go after it.

Dianna: How do you deal with the lows? Because if there is a rush and a high, there has to be a low.

Stephanie: We call it post-concert let-down in our household. A very good way to deal with it actually is to go swimming . . . then you get on with the next thing, I suppose, is the way I deal with it.

Dianna: So you just accept that that's part of the high. There's going to be a low and then you return to equilibrium.

Stephanie: Mmm. One thing I've found with solo recitals is the importance of rest, absolute rest. I go to bed beforehand. So, usually by the time I finish a concert at 10.30 at night, I'm wide awake, the adrenaline levels are sky high, so I have two or three glasses of wine and go to bed at 3 am. I'll get up at 6 am the next day perfectly normal.

Dianna: Do you need an early night that night?

Stephanie: Yes, I feel a bit down in the dumps or a bit wrung out. It's a big thing.

Dianna: And this interview has been a big thing. Thanks so much for talking with me about your musical life.

Stephanie: Thank you . . . it's been fascinating . . .

Summary

This final chapter is devoted to some thoughts about prevention of severe forms of music performance anxiety and the psychological aspects that need to be attended to in the raising and pedagogy of gifted music students. We face many challenges throughout life by virtue of being human in a complex world; those challenges are best negotiated by those who have secure attachments and have developed the resilience to confront obstacles with maturity and equanimity, including their music performance anxiety. First and foremost, the importance of understanding that while gifted children have a particular gift in a specific domain, they have in common with all children of their age the need for secure attachment to primary caregivers, love, acceptance and support for their overall development, in addition to an environment that supports the development of their special talent. Children whose gifts are nurtured more than the person with the gifts may experience significant difficulties with their sense of self and self-esteem, as we heard from musicians in the previous chapter. Teachers occupy a very important role with respect to gifted music students; hence, they must not only be excellent practitioners in their musical craft but also sensitive to the complexities that arise in the student–teacher relationship by virtue of the fact that musical performance is at the center of their interactions. This section concluded with strategies to enhance the student's sense of competence and control. The next section focused on that most dreaded of all events in a musician's life—the audition, for which careful physical and psychological preparation is required. I concluded the chapter with excerpts from an interview with Stephanie McCallum, concert pianist and piano pedagogue at the Sydney Conservatorium of Music, Sydney, Australia.

Conclusion

It would be tempting to conclude this book with a list of theory- and research-driven recommendations for the prevention, management, and treatment of music performance anxiety. Unfortunately, this is a young field and the current state of our knowledge is such that we are not yet able to engage in such synthesis. However, I hope this book has provided the needed links between the vast literature on performance, anxiety, the anxiety disorders and performance anxiety contained in the psychology, philosophy, psychoanalysis, psychotherapy, medicine, and pharmacotherapy literatures outside the specific domain of music performance anxiety, such that it will stimulate a new generation of music researchers to apply, modify, develop, and test new hypotheses that will move the field forward.

References

Abbass, A. A., Hancock, J. T., Henderson, J., & Kisely, S. R. (2009). Short-term psychodynamic psychotherapies for common mental disorders. *Cochrane Database of Systematic Reviews, 1*, 1.

Abbott, M. J., & Rapee, R. M. (2004). Post-event rumination and negative self-appraisal in social phobia before and after treatment. *Journal of Abnormal Psychology, 113*(1), 136–44.

Ablon, J. S., & Jones, E. E. (1998). How expert clinicians' prototypes of an ideal treatment correlate with outcome in psychodynamic and cognitive-behavioral therapy. *Psychotherapy Research, 8*, 71–83.

Achenbach, T. M., Howell, C. T., McConaughy, S. H., & Stanger, C. (1995). Six-year predictors of problems in a national sample of children and youth: 1. Cross informant syndromes. *Journal of the American Academy of Child and Adolescent Psychiatry, 34*(3), 336–47.

Ackermann, B. (2002). Managing the musculoskeletal health of musicians on tour. *Medical Problems of Performing Artists, 17*(2), 63–7.

Ackermann, B., & Adams, R. (2004). Perceptions of causes of performance-related injuries by music health experts and injured violinists. *Perceptual and Motor Skills, 99*, 669–78.

Ackermann, B., Kenny, D. T., & Driscoll, T. (unpublished). Preliminary report on the physical and psychological well being of professional musicians in the eight orchestras of Australia.

Adan, A., & Serra-Grabulosa, J. M. (2010). Effects of caffeine and glucose, alone and combined, on cognitive performance. *Human Psychopharmacology, 25*(4), 310–17.

Addicott, M. A., & Laurienti, P. J. (2009). A comparison of the effects of caffeine following abstinence and normal caffeine use. *Psychopharmacology, 207*(3), 423–31.

Ainsworth, M. D., & Bell, S. M. (1970). Attachment, exploration and separation: Illustrated by the behavior of one-year-olds in a strange situation. *Child Development, 41*, 49–67.

Ainsworth, M. D. (1963). The development of mother–infant interaction among the Ganda. In B. M. Foss (Ed.), *Determinants of infant behaviour* (Vol. 2, pp. 67–112). New York, NY: Wiley.

Albano, A. M., & Kendall, P. C. (2002). Cognitive behavioural therapy for children and adolescents with anxiety disorders: Clinical research advances. *International Review of Psychiatry, 14*, 129–34.

Alden, L. E., Ryder, A. G., & Mellings, T. M. (2002). Perfectionism in the context of social fears: Toward a two-component model. In G. L. Flett & P. L. Hewitt (Eds.), *Perfectionism: Theory, research, and treatment* (pp. 373–91). Washington, DC: American Psychological Association.

Allami, N., Paulignan, Y., Brovelli, A., & Boussaoud, D. (2008). Visuo-motor learning with combination of different rates of motor imagery and physical practice. *Experimental Brain Research, 84*(1), 105–13.

Allen, L. B., McHugh, R. K., & Barlow, D. H. (2008). Emotional disorders: A unified protocol. In D. H. Barlow (Ed.), *Clinical handbook of psychological disorders: A step-by-step treatment manual* (4th ed., pp. 216–49). New York, NY: Guilford Press.

Alloy, L. B., Kelly, K. A., Mineka, S., & Clements, C. M. (1990). *Comorbidity of anxiety and depressive disorders: A helplessness–hopelessness perspective.* Washington, DC: American Psychiatric Press.

Allport, G. W. (1955). *Becoming: Basic considerations for a psychology of personality*. New Haven, CT: Yale University Press.

Almqvist, F., Puura, K., Kumpulainen, K., Tuompo-Johansson, E., Henttonen, I., Huikko, E., *et al.* (1999). Psychiatric disorders in 8–9-year-old children based on a diagnostic interview with the parents. *European Child and Adolescent Psychiatry, 8*, 17–28.

Alonso, J., Angermeyer, M. C., Bernert, S., Bruffaerts, R., Brugha, T. S., Bryson, H. (2004). Prevalence of mental disorders in Europe: Results from the European study of the epidemiology of mental disorders (ESEMeD) project. *Acta Psychiatrica Scandinavica, 109*, 21–7.

Alpert, R., & Haber, R. N. (1960). Anxiety in academic achievement situations. *Journal of Abnormal Social Psychology, 61*, 207–15.

Altenmüller, E., Gruhn, W., Liebert, G., & Parlitz, D. (2000). The impact of music education on brain networks: Evidence from EEG studies. *International Journal of Music Education, 35*, 47–53.

Altenmüller, E., & Gruhn, W. (2002). Brain mechanisms. In R. Parncutt & G. E. McPherson (Eds.), *The science and psychology of music performance: Creative strategies for teaching and learning*. (pp. 63–81). Oxford: Oxford University Press.

Altenmüller, E., Wiesendanger, M., & Kesselring, J. (Eds.). (2006). *Music, motor control and the brain*. Oxford: Oxford University Press.

American College of Sports Medicine. (1998). The recommended quantity and quality of exercise for developing and maintaining cardiorespiratory and muscular fitness and flexibility in healthy adults. *Medicine, Science, Sport and Exercise, 30*, 975–91.

American Psychiatric Association. (1980). *Diagnostic and Statistical Manual of Mental Disorders (DSM-III-R)*. Washington, DC: American Psychiatric Association.

American Psychiatric Association. (1994). *Diagnostic and Statistical Manual of Mental Disorders (DSM-IV)* (4th ed.). Washington, DC: American Psychiatric Association.

American Psychiatric Association. (2000). *Diagnostic and Statistical Manual of Mental Disorders (DSM-IV-TR)*. Washington: American Psychiatric Association.

Andersen, M. B. (2009). *The 'canon' of psychological skills training for enhancing performance*. Washington, DC: American Psychological Association.

Anderson, J., Williams, S., McGee, R., & Silva, P. A. (1987). DSM-III disorders in preadolescent children: Prevalence in a large sample from the general population. *Archives of General Psychiatry, 44*(1), 69–76.

Andrews, G., Henderson, S., & Hall, W. (2001). Prevalence, comorbidity, disability and service utilisation: Overview of the Australian national mental health survey. *British Journal of Psychiatry, 178*(2), 145–53.

Antony, M. M., & Rowa, K. (2008). *Social anxiety disorder*. Toronto: Hogrefe & Huber.

Antony, M. M., & Stein, M. B. (Eds.). (2009). *Oxford handbook of anxiety and related disorders* Oxford: Oxford University Press.

Antony, M. M., & Swinson, R. P. (2000a). Exposure-based strategies and social skills training. In M. M. Antony & R. P. Swinson (Eds.), *Phobic disorders and panic in adults: A guide to assessment and treatment* (pp. 191–238). Washington, DC: American Psychological Association.

Antony, M. M., & Swinson, R. P. (2000b). Social phobia. In M. M. Antony & R. P. Swinson (Eds.), *Phobic disorders and panic in adults: A guide to assessment and treatment* (pp. 49–77). Washington, DC: American Psychological Association.

Antony, M. M., & Swinson, R. P. (2000c). Specific phobia. In M. M. Antony & R. P. Swinson (Eds.), *Phobic disorders and panic in adults: A guide to assessment and treatment* (pp. 79–104). Washington, DC: American Psychological Association.

Appel, S. S. (1976). Modifying solo performance anxiety in adult pianists. *Journal of Music Therapy, 13*(1), 2–16.

Apter, M. J. (1982). *The experience of motivation: The theory of psychological reversals.* London: Academic Press.

Armfield, J. M. (2006). Cognitive vulnerability: A model of the etiology of fear. *Clinical Psychology Review, 26*(6), 746–68.

Arntz, A. (2002). Cognitive therapy versus interoceptive exposure as treatment of panic disorder without agoraphobia. *Behaviour Research and Therapy, 40*(3), 325–41.

Ashcraft, M. H., & Faust, M. W. (1994). Mathematics anxiety and mental arithmetic performance: An exploratory investigation. *Cognition and Emotion, 8*, 97–125.

Astorino, T. A., & Roberson, D. W. (2010). Efficacy of acute caffeine ingestion for short-term high-intensity exercise performance: a systematic review. *Journal of Strength & Conditioning Research, 24*(1), 257–65.

Auerbach, J. S. (1990). Narcissism: Reflections on others' images of an elusive concept. *Psychoanalytic Psychology, 7*(4), 545–64.

Auerbach, S. M., & Gramling, S. E. (1998). *Stress management: Psychological foundations.* England Cliffs, New Jersey: Prentice Hall.

Bandura, A. (1969). *Principles of behavior modification.* Oxford, England: Holt, Rinehart, & Winston.

Bandura, A. (1977a). Self-efficacy: Toward a unifying theory of behavioral change. *Psychological Review, 84*(2), 191–215.

Bandura, A. (1977b). *Social learning theory.* Englewood Cliffs, N. J.: Prentice Hall.

Bandura, A. (1991). Self-efficacy conception of anxiety. In S. Schwarzer & R. A. Wicklund (Eds.), *Anxiety and self-focused attention* (pp. 89–110). Amsterdam, Netherlands: Harwood Academic Publishers.

Bandura, A., Cioffi, D., Taylor, C., & Brouillard, M. E. (1988). Perceived self-efficacy in coping with cognitive stressors and opioid activation. *Journal of Personality and Social Psychology, 55*(3), 479–88.

Bandura, A., Taylor, C. B., Williams, S. L., Mefford, I. N., & Barchas, J. D. (1985). Catecholamine secretion as a function of perceived coping self-efficacy. *Journal of Consulting and Clinical Psychology, 53*(3), 406–14.

Bargh, J. A., & Morsella, E. (2008). The unconscious mind. *Perspectives on Psychological Science, 3*(1), 73–9.

Barlow, D. H. (1988). *Anxiety and its disorders: The nature and treatment of anxiety and panic.* New York, NY: Guilford Press.

Barlow, D. H. (2000). Unravelling the mysteries of anxiety and its disorders from the perspective of emotion theory. *American Psychologist, 55*(11), 1247–63.

Barlow, D. H. (2002a). *Anxiety and its disorders. The nature and treatment of anxiety and panic* (2nd ed.). New York, NY: Guilford Press.

Barlow, D. H. (2008a). *Clinical handbook of psychological disorders: A step by step treatment manual* (4th ed.). New York, NY: Guilford Press.

Barlow, D. H. (Ed.). (2002b). *Anxiety and its disorders: The nature and treatment of anxiety and panic* (2nd ed.). New York, NY: Guilford Press.

Barlow, D. H. (Ed.). (2008b). *Clinical handbook of psychological disorders: A step-by-step treatment manual* (4th ed.). New York, NY: Guilford Press.

Barlow, D. H., & Nock, M. K. (2009). Why can't we be more idiographic in our research? *Perspectives on Psychological Science, 4*(1), 19–21.

Barney Dews, C. L., & Williams, M. S. (1989). Student musicians' personality styles, stresses, and coping patterns. *Psychology of Music, 17*, 37–47.

Barr, K., & Hall, C. (1992). The use of imagery by rowers. *International Journal of Sport Psychology, 23*, 243–61.

Barrett, P. M., Rapee, R. M., Dadds, M. M., & Ryan, S. M. (1996). Family enhancement of cognitive style in anxious and aggressive children. *Journal of Abnormal Child Psychology, 24*(2), 187–203.

Bartel, L. R., & Thompson, E. G. (1994). Coping with performance stress: A study of professional orchestral musicians in Canada. *The Quarterly Journal of Music Teaching and Learning, 5*(4), 70–8.

Bartley, J., & Clifton-Smith, T. (2006). *Breathing matters.* Auckland, NZ: Random House.

Bateman, A., & Fonagy, P. (2004). *Psychotherapy for borderline personality disorder.* Oxford: Oxford University Press.

Baumeister, R. F. (1984). Choking under pressure: Self consciousness and paradoxical effects of incentives on skillful performance. *Journal of Personality and Social Psychology, 46*(3), 610–20.

Baumeister, R. F., Dale, K., & Sommer, K. L. (1998). Freudian defense mechanisms and empirical findings in modern social psychology: Reaction formation, projection, displacement, undoing, isolation, sublimation, and denial. *Journal of Personality and Social Psychology, 66*, 1081–124.

Baumrind, D. (1971). Current patterns of parental authority. *Developmental Psychology Monograph, 4* (1, Part 2).

BBC News. (2006). Streisand makes stage comeback. *BBC News: International Version*, from http://news.bbc.co.uk/2/hi/entertainment/5405166.stm.

Beattie, H. J. (2005). Revenge. *Journal of the American Psychoanalytic Association, 53*(2), 513–24.

Beck, A. T. (1976). *Cognitive therapy and the emotional disorders*: Oxford: International Universities Press.

Beck, A. T., & Clark, D. A. (1988). Anxiety and depression: An information processing perspective. *Anxiety Research, 1*, 23–6.

Beck, A. T., & Clark, D. A. (1997). An information processing model of anxiety: Automatic and strategic processes. *Behaviour Research and Therapy, 35*(1), 49–58.

Beck, A. T., Emery, G., & Greenberg, R. L. (1985). *Anxiety disorders and phobias: A cognitive perspective.* New York, NY: Basic Books.

Beck, J. (1995). *Cognitive therapy: Basics and beyond.* New York, NY: Guilford Press.

Behar, E., DiMarco, I. D., Hekler, E. B., Mohlman, J., & Staples, A. M. (2009). Current theoretical models of generalized anxiety disorder (GAD): Conceptual review and treatment implications. *Journal of Anxiety Disorders, 23*(8), 1011–23.

Beidel, D. C., Turner, S. M., & Morris, T. L. (1995). A new inventory to assess childhood social anxiety and phobia: The social phobia and anxiety inventory for children. *Psychological Assessment, 7*(1), 73–9.

Beidel, D. C., Turner, S. M., & Morris, T. L. (1998). *Social Phobia and Anxiety Inventory for Children (SPAI-C).* North Tonawanda, NY: Multi-Health Systems Inc.

Beidel, D. C., Turner, S. M., & Morris, T. L. (2000). Behavioral treatment of childhood social phobia. *Journal of Consulting and Clinical Psychology, 68*(6), 1072–80.

Beilock, S. L., & Carr, T. H. (2001). On the fragility of skilled performance: What governs choking under pressure? *Journal of Experimental Psychology: General, 130*(4), 701–25.

Bentz, B. G., & Williamson, D. A. (1998). Worry and the prediction of future threatening events: Association with gender and trait anxiety. *Journal of Gender, Culture and Health, 3*(1), 41–9.

Berens, P. L., & Ostrosky, J. D. (1988). Use of beta-blocking agents in musical performance induced anxiety. *Drug Intelligence and Clinical Pharmacy, 22*, 148–9.

Berglund, B., & Stafstom, H. (1994). Psychological monitoring and modulation of training load of world class canoeists. *Medicine & Science in Sports & Exercise, 26*, 1036–40.

Bertollo, M., Saltarelli, B., & Robazza, C. (2009). Mental preparation strategies of elite modern pentathletes. *Psychology of Sport and Exercise, 10*(2), 244–54.

Billig, M. (2006). A psychoanalytic discursive psychology: From consciousness to unconsciousness. *Discourse Studies, 8*(1), 17–24.

Birk, L. (2004). Pharmacotherapy for performance anxiety disorders: Occassionally useful but typically contraindicated. *Journal of Clinical Psychology, 60*(8), 867–79.

Birmaher, B., Axelson, D. A., Monk, K., Kalas, C., Clark, D. B., Ehmann, M., Bridge, J., Heo, J., & Brent, D. A. (2003). Fluoxetine for the treatment of childhood anxiety disorders. *Journal of the American Academy of Child & Adolescent Psychiatry, 42*(4), 415–23.

Birmaher, B., Brent, D. A., & Benson, R. S. (1998). Summary of the practice parameters for the assessment and treatment of children and adolescents with depressive disorders. *Journal of the American Academy of Child and Adolescent Psychiatry, 37*(11), 1234–38.

Bishop, S. R. (2002). What do we really know about mindfulness based stress reduction? *Psychosomatic Medicine, 64*, 71–82.

Bisley, J. W., & Goldberg, M. E. (2010). Attention, intention, and priority in the parietal lobe. *Annual Review of Neuroscience, 33*, 1–21.

Bitran, S., & Barlow, D. H. (2004). Etiology and treatment of social anxiety: A commentary. *Journal of Clinical Psychology, 60*(8), 881–6.

Blagys, M. D., & Hilsenroth, M. J. (2002). Distinctive activities of cognitive-behavioral therapy: A review of the comparative psychotherapy process literature. *Clinical Psychology Review, 22*, 671–706.

Blalock, J. E., & Smith, E. M. (2007). Conceptual development of the immune system as a sixth sense. *Brain, Behavior, and Immunity, 21*, 23–33.

Blanchard, R. J., Griebel, G., Henrie, J. A., & Blanchard, D. C. (1997). Differentiation of anxiolytic and panicolytic drugs by effects on rat and mouse defense test batteries. *Neuroscience and Biobehavioural Review, 21*, 783–9.

Blanco, C., Antia, S. X., & Liebowitz, M. R. (2002). Pharmacotherapy of social anxiety disorder. *Biological Psychiatry, 51*, 109–20.

Blote, A. W., Kint, M. J., Miers, A. C., & Westenberg, P. M. (2009). The relation between public speaking anxiety and social anxiety: A review. *Journal of Anxiety Disorders, 23*(3), 305–313.

Booth, R. J. (2007). Are there meaningful relationships between psychosocial self and physiological self? *New Directions in Psychotherapy and Relational Psychoanalysis 2*, 165–78.

Borkovec, T. (1976). Physiological and cognitive processes in the regulation of anxiety. In G. E. Schwartz & S. Shapiro (Eds.), *Consciousness and self-regulation* (Vol. 1, pp. 261–312). New York, NY: Plenum Press.

Borkovec, T. D. (1994). The nature, functions, and origins of worry. In G. D. & F. Tallis (Eds.), *Worrying: Perspectives on theory assessment and treatment* (pp. 5–33). Sussex, UK: Wiley & Sons.

Borkovec, T. D., Robinson, E., Pruzinsky, T., & DePree, J. A. (1983). Preliminary exploration of worry: Some characteristics and processes. *Behavior Research and Therapy, 21*, 9–16.

Bowlby, J. (1980). *Attachment and loss.* New York: Basic Books.

Bowlby, J. (1987). Defensive processes in the light of attachment theory. In D. P. Schwartz, J. Sacksteder & Y. Akabane (Eds.), *Attachment and the therapeutic process: Essays in honor of Otto Allen Will, Jr., M.D.* (pp. 63–79). Madison, CT, US: International Universities Press.

Bowlby, J. (1988). *A secure base: Parent-child attachment and healthy human development.* New York, NY: Basic Books.

Bowlby, J. (1988). *A secure base: Clinical applications of attachment theory.* London: Routledge.

Brandchaft, B. (2007). Systems of pathological accommodation and change in analysis. *Psychoanalytic Psychology, 24*(4), 667–87.

Brandfonbrener, A. (1999). Performance anxiety: Different strokes for different folks. *Medical Problems of Performing Artists, 14*(3), 101–2.

Brandfonbrener, A. (2000). Epidemiology and risk factors. In R. Tubiana & P. C. Amadio (Eds.), *Medical problems of the instrumentalist musician.* London: Martin Dunitz.

Brandfonbrener, A. G. (1990). Beta blockers in the treatment of performance anxiety. *Medical Problems of Performing Artists, 5*(1), 23–6.

Brantigan, C. O., Brantigan, T. A., & Joseph, N. (1982). Effect of beta blockade and beta stimulation on stage fright. *The American Journal of Medicine, 72*, 88–94.

Britsch, L. (2005). Investigating performance-related problems of young musicians. *Medical Problems of Performing Artists, 20*, 40–7.

Broadhurst, P. L. (1957). Emotionality and the Yerkes–Dodson law. *Journal of Experimental Psychology, 54*, 345–52.

Brodsky, W. (1996). Music performance anxiety reconceptualised: A critique of current research practice and findings. *Medical Problems of Performing Artists, 11*(3), 88–98.

Brodsky, W., & Sloboda, J. A. (1997). Clinical trial of a music generated vibrotactile therapeutic environment for musicians: Main effects and outcome differences between therapy subgroups. *Journal of Music Therapy, 34*, 2–32.

Brotons, M. (1994). Effects of performing conditions on music performance anxiety and performance quality. *Journal of Music Therapy, 31*(1), 63–81.

Brown, T. A., & Barlow, D. H. (2005). Dimensional versus categorical classification of mental disorders in the fifth edition of the Diagnostic and Statistical Manual of Mental Disorders and beyond: Comment on the special section. *Journal of Abnormal Psychology, 114*(4), 551–6.

Brown, T. A., Campbell, L. A., Lehman, C. L., Grisham, J. R., & Mancill, R. B. (2001). Current and lifetime cormorbidity of the DSM-IV anxiety and mood disorders in a large clinical sample. *Journal of Abnormal Psychology, 110*(4), 585–99.

Bruce, T. J., & Barlow, D. H. (1990). The nature and role of performance anxiety in sexual dysfunction. In H. Leitenberg (Ed.), *Handbook of social anxiety.* New York: Plenum Press.

Brunye, T. T., Mahoney, C. R., Lieberman, H. R., & Taylor, H. A. (2010). Caffeine modulates attention network function. *Brain & Cognition, 72*(2), 181–8.

Buccino, G., & Riggio, L. (2006). The role of the mirror neuron system in motor learning. *Kinesiology, 38*(1), 5–15.

Burgin, J. (1973). *Teaching singing.* Metuchen, NJ: The Scarecrow Press, Inc.

Burke, R. J., & Greenglass, E. R. (2000). Organizational restructuring: Identifying effective hospital downsizing processes. In R. J. Burke & C. L. Cooper (Eds.), *The organization in crisis* (pp. 284–303). London: Blackwell.

Butler, A. C., Chapman, J. E., Forman, E. M., & Beck, A. T. (2006). The empirical status of cognitive-behavioral therapy: A review of meta-analyses. *Clinical Psychology Review, 26*(1), 17–31.

Butor, M. (1969). *Passing time: A change of heart* . (Trans. Jean Stewart). New York, NY: Simon & Schuster.

Calvo, M. G., Ramos, P. M., & Estevez, A. (1992). Test anxiety and comprehension efficiency: The role of prior knowledge and working memory deficits. *Anxiety, Stress and Coping, 5*(2), 125–38.

Cannon, W. B. (1929). *Bodily changes in pain, hunger, fear and rage: An account of recent researches into the function of emotional excitement.* New York, NY: Appleton.

Cantril, H. (1956). The qualities of being human. *American Quarterly, 6*(1), 3–18.

Cartwright-Hatton, S., McNicol, K., & Doubleday, E. (2006). Anxiety in a neglected population: Prevalence of anxiety disorders in pre-adolescent children. *Clinical Psychology Review, 26*(7), 817–33.

Carver, C. S., & Scheier, M. F. (1999). Optimism. In C. R. Snyder (Ed.), *Coping: The psychology of what works* (pp. 182–204). New York, NY: Oxford University Press.

Carver, C. S., Scheier, M. F., & Weintraub, J. K. (1989). Assessing coping strategies: A theoretically based approach. *Journal of Personality and Social Psychology, 56*, 267–83.

Case, R. (1991). Stages in the development of the young child's sense of self. *Developmental Review, 11*, 210–30.

Cassidy, J., & Shaver, P. R. (Eds.). (2008). *Handbook of attachment: Theory, research, and clinical applications* (2nd ed.). New York, NY: Guilford Press.

Castonguay, L. G., Goldfried, M. R., Wiser, S. L., Raue, P. J., & Hayes, A. M. (1996). Predicting the effect of cognitive therapy for depression: A study of unique and common factors. *Journal of Consulting and Clinical Psychology, 64*, 497–504.

Chambless, D. L., Caputo, G., Bright, P., & Gallagher, R. (1984). Assessment of fear of fear in agoraphobics: The Body Sensations Questionnaire and the Agoraphobic Cognitions Questionnaire. *Journal of Consulting and Clinical Psychology, 52*(6), 1090–7.

Champion, R. A. (1969). *Learning and activation.* Sydney: John Wiley and Sons Australasia.

Chang, J. C. (2001). An examination of performance anxiety associated with solo performance of college-level music majors. *Dissertation Abstracts International, 62*, 1765A–6A.

Chang, J. C., Midlarsky, E., & Lin, P. (2003). The effects of meditation on music performance anxiety. *Medical Problems of Performing Artists, 18*(3), 126–30.

Chavira, D. A., & Stein, M. B. (2002). Combined psychoeducation and treatment with selective serotonin reuptake inhibitors for youth with generalized social anxiety disorder. *Journal of Child and Adolescent Psychopharmacology, 12*, 47–54.

Chesky, K. S., & Hipple, J. (1997). Performance anxiety, alcohol-related problems, and social/emotional difficulties of college students: A comparative study between lower-division music and non-music majors. *Medical Problems of Performing Artists, 12*, 126–32.

Chesky, K. S., Kondraske, G., & Rubin, B. (2000). Effect of elastic neck strap on right thumb force and force angle during clarinet performance. *Journal of Occupational & Environmental Medicine, 42*(8), 775–6.

Cho, C. K. (2007). Motivated goal setting and affect: Expectations and reality. *Dissertation Abstracts International, 68*(6-A), 2254.

Chorpita, B. F., Albano, A. M., & Barlow, D. H. (1996). Cognitive processing in children: Relation to anxiety and family influences. *Journal of Clinical Child Psychology, 25*(2), 170–6.

Chorpita, B. F., & Barlow, D. H. (1998). The development of anxiety: The role of control in the early environment. *Psychological Bulletin, 124*(1), 3–21.

Chorpita, B. F., Brown, T. A., & Barlow, D. H. (1998). Perceived control as a mediator of family environment in etiological models of childhood anxiety. *Behavior Therapy, 29*, 457–76.

Cicchetti, D., & Cohen, D. J. (1995). Perspectives on developmental psychopathology. In D. Cicchetti & D. J. Cohen (Eds.), *Developmental psychopathology: Theory and methods* (Vol. 1, pp. 3–20). New York, NY: Wiley.

Clark, A. (2008). *Supersizing the mind: Embodiment, action, and cognitive extension.* New York, NY: Oxford University Press.

Clark, D. B., & Agras, W. S. (1991). The assessment and treatment of performance anxiety in musicians. *American Journal of Psychiatry, 148*(5), 598–605.

Cobham, V. E., Dadds, M. R., & Spence, S. H. (1998). The role of parental anxiety in the treatment of childhood anxiety. *Journal of Consulting and Clinical Psychology in the Schools, 66*(6), 893–905.

Coffman, D. D. (1990). Effects of mental practice, physical practice, and knowledge of results on piano performance. *Journal of Research in Music Education, 38*(3), 187–96.

Cohen, A., Pargman, D., & Tenenbaum, G. (2003). Critical elaboration and empirical investigation of the cusp catastrophe model: A lesson for practitioners. *Journal of Applied Sport Psychology, 15*(2), 144–59.

Collier, J. L. (1983). *Louis Armstrong: An American genius.* New York, NY: Oxford University Press.

Compton, S. N., March, J. S., Brent, D., Albano, A. M., Weersing, V. R., & Curry, J. (2004). Cognitive-behavioral psychotherapy for anxiety and depressive disorders in children and adolescents: An evidence-based medicine review. *Journal American Academy of Child Adolescenct Psychiatry 43*, 930–59.

Connolly, S. D., & Bernstein, G. A. (2007). Practice parameter for the assessment and treatment of children and adolescents with anxiety disorders. *Journal of American Academy of Child & Adolescent Psychiatry, 46*(2), 267–83.

Cooper, C. L. (1983). Identifying stressors at work: Recent research developments. *Journal of Psychosomatic Research, 27*(5), 369–76.

Cooper, C. L. (1985). The stress of work: An overview. *Aviation, Space and Environmental Medicine, 56*(7), 627–32.

Cooper, C. L., & Payne, R. L. (1992). International perspectives on research into work, well being and stress management. In J. C. Quick, L. R. Murphy & H. J. J. (Eds.), *Stress and wellbeing at work.* American Psychology Association.

Cooper, C. L., & Willis, G. I. D. (1989). Popular musicians under pressure. *Psychology of Music, 17*(1), 22–36.

Corbetta, M., & Shulman, G. L. (2002). Control of goal-directed and stimulus-driven attention in the brain. *Nature Reviews Neuroscience, 3*, 201–15.

Costello, E. J., Mustillo, S., Erkanli, A., Keeler, G., & Angold, A. (2003). Prevalence and development of psychiatric disorders in childhood and adolescence. *Archives of General Psychiatry, 60*(8), 837–44.

Cotterill, S. T., Sanders, R., & Collins, D. (2010). Developing effective pre-performance routines in golf: Why don't we ask the golfer? *Journal of Applied Sport Psychology, 22*(1), 51–64.

Cousineau, T. M., & Shedler, J. (2006). Predicting physical health: Implicit mental health measures versus self-report scales. *The Journal of Nervous and Mental Disease, 194*(6), 427–32.

Cox, M. J., Owen, M. T., Henderson, V. K., & Margand, N. A. (1992). Prediction of infant–father and infant–mother attachment. *Developmental Psychology, 28,* 474–83.

Cox, R. (2007). *Sport psychology: Concepts and applications* (6th ed.). New York, NY: McGraw Hill.

Cox, R. H. (2006). To your health: An holistic approach to performance preparation. *International Musician, 104*(9), 12.

Cox, W. J., & Kenardy, J. (1993). Performance anxiety, social phobia, and setting effects in instrumental music students. *Journal of Anxiety Disorders, 7*(1), 49–60.

Coyle, S. (2006). Conquer stage fright. *Acoustic Guitar, 16*(7), 40–1.

Cramer, J. (1998). Freshman to senior year: A follow-up study of identity, narcissism and defense mechanisms. *Journal of Research in Personality, 32,* 156–72.

Craske, M., & Craig, K. (1984). Musical performance anxiety: The three-systems model and self-efficacy theory. *Behaviour Research and Therapy, 22*(3), 267–80.

Crawford, M. (2003). Sight-reading, learning a new piece, memorizing and playing by ear. *Flute Australasia* (Spring–Summer).

Creed, P. A., & Evans, B. M. (2002). Personality, well-being and deprivation theory. *Personality and Individual Differences, 33*(7), 1045–54.

Crippa, J. A., Zuardi, A. W., Martín-Santos, R., Bhattacharyya, S., Atakan, Z., & McGuire, P. (2009). Cannabis and anxiety: A critical review of the evidence. *Human Psychopharmacology, 24,* 515–23.

Crippa, J. A. S. (2011). Neural basis of anxiolytic effects of cannabidiol (CBD) in generalized social anxiety disorder: A preliminary report. *Journal of Psychopharmacology, 25*(1), 121–30.

Cromer, J., & Tenenbaum, G. (2009). Meta-motivational dominance and sensation-seeking effects on motor performance and perceptions of challenge and pressure. *Psychology of Sport and Exercise, 10*(5), 552–8.

Csikszentmihalyi, M. (1975). *Beyond boredom and anxiety*. San Francisco: Jossey-Bass Publishers.

Csikszentmihalyi, M. (1999). If we are so rich, why aren't we happy? *American Psychologist, 54*(10), 821–7.

Culf, N. (1998). *Musician's injuries. A guide to their understanding and prevention*. Guildford: Parapress.

Cushway, D., & Tyler, P. A. (1994). Stress and coping in clinical psychologists. *Stress Medicine, 10,* 35–42.

D'Zurilla, T. J., & Goldfried, M. R. (1971). Problem solving and behavior modification. *Journal of Abnormal Psychology, 78*(1), 107–26.

Dadds, M. R., Davey, G. C. L., & Field, A. P. (2001). Developmental aspects of conditioning processes in anxiety disorders. In M. W. Vasey & M. M. Dadds (Eds.), *The developmental psychopathology of anxiety* (pp. 205–30). New York, NY: Oxford University Press.

Dalrymple, G. V. (2005). Medical issues and horn playing: Beta blockers and stage fright (performance anxiety). *The Horn Call—Journal of the International Horn Society, 35*(2), 69–70.

Damasio, A. (1994). *Descartes' error: Emotion, reason and the human brain*. New York, NY: Avon books.

Danner, D. D., Snowdon, D. A., & Friesen, W. V. (2001). Positive emotions in early life and longevity: Findings from the nun study. *Journal of Personality and Social Psychology, 80,* 804–13.

Danzinger, K. (1997). The historical formation of selves. In R. D. Ashmore & L. Jussim (Eds.), *Self and identity: Fundamental issues* (Vol. 1, pp. 137–59). New York, NY: Oxford University Press.

Darwin, C. R. (1859). *On the origin of species by means of natural selection, or the preservation of favoured races in the struggle for life.* (1st ed.). London: John Murray.

Darwin, C. R. (1872). *The expressions of the emotions in man and animals.* London: John Murray.

Davanloo, H. (1990). *Unlocking the unconscious: Selected papers of Habib Davanloo.* Oxford: Wiley and Sons.

Davanloo, H. (2005). Intensive short-term dynamic psychotherapy. In B. Sadock & V. A. Sadock (Eds.), *Kaplan and Sadock's comprehensive textbook of psychiatry* (Vol. 2). New York, NY: Lippincott Williams Wilkins.

Davidson, J. (2002). Developing the ability to perform. In J. Rink (Ed.), *Musical performance: A guide to understanding* (pp. 89–101). Cambridge, UK: Cambridge University Press.

Davidson, J. W. (2004). *The music practitioner: Research for the music performer, teacher, and listener.* Hampshire, UK: Ashgate Publishing.

Davis, E. P., Donzella, B., Krueger, W. K., & Gunnar, M. R. (1999). The start of a new school year: Individual differences in salivary cortisol response in relation to child temperament. *Developmental Psychobiology, 35,* 188–96.

Davison, G. C., Vogel, R. S., & Coffman, S. G. (1997). Think-aloud approaches to cognitive assessment and the articulated thoughts in simulated situations paradigm. *Journal of Consulting and Clinical Psychology, 65*(6), 950–8.

Dawson, W. J., Charness, M. E., Goode, D. J., Lederman, R. J., & Newmark, J. (1998). What's in a name? Terminologic issues in performing arts medicine. *Medical Problems of Performing Artists, 13*(2), 45–50.

Day, T. (2005). Teachers' craft knowledge: A constant in times of change? *Irish Educational Studies, 24*(1), 21–30.

De Francesco, C., & Burke, K. (1997). Performance enhancement strategies used in a professional tennis tournament. *International Journal of Sport Psychology, 28,* 185–95.

Debiec, J., Diaz-Mataix, L., Bush, D. E., Doyere, V., & LeDoux, J. E. (2010). The amygdala encodes specific sensory features of an aversive reinforcer. *Nature Neuroscience, 13*(5), 536–7.

Deci, E. L., & Ryan, R. M. (1995). Human autonomy: The basis of true self-esteem. In M. H. Kernis (Ed.), *Efficacy, agency and self-esteem* (Vol. 2, pp. 31–46). New York, NY: Plenum Press.

Deen, D. R. (2000). Awareness and breathing: Keys to the moderation of musical performance anxiety. *Dissertation Abstracts International, 60,* 4241A.

Deffenbacher, J. L. (1986). Cognitive and physiological components of test anxiety in real-life exams. *Cognitive Therapy and Research, 10*(6), 1573–2819.

Dienstbier, R. A. (1989). Arousal and physiological toughness: Implications for mental and physical health. *Psychological Review, 96*(1), 84–100.

Dollard, J., & Miller, N. E. (1950). *Personality and psychotherapy: An analysis in terms of learning, thinking, and culture.* New York, NY: McGraw-Hill.

Dugas, M. J., Letarte, H., Rheaume, J., Freeston, M. H., & Ladouceur, R. (1995). Worry and problem solving: Evidence of a specific relationship. *Cognitive Therapy and Research, 19,* 109–20.

Dunbar-Wells, R. (1999). The relevance of metaphor to effective voice teaching strategies. *Australian Voice, 5*, 50–9.

Durbin, P. G. (2006). Therapist: Beware of false memories. *Australian Journal of Clinical Hypnotherapy and Hypnosis, 24*(1), 35–44.

Dvorak-Bertsch, J. D., Curtin, J. J., Rubinstein, T. J., & Newman, J. P. (2007). Anxiety moderates the interplay between cognitive and affective processing. *Psychological Science, 18*(8), 699–705.

Dworkin, B. R. (1993). *Learning and physiological regulation*. Chicago: University of Chicago Press.

Easterbrook, J. A. (1959). The effect of emotion on cue utilization and the organization of behavior. *Psychological Review, 66*, 183–201.

Eckman, P. S., & Shean, G. D. (1997). Habituation of cognitive and physiological arousal and social anxiety. *Behaviour Research and Therapy, 35*(12), 1113–21.

Ehlers, A. (1993). Somatic symptoms and panic attacks: A retrospective study of learning experiences. *Behaviour Research and Therapy, 31*(3), 269–78.

Eifert, G. H., & Forsyth, J. P. (2005). *Acceptance and commitment therapy for anxiety disorders: A practionier's treatment guide to using mindfulness, acceptance and value-based behavior change strategies*. Oakland, CA: New Harbinger.

Eilam, D., Izhara, R., & Mort, J. (2011). Threat-detection and precaution: Neurophysiological, behavioral, cognitive and psychiatric aspects. *Neuroscience & Biobehavioral Reviews, 35*(4), 999–1006.

Ein-Dor, T., Mikulincer, M., Doron, G., & Shaver, P. R. (2010). The attachment paradox: How can so many of us (the insecure ones) have no adaptive advantages? *Perspectives on Psychological Science, 5*(2), 123–41.

Ekman, P. (2003). *Emotions revealed: Understanding faces and feelings*. London: Weidenfeld & Nicholson.

Ekman, P., Levenson, R. W., & Friesen, W. V. (1983). Automatic nervous system activity distinguishes among emotions. *Science, 221*, 1208–10.

Elicker, J., Englund, M., & Sroufe, L. A. (1992). Predicting peer competence and peer relationships in childhood from early parent–child relationships. In R. D. Parke & G. W. Ladd (Eds.), *Family–peer relationships: Modes of linkage* (pp. 77–106). Hillsdale, NJ: Erlbaum.

Elliot, A. J., & McGregor, H. A. (1999). Test anxiety and the hierarchical model of approach and avoidance achievement motivation. *Journal of Personality and Social Psychology, 76*(4), 628–44.

Elliot, A. J., & Thrash, T. M. (2002). Approach–avoidance motivation in personality, approach and avoidance temperaments and goals. *Journal of Personality and Social Psychology, 82*, 804–18.

Elliott, R. (1998). Editor's introduction: A guide to the empirically supported treatments controversy. *Psychotherapy Research, 8*, 115–25.

Ellis, A. (1984). *Rational-emotive therapy and cognitive behaviour therapy*. New York, NY: Springer.

Ellis, A. (2002). The role of irrational beliefs in perfectionism. In G. L. Flett & P. L. Hewitt (Eds.), *Perfectionism: Theory, research, and treatment* (pp. 217–29). Washington, DC: American Psychological Association.

Emerick, G. (2006). *Here, there and everywhere*. New York, NY: Gotham Books.

Emmons, R. A. (1987). Narcissism: Theory and measurement. *Journal of Personality and Social Psychology, 52*, 11–17.

Eng, W., Heimberg, R. G., Coles, M. E., Schneier, F. R., & Liebowitz, M. R. (2000). An empirical approach to subtype identification in individuals with social phobia. *Psychological Medicine, 30,* 1345–57.

Erickson, K., Drevets, W., & Schulkin, J. (2003). Glucocorticoid regulation of diverse cognitive functions in normal and pathological emotional states. *Neuroscience and Biobehavioral Reviews, 27,* 233–46.

Ericsson, K. A., Krampe, R. T., & Tesch-Romer, C. (1993). The role of deliberate practice in the acquisition of expert performance *Psychological Review, 100*(3), 363–406.

Ericsson, K. A., & Lehmann, A. C. (1996). Expert and exceptional performance: Evidence of maximal adaptation to task constraints. *Annual Reviews in Psychology, 47,* 273–305.

Erikson, E. H. (1968). *Identity: Youth and crisis.* New York, NY: W. W. Norton.

Essau, C. A., Conradt, J., & Petermann, F. (1999). Frequency and comorobidity of social phobia and social fears in adolescents. *Behaviour Research and Therapy, 37,* 831–43.

Evans, A. (1994). *The secrets of musical confidence: How to maximize your performance potential.* Sydney, Australia: HarperCollins.

Eysenck, H. J. (1960). *Behaviour therapy and the neuroses: Readings in modern methods of treatment derived from learning theory.* Oxford; New York, NY: Symposium Publications Division, Pergamon Press.

Eysenck, H. J. (1988). Personality, stress and cancer: Prediction and prophylaxis. *British Journal of Medical Psychology, 61,* 57–75.

Eysenck, M. W. (1991). Anxiety and attention. In R. Schwarzer & R. A. Wicklund (Eds.), *Anxiety and self-focused attention.* Chur, Switzerland: Harwood Academic Publishers.

Eysenck, M. W. (1997). *Anxiety and cognition: A unified theory.* Hove, UK: Psychology Press.

Eysenck, M. W., Derakshan, N., Santos, R., & Calvo, M. G. (2007). Anxiety and cognitive performance: Attentional control theory. *Emotion, 7*(2), 336–53.

Falk, Q. (1989). *Anthony Hopkins: Too good to waste.* London: Columbus Books.

Fehm, L., & Schmidt, K. (2005). Performance anxiety in gifted adolescent musicians. *Journal of Anxiety Disorders, 20*(1), 98–109.

Feldner, M. T., Zvolensky, M. J., Stickle, T. R., Bonn-Miller, M. O., & Leen-Feldner, E. W. (2006). Anxiety sensitivity—physical concerns as a moderator fo the emotional consequences of emotion suppression during biological challenge: An experimental test using individual growth curve analysis. *Behaviour Research and Therapy, 44,* 249–72.

Field, A. P. (2006). Is conditioning a useful framework for understanding the development and treatment of phobias? *Clinical Psychology Review, 26*(7), 857–75.

Field, T. (1996). Attachment and separation in young children. *Annual Review of Psychology, 47,* 541–61.

Filimon, F., Nelson, J. D., Hagler, D. J., Sereno, M. I., Filimon, F., Nelson, J. D., Hagler, D. J., & Sereno, M. I. (2007). Human cortical representations for reaching: Mirror neurons for execution, observation, and imagery. *Neuroimage, 37*(4), 1315–28.

Fishbein, M., Middlestadt, S. E., Ottati, V., Strauss, S., & Ellis, A. (1988). Medical problems among ICSOM musicians: Overview of a national survey. *Medical Problems of Performing Artists, 3,* 1–8.

Fitousi, D., & Wenger, M. J. (2011). Processing capacity under perceptual and cognitive load: A closer look at load theory. *Journal of Experimental Psychology: Human Perception and Performance* (18 April 2011: Epub ahead of print).

Fjellman-Wiklund, A., Brulin, C., & Sundelin, G. (2003). Physical and psychosocial work-related risk factors associated with neck–shoulder discomfort in male and female music teachers. *Medical Problems of Performing Artists, 18*(1), 33–41.

Flannery-Schroeder, E. C., & Kendall, P. C. (2000). Group and individual cognitive-behavioral treatments for youth with anxiety disorders: A randomized clinical trial. *Cognitive Therapy and Research, 24*, 251–78.

Fleege, P. O., Charlesworth, R., Burts, D. C., & Hart, C. H. (1992). Stress begins in kindergarten: A look at behavior during standardized testing. *Journal of Research in Childhood Education, 7*, 20–6.

Flesch, C. (1939). *The art of violin playing* (revised ed.). New York, NY: Carl Fischer.

Flett, G. L., Endler, N. S., Tassone, C., & Hewitt, P. L. (1994). Perfectionism and components of state and trait anxiety. *Current Psychology, 13*(4), 326–50.

Flett, G. L., Greene, A., & Hewitt, P. L. (2004). Dimensions of perfectionism and anxiety sensitivity. *Journal of Rational Emotive and Cognitive Behaviour Therapy, 22*(1), 39–57.

Flett, G. L., & Hewitt, P. L. (2005). The perils of perfectionism in sports and exercise. *Current Directions in Psychological Science, 14*(1), 14–18.

Flett, G. L., & Hewitt, P. L. (Eds.) (2002). *Perfectionism: Theory, research, and treatment*. Washington, DC: American Psychological Association.

Flint, A. J. (1994). Epidemiology and comorbidity of anxiety disorders in the elderly. *American Journal of Psychiatry, 151*(5), 640–9.

Foa, E. B., Cahill, S. P., Boscarino, J. A., Hobfoll, S. E., Lahad, M., McNally, R. J., & Solomon, Z. (2005). Social, psychological, and psychiatric interventions following terrorist attacks: Recommendations for practice and research *Neuropsychopharmacology, 30*(10), 1806–17.

Foa, E. B., & Kozak, M. (1986a). Emotional processing of fear: Exposure to corrective information. *Psychological Bulletin, 99*, 20–35.

Foa, E. B., & Kozak, M. J. (1986b). Emotional processing of fear: Exposure to corrective information. *Psychological Bulletin, 99*(1), 20–35.

Folkman, S., & Moskowitz, J. T. (2000). Positive affect and the other side of coping. *American Psychologist, 55*, 647–54.

Fonagy, P., Gergely, G., Jurist, E., & Target, M. (2002). *Affect regulation, mentalization, and the development of the self*. New York, NY: Other Press.

Fonagy, P., Steele, H., & Steele, M. (1991). Maternal representations of attachment during pregnancy predict the organization of infant–mother attachment at one year of age. *Child Development, 62*, 891–905.

Fonteyn, M. (1976). *Margot Fonteyn: Autobiography*. Sydney, Australia: Random House.

Ford, T., Goodman, R., & Meltzer, H. (2003). The British child and adolescent mental health survey 1999: The prevalence of DSM-IV disorders. *Journal of the American Academy of Child and Adolescent Psychiatry, 42*(10), 1203–11.

Fortune, J. M. (2007). *Performance related musculoskeletal disorders in university flute students and relationships with muscle tension, music performance anxiety, musical task complexity and musical ability*. Unpublished Master in Music, University of Sydney, Australia.

Foster, D. J., Weigand, D. A., & Baines, D. (2006). The effect of removing superstitious behavior and introducing a pre-performance routine on basketball free-throw performance. *Journal of Applied Sport Psychology, 18*(2), 167–71.

Fox, E., Russo, R., Bowles, R., & Dutton, K. (2001). Do threatening stimuli draw or hold visual attention in subclinical anxiety? *Journal of Experimental Psychology: General, 130*(4), 681–700.

Fox, N. A., Henderson, H. A., Marshall, P. J., Nichols, K. E., & Ghera, M. M. (2005). Behavioral inhibition: Linking biology and behavior within a developmental framework. *Annual Review of Psychology, 56*, 235–62.

Fredrickson, W. E. (2002). Review of the science and psychology of music performance: Creative strategies for teaching and learning. *Psychomusicology, 18*(1–2), 147–8.

Fredrikson, M., Annas, P., Fischer, H., & Wik, G. (1996). Gender and age differences in the prevalence of specific fears and phobias. *Behaviour Research and Therapy, 34*(1), 33–9.

Fredrikson, M., & Gunnarsson, R. (1992). Psychobiology of stage fright: The effect of public performance on neuroendocrine, cardiovascular and subjective reactions. *Biological Psychology, 33*(1), 51–61.

Freud, S. (1914). On narcissism: An introduction. In *The standard edition of the complete psychological works of Sigmund Freud*, Vol *14*, 73–102. London: Hogarth Press.

Freud, S. (1923). Two encyclopaedia articles: Psycho-analysis and the libido theory. In *The standard edition of the complete psychological works of Sigmund Freud*. Vol *18*, 233–59.

Freud, S. (1926). Inhibitions, symptoms and anxiety. In J. Strachey (Ed.), *The standard edition of the complete psychological works of Sigmund Freud*. Vol. 20 (pp. 75–176).

Freud, S. (1962). The ego and the id. In J. Strachey (Ed.), *The standard edition of the complete psychological works of Sigmund Freud* (pp. 3–62). New York, NY: W. W. Norton.

Freud, S. (1916-1917/1973). *Introductory lectures on psychoanalysis* (J. Strachey, Trans. Vol. 1, 15, 16). Middlesex, UK: Penguin.

Frost, R. O., Lahart, C. M., & Rosenblate, R. (1991). The development of perfectionism. *Cognitive Therapy and Research, 14*, 559–72.

Frost, R. O., Marten, P., Lahart, C., & Rosenblate, R. (1990). The dimensions of perfectionism. *Cognitive Therapy and Research, 14*, 449–68.

Furmark, T., Tillfors, M., Stattin, H., Ekselius, L., & Fredrikson, M. (2000). Social phobia subtypes in the general population revealed by cluster analysis. *Psychological Medicine, 30*, 1335–44.

Gaab, J., Sonderegger, L., Scherrer, S., & Ehlert, U. (2006). Psychoneuroendocrine effects of cognitive-behavioral stress management in a naturalistic setting—a randomized controlled trial. *Psychoneuroendocrinology, 31*(4), 428–38.

Gabbard, G. O. (1979). Stage fright. *International Journal of Psychoanalysis, 60*, 383–92.

Gabbard, G. O. (1983). Further contributions to the understanding of stage fright: Narcissistic issues. *Journal of the American Psychoanalytic Association, 31*, 423–41.

Gabbard, G. O. (1994). The vicissitudes of shame in stage fright in work. In C. W. Socarides & S. Kramer (Eds.), *Work and its inhibitions: Psychoanalytic essays* (pp. 209–20). Madison, CT: International Universities Press.

Gabbard, G. O. (2006). When is transference work useful in dynamic psychotherapy? *American Journal of Psychiatry, 163*(10), 1667–9.

Gabrielsson, A. (1999). The performance of music. In D. Deutsch (Ed.), *The psychology of music* (pp. 501–601). San Diego, California: Academic Press.

Gaetani, S., Dipasquale, P., Romano, A., Righetti, L., Cassano, T., Piomelli, D., *et al.* (2009). The endocannabinoid system as a target for novel anxiolytic and antidepressant drugs. *International Review of Neurobiology, 85*, 57–72.

Gardner, W. N. (1996). The pathophysiology of hyperventilation disorders. *Chest, 109*, 516–19.

Garfield, C. A., & Bennett, H. Z. (1984). *Peak performance: Mental training techniques of the world's greatest athletes*. Los Angeles: Tarcher.

Gater, R., Tansella, M., Korten, A., Tiemens, B. G., Mavreas, V. G., & Olatawura, M. O. (1998). Sex differences in the prevalence and detection of depressive and anxiety disorders in general health care settings: Report from the World Health Organization collaborative study on psychological problems in general health care 10.1001/archpsyc.55.5.405. *Archives of General Psychiatry, 55*(5), 405–13.

Gates, G. A., Saegert, J., Wilson, N., Johnson, L., Shepherd, A., & Hearne, E. (1985). Effect of beta blockade on singing performance. *Annals of Otolaryngology, Rhinology and Laryngology, 94*, 570–4.

Gaudry, E., & Spielberger, C. D. (1971). *Anxiety and educational achievement.* New York, NY: Wiley.

Gill, A., Murphy, F., & Rickard, N. S. (2006). A preliminary examination of the roles of perceived control, cortisol and perception of anxiety in music performance. *Australian Journal of Music Education*(1), 32–47.

Ginsberg, D. L. (2004). Women and anxiety disorders: Implications for diagnosis and treatment. *CNS Spectrums, 9*(9), 1–16.

Gleitman, H., Fridlund, A. J., & Reisber, D. (2004). *Psychology* (6th ed.). New York, NY: Norton.

Goffman, E. (1959). *The presentation of self in everyday life.* New York, NY: Doubleday Anchor.

Goleman, D. J., & Schwartz, G. E. (1976). Meditation as an intervention in stress reactivity. *Journal of Consulting and Clinical Psychology, 44*, 456–65.

Gorges, S., Alpers, G. W., & Pauli, P. (2007). Musical performance anxiety as a form of social anxiety? In A. Williamon & D. Coimbra (Eds.), *International Symposium on Performance Science* (Vol. 1, pp. 67–72). Porto, Portugal: European Association of Conservatoires (AEC): Utrecht, The Netherlands.

Gosch, E. A., Flannery-Schroeder, E., Mauro, C. F., & Compton, S. N. (2006). Principles of cognitive-behavioral therapy for anxiety disorders in children. *Journal of Cognitive Psychotherapy, 20*(3), 247–62.

Goubet, N., Rochat, P., Marie-Leblond, S., & Poss, S. (2006). Learning from others in 9–18-month-old infants. *Infant and Child Development, 15*(2), 161–77.

Gould, D., Greenleaf, C., & Krane, V. (2002). Arousal anxiety and sport behaviour. In T. S. Horn (Ed.), *Advances in sport psychology* (2nd ed., pp. 207–41). Champaign, IL: Human Kinetics.

Gramzow, R. H., Sedikides, C., Panter, A. T., Sathy, V., Harris, J., & Insko, C. A. (2004). Patterns of self-regulation and the Big Five. *European Journal of Personality, 18*(5), 367–85.

Gratto, S. D. (1998). The effectiveness of an audition anxiety workshop in reducing stress. *Medical Problems of Performing Artists, 13*(1), 29–34.

Gray, J. A., & McNaughton, N. (2000). *The neuropsychology of anxiety: An enquiry into the functions of the septo-hippocampal system* (2nd ed.). Oxford: Oxford University Press.

Green, A., Garrick, T., Sheedy, D., Blake, H., Shores, E., & Harper, C. (2010). The effect of moderate to heavy alcohol consumption on neuropsychological performance as measured by the repeatable battery for the assessment of neuropsychological status *Alcoholism: Clinical & Experimental Research, 34*(3), 443–50.

Greenacre, P. (1971). The childhood of the artist: Libidinal phase development and giftedness. In P. Greenacre (Ed.), *Emotional development* (Vol. 2, pp. 479–504). New York, NY: International Universities Press.

Greenberg, N., & Wessely, S. (2009). The dangers of inflation: Memories of trauma and post-traumatic stress disorder. *British Journal of Psychiatry, 194*(6), 479–80.

Greenfield, S. (2000). *The private life of the brain*. Canada: John Wiley and Sons.

Greenwald, A. G. (1992). Unconscious cognition reclaimed. *American Psychologist, 47*, 766–79.

Greiff, S., & Funke, J. (2008). What makes a problem complex? Factors determining difficulty in dynamic situations and implications for diagnosing complex problem solving competence. In J. Zumbach, N. Schwartz, T. Seufert, & L. Kester (Eds.), *Beyond knowledge: The legacy of competence* (pp. 199–200). Dordrecht, The Netherlands: Springer.

Grishman, A. (1989). Musicians' performance anxiety: The effectiveness of modified progressive muscle relaxation in reducing physiological, cognitive, and behavioral symptoms of anxiety. *Dissertation Abstracts International, 50*(6-B), 2622.

Grossmann, K. E., & Grossmann, K. (2005). Universality of human social attachment as an adaptive process. From http://www.brown.edu/Departments/Human_Development_Center/Roundtable/Grossman2.pdf.

Gullone, E., & King, N. J. (1992). Psychometric evaluation of a Revised Fear Survey Schedule for Children and Adolescents. *Journal of Child Psychology and Psychiatry Research, 33*(6), 987–98.

Gullone, E., King, N. J., Tonge, B., Heyne, D., & Ollendick, T. H. (2000). The Fear Survey Schedule for Children—II (FSSC-II): Validity data as a treatment outcome measure. *Australian Psychologist, 35*(3), 238–43.

Gunnar, M. R., & Donzella, B. (2002). Social regulation of the cortisol levels in early human development. *Psychoneuroendocrinology, 27*(1–2), 199–220.

Günter, H. (1992). Mental concepts in singing: A psychological approach. *The NATS Journal, Part 1*, 4–8, 46.

Hall, H. K., & Kerr, A. W. (1998). Predicting achievement anxiety: A social-cognitive perspective. *Journal of Sport and Exercise Psychology, 20*, 98–111.

Hall, H. K., Kerr, A. W., & Matthews, J. (1998). Precompetitive anxiety in sport: The contribution of achievement goals and perfectionism. *Journal of Sport and Exercise Psychology, 20*, 194–217.

Hamann, D. L. (1982). An assessment of anxiety in instrumental and vocal performances. *Journal of Research in Music Education, 30*(2), 77–90.

Hamburger, M. (1966). *Beethoven: Letters, journals and conversations*. London: Jonathan Cape.

Hammond, C. J., & Gold, M. S. (2008). Caffeine dependence, withdrawal, overdose and treatment: A review. *Directions in Psychiatry, 28*(3), 177–90.

Hanin, Y. L. (1986). State–trait anxiety research on sports in the USSR. In C. D. Spielberger & R. Diaz (Eds.), *Cross-cultural anxiety* (pp. 45–64). New York, NY: Hemisphere Publishing Corp/Harper & Row Publishers.

Hanin, Y. L. (2000a). Individual zones of optimal functioning (IZOF) Model. In Y. L. Hanin (Ed.), *Emotions in sport* (pp. 65–89). Champaign, IL: Human Kinetics.

Hanin, Y. L. (Ed.). (2000b). *Emotions in sport*. Champaign, IL: Human Kinetics.

Hanoch, Y., & Vitouch, O. (2004). When less is more: Information, emotional arousal and the ecological reframing of the Yerkes–Dodson law. *Theory & Psychology, 14*(4), 427–52.

Hanton, S., O'Brien, M., & Mellalieu, S. D. (2003). Individual differences, perceived control and competitive trait anxiety. *Journal of Sport Behavior, 26*(1), 39–55.

Hanton, S., Wadey, R., & Mellalieu, S. D. (2008). Advanced psychological strategies and anxiety responses in sport. *The Sport Psychologist, 22*(4), 472–90.

Hardy, L. (1990). A catastrophe model of performance in sport. In J. G. Jones & L. Hardy (Eds.), *Stress and Performance in Sport* (pp. 81–106). Chichester, UK: Wiley.

Hardy, L., Beattie, S., & Woodman, T. (2007). Anxiety-induced performance catastrophes: Investigating effort required as an asymmetry factor. *British Journal of Psychology, 98*(1), 15–31.

Hardy, L., Jones, G., & Gould, D. (1996a). *Understanding psychological preparation for sport.* Chichester, UK: John Wiley and Sons.

Hardy, L., Jones, G., & Gould, D. (1996b). A unifying model of psychological preparation for peak performance. In L. Hardy (Ed.), *Understanding psychological preparation for sport: Theory and practice of elite performers.* Chichester, UK: Wiley.

Hardy, L., & Parfitt, G. (1991). A catastrophe model of anxiety and performance. *British Journal of Psychology, 82*(2), 163–78.

Harlow, H. F., & Zimmerman, R. (1959). Affectional responses in the infant monkey. *Science, 130*, 421–32.

Harmison, R. J. (2006). Peak performance in sport: Identifying ideal performance states and developing athletes' psychological skills. *Professional Psychology: Research and Practice, 37*(3), 233–43.

Harrell, P. T., & Juliano, L. M. (2009). Caffeine expectancies influence the subjective and behavioral effects of caffeine. *Psychopharmacology, 207*(2), 335–42.

Harris, D. A. (2001). Using B-blockers to control stage fright: A dancer's dilemma. *Medical Problems of Performing Artists, 16*(2), 72–6.

Harter, S. (1997). The personal self in social context. In R. D. Ashmore & L. Jussim (Eds.), *Self and identity: Fundamental issues* (Vol. 1, pp. 81–105). Oxford: Oxford University Press.

Hartmann, F. (1973). *Paracelsus: Life & prophecies (1493–1541).* Blauvett, NY: Steinerbooks.

Hayes, A. M., & Strauss, J. L. (1998). Dynamic systems theory as a paradigm for the study of cognitive change in psychotherapy: An application of cognitive therapy for depression. *Journal of Consulting and Clinical Psychology, 66*, 939–47.

Hayes, D. (1975). The archetypal nature of stage fright. *Arts and Psychotherapy*(2), 279–81.

Hayes, S. C. (2004). Acceptance and commitment therapy, relational frame theory, and the third wave of behavioral and cognitive therapies. *Behavior Therapy, 35*, 639–65.

Hayes, S. C., Strosahl, K. D., & Wilson, K. G. (1999). *Acceptance and commitment therapy: An experiential guide to behavior change.* New York, NY: Guilford Press.

Hayward, C., Killen, J. D., Kraemer, H. C., & Taylor, C. B. (2000). Predictors of panic attacks in adolescents. *Journal of the American Academy of Child and Adolescent Psychiatry, 39*(2), 207–14.

Heaven, P. C. (2001). *The social psychology of adolescence.* Hampshire, UK: Palgrave.

Hebb, D. O. (1955). Drives and the C.N.S. (central nervous system). *Psychological Review, 62*, 243–54.

Hecker, J. E., Fink, C. M., Vogeltanz, N. D., Thorpe, G. L., & Sigmon, S. T. (1998). Cognitive restructuring and interoceptive exposure in the treatment of panic disorder: A crossover study. *Behavioural and Cognitive Psychotherapy, 26*, 115–31.

Heidegger, M. (1962). *Being and time* (J. Macquarrie & E. Robinson, Trans.). London: SCM Press.

Heimberg, R. G., Hope, D. A., Dodge, C. S., & Becker, R. E. (1990). DSM-III-R subtypes of social phobia: Comparison of generalized social phobics and public speaking phobics. *Journal of Nervous and Mental Disease, 178*, 172–9.

Heimberg, R. G., Liebowitz, M. R., Hope, D. A., Schneier, F. R., Holt, C. S., Welkowitz, L. A., et al. (1998). Cognitive behavioural group therapy vs phenelzine therapy for social phobia. *Archives of General Psychiatry, 55*, 1133–41.

Heimerdinger, S. R., & Hinsz, V. B. (2008). Failure avoidance motivation in a goal-setting situation. *Human Performance, 21*(4), 383–95.

Heishman, S. J., Kleykamp, B. A., & Singleton, E. G. (2010). Meta-analysis of the acute effects of nicotine and smoking on human performance. *Psychopharmacology 210*, 453–69.

Hembree, R. (1988). Correlates, causes, effects, and treatment of test anxiety. *Review of Educational Research, 58*(1), 47–77.

Hewitt, P. L., & Flett, G. L. (1991). Perfectionism in the self and social contexts: Conceptualization, assessment, and association with psychopathology. *Journal of Personality and Social Psychology, 60*(3), 456–70.

Hewitt, P. L., Flett, G. L., Sherry, S. B., Habke, A. M., Parkin, M., Lam, R. W., *et al.* (2003). The interpersonal expression of perfectionism: Perfectionistic self-presentation and psychological distress. *Journal of Personality and Social Psychology, 84*, 1303–25.

Himle, J. A., Abelson, J. L., Haghightgou, H., Hill, E. M., Nesse, R. M., & Curtis, G. C. (1999). Effect of alcohol on social phobic anxiety. *American Journal of Psychiatry, 156*(8), 1237–43.

Hobson, R. F. (1953). Prognostic factors in electroconvulsive therapy. *Journal of Neurology, Neurosurgery & Psychiatry, 16*, 275.

Hoehn-Saric, R., Hazlett, R. L., & McLeod, D. R. (1993). Generalized anxiety disorder with early and late onset of anxiety symptoms. *Comprehensive Psychiatry, 34*(5), 291–8.

Hofmann, S. G., & Barlow, D. H. (2002). Social phobia (social anxiety disorder). In D. H. Barlow (Ed.), *Anxiety and its disorders: The nature and treatment of anxiety and panic* (2nd ed., pp. 454–76). New York, NY: Guilford Press.

Hofmann, S. G., Gerlach, A. L., Wender, A., & Roth, W. T. (1997). Speech disturbances and gaze behavior during public speaking in subtypes of social phobia. *Journal of Anxiety Disorders, 11*(6), 573–85.

Hofmann, S. G., Heinrichs, N., & Moscovitch, D. A. (2004). The nature of social phobia: Toward a new classification *Clinical Psychology Review, 24*, 769–97.

Holden, R. R., & Passey, J. (2009). Social desirability. In M. R. Leary & R. H. Hoyle (Eds.), *Handbook of individual differences in social behavior* (pp. 441–54). New York, NY: Guilford Press.

Holmes, P. (2005). Imagination in practice: A study of the integrated roles of interpretation, imagery and technique in the learning and memorisation processes of two experienced solo performers. *British Journal of Music Education, 22*(3), 217–35.

Hook, J. N., & Valentiner, D. P. (2002). Are specific and generalized social phobias qualitatively distinct? *Clinical Psychology: Science and Practice, 9*(4), 379–95.

Horesh, N., Amir, M., Kedem, P., Goldberger, Y., & Kotler, M. (1997). Life events in childhood, adolescence and adulthood and the relationship to panic disorder. *Acta Psychiatrica Scandinavica, 96*(5), 373–8.

Horney, K. (1937). *The neurotic personality of our time.* London: Kegan Paul, Trench, Trubner.

Horowitz, J. (1982). *Conversations with Arrau.* New York, NY: Knopf, Random House.

Horvath, J. (2002). *Playing (less) hurt.* Kearney, NE: Morris Publishing.

Horvath, M., Herleman, H. A., & McKie, R. (2006). Goal orientation, task difficulty, and task interest: A multilevel analysis. *Motivation and Emotion, 30*(2), 171–8.

Hudson, J., & Walker, N. C. (2002). Metamotivational state reversals during matchplay golf: An idiographic approach. *The Sport Psychologist, 16*(2), 200–17.

Ihasz, D., & Parmer, D. (2006). Practical pedagogy and voice spectrography: A proposal for using technology in pursuit of artistic excellence. *Journal of Singing, 63*(1), 65–70.

Iñesta, C., Terrados, N., García, D., & Pérez, J. A. (2008). Heart rate in professional musicians. *Journal of Occupational Medicine and Toxicology, 3*(16), 1–11.

Ingurgio, V. J. (1999). The effect of state anxiety upon a motor task: An application of the cusp catastrophe model. *Dissertation Abstracts International, 60*(6-B), 3017.

Insel, T. R., & Fenton, W. S. (2005). Psychiatric epidemiology: It's not just about counting anymore. *Archives of General Psychiatry, 62*(6), 590–5.

Ipser, J. C., Kariuki, C. M., & Stein, D. J. (2008). Pharmacotherapy for social anxiety disorder: A systematic review. *Expert Review of Neurotherapeutics, 8*(2), 235–57.

Izard, C. E. (1977). *Human emotions.* New York, NY: Plenum Press.

Izard, C. E. (1993). Four systems for emotion activation: Cognitive and noncognitive processes. *Psychological Review, 100*(1), 68–90.

Izard, C. E., & Blumberg, M. A. (1985). Emotion theory and the role of emotionsin anxiety in children and adults. In A. H. Tuma & J. D. Maser (Eds.), *Anxiety and the anxiety disorders.* Hillsdale, NJ: Erlbaum.

Jackson, B., & Lurie, S. (2006). Adolescent depression: Challenges and opportunities: A review and current recommendations for clinical practice. *Advances in Pediatrics, 53*(1), 111–63.

Jackson, J. M., & Latane, B. (1981). All alone in front of all those people: Stage fright as a function of number and type of co-performers and audience. *Journal of Personality and Social Psychology, 40*(1), 73–85.

Jackson, R. C., & Masters, R. S. (2006). Ritualized behavior in sport. *Behavioral and Brain Sciences, 29*(6), 621–2.

James, I. (1997). *Federation Internationale des Musiciens 1997 Survey of 56 orchestras worldwide.* London: British Association for Performing Arts Medicine.

James, I. (1998). Western orchestral musicians are highly stressed. *Resonance: International Music Council, 26,* 19–20.

James, I., & Savage, I. (1984). Beneficial effect of nadolol on anxiety-induced disturbances of performance in musicians: A comparison with diazepam and placebo. *American Heart Journal, 108,* 1150–5.

James, I. M., Burgoyne, W., & Savage, I. T. (1983). Effect of pindolol on stress-related disturbances of musical performance: Preliminary communication. *Journal of the Royal Society of Medicine, 76,* 194–6.

Jiang, W., Zhang, Y., Xiao, L., Van Cleemput, J., Ji, S. P., Bai, G., *et al.* (2005). Cannabinoids promote embryonic and adult hippocampus neurogenesis and produce anxiolytic- and antidepressant-like effects. *Journal of Clinical Investigation, 115*(11), 3104–16.

Joseph, S. (2001). Caffeine addiction and its effects. *Nursing Times, 97*(31), 42–3.

Judge, T. A. (2009). Core self-evaluations and work success. *Current Directions in Psychological Science, 18*(1), 58–62.

Jung, C. G. (1952). *Symbols of transformation* (Vol. Collected works V). London: Routledge & Kegan Paul.

Jung, C. G. (1963). *Memories, dreams and reflections.* London: Collins & Routledge.

Kabat-Zinn, J. (2005). *Full catastrophe living; Using the wisdom of your body and mind to face stress, pain and illness: Fifteenth anniversary edition.* New York, NY: Cambridge University Press.

Kahneman, D. (1973). *Attention and effort.* Englewood Cliffs, NJ: Prentice-Hall.

Kaplan, K. (2009). Unmasking the impostor. *Nature Neuroscience, 459*(21 May), 468–9.

Kashani, J. H., & Orvaschel, H. (1990). A community study of anxiety in children and adolescents. *American Journal of Psychiatry, 147,* 313–18.

Kashani, J. H., Orvaschel, H., Rosenberg, T. K., & Reid, J. C. (1989). Psychopathology in a community sample of children and adolescents. *Journal of the American Academy of Child & Adolescent Psychiatry, 28*(5), 701–6.

Kaspersen, M., & Gotestam, K. G. (2002). A survey of music performance anxiety among Norwegian music students. *European Journal of Psychiatry, 16*(2), 69–80.

Kass, R. G., & Gish, J. M. (1991). Positive reframing and the test performance of test anxious children. *Psychology in the Schools, 28*, 43–52.

Kawamura, K. Y., Hunt, S. L., Frost, R. O., & DiBartolo, P. M. (2001). Perfectionism, anxiety, and depression: Are the relationships independent? *Cognitive Therapy and Research, 25*, 291–301.

Kazdin, A. E. (2007). Mediators and mechanisms of change in psychotherapy research. *Annual Review of Clinical Psychology, 3*, 1–27.

Keating, P. (2009). Eulogy for Geoffrey Tozer. *The Age, reproduced in Sydney Morning Herald*, from http://www.smh.com.au/opinion/society-and-culture/we-should-never-again-neglect-artists-like-the-late-geoffrey-tozer-20091002-gez6.html.

Kemeny, M. E. (2003). The psychobiology of stress. *Current Directions in Psychological Science, 12*(4), 124–9.

Kemp, A. E. (1996). *The musical temperament: Psychology and personality of musicians*. USA: Oxford University Press.

Kemper, K. J., & Shannon, S. (2007). Complementary and alternative medicine therapies to promote healthy moods. *Pediatric Clinics of North America, 54*(6), 901–26.

Kendrick, M. J., Craig, K. D., Lawson, D. M., & Davidson, P. O. (1982). Cognitive and behavioural therapy for musical-performance anxiety. *Journal of Consulting and Clinical Psychology, 50*(3), 353–62.

Kenny, D. T. (2000a). Occupational stress: Reflections on theory and practice. In D. T. Kenny, J. G. Carlson, F. J. McGuigan & J. L. Sheppard (Eds.), *Stress and health: Research and clinical applications* (pp. 375–96). Ryde, NSW: Gordon Breach Science/Harwood Academic Publishers.

Kenny, D. T. (2000b). Psychological foundations of stress and coping: A developmental perspective. In D. T. Kenny, J. G. Carlson, F. J. McGuigan & J. L. Sheppard (Eds.), *Stress and health: Research and clinical applications* (pp. 73–104). Ryde, NSW: Gordon Breach Science/Harwood Academic Publishers.

Kenny, D. T. (2004). Music performance anxiety: Is it the music, the performance or the anxiety? *Music Forum, 10*(4), 38–43.

Kenny, D. T. (2005a). Performance anxiety: Multiple phenotypes, one genotype? Introduction to the special edition on performance anxiety. *International Journal of Stress Management, 12*(4), 307–11.

Kenny, D. T. (2005b). Special edition: Performance anxiety in human endeavour. *International Journal of Stress Management, 12*(4).

Kenny, D. T. (2005c). A systematic review of treatment for music performance anxiety. *Anxiety, Stress and Coping, 18*(3), 183–208.

Kenny, D. T. (2006). Music performance anxiety: Origins, phenomenology, assessment and treatment. In Special issue: Renegotiating musicology. *Context: Journal of Music Research, 31*, 51–64.

Kenny, D. T. (2009a). *The factor structure of the revised Kenny Music Performance Anxiety Inventory*. Paper presented at the International Symposium on Performance Science, Auckland, New Zealand.

Kenny, D. T. (2009b). Negative emotions in music making: Performance anxiety. In P. Juslin & J. Sloboda (Eds.), *Handbook of music and emotion: Theory, research, applications*. Oxford, UK: Oxford University Press.

Kenny, D. T., & Ackermann, B. (2009). Optimizing physical and psychological health in performing musicians. In S. Hallam, I. Cross & M. Thaut (Eds.), *Oxford Handbook of Music Psychology* (pp. 390–400). Oxford, UK: Oxford University Press.

Kenny, D. T, Ackermann , B, & Driscoll, T. (2009). Questionnaire on physical and psychological well-being of professional orchestral musicians. Unpublished.

Kenny, D. T., Davis, P., & Oates, J. M. (2004). Music performance anxiety and occupational stress amongst opera chorus artists and their relationship with state and trait anxiety and perfectionism. *Journal of Anxiety Disorders, 18*(6), 757–77.

Kenny, D.T., & McIntyre, D. (2005). Constructions of occupational stress: Nuisance, nuance or novelty? In A.-S. Antoniou and Cary Cooper (Eds.), *Research Companion to Organizational Health Psychology* (Chapter 2, pp. 20–58). Cheltenham, UK: Edward Elgar Publishing.

Kenny, D. T., & Mitchell, H. F. (2007). *Vocal quality in female classical singers: The role of acoustics, perception and pedagogy.* Paper presented at the Proceedings of the Third International Conference on Interdisciplinary Musicology (CIM07). From www-gewi.uni.graz.at/cim07.

Kenny, D. T., & Osborne, M. S. (2006). Music performance anxiety: New insights from young musicians. *Advances in Cognitive Psychology, 2*(2–3), 103–12.

Kerr, J. H. (1997). *Motivation and emotion in sport: Reversal theory.* East Sussex, UK: Psychology Press.

Kessler, R. C., Berglund, P., Demler, O., Jin, R., Merikangas, K. R., & Walters, E. E. (2005a). Lifetime prevalence and age-of-onset distributions of DSM-IV disorders in the National Comorbidity Survey replication. *Archives of General Psychiatry, 62*(6), 593–602.

Kessler, R. C., Chiu, W. T., Demler, O., & Walters, E. E. (2005b). Prevalence, severity, and comorbidity of 12-month DSM-IV disorders in the National Comorbidity Survey replication. *Archives of General Psychiatry, 62*(6), 617–27.

Kessler, R. C., McGonagle, K. A., Zhao, S., Nelson, C. B., Hughes, M., & Eshleman, S. (1994). Lifetime and 12-month prevalence of DSM-III-R psychiatric disorders in the United States. *Archives of General Psychiatry, 51*, 8–19.

Kessler, R. C., Stang, P., Wittchen, H. U., Stein, M., & Walters, E. E. (1999). Lifetime comorbidities between social phobia and mood disorders in the US National Comorbidity Survey. *Psychological Medicine, 29*, 555–67.

Khalsa, S. B., Shorter, S. M., Cope, S., Wyshak, G., & Sklar, E. (2009). Yoga ameliorates performance anxiety and mood disturbance in young professional musicians. *Applied Psychophysiology & Biofeedback, 34*(4), 279–89.

Khawaja, N. G., & Armstrong, K. A. (2005). Factor structure and psychometric properties of the Frost Multidimensional Perfectionism Scale: Developing shorter versions using an Australian sample. *Australian Journal of Psychology, 57*(2), 129–38.

Kilborne, B. (2004). Superego dilemmas. *Psychoanalytic Inquiry, 24*(2), 175–82.

Kim, Y. (2005). Combined treatment of improvisation and desensitization to alleviate music performance anxiety in female college pianists: A pilot study. *Medical Problems of Performing Artists, 20*(1), 17–24.

Kindt, M., Soeter, M., & Vervliet, B. (2009). Beyond extinction: Erasing human fear responses and preventing the return of fear. *Nature Neuroscience, 12*(3), 256–8.

Kinrys, G., Coleman, E., & Rothstein, E. (2009). Natural remedies for anxiety disorders: potential use and clinical applications. *Depression and Anxiety, 26*, 259–65.

Kirchner, J. M. (2003a). Performance anxiety in solo piano playing. Dissertation Abstracts International, 63(10-A), 3503.

Kirchner, J. M. (2003b). A qualitative inquiry into musical performance anxiety. *Medical Problems of Performing Artists, 18*(2), 78–82.

Kivimaki, M., & Jokinen, M. (1994). Job perceptions and well-being among symphony orchestra musicians: A comparison with other occupational groups. *Medical Problems of Performing Artists, 9*, 73–6.

Knott, V. J., Bolton, K., Heenan, A., Shah, D., Fisher, D. J., & Villeneuve, C. (2009). Effects of acute nicotine on event-related potential and performance indices of auditory distraction in nonsmokers. *Nicotine & Tobacco Research, 11*(5), 519–30.

Kohut, H. (1971). *The analysis of self.* New York, NY: International Universities Press.

Kohut, H. (1977). *The restoration of the self.* New York, NY: International Universities Press.

Kohut, H. (1984). *How does analysis cure?* Chicago: University of Chicago Press.

Kokotsaki, D., & Davidson, J. W. (2003). Investigating musical performance anxiety among music college singing students: A quantitative analysis. *Music Education Research, 5*(1), 45–59.

Kozma, A., Stone, S., & Stones, M. J. (1999). Stability in components and predictors of subjective well-being (SWB): Implications for SWB structure. *Journal of Personality and Social Psychology, 69*(1), 152–61.

Krane, V., & Williams, J. M. (2006). Psychological characertistics of peak performance. In J. M. Williams (Ed.), *Applied sport psychology: Personal growth to peak performance* (pp. 207–27). New York, NY: McGraw-Hill.

Krisanaprakornkit, T., Krisanaprakornkit, W., & Piyavhatkul, N. (2007). Meditation therapy for anxiety disorders. *Cochrane Database Systematic Review, 3*(CD004998).

Krueger, R. F., Watson, D., & Barlow, D. H. (2005). Toward a dimensionally based taxonomy of psychopathology. *Journal of Abnormal Psychology, 114*(4), 491–3.

Lacaille, N., Whipple, N., & Koestner, R. (2005). Reevaluating the benefits of performance goals: The relation of goal type to optimal performance for musicians and athletes. *Medical Problems of Performing Artists, 20*(1), 11–16.

Lakhan, S. E., & Vieira, K. F. (2010). Nutritional and herbal supplements for anxiety and anxiety-related disorders: systematic review. *Nutrition Journal, 9*(42).

Landers, D. M., & Lochbaum, M. (1998). Is the inverted-U hypothesis really a 'catastrophe'? [1998 NASPSPA Abstracts]. *Journal of Sport & Exercise Psychology, 20* (June Supplement), S16.

Lang, P. J. (1971). Phsyiological assessment of anxiety and fear. In J. Cone & R. Hawkins (Eds.), *Behavioural assessment: New directions in clinical psychology.* New York, NY: Brunner-Mazel.

Lang, P. J. (1979). A bio-informational theory of emotional imagery. *Psychophysiology, 16*, 495–512.

Lang, P. J., Cuthbert, B. N., & Bradley, M. M. (1998). Measuring emotion in therapy: Imagery, activation, and feeling. *Behavior Therapy, 29*(4), 655–74.

Lang, P. J., Davis, M., & Ohman, A. (2000). Fear and anxiety: Animal models and human cognitive psychophysiology. *Journal of Affective Disorders, 61*(3), 137–59.

Lankton, S. R. (1983). *The answer within: A clinical framework of Ericksonian hypnotherapy.* New York, NY: Brunner/Mazel.

Lara, D. R. (2010). Caffeine, mental health, and psychiatric disorders. *Journal of Alzheimer's Disease, 20 Suppl 1,* S239–48.

Last, C. G., Hansen, C., & Franco, N. (1998). Cognitive-behavioral treatment of school phobia. *Journal of the American Academy of Child and Adolescent Psychiatry, 37*(4), 404–11.

Latham, G. P., & Locke, E. A. (2007). New developments in and directions for goal-setting research. *European Psychologist, 12*(4), 290–300.

Layne, A. E., Bernstein, G. A., Egan, E. A., & Kushner, M. G. (2003). Predictors of treatment response in anxious-depressed adolescents with school refusal. *Journal of the American Academy of Child and Adolescent Psychiatry, 42*, 319–26.

Lazarus, R. S. (1984). On the primacy of cognition. *American Psychologist, 39*(2), 124–9.

Lazarus, R. S. (1991a). Cognition and motivation in emotion. *American Psychologist, 46*(4), 352–67.

Lazarus, R. S. (1991b). Progress on a cognitive-motivational-relational theory of emotion. *American Psychologist, 46*(8), 819–34.

Lazarus, R. S. (1999). The cognition–emotion debate: A bit of history. In T. Dalgliesh & M. J. Power (Eds.), *Handbook of cognition and emotion* (pp. 3–19). Chichester, UK: Wiley.

Lazarus, R. S. (2000a). Cognitive-motivational-relational theory of emotion. In Y. L. Hanin (Ed.), *Emotions in Sport* (pp. 39–63). Champaign, IL: Human Kinetics.

Lazarus, R. S. (2000b). How emotions influence performance in competitive sports. *The Sport Psychologist, 14*, 229–52.

Lazarus, R. S., & Abramovitz, A. A. (2004). A multimodal behavioral approach to performance anxiety. *Journal of Clinical Psychology, 60*(8), 831–40.

Lazarus, R. S., & Folkman, S. (1984). *Stress, appraisal, and coping*. New York, NY: Springer.

LeDoux, J. (1996). *The emotional brain: The mysterious underpinnings of emotional life*. New York, NY: Simon and Shuster.

Leary, M. R. (1983). Social anxiousness: The construct and its measurement. *Journal of Personality Assessment, 47*(1), 66–75.

LeBlanc, A., Jin, Y. C., Obert, M., & Siivola, C. (1997). Effect of audience on music performance anxiety. *Journal of Research in Music Education, 45*(3), 480–96.

LeCroy, D. (2000). Freud: The first evolutionary psychologist? *Annals of the New York Academy of Sciences, 907* (Evolutionary perspectives on human reproductive behavior: Part III. Commentaries), 182–90.

Lederman, R. J. (1999). Medical treatment of performance anxiety: A statement in favor. *Medical Problems of Performing Artists, 14*(3), 117–21.

LeDoux, J. (1998). *The emotional brain*. London: Weidenfeld & Nicolson.

Lee, S. H., Ahn, S. C., & Lee, Y. J. (2007). Effectiveness of a meditation-based stress management program as an adjunct to pharmacotherapy in patients with anxiety disorder. *Journal of Psychosomatic Research, 62*, 189–95.

Lehrer, P. M. (1987). A review of the approaches to the management of tension and stage fright in music performance. *Journal of Research in Music Education, 35*, 143–53.

Lehrer, P. M., Goldman, N., & Strommen, E. (1990). A principal components assessment of performance anxiety among musicians. *Medical Problems of Performing Artists, 5*, 12–18.

Lester, D., & Yang, B. (2009). Two sources of human irrationality: Cognitive dissonance and brain dysfunction. *The Journal of Socio-Economics, 38*(4), 658–662.

Levi, L. (1999). Stress management and prevention on a European community level: Options and obstacles. In D. T. Kenny, J. G. Carlson, F. J. McGuigan & J. L. Sheppard (Eds.), *Stress and health: Research and clinical applications* (pp. 229–42). Sydney: Harwood Academic.

LeVine, W. R., & Irvine, J. K. (1984). In vivo EMG biofeedback in violin and viola pedagogy. *Biofeedback and Self-regulation, 9*, 161–8.

Lewinsohn, P. M., Gotlib, I. H., Lewinsohn, M., Seeley, J. R., & Allen, N. B. (1998). Gender differences in anxiety disorders and anxiety symptoms in adolescents. *Journal of Abnormal Psychology, 107*, 109–17.

Lewinsohn, P. M., Hops, H., Roberts, R. E., Seeley, J. R., & Andrews, J. A. (1993). Adolescent psychopathology: I. Prevalence and incidence of depression and other DSM-III-R disorders in high school students. *Journal of Abnormal Psychology, 102*(1), 133–44.

Lewinsohn, P. M., Zinbarg, R., Seeley, J. R., Lewinsohn, M., & Sack, W. H. (1997). Lifetime comorbidity among anxiety disorders and between anxiety disorders and other mental disorders in adolescents. *Journal of Anxiety Disorders, 11*(4), 377–94.

Libkuman, T. M., Stabler, C. L., & Otani, H. (2004). Arousal, valence, and memory for detail. *Memory, 12*(2), 237–47.

Lieberman, J. L. (1991). *You are your instrument.* New York, NY: Huiksi Music.

Lin, P., Chang, J., Zemon, V., & Midlarsky, E. (2008). Silent illumination: A study on Chan (Zen) meditation, anxiety, and musical performance quality. *Psychology Of Music, 36*(2), 139–55.

Linehan, M. M. (1993). *Cognitive-behavioral treatment of borderline personality disorder.* New York, NY: Guilford Press.

Linford, L., & Arden, J. B. (2009). Brain-based therapy and the *Pax Medica. Psychotherapy in Australia, 15*(3), 16–23.

Liston, M., Frost, A. A. M., & Mohr, P. B. (2003). The prediction of musical performance anxiety. *Medical Problems of Performing Artists, 18*(3), 120–5.

Locke, E. A. (2009). It's time we brought introspection out of the closet. *Perspectives on Psychological Science, 4*(1), 24–5.

Lockwood, A. H. (1989). Medical problems of musicians. *New England Journal of Medicine, 320*, 221–7.

Lonsdale, C., & Tam, J. T. (2008). On the temporal and behavioural consistency of pre-performance routines: An intra-individual analysis of elite basketball players' free throw shooting accuracy. *Journal of Sports Sciences, 26*(3), 259–66.

Lyubomirsky, S., Tucker, K. L., Caldwell, N. D., & Berg, K. (1999). Why ruminators are poor problem solvers: Clues from the phenomenology of dysphoric rumination. *Journal of Personality and Social Psychology, 77*(5), 1041–60.

Maas, E., Robin, D. A., Hula, S., Freedman, S., Wulf, G., & Ballard, K. (2008). Principles of motor learning in treatment of motor speech disorders. *American Journal of Speech–Language Pathology, 17*, 277–98.

Maddox, W. T., & Ashby, F. G. (2004). Dissociating explicit and procedural-learning based systems of perceptual category learning. *Behavioural Processes 66*, 309–32.

Magrath, J. (2003–2004). Polyphony: Visualization and music study. *The American Music Teacher, 53*(3), 48.

Mahl, G. F. (1968). Gestures and body movements in interviews. In J. M. Shlien (Ed.), *Research in psychotherapy* (Vol. 1, pp. 295–346). Washington, DC: American Psychological Association.

Mahler, M., Pine, F., & Bergmann, A. (1975). *The psychological birth of the human infant.* New York, NY: Basic Books.

Mahler, M. S. (1972). On the first three phases of the separation–individuation process. *International Journal of Psychoanalysis, 53*, 333–8.

Mahoney, M. J. (1992). Performing under pressure. *American Psychological Association, 37*(4), 312.

Main, M. (1995). Attachment: Overview and implications for clinical work. In S. Goldberg, R. Muir & J. Kerr (Eds.), *Attachment theory: Social, developmental and clinical perspectives* (pp. 404–74). Hillsdale, NJ: Analytic Press.

Main, M., Hesse, E., & Kaplan, N. (2005). Predictability of attachment behaviour and representational processes. In K. E. Grossman, K. Grossman & E. Waters (Eds.), *Attachment from infancy to adulthood: Lessons from longitudinal studies* (pp. 245–304). New York, NY: Guilford Press.

Malan, D. H. (1979). *Individual psychotherapy and the science of psychodynamics* (2nd ed.). Oxford: Butterworth-Heinemann.

Malan, D. H., & Osimo, F. (1992). *Psychodynamics, training, and outcome in brief psychotherapy.* Oxford: Butterworth-Heinemann.

Manassis, K., Mendlowitz, S. L., & Scapillato, D. (2002). Group and individual cognitive-behavioral therapy for childhood anxiety disorders: A randomized trial. *Journal of the American Academy of Child and Adolescent Psychiatry, 41,* 1423–30.

Manchester, R. (2006). Toward better prevention of injuries among performing artists. *Medical Problems of Performing Artists 21*(1), 1–2.

Mandler, G. (1984). *Mind and body: Psychology of emotion and stress.* New York, NY: W. W. Norton.

Mann, T. (1927). *The magic mountain.* New York, NY: Knopf.

Mansberger, N. B. (1988). *The effects of performance anxiety management training on musicians' self-efficacy, state anxiety and musical performance quality.* Unpublished Master of Music thesis, Western Michigan University, Kalamazoo, Michigan.

Mantel, G. (2003). *Mut zum Lampenfieber. Mentale Strategien für Musiker zur Bewältigung von Auftritts-und Prüfungsangst*: Mainz: Schott Musik International.

Marco, E. M., & Viveros, M. P. (2009). Functional role of the endocannabinoid system in emotional homeostasis. *Revista de Neurologia, 48*(1), 20–6.

Marieb, E. N. (2001). *Human anatomy and physiology* (5th ed.). New York, NY: Benjamin Cummins.

Marks, I. M. (1978). *Living with fear: Understanding and coping with anxiety.* New York, NY: McGraw-Hill.

Marmot, M. (1986). Social inequalities in mortality; the social environment. In R. Wilkinson (Ed.), *Class and Health: Research and Longitudinal Data.* London: Tavistock.

Maroon, M. T. J. (2003). Potential contributors to performance anxiety among middle school students performing at solo and ensemble contest. *Dissertation Abstracts International, 64*(2-A), 437.

Marr, J. (2000). Commentary: Flow, intrinsic motivation, and 2nd generation cognitive science. *The Online Journal of Sport Psychology, 2*(3).

Martens, R., Burton, D., Vealey, R., Bump, L., & Smith, D. (1990). The development of the competitive state anxiety inventory-2 (CSAI-2). In R. Martens., R. S. Vealey. & D. Burton. (Eds.), *Competitive anxiety in sport* (pp. 117–90). Champaign, IL: Human Kinetics.

Martin, R. (2007). *The effect of a series of guided music imaging sessions on music performance anxiety.* Unpublished Master of Music thesis, University of Melbourne.

Martin, R. A., Kuiper, N. A., Olinger, L. J., & Dobbin, J. (1987). Is stress always bad?: Telic versus paratelic dominance as a stress-moderating variable. *Journal of Personality & Social Psychology, 53*(5), 970–82.

Maser, J. D., & Akiskal, H. S. (2002). Spectrum concepts in major mental disorders. *Psychiatric Clinics of North America, 25*(4), xi–xiii.

Masi, G., Toni, C., Mucci, M., Millepiedi, S., Mata, B., & Perugi, G. (2001). Paroxetine in child and adolescent outpatients with panic disorder. *Journal of Child & Adolescent Psychopharmacology, 11*(2), 151–7.

Masters, R. S. (1992). Knowledge, nerves and know-how: The role of explicit versus implicit knowledge in the breakdowns of a complex motor skill under pressure. *British Journal of Psychology, 83*, 343–58.

Mather, M., Mitchell, K. J., Raye, C. L., Novak, D. L., Greene, E. J., & Johnson, M. K. (2006). Emotional arousal can impair feature binding in working memory. *Journal of Cognitive Neuroscience, 18*(4), 614–25.

Mathews, A., & MacLeod, C. (2005). Cognitive vulnerability to emotional disorders. *Annual Review of Clinical Psychology, 1*, 167–95.

Maturana, H. R., & Varela, F. J. (1987). *The tree of knowledge: The biological roots of understanding*. Boston, MA: Shambhala.

May, J. R., Veach, T. L., & Reed, M. W. (1985). A psychological study of health, injury and performance in athletes on the US alpine ski team. *Physical and Sports Medicine, 13*, 111–15.

May, R. (1977). *The meaning of anxiety* (revised ed.). New York, NY: Norton, Washington Square.

Mayer, J. D. (2001). Primary divisions of personality and their scientific contributions: From the trilogy-of-minds to the systems set. *Journal for the Theory of Social Behaviour, 31*(4), 449–77.

Maykut, P., & Morehouse, R. (1994). *Beginning qualitative research: A philosophical and practical guide*. London: Falmer Press.

McAdams, D. P. (1997). The case for unity in the post-modern self. In R. D. Ashmore & L. Jussim (Eds.), *Self and identity: Fundamental issues* (Vol. 1, pp. 46–78). New York, NY: Oxford University Press.

McCauley, R. J., & Swisher, L. (1984). Psychometric review of language and articulation tests for preschool children. *Journal of Speech and Hearing Disorders, 49*, 34–42.

McCormick, J., & McPherson, G. (2003). The role of self-efficacy in a musical performance examination: An exploratory structural equation analysis. *Psychology of Music, 31*(1), 37–50.

McCoy, L. H. (1999). Musical performance anxiety among college students: An integrative approach. *Dissertation Abstracts International, 60*(4-A), 1059.

McCrae, R. R., & Costa, P. T. (1991). Adding liebe & arbeit: The full five factor model and well-being. *Bulletin of Personality and Social Psychology, 17*, 227–32.

McEwen, B. S. (2003). Early life influences on life-long patterns of behavior and health. *Mental Retardation and Developmental Disabilities Research Reviews, 9*(3), 149–54.

McGinnis, A. M., & Milling, L. S. (2005). Psychological treatment of musical performance anxiety: Current status and future directions. *Psychotherapy: Theory, Research, Practice, Training, 42*(3), 357–73.

McKinney, H. V. (1984). The effects of thermal biofeedback training on musical performance and performance anxiety. *Dissertation Abstracts International, 45*(5-A), 1328.

McLaughlin, T., Geissler, E. C., & Wan, G. J. (2003). Comorbidities and associated treatment charges in patients with anxiety disorders. *Pharmacotherapy, 23*(10), 1251–6.

McMahon, C. (1973). Images as motives and motivators: A historical perspective. *American Journal of Psychology, 86*, 465–90.

McNally, I. (2002). Contrasting concepts of competitive state-anxiety in sport: Multidimensional anxiety and catastrophe theories. *Athletic Insight, 4*(2). Retrieved from http://www.athleticinsight.com/Vol2Iss3/Commentary_2.htm.

McNally, R. J. (2003). Psychological mechanisms in acute response to trauma. *Biological Psychiatry, 53*(9), 779–88.

McNaughton, N., & Gray, J. A. (2000). Anxiolytic action on the behavioural inhibition system implies multiple types of arousal contribute to anxiety. *Journal of Affective Disorders, 61*(3), 161–76.

McWilliams, N. (1994). *Psychoanalytic diagnosis*. New York, NY: Guilford Press.

Mead, G. H. (1934). *Mind, self and society from the standpoint of a social behaviorist*. Chicago: University of Chicago Press.

Mechoulam, R., Parker, L. A., Gallily, R., Mechoulam, R., Parker, L. A., & Gallily, R. (2002). Cannabidiol: an overview of some pharmacological aspects. *Journal of Clinical Pharmacology, 42* (11 Suppl), 11S–9S.

Meichenbaum, D. (1985). *Stress inoculation training*. New York, NY: Pergamon Press.

Meichenbaum, D. H. (1977). *Cognitive behaviour modification: An integrative approach*. New York, NY: Plenum.

Melhorn, M. J. (1998). Cumulative trauma disorders and repetitive strain injuries: The future. *Clinical Orthopaedics and Related Research, 351*, 107–26.

Mennin, D. S., Heimberg, R. G., Turk, C. L., & Fresco, D. M. (2002). Applying an emotion regulation framework to integrative approaches to generalized anxiety disorder. *Clinical Psychology: Science and Practice, 9*, 85–90.

Merritt, L., Richards, A., & Davis, P. (2001). Performance anxiety: Loss of the spoken edge. *Journal of Voice, 15*, 257–69.

Mesagno, C., & Mullane-Grant, T. (2010). A comparison of different pre-performance routines as possible choking interventions. *Journal of Applied Sport Psychology, 22*(3), 343–60.

Meyers, A. W., Whelan, J. P., & Murphy, S. M. (1996). Cognitive-behavioral strategies in athletic performance enhancement. In M. Hersen, R. M. Eisler & P. M. Miller (Eds.), *Progress in behavior modification* (Vol. 30, pp. 137–64). Pacific Grove, CA: Brooks/Cole.

Miller, A. (1975). *Prisoners of childhood: The drama of the gifted child and the search for the true self*. New York, NY: Basic Books.

Miller, N., & Dollard, J. (1941). *Social learning and imitation*. New Haven, NJ: Yale University Press.

Miller, S. M. (1992). Individual differences in the coping process: What to know and when to know it. In B. N. Carpenter (Ed.), *Personal coping: Theory, research, and application* (pp. 77–91). New York, NY: Praeger.

Miller, S. R., & Chesky, K. (2004). The multidimensional anxiety theory: An assessment of and relationships between intensity and direction of cognitive anxiety, somatic anxiety, and self-confidence over multiple performance requirements among college music majors. *Medical Problems of Performing Artists, 19*(1), 12–20.

Milton, J., Solodkina, A., Hluštík, P., & Smalla, S. L. (2007). The mind of expert motor performance is cool and focused. *NeuroImage, 35*(2), 804–13.

MIMS Australia (2010). *St Leonards*. Australia: UBM Medica.

Mineka, S. (1987). A primate model of phobic fears. In H. J. Eysenck & I. Martin (Eds.), *Theoretical foundations of behavior therapy* (pp. 81–111). New York, NY: Plenum Press.

Mineka, S., & Zinbarg, R. (1996). *Conditioning and ethological models of anxiety disorders: Stress-in-dynamic-context anxiety*. Paper presented at the Nebraska Symposium on Motivation, Lincoln, Neb.

Mineka, S., & Zinbarg, R. (2006). A contemporary learning theory perspective on the etiology of anxiety disorders: It's not what you thought it was. *American Psychologist, 61*(1), 10–26.

Mitchell, S. A. (1993). *Hope and dread in pychoanalysis.* New York, NY: Basic Books.

Mitchell, S. A., & Black, M. J. (1995). *Freud and beyond: A history of modern psychoanalytic thought.* New York, NY: Basic Books.

Miyake, A., Friedman, N. P., Emerson, M. J., Witzki, A. H., Howerter, A., & Wager, T. D. (2000). The unity and diversity of executive functions and their contributions to complex 'frontal lobe' tasks: A latent variable analysis. *Cognitive Psychology, 41*, 49–100.

Molenaar, P. C. M., & Campbell, C. G. (2009). The new person-specific paradigm in psychology. *New Directions in Psychological Science, 18*(2), 112–17.

Montello, L. (1989). Utilizing music therapy as a mode of treatment for performance stress of professional musicians. *Dissertation Abstracts International, I-A*(50/10).

Montello, L., Coons, E. E., & Kantor, J. (1990). The use of group music therapy as a treatment for musical performance stress. *Medical Problems of Performing Artists, 5*, 49–57.

Moorcroft, L. (2011). Pre-performance practices: Breathing imagery and warm-up for singers. Unpublished doctoral thesis, The University of Sydney, Sydney.

Moore, P. J., Chung, E., Peterson, R. A., Katzman, M. A., & Vermani, M. (2009). Information integration and emotion: How do anxiety sensitivity and expectancy combine to determine social anxiety? *Cognition and Emotion, 23*(1), 1237–51.

Mor, S., Day, H. I., Flett, G. L., & Hewitt, P. L. (1995). Perfectionism, control, and components of performance anxiety in professional artists. *Cognitive Therapy and Research, 19*, 207–25.

Morasky, R. L., Reynolds, C., & Sowell, L. E. (1983). Generalization of lowered EMG levels during musical performance following feedback training. *Biofeedback and Self-regulation, 8*, 207–16.

Moreira, F. A., Aguiar, D. C., Guimaraes, F. S., Moreira, F. A., Aguiar, D. C., & Guimaraes, F. S. (2006). Anxiolytic-like effect of cannabidiol in the rat Vogel conflict test. *Progress in Neuro-Psychopharmacology & Biological Psychiatry, 30*(8), 1466–71.

Morgan, W. P. (1980). The trait psychology controversy. *Research Quarterly for Exercise and Sport, 51*, 50–76.

Moritz, S., Hall, C., Martin, K., & Vadocz, E. (1996). What are confident athletes imaging?: An examination of image content. *The Sport Psychologist, 10*, 171–9.

Mornell, A. (2002). *Lampenfieber und Angst bei ausübenden Musikern.* Frankfurt am Main: Peter Lang GmbH Europäischer Verlag der Wissenschaften.

Morris, T. L. (2001). Social phobia. In M. W. Vasey & M. R. Dadds (Eds.), *The developmental psychopathology of anxiety* (pp. 435–58). New York, NY: Oxford University Press.

Mowrer, O. H. (1939). A stimulus–response theory of anxiety and its role as a reinforcing agent. *Psychological Review, 46*, 553–65.

Mowrer, O. H. (1947). On the dual nature of learning: A reinterpretation of 'conditioning' and 'problem solving.' *Harvard Educational Review, 17*, 102–48.

Mozart, W. A. (1778/1985). *The letters of Mozart and his family* (E. Anderson, S. Sadie & F. Smart, Trans. 3rd ed.). London: Macmillan.

Muhlberger, A., Wieser, M. J., & Pauli, P. (2008). Visual attention during virtual social situations depends on social anxiety. *CyberPsychology & Behavior, 11*(4), 425–30.

Muran, J. C., Safran, J. D., Samstag, L. W., & Winston, A. (2005). Evaluating an alliance-focused treatment for personality disorders. *Psychotherapy: Theory, Research, Practice, 42*(4), 532–45.

Muratori, F., Picchi, L., Bruni, G., Patarnello, M., & Romagnoli, G. (2003). A two-year follow-up of psychodynamic psychotherapy for internalizing disorders in children. *Journal of the American Academy of Child and Adolescent Psychiatry, 42*, 331–9.

Myers, E. (2002). Fever pitch. *Opera News, 67*(5), 36–42.

Nagel, J. J. (1990). Performance anxiety and the performing musician: A fear of failure or a fear of success? *Medical Problems of Performing Artists, 5*, 37–40.

Nagel, J. J. (1993). Stage fright in musicians: A psychodynamic perspective. *Bulletin of the Menninger Clinic, 57*(4), 492–503.

Nagel, J. J. (2004). Performance anxiety theory and treatment: One size does not fit all. *Medical Problems of Performing Artists, 19*(1), 39–43.

Nagel, J. J., Himle, D. P., & Papsdorf, J. D. (1989). Cognitive-behavioural treatment of musical performance anxiety. *Psychology of Music, 17*(1), 12–21.

Nash, J., & Potokar, J. (2004). Anxiety disorders. *Medicine, 32*(7), 17–21.

Neftel, K., Adler, R., Käppeli, L., Rossi, M., Dolder, M., Käser, H., *et al.* (1982). Stage fright in musicians: A model illustrating the effect of beta blockers. *Psychosomatic Medicine, 44*, 461–9.

Nehlig, A. (2010). Is caffeine a cognitive enhancer? *Journal of Alzheimer's Disease, 20 Suppl 1*, S85–94.

Newman, C. F., & Beck, A. B. (2010). Cognitive therapy. In K. Sadock (Ed.), *Comprehensive textbook of psychiatry.*

News, A. (20 September 05, 22). Barbra Streisand Looks Back on 25 Years: Legendary Singer, Actress, Director Talks to Sawyer About New Album, New Attitude. Retrieved from http://abcnews.go.com/Primetime/Entertainment/story?id=1147020&page=1.

Nicholson, K. C., & Torrisi, J. (2006, Fall). Performance Anxiety. *Theme Magazine, 7.*

Niemann, B. K., Pratt, R. R., & Maughan, M. L. (1993). Biofeedback training, selected coping strategies, and music relaxation interventions to reduce debilitative musical performance anxiety. *International Journal of Arts Medicine, 2*(2), 7–15.

NIOSH. (1999). *Stress at work* (DHHS Publication No. 99–101), Cincinnati, OH.

Nolen-Hoeksema, S. (2000). The role of rumination in depressive disorders and mixed anxiety-depressive symptoms. *Journal of Abnormal Psychology, 109*, 504–11.

Nolen-Hoeksema, S., Wisco, B. E., & Lyubomirsky, S. (2008). Rethinking rumination. *Perspectives on Psychological Science, 3*(5), 400–24.

Norris, R. (1993). *The musician's survival manual: A guide to preventing and treating injuries in instrumentalists.* Saint Louis, MO: MMB Music Inc.

Norris, R. N. (2000). Applied ergonomics. In R. Tubiana & P. C. Amadio (Eds.), *Medical problems of the instrumentalist musician* (pp. 595–613). London: Martin Dunitz Ltd.

Nubé, J. (1991). Beta-blockers: Effects on performing musicians. *Medical Problems of Performing Artists, 6*, 61–8.

Ohman, A. (1986). Face the beast and fear the face: Animal and social fears as prototypes for evolutionary analyses of emotion. *Psychophysiology, 23*(2), 123–45.

Olatunji, B. O., Forsyth, J. P., & Feldner, M. T. (2007). Implications of emotion regulation for the shift from normative fear-relevant learning to anxiety-related psychopathology. *American Psychologist, 62*(3), 257–9.

Ollendick, T. H. (1995). Cognitive-behavioral treatment of panic disorder with agoraphobia in adolescents: A multiple baseline design analysis. *Behavior Therapy, 26*, 517–31.

Ollendick, T. H., King, N. J., & Chorpita, B. F. (2006). Empirically supported treatments for children and adolescents. In P. C. Kendall (Ed.), *Child and adolescent therapy: Cognitive-behavioral procedures* (pp. 492–520). New York, NY: Guilford Press.

Ollendick, T. H., Yang, B., Dong, Q., Xia, Y., & Lin, L. (1995). Perceptions of fear in other children and adolescents: The role of gender and friendship status. *Journal of Abnormal Child Psychology, 23*, 439–52.

Olsson, A., & Phelps, E. (2004). Learned fear of unseen faces after Pavlovian, observational and instructed fear. *Psychological Science, 15*(12), 822–8.

Orbach, I. (1999). The relationship between self-confidence and competitive anxiety in influencing sport performance. *Dissertation Abstracts International*, 60(2-B), 0874.

Orman, E. K. (2003). Effect of virtual reality graded exposure on heart rate and self-reported anxiety levels of performing saxophonists. *Journal of Research in Music Education, 51*(4), 302–15.

Orman, E. K. (2004). Effect of virtual reality graded exposure on anxiety levels of performing musicians: A case study. *Journal of Music Therapy, 41*(1), 70–8.

Osborne, M. S. (1998). *Determining the diagnostic and theoretical adequacy of conceptualising music performance anxiety as a social phobia.* Unpublished Honours thesis, Macquarie University, Sydney.

Osborne, M. S., & Franklin, J. (2002). Cognitive processes in music performance anxiety. *Australian Journal of Psychology, 54*(2), 86–93.

Osborne, M. S., & Kenny, D. T. (2005). Development and validation of a music performance anxiety inventory for gifted adolescent musicians. *Journal of Anxiety Disorders, 19*(7), 725–51.

Osborne, M. S., & Kenny, D. T. (2008). The role of sensitising experiences in music performance anxiety in adolescent musicians. *Psychology of Music, 36*(4), 447–62.

Osborne, M. S., Kenny, D. T., & Cooksey, J. (2007). Impact of a cognitive-behavioural treatment program on music performance anxiety in secondary school music students: A pilot study. *Musicae Scientiae* (Special Issue), 53–84.

Osborne, M. S., Kenny, D. T., & Holsomback, R. (2005). Assessment of music performance anxiety in late childhood: A validation study of the Music Performance Anxiety Inventory for Adolescents (MPAI–A). *International Journal of Stress Management, 12*(4), 312–30.

Osmond, D. (1999). Interview with Donny Osmond. *People Magazine*, 109–11.

Osmond, D., & Romanowski, P. (1999). *Life is just what you make it, my life so far.* New York, NY: Hyperion Books.

Ost, L.-G. (1985). Mode of acquisition of phobias. *Acta Universitatis Uppsaliensis (Abstracts of Uppsala Dissertations from the Faculty of Medicine), 529*, 1–45.

Ost, L.-G. (2008). Efficacy of the third wave of behavioral therapies: A systematic review and meta-analysis. *Behaviour Research and Therapy 46*, 296–321.

Ostwald, P. F. (1987). Psychotherapeutic strategies in the treatment of performing artists. *Medical Problems of Performing Artists 2* (4), 131–6.

Ostwald, P. F. (1994). Historical perspectives on the treatment of performing and creative artists. *Medical Problems of Performing Artists, 9*(4), 113–18.

Pacheco-Unguetti, A. P., Acosta, A., Callejas, A., & Lupiáñez, J. (2010). Attention and anxiety: Different attentional functioning under state and trait anxiety. *Psychological Science, 21*(1), 1–10.

Packer, C. D., & Packer, D. M. (2005). Beta-blockers, stage fright, and vibrato: A case report. *Medical Problems of Performing Artists, 20*(3), 126–30.

Paolino, T. J. (1981). *Psychoanalytic psychotherapy: Theory, technique, therapeutic relationship, and treatability*. New York, NY: Brunner/Mazel.

Papageorgi, I., Hallam, S., & Welch, G. F. (2007). A conceptual framework for understanding musical performance anxiety. *Research Studies In Music Education, 28*(1), 83–107.

Parkes, K. R. (1994). Personality and coping as moderators of work stress processes: Models, methods and measures. *Work and Stress, 8*(2), 110–29.

Pascarelli, E. F., & Hsu, Y. P. (2001). Understanding work-related upper extremity disorders: Clinical findings in 485 computer users, musicians, and others. *Journal of Occupational Rehabilitation, 11*(1), 1–21.

Passer, M. W. (1983). Fear of failure, fear of evaluation, perceived competence, and self-esteem in competitive-trait-anxious children. *Journal of Sport Psychology, 5*, 172–88.

Patenaude-Yarnell, J. (2003). The role of imagination in teaching voice. *NATS Journal of Singing, 59*(5), 425–30.

Paul, G. L. (1966). *Insight vs. desensitization in psychotherapy: An experiment in anxiety reduction*. Stanford: Stanford University Press.

Paulhus, D. L., Fridhandler, B., & Hayes, S. (1997). Psychological defense: Contemporary theory and research. In R. Hogan, J. Johnson & S. Briggs (Eds.), *Handbook of personality* (pp. 236–59). New York, NY: Guilford Press.

Pauli, P., Dengler, W., Wiedemann, G., Montoya, P., Flor, H., Birbaumer, N., & Buchkremer, G. (1997). Behavioral and neurophysiological evidence for altered processing of anxiety-related words in panic disorder. *Journal of Abnormal Psychology, 106*(2), 213–20.

Pavlov, I. P. (1927). *Conditioned reflexes: An investigation of the physiological activity of the cerebral cortex* (G. V. Anrep, Trans.). London: Oxford University Press.

Pessoa, L. (2008). On the relationship between emotion and cognition. *Nature Reviews Neuroscience 9*, 148–58.

Peter, R., & Siegrist, J. (1997). Chronic work stress, sickness absence, and hypertension in middle managers: General or specific sociological explanations? *Social Science Medicine, 45*, 1111–20.

Peterson, C. (2000a). The future of optimism. *American Psychologist, 55*, 44–55.

Peterson, C., Seligman, M. E., & Vaillant, G. E. (1988). Pessimistic explanatory style is a risk factor for physical illness: A thirty-five year longitudinal study. *Journal of Personality and Social Psychology, 55*, 23–7.

Peterson, L. (2000b). Dietrich Fischer-Dieskau and the art of song. *NATS Journal of Singing, 57*(1), 4–11.

Peterson, R. A., & Reiss, S. (1992). *Anxiety Sensitivity Index manual* (2nd ed. revised). Worthington, Ohio: International Diagnostic Systems.

Phan, K. L., Angstadt, M., Golden, J., Onyewuenyi, I., Popovska, A., & de Wit, H. (2008). Cannabinoid modulation of amygdala reactivity to social signals of threat in humans. *Journal of Neuroscience, 28*(10), 2313–19.

Phelps, E. A. (2006). Emotion and cognition: Insights from studies of the human amygdala. *Annual Review of Psychology, 57*, 27–53.

Piaget, J. (1970). Piaget's theory. In P. H. Mussen (Ed.), *Carmichael's manual of child psychology* (pp. 703–32). New York, NY: Wiley.

Piantanida, M., Tananis, C. A., & Grubs, R. E. (2004). Generating grounded theory of/for educational practice: The journey of three epistemorphs. *International Journal of Qualitative Studies in Education, 17*(3), 325–46.

Piqueras, J. A., Olivares, J., & Lopez-Pina, J. A. (2008). A new proposal for the subtypes of social phobia in a sample of Spanish adolescents. *Journal of Anxiety Disorders, 22*, 67–77.

Plaut, E. A. (1990). Psychotherapy of performance anxiety. *Medical Problems of Performing Artists, 5*(1), 58–63.

Porges, S. W. (2001). The polyvagal theory: Phylogenetic substrates of a social nervous system. *International Journal of Psychophysiology, 42*, 123–46.

Porges, S. W. (2007). The polyvagal perspective. *Biological Psychology, 74*, 116–43.

Powell, C. (2010). *The analytic method*. Paper presented at the 2010 seminar series of the Sydney Institute of Psychoanalysis.

Powell, D. H. (2004a). Behavioral treatment of debilitating test anxiety among medical students. *Journal of Clinical Psychology, 60*(8), 853–65.

Powell, D. H. (2004b). Treating individuals with debilitating performance anxiety: An introduction. *Journal of Clinical Psychology/In Session, 60*(8), 801–8.

Prior, V., & Glaser, D. (2006*). Understanding attachment and attachment disorders: Theory, evidence and practice. Child and adolescent mental health*. London and Philadelphia: Jessica Kingsley Publishers.

Pruett, K. D. (1987). A longitudinal view of the musical gift: Clinical studies of the blessings and curses of precocious talent. *Medical Problems of Performing Artists, 2*(1), 31–8.

Pruett, K. D. (2004). First patrons: Parenting the musician. *Medical Problems of Performing Artists, 19*(4), 154–9.

Puliafico, A. C., & Kendall, P. C. (2006). Threat-related attentional bias in anxious youth: A review. *Clinical Child and Family Psychology Review, 9*(3–4), 162–80.

Quarrier, N. F., & Norris, R. N. (2001). Adaptations for trombone performance: Ergonomic interventions. *Medical Problems of Performing Artists, 16*(2), 77–80.

Rachman, S. (1991). Neo-conditioning and the classical theory of fear acquisition. *Clinical Psychology Review, 11*(2), 155–73.

Rachman, S. J., & Hodgson, R. (1974). Synchrony and desynchrony in fear and avoidance. *Behaviour Research and Therapy, 12*, 311–18.

Rae, G., & McCambridge, K. (2004). Correlates of performance anxiety in practical music exams. *Psychology of Music, 32*(4), 432–9.

Raeburn, S. D. (1999). Psychological issues and treatment strategies in popular musicians: A review, part 1. *Medical Problems of Performing Artists, 14*, 171–9.

Raeburn, S. D. (2000). Psychological issues and treatment strategies in popular musicians: A review, part 2. *Medical Problems of Performing Artists, 15*, 6–16.

Raeburn, S. D. (2007). The ring of fire: Shame, fame, and rock 'n' roll (Johnny Cash's drug addiction). *Medical Problems of Performing Artists, 22*(1), 3–9.

Raglin, J. S. (2001). Psychological factors in sport performance: The mental health model revisited. *Sports Medicine, 31*(12), 875–90.

Rapee, R. M. (1991). Generalized anxiety disorder: A review of clinical features and theoretical concepts. *Clinical Psychology Review, 11*(4), 419–40.

Rapee, R. M., Craske, M. G., Brown, T. A., & Barlow, D. H. (1996). Measure of perceived control over anxiety related events. *Behavior Therapy, 27*, 279–93.

Rapee, R. M., & Heimberg, R. G. (1997). A cognitive-behavioral model of social phobia. *Behaviour Research and Therapy, 35*(8), 741–56.

Rapee, R. M., & Medoro, L. (1994). Fear of physical sensations and trait anxiety as mediators of the response to hyperventilation in nonclinical subjects. *Journal of Abnormal Psychology, 103*(4), 693–9.

Raskin, R. N., & Hall, C. S. (1981). The Narcissistic Personality Inventory: Alternate form reliability and further evidence of construct validity. *Journal of Personality Assessment, 45*, 149–62.

Rasmussen, S. A., & Eisen, J. L. (1994). The epidemiology and differential diagnosis of obsessive compulsive disorder. *Journal of Clinical Psychiatry, 55*, 5–10.

Reiss, S., Peterson, R. A., Gurskya, D. M., & McNally, R. J. (1986). Anxiety sensitivity, anxiety frequency and the prediction of fearfulness. *Behaviour Research and Therapy, 24*(1), 1–8.

Reitman, A. D. (2001). The effects of music-assisted coping systematic desensitization on music performance anxiety. *Medical Problems of Performing Artists, 16*(3), 115–25.

Rendi, M., Szabo, A., Szabo, T., Velenczei, A., & Kovacs, A. (2008). Acute psychological benefits of aerobic exercise: A field study into the effects of exercise characteristics *Psychology Health & Medicine, 13*(2), 180–4.

Rescorla, R. A. (1988). Pavlovian conditioning: It's not what you think it is. *American Psychologist, 43*(3), 151–60.

Reubart, D. (1985). *Anxiety and musical performance.* New York, NY: Da Capo.

Richard, J. J., Jr. (1992). The effects of Ericksonian resource retrieval on musical performance anxiety. *Dissertation Abstracts International, 55*(2-B), 604.

Rink, J. (Ed.). (2002). *Musical performance: A guide to understanding.* Cambridge, UK: Cambridge University Press.

Robazza, C., Bortoli, L., & Nougier, V. (1998). Physiological arousal and performance in elite archers: A field study. *European Psychologist, 3*(4), 263–70.

Robson, B., Davidson, J., & Snell, E. (1995). 'But I'm not ready, yet': Overcoming audition anxiety in the young musician. *Medical Problems of Performing Artists, 10*(1), 32–7.

Rodebaugh, T. L. (2007). The effects of different types of goal pursuit on experience and performance during a stressful social task. *Behaviour Research and Therapy, 45*(5), 951–63.

Rodebaugh, T. L., Holaway, R. M., & Heimberg, R. G. (2004). The treatment of social anxiety disorder. *Clinical Psychology Review, 24*(7), 883–908.

Roemer, L., & Orsillo, S. M. (2002). Expanding our conceptualization of and treatment for generalized anxiety disorder: integrating mindfulness/acceptance-based approaches with existing cognitive behavioral models. *Clinical Psychology: Science and Practice, 9*, 54–68.

Rosen, J. B., & Schulkin, J. (1998). From normal fear to pathological anxiety. *Psychological Review, 105*(2), 325–50.

Ross, S. L. (1985). The effectiveness of mental practice in improving the performance of college trombonists. *Journal of Research in Music Education, 33*(4), 221–30.

Rotter, J. B. (1966). Generalized expectancies for internal versus external control of reinforcement. *Psychological Monographs, 80*, 1–28.

Ruscio, A. M., Brown, T. A., Chiu, W. T., Sareen, J., Stein, M. B., & Kessler, R. C. (2008). Social fears and social phobia in the USA: Results from the National Cormorbidity Survey Replication. *Psychological Medicine, 38*, 15–28.

Rushmore, R. (1971). *The singing voice.* New York: Dodd, Mead & Company.

Rushall, B., & Lippman, L. (1998). The role of imagery in physical performance. *International Journal of Sport Psychology, 29*, 57–72.

Rutter, M. (1980). *Changing youth in a changing society*. Cambridge, MA: Harvard University Press.

Ryan, C. (1998). Exploring musical performance anxiety in children. *Medical Problems of Performing Artists, 13*, 83–8.

Ryan, C. (2003). A study of the differential responses of male and female children to musical performance anxiety. *Dissertation Abstracts International, 63*(7-A), 2487.

Ryan, C. (2004). Gender differences in children's experience of musical performance anxiety. *Psychology of Music, 32*(1), 89–103.

Ryan, C. (2005). Experience of musical performance anxiety in elementary school children. *International Journal of Stress Management, 12*(4), 331–42.

Ryan, C., & Andrews, N. (2009). An investigation into the choral singer's experience of music performance anxiety. *Journal of Research in Music Education, 57*(2), 108–26.

Ryan, C., & Boucher, H. (2011). Performance stress and the very young musician. *Journal of Research in Music Education, 58*(4), 329–45.

Ryan, M., & Kenny, D. T. (2009). Perceived effects of the menstrual cycle on young female singers in the Western classical tradition. *Journal of Voice, 23*(1), 99–108.

Sabbe, B., Hulstijn, W., & Van Hoof, J. (1996). Fine motor retardation and depression. *Journal of Psychiatric Research, 30*, 295–306.

Sadock, B. J., Sadock, V. A., & Ruiz, P. (Eds.). (2009). *Kaplan & Sadock's comprehensive textbook of psychiatry* (9th ed.). Philadelphia, PA: Lippincott Williams & Wilkins.

Sakolsky, D., & Birmaher, B. (2008). Pediatric anxiety disorders: Management in primary care. *Current Opinion in Pediatrics 20* (5), 538–43.

Salmon, P. (1990). A psychological perspective on musical performance anxiety: A review of the literature. *Medical Problems of Performing Artists, 5*(1), 2–11.

Salmon, P. (1991). A primer on performance anxiety for organists: Part I. *The American Organist, 25*, 55–9.

Samuels, M., & Samuels, N. (1987). *Seeing with the mind's eye: The history, techniques and uses of visualisation*. New York, NY: Random House Inc.

Sanderson, W. C., DiNardo, P. A., Rapee, R. M., & Barlow, D. H. (1990). Symptom comorbidity in patients diagnosed with DSM-III-R anxiety disorders. *Journal of Abnormal Psychology, 99*, 308–12.

Sasso, D. A. (2010). Psychiatric issues and performing artists. In R. T. Sataloff, A. G. Brandfronbrenner & R. J. Lederman (Eds.), *Performing arts medicine* (3rd ed.), Narberth, PA: Science and Medicine Inc.

Sataloff, R., Rosen, D. C., & Levy, S. (2000). Performance Anxiety: What Singing Teachers Should Know. *Journal of Singing, 56*, 33–40.

Sauser, E. L., & Billard, A. G. (2006). Parallel and distributed neural models of the ideomotor principle: An investigation of imitative cortical pathways. *Neural Networks, 19*(3), 285–98.

Sauter, D., Eisner, F., Ekman, P., & Scott, S. (2010). Cross-cultural recognition of basic emotions through nonverbal emotional vocalizations. *PNAS, Proceedings of the National Academy of Sciences of the United States of America, 107*(6), 2408–12.

Scanlan, T. K., & Lewthwaite, R. (1984). Social psychological aspects of competition for male youth sport participants: Predictors of competitive stress. *Journal of Sport Psychology, 6*, 208–26.

Schafer, R. (1978). *Language and insight*. New Haven, CT: Yale University Press.

Schlenker, B. R., & Leary, M. R. (1982). Social anxiety and self-presentation: A conceptualization and model. *Psychological Bulletin, 92*(3), 641–69.

Schmidt, R. (2003). Motor schema theory after 27 years: Reflections and implications for a new theory. *Research Quarterly for Exercise and Sport, 74*(4), 366–75.

Schneier, F. R., Foose, T. E., Hasin, D. S., Heimberg, R. G., Liu, S.-M., Grant, B. F., *et al.* (2010). Social anxiety disorder and alcohol use disorder co-morbidity in the national epidemiologic survey on alcohol and related conditions. *Psychological Medicine: A Journal of Research in Psychiatry and the Allied Sciences, 40*(6), 977–88.

Schonberg, H. C. (1963). *The great pianists.* New York, NY: Simon and Schuster.

Schore, A. N. (2003). *Affect regulation and the repair of the self.* New York, NY: Norton.

Schore, J., & Schore, A. (2008). Modern attachment theory: The central role of affect regulation in development and treatment. *Clinical Social Work Journal, 36*(1), 9–20.

Schroeder, H., & Liebelt, P. (1999). Psychologische Phaenomen- und Bedingungsanalysen zur Podiumsangst von Studierenden an Musikhochschulen. *Musikphysiologie und Musikermedizin, 6*(1), 1–6.

Schulz, W. (1981). Analysis of a symphony orchestra. In M. Piperek (Ed.), *Stress and music: Medical, psychological, sociological, and legal strain factors in a sympony orchestra musician's profession* (pp. 35–56). Vienna: Wilhelm Branmuller.

Schurman, C. L. (2001). *Social phobia, shame and hypersensitive narcissism. Dissertation Abstracts International, 61*(9-B), 5004.

Schwartz, G. E., Davidson, R. J., & Goleman, D. J. (1978). Cognitive and somatic processes in anxiety. *Psychosomatic Medicine, 40*, 321–8.

Seligman, M. E. (1991). *Learned optimism: How to change your mind and your life.* New York, NY: Pocket Books.

Selye, H. (1955). Stress and disease. *Science, 122*, 625–31.

Senyshyn, Y. (1999). Perspectives on performance and anxiety and their implications for creative teaching. *Canadian Journal of Education, 24*(1), 30–41.

Shafran, R., & Mansell, W. (2001). Perfectionism and psychopathology: A review of research and treatment. *Clinical Psychology Review, 21*(6), 879–906.

Shedler, J. (2010). The efficacy of psychodynamic psychotherapy. *American Psychologist, 62*(2), 98–108.

Shedler, J., Mayman, M., & Manis, M. (1993). The illusion of mental health. *American Psychologist, 48*(11), 1117–31.

Silverman, W. K., Fleisig, W., Rabian, B., & Peterson, R. A. (1991). Child Anxiety Sensitivity Index. *Journal of Clinical Child Psychology, 20*, 162–8.

Simon, J. A., & Martens, R. (1979). Children's activity in sport and nonsport evaluative activities. *Journal of Sport Psychology, 1*, 160–9.

Sinden, L. M. (1999). Music performance anxiety: Contributions of perfectionism, coping style, self-efficacy, and self-esteem. *Dissertation Abstracts International, 60*(3-A), 0590.

Sisterhen, L. (2004). Enhancing your musical performance abilities. *The American Music Teacher, 54*(1), 32–5.

Skinner, B. F. (1953). *Science and human behavior.* New York, NY: Macmillan.

Skinner, B. F. (1969). *Contingencies of reinforcement: A theoretical analysis.* New York, NY: Appleton-Century-Crofts.

Slaney, R. B., Rice, K. G., & Ashby, J. S. (2002). A programmatic approach to measuring perfectionism: The almost perfect scales. In G. L. Flett & P. L. Hewitt (Eds.), *Perfectionism: Theory, research, and treatment* (pp. 63–88). Washington, DC: American Psychological Association.

Sloboda, R. (1993). Musical ability. In G. Bock & K. Ackrill (Eds.), *The origins of high ability* (pp. 106–18). Chichester, UK: Wiley.

Smith, A. M., Maragos, A., & van Dyke, A. (2000). Psychology of the musician. In R. Tubiana & C. P. Amadio (Eds.), *Medical problems of the instrumentalist musician* (pp. 135–70). London: Martin Dunitz Ltd.

Smith, E. E., & Jonides, J. (1999). Storage and executive processes in the frontal lobes. *Science, 283*, 1657–61.

Smith, J., Harré, R., & van Langenhove, L. (Eds.). (1995). *Rethinking psychology: Conceptual foundations* (Vol. 1). London: Sage.

Smith, R. E., Smoll, F. L., & Barnett, N. P. (1995). Reduction of children's sport anxiety through social support and stress-reduction training for coaches. *Journal of Applied Developmental Psychology, 16*, 125–42.

Smith, R. J., Amkoff, D. B., & Wright, T. I. (1990). Test anxiety and academic competence: A comparison of alternative models. *Journal of Counseling Psychology, 37*(3), 313–21.

Sowell, E. R., Thompson, P. M., Tessner, K. D., & Toga, A. W. (2001). Mapping continued brain growth and gray matter density reduction in dorsal frontal cortex: Inverse relationships during postadolescent brain maturation. *Journal of Neuroscience, 15, 21*(22), 8819–29.

Spahn, C., Nikolaus, E., & Seidenglzanz, K. (2001). Psychosomatic findings in musician patients at a department of hand surgery. *Medical Problems of Performing Artists, 16*, 144–51.

Spangler, G., & Grossmann, K. E. (1993). Biobehavioural organization in securely and insecurely attached infants. *Child Development, 64*, 1439–50.

Sparrow, W. A., & Newell, K. M. (1998). Metabolic energy expenditure and the regulation of movement economy. *Psychonomic Bulletin and Review, 5*(2), 173–96.

Spence, D. (1986). Narrative smoothing and clinical wisdom. In T. S. Sarbin (Ed.), *Narrative psychology: The storied nature of human conduct*. New York, NY: Praeger.

Spence, J. T., & Spence, K. W. (1966). The motivational components of manifest anxiety: Drive and drive stimuli. In C. D. Spielberger (Ed.), *Anxiety and behaviour* (pp. 291–326). New York, NY: Academic Press.

Spence, S. H., Donovan, C., & Brechman-Toussaint, M. (2000). The treatment of childhood social phobia: the effectiveness of a social skills training-based, cognitive-behavioural intervention, with and without parental involvement. *Journal of Child Psychology and Psychiatry, 41*, 713–26.

Spielberger, C. D. (1972). Anxiety as an emotional state. In C. D. Spielberger (Ed.), *Anxiety: Current trends in theory and research* (pp. 23–49). New York, NY: Academic Press.

Spielberger, C. D. (1983). *State–Trait Anxiety Inventory STAI (Form Y)*. Palo Alto, CA: Consulting Psychologists Press, Inc.

Spielberger, C. D. (1985). Anxiety, cognition, and affect: A state–trait perspective. In A. H. Tuma & J. D. Maser (Eds.), *Anxiety and the anxiety disorders* (pp. 171–82). Hillsdale, NJ: Lawrence Erlbaum Associates.

Spitzer, R. L., & Wakefield, J. C. (1999). DSM-IV diagnostic criterion for clinical significance: Does it help solve the false positives problem? *American Journal of Psychiatry, 156*(12), 1856–64.

Spohr, L. (1833). *Spohr's violin school*. London: Boosey & Co.

Sroufe, L. A., & Waters, E. (1977). Attachment as an organizational construct. *Child Development, 48*, 1184–99.

Stangier, U., & Heidenreich, T. (2004). Die Liebowitz Soziale Anngst-Skala (LSAS). In C.I.P. Scalarum (Ed.), *Collegium Internationale Pscyhiatriae Scalarum*: Weinhelm: Beltz.

Stanislavski, C., & Rumyantsev, P. (1975). *Stanislavski on opera* (E. R. Hapgood, Trans.). New York, NY: Theatre Arts Books.

Stankov, L., & Crawford, J. D. (1993). Ingredients of complexity in fluid intelligence. *Learning and Individual Differences, 5*(2), 73–111.

Stanton, H. E. (1994). Reduction of performance anxiety in music students. *Australian Psychologist, 29*(2), 124–7.

Steffenmeir, J. J., Ernst, M. E., Kelly, M., & Hartz, A. J. (2006). Do randomized controlled trials always trump case reports? A second look at propranolol and depression. *Pharmacotherapy, 26*(2), 162–7.

Stein, M. B., & Stein, D. J. (2008). Social anxiety disorder. *The Lancet, 371*(9618), 1115–25.

Steinberg, L. D., Darling, N. E., & Fletcher, A. C. (1995). Authoritative parenting and adolescent development: An ecological journey. In P. Moen, G. H. Elder & K. Luscher (Eds.), *Examining lives in context* (pp. 423–66). Washington DC: American Psychological Association.

Stephenson, H., & Quarrier, N. F. (2005). Anxiety sensitivity and performance anxiety in college music students. *Medical Problems of Performing Artists, 20*(3), 119–25.

Steptoe, A. (1989). Stress, coping and stage fright in professional musicians. *Psychology of Music, 17*(1), 3–11.

Steptoe, A. (2001). Negative emotions in music making: The problem of performance anxiety. In P. N. Juslin & J. A. Sloboda (Eds.), *Music and emotion: Theory and research* (pp. 291–307). Oxford, UK: Oxford University Press.

Steptoe, A., & Fidler, H. (1987). Stage fright in orchestral musicians: A study of cognitive and behavioral strategies in performance anxiety. *British Journal of Psychology, 78*(2), 241–9.

Sternbach, D. J. (1995). Musicians: A neglected working population in crisis. In S. L. Sauter & L. R. Murphy (Eds.), *Organizational risk factors for job stress* (pp. 283–302). Washington, DC: American Psychological Association.

Stewart, S. H., Taylor, S., & Baker, J. M. (1997). Gender differences in dimensions of anxiety sensitivity. *Journal of Anxiety Disorders, 11*(2), 179–200.

Stocker, C., & Hoffmann, J. (2004). The ideomotor principle and motor sequence acquisition: Tone effects facilitate movement chunking. *Psychological Research/Psychologische Forschung, 68*(2–3), 126–37.

Stoeber, J., & Eismann, U. (2007). Perfectionism in young musicians: Relations with motivation, effort, achievement, and distress. *Personality and Individual Differences, 43*(8), 2182–92.

Stoeber, J., & Eysenck, M. W. (2008). Perfectionism and efficiency: Accuracy, response bias, and invested time in proof-reading performance. *Journal of Research in Personality, 42*(6), 1673–8.

Stolorow, R. (2006). The relevance of Freud's concept of danger-situation for an intersubjective-systems perspective. *Psychoanalytic Psychology, 23*(2), 417–19.

Stolorow, R. D. (2007). Anxiety, authenticity and trauma: The relevance of Heidegger's existential analytic for psychoanalysis. *Psychoanalytic Psychology, 24*(2), 373–83.

Strauman, T. J. (1989). Self-discrepancies in clinical depression and social phobia: Cognitive structures that underlie emotional disorders? *Journal of Abnormal Psychology, 98*(1), 14–22.

Studer, R. K., Danuser, B., Hildebrandt, H., Arial, M., & Gomez, P. (2011). Hyperventilation complaints in music performance anxiety among classical music students. *Journal of Psychosomatic Research* (19 January 2011: Epub ahead of print).

Su, Y.-H., Luh, J.-J., Chen, H.-I., Lin, C.-C., Liao, M.-J., & Chen, H.-S. (2010). Effects of using relaxation breathing training to reduce music performance anxiety in 3rd to 6th graders. *Medical Problems of Performing Artists, 25*(1), 82–6.

Sugawara, M., Mukai, T., Kitamura, T., Toda, M., Shima, S., & Tomoda, A. (1999). Psychiatric disorders among Japanese children. *Journal of the American Academy of Child and Adolescent Psychiatry, 38*(4), 444–52.

Suinn, R. M. (1990). *Anxiety management training: A behavior therapy.* New York, NY: Plenum Press.

Suinn, R. M. (2005). Behavioral intervention for stress management in sports. *International Journal of Stress Management, 12*(4), 312–20.

Sweeney-Burton, C. (1997). Effects of self-relaxation techniques training on performance anxiety and on performance quality in a music performance condition. *Dissertation Abstracts International, 58*(7-A), 2581.

Sweeney, G. A., & Horan, J. J. (1982). Separate and combined effects of cue-controlled relaxation and cognitive restructuring in the treatment of musical performance anxiety. *Journal of Counselling Psychology, 29*(5), 486–97.

Tamborrino, R. A. (2001). An examination of performance anxiety associated with solo performance of college-level music majors. *Dissertation Abstracts International, 62* (5A): 1636.

Tangney, J. P. (2002). Perfectionism and the self-conscious emotions: Shame, guilt, embarrassment, and pride. In G. L. Flett & P. L. Hewitt (Eds.), *Perfectionism: Theory, research, and treatment* (pp. 199–215). Washington, DC: American Psychological Association.

Target, M., & Fonagy, P. (1994). Efficacy of psychoanalysis for children with emotional disorders. *Journal of the American Academy of Child and Adolescent Psychiatry, 33*, 361–71.

Taskforce, P. (2006). *Psychodynamic Diagnostic Manual.* Silver Spring: MD: Alliance of Psychoanalytic Organizations.

Tassi, P., Bonnefond, A., Hoeft, A., Eschenlauer, R., & Muzet, A. (2003). Arousal and vigilance: Do they differ? Study in a sleep inertia paradigm. *Sleep Research Online, 5*(3), 83–7.

Taubman-Ben-Ari, O., Mikulincer, M., & Gillath, O. (2005). From parents to children—similarity in parents and offspring driving styles. *Transportation Research Part F: Traffic Psychology and Behaviour, 8*(1), 19–29.

Taylor, S. (1999). *Anxiety sensitivity: Theory, research and treatment of the fear of anxiety.* Mahwah, NJ: Lawrence Erlbaum Associates.

Taylor, S., Jang, D. L., Stewart, S. H., & Stein, M. B. (2008). Etiology of the dimensions of anxiety sensitivity: A behavioral–genetic analysis. *Journal of Anxiety Disorders, 22*, 899–914.

Taylor, S. E., & Brown, J. D. (1988). Illusion and well-being: A social psychological perspective on mental health. *Psychological Bulletin, 103*, 193–210.

Taylor, S. E., & Brown, J. D. (1994). Positive illusions and well-being revisited: Separating fact from fiction. *Psychological Bulletin, 116*, 21–7.

Templeton, D. (2003). Stressed for success. *Strings, 18*(3), 28.

Terry, P., Coakley, L., & Karageorghis, C. (1995). Effects of intervention upon precompetition state anxiety in elite junior tennis players: The relevance of the matching hypothesis. *Perceptual and Motor Skills, 81*, 287–96.

The Band. (19 August 70, 17). Stage fright (album). *Capitol Records.* Retrieved from http://en.wikipedia.org/wiki/Stage_Fright_(album).

Thomas, C., Turkheimer, E., & Oltmans, T. F. (2003). Factorial structure of pathological personality evaluated by peers. *Journal of Abnormal Psychology, 112*, 81–91.

Thomsen, D. K. (2006). The association between rumination and negative affect: A review. *Cognition and Emotion, 20*(8), 1216–35.

Thurber, M. R. (2007). Effects of heart-rate variability biofeedback training and emotional regulation on music performance anxiety in university students. *Dissertation Abstracts International, 68*(3-A), 889.

Tindall, B. (20 October 04, 17). Better playing through chemistry. *New York Times*. Retrieved from http://www.nytimes.com/2004/10/17/arts/music/17tind.html?_r=1&ex=1270785600 &en=37bef79604f97228&ei=5090&partner=rssuserland.

Tindall, B. (2005). Medical issues and horn playing: Better playing through chemistry. *The Horn Call—Journal of the International Horn Society, 35*(2), 67–9.

Toneatto, T. T., & Nguyen, L. L. (2007). Does mindfulness meditation improve anxiety and mood symptoms? A review of the controlled research. *Canadian Journal of Psychiatry, 52*, 260–66.

Tracy, J., Madi, S., Laskas, J., Stoddard, E., Pyrros, A., Natale, P., *et al.* (2003). Regional brain activation associated with different performance patterns during learning of a complex motor skill. *Cerebral Cortex, 13*(9), 904–10.

Tracy, J., & Robins, R. (2008). The nonverbal expression of pride: Evidence for crosscultural recognition. *Journal of personality and social psychology, 94*(3), 516–30.

Trippany, R. L., Helm, H. M., & Simpson, L. (2006). Trauma reenactment: Rethinking borderline personality disorder when diagnosing sexual abuse survivors. *Journal of Mental Health Counseling, 28*(2), 95–110.

Turkington, D., Dudley, R., Warman, D. M., & Beck, A. T. (2006). Cognitive-behavioral therapy for schizophrenia: A review. *Focus, 4*, 223–33.

Turner, G., & Kenny, D. T. (2010). A preliminary investigation into the association between body movement patterns and dynamic variation in western contemporary popular singing. *Musicae Scientiae, 14, 1*, 143–164.

Turner, P. E., & Raglin, J. S. (1991). Anxiety and performance in track and field athletes: A comparison of ZOFR and inverted-U hypothesis. *Medial Science in Sport and Exercise, 23*, s119.

Turner, S. M., Beidel, D. C., Borden, J. W., Stanley, M. A., & Jacob, R. G. (1991). Social phobia: Axis I and II correlates. *Journal of Abnormal Psychology, 100*, 102–6.

Turner, S. M., Johnson, M. R., Beidel, D. C., Heiser, N. A., & Lydiard, R. B. (2003). The social thoughts and beliefs scale: A new inventory for assessing cognitions in social phobia. *Psychological Assessment, 15*(384–91).

Valentine, E. (2002). The fear of performance. In J. Rink (Ed.), *Musical performance: A guide to understanding* (pp. 168–82). Cambridge, UK: Cambridge University Press.

Valentine, E., Fitzgerald, D., Gorton, T., Hudson, J., & Symonds, E. (1995). The effect of lessons in the Alexander technique on music performance in high and low stress situations. *Psychology of Music, 23*(2), 129–41.

van der Watt, G., Laugharne, J., & Janca, A. (2008). Complementary and alternative medicine in the treatment of anxiety and depression. *Current Opinion in Psychiatry 21*, 37–42.

van Dixhoorn, J., & Duidenvoorden, H. J. (1985). Efficacy of Nijmegen questionnaire in recognition of the hyperventilation syndrome. *Journal of Psychosomatic Research, 29*, 199–206.

van IJzendoorn, M. H., & Sagi, A. (1999). Cross-cultural patterns of attachment: Universal and cultural dimensions. In J. Cassidy & P. R. Shaver (Eds.), *Handbook of attachment: Theory, research, and clinical applications* (pp. 713–34). New York, NY: Guilford Press.

van Kemenade, J. F., van Son, M. J., & van Heesch, N. C. (1995). Performance anxiety among professional musicians in symphonic orchestras: A self-report study. *Psychological Reports, 77,* 555–62.

Vasey, M. W., & Dadds, M. R. (Eds.). (2001). *The developmental psychopathology of anxiety.* New York, NY: Oxford University Press.

Velting, O. N., Setzer, N. J., & Albano, A. M. (2004). Update on and advances in assessment and cognitive-behavioral treatment of anxiety disorders in children and adolescents. *Professional Psychology: Research and Practice, 35*(1), 42–54.

Vennard, W. (1958). Philosophies of vocal pedagogy. *American Music Teacher, May–June.*

Wallace, S., & Alden, L. (1997). Social phobia and positive social events: The price of success. *Journal of Abnormal Psychology, 106,* 416–24.

Wallin, D. J. (2007). *Attachment in psychotherapy.* New York, NY: Guilford Press.

Walsh, R. (1995). Phenomenological mapping: A method for describing and comparing states of consciousness. *Journal of Transpersonal Psychology, 27,* 25–56.

Wan, C. Y., & Huon, G. F. (2005). Performance degradation under pressure in music: An examination of attentional processes. *Psychology of Music, 33*(2), 155–72.

Wang, J. C. (2001). A study of performance anxiety in talented music students. *Bulletin for Research in Elementary Education, 7,* 1–67.

Wardle, A. (1975). Behavior modification by reciprocal inhibition of instrumental music performance anxiety. In C. K. Madsen, C. H. Madsen & R. D. Greer (Eds.), *Research in music behavior: Modifying music behavior in the classroom* (pp. 191–205). New York, NY: Teachers College Press.

Warrington, J., Winspur, I., & Steinwede, D. (2002). Upper-extremity problems in musicians related to age. *Medical Problems of Performing Artists, 17*(3), 131–40.

Watson, D., Clark, L. A., & Carey, G. (1988). Positive and negative affectivity and their relation to anxiety and depressive disorders. *Journal of Abnormal Psychology, 97,* 346–53.

Watson, D., & Kendall, P. C. (1989). Understanding anxiety and depression: Their relation to negative and positive affective states. In P. C. Kendall & D. Watson (Eds.), *Anxiety and depression: Distinctive and overlapping features. Personality, psychopathology and psychotherapy* (pp. 3–26). San Diego: Academic Press.

Watson, J. B., & Rayner, R. (1920). Conditioned emotional reactions. *Journal of Experimental Psychology, 3,* 1–14.

Weber, H. (1997). Sometimes more complex, sometimes more simple. *Journal of Health Psychology, 2,* 170–1.

Weinberger, D. A., Schwartz, G. E., & Davidson, J. R. (1979). Low anxious, high anxious and repressive coping styles: Psychometric patterns and behavioral and physiological responses to stress. *Journal of Abnormal Psychology, 88,* 369–80.

Weisblatt, S. (1986). A psychoanalytic view of performance anxiety. *Medical Problems of Performing Artists, 1,* 64–7.

Wells, A. (2002). Worry, metacognition, and GAD: Nature, consequences, and treatment. *Journal of Cognitive Psychotherapy, 16*(2), 179–92.

Wesner, R. B., Noyes, R., & Davis, T. L. (1990). The occurrence of performance anxiety among musicians. *Journal of Affective Disorders, 18*(3), 177–85.

Westen, D. (1998). The scientific legacy of Sigmund Freud: Toward a psychodynamically informed psychological science. *Psychological Bulletin, 124*(3), 333–71.

Westen, D. (2002a). The language of psychoanalytic discourse. *Psychoanalytic Dialogues, 12*(6), 857–98.

Westen, D. (2002b). The search for objectivity in the study of subjectivity: Reply to commentary. *Psychoanalytic Dialogues, 12*(6), 915–20.

Westen, D., & Morrison, K. (2001). A multidimensional meta-analysis of treatments for depression, panic, and generalized anxiety disorder: An empirical examination of the status of empirically supported therapies. *Journal of Consulting and Clinical Psychology, 69*(6), 875–99.

Williams, J. M. G., Watts, F. N., MacLeod, C., & Mathews, A. (1997). *Cognitive psychology and emotional disorders* (2nd ed.). Chichester, UK: Wiley.

Wilson, G. D. (2002). *Psychology for performing artists* (2nd ed.). London, UK: Whurr.

Wilson, G. T. (1995). Behavior therapy. In R. J. Corsini & D. Wedding (Eds.), *Current psychotherapies* (5th ed.). Itasca, IL: F.E. Peacock.

Wilson, T. D., Lindsey, S., & Schooler, T. Y. (2000). A model of dual attitudes. *Psychological Review, 107*, 101–26.

Wine, J. (1971). Test anxiety and direction of attention. *Psychological Bulletin, 76*(2), 92–104.

Winnicott, D. (1965). *The maturational processes and the facilitating environment.* New York, NY: International Universities Press.

Winnicott, D. (1974). Fear of breakdown. In D. Goldman (Ed.), *In one's bones: The genius of Winnicott* (pp. 39–47). Northvale, New Jersey: Jason Aranson Inc.

Wittchen, H.-U., Stein, M. B., & Kessler, R. C. (1999). Social fears and social phobia in a community sample of adolescents and young adults: Prevalence, risk factors and comorbidity. *Psychological Medicine, 29*(2), 309–23.

Wolfe, M. L. (1989). Correlates of adaptive and maladaptive musical performance anxiety. *Medical Problems of Performing Artists, 4*(1), 49–56.

Wolpe, J. (1958). *Psychotherapy by reciprocal inhibition.* Stanford, CA: Stanford University Press.

Wolpe, J., & Lazarus, A. A. (1966). *Behavior therapy techniques: A guide to the treatment of neuroses.* New York, NY: Pergamon Press.

Wolverton, D. T., & Salmon, P. (1991). Attention allocation and motivation in music performance anxiety. In G. D. Wilson (Ed.), *Psychology and performing arts* (pp. 231–37). Amsterdam: Swets & Zeitlinger.

Woodruff-Borden, J., Morrow, C., Bourland, S., & Cambron, S. (2002). The behavior of anxious parents: Examining mechanisms of transmission of anxiety from parent to child. *Journal of Clinical Child and Adolescent Psychology, 31*, 364–74.

World Health Organization Study Group. (2007). *The scientific basis of tobacco product regulation.* World Health Organization Technical Report Series.

Wulf, G., McNevin, N., & Shea, C. H. (2001). The automaticity of complex motor skill learning as a function of attentional focus. *Quarterly Journal of Experimental Physiology, 54*(4), 1143–54.

Wulf, G., & Prinz, W. (2001). Directing attention to movement effects enhances learning: A review. *Psychonomic Bulletin & Review, 8*(4), 648–60.

Wynn Parry, C. B. (1998). The interface. In I. Winspur & C. B. Wynn Parry (Eds.), *The musician's hand: A clinical guide.* London: Martin Dunitz Ltd.

Yerkes, R. M., & Dodson, J. D. (1908). The relation of strength of stimulus to rapidity of habit formation. *Journal of Comparative Neurology and Psychology, 18*, 459–82.

Yonkers, K. A., Massion, A. O., Warshaw, M. G., & Keller, M. B. (1996). Phenomenology and course of generalised anxiety disorder. *British Journal of Psychiatry, 168*(3), 308–13.

Yoshie, M., Kudo, K., Murakoshi, T., & Ohtsuki, T. (2009). Music performance anxiety in skilled pianists: Effects of social-evaluative performance situation on subjective, autonomic, and electromyographic reactions. *Experimental Brain Research, 199*(2), 117–26.

Young, J. A., & Pain, M. D. (1999). The zone: Evidence of a universal phenomenon for athletes across sports. *The Online Journal of Sport Psychology, 1*(3), 21–30.

Youngshin, K. (2008). The effect of improvisation-assisted desensitization, and music-assisted progressive muscle relaxation and imagery on reducing pianists' music performance anxiety. *Journal of Music Therapy, 45*(2), 165–91.

Zatz, S., & Chassin, L. (1985). Cognitions of test-anxious children under naturalistic test-taking conditions. *Journal of Consulting and Clinical Psychology, 53*, 393–401.

Zaza, C. (1994). Research-based prevention for musicians. *Medical Problems of Performing Artists, 9*, 3–6.

Zaza, C., Fleiszer, M. S., Main, F. W., & Mechefske, C. (2000). Beating injury with a different drumstick: A pilot study. *Medical Problems of Performing Artists, 15*(1), 39–44.

Zdzisław Jachimecki, Z. (1937). *Chopin, Fryderyk Franciszek*: Polski słownik biograficzny. Kraków, Polska Akademia Umiejętności, (Vol. III).

Zeanah, C. H. (1996). Beyond insecurity: A reconceptualisation of attachment disorders of infancy. *Journal of Consulting and Clinical Psychology, 64*(1), 42–52.

Zeanah, C. H., & Fox, N. A. (2004). Temperament and attachment disorders. *Journal of Clinical Child & Adolescent Psychology, 33*(1), 32–41.

Zinn, M., McCain, C., & Zinn, M. (2000). Musical performance anxiety and the high-risk model of threat. *Medical Problems of Performing Artists, 15*(2), 65–71.

Author Index

Subject Index

Note: The suffix 'f' following a page locator indicates a figure, 'n' indicates a footnote, and 't' a table.